Exterior Building Enclosures

Design Process and Composition for Innovative Facades

C. KEITH BOSWELL, FAIA

WILEY

Cover Design: Wiley
Cover Photograph: © Tim Griffith

Published by John Wiley & Sons, Inc., Hoboken, New Jersey
Published simultaneously in Canada

For general information about our other products and services, please contact our Customer
Care Department within the United States at (800) 762-2974, outside the United States at
(317) 572-3993 or fax (317) 572-4002.

Wiley publishes in a variety of print and electronic formats and by print-on-demand. Some
material included with standard print versions of this book may not be included in e-books or in
print-on-demand. If this book refers to media such as a CD or DVD that is not included in the
version you purchased, you may download this material at http://booksupport.wiley.com. For
more information about Wiley products, visit www.wiley.com.

Library of Congress Cataloging-in-Publication Data:

Boswell, C. Keith.
   Exterior building enclosures: design process and composition for innovative facades / C. Keith
Boswell.
      pages   cm
   Includes index.
   ISBN 978-0-470-88127-9 (hardback); 978-1-118-33006-7 (ebk.); 978-1-118-33200-9 (ebk);
   978-1-118-33279-5 (ebk)
      1. Exterior walls. 2. Buildings—Protection. 3. Architectural design. I. Title.
NA2940.B37   2013
721'.8—dc23
                                                                    2012047064

Printed in the United States of America
10 9 8 7 6 5 4 3 2 1

Contents

Acknowledgments

Many very talented people have directly and indirectly contributed to the thought development, problem solving process, and built examples presented in the content of this book. This is the result of being fortunate, beyond my imagination, to be surrounded by talented and quality driven professionals throughout my career. To all of them I say thank you. I am particularly grateful to the clients—mine and those responsible for buildings completed by other architects—for their support and vision of high performance and finely crafted buildings and exterior enclosures.

There are a select group of individuals who have participated directly with a steady and positive influence during the development and gestation of the writing and graphics presented.

Much of the design fundamentals presented have been the result of my exposure to the creative genius of John Walker III. What started as an architect subcontractor interaction many years ago developed into a fantastic collaboration between an architect and enclosure designer. Exchanging sketches of systems and details with dialogue and critiques on how to effectively develop a successful solution is enormously beneficial and educational. It is a privilege to call you a mentor and friend. All issues have an answer and the joy is the journey during design, detail and construction. Every design problem is a design opportunity

Many of the line drawings presented were drawn freehand by me and graphically composed by Cortney Cassidy. Her patience, care, and attention to each line and word made this effort enjoyable.

To Michael Flynn and Emma Cobb from Pei Cobb Freed & Partners LLP (PCF) a hearty thank you for your reviews of the PCF Case Studies and the use of the drawings provided. I have always respected your work with a special admiration of the design consistency and resulting building enclosures. I am grateful to Charles Bloomberg and Andrea Lamberti from Rafael Vinoly Architects for contributing your design thought process for the HHMI case study. Brad Feinknopf, Paul Fetters, Tim Griffith, Jeff Goldberg, Timothy Hursley, Nathaniel Liebermann, Nick Merrick, Cesar Rubio, Nathaniel Liebermann, and Peter Vanderwarker, graciously allowed me access to their stunning photos for many of the completed enclosures presented in the case studies.

To my talented colleagues at Skidmore, Owings & Merrill LLP San Francisco, present and past, you make work fun. What started as an idea of working at SOM for a few years to gain experience has grown into 33 years of collaboration with the most talented interdisciplinary designers with the hopes of many more years and design opportunities to come. Particularly, thanks to Diane Hernandez, for all of your assistance, work, and support in this effort and every day.

Finally and most of all, thank you to Cathy Boswell. You are my biggest supporter and critic. Your patience, encouragement, and unwavering commitment are the reason I get up every morning.

Chapter 1

Basics

You have to learn the rules of the game. And then you have to play better than anyone else.

ALBERT EINSTEIN

Good building design and good exterior building enclosure design don't just happen. "Good" is a broad, subjective, and sometimes overused term, used primarily to describe the visual aspects of design. It is open to many interpretations. In exterior building enclosure design, visual appearance is generally considered the major component of good design. It has been said before that beauty is in the eye of the beholder. Exterior appearance is very important; however, exterior building enclosure design is more than just visual appearance. It is the integration of the science of physics with the science of materials. It is the integration of materials, material properties, and performance design principles. It requires a basic understanding of building and construction sequencing. It is the application of science and design principles with the art of composition. It is in this intersection of science, art, materials, construction, and many other factors where design and technology, art, and science become architecture. In complete design of exterior building enclosures, beauty is more than skin deep.

Understanding the Basics

Every building design and the associated exterior enclosure design are unique for the particular project. This is the case no matter the size or location of the project. Large or small or any size in between, exterior building enclosures are planned, researched, designed, detailed, and executed to look good and achieve defined performance levels per criteria established for the specific project. Before beginning exterior enclosure design for a project, it is imperative that the architect possess or acquire a basic understanding of the intended and necessary functions of the enclosure, the elements and forces acting on and influencing the enclosure design, performance design principles and associated physics, and the basic types of exterior building enclosures. In conjunction with these items noted, project delivery methods will determine the extent of detailed design to be performed by the architect and design team or by delegated detailed design to participants of the construction team. This embedded or acquired knowledge and identification of design responsibility, coupled with the design intent, is required to provide complete enclosure design.

Some exterior building enclosures are fairly simple. However, with higher performance expectations, emerging technologies, and regulatory standards, proposed designs may require a higher level of detail, documentation, and construction technology to execute. As the old English proverb states: "You have to crawl before you can walk, and walk before you can run." So, getting exterior enclosure basics defined and understood is the first step. The moral is that you have to understand the basics in order to advance to more sophisticated levels of design performance and execution. This is paramount. For those unfamiliar with the basics outlined above, these principles will be presented initially at a foundation level and then applied to enclosure systems and types later, in the system case study sections. For those who are familiar with these basics, read on. You may find the foundation descriptions useful for their application to the design process discussed in subsequent chapters and the systems/case studies where the basics are applied.

Process

Architectural design is a process-oriented profession and activity. Exterior building enclosure design is also a process. Exterior building enclosures are one of the most visible and technically complex aspects of architecture. Enclosure design intent, performance design principles, system design, fabrication and construction methodologies, and completed exterior enclosures must be studied, researched, and articulated in a meaningful and systematic way or inevitably something will be missed and/or left out. As an architecture student during an interview for a summer intern job, I received some valuable advice when showing my modest portfolio of student work. "You can't learn it all, you can't memorize it all, and you will never know it all. What you can do is develop, implement, and practice a problem-solving process." I have carried this with me during my years of practice.

Enclosure design process has its "Do's" and "Do Not's."

DO'S:
1. Research and continue learning.
2. Listen.
3. Keep an open mind.
4. Accept criticism, and determine what to accept and what to reject.
5. Understand the basics of materials, structural principles, natural elements, natural and human-created forces, thermal transfer and properties, and acoustics.
6. Study manufacturing processes.
7. Distill information.
8. Think with graphics.

DO NOT'S:
1. Do not be afraid to try multiple ideas.
2. Do not be too proud to redesign and redraw.
3. Do not limit your imagination.
4. Do not forget for whom or what the building design and exterior enclosure is designed.

Exterior design is a process that is tailored to the specific needs of the project. In order to be a complete design process, the process must define and answer the five W's: What, Why, Who, Where, and When, as well as one H: How. This chapter discusses the "What" (basics and topics of exterior enclosures) and "Why" each topic is applicable. For example: What is the extent of the exterior building enclosure? What are the intended functions, and why do they influence design? What are the forces on the exterior enclosure, and what do they influence? What are some of the performance design principles, and why are they applied within enclosure systems and system interfaces? What are some of the types of exterior enclosure systems?

The topics identified are applicable, in part or whole, to all exterior enclosures and their design. These may appear abstract in some cases, until they are applied. Subsequent chapters will address: Who are the participants, and what are their roles? What levels of design are addressed, and when does each occur in the design process? What levels of documentation, collaboration, and coordination occur, and when does each occur in the process? What is expected by builders in the construction process? Why is a particular enclosure system selected, and how is it used? Where are the design basics and performance principles applied to actual case studies? How does it all come together in architecture?

The design process can be creative and lead to innovative solutions faster, and with more joy than pain, if you imagine, research, analyze, collaborate, imagine again, test solutions, refine solutions, document, and execute.

Definition

Prior to initiating a discussion of the basics, it is necessary to define—for the purposes of this book—the exterior building enclosure. It is the enclosing membrane in vertical, sloped, horizontal, or other geometric configurations separating exterior elements and forces from interior occupied areas. The exterior building enclosure begins either at grade or within the height of the building and terminates either on itself or at a roofing system. Roofing systems perform similar functions as the exterior enclosure, but are not described or discussed here. Similar design concepts, principles, design/detailing approaches, and performance functions apply to roofing systems; however, only the interfaces of the exterior building enclosure to roofing systems will be reviewed in this book.

Exterior enclosure systems may be load-bearing or non-load-bearing. A load-bearing exterior enclosure provides enclosure and is also the primary or secondary building structural system. A non-load-bearing enclosure provides a cladding envelope but is not the building primary or secondary structural system. Non-load-bearing cladding systems are often suspended from or contained within and supported by the primary building structural system or other structural supporting elements or systems. Load-bearing and non-load-bearing enclosures are designed to accommodate elements such as air, water, and sun, and withstand applied loads created by natural forces such as wind, seismic, thermal (expansion and contraction), and other forces. Load-bearing and non-load-bearing exterior building enclosure systems must include methods to control and prevent water intrusion, limit air infiltration, admit and control sunlight, control thermal transfer, control acoustics, and perform for a long period of time with minimal maintenance or repair. The term "enclosure system" is a key word and a central concept. An enclosure system is an assembly or combination of parts, components and materials forming a complete or unified whole. An exterior building enclosure is a system made of connections, anchorage components, framing elements, weatherproofing materials, insulation materials and components, and infill materials. All of these materials and components must be researched and understood to ascertain their respective characteristics, strengths, weaknesses, and compatibilities then arranged and ordered in a working combination with principles of physics.

Functions

Whether load-bearing or non-load-bearing, exterior enclosure systems perform multiple functions. While each of these functions can be discussed and reviewed as an individual topic, the multiple functions are interrelated and influence each other. Each exterior building enclosure has primary functions that include:

1. **Structural function:** The ability of the system to support itself and the applied loads.
2. **Weathertightness:** Keeping natural elements outside.
3. **Energy efficiency:** Performing to high levels by reducing energy consumption. Energy efficiency goes hand in hand with weathertightness.
4. **Accommodating building movements.** This goes hand in hand with structural.

Additional functions, depending on the design requirements, may include acoustics, blast/threat resistance, and other force resistance or performance features.

STRUCTURAL

Owners, architects, engineers, and builders agree that a building is only as good as the strength of its foundation. If the foundation is weak or faulty, the building is doomed. If the foundation is solid and strong, the building will stand for a long time. This concept applies to exterior building enclosure systems as well. The enclosure system must be of sufficient strength and appropriate system depth to support its own weight, accommodate and transfer exterior forces, and span the necessary distances, vertically and horizontally, to supporting building structural elements. In load-bearing conditions, the exterior enclosure system must be of sufficient strength to accommodate the supporting primary building structural demands and transfer applied exterior loads and forces to the foundation. In exterior enclosure cladding applications, the exterior enclosure system must be of sufficient strength to accommodate its own loads (self-weight, often referred to as dead load), applied loads, and forces, and to transfer these through enclosure anchorage assemblies to the primary building structural system. The enclosure must be fully functional during and after the loads are removed. Elements and forces that impose the applied loads are discussed in this chapter.

To withstand exterior forces and support its own loads, the exterior enclosure is designed as a system. The

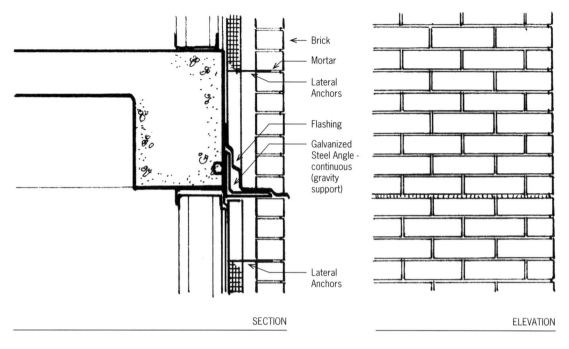

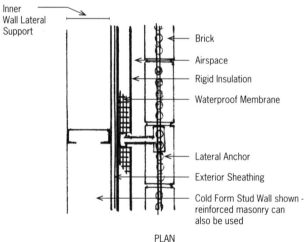

FIGURE 1.1 Materials and components must work together as an assembly in an exterior enclosure system. Brick masonry wall systems rely on a gravity support for the brick self load, the inner wall for lateral support, lateral anchors spaced appropriately, and the brick and mortar for the enclosure system structural integrity.

system consists of components, and using the chain analogy, the enclosure structural integrity is only as good as the weakest link or component. Whether the enclosure is an opaque and planar composition such as brick masonry wall (Figure 1.1), a framed masonry natural stone wall (Figure 1.2), or an opaque and trans-parent composition such as curtain wall (Figure 1.3), the systematic design approach is similar. The structural performance characteristics of each of the components within the system must be understood in order to develop the basic system structural design approach. Materials performing as supports in the system structure

Exterior Building Enclosures

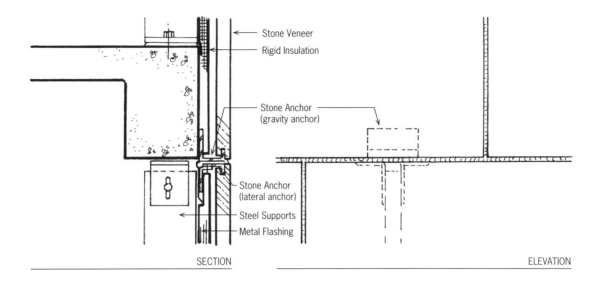

SECTION

ELEVATION

- Stone Veneer
- Rigid Insulation
- Stone Anchor (gravity anchor)
- Stone Anchor (lateral anchor)
- Steel Supports
- Metal Flashing

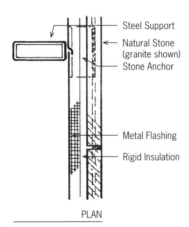

PLAN

- Steel Support
- Natural Stone (granite shown)
- Stone Anchor
- Metal Flashing
- Rigid Insulation

FIGURE 1.2 Framed masonry natural stone wall systems rely on the primary building structure and the steel supports illustrated for gravity and lateral support. The stone itself accommodates and transfers lateral loads to the stone anchors, and the stone anchors support the stone self/dead and lateral loads. The stone cladding itself accommodates and transfers loads for the enclosure system structural integrity.

have inherent strengths and weaknesses. The goal is to accentuate the strengths and minimize—or eliminate—the weaknesses. Superimposed on the enclosure system is the behavior of the building structural system. Under loading, beams and slabs deflect, columns shorten, and the primary structural frame may "drift" or lean when lateral wind or seismic loads are applied. Primary building structure deflection movements are illustrated by the diagrams in Figure 1.4. Primary building structural movements are covered in more detail

later in this chapter. It is important to note that the enclosure structural characteristics and the supporting primary structure characteristics must be evaluated, reviewed, and designed in concert with each other.

Each component within the enclosure system has certain and distinct structural properties. The structural capacity of a component is dependent upon material properties, size, thickness, orientation, method of attachment, and geometry. Components within a system will deflect from their own weight

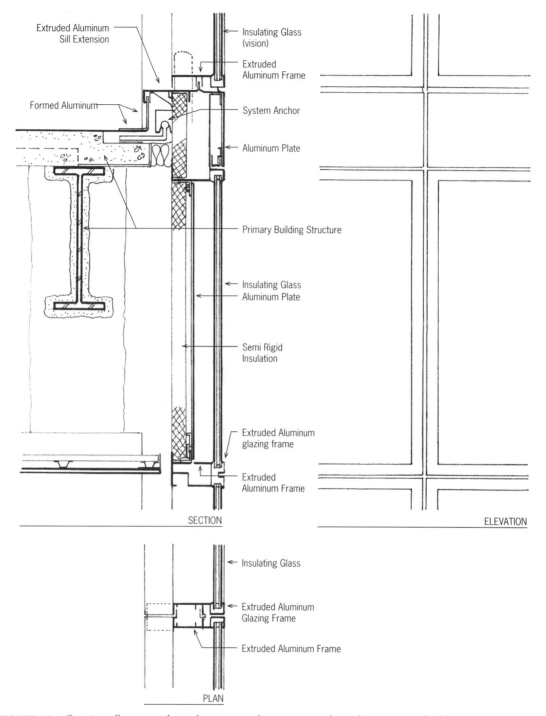

FIGURE 1.3 Curtain wall systems rely on the system anchor to support the enclosure system dead load. The glass and aluminum plate accommodates and transfers lateral loads to the extruded aluminum frame for the enclosure system structural integrity. The extruded aluminum frame carries the dead load of the glass and other infill or cladding materials, and transfers lateral loads to the system anchor, which transfers loads to the primary building structure.

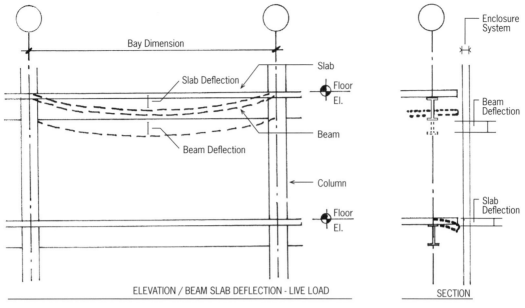

Bay Dimension

Slab Deflection

Slab

Floor
El.

Beam

Beam Deflection

Column

Floor
El.

ELEVATION / BEAM SLAB DEFLECTION - LIVE LOAD

Enclosure
System

Beam
Deflection

Slab
Deflection

SECTION

Note: Deflections are graphically
exaggerated for clarity

FIGURE 1.4   Primary building structural elements react to loads imposed. Imposed loads include dead loads and live loads that create structural deflections that must be addressed in the enclosure design. Note both deflections shown in elevation and section can occur simultaneously.

(dead load) and the location and magnitude of the applied loads. The material, size of the components, connections between components, and deflection direction and magnitude when subjected to applied loads must be addressed in the enclosure design. Enclosure structural components consist of framing, connections, infill, cladding and system anchorage. Enclosure system framing support elements are typically designed with stiffness as the primary criterion. The stiffness design criterion, which is stated in terms of deflection, varies depending on the infill or cladding material being supported, joinery size, system assembly, and other factors. Stiffness and deflection are usually defined as $X = L/number$. X is the deflection and is usually stated in inches (or fractions of an inch) or millimeters. L is the span length or distance between points of support or anchorage. This length is typically stated in inches or millimeters. The denominator "number" is dependent on the cladding or infill material being supported or the desired criterion established as the maximum bending (deflection) allowed. A higher denominator results in a

lower resulting deflection X. Industry standards and building codes are valuable sources to review for suggested allowable deflections. Simplified diagram examples of supporting framing elements, type of cladding, and the resulting deflections are shown in Figures 1.5a, 1.5b, 1.5c. Deflection criteria are dependent on the type of system. System deflection specifics are covered in more detail in the systems descriptions/case study sections. This is a point that was made clear in an early design studio critique between an architecture student and professor at a jury critique. The professor was reviewing a building section of the student's proposed design. An exterior enclosure wall was shown spanning from one floor to approximately four floors above and was drawn with two lines representing approximately 3 inches (76 mm) in system depth. The student, who, for the purposes of anonymity, will be referred to as Mr. Smith, was challenged by the professor's observation. "Mr. Smith, this wall looks to be about 60 feet (18.28 m) tall and is illustrated as very thin. Looks to be—ummm—3 inches (76 mm) deep or so." The

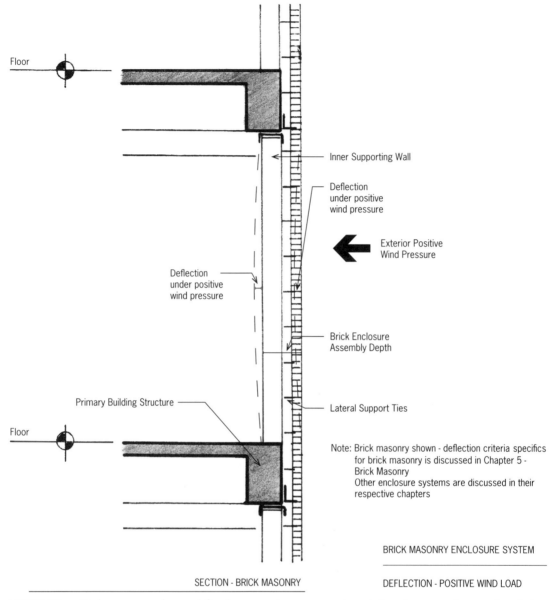

Floor

Inner Supporting Wall

Deflection under positive wind pressure

Exterior Positive Wind Pressure

Deflection under positive wind pressure

Brick Enclosure Assembly Depth

Primary Building Structure

Floor

Lateral Support Ties

Note: Brick masonry shown - deflection criteria specifics for brick masonry is discussed in Chapter 5 - Brick Masonry
Other enclosure systems are discussed in their respective chapters

BRICK MASONRY ENCLOSURE SYSTEM

SECTION - BRICK MASONRY

DEFLECTION - POSITIVE WIND LOAD

FIGURE 1.5a Brick masonry enclosures deflect between primary support boundaries when exposed to exterior wind pressure loads.

professor paused for a moment and then stated: "It must be made of the revolutionary new material called 'Smithite,' which can span infinite distances in minimal thickness." The professor then moved on to the next critique. The point that any system requires a certain depth to span ratio—however blunt and brutal in its delivery—was made.

WEATHERTIGHTNESS

The exterior building enclosure system is the enclosing membrane separating the exterior elements and forces from the interior spaces and occupants, and is required to be weathertight. For purposes of defining weathertightness, air and water are considered here. Sunlight,

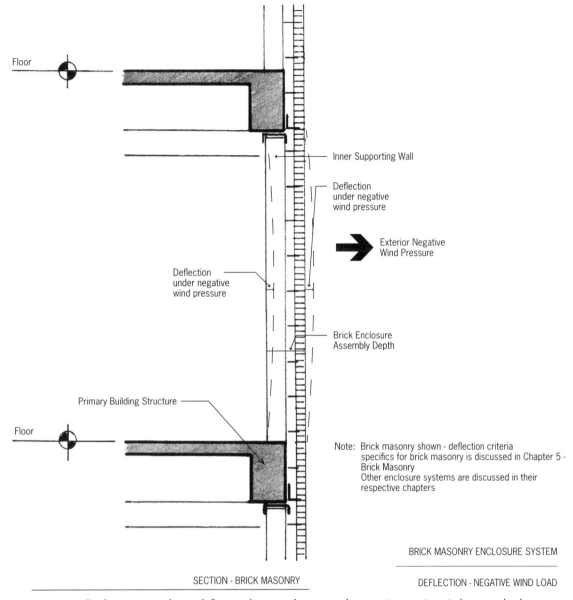

Floor

Inner Supporting Wall

Deflection
under negative
wind pressure

Exterior Negative
Wind Pressure

Deflection
under negative
wind pressure

Brick Enclosure
Assembly Depth

Primary Building Structure

Floor

Note: Brick masonry shown - deflection criteria
specifics for brick masonry is discussed in Chapter 5 -
Brick Masonry
Other enclosure systems are discussed in their
respective chapters

BRICK MASONRY ENCLOSURE SYSTEM

SECTION - BRICK MASONRY

DEFLECTION - NEGATIVE WIND LOAD

FIGURE 1.5b Brick masonry enclosure deflection diagram when exposed to negative exterior wind pressure loads.

temperature, wind, and other forces influence weathertightness. These are discussed in the energy efficiency section. To achieve a weathertight building enclosure, water intrusion and air filtration must be controlled. Water must be managed and discharged to the exterior without penetration of water to the interior occupied spaces or to portions of the enclosure designed as dry, allowing the enclosure system to dry after the source of the water is removed. Excessive air infiltration must also be prevented. Weathertightness is the enclosure's ability to protect against air infiltration within prescribed limits and to prevent water leakage. Air and water act together, so both must be considered together in weathertight enclosure design. Weathertightness is a

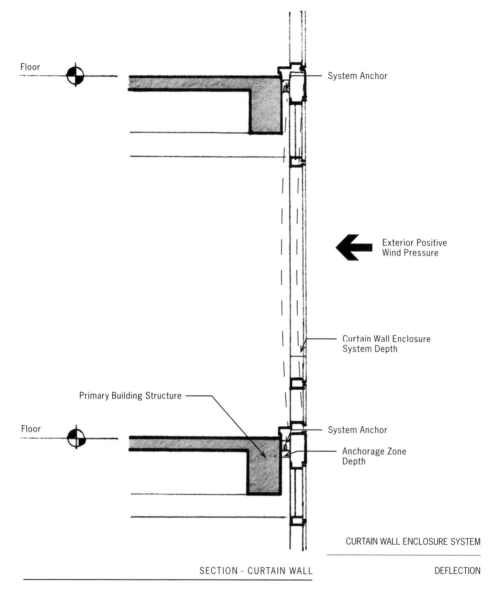

Floor

System Anchor

Exterior Positive
Wind Pressure

Curtain Wall Enclosure
System Depth

Primary Building Structure

Floor

System Anchor

Anchorage Zone
Depth

CURTAIN WALL ENCLOSURE SYSTEM

SECTION - CURTAIN WALL

DEFLECTION

FIGURE 1.5c Curtain wall systems utilize the infill and/or cladding materials and the system framing material and depth to accommodate and transfer wind loads to the system anchor. The system anchor transfers loads to the primary building structure. Negative wind pressure creates deflection in the opposite direction. Note infill materials also deflect when subjected to lateral loads.

function whose importance is obvious, but the methods to actually achieve a weathertight enclosure are often not fully understood or thoroughly tracked through the building enclosure system(s) design and associated graphic details. Graphic details must define

materials and connections of materials, therefore defining layers to control and manage air and water.

Enclosure system materials and the associated joinery within and between materials greatly influence how a weathertight enclosure is achieved and maintained.

Enclosure system materials and components—framing and infill—are inherently either weatherproof or porous. Materials such as glass and metal are impervious to air and water penetration, so when one is designing with these materials, the focus is on the joinery method, location of the joinery within the system, and the type of joinery materials used when one material or one system meets another. Materials such as concrete, masonry, wood, and stone have levels of porosity. When these materials are present in the enclosure design, additional material(s) must be incorporated in conjunction with these cladding materials. Either porous materials must allow storage of water, which can be released to the exterior after the water source is removed, or the enclosure system must contain a combination of water impervious flashings, gutters, and drainage openings to control and discharge water to the exterior when these materials are present.

Local climate and geography can greatly influence the action and effect of air and water on the exterior enclosure. It is easier to observe when an exterior enclosure system is not watertight than when there is air leakage. Obvious evidence of water such as leaks or moisture in the form of condensation can be visually detected in accessible areas. Water or moisture that occurs in nonaccessible areas often results in significant damage. Air infiltration and exfiltration—also known as leakage in and out—is a little more difficult to observe. The intended function of the exterior enclosure is to control the water and to eliminate or minimize the air infiltration to the interior to an acceptable level. This is a bit more challenging to observe and quantify. Water control is achieved by either keeping water to the exterior or controlling the water through layers in the enclosure and removing it to the exterior, allowing drying. Where air goes, water generally follows and can be observed.

To achieve a weathertight building enclosure design approach, it is best to establish a primary line of defense against air whose location is defined within the enclosure system, preventing air leakage. This primary air line is often the primary water protection line as well. Water can be controlled using multiple layers to reduce the quantity of water reaching each succeeding layer. Air, on the other hand, cannot be diminished or reduced in quantity using the multiple layer approach, as it follows the water path until it reaches the primary air line and stops. So the design of the primary air line is imperative and key.

You can't fool Mother Nature. You also can't beat Mother Nature. However, if you understand the functional need to provide a weathertight enclosure system, and the basics of what moves air and water from one place to another, you can control these elements and peacefully coexist with Mother Nature. The forces that move the elements of air and water and the design principles that provide the primary and secondary lines of control are discussed later in this chapter.

ENERGY EFFICIENCY

Enclosures consist of opaque (spandrels, column covers, etc.) and transparent (vision glass with or without frames) areas. No matter the style, composition, or specific cladding material, the basics are opaque and transparent areas. Transparent areas allow views in and out and admit natural daylight into interior spaces. An energy-efficient exterior building enclosure entails admitting natural light in vision areas, while minimizing the heat gain or heat loss and maximizing insulation values in the opaque areas to control temperature and condensation. Energy efficiency in the enclosure is also influenced by minimizing air leakage, because energy is required to heat or cool interior air. The goal is to maximize energy efficiency and occupant comfort. There are several "big picture" considerations and resulting analyses that inform the design and the functional requirements of an energy-efficient enclosure. These are:

1. Local climate and geography
2. Building shape and orientation
3. Material selections, quantity, and placement

Local Climate and Geography

Architects must understand (or in some cases be reeducated about) and interpret the natural characteristics of the micro and macro climates of the region and local site in which a building and its exterior building enclosure are being designed. Some architects work locally and regionally. Some projects are far removed from the daily environment of the architect. When the architect is designing in a location where he or she is a visitor or invited guest, it is essential to achieve an understanding of the natural and man-made environment in which each building is designed. Time must be spent on-site obtaining the "feel" for the climate. This can be accomplished on two levels. First, appropriate and sometimes exhaustive research should be made into daily and seasonal weather patterns. Second, physically visit the site and experience firsthand the heat, cold, humidity, sunlight, and breezes. First-hand experience is invaluable. When designing an exterior building enclosure "in your own backyard" (i.e., a location with which the architect is familiar), weather patterns and the natural environment are known through personal experiences.

There is reliable empirical climate data to evaluate seasonal variations in solar, temperature and diurnal temperature variations, humidity, and air movement/wind that can be obtained through dependable sources. There is no substitute for experiencing and breathing the local environment and microclimate effects of sun, wind, temperature, shade, water, and topography. Excellent lessons can be learned by studying indigenous

architecture and buildings. Air travel has reduced the size of our planet by making travel easy. Local building customs, materials, massing, and orientation evolved as a result of the local inhabitants' intimate knowledge of and responses to the local environment. Indigenous architecture provides valuable clues, lessons, and real-life solutions to practical exterior building enclosure concepts and systems that have provided shelter for generations. These can be interpreted into a new building enclosure design vocabulary in multiple and often innovative ways. The moral is: Learn from the past.

Local climate is the prevailing weather conditions of a region. These include temperature, humidity, precipitation, sunshine, clouds, and wind throughout the year, averaged over a series of years. Geography will influence climate conditions of regions into microclimates. Temperature is arguably the most recognized and easily understood. Regional climate maps divided by temperature-oriented climate zones are available through the International Energy Conservation Code (IECC), ASHRAE, US Department of Energy, and others. An example of a climate map for the continental United States is shown in Figure 1.6.

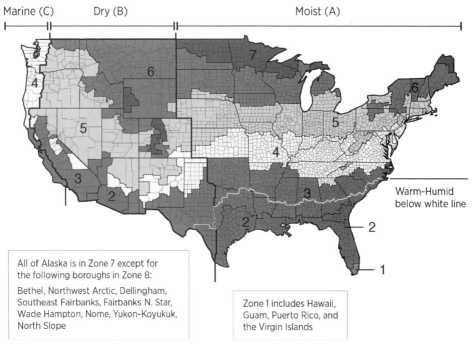

FIGURE 1.6 ASHRAE climate zone map. Climate maps outline performance basics per region. A continental U.S. example is shown.

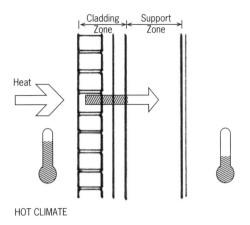

HOT CLIMATE

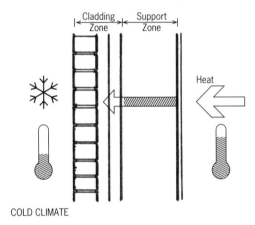

COLD CLIMATE

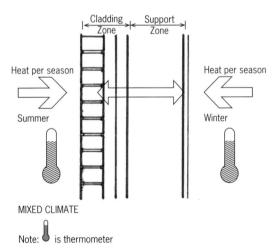

MIXED CLIMATE

Note: ⬤ is thermometer

FIGURE 1.7 Enclosure heat flow profile. Heat flows from hot to cold. Climate and interior design conditions determine heat flow direction through the enclosure.

Following basic physics, heat transfer moves from hot (or warm) to cold. Moisture also moves from hot to cold. Moisture also moves from more to less. Therefore, in colder climates where interior heating is predominant, moisture will move from the building interior toward the exterior. Conversely, in hot climates and hot/humid climates, moisture moves from the exterior towards the interior. In mixed climates with hot and/or hot/humid seasons and cold seasons, the flow of heat and moisture moves out-to-in or in-to-out, depending on the exterior climate seasonal conditions and interior space conditions. This recognition of climate and the resulting thermal, air, and moisture physics determines design locations for air and water defense lines, discussed earlier, and drying areas within the enclosure system. Example diagrams are shown in Figure 1.7.

Building Shape and Orientation

Building shape and orientation have a direct impact on the energy efficiency of the exterior enclosure. Shape and orientation also influence an appropriate ratio of transparent area to opaque insulated area. Thoughtful and informed orientation can maximize opportunities for innovative exterior building enclosures to respond to and coexist with the natural climate and environment. This is a basic premise of passive energy efficient design. Farmers and others who rely on the land and on nature for their existence refer to this type of design as common sense. Building orientation can maximize passive solar heating when needed and avoid or minimize heat gain when cooling is needed. It can also provide opportunities for natural ventilation and daylighting throughout most of the year by utilizing and maximizing the characteristics of the local climate.

Appropriate building orientation is geographic and site specific. Most architects recognize that southern exposure is a key physical orientation option for passive solar energy design strategies in the northern hemisphere. Building orientation in the northern and southern hemispheres has different "rules of the game," as indicated in Figures 1.8a–d. Site-specific features such as topography, trees, bodies of water, breezes, and other local factors create site-specific design opportunities. Building shape and orientation influence the type and quantity of vision glass area, type and thickness of insulation required in opaque areas, and opportunities

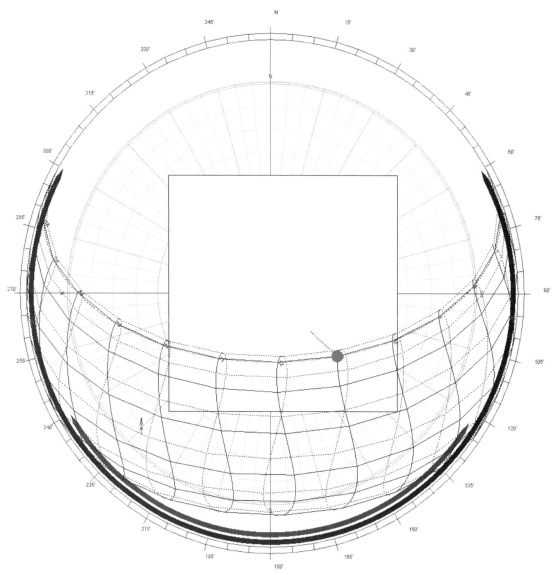

FIGURE 1.8a Solar path is three dimensional (altitude [vertical] and azimuth [plan]) and provides enclosure design information and opportunities through understanding sun angles during the year. Example shown is for San Francisco, California, in the northern hemisphere at 37.775 degrees North Latitude.

for overhangs, sunshades, wind deflectors/baffles, or other solar/daylight control or mitigating devices, as well as solar and/or wind generation design options.

Material Selection, Quantity, and Placement

Each material in the enclosure assembly design has its own specific qualities as an insulator or a conductor for thermal transfer. Research is required for every enclosure design in order to understand the performance characteristics of building materials. There are several basic units of measure used to define a material's thermal qualities. These are: R-value, U-value, solar heat gain coefficient, and visible transmittance.

R-value is a measure of the thermal resistance of building materials (resistance as R) to the flow of heat

Exterior Building Enclosures

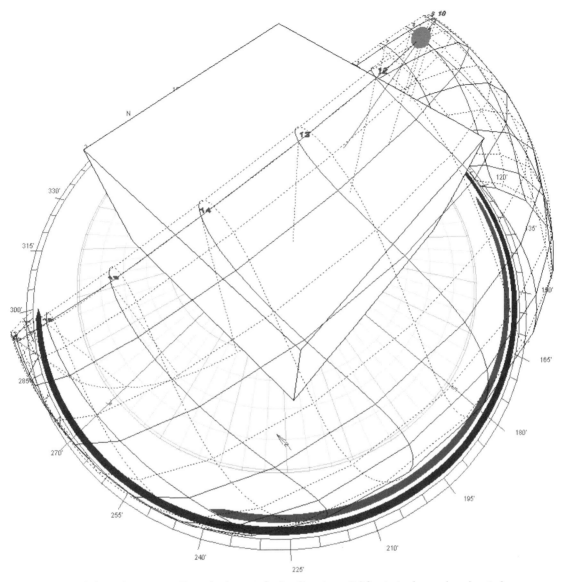

FIGURE 1.8b Solar path isometric. Example shown is for San Francisco, California, in the northern hemisphere.

and cold. The higher the R-value, the better the material is as an insulator. R-values for materials in the United States are typically provided in R-value per inch. To establish the overall R-value of an exterior building enclosure system, add together the R-values of each of the materials within the enclosure system. The determination of a total R-value for an exterior enclosure is typically performed using a steady state calculation. Temperature and exterior climate are not consistent (steady); however, this calculation is an essential basic first step in exterior design. An example of a total R-value for an enclosure system is illustrated in Figure 1.9. This is a very straightforward example. Each material shown remains in the same plane and location in the enclosure assembly. The R-value can be easily calculated and increased by increasing the

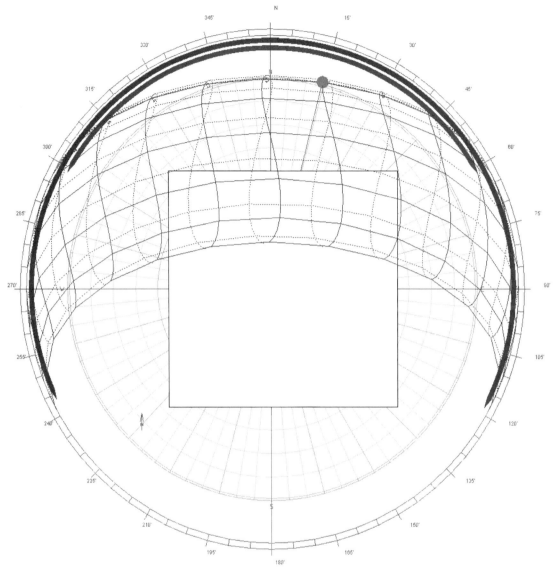

FIGURE 1.8c   Solar path for Sydney, Australia, in the southern hemisphere at 33.868 South Latitude..

thickness of insulation. Additional interior layers can be added—carefully—to increase the R-value. Beware of potential thermal weak links at primary building structure locations. It is important to consider and remember that in some cases the cross section of an enclosure may not consist of the same thickness of materials across the entire enclosure. This is an instance where three-dimensional design thinking must be applied. It is best when insulation is continuous and—depending on climate—often toward the exterior of the primary air and water line. Insulation location in the enclosure assembly is also climate based. However, there are designs where the insulation is contained between framing members such as studs, framing supports, or similar elements. When this occurs, care must be exercised in mitigating or preventing thermal breaches or "bridges" by continuing the insulation material. Insulation should be wrapped

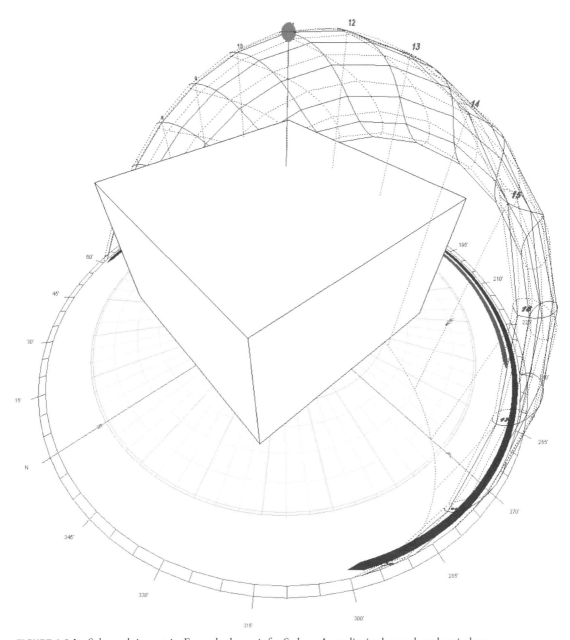

FIGURE 1.8d Solar path isometric. Example shown is for Sydney, Australia, in the southern hemisphere.

either behind or in front of the framing. Design and construction of enclosure systems where the insulation is contained between framing members will result in a reduction of the overall R-value because of thermal discontinuities between framing members.

U-value, or U-factor, is the inverse of the R-value, $U = 1/R$. In the U.S., this is expressed in units of BTU/(h°F ft²). It is different in Europe and other parts of the world where Kelvin temperature is used in lieu of Fahrenheit, and metric measurements in lieu of imperial. The U-factor is the overall heat transfer coefficient in a nonsolar (i.e. exterior and interior temperatures) condition. The U-factor defines how well the material functions as a conductor. U-values are

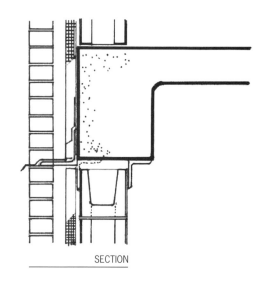

SECTION

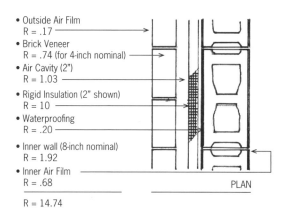

- Outside Air Film
  R = .17
- Brick Veneer
  R = .74 (for 4-inch nominal)
- Air Cavity (2")
  R = 1.03
- Rigid Insulation (2" shown)
  R = 10
- Waterproofing
  R = .20
- Inner wall (8-inch nominal)
  R = 1.92
- Inner Air Film
  R = .68

R = 14.74

PLAN

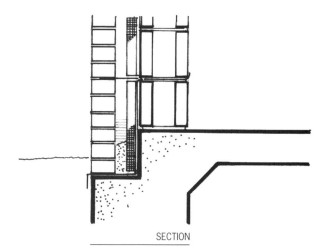

SECTION

FIGURE 1.9 Overall thermal resistance (R-value) is defined by the composite of the enclosure component material R-values.

Exterior Building Enclosures

often provided in lieu of R-values for glass and metals. Glass infill is not a very good insulator compared with insulation materials in insulated opaque areas. So when using glass, use high-performance glass appropriately. U-factors indicate the rate of heat flow due to conduction, convection, and radiation resulting from temperature differences between the exterior and interior.

For transparent materials such as glass, the solar heat gain coefficient (SHGC) measures how glass blocks heat generated by sunlight from entering through transparent glazed portions of a building enclosure. Stated in a slightly different way, the SHGC is the fraction of solar radiation from sunlight that passes through the glass and becomes heat inside the building. SHGC is expressed as a number between 0 and 1. The lower the SHGC number, the less solar heat the glass transmits. The less the solar heat gain in a hot climate, the smaller the cooling system. The smaller the cooling system, the less energy is consumed. There may be design opportunities where heat gain is desired, so the reverse application may apply. Glass and glass framing (window frames) utilize both U-factors and SHGC numbers. Glass products have performance criteria established by the manufacturers after these products have been tested by accredited independent testing laboratories using standardized tests. The performance of glass assemblies has a direct influence on the quantity of glass that should be included in the enclosure design to achieve energy efficiency and the resulting size of the building mechanical system to compensate for the solar heat gain or heat loss.

Requirements to reduce energy consumption and provide increased energy conservation have been elevated over recent years and have a direct influence on glass and insulation material selection, quantity, and placement. Exterior enclosure designs are required to comply with requirements of local code jurisdictions. The International Energy Conservation Code (IECC) has been adopted by many local jurisdictions. Several states such as California have their own energy codes. Many states recently expanded their model codes to include specific energy codes. For commercial buildings there are two compliance methods to use to determine an acceptable extent of glass in the enclosure design. One is to utilize ASHRAE 90.1, and the other method is Design by Acceptable Practice. The latter is a prescriptive method that defines enclosure requirements for seventeen (17) climate zones

and designates percentages of allowable glass in four (4) fenestration area tables. Each method establishes a minimum standard which is sometimes referred to as "less bad". The challenge is how to efficiently make enclosures perform to high(er) energy goals.

Visible light transmittance (VLT) is the percentage of visible light that is transmitted through glass. The VLT is expressed as a number between 0 and 1. The higher the number, the more visible light is transmitted through the glass. Coupled with light transmittance is the solar heat gain coefficient (SHGC). Glass type, glass performance, quantity of glass, orientation of the glass, and the project's requirements for energy consumption and conservation are all early evaluation factors in building enclosure design efforts.

Composing the design of the exterior building enclosure requires a balance of material selections, material location and the resulting R values, U factors, SHGC, and VLT selections will be discussed in the design process section in later chapters.

ACCOMMODATE SYSTEM MOVEMENT AND STRUCTURE MOVEMENT

The location and size of each material (framing or infill cladding) within the system have a direct effect on joinery, joinery materials, and joinery details. Details at material joinery within an enclosure system and systems interfaces are important. There are many opinions as to what constitutes a detail. A detail is defined as a condition where two or more materials come together. Joinery and movement are analogous to the chicken and egg—which comes first? Types and mechanics of movement influence joinery design. Joinery design accommodates certain types of movement and determines the type, size, and materials in the joint.

There is a quote from the film *The Wizard of Oz*: "It is always best to start at the beginning." Buildings are dynamic; they move. Exterior enclosure systems are dynamic; they move. Beginning with the primary building superstructure: Columns, beams, slabs, and the like, deflect, sway, and drift. Similar to the human body, the primary building superstructure is the bones, and the exterior building enclosure system is the skin. As the bones move, the skin reacts in kind. Discussions with a building's structural engineer can be enlightening and occasionally discouraging. Structural beams spanning between columns deflect when superimposed dead loads are applied. Dead loads are items that are physically attached to the superstructure, including superstructure self-weight, enclosure cladding, and so forth. Beams also deflect when live loads, such as occupants, are applied. The conventional engineering live load deflection standard for beam design is L (the span length) divided by 360. The formula is simple: $L/360$. For a beam supporting an exterior enclosure spanning $30'0''$ the resulting deflection would be: L ($30'0'' \times 12'' = 360''$)$/360 = 1''$. In an exterior enclosure that utilizes sealant in a horizontal joint to accept structural movement which has a maximum movement capacity for expansion and contraction of +/- 50%, the resulting correct joint size would be $2''$. This $2''$ dimension does not include the enclosure fabrication and installation tolerances, which will increase the joint size slightly. Imagine the joint size, following the $L/360$ approach for beams that span longer dimensions such as $40'0''$ to $50'0''$ and the resulting joinery. A diagram of structural beam deflection parallel to the enclosure is shown in Figure 1.10. Examples of joinery design by enclosure systems are discussed in the enclosure systems/case study chapters.

There are several approaches to joinery design utilizing joinery materials between enclosure materials. The use of sealant materials in the joints is one. Another approach in movement joint design utilizes concealed gaskets. This approach results in an open joint appearance (no sealant, since the gaskets are often integral to the system, accommodating the movement and providing weathertightness capability). This allows the movement in a smaller exterior visual joint size than the sealant approach. However, the concealed gasket assembly will occur either above or below the joint and does have an influence on the supporting profile size when viewed in section. An example of a sealant joint and gasketed joint is shown in Figure 1.11. Often in discussion with a structural engineer, tighter deflection limits can be established to "tune" the structure and the joinery sizes to comply with the visual and performance design requirements. Similar structural movements apply to structural slabs for horizontal joinery design.

Wind loads are applied to a building, resulting in sway or "drift" in the primary structure. This is typically expressed as the displacement of one floor in relation to the next floor above or below. Columns deflect and impart movement to vertical and horizontal joinery. A diagram example of building drift due to wind is shown in Figure 1.12. Seismic movement also creates building drift, and, depending on the primary structural system design, earthquake magnitude and building height can impose significant drift values from floor to floor. This is illustrated in the seismic force section of this chapter. The enclosure system (the skin) must be designed to accommodate the movement of the building structural frame (the bones).

Moving outward from the primary building structural system, the exterior building enclosure system itself is dynamic when forces act on the enclosure. A variety of forces including temperature and sunlight, discussed later in this chapter, influence the functions and size of the joinery. Wind forces acting on an enclosure will create deflections perpendicular to the plane of the enclosure on both horizontal and vertical cladding infill and supporting elements. The extent of deflections and the location of the movement will influence the type and size of joinery. Temperature variations and changes will create expansion or contraction. Each material has its own inherent expansion/contraction properties. For example, metals exhibit higher coefficients of expansion than masonry. The common denominator is that all materials expand and contract, which contribute to joinery design considerations. The greater the temperature change, and the larger the size or length of material, the greater the movement will be, and the larger the required joint size to accommodate the thermal expansion or contraction. It is also important to note that movement due to thermal changes occurs vertically and horizontally.

Movement not recognized and accommodated in enclosure design by properly located, sized, and designed joinery results in stresses that have to go somewhere other than the joint. Stresses that are not relieved through joinery create increased stresses within the enclosure materials themselves. When this occurs, material bending or buckling may, and usually does, occur. Imparting undesired stresses into cladding, infill and framing elements is not advisable in exterior enclosure design.

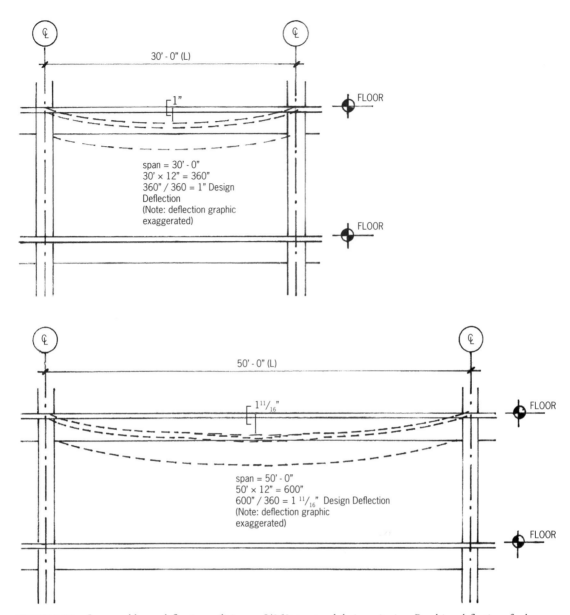

FIGURE 1.10 Structural beam deflection utilizing an *L*/360 structural design criterion. Resulting deflections for longer spans require larger enclosure joinery or enhanced specific structural design criteria to reduce beam deflections.

The movement acting on the exterior enclosure by the structural system and exterior forces varies for every project. However, both types do occur in every exterior building enclosure. The important fact is that these movements will occur. Once identified, the extent, location, and quantity of movement can be defined and established. Once movement is quantified, movement joinery can be sized for the location in the system joinery. Once location is established, the appropriate type of joinery design and materials can be applied to the enclosure design.

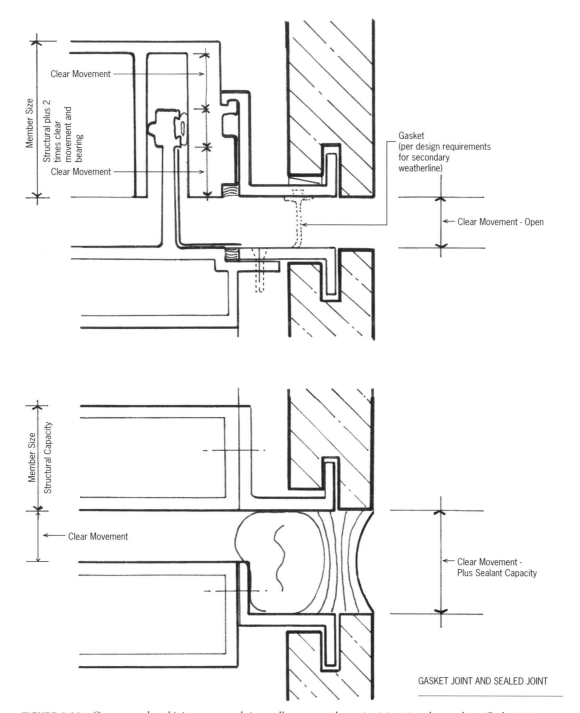

FIGURE 1.11 Open or gasketed joints may result in smaller expressed exterior joint sizes than sealant. Gasket joinery systems often require a larger amount of space in concealed areas to accommodate the concealed gasket components.

Exterior Building Enclosures

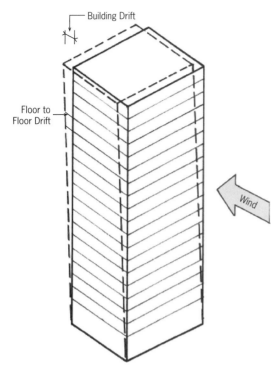

Building Drift

Floor to
Floor Drift

Wind

FIGURE 1.12 Lateral wind forces create building drift. Drift per floor influences enclosure design items such as materials, materials size, shape, joinery, and other issues.

Elements and Forces on the Exterior Enclosure

Prior to beginning enclosure schematic design, and definitely before the more detailed design development effort, there must be an assessment and evaluation of the natural elements (air, water, and sun) discussed earlier, natural forces, and human-created forces that will act on the enclosure. With a fundamental understanding of the forces and their magnitude, design methodologies and performance design principles can be applied and integrated into the enclosure system design, to achieve the necessary performance.

Newton's third law of motion is: "To every action there is always an equal and opposite reaction." An enclosure system design needs to accommodate each and every force: the action. This accommodation and response is the equal and opposite reaction. Forces are identified in two groups:

1. Exterior forces
2. Interior forces

Natural exterior elements and their associated forces include wind, precipitation, air, temperature, sunlight, gravity, and seismic force. These can be studied and examined independently; however, multiple elements and forces usually act concurrently on the enclosure. For the majority of building types, natural forces are applicable in the design of the exterior enclosure. In specialized building types, higher force levels or other additional human-made forces create more case-specific design parameters. Human-created exterior forces and conditions include noise, forced entry, ballistic impact, explosive blasts, and built surroundings that must be addressed in the enclosure design.

There are interior forces that influence the enclosure design. These interior forces include primary building structural system movement created by live loads, dead loads, column shortening, and wind or seismic drift; temperature control requirements; humidity control requirements; and noise.

Many papers and publications have used the analogy of a selective filter to describe the exterior building enclosure. This is an interesting conceptual abstract. Most architects have difficulty translating this to reality. The exterior enclosure is a selective filter used to moderate conditions between the exterior and the interior environments. The enclosure as selective filter provides a barrier to some elements and forces or allows passage of others. The enclosure must be a barrier to air, water in its multiple states, and unauthorized people, and it must be a selective filter for light, temperature, and air. The filter serves the multiple functions of (1) withstanding the exterior forces of nature and human beings, (2) controlling and filtering the inward and outward flow of heat, cold, water, air, light, and sound, and (3) providing a weathertight and safe enclosure that protects the building occupants and the enclosure itself.

The matrix presented in Figure 1.13 identifies natural and human-created forces along one axis, and design requirements along the other axis. Forces that influence design as a primary consideration are indicated by the symbol "P" in the matrix. Forces that influence enclosure design as a secondary

EXTERIOR ELEMENTS AND FORCES

DESIGN	NATURAL							NATURAL & HUMAN		HUMAN CREATED
	WIND	PRECIPITATION (INCL HUMIDITY)	AIR INFILTRATION	TEMPERATURE	SUNLIGHT	SEISMIC	GRAVITY	NOISE	BLAST	BALLISTIC
STRUCTURAL	P	S	S	S	-	P	P	S	P	P
WEATHERTIGHTNESS	P	P	P	P	P	P	S	S	-	-
THERMAL COMFORT	S	P	P	P	P	S	-	S	-	-
MOVEMENT	P	P/S	P/S	P	P	P	P	-	S	S
LIGHT TRANSMISSION	-	-	-	P	P	-	-	-	S	S
ACCOUSTICS	S	S	S	S	S	-	-	P	S	S
SECURITY	-	-	-	S	S	-	-	-	P	P

P = Primary
S = Secondary
- = Not Applicable

FIGURE 1.13 The table identifies primary exterior elements and forces and their influence on the enclosure design. Note: Fire resistance is not shown, however, this is a primary enclosure design consideration. Specific building types and their enclosure design may involve other forces not illustrated here.

24

consideration are indicated by the symbol "S." Where forces have little or no influence, the symbol "-" is used.

Following are descriptions of the natural and human-created forces identified in Figure 1.13. Included with each force listing are some methods to define and determine the magnitude of the force and the resulting design performance criteria to address the force. The matrix illustrated is general. It should be fine-tuned specifically for the enclosure design opportunity.

FORCE TYPE: WIND

Wind is one of the primary exterior forces: it reacts on the exterior enclosure as a lateral load for vertical, horizontal, or sloping exterior enclosures. Wind forces significantly influence the structural design of the enclosure. Wind speed is expressed on the enclosure as a pressure. Cladding, infill materials, and framing members' sizes and thickness, as well as connections and anchorages, are determined by the maximum wind loads and the resulting pressures exerted on the enclosure. The primary goal is to transfer the lateral wind load pressures from the enclosure system through the enclosure system anchorage into the primary building superstructure. Wind creates positive and negative (suction) pressures. The shape and height of the building also influence the magnitude and location of the pressures. An example of a tall building with pressure contours is shown in Figure 1.14a, and with wind pressure contours converted to blocks of pressure areas in Figure 1.14b. An example of a building with an irregular floor plan and the resulting pressures is shown in Figure 1.15. Wind speeds result from climate and microclimate. These vary by region, topography, and surroundings. Wind forces must be determined for the maximum positive pressure and the maximum negative pressure to determine the higher—and therefore governing—design pressure value. In addition to the enclosure structure considerations; created by wind pressure, wind also drives water.

Defining Wind Speeds and Pressures

There are two primary methods to determine the wind speed and the resulting pressures on the exterior enclosure. These are (1) building code and related standards, and (2) wind tunnel testing.

Building Code and Related Standards

In the United States, the building code method utilizes a combination of the applicable building code used by the authority having jurisdiction (AHJ) and the American Society of Civil Engineers (ASCE) 7 Section 1609. These two documents determine the basic wind speed and the exposure category. For discussion purposes, the applicable building code will be the 2009 International Building Code (IBC). Each locale has its own applicable code. Which code or standard to follow should be determined early in the design. The basic wind speed is indicated in region maps in the building code. The basic wind speed is associated with annual probabilities and adjusted for wind gusts. There are some specifics and exceptions for special wind speed areas such as hurricane zones and mountains or gorges. These are determined by local jurisdictions on a local case-by-case basis. The basic wind speed is provided in MPH in the U.S. for the determination of the wind load on the structure and the enclosure. The wind directions have an exposure category assigned to reflect the characteristics of the ground surface irregularities upwind of the site. Natural topography, vegetation, and constructed features are factored into the surface roughness category. The building code method to determine exterior cladding pressures is a relatively simple procedure to calculate loads based on height, shape, and location. For buildings with irregular shapes, high rise, or other special conditions, a more project-specific wind tunnel test should be conducted.

Wind Tunnel Testing

Another method to determine wind speeds and the resulting pressures on the exterior enclosure is wind tunnel testing. In wind tunnel testing, a massing model is built, usually in acrylic, and is placed in a wind tunnel. The wind tunnel has a long tunnel section to model the upwind terrain. The model of the terrain is done in more detail closer to the building site. The wind tunnel air flow exhibits characteristics similar to the actual wind conditions over the terrain approaching the building. A scale model of the

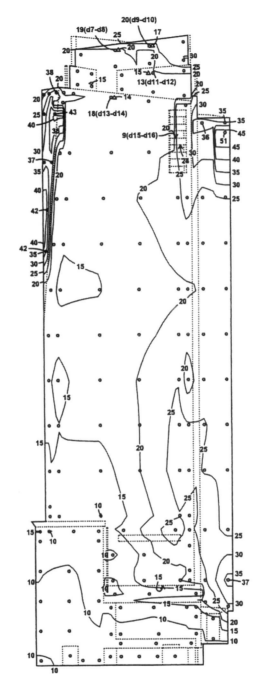

**PEAK NEGATIVE EXTERNAL
CLADDING PRESSURES (PSF)**

WEST ELEVATION

Local peak negative pressure distribution.

FIGURE 1.14a Building elevation with wind pressure contours (negative pressure shown). The building shown is the St. Regis Hotel and Residences in San Francisco, CA. *CPP Wind Engineering*

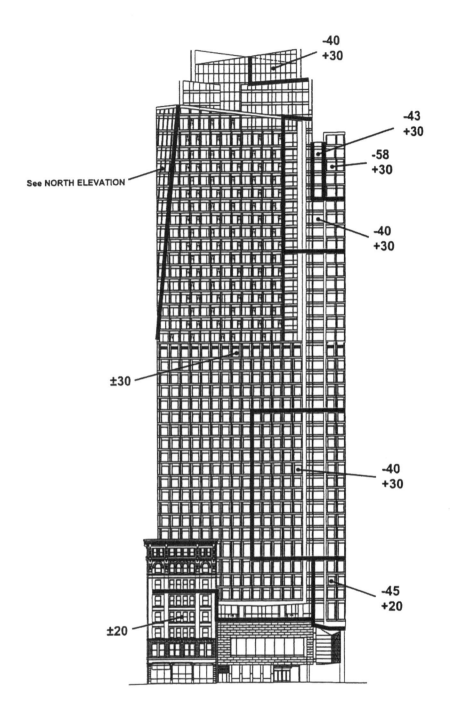

WEST ELEVATION

Peak cladding zones.

FIGURE 1.14b Building elevation with wind pressure contours converted to block pressure areas per elevation. *CPP Wind Engineering*

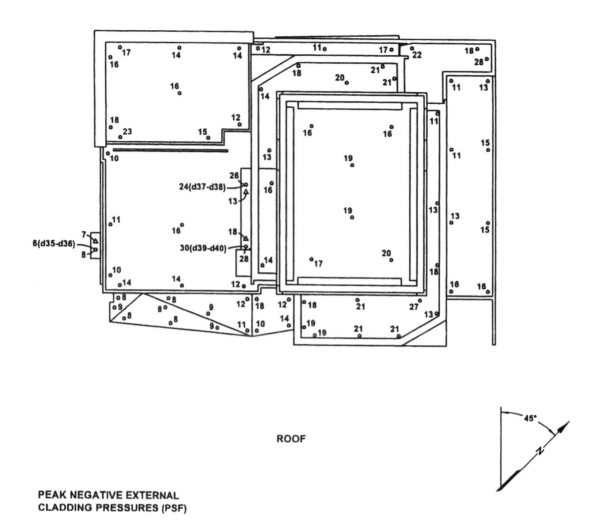

ROOF

45°

PEAK NEGATIVE EXTERNAL CLADDING PRESSURES (PSF)

Local peak negative pressure distribution.

FIGURE 1.15 Roof plan, shapes, height, and other features create project-case-specific wind pressures for horizontal enclosures and parapets. The wind tunnel plan shown is the St. Regis Hotel and Residences in San Francisco, CA. *CPP Wind Engineering*

proposed design is built with numerous holes, often referred to as "taps." The taps are connected by tubing to pressure transducers and record the pressure on the faces of the massing model. The model is placed in the wind tunnel and is rotated in increments of 10 degrees for a full 360 degrees where measurements are made at each increment of rotation. The scale building model with taps and the surrounding environment, including topography and other buildings, is tested using wind speeds and directions obtained from local weather sources. The recorded pressures are provided, with a report and graphics illustrating the tap locations and pressures. A photo of a high-rise project in the wind tunnel is shown in Figure 1.16.

The corresponding tap pressure results from this wind tunnel model and testing are shown in Figure 1.17. Wind pressure contours and pressure block diagrams are derived from the tap pressure readings.

The resulting wind pressure to be used in the design may be a single value for the exterior building enclosure. For larger buildings, the wind pressures may be identified in pressure zones. After identifying the singular pressure or multiple pressure zones and the location on the enclosure surfaces, determinations can be made regarding what pressure will be used for the design of the enclosure system(s). Enclosures can be designed to a selected pressure and strategically reinforced for higher pressures, referred to as "hot spots."

An additional design evaluation is the resulting drift of the primary building structure due to wind loads. The magnitude of drift is influenced by surface area, height of the building, and the type and stiffness of the primary building structure. Structural engineers provide the architect with the design drift to be used in the evaluation and design of the enclosure.

With definition and understanding of the wind pressure results, design performance criteria can be established for framing, infill, cladding, cladding attachments, system anchorage, and enclosure surface areas. Each enclosure system type has its own unique standards and criteria. Enclosure performance criteria to accommodate wind pressure loads are identified in the systems descriptions and associated case study chapters in this book.

Design Performance Criteria: Framing and Cladding Combined

The deflections of the framing members and enclosure plane must recognize the type of infill or cladding material (glass, metal, stone, brick, etc.) and the method of attachment and clearances required. The cladding materials, like the framing or supporting elements, also deflect under wind load, and the boundary conditions of the cladding infill at the framing members must be reviewed and designed together. Deflection criteria is dependent on the enclosure system and associated materials within the system.

FIGURE 1.16 Scale model of the St. Regis Hotel and Residences and surroundings in a wind tunnel. *CPP Wind Engineering*

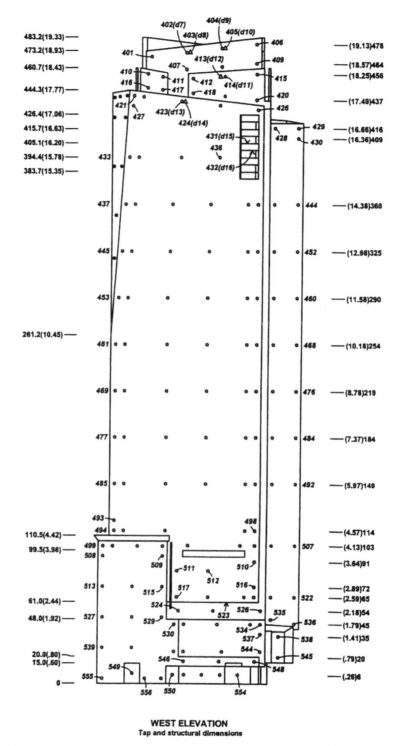

FIGURE 1.17 Building elevations with pressure "tap" locations and results. *CPP Wind Engineering*

Deflection performance criteria is discussed in chapters 5 through 9 for specific enclosure systems.

Design Performance Criteria: Wind Drift

Wind drift is the amount of sway, off-center, in a structure when subjected to the maximum wind pressure. This drift value is typically given in inches or fractions of inches per floor, and is determined by the structural engineer. It is important to evaluate the drift for typical floor-to-floor heights, and if there are taller atypical floors, consult the structural engineer for drift values on these floors as well.

The wind drift value per floor, the framing system, the infill or cladding attachment method, and the type of system anchorage connection of the enclosure to the primary building structure are factors in the system and joinery design. The drift value should be evaluated both parallel and perpendicular to the plane of the enclosure. Cladding or infill is generally considered to be rigid. Therefore, the attachment of the cladding or infill to the framing is typically evaluated as slipping in a pocket or rabbet (such as glass "captured" and glazed into a mullion frame) or fixed (such as glass that is adhered with structural silicone). Other cladding or infill materials have similar slip or fixed attachment conditions.

The framing components assembled as a framing system can be viewed as a rigid framing system or a deforming framing system. "Rigid" is defined as the framing configuration remaining in its original shape under loading. "Deforming" is defined as either the framing members bending or the connectors allowing movement, both of which allow the framing configuration to change to a shape other than the original. A rigid framing system is used where cladding or infill is fixed. A deforming framing system is used where cladding or infill is attached in a captured method, allowing cladding or infill to move within a frame or at a cladding connection without damage. System anchorage connections of the framing to the structure should be designed and specified to accommodate movement both parallel to the plane of the enclosure and perpendicular to the plane of the enclosure. For a rigid frame, the connections should allow for tipping or sliding parallel to the plane and rotation or

stairstepping perpendicular to the plane. The drift of the primary building structure frame parallel and perpendicular to the enclosure plane is illustrated in Figure 1.18a. An enclosure movement diagram of a rigid frame is superimposed on the structural drift. This is illustrated in Figures 1.18b and 1.18c. In deforming frames, the movement parallel to the plane of the enclosure results in the frames deforming to a parallelogram or other shape without damage to the cladding or infill. Deforming frames are illustrated in Figure 1.19.

Drift perpendicular to the enclosure results in system rotation perpendicular to the plane. The enclosure tips or leans inward or outward in relationship to the gravity and lateral system connection locations. Each method has its own design and detail implications at typical conditions and at inside and outside corners. Examples of outside-corner diagrams are shown in Figure 1.20. Inside-corner frame movement conditions are similar. These diagrams are illustrated to a conceptual level. Drift movements are discussed in detail by enclosure system in the systems/case study chapters 5 through 9.

ELEMENT AND FORCE TYPE: PRECIPITATION/WATER

Precipitation, in the form of rain, snow, sleet, hail, and humidity, is various states of water, and water must be managed in the exterior enclosure. The term "managed" is key. Water management includes water penetration and discharge. As noted earlier, most forces act concurrently. Water in the absence of other forces is influenced by gravity. When water contacts an exterior enclosure, it will follow the influence of gravity and flow in a downward direction. Water combined with the force of wind will flow in multiple directions, even upwards. Water can also be moved by surface tension and capillary action across surfaces and joints. Water can be moved by pressure differences, air movements, and kinetic energy. A diagram illustrating methods of water movement and transfer is shown in Figure 1.21.

Water combined with the wind forces previously described can enter very small openings. Establishing a design and the resulting detail methodology to prevent water migration through the exterior enclosure

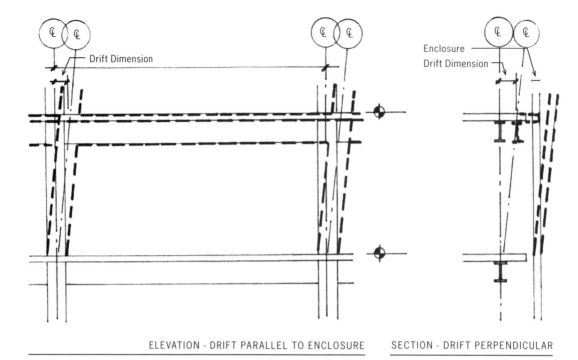

ELEVATION - DRIFT PARALLEL TO ENCLOSURE   SECTION - DRIFT PERPENDICULAR

FIGURE 1.18a The primary building structure displaces, or "drifts," under lateral loads. These drifts are defined as wind or seismic induced. The primary building structure "leans" parallel and perpendicular to the enclosure. Seismic drift creates similar and often more significant drift, depending on the floor-to-floor height, building height, and structural system.

to the building interior can be accomplished in a variety of ways. Again, it is important to first understand the fundamentals of the forces in order to select the most appropriate design solution. For water to enter an enclosure, three conditions must be present. These are: (1) a water source, (2) an opening, and (3) some type of force to move the water through the opening. All three must be present. If any one of the three is removed, there can be no transfer of water through an enclosure.

One approach is to design an impervious enclosure to keep the water completely to the exterior. This theory means exterior and interior are completely separated. Another approach reduces water quantity through multiple layers in the enclosure. The layers reduce water quantity; reduce the pressure differ-

ences between the enclosure and interior; allow storage, then drainage; and allow drying. This is the concept of water management.

Defining Water (Rain) Quantities and Directions

Historical weather data can be obtained through a number of sources and agencies. Some of these are: NASA, EnergyPlus, the U.S. Department of Energy, and the National Oceanic and Atmospheric Administration (NOAA) National Weather Service. There are many other available sources. The primary objective is to ascertain weather trends and patterns. Local meteorological data are compiled at airports and are available with historical

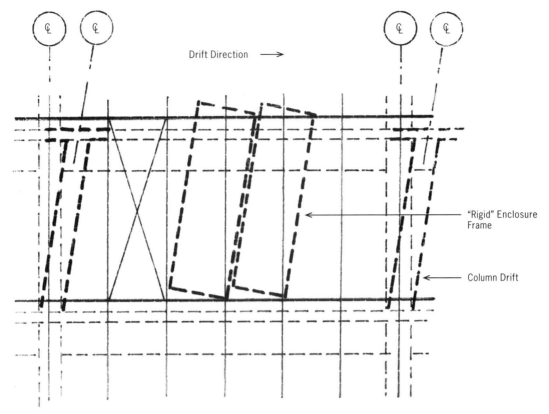

Drift Direction →

"Rigid" Enclosure Frame

Column Drift

FIGURE 1.18b A drift diagram of a curtain wall with the fixed infill creating a rigid frame. The movement shown is a "tipping" enclosure condition parallel to the enclosure plane.

background to establish reliable local weather patterns relating to the regional climate or microclimate of the area. In addition to annual rainfall, or depending on the location, other important design parameters are snow amounts, the quantity of rainfall in a one-hour time frame, and daily amounts of precipitation.

No matter the climate, water in some form or quantity will be present. In most, if not all, enclosure designs, there will be openings. The openings may be windows or joints between cladding or infill materials. In either case, both create potential openings for water penetration and leakage. As stated earlier, three

items are required for water to enter through an enclosure. Since water will be present and openings will occur, the last item that can be evaluated in the design is how to remove the force that drives water or how to disassociate or decouple the water and the transportation force. This will be reviewed in the "Design Principles" section of this chapter. Enclosures are designed with either water-impermeable (glass, metals, etc.) or permeable (stone, concrete, brick, etc.) exterior cladding. Methods to control and manage water depending on the type of enclosure material and system are reviewed in the systems/case study chapters 5 through 9.

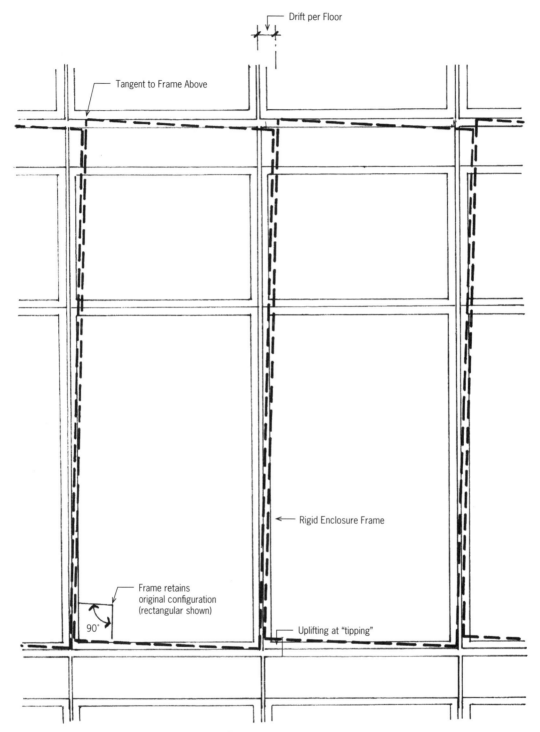

Drift per Floor

Tangent to Frame Above

Rigid Enclosure Frame

Frame retains
original configuration
(rectangular shown)

90°

Uplifting at "tipping"

FIGURE 1.18c   An enlarged view of a unitized curtain wall with the cladding infill in a rigid frame. The structural frame drift is parallel to the enclosure plane. The horizontal enclosure at the perimeter mullion frame-to-frame is sized so the frames do not touch when one floor is displaced in relation to the adjacent floor.

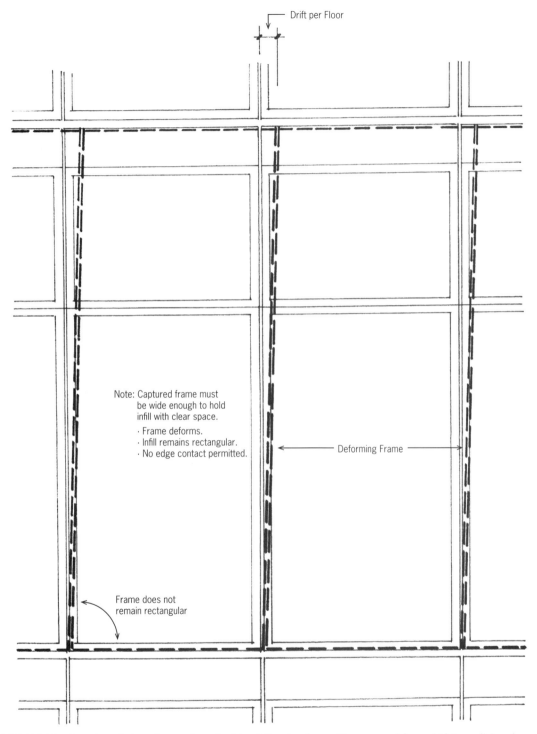

FIGURE 1.19 An enlarged view of a curtain wall with a deforming frame. The structural frame drift is parallel to the enclosure plane. The frame must be wide enough to prevent contact of the glass infill inside the captured glazing pocket, to avoid creating damage to the glass.

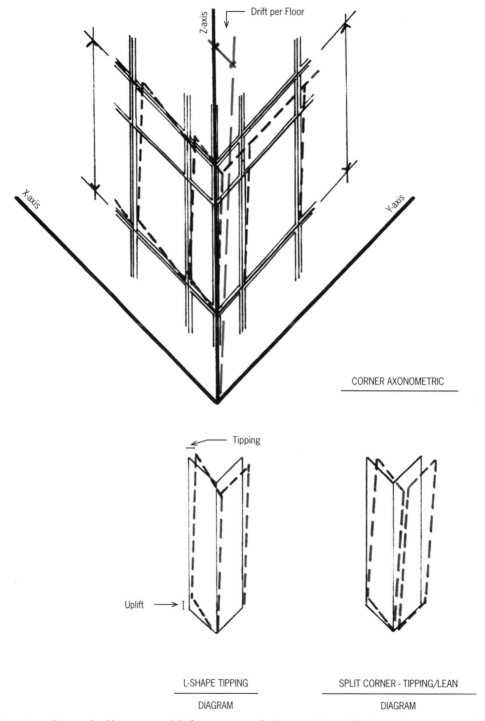

Drift per Floor

Z-axis

X-axis

Y-axis

CORNER AXONOMETRIC

Tipping

Uplift → I

L-SHAPE TIPPING

DIAGRAM

SPLIT CORNER - TIPPING/LEAN

DIAGRAM

FIGURE 1.20 Primary building structural drift requires specific design and details for the enclosure corners. The diagram illustrates two options. The L-shaped corner tips and leans like an open book tipping on its binding. The "split" corner allows slipping at the corner seam when tipping on one side and leaning on the adjacent side. There are other methods to accommodate drift at corners.

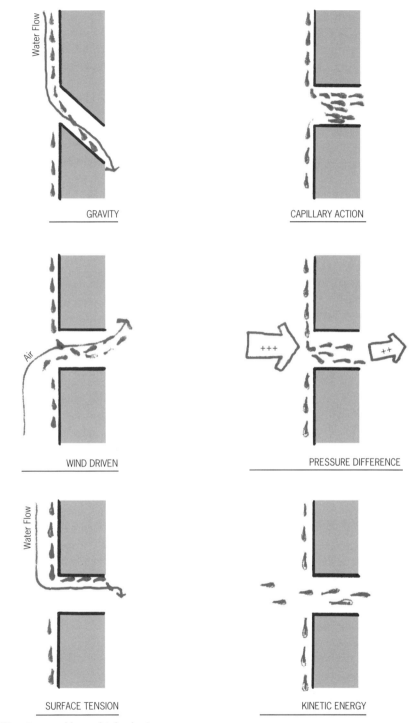

FIGURE 1.21 Water is moved by multiple physics.

ELEMENT TYPE: AIR, FORCE TYPE: INFILTRATION AND EXFILTRATION

Air infiltration and exfiltration are forces created by pressures resulting from the exterior wind pressure, stack effect, and the project's mechanical system. These may act independently, but they usually act in combination. Air movement and the enclosure's ability to be a barrier to air transfer from exterior to interior are interrelated with water control. Air contains water, and to keep the water out you need to keep the air out.

Air moves from higher pressure to lower pressure. If there is a pressure difference, air will move, carrying water in the process. Pressure-equalization is the principle of reducing air/wind pressure on the weatherproofing components of the enclosure, which is explained in more detail later in this chapter. This works to reduce the amount of water and the air/wind pressure, but not the quantity of air. Enclosures are designed with air barriers in a variety of ways. The air barrier must be continuous in three dimensions, be of a material or combination of materials of sufficient stiffness and strength to resist the air pressure differential, and be durable to withstand the construction process and perform during the enclosure service life. The location of the air barrier varies depending on the climate and the enclosure system design principle. This is explained in more detail in the "Design Principles" section of this chapter.

Defining Air Quantities and Direction

Defining air quantity is complex because of the dynamic nature of the exterior wind force and the multiple and varied pressures at locations on the exterior and interior of the enclosure. Air quantities used in the design of exterior enclosures are focused on an allowable amount of air leakage. All enclosures will have some air infiltration and exfiltration. The key is defining the acceptable level and developing a system that can meet that level or limit leakage to an amount below the allowable level. Referring to the filter analogy, air is more often selectively filtered from exterior to interior transfer. This is due to "real-world" design and construction inability to create a perfect air barrier in built reality. To determine an acceptable level of air infiltration, an allowable leakage is determined based on the linear length of openings in designs with air-impervious materials, and lengths of openings and material porosity in designs with air-pervious materials. There are multiple standards for design and for laboratory and field testing. This can be validated through testing for custom enclosures. Manufacturers of standard window and enclosure systems offer air leakage criteria that have been laboratory tested with their respective systems.

FORCE TYPE: TEMPERATURE

Exterior temperature ranges created by solar heat or cold are a dynamic force on the exterior enclosure. Temperature differences between the exterior and interior create heat flow through the enclosure. Heat flows by either: (1) conduction: direct transfer through materials, (2) convection: transfer by movement of heated gas (air) or liquid, or (3) radiation: transfer by waves through a medium such as gas (air) or a vacuum. Exterior and interior temperatures, along with thermal performance criteria specific to the building use, influence the type of cladding materials selected, the layers of materials in the enclosure assembly, and the type of insulation (R-value) required for controlling heat flow and therefore heat gain/heat loss. Temperature ranges also affect material expansion and contraction and the associated joinery design. Heat moves from hot/warm to cold. This is basics physics, so the exterior climate will determine whether the enclosure is transferring heat from the exterior to interior, or vice versa. Associated with temperature is condensation. As temperatures increase or decrease, there is the potential to achieve the dew point temperature on the enclosure assembly material surfaces. The enclosure materials selected for use and their placement in the system must be appropriate to the exterior to interior temperature differential.

Glass in vision areas functions more as a filter than a barrier to the temperature. Glass allows a percentage of daylight into the interior based on the glass assembly (single, multiple layers, or multiple layers with air space(s)) and coatings. Glass has a low R-value and is more conducive to heat gain/heat loss. This is more evident at the edges than in the center.

Glass also transmits heat through convection and radiation via air. Enclosure opaque areas offer opportunities for higher R-values with air space(s) and insulation and therefore a higher resistance to heat gain/heat loss. Metal framing components such as steel and aluminum are highly conductive and are the weakest thermal link in the enclosure system. Introducing thermal breaks in metals such as aluminum is a means to isolate the metal framing from direct exterior to interior temperatures. Thermal break locations determine a "thermal line" in metal, delineating exterior and interior. The goal is to locate as much metal mass to the interior of the thermal break line. This can improve the enclosure system's ability to resist or slow down temperature flow and energy transfer.

Exterior enclosures typically have transparent and opaque areas, so each must be evaluated and designed to determine the necessary R-value for each cross section, to address temperature. The exterior enclosure's ability to resist temperature differences between interior and exterior is related to the overall U $(1/R)$ factors of the enclosure assembly. This is determined by the formula: $Uw = UiAi/Ag$, where Ui is the U value of a particular element or zone, Ai is the area of a particular element or zone, and Ag is the total wall area. This calculation is for conductance only and does not address convection or radiation due to solar effects.

Defining Temperature Range

To control heat gain or heat loss through the exterior enclosure system, exterior temperature ranges are established for heating and cooling seasons, on the basis of local climate data. Interior temperature and relative humidity design ranges are also established. These are relatively small ranges. Specific interior temperature and humidity range is linked to the building type and use. These are determined in consultation with the owner and the mechanical engineer. Once exterior temperatures for the building location and orientation and interior design temperature and humidity are established, the insulation R-value (and/or U-value) for the enclosure system can be established.

Each material and layer in the enclosure has some resistance to heat flow and its own unique insulation qualities. The variable is typically material density, thickness, and the location of the material within the system. Typically, heat flow is designed in a steady state one-dimensional flow. Heat flow, like design, is three dimensional. Daily ambient temperature ranges of 40°F +/− (4.44°C) and yearly temperature ranges between seasons of 100°F (37.78°C) are fairly common. Enclosure surface temperatures generated from direct solar exposure are much higher and are influenced by solar orientation and surface color. Surface temperature may range between 150° and 200°F (65.55°−93.33°C). For many materials such as metals with higher expansion/contraction coefficients, this has a definitive impact on joinery sizes. It is important to keep in mind that the larger or longer the material, the greater the expansion/contraction that each joint must accommodate.

Establish Design Performance Criteria: Temperature

Exterior temperature ranges create two design evaluations to determine the design criteria. These are: (1) controlling the passage of heat or cold through the exterior enclosure and (2) expansion and contraction of materials within the enclosure system.

Exterior temperatures are local climate dependent. Interior temperatures are building-use dependent. Local climate will determine if the performance criteria is to control heat gain, heat loss, or both. In hot climates the heat flow is from exterior to interior. In cold climates it is from interior to exterior. In mixed climates with both cold and hot seasons, heat flow is dependent on the time of year. Air flow through materials or at material intersections increases heat flow by bypassing materials. Joints or gaps between materials create thermal bridges. Design criteria are based on heat flow through full material cross sections, so gaps and discontinuities in materials must be avoided. Interior temperature and humidity are also influenced by quantity of occupants and other building systems such as lighting and equipment loads. These must be factored into the design criteria. Control of heat or cold through the enclosure influences enclosure design in the selection of materials, thickness in enclosure opaque areas, the extent and type of glass in the vision areas, and the joinery and attachment method of cladding and materials within the enclosure. To establish the extent of vision to insulated opaque areas, the R-value (thermal resistance) or the U-value (overall heat transfer coefficient, 1/R) must be defined in collaboration with the building mechanical engineer.

ELEMENT AND FORCE TYPE: SUNLIGHT

Sunlight consists of electromagnetic radiation in wavelengths of infrared light, visible light, and ultraviolet light, and it is a dynamic force on the exterior enclosure. Much of the energy from the sun consists of infrared radiation. This wavelength accounts for approximately half of the heating of the earth. Sunlight creates exterior temperature ranges, associated heat gain through the enclosure materials, and material surface temperatures discussed in the previous sections.

Sunlight incident on the enclosure determines the amount of light transmission through transparent openings by either direct or diffuse light. The design goal is to admit natural light and, depending on climate, to maximize or minimize the solar temperature heat gain/loss effects. Sunlight is a force for which the enclosure acts as a selective filter. Allowing natural light into a building through the exterior building enclosure is a design balance of light transmission and heat/glare control.

Sunlight ultraviolet (UV) wavelengths have distinct effects on materials, ranging from color loss to material degradation. Finishes will fade, chalk, and discolor with prolonged exposure to sun. Sealants and gaskets will dry and deteriorate at more rapid rates with prolonged exposure to sun.

Sunlight and the effects of shading and partial shading are particular design considerations for glass. Partial shading for tinted, coated, and annealed glass can create glass stress and the potential for breakage. Sunlight and shade exposure should be carefully considered as glass selection criteria.

Defining Sunlight Control

Determining sunlight and light incident on and entering the enclosure can be done through solar angle studies for the enclosure orientation. These can be evaluated at select seasonal times for sunlight altitude and azimuth as shown in earlier figures of this chapter. Computer programs have expanded the capacity to analyze multiple design options for glass type selection and the viability of exterior and interior shading controls.

Defining the amount of natural light is directly linked to temperature control. Building orientation and the location of transparent areas of the enclosure are the most direct means to achieve natural light levels within the building. Sunlight transmitted to the interior is measured in foot candles (FC). Building use determines design foot candle levels for natural light.

FORCE TYPE: SEISMIC

Seismic movement creates ground motion. This ground motion creates forces that are transferred through foundations and into the primary building structure, creating a sway or "drift" in the building structure during a seismic event. Seismic drift is similar to wind drift in that the primary building structure—and therefore the enclosure—will move. For exterior enclosure design in seismic zones, the larger of the wind or seismic drift will govern. The enclosure drift design is similar to the illustrations shown previously for wind drift.

Defining Seismic Drift

Seismic drift is defined as the differential movement of one floor over another above or below. Seismic drift is defined by the structural engineer. Drift can be defined as a percentage of movement over a height, or as a numerical value off-center over a height. It is more effective for the structural engineer to define numerical movements from floor to floor rather than a span/number. There are two levels of drift. These are (1) Delta "S" for serviceability drift and (2) Delta "M" for maximum drift.

Seismic Performance Criteria

Enclosure performance criteria for seismic event levels are different. Delta "S" (serviceability) means that the enclosure should be fully functional after this level of seismic event and the resulting building and enclosure movement. Delta "M" (maximum) means that the enclosure may have minor deformation damage with no breakage or structural disengagement. Framing and anchorage may experience slight deformation, but should remain intact. Infill materials may be damaged but are not designed or permitted to evacuate the openings.

FORCE TYPE: BLAST

Blast events create large pressures on the enclosure for very short durations. The pressures are positive shock waves followed by negative shock waves. In addition to the blast pressure, there are fragments and projectiles propelled by the blast.

Defining Blast Pressures

The actual characteristics of blast waves are complex. Specialty consulting structural engineers are required to provide the design blast pressures. The size of the blast charge and the distance from the charge to the enclosures will determine the pressure and the duration. While similar to wind pressure, the pressure magnitudes are extremely high and the duration is extremely short. Wind pressures are measured in lb./sq. ft. (kg/sq. m), while blast is measured in lb./sq. in. (kg/sq. mm), and the duration or impulse is measured in milliseconds for blast and seconds for wind.

Defining Blast Performance Criteria

In contrast to the effect of wind forces, the exterior enclosure will suffer damage in a blast event. This is due to much higher pressures than those created by wind pressure, and to damage from projectiles and debris generated by the blast. The performance goal for the enclosure is to protect the occupants. The enclosure framing will deform but cannot disengage. The infill, glass, or other materials can crack or experience damage but are not permitted to evacuate the openings, leaving the occupants vulnerable. System anchorage is designed for strength and cannot fail or disengage in a blast event.

FORCE TYPE: WATER VAPOR/ CONDENSATION

Control of water vapor and prevention of condensation are interrelated with temperature and heat flow. After water penetration, condensation is the most often reported enclosure performance issue. Just as heat flows from warm to cold, so does moisture. Air goes from higher to lower pressure, and air carries water and water vapor.

Defining Water Vapor/Condensation

Climate and the interior temperature and humidity design requirements influence water vapor transfer physics and the potential for condensation. Condensation is the change of vapor to liquid. Condensation occurs on surfaces which are cooler than the dew point temperature of the air containing vapor. As the air cools due to the cooler surface, the air is unable to retain the moisture, thereby releasing it in the form of water. Materials are either impervious or permeable to liquid water and to water vapor flow. Enclosure materials should be selected and located in the assembly with an understanding of vapor resistance or permeability. The location of an air barrier or vapor barrier should be based on climate, interior humidity and temperature, an understanding of the enclosure layers and the temperature in relation to the dew point, and consultation with the project's mechanical engineer.

Defining Water Vapor/Condensation Criteria

Design for condensation resistance is effectively a design to minimize the frequency and extent of condensation formation. There will be extreme conditions beyond the project's and building enclosure's basis of design, where some condensation may occur. The enclosure composition and materials should be arranged and designed to minimize the possibility of condensation and to allow drying of materials as temperatures and humidity return to the design range.

Condensation design criteria is related to temperature changes, which is related to moisture content in the air, which is inextricably linked to regional climate and building use. The base criteria is simple—no condensation—particularly internally within areas of the enclosure that are not vented and drained. In consultation with the mechanical engineer, determine the dew point temperature. After review of the climate data, select a location for the air/vapor barrier. This is located toward the warm side. Test thermal gradients through the enclosure section to determine if the dew point temperature occurs on surfaces of materials within the enclosure. Allow for a drying profile. Example wall section diagrams are shown in Figure 1.22.

FORCE TYPE: NOISE/ACOUSTICS

Traditionally, noise transmission is identified with exterior traffic, aircraft, railway, or other human-created noise. Natural noise generation can originate from water, wind, and thermal exposure; the latter creates sounds as a result of material expansion and contraction.

Defining Noise/Acoustics

Noise is defined in decibel ratings. The higher the decibel rating, the higher the noise level. The enclosure can be designed to a minimum acceptable transmission loss (TL) or Sound Transmission Class (STC). STC is the noise reduction of a material or an assembly of materials measured in a reverberation chamber. The TL or STC rating can be established in different ways, ranging from simple handbook approaches to more sophisticated analysis. In designs where the enclosure exterior encloses sound/noise-sensitive uses, it is advisable to engage an acoustic consultant to collaborate on determining the enclosure minimum performance criteria values.

Acoustical characteristics of the enclosure system and components include sound absorption and transmission loss. Sound absorption is the ability to control reflected sound through a material's or assembly's capacity to absorb noise. Noise reduction

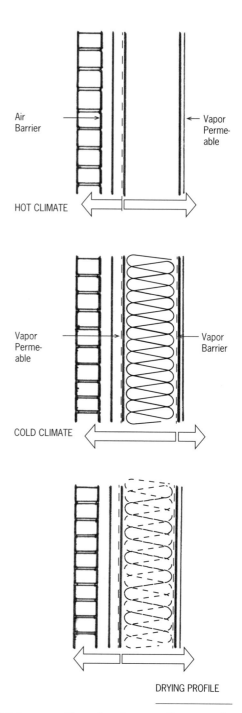

FIGURE 1.22 Vapor flow drying profiles. Vapor flow will influence the design and location of the vapor barrier. The enclosure materials must allow drying. Note: These are just a few basic examples. Each climate and enclosure assembly will yield specific design information.

coefficient (NRC) is the percentage of sound absorbed by a material under specific test procedures. Transmission loss is a measure of attenuation through an enclosure material or system.

Defining Noise/Acoustic Performance Criteria

The TL, STC, or NRC is dependent on the building's interior functional requirements and the composition of the enclosure. The design noise/acoustic level for the interior should be established in collaboration with the owner, acoustic consultant, and architect.

To determine the TL, STC or NRC enclosure value, the opaque and vision areas are typically considered separately and evaluated as a unified system. The vision area TL or STC is dependent on the glass thickness, the glass assembly, and the method of glass attachment. Glass thickness and its sound reduction capacity are mass dependent. Stated simply, the more mass and more flexible the material, the better it performs at reducing sound transmission. Thicker glass will transmit less sound than thinner. Laminated glass with polyvinyl butyral (PVB) or other types of interlayers aids in reducing noise transmission. Asymmetrical laminated glass assemblies utilize mass, the interlayer material, and variable mass to further reduce noise transmission. Opaque areas utilize a similar approach with usually thicker materials and the opportunity for insulation, which can perform dual roles of thermal and sound control. Specific STC rating levels can be approximated. To obtain actual STC rating levels on custom or standard system enclosures, testing mock-ups must be performed at certified testing laboratories.

Design Principles

There are performance design principles that can be utilized to control air infiltration and manage water penetration. Other elements and forces such as temperature, sunlight, condensation, and noise are controlled by cladding materials, glass selection, insulation, material type/placement/thickness/quantity, material and component placement and spacing, and building orientation. These elements and forces should be evaluated in concert with air and water management. Each principle described below has its own merits, complexities, and sometimes shortcomings. Certain enclosure systems and materials will influence which principle or which combination of design principles is appropriate. The following enclosure performance design principles focus primarily on air control and water management. These are: barrier, mass, rain screen, and pressure-equalized rain screen.

BARRIER

The barrier design principle relies on an assembly of water-impermeable exterior materials and sealed joints. This means every surface, recess, opening, joint, and joint intersection is completely and continuously sealed to keep air and water to the exterior of the enclosure. This method relies on perfection. No design is perfect, and construction is not perfect either. While the openings, joints, and their intersections may initially be installed to provide a consistent and continuous barrier of air- and water-impermeable materials, natural forces such as ultraviolet sunlight, wind, or resulting movements will eventually degrade the barrier usually at the joinery. Barrier designs usually rely on sealants as the primary material to provide the weather protection continuity at cladding material joinery. It should be noted that, strictly speaking, porous materials such as natural stone, concrete, and wood are not primary candidates for a barrier method; they serve only as the secondary water control, since these materials may allow the passage of water or moisture to the interior surface through the material. Gutter and other collection methods on the interior of the exterior material are discussed in the Rain Screen section. The joinery, joinery material, and intersections, when properly detailed and installed, are a continuous barrier. However, if the primary enclosure material is a porous cladding material, the system utilizing a barrier principle is not weathertight. Two examples of the barrier principle are illustrated in Figure 1.23.

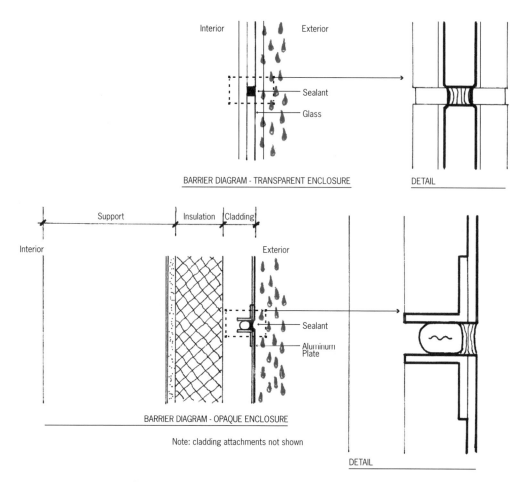

Interior   Exterior

Sealant

Glass

BARRIER DIAGRAM - TRANSPARENT ENCLOSURE   DETAIL

Support   Insulation   Cladding

Interior   Exterior

Sealant

Aluminum
Plate

BARRIER DIAGRAM - OPAQUE ENCLOSURE

Note: cladding attachments not shown

DETAIL

FIGURE 1.23 Two examples of the barrier design principle. Cladding materials shown are impervious to water penetration. Seals at joints must be continuous with no irregularities or openings, to achieve a successful barrier design.

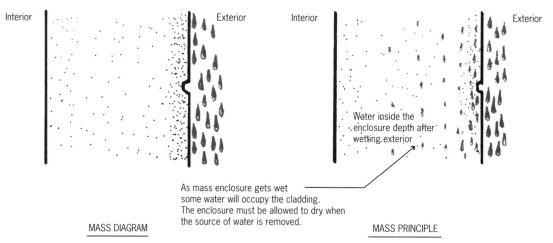

Interior   Exterior   Interior   Exterior

Water inside the
enclosure depth after
wetting exterior

As mass enclosure gets wet
some water will occupy the cladding.
The enclosure must be allowed to dry when
the source of water is removed.

MASS DIAGRAM   MASS PRINCIPLE

FIGURE 1.24 The mass design principle relies on the exterior enclosure material density and thickness. Exposed architectural concrete and architectural precast are examples of materials that employ a mass design principle.

MASS

The mass design principle relies on a combination of material thickness, storage capacity, and material density to resist air infiltration and water penetration. Architectural concrete, precast architectural concrete, and natural stone in thicker cross sections will often employ a mass principle. Joinery between mass materials or between mass materials and systems such as glass in openings typically utilizes a barrier principle in the form of sealant or gaskets. Joints in thicker mass-principle enclosures often utilize a dual line of sealants or gaskets. These may be continuous or have openings in the exterior line to pressure-equalize the cavity between seal lines. Pressure-equalization is discussed later in this section. When implementing the mass principle, attention should be paid to rainwater penetration, potential storage capacity of moisture in the mass material, air/water ingress at cracks, and the drying effects to the interior and the exterior. An example of the mass design principle is illustrated in Figure 1.24.

RAIN SCREEN

The rain screen design principle establishes two separate and distinct planes with a cavity between the planes. The outer exterior plane is a cladding material keeping the majority of the water on the exterior side of the enclosure. Joints between exterior cladding materials are either sealed or gasketed with sufficient openings and baffles (protection) to prevent significant water penetration. The inner plane is the barrier plane resisting air infiltration and the reduced amount of water. In a rain screen design approach, the design must provide layers and zones to reduce the quantity of water infiltrating from the exterior plane to the interior air (and water) barrier plane. The planes and zones are:

1. An exterior control plane sheds the majority of water. This plane is considered the secondary line of water protection.
2. The joinery in the exterior plane—both horizontal and vertical—is designed to minimize water penetration. The water that does penetrate the joinery is controlled and collected in the cavity zone, usually at horizontal locations and drained to the exterior.
3. A cavity zone between the exterior plane and the inner plane, of sufficient width to allow air circulation between the two planes. The depth of the cavity is dependent on the exterior plane material and on the presence or absence of insulation within the cavity zone. This cavity zone is considered a "wet cavity area," and the materials selected and located in the cavity must be capable of performing properly when wet.
4. A primary inner plane provides a continuous air and water barrier separating the cavity zone from the interior building spaces. This plane is considered the primary line of air and water protection.

When viewed in plan or section, as shown in Figure 1.25, the concept is direct and easily understandable. Architectural design and detailing is a three-dimensional effort. The joinery material configuration and size in plan and section of the exterior rain screen plane and the joinery intersections determine the quantity of water in the cavity. The inner plane providing a continuous air and water barrier must also be designed to accommodate building movement. The resulting building movement joinery must continue the primary air/water barrier, accommodate movement, and, because of the difficulty of maintenance access, have a long service life. All of these requirements can be achieved, but the importance of proper material selection, detailing, and installation is critical.

Publications, papers, and other printed material utilize a variety of descriptive terms such as "primary barrier" and "secondary barrier," and interchangeably assign these to either the exterior plane or inner plane. For the rain screen design principle described, the primary line of protection for air and water control is defined as the inner plane. This plane is a continuous separation of air and water between the interior building spaces and the exterior. The secondary line for water control is the exterior plane and the associated joinery with baffles or openings to allow drainage of the cavity. The secondary line deflects the majority of rain and allows air within the cavity zone. The delineation of the primary and secondary line is

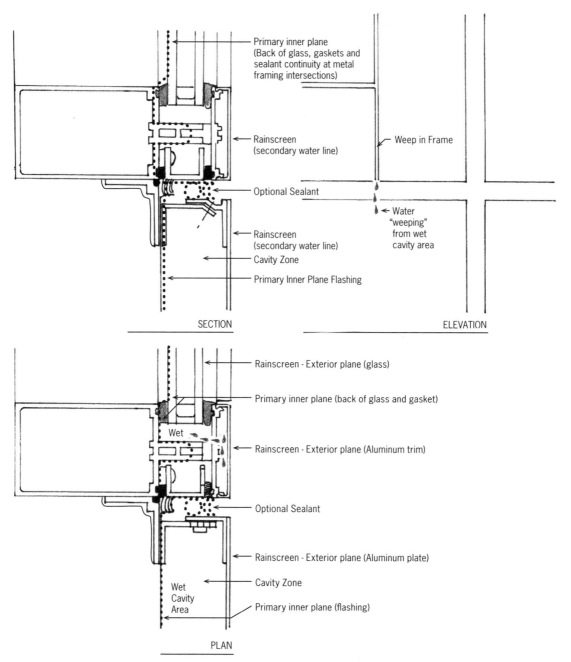

FIGURE 1.25 The rain screen principle relies on a continuous inner air and water barrier plane, a cavity space, and an outer rain screen plane with joints designed to allow water to evacuate the cavity space. The joinery material is shown as "optional sealant". The greater the opening area in the rain screen plane, the greater quantity of water on the primary plane and cavity area.

shown on an opaque and transparent enclosure wall in Figure 1.26 and 1.27.

PRESSURE-EQUALIZED RAIN SCREEN

The pressure-equalized rain screen assembly combines the rain screen principle with a compartmentalized air chamber space in order to achieve an equal or near equal pressure between the exterior side of the enclosure and the cavity or air space separating the primary inner air and water line and the secondary (exterior) water line. The reason for the compartmentalized air space is that pressure-equalization can only occur within limited periods of time. Compartmentalization is essential since wind pressures across the face of the enclosure are dynamic and constantly changing. Reducing or removing the force moving water through the joints means that the materials and joinery of the inner layer "see," and therefore have to resist, less water. The reason for saying "less" instead of "no" water is that often the outer, or secondary, layer is a porous material that allows some moisture migration through the material itself or through joints in the exterior enclosure material into the cavity.

The pressure-equalized rain screen assembly consists of an outer layer (the rain screen), an air space, compartments within the cavity, and an inner wall or material that is impermeable with joints sealed, gasketed, or lapped and sealed. The air space cavity and the edge compartments define the pressure-equalized chamber. An example of this assembly is shown in Figure 1.28. The pressure in the cavity space is maintained to an equal or almost equal pressure with the air pressure toward the exterior of the rain screen. This equal pressure removes the force; therefore, a high percentage of the water remains on the exterior side of the rain screen. Since water may occasionally penetrate the rain screen through joints or the rain screen layer, the air space should allow drainage to the exterior. Insulation that is capable of withstanding moisture may be included in the cavity of a pressure-equalized assembly.

There are several familiar examples of rain screen/pressure-equalized assemblies, such as some wood-frame construction with a waterproof material on the exterior face of the framing and wood siding as the rain screen and blocking in vertical locations, some metal-framed or masonry inner wall with waterproofing, and a masonry veneer of brick or natural stone with air chamber compartments defined with horizontal and vertical definition; and certain window wall or curtain wall systems. Each of these assemblies has an air/water barrier on the inner surface of the air cavity. The inner wall is the primary air and water line, and the rain screen is the outer secondary cladding water line. Each pressure-equalized cavity assembly is drained to the exterior. The extent of the air cavity is determined by the placement of the primary line, the depth of the system, the boundary or delimiter edges that define the chamber, and the placement of the secondary rain screen line. An example of a pressure-equalized rain screen window wall is shown in Figure 1.28. The transition of the primary line in the window wall example to the spandrel at the head and sill requires knowledgeable and sometimes clever detailing to maintain the continuity of the primary line. An example of a unitized curtain wall that employs the rain screen pressure-equalized principle is shown in Figure 1.29. The primary difference is the size of the pressure-equalized chamber.

Corner intersections at both outside and inside conditions provide tremendous design opportunities and detailing challenges. Corner joinery has significant visual implications on and for the design intent. Examples of multiple corner configurations utilizing this principle are illustrated in the systems/case studies in chapter 8—Metal Framing and Glass. In addition to the visual composition of the corner and its design implications (performance principle and visual), the internal workings of insulation (thermal protection and R-value), air and water protection, and glazing (for solar control) must have a consistent detailing approach for the primary and secondary lines of protection defined in the enclosure wall plane.

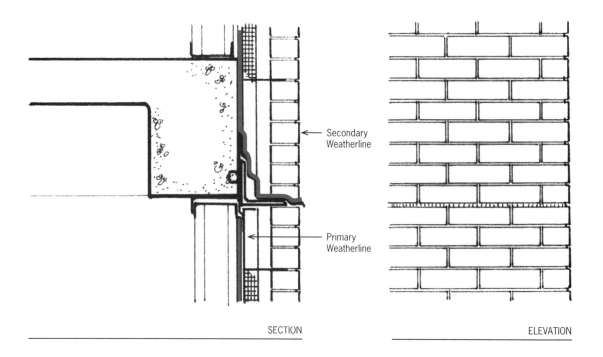

SECTION

ELEVATION

→ Secondary
Weatherline

→ Primary
Weatherline

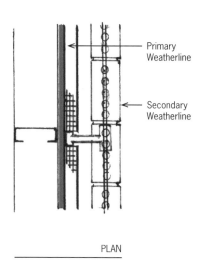

→ Primary
Weatherline

→ Secondary
Weatherline

PLAN

FIGURE 1.26 Brick masonry wall enclosures utilize primary and secondary weather protection lines.

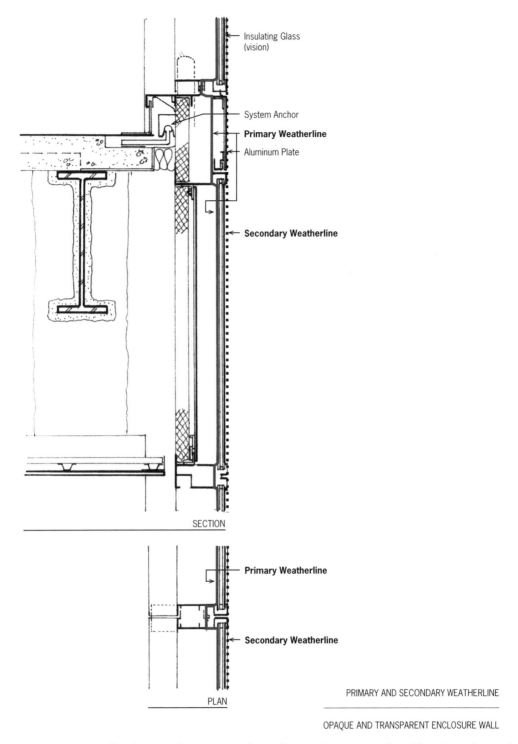

Insulating Glass
(vision)

System Anchor

Primary Weatherline

Aluminum Plate

Secondary Weatherline

SECTION

Primary Weatherline

Secondary Weatherline

PLAN

PRIMARY AND SECONDARY WEATHERLINE

OPAQUE AND TRANSPARENT ENCLOSURE WALL

FIGURE 1.27 Curtain wall enclosures utilize primary and secondary weather protection lines. The primary (or inner) line can be located in various locations, depending on the system design.

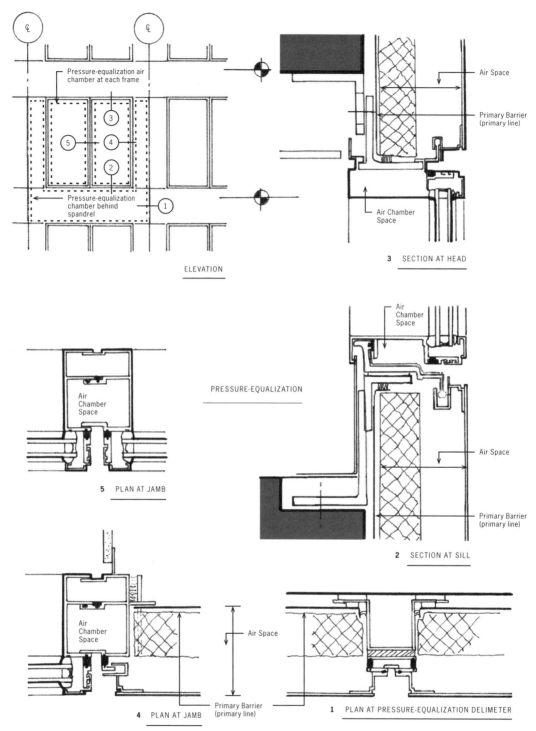

ELEVATION

Pressure-equalization air chamber at each frame

Pressure-equalization chamber behind spandrel

3 SECTION AT HEAD

Air Space

Primary Barrier (primary line)

Air Chamber Space

PRESSURE-EQUALIZATION

Air Chamber Space

5 PLAN AT JAMB

Air Chamber Space

2 SECTION AT SILL

Air Space

Primary Barrier (primary line)

Air Chamber Space

Air Space

Primary Barrier (primary line)

4 PLAN AT JAMB

Air Space

1 PLAN AT PRESSURE-EQUALIZATION DELIMETER

FIGURE 1.28 The pressure-equalization principle relies on a continuous primary weather protection line with ends—or delimiters—to define the pressure-equalization chamber.

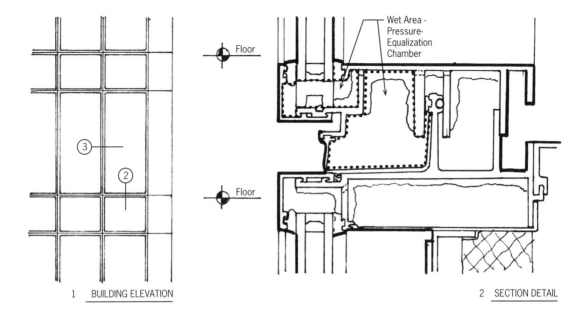

1   BUILDING ELEVATION

Floor

Floor

Wet Area -
Pressure-
Equalization
Chamber

2   SECTION DETAIL

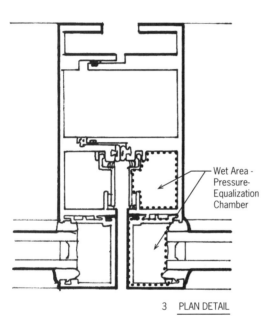

Wet Area -
Pressure-
Equalization
Chamber

3   PLAN DETAIL

FIGURE 1.29 The pressure-equalization principle in a unitized curtain wall.

Basic Types

The visual character, compositions, and materials in exterior enclosure systems are too numerous to count or classify. There are, however, three basic types of enclosures:

1. Standard
2. Customized standard
3. Custom

All of these three types can provide the intended functions, withstand the elements and forces, and adhere to one of, or a combination of, the weather protection design principles discussed earlier. Building designs often include multiple enclosure types where two or all three types will occur. While each must be designed and detailed with its own composition, materials, and performance requirements, the intersection of one system to another offers unique design and technical challenges and opportunities.

STANDARD ENCLOSURE SYSTEM

A standard exterior enclosure system is composed of materials, components, and details that have been designed and tested to certain performance criteria by a manufacturer. The composition of the materials can be modified to comply with the architectural design intent, within the qualifying parameters of the manufacturer. There are hundreds, if not thousands, of manufacturers' standard exterior enclosures. Standard enclosure systems have been developed by manufacturers to optimize repetition, manufacturing, or any number of efficiencies. Discussions with manufacturers regarding the specifics of their systems, to ascertain if the standard system can comply with the intended functions, accommodate the elements and forces defined for the project, and meet the visual design intent, are essential.

CUSTOMIZED STANDARD

There are times when a custom-designed enclosure may be above the project performance requirements, exceed the project budget, or simply not be applicable. There are times when a manufacturer's standard enclosure system meets several, but not all, of the project requirements. In these "in-between" scenarios, customizing a standard system may offer the most applicable and advantageous solution. When customizing a system, the extent of customization should be discussed and reviewed with the manufacturer. Some offer "stock customized" options. These are modifications that have little or no effect on performance, and are similar to options available on an automobile that can be incorporated, with the associated costs related to the level of customization. Further customization can be either modifications to visual components, such as trims, features, colors, and the like, or

performance modifications to enhance the structural or weathertight performance to which the system has been previously tested or engineered to achieve.

CUSTOM ENCLOSURE SYSTEM

A custom exterior enclosure system is exactly what its name states. The materials, components, assembly, composition, and performance requirements are designed, fabricated, assembled, and installed specifically for a project. Custom enclosure walls range from familiar and recognizable systems such as brick masonry to exotic custom glass and curtain wall enclosure systems. There are many factors in the selection and design of a custom enclosure. The performance requirements necessary to resist the anticipated forces may exceed what is available from a standard manufacturer's system. The intended functions of specialized building types may require a project-specific solution. In many instances, a custom enclosure may be necessary to achieve the design intent.

Examples of all three enclosure system types are included in the system descriptions and case study sections of chapters 5 through 9.

Interfaces of Enclosure Types

There are occasions in building designs when a single enclosure system—whether custom, standard, or a customized standard—will suffice for the full extent of the enclosure. More often, building design solutions require multiple enclosure systems to achieve the visual, performance, and cost requirements of the project. The design challenges and opportunities occur in the interface between systems.

In these cases, individual requirements of each enclosure must be studied, identified, and documented with the additional level of design and detail on the system interfaces. The continuity of the primary air and water line must be maintained through the interface and transition. The location of the primary line may shift, but it must be continuous. It is helpful to design and detail this continuity by "tracking" a line where the pen or computer line never leaves the surface of the paper. If the "pen line" has to be picked up or can't bridge the transition, there is a discontinuity, which will allow air, water, sound, or other exterior elements and forces to penetrate the enclosure. It is also helpful to remember that any shifts in location are three-dimensional. This means that a plan shift often results in a section shift, and there is always a corner transition, which requires careful thought on material selection and constructability. Examples of continuous plane transition (no shift) and shifts in the plane of the primary air/ water line are shown in the systems/case study chapters 5 through 9.

Summary

Exterior enclosure design, like building design, is a process. The process is tailored to the specific needs of the project, but it must define and answer the five W's: What, Why, Who, Where, and When, as well as one H: How, in order to be a complete process. This chapter has begun to define What and Why. What is the extent of the exterior building enclosure? What are the intended functions, and why do they influence design? What are the elements and forces acting on the exterior enclosure, and what do they influence? What are some performance principles? What are the types of exterior enclosure systems?

The topics identified are applicable in part or whole to all exterior enclosures and their design. These are the basics and may still appear abstract until applied. Subsequent chapters will address: Who are the participants, and what are their roles? What levels of design are addressed, and when do they occur in the design process? What are the levels of collaboration, documentation, and coordination, and when do they occur in the process? What occurs in the construction phase, and who is responsible for what? Why were certain enclosures selected for the building design? Where are examples of the basics applied to actual case studies? How does it all come together in architecture?

Chapter 2

Participants

It takes all kinds to make the world go round.

PROVERB—FIRST HEARD FROM MY GRANDMOTHER

The design and construction process for buildings and exterior enclosures involves many participants. Each is a stakeholder and has "skin in the game." Interaction among participants is complex, interactive, and iterative. This creates dynamic relationships in the design and construction process. Each participant has individual responsibilities and a shared obligation to engage, collaborate, and coordinate with others. The importance of this obligation cannot be overstated. Participants' involvement may be continual or "as required," depending on their respective roles.

Exterior enclosure design is analogous to a team sport. Composing the appropriate project team for the design and construction phases is a key objective. Selection criteria include applicable talent, experience, resources, ingenuity, and the required level of participation. Equally important are the intangible qualities of ability to exchange ideas and information, appreciation of the needs of other team members, responsiveness, and attention to what is really being said and what goals are to be achieved. This goes beyond playing well with others. As in team sports, each team participant must know what is expected of him or her and what this means to the work of others. Aligning expectations and then delivering is a key for success. Participants may not always see eye to eye, and often team tensions can spur creativity, intensity,

and innovation. The focus should always remain on the design and implementation of a high-quality finished enclosure, incorporating applicable comments and critique by inclusion instead of resistance.

Exterior enclosure design requires the assimilation, synthesis, and integration of information from multiple participants into a unified solution. Participants in the exterior enclosure design and construction process are:

1. Owner
2. Architect
3. Prime-tier consultants
   a. Structural engineer (engineer of record and sometimes specialty structural)
   b. Building service engineers (mechanical, electrical, and plumbing)
4. Second-tier consultants
   a. Specialty building consultants and engineers, i.e., acoustical, wind tunnel, blast
   b. Specialty consultants and/or engineers, i.e., exterior wall or other specialty consultants, if required
5. General contractor (participant's official title may vary, depending on the delivery method)
6. Enclosure contractor(s), with specialty engineers if there are delegated design responsibilities
7. Fabricators/suppliers/vendors

Each participant's role usually remains constant; however, participants' responsibilities will vary depending on the project delivery method. The defining line between role and responsibilities is a fine one. Role is defined as: "proper or customary function." Role establishes "who" is "what" of the five W's. Responsibility is defined as: "being answerable or accountable." Responsibility is the "who" does "what, when, where, and why." To benefit from the input of each team member, every effort should be made to minimize or eliminate compartmentalization of responsibilities.

In team sports, a productive team has an effective, involved, motivated, and knowledgeable leader. Enclosure design and construction is no different. This leader is usually a constant participant. It is highly likely that a team leader may spearhead a phase or group of phases of the enclosure process, and then, in other phases, rotate to a supporting role while another team member acquires the leadership role. The design team must have a constant leader. Likewise, the construction team must also have a constant leader. Along the phases of the enclosure process, one will lead certain phases, and the other will support. Depending on the delivery method, lead/support roles may reverse. Responsibility for documentation is also dependent on the project delivery method. When this symbiotic relationship is defined, developed, and accepted, the seed for collaboration is planted.

Most participants, no matter the level of experience, have their own notional ideas of participants' traditional roles and responsibilities. It is helpful and advisable to step back and take a fresh look at these in the particular enclosure design/construction context. Following this advice, a questionnaire was developed by the author to solicit input and commentary from each participant "group" to obtain descriptions, roles, responsibilities, insights, and expectations of themselves and other participants. The questionnaire was the same for each group representative interviewed, with a few customized questions per group. Some of the responses were expected. Many were extremely enlightening. In particular, the response to what is expected of them and what is expected of others yielded fresh insights into the team dynamic. The questionnaire led to a dialogue with each interviewee and is included in Figure 2.1.

GENERAL QUESTIONNAIRE

(TAILORED FOR EACH PARTICIPANT)

EXTERIOR ENCLOSURES—DESIGN PROCESS

Name:
Organization:
Participant Type:
Participant Company:
Date of Interview:
Years in the Profession:

QUESTIONS:

1. What is your description or definition of (participant)
2. Can you describe "types" of (participant)
3. What is your definition of the (participant)'s roles and responsibilities?
4. What are your primary responsibilities (3 items min)?
   a.
   b.
   c.
   d.
5. What are your expectations of what the (participant) does?
6. What are your expectations of the architect in the design process?
7. Provide your description of the design process:

8. Provide your description of design process for exterior enclosures:
9. What is your role in the design process?
10. What are some of your goals in the design for exterior enclosure?
11. Do you expect the architect to establish the objectives to achieve your goals?
12. When do you have most influence on the process?
13. When do you have the least influence?
14. Who do you interact with the most?
15. Do you enjoy the process?

IF YES, WHY?

IF NO, WHY?

16. List the participants in the exterior enclosure design process:
17. What are some of your favorite building / exterior enclosures (and why)?
18. What are some of your least favorite buildings / exterior enclosures (and why)?
19. What is your role in:
    a. Concept/ Preliminary Design
    b. Schematic Design
    c. Design Development
    d. Construction Documents
    e. Bidding
    f. Construction Administration

20. What do you expect of the architect in:
    a. Overall
    b. Concept / Preliminary Design
    c. Schematic Design
    d. Design Development
    e. Construction Documents
    f. Bidding
    g. Construction Phase Services

21. What level of design / documentation do you expect from an architect?
22. Do you believe an architect can design an exterior wall?
23. What do you see as trends in exterior enclosure design construction in:
    5 years
    10 years
    20 years

24. Are new design technologies assisting/enhancing or hindering the design and construction process?
25. Interview comments
26. Interviewees' additive comments

FIGURE 2.1 Interview questionnaire form provided to exterior enclosure design participants.

Project delivery methods inform the participants' roles and responsibilities. Some project delivery methods are:

1. Design-bid-build, sometimes referred to as design-award-build: The owner develops contract documents with an architect, engineer, and design consultant team. Competitive bids are solicited from contractors based on the contract documents. A contract is awarded for construction.

2. Design-build, sometimes referred to as design-construct: The owner engages the architect, engineering, and consultant design team to prepare drawings and specifications to profile and performance levels. The contractor and enclosure contractor are awarded the enclosure work after review and general acceptance of the contractor's system proposal drawings and cost. There are many other interpretations of the design-build delivery system, so it is helpful to define it per project.

3. Design-assist: A general contractor and often an enclosure contractor are engaged in the early design phases, to assist the owner, architect, and design team in developing the enclosure design and performance-related details.

4. Construction manager: A construction manager (CM) "holds" the contracts of multiple trade contractors, including the exterior enclosure contractor. The CM manages the work and interdependencies of each trade.

5. Integrated project delivery: Project team participants—architect, engineer, contractor, and subcontractors—are engaged (hired) at key and often early points in the design process, to contribute their knowledge and expertise. This process is similar to design-assist.

These are some delivery methods. There are often permutations and combinations resulting from negotiations among all involved participants. Each has his or her specific definitions and understanding of the delivery methods noted. Most are typically very passionate with their opinions and will "wordsmith," nitpick, or even disagree. This is fine. The key concept is to establish and define the project delivery method to determine:

1. Who is responsible for what?
2. What are the relationships?

3. When is each participant involved, and to what extent?
4. Why is this delivery method appropriate?
5. What does each participant do?
6. Where and when will activities occur?

The goal is to establish and align expectations.

As with the earlier statement that each exterior enclosure design is unique and specific to a project, most enclosure design and construction delivery methods are tailored specifically to a project. The owner's, and often the project team's, initial task is identifying the appropriate delivery method and establishing an organizational structure that defines each team member's responsibilities. The second task is for each participant to understand how his or her work affects others, and vice versa, and to achieve a collective buy-in from all.

The following pages provide a general definition of each participant, participant groups or types, traditional roles and responsibilities in the exterior enclosure design process, and the construction process with expectations and interdependencies between participant team members.

Owner

Great artists need great clients.

I. M. PEI

No matter the project type, size, or delivery method, the pinnacle of the project team structure is the owner. The owner's position is key and pivotal with respect to the enclosure design and construction team, whether separate or combined. The term "owner" is used throughout. Similar titles are client and owner's representative. A diagram of a project's enclosure team structure with the primary team members, independent of the contract type or delivery method, is shown in Figure 2.2.

DEFINITION

The American Institute of Architects' (AIA) definition of the owner, from AIA Document A201-2007, is:

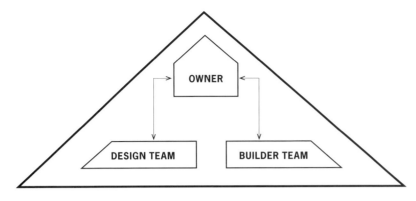

FIGURE 2.2 The owner is the pinnacle of the enclosure project team.

The owner is the person or entity indentified as such in The Agreement and is referred to throughout the Contract Documents as if singular in number. The owner shall designate in writing a representative who shall have express authority to bind the owner with respect to all matters requiring the owner's approval or authorization. The term "Owner" means the owner or the owner's authorized representative.

The AIA definition is broad. The AIA suite of documents has further delineated roles and responsibilities depending on the type of contract. A dictionary definition of "owner" is: "person or entity who awards a contract for a project and undertakes to pay for services of the contract."

GROUPS AND TYPES

There are multiple groups of owners, generally defined by their operational methods, the type of buildings they execute, or the organizations they own or represent. Owner groups include, but are not limited to:

1. Governmental
2. Educational (schools, universities, etc.)
3. Commercial (developer, investor, etc.)
4. Residential
5. Institutional (public or private companies)
6. "First timer"

These are a few groups. There are several others and multiple subclassifications within the groups. Building owner groups interviewed include:

1. Governmental professional owners: those who represent governmental agencies or other branches of federal, state, or local governments in the procurement of design and construction services
2. Private professional owners: those who develop and build as their business model
3. Educational owners: those who represent higher education facilities or primary or secondary schools
4. Individuals who have been building owners or who are in this role for the first time

In interviews and discussions with multiple owners and owners' representatives, there were several types and characteristics that were consistently identified. These are:

1. Hands-on and involved in a detailed manner vs. deferential
2. Active vs. passive
3. Knowledgeable vs. inexperienced
4. Sophisticated vs. unsophisticated
5. Plays fair vs. manipulates everyone

These are owners' descriptions, from varying backgrounds and groups, obtained directly from interviews.

The owner sets the management tone for the project and therefore the environment for the design and development of the exterior enclosure. The own-er's management style and technique ultimately influence the performance of the project team. Owners who are passive or have little or no experi-ence in the role should, and usually do, supplement their role with a professional program manager and/or a construction manager.

ROLE

The owner or the owner's authorized representative provides the financial arrangements to fulfill the own-er's obligations. Additionally, the owner establishes the project budget; sets the project requirements; establishes, with the design team, the project's goals and objectives; and champions the project's cause throughout the process. There are literally hundreds of decisions rendered by owners during the design and construction phases. Owners evaluate input from design and construction professionals and balance this information with the project's budget and goals to provide concise direction and guidance. As one owner stated, "A well-informed and involved owner is the project's enabler."

RESPONSIBILITIES

A primary responsibility of the owner is to pay the bills. Few openly state or discuss this point—but, face it, it is a big responsibility. The majority of owners interviewed are active owners who have served in the owner's role on multiple building design projects. The interviews yielded the following owner responsibilities:

1. Develop and enter into clear contracts, depend-ing on the delivery method, with all design and construction team members, so that all mem-bers understand their roles and what is expected from them and others.
2. Analyze the contract thoroughly to make sure that it is reasonable, but not excessive or loaded, and that coverage is included.
3. Make sure that all team members perform their duties and obligations in a timely manner.
4. Monitor team performance.
5. Make timely and clear owner decisions, particu-larly in the design process.
6. Provide approvals for the visual design aspects.

7. Advise and guide the architect through the design process.
8. Develop sufficient owner/design contingency to cover unexpected/unanticipated costs normal to the project.
9. Pay the bills.
10. Be actively engaged in the design process—not just getting through it.
11. Establish the goals and expectations of the design.
12. Establish the goals and expectations of the design and construction team.
13. Act as a conduit/interpreter between the owner's "big boss" and the architect/design team.
14. Once the project is in construction, adhere to the documents.
15. Provide availability of project resources.
16. Take ultimate authority and responsibility for the project.

Many of the responses from interviews are very similar. These have been generally grouped sequen-tially. The purpose of retaining similar comments is to illustrate a common theme and understanding between different owner groups. These points should be discussed and expanded in the context of the spe-cific project assignment. The responses have a bias toward the design team because the interview was con-ducted by an architect. A highlight stated in each inter-view and discussion is that the owner retains an active role throughout all phases—design and construction—of the building and the exterior enclosure.

In addition to the owner's roles and responsibili-ties discussed in the interviews, there are the owner's expectations of the architect, design team members, and the contractor and subcontractors or trades. Understanding the owner's expectations for quality and extent of design services of the exterior building enclosure is essential.

The owner is why there is a project. For this rea-son alone, the building and the exterior enclosure are designed for the owner, to meet the owner's needs, goals, and requirements. The responsibilities of archi-tects are elaborated in their respective sections, but there are several owner expectations of the architect's responsibilities worth noting. These are:

1. The architect must be knowledgeable and experi-enced in projects of the nature being performed.

2. The architect should be knowledgeable in the subject area (enclosure).
3. The architect should work "arm in arm" with the owner to establish the goals.
4. The architect should provide plans, details, and specifications tailored to the needs of the project—not standard or canned information.
5. The architect should lead the design effort for the project consultant team.
6. The architect should collaborate across disciplines in the design phases and coordinate across disciplines in the documentation phases.
7. The architect should provide timely information to the other design team disciplines to permit them to provide their designs on schedule.
8. The architect must provide thorough drawings and specifications.
9. The architect must provide a sufficient level of detail.
10. Each team member must provide thorough and timely responses.
11. The architect should provide sufficient detailed information to the general contractor and the subcontractors.

Each owner interviewed expected the architect to be the lead for the enclosure design process. Commercial and government owners in particular expressed that the architect should be the clearinghouse for the enclosure "paper" construction efforts, such as shop drawing reviews, field reviews, reports, and so forth. All owners interviewed consistently expected the contractor to be the lead and clearinghouse for construction-related items.

DESIGN PROCESS AND EXPECTATIONS

Each owner provided his or her description of the design process for exterior enclosures. A consistent response is that the exterior enclosure is the project's identification to the public. The owner and the architect collaboratively determine a design direction in the earliest design stages. Typical responses included "big picture" considerations, such as: Should the enclosure be visually lightweight or heavy, light or dark, corporate or flashy? A budget must then be established using metrics such as cost/sq. ft. or other

cost/budget criteria and parameters. One owner stated: "The owner should be prepared to spend more than the amount stipulated to the architect for the enclosure design." This particular owner stated: "It always happens," and added, "This is one of the places where additional money is usually well spent."

Owners consistently noted that the architect should develop several concepts for the owner's review. Each concept should express the stated design goals. The concept or schematic presentations must include sufficient visual materials, such as models, renderings, or other materials, to allow the owner and/or the lead user or tenant to understand the enclosure design intent. Owners provided the following insights and descriptions of the exterior enclosure per project phase:

SCHEMATIC DESIGN:

1. Once the enclosure concept has been approved, the architect must develop sufficient enclosure profiles, typical elevations and sections, and an outline specification to permit budget confirmation, which should include general contractor and subcontractor budget input.
2. The enclosure must establish a recognizable building identity.
3. The architect must provide plans and elevations that respond to and address the building program.
4. The architect must demonstrate how the enclosure design reinforces the project's goals. If this is expressed in the exterior enclosure, define how and why.

DESIGN DEVELOPMENT:

1. The architect must provide further defined plans, elevations, section, typical system details, and in-progress specifications. At 50% design development, the architect should provide an enclosure "in-progress package" for owner review and—if involved—contractor/subcontractor pricing.
2. The architect must provide sufficient information on proposed materials and systems.
3. The architect must collaborate with the other design consultants to establish how the enclosure and other building systems work together.

CONSTRUCTION DOCUMENTS:

1. At the 50% stage of construction documents, the architect must provide drawings and specifications for competitive review and lump sum pricing to qualified contractors. The drawings and specifications must be sufficiently complete without scope gaps, and must be specifically tailored to the project. This is particularly true of the specifications. If specifications are simply "spit out" as a standard canned version, the contractor and subcontractors cannot be expected to figure out what is required.
2. The architect must develop details appropriate to the delivery method and enclosure type required for the contractor and their subcontractor(s) to further the documents for construction.
3. The architect must provide an organized package of drawings and specifications with an intimate knowledge of how the enclosure drawings (plans, elevations, sections, and details) and the specifications reinforce the approved schematic design.

BIDDING:

1. The architect must provide quick and complete responses to bidders' questions.
2. The architect must be open to material specifications without proprietary materials or systems.

CONSTRUCTION PHASE:

1. A thorough and quick turnaround of submittals is essential.
2. There should be no changing the design intent during submittal reviews.
3. Revisions must be limited to those requested by the owner.

THE BUILDING OWNERS INTERVIEWED WERE ASKED THEIR EXPECTATIONS OF THEMSELVES OR THEIR ORGANIZATIONS IN THE ENCLOSURE DESIGN PROCESS. THE RESPONSES WERE:

1. Provide clarity of performance expectations of the architect/design team and contractors.
2. Advise and guide the design process.
3. Conduct regular reviews for design and technical items.
4. Be intimately engaged in the process.

5. Maximize the relationship with the architect, but do not abuse it for "pesky" items that are not expressed in the contract.

The AIA Standard Form of Agreement between owner and architect states at the beginning of each phase of design services: "Based on the owner's approval of the (preceding task or phase) and on the owner's authorization of any adjustments in the project requirements and the budget, the architect shall prepare the (next phase of services)." This establishes the owner as the primary decision maker. In matters pertaining to exterior enclosure design, the owner must be presented with concise and understandable information, well organized and prepared to the appropriate level of completion, dependent on the design phase, in order to make informed decisions.

Architects and contractors, the two primary entities contracted to the owner, have often been quoted as stating: "It takes a great client to make a great building." Each of the owner's comments and responses was very clear and deliberate. A comment made by one interviewed owner eloquently summed up the owner's role in relationship to the design and construction team construct: "The ideal project structure is where the owner has confidence in the design and construction groups—the team."

Architect

In architecture as in all other operative arts, the end must direct the operation. The end is to build well. Well-built buildings have three conditions: commodity, firmness, and delight.

SIR HENRY WOTTON

The architect's involvement in the design and execution of the exterior enclosure is usually more continuous than that of other team members, and often with a longer duration, with the exception of the ongoing exterior enclosure maintenance provided by the owner. Using a musical analogy, the architect is to

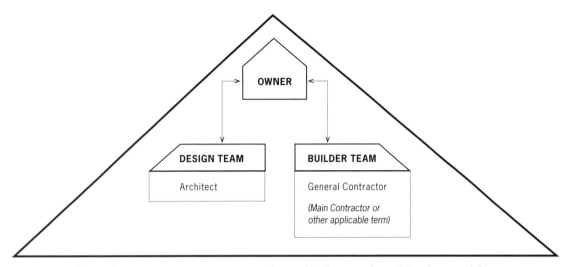

FIGURE 2.3 The enclosure team primary participants. The graphic illustrates the traditional responsibility structure, with design and builder participants responsible directly to the owner.

the enclosure design and construction process as the conductor is to an orchestra. The architect is the conductor who may and often plays several instruments. Simply stated, the architect needs to understand what is required of the architect and other participants to be the lead conductor in enclosure design. A diagram of a project enclosure team structure, illustrating the relationship of the architect to the owner and design team, is shown in Figure 2.3.

DEFINITION

The American Institute of Architects (AIA) refers to the architect in AIA document A201-2007 as: "the person lawfully licensed to practice architecture or an entity lawfully practicing architecture in the jurisdiction where the project is located." Architects often describe themselves as generalists and not specialists.

In exterior enclosure design, this description is naïve and frankly unhealthy for the profession and the craft of enclosure design. Rather, the architect should be general in the early phases and develop specifics as the design progresses. This method and skill set enable and require the architect to collaborate and communicate with design team disciplines in the design phases (concept, schematic design, and design development), coordinate and detail in the documentation phases (construction documents), and provide the contractor and exterior enclosure contractor(s) with organized and clear documents for construction. There are projects where design and documentation are performed by the architect, and projects where detailed design is performed by or delegated to the contractor, enclosure contractor, and specialty engineers.

Quantity of detail, extent of details, and the level of information contained in details are typically a discussion point. There is no standard answer. The level of detail developed by the architect is definitely tied to the project delivery method and the experience level of the architect and design team. In the end, prior to fabrication or construction, no matter who provides them, the level of detail is essentially the same. Details are developed by the architect while maintaining a "big picture" view of the project and the project's exterior enclosure design vision. As the design team lead, the architect must be conversant, knowledgeable, and definitive in visual and technical design issues. No one is born with the knowledge required in exterior enclosure design. It is an acquired talent that includes x parts design intent, x parts research, x parts clear and understandable detail, x parts knowing how the enclosure can be built, x parts collaboration, x parts common sense, and x parts knowing how the enclosure can thrive and survive the test of time.

GROUPS AND TYPES

There are several groups of architects. Groups are generally organized by:

1. The size of the practice, which may range from an individual to an office of several hundred
2. Expertise in particular business sectors
3. Expertise in particular building types
4. Expertise in particular building enclosure systems

The expertise groups shoot another hole in the "architect as generalist" theory. These are a few groups as identified in interviews. Architects interviewed range from small office practitioners to practitioners in larger offices, practitioners in different regions in the United States, and practitioners who work internationally.

In interviews and discussions, architects were asked their level of exterior enclosure expertise and views on the profession's expertise in enclosure design. Responses include:

1. Knowledgeable on standard enclosure design—custom enclosures require assistance on some levels
2. Design documentation process that varies by project and enclosure envelope type
3. Knowledge that is fine-tuned per project, regarding what and which discipline provides detailed design and extent of detail intricacy.
4. Imaginative vs. standardized
5. Experienced vs. inexperienced
6. Understanding what they know and do not know, and how they fill the knowledge gaps
7. Research to solve design opportunities vs. enlisting previously used solutions

These are architect's responses from interviews. The defining characteristic each architect mentioned is level of in-house experience, or requiring access to additional participants with enclosure design experience. Every architect has to do something the first time—once. This holds true in the design and execution of exterior enclosures. In many offices, no matter the size, there is usually the opportunity to learn, one on one, in a project-based setting, from those who have performed similar work before. The objective is to understand what to draw and specify and how to convey the concepts through systems and details to achieve the desired imagery and required performance.

ROLE

The architect is the person or entity responsible for developing, in conjunction with the owner, the design that defines the project and responds to the programmatic and performance requirements. There are opinions, real or perceived, that in "today's world" the architect cannot possess the required legal, technical, and cultural knowledge base, as did the "master builders" of previous generations. There are projects where the architect's involvement in the exterior enclosure is limited to only the composition and visual aspects of design. At the other end of the spectrum, the architect, in collaboration with design team participants, fully designs, details, specifies, and documents the exterior enclosure. There are passionate and convincing arguments to both approaches. In any enclosure design effort, the approach should follow the old carpenter's saying: "The right tool for the job at hand." This means if the architect-led design team has the in-house talent and expertise, then the architect should proceed with full design, documentation, and construction phase services. If the architect-led design team does not possess the in-house talent and expertise, then it may be necessary to either supplement the design team with consultant(s) who possess the appropriate skill set(s), or enlist a project delivery method that includes team members traditionally associated with the construction-oriented team that does possess the technical capabilities for the design and documentation phases.

RESPONSIBILITIES

The full spectrum of the architect's responsibilities in exterior enclosure design includes a design, documentation, and construction role. A nonexhaustive list of responsibilities includes:

1. Manage and lead the project team in the design and documentation.
2. Provide project deliverables in line with the contracted services.
3. Foster and practice interdisciplinary collaboration.
4. Develop design solutions that address and respond to the project scope.
5. Coordinate design and detail work with consultants to the level agreed, with specifications that

state the basis of design in a fully detailed approach, or performance requirements if the delivery requires delegated design, by the construction team participants.

6. Develop case-specific project specifications.
7. Perform review of contractor submittals with detailed responses. For shop drawing reviews, the responses should be weighted toward graphic commentary.
8. Perform review of contractor construction progress for adherence to the contract documents.

In the design phases—schematic design and design development—the architect generates and establishes the design concept(s), and develops form to the concept(s). Enclosure system details are developed to a profile level with interface conditions addressed between adjacent systems. This effort is done in collaboration and consultation with the owner and the engineering/consultant discipline participants. In the documentation phase—construction documents—the architect, with the project engineering and consultant design team disciplines, produces the necessary drawings, specifications, and other products to the agreed detailed design level, to illustrate the design, project components, building materials, performance requirements, and building systems. The enclosure system and complexity may be fully detailed or may be defined through profiles and performance specifications in a delegated design. In the construction phase—bidding and construction—the architect and design team administer construction phase services for the project.

Architects' skill levels in the design of exterior building enclosures range from the novice to the seasoned professional. Despite their previous experience or knowledge base, architects interviewed commented, as did the owners, that the exterior enclosure is the most publicly visible aspect of the building and often one of the most technically challenging. For this reason the enclosure design should be embraced as a challenge and opportunity—not an obstacle.

For architects to provide full enclosure design and documentation requires a high level of "want to." As stated previously, no one is born with this requisite knowledge. It is also not a primary study focus of most architectural school curricula. Architects are taught the design process. Architects who research materials, enclosure systems, and methods of how to build enclosures can become "enclosure multilingual," meaning that they will speak three languages: the language of design, the language of engineering, and ultimately the language of the builder. Most architects who design enclosures have obtained their knowledge base and expertise through experience and "want to." Many architects possess parts of the basic understanding of the principles of enclosure design. An architect should be knowledgeable about how to merge the basic understanding of performance principles and design intent with research and construction industry consultation, to fill in the knowledge gaps. The necessary documents can then be developed in a manner, and to a level of detail, that can be understood by contractors and exterior enclosure subcontractors. Rephrasing this more directly: The documents, including drawings and specifications, are developed for someone else—not the architect.

A SIMPLIFIED WAY OF VIEWING ENCLOSURE DETAILED DESIGN IS:

1. "A way" and
2. "The way"

Architects who fully design exterior enclosures make every attempt to design, detail, and specify "a way" for the construction team participants to build. This includes materials, systems, and interfaces between enclosure(s) and other building systems. A large majority of enclosure details are implemented as drawn and specified by the architect. As an example, most architects who work in areas where brick masonry is widely used have developed an understanding of how this works and what needs to be drawn. There are conditions and situations where alternative enclosure approaches are suggested, usually by a contractor or subcontractor. This may be due to contractor preference, or it may be a "better mousetrap." A responsibility of the architect in enclosure design is to have thought through "a way" to build the enclosure. An equal responsibility is to have the confidence and the common sense to recognize the merits or shortcomings of the alternative better mouse trap and be able to either adopt it or explain—in a manner that is understood by all—how the original proposed details have more merit.

When the architectural drawings and builder methods are aligned, "a way" to build becomes "the way."

Building owners were asked: "Do you believe an architect can design an exterior enclosure?" Most responded that an architect can design a "simple wall." Each further commented that, in his or her experience, only a few architects possess the knowledge to fully design an exterior enclosure. For complex buildings and complex enclosures, the owners felt that an architect could not do it alone and required the assistance from either specialty consultants or the construction industry. On the heels of this response, each owner stated that the responsibility of the enclosure design lies with the architect.

To address this contradiction between expectation and responsibility, architects should ascertain the following, in order to define their role and responsibilities in exterior enclosure design:

1. Determine what the architect knows and therefore the extent of what or how much they can design.
2. Establish how much their knowledge base can be expanded in the design process without compromising the success of the project.
3. Identify "knowledge gaps" and solutions to those gaps.
4. Identify additional design team members to supplement and fill the knowledge gaps.
5. Identify how much the architect "wants to" or "can do" in the enclosure design.

Building design and exterior enclosure design is an evolutionary approach. It is a layering process, both additive and subtractive. It is not a perfectly linear process; however, it does progress from the fundamental concept(s), and through each progressive step or phase it increases the level of definition and detail, resulting in a complete set of enclosure drawings and specifications.

DESIGN PROCESS AND EXPECTATIONS

What are the architect's expectations of the other design disciplines and construction team participants? Although the architect is the primary enclosure design leader, each design discipline is expected to collaborate, challenge, and contribute in the schematic and design development phases. In the construction document phase, the expectations shift to coordination among the architectural and disciplines work, to be sure that what is designed is thoroughly documented across each discipline. There are customary interface points between the enclosure and the design work of other discipline participants. These include: attachments to structure, thermal performance with mechanical systems, and daylight with electrical and lighting systems. These are discussed in more detail under each discipline and the systems and case studies sections in chapters 5 through 9.

In many projects, it is not practical to expect an architect—even one who possesses significant experience in enclosure design and a broad understanding of multidisciplinary interfaces—to execute the multiple requirements for the enclosure design on his or her own. This is where collaboration among design and construction team professionals is paramount. Increased demand by building owners and the public for occupant comfort and energy conservation has led to the increased complexity of new exterior building materials, enclosure systems, and case-specific designs for higher-performing exterior enclosures. This presents significant challenges and opportunities. This increased complexity can and does influence the types and number of consultant participants necessary for design collaboration.

Architects consistently state that design is a three-dimensional process. This is a truism that predates computers and the more sophisticated analysis tools now available. Models, isometrics, mock-ups, and other three-dimensional design tools have traditionally been the architect's and the project team's most thought-provoking and advantageous problem-solving tools. A recurring question arises in every enclosure design: "What are the impacts of advances in technology, particularly the use of computer programs for analysis and documentation, on enclosure design and construction?" Computer design and documentation technology has advanced at breakneck speed since the early 1980s. Building Information Modeling (BIM) has increased the ability to visualize design and detail in three dimensions. This allows multiple views to be generated and studied in three dimensions, increasing coordination between design participants. It allows contractors and subcontractors the opportunity for more detailed information on materials and quantities. Computer-aided efforts are definitely advancements. The manner in which information is shared and utilized determines how advantageous it can be in design and detail.

However, BIM and other computer technology advancements do not change physics or the level of detail or who draws what. BIM also does not allow an enclosure or any other building material or system to be fabricated or installed in smaller dimensions, just because it can be modeled. This is another supporting point for "the right tool for the job at hand." BIM and other technology advances, when used on a shared collaboration platform, can narrow the communication gap between the architect/design team and construction professionals. Understanding the most advantageous documentation application of technology is also a key responsibility of the architect.

Architects were asked to comment on expectations of contractors. Some responses are:

1. Provide input on constructability. Builders are the ones who actually do the work, so their insights, when they understand the design intent and performance requirements, are invaluable.
2. Cost input. Builders have the only legitimate input on costs, since it is their effort and materials used in the work.
3. Builders provide the possibility for highly specific new methods of fabrication and new materials.
4. Builder required time to fabricate and construct.

Although the architect's responsibilities should be tailored to fit the specifics of each enclosure design, I am a proponent that the architect's role remains constant, and responsibilities in exterior enclosure design increase as subsequent design and documentation phases commence. Involvement continues through construction. Each successive action, decision, and detail is layered on the previous ones. Each is important, each provides refinement of the design through details and specifications, and each benefits from interaction between enclosure creator and builder. The result, when all are engaged, is richer and more fulfilling.

In addition to the architect's role and responsibilities, a few guiding principles for the architect in design, documentation, and construction are:

- Design, detail, and specify in "a way" to execute the enclosure. Simply put: "If the architect had a really good set of tools, how would he or she build the enclosure?" This may be "the way," or it may be altered or modified if other design or construction team participants have a better way.
- Don't request or require a contractor (general or building enclosure) to do something you can't or don't have a viable method to achieve. This is not intended to be a "know-it all" comment or to squelch creativity. This is a challenge for the architect to think holistically about the A–Z of the enclosure.
- Ask questions—lots of questions—in each phase, of each participant.

Owners expect the architect to be knowledgeable. Consultant engineering disciplines expect the architect to identify interface conditions with the engineering system design. Contractors expect the architect to produce a thorough set of enclosure documents and be able to answer questions concisely when they arise. All team members desire that the finished enclosure looks good and performs to the specified levels. Design team disciplines expect the architect to lead the enclosure design effort and collaborate/coordinate with each participant. These multiple expectations and the architect's ability must be considered, to determine the appropriate level of involvement and documentation.

Engineers

Scientists dream about doing great things. Engineers do them.

JAMES A. MICHENER

Prime-tier structural, mechanical, electrical, and plumbing discipline participants, whether contracted directly to the architect or the owner, provide design

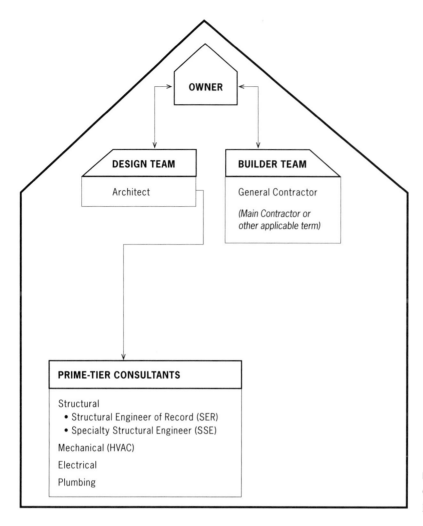

FIGURE 2.4 The enclosure design team structure with prime-tier design consultants.

services for their respective systems and collaborate with the architect and design team on interfaces between their systems and the enclosure. Depending on the contract and the nature of the project, these participants may provide design services for exterior building enclosures. Prime-tier engineering disciplines are typically the engineer of record (EOR) for their respective system designs. It is important, if not essential, for the architect to understand the engineering disciplines' basic scope of services under the agreement and their capabilities. A diagram of the prime-tier consultants contracted to the architect is shown in Figure 2.4, and those contracted to the owner are shown in Figure 2.5.

The complexity of the enclosure design may require engineering beyond the prime-tier engineer's basic services. This is an important distinction for the architect and owner to understand. The prime-tier engineer's design capabilities may suffice for these tasks or may require the additional design services of specialty consulting engineers.

Prime-tier engineering disciplines should be actively engaged and involved, beginning at design inception. For select projects with specialized or

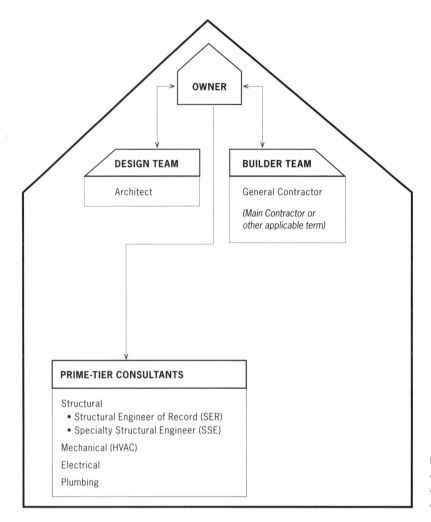

FIGURE 2.5 The enclosure design team with prime-tier consultants responsible to the owner.

complex enclosure design, specialty engineers should also be involved in the early design phases. Exterior enclosure design requires integration of most if not all engineering disciplines. Enclosure performance design and documentation is a multidisciplinary collaboration and coordination effort.

The primary roles and responsibilities of the engineering disciplines identified in this text are described briefly for reference. Their roles and responsibilities related to the enclosure design are described in more detail, with extended services described as applicable.

STRUCTURAL ENGINEERS

Definition and Types

Structural engineering deals with analysis, design, and documentation of structures that support or resist loads. The Council of American Structural Engineers (CASE) defines a structural engineer as: "an engineer with specialized knowledge, training, and experience in the sciences and mathematics relating to analyzing and designing force-resisting systems for buildings and other structures."

Groups

There are two primary groups of structural engineers in the design of buildings and exterior enclosures. These are:

1. Structural engineers of record
2. Specialty structural engineers

In discussions with structural engineers, types were identified within the groups. These are:

1. Structural engineers with experience in working with architects in enclosure design
2. Specialized building types
3. Specialized forces (seismic, wind, blast, etc.)
4. Theoretical
5. Size of practice

Roles

Structural engineers have definitive roles in building and enclosure design, depending on their group.

Structural Engineer of Record

The structural engineer of record (SER) is an entity lawfully licensed to practice engineering in the jurisdiction where the project is located, and is primarily responsible for performing or supervising the analysis, design, and documentation of the building primary structural system and frame. The primary structural system is typically the completed combination of elements, including but not limited to foundations; columns; walls; beams; floor and roof slab assemblies, which serve to support the building's self-weight; applicable live loads, based on the occupancy and use of the spaces; and forces such as wind, seismic, thermal, and others.

To accomplish the primary structural system design, performance requirements and design criteria are reviewed and examined in conjunction with enclosure performance requirements. Performance criteria for the primary structural system are influenced by:

1. Building type and use
2. Building occupancy
3. Building massing and geometry
4. Site/geotechnical conditions
5. Climatic conditions

6. Adjacent environments such as existing buildings
7. Local and national building codes, standards, and requirements
8. Gravity loads
   a. Dead loads
   b. Live loads
9. Dynamic loads
   a. Wind
   b. Seismic, if applicable
   c. Snow, if applicable

Each of these has consequences for enclosure design.

Specialty Structural Engineer

Some enclosure designs require the services of a specialty structural engineer (SSE). CASE defines a specialty structural engineer as one who: "performs structural engineering functions necessary for the structure to be completed and who has shown experience and/or training in the specific specialty." Specialty structural engineers may be included in the design team structure or may be retained by suppliers, subcontractors, or the general contractor for design, engineering, fabrication, and sometimes the installation of delegated contractor-designed items.

The distinction of who does what identifies design responsibility and design delegation. This is the determination of which participant has responsibility for the design of a specific system or component. The objective is to determine whether the SER scope of services includes some or all components in enclosure engineering design required by contract or a national standard, or whether it delegates certain portions of the design either to an SSE within the design team or to the contractor who would employ an SSE.

Responsibilities

The SER's primary responsibilities are analysis, design, and documentation of the primary structural system. Communication of the primary structural system performance characteristics to the architect is essential.

The SSE's primary responsibilities are analysis, design, and documentation of components or systems that are more unique, usually associated with a specific expertise and depth of knowledge. Often a specialty engineer can guide design of specific system(s) or component(s) to a more efficient design.

The previously noted design responsibilities of the SER—and, if required, an SSE—identify services and extent of structural system design. It is customary design practice for the SER discipline to design the structural frame in collaboration with the architect and to arrive at a mutually agreeable structural design solution whereby the performance of the columns, beams, slabs, and major structural components perform in concert with the exterior building enclosure system and joinery.

SERs need to know, from the architect, locations where enclosure loads and reactions are received by the primary structural system. The SER can then proceed to design columns, beams, and slabs to receive and transfer enclosure loads and reactions through the structural system. They also detail specifics of how and where the primary structure materials and components can accept the enclosure anchorage. Rarely do structural engineers design the enclosure anchorage device within their basic services. In some enclosures, the anchorages can be fully detailed by the architect and the structural engineer. In certain enclosures, anchorage design and detail is a design responsibility delegated to a contractor or a subcontractor. In either case, the primary building structure is designed to accommodate the enclosure system self-loads and reactions at designated locations created by dynamic forces such as wind, thermal, or seismic forces.

Responsibilities in Enclosure Design

A project's SER extent of involvement is contract-dependent. Levels of enclosure design involvement are:

1. Performance of the primary structure
2. Connection locations and loads between the enclosure and the primary structure
3. Intermediate enclosure substructure—structural elements in addition to the primary building structure
4. Preliminary design of enclosure integrated structural components

Performance of the Primary Structure

Design by each discipline is not performed in isolation. The building primary structure design has distinct physical and performance characteristics, including member sizes, deflection magnitudes, and locations. The iterative process of structural design and enclosure design will yield a "sweet spot" where the primary structure performance is efficient, safe, and economical, and the enclosure system materials organization and joinery design reflects the ability of the enclosure to accommodate the structural system's performance. This is often a back-and-forth effort, with all of the disciplines refining their design in collaboration with each other.

Connections and Loads between the Enclosure and the Primary Structure

This begins with a concept and evolves to specifics. The architect identifies expected locations for the enclosure connection points. The connection points may be for self-load, lateral load, or both. The SER, in collaboration with the architect, designs and documents where these occur, on the basis of information provided by the architect. The SER develops details of the primary structure to receive the enclosure connections. The particulars of the enclosure connections for tolerances, adjustments, anchorages, compatibility, access, and other factors should be defined graphically and by specification. Anticipated loads imparted at the connection points can be determined by the SER on the basis of the enclosure system layout, geometry, and forces identified for the particular design.

Intermediate Substructure for the Enclosure

In some designs, there is a supporting structure "gap" between the enclosure and the primary building structure. This may occur as the result of tall floor-to-floor heights, long beam spans, or other building design features. Design and engineering for this type of intermediate or secondary structure can be performed by the SER or an SSE. This is contract and expertise-dependent. These types of substructures typically occur inboard of the enclosure plane at defined heights or at locations in plan that coincide with enclosure connection opportunities. The intermediate substructure connects the enclosure to the primary building structure. Examples of intermediate substructures are included in several of the case studies.

Design of Enclosure Integrated Structural Components

Like the intermediate substructures noted above, several enclosure systems require structural components within the enclosure. These may be in the form of steel or aluminum sections for long-span curtain wall systems, cables within systems, ledger angles or lintels in masonry, or other elements and conditions. These may be designed by the SER or the SSE in the design team, or delegated to the contractor or subcontractor with specified performance criteria. Examples of enclosure integrated structural components are included in several of the case studies.

Interdependencies and Expectations

Information flow and specifics between design disciplines are a vital part of the design process. Understanding the information exchanged and providing thorough responses creates a truly integrated design team. Enclosure design is a language with multiple dialects. The architect must speak basic engineering, and the engineer must speak basic architecture. An information-rich design environment is fantastic if you take the time to understand the information.

Further Structural Engineer Design Responsibilities

Some exterior enclosure designs, whether by system approach, contractual requirements, or local jurisdiction, may require more detailed design of the enclosure system and anchorage by the design team. This further design and documentation may be performed by the SER or may require an SSE, depending on the skill sets. As an example, the supporting structure for a stone veneer enclosure and the associated connection between the enclosure system structure and the building structural frame are shown with member sizes and connections on the contract documents. In this case,

because of the contract requirements, the connections and supporting structure were required to be fully engineered and detailed as part of the architectural/engineering contract documents and provided to the builder. This is a higher level of design deliverable than is typically envisioned by the SER as a basic service.

Understanding team member expectations and scope of services at project inception is paramount. Both the architect and the structural engineer have expectations of each other. Collaboration and the resulting design and documentation must be tailored to the project's needs, to determine the best solution. The involvement of the architect and the SER responsible for building primary structure, and, if required, design work by an SSE, must continue through design, into construction, to project completion.

BUILDING SERVICES ENGINEERS

Building services include mechanical, electrical, and plumbing engineering. These participants have experienced an awakening and re-imaging in recent years with a focus on integration of building service system designs with the performance of the enclosure. This is the result of multiple factors, including an increased awareness by owners, architects, the public, and the engineers themselves of the way that their system designs and expertise influence energy consumption, conservation, occupant comfort, and quality of the built environment. This began in the United States with the oil embargo of the early 1970s and has increased significantly ever since. These engineering disciplines are in the process of redefining themselves from individual silos of expertise to a broader and more holistic application of building services and climate engineering. This is more than a marketing strategy using a catchy name. It is a paradigm shift born out of necessity. The building services engineers need to be an ally of the architect in the design process.

Buildings are credited (or reviled) as being responsible for approximately 40 percent of all energy consumption, and significantly more when only electrical use is considered. Actual consumption numbers vary depending on the information source, but the undeniable fact remains that buildings are very large consumers of natural resources. Building energy consumption is due in large part to heating, cooling, lighting, electrical distribution, electrical use by occupants, information technology, water use, water discharge, and other similar services. The exterior enclosure is a large factor contributing either positively or negatively to building heating, ventilating, and air-conditioning (HVAC) requirements. The interrelationship of the exterior enclosure and the mechanical, electrical, plumbing, and other building services system designs can have a significant and positive influence on the overall building efficiency.

Building service engineering and the resulting systems determine the operational efficiency of the building and the quality of the occupied environment. The design and implementation goal is to maximize, through a collaborative process, passive systems and cleverly designed active systems. Passive enclosure system approaches include building massing, siting, orientation, extent of transparent/opaque enclosure surfaces, daylighting, natural ventilation, shading, thermal mass, and other strategies. These approaches, in conjunction with building service systems, cannot be defined, designed, or implemented in isolation—they work together.

To maximize these "big picture design moves," building service design disciplines must be involved at the start of the design process. The local environment is evaluated, considering fundamentals such as climate, physics, and thermodynamics. For architects, it is no longer a matter of a phone call to ask, "How deep are the ducts?" or "How much glass can the mechanical system accommodate?" Building service systems design still results in equipment, distribution, fixtures, and controls. However, interdependencies of the enclosure and building service system designs must be done with a common sense understanding of, and a closer connection with, the environment and an awareness of ever-limited natural resources.

Definition

Traditional definitions for mechanical, electrical, and plumbing engineers of record are noted in the following sections:

Mechanical Engineering

Mechanical engineering for buildings is traditionally referred to as heating, ventilation, and air conditioning (HVAC). HVAC is a subdiscipline of mechanical engineering focused on the technology of indoor environmental comfort. HVAC engineering involves application of the principles of thermodynamics and heat transfer, fluid mechanics, and physics. HVAC and mechanical engineering are disciplines of engineering that apply the aforementioned principles for analysis, design, documentation, manufacturing, and maintenance of mechanical systems. The traditional definition requires expanding. "Mechanical" engineering should be broadened to include interior and exterior climate engineering.

Electrical Engineering

Electrical engineering is a branch of engineering that deals with the technology of electricity, especially the design and application of circuitry and equipment for power generation and distribution. This discipline specializes in the design, construction, and practical uses of electrical systems.

Plumbing Engineering

Plumbing engineering is a branch of engineering that is involved with systems that overlap into the mechanical, electrical, and civil engineering disciplines. Plumbing engineering includes calculations, design, equipment sizing, and documentation of water, waste, and other hydraulic building systems.

THE ROLE OF BUILDING SERVICES ENGINEERS

Mechanical Engineers

A primary role of the mechanical engineer of record is the design of the building's HVAC system equipment and distribution. The mechanical engineer is a prime collaborator with the architect at the genesis of the exterior building enclosure concept design. Increased requirements and complexities of energy performance regulations and criteria necessitate involvement at project inception in a more prevalent and participatory manner than ever. Exterior climate factors of summer temperature, winter temperature, humidity, and solar exposure; occupant loads, and the performance parameters must be clearly defined and made understandable to the design team. This allows options and potential solutions to be addressed in the building enclosure design. In addition to the basics of required insulation values and the quantity of glass to opaque areas of the exterior enclosure, the mechanical engineer contributes a knowledge of physics and computational analysis to the enclosure design thought process.

Electrical Engineers

The primary role of the electrical engineer of record is the design and documentation of the building's primary electrical equipment and the distribution system. The role of the electrical engineer is often overlooked in the design of the exterior enclosure. Beyond the more obvious collaboration between the architect and the mechanical engineer, the enclosure design interface between architect and electrical engineer includes electrical requirements for the mechanical system, lighting, and opportunities to generate building power through passive and active electrical devices within the enclosure or other more straightforward applications.

Plumbing Engineers

The primary role of the plumbing engineer of record is the design and documentation of the building's primary plumbing equipment (water tanks, pumps, fixtures, etc.) and the water and sewer distribution system. The role of the plumbing engineer is also often overlooked in the design of the exterior enclosure. Passive and active hydraulic systems integral to the enclosure design require the plumbing engineer and architect to collaborate in often uncharted design opportunities beyond typical plumbing systems.

RESPONSIBILITIES

THE MECHANICAL ENGINEER'S PRIMARY RESPONSIBILITIES INCLUDE:

1. Heating: adding thermal energy to occupied space in response to heat loss
2. Cooling: removal of thermal energy from occupied space in response to heat gain
3. Humidification: adding water vapor to occupied space to increase moisture content; working

with the architect to evaluate thermal performance of the envelope and thermal mitigation
4. Dehumidification: removing water vapor from occupied space to decrease moisture content; working with the architect to evaluate thermal efficiencies in the enclosure and related issues of vapor barrier and insulation
5. Ventilation: providing adequate quantity of fresh outside air to occupied spaces
6. Cleaning air: removal of particulates and contaminants from occupied spaces

THE ELECTRICAL ENGINEER'S PRIMARY BUILDING DESIGN RESPONSIBILITIES INCLUDE:

1. Main power equipment: primary electrical equipment that receives off-site power and transforms to building-usable power
2. Power to other building systems
3. Distribution systems: risers and distribution lines
4. Outlets and connections
5. Building grounds
6. Building communication

THE PLUMBING ENGINEER'S PRIMARY BUILDING DESIGN RESPONSIBILITIES INCLUDE:

1. Design and process of main equipment
2. Design of distribution and collection systems
3. Design of heat and energy transfer piping systems

RESPONSIBILITIES IN ENCLOSURE DESIGN

In a traditional team organization, the mechanical engineer will assist and collaborate with the architect to establish the "big picture" items. The exterior enclosure's performance characteristics must be defined to comply with jurisdictional prescribed energy consumption or project-specific performance requirements, and then fine-tuned as the design evolves. Occupant comfort and the performance of the exterior enclosure have the highest influence on the mechanical engineer's design of the primary heating, cooling, and ventilation systems.

The built environment should respect and understand the natural environment. This is a fundamental principle in passive design. The size, performance, and energy efficiency of the building in total are inextricably linked to the performance of the exterior building enclosure. Extent of glazing, type of glazing, solar orientation, insulating value of opaque enclosure areas, and other enclosure or building system features must be carefully considered by the mechanical engineer and architect together in the earliest project phases. Through either prescriptive or performance-oriented design, the mechanical system design parameters that are established will directly inform the exterior enclosure design.

Technologies blended with traditional knowledge and engineering practices are being applied to low-energy design solutions. Building mechanical systems and the exterior building enclosure should be considered in tandem, as opposed to one influencing the other. Design collaboration between architect and mechanical engineer on heat transfer, condensation analysis, and integration of the multiple HVAC/ enclosure design, material, and systems is more critical and more expected than ever before. Utilizing engineering training, the mechanical engineer needs to make certain that the physics of thermal gradient, moisture, and air pressure can be understood by architects, so they can incorporate appropriate response to the local climate in enclosure design. New design tools such as heat transfer computer programs, computational fluid dynamics programs, and simulation computer programs for daylighting/glare analysis offer the design team increased information on the viability of exterior enclosure designs for achieving or exceeding the minimum requirements and project goals while in the design phase.

Electrical

Today's buildings have different and often higher electrical load requirements than previous building generations. However, building codes have continued to reduce the allowable use and consumption of power. Optimal electrical design is not only directly linked to power use by occupants, but is also significantly influenced by the power requirements for mechanical and building service system equipment.

New and innovative exterior enclosures are exploring dynamic sun-shading devices, integrated photovoltaic systems, switchable glazing (electrochromic), and other systems with electrical design

components integrated within the enclosure design. These new technologies integrated into enclosure design require electrical engineering for power and monitoring controls necessary to design a complete system. Integrating electrical generation technology for enhanced enclosure performance is a newer responsibility of the electrical engineer.

Interdependencies and Expectations

With the need—not goal—to create higher performing buildings that reduce consumption of natural resources, the enclosure design is inextricably linked to the building service systems. This creates the requirement to conceptualize real and achievable enclosure and building service strategies in the earliest design phases. This is the easy part. Conceptualization—or blue sky thinking—is invigorating. The harder part is developing systems to implement the concept. This requires pieces, parts, valves, equipment, materials and the like. It is not enough to simply diagram this and expect it to get built. It requires architects and building service engineers to research and engage suppliers and manufacturers to push existing boundaries and in some cases, break down boundaries to design, document and implement new equipment and systems. The work doesn't stop there. Once a system—or in the best case—integrated or inter-related enclosure and building service system— are implemented, they must be measured. Learn from what works and what can be designed and built to perform better at higher efficiencies with lower use of natural resources.

SPECIALTY ENGINEERS AND CONSULTANTS

This is a specialty category of second-tier consultants with a primary focus on design services for the exterior enclosure. The term "specialty engineer" comprises structural, materials, façade, environmental, or disciplines that offer a particular design or engineering expertise. Specialty consultants include participants who are knowledgeable in the design, fabrication, assembly, or installation of enclosures. Many specialty consultants have experience as contractors or fabricators. This tier of consultants may include curtain wall, blast, or energy specialists, acousticians, material scientists, and others. The project team organization chart with these consultants is presented in Figure 2.6.

Architects continually strive to create innovative designs. These design efforts often involve application of new materials, new systems, or using a known material or system in a manner that has not been previously attempted. Often enclosure designs may involve all three.

The architect is not and cannot be an expert in all fields. Architects cannot be expected to know as much about specific material properties, performance requirements, or fabrication techniques as those who specialize in this design effort as their line of work. Architects do recognize that enclosure design that elevates technical levels of sophistication and intricacy will often require the design and detail assistance of specialized engineering disciplines. This participant works closely with the architect on specific custom designs, providing advice, consultation, and often documentation.

The engagement of an enclosure design consultant or engineer usually accompanies a custom design where material science or engineering knowledge for materials goes beyond the traditional uses. Custom designs of this type require a higher level of detailing and specification by the architect/specialty consulting engineer than a standard or customized standard enclosure or delegated design requires. Specialty engineers provide engineering services, advice, specifications, and documentation to an appropriately advanced level to convey the design intent and the required material characteristics, system performance, tolerances, and construction specifics that extend beyond the exterior enclosure industry's accepted norms.

The engagement of a specialty consultant or engineer is appropriate when required to supplement the architect's expertise, or supplement or provide engineering to the traditional core of consulting engineers, such as structural and building services, to provide engineering independent and interdependent of the traditional consulting design services for atypical and custom enclosures. Occasionally, specialty consultants or engineers are the "engineer of record" on the exterior enclosure portion of the project.

Design Team Resources: Material Suppliers, System Fabricators, and Specialty Fabricators

As architectural concepts or schematic designs begin to take an overall form and character, research into materials, systems, details, and construction techniques begins. Questions arise that can only be answered if the architect understands the materials, material properties, systems, availability, associated suppliers, manufacturers, and fabricators. Researching and discussing materials and/or systems directly with the fabrication source is a primary "must do," whether the materials and systems are known or new. There is nothing that can elevate an architect's understanding more than actually holding, reviewing, simple testing, and discussion of materials with the source provider. In the process of material selection and system design development, material suppliers and system fabricators are excellent resources for the architect and consulting team participants. The relationship of these resources to the architect and design team is illustrated in Figure 2.7.

MATERIAL SUPPLIERS

Doing research and assembling material samples and product technical data are essential steps to provide the architect with a working knowledge of—and a "feel" for—a material and its properties, and how these may be introduced in the enclosure design. Most material suppliers have in-house technical staff who can offer advice on their products and suggestions on availability, limitations, applicability, and compatibility with adjacent materials. Collecting samples and data, and then evaluating a material's application to the design, enables the architect to design and detail components into the enclosure system design with an informed understanding of how it should and will perform to an optimal level. Doing this allows the architect and specification writer to include the material's pertinent information in the project specifications. There are few instances that can either elevate or diminish the attitude of an owner or builder more than the evidence (or lack) of product research and the understanding of a material's limitations and availability. Illustrating and documenting a

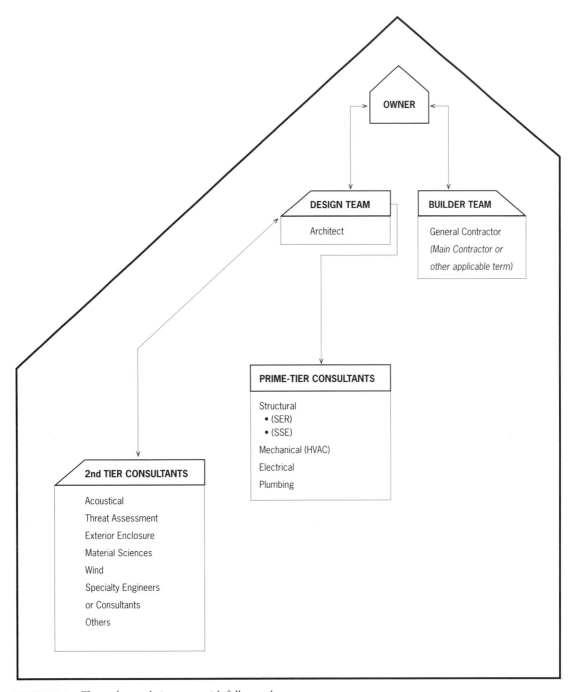

FIGURE 2.6 The enclosure design team with full consultant team.

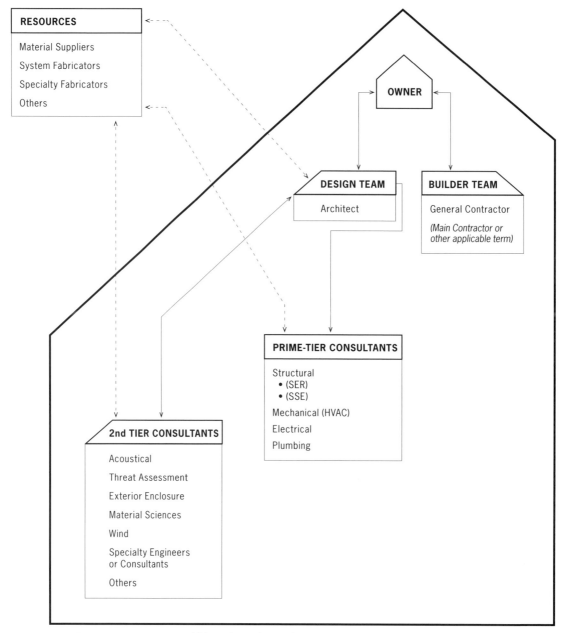

FIGURE 2.7 Resource participants available to the enclosure design team. These are also available to the builder team.

material through samples, technical data, availability, and fabrication contacts—coupled with the architect's ability to describe how and why a material is appropriate for use—can turn a "nonbeliever" into a supporter.

SYSTEM FABRICATORS

As the design evolves to initial system details, system fabricators can offer insights for performance and constructability that can inform the architect's enclosure design. System fabricators/manufacturers often can suggest minor changes or alterations to the details, using their expertise and experience, that may lead to improvements and often a more cost-efficient solution. Early consultation with system fabricators on size and depth requirements allows the architect to more accurately coordinate the evolving enclosure design with the project team of engineers—structural and building services—for clearances, points of attachment of the exterior enclosure to the primary structure or primary building services system, and the type of connections required. System fabricators will often offer constructability suggestions that can influence the profiles, thicknesses, and joinery of the enclosure. The level of interaction with system fabricators varies with the size and complexity of the design. For designs that utilize a single system, consultation with several fabricators of systems similar to the envisioned design will yield recurring comments that the architect can interpret and integrate into the design and documentation. Designs that utilize multiple enclosure systems require the same investigations already noted, along with advice on how to interface multiple systems for desired visual design objectives and performance requirements, such as air infiltration, water penetration, thermal control, acoustics, and continuity of basic system performance objectives and requirements.

SPECIALTY FABRICATORS

Specialty fabricators' work ranges from highly custom connections such as those used in tension and cable type structures, to carbon fiber, photovoltaic, polymer resinous panels, pultrusions, and many others. Several of the case studies presented in later chapters illustrate the role and products produced by specialty fabricators. As with material suppliers and fabricators, specialty fabricators combine materials science, engineering, and fabrication for custom assemblies in exterior enclosures. Usually reserved for highly technical and project-specific designs, specialty fabricators have a wide range of clients, from the architect or engineer when assisting in the design to builders when contracted as a member of the construction team.

Specialty fabricators possess a depth of knowledge in engineering coupled with hands-on experience in

fabrication and construction. Components and assemblies that are designed and fabricated by specialty fabricators are often a key link in the architect's vision and documentation of the enclosure. Specialty fabricators' expertise is applicable when designs require nontraditional materials and the application of these materials in the architectural enclosure designs. Limitations of specialty fabricators' knowledge of the complete building process should be considered within the context of their specialty and its relation to the entire project.

Builders

The main ingredient of stardom is the rest of the team.

JOHN WOODEN

Participants listed under "builders" include the general contractor, exterior enclosure contractor, material suppliers, special engineering consultants to exterior contractors, sub-subcontractors, and vendors involved in the enclosure construction process. These participants may be involved during the design process or during the paper phase of construction. In any case, builders are team members who are responsible for taking graphic information and transforming it into enclosure reality.

Project delivery methods initially outline and define the expectations of design and construction team participants. Many delivery methods in recent years include the term "alternative delivery method," in an attempt to address perceived shortcomings in the traditional design-bid-build method. No matter the delivery method, specifics of what each team member—design or construction—is expected to deliver, and to what level of detail, must be discussed and agreed upon. The opinions and debates over the merits and shortcomings of any delivery method are a treatise unto itself. The objective here is to identify the positives in the relationship of the builders, the owner, and the design team in the design process of exterior enclosures, no matter which delivery method is employed. As with the collaboration of design team participants, the relationship between builders and design team members must be built on an earned respect. In that spirit, the definitions for builders will use the more traditional names of general contractor, subcontractor, and vendors/engineering consultants. The builder team in relationship to other enclosure team members is shown in Figure 2.8.

GENERAL CONTRACTOR

Definition

"General contractor" is a term widely used in the United States. The general contractor is sometimes referred to as the prime or main contractor in other countries. AIA document A201 (2007 ed.) uses the term "contractor." The AIA definition is:

> The contractor is the person or entity identified in the agreement and is referred to throughout the contract documents as if singular in number. The contractor shall be lawfully licensed, if required in the jurisdiction where the project is located. The contractor shall designate in writing a representative who shall have express authority to bind the contractor with respect to all matters under the Contract.

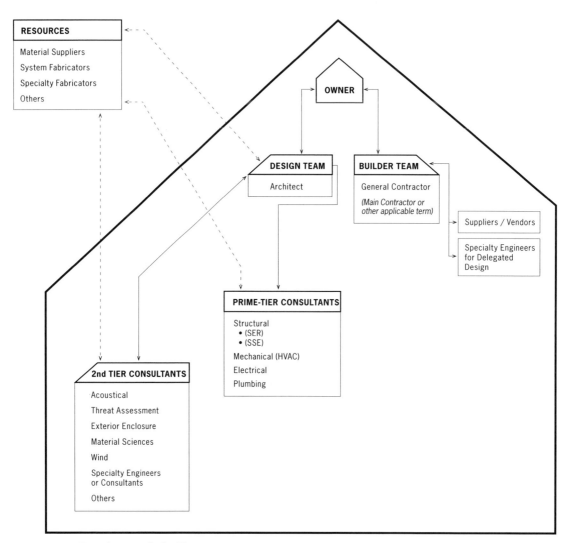

FIGURE 2.8 Consultants to the builder team.

The term "contractor" means "the contractor or the contractor's authorized representative." Another definition used is: "The contractor is the person or entity lawfully licensed in the jurisdiction where the project is located."

Role

The general contractor supervises and directs the work, using the contractor's best skill and attention. The contractor is solely responsible for, and has control over, construction means, methods, techniques, sequences, and procedures, and for coordinating all portions of the work under the contract. General contractors, depending on type of contract and project type, perform certain scopes of the work and subcontract work to other contractors and companies that specialize, such as exterior enclosure contractors.

Responsibility

The contractor has a number of responsibilities relating to the execution of the work. These are:

1. Day-to-day oversight of the construction site
2. Management of trades and vendors involved in the construction
3. Providing material, labor, equipment, and services necessary for the construction
4. Coordination of the work of trades and subcontractors
5. Providing construction pricing for the work
6. Application of craft necessary to achieve the owner's vision
7. Payments to various entities working on the construction

Depending on the type of contract, the contractor may be involved in the project during the design phases. When this opportunity is available, the project can usually benefit from the contractor's input on issues ranging from cost to schedule, constructability, and other topics.

Responsibility in Exterior Enclosure

The general contractor will usually employ one or multiple subcontractors to execute the exterior enclosure. The tasks associated with this are:

1. Paper phase of construction (shop drawings, catalogue cuts, samples, and calculations if required by contract)
2. Providing design assistance in a design-assist contract agreement
3. Testing: sample, material, component, or overall system
4. Bricks and mortar: actual physical construction
5. Completion and finishes
6. Final review
7. Final testing
8. Commissioning

The contractors' role(s) for coordination of their work and their subcontractors occurs on an administrative level, such as contract document reviews, shop drawing reviews and submissions, coordination sessions between subcontractors, and coordination sessions with owners, architects, and engineers. On the construction site, coordination includes sequence of work, interfaces with multiple subcontractor trades, and overall supervision of the work on-site.

Actual on-site construction work for exterior enclosures is very dependent on the type of enclosure system. Some enclosures may be constructed to a large extent on the basis of information contained in the contract documents. In this scenario, the extent of shop drawings is less, and the extent of material, details, and systems shown on the contract documents is high. In other types of enclosure systems, the level of enclosure construction work is heavily dependent on shop drawings. In this scenario, the extent of shop drawing reviews by the design and construction team members is high, with the contract documents illustrating profiles, performance criteria, and interface points between the enclosure and other building systems, for guidance in the development of the shop drawings.

Coordination during Shop Drawings

Just as the architect coordinates exterior enclosure anchorage types and locations with the structural engineer in the design and documentation phases, the general contractor coordinates anchorage placement, via shop drawings, between the exterior enclosure contractors and the subcontractors performing the primary superstructure work. Shop drawings are a set of drawings produced by the contractor or subcontractor for fabricated items and systems. Other primary coordination interfaces occur with interior finish subcontractors in placement and sequence of construction. General contractors recognize interface coordination activities required for the site through working reviews of shop drawing submittals. The general contractor should provide (1) notations on shop drawings indicating the coordination activities required between subcontractors and (2) notations to the architect, highlighting specific areas or questions that require the architect's input, in addition to the architect's review for general conformance with the contract documents.

Coordination on the Construction Site

Coordination of activities on a construction site requires a high degree of planning, logistics, and firm guidance to allow multiple subcontractors and trades to perform their work and interface with the work of others. The first step in on-site coordination preparation work for the exterior enclosure is the placement of anchorage devices within the specified tolerances. This involves the exterior wall contractor(s), concrete or steel contractor, and usually several other trades.

Once the anchorage devices are installed and surveyed to check accuracy, the logistics of receiving exterior enclosure components or fabricated assemblies begins. Transportation access, layout space, hoisting, and storage are established. During installation, different exterior enclosure systems require their own specific time periods and access/installation space, to allow the installation operations. Component-type enclosures (brick masonry, stone, stick-type curtain or window walls) usually require lay-down space, assembly or fabrication areas, and a longer time frame to install. Comparatively, prefabricated assemblies (precast, unitized curtain or window walls, stone panels, etc.) require lay-down areas (unless hoisted directly upon arrival to the site) and shorter installation times. All of these activities are orchestrated by the general contractor.

After erection and installation of the exterior enclosure, the general contractor's coordination efforts focus on site testing (if specified and required) and protection of the enclosure during construction from adjacent subcontractors' work. Final cleaning, punch list, and commission round out the construction coordination activities prior to project turnover to the owner.

EXTERIOR ENCLOSURE CONTRACTOR(S)

Exterior enclosure contractors are traditionally subcontractors. Depending on the design and number of exterior enclosure systems, the exterior enclosure contractor can be a single contractor entity or multiple contractors. The subcontractor's(s') relationship to the enclosure project team is illustrated in Figure 2.9. Just as the level of detail developed by the architect is dependent on whether the enclosure system is standard, customized standard, or custom—and on interface details between systems as well—a similar level of time, detail, and labor effort is incumbent on the exterior enclosure contractors to develop their system and collaborate on connection points to the structure and on connection of performance interfaces (structural, weatherproofing, etc.) with adjacent exterior enclosure systems.

Definition

A subcontractor is: "One who takes a portion of a contract from the principal contractor or from another subcontractor." Whether for a small- or large-scale project, the exterior enclosure is typically performed by subcontractor(s). Subcontractors range from masons (brick, stone, etc.) to carpenters (concrete), sealing, framers, ironworkers, curtain wall, and many others. These subcontractors often supply and install enclosure work based on the design and details provided in the contract documents. There are instances in these trades where specialty engineers are a subcontractor team participant. Subcontractors who perform glass, glass and metal, and metal enclosures refer to themselves as subcontractors and often as exterior subcontractors/designers. These types of enclosure building participants employ very specific and custom design, fabrication, assembly, and installation techniques and methods used in metal and glass and all-glass enclosures.

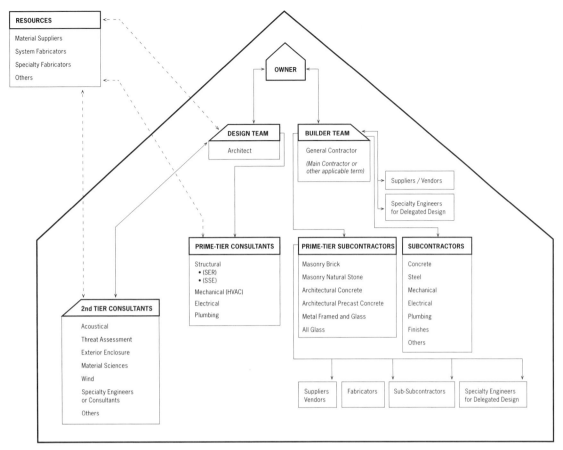

FIGURE 2.9 Enclosure team structure: enclosure subcontractors.

Groups

EXTERIOR ENCLOSURE SUBCONTRACTORS, FOR THE PURPOSES OF THIS BOOK, INCLUDE:

1. Brick masons
2. Stonemasons
3. Architectural concrete carpenters
4. Metal and glass fabricators, designers and builders
5. All-glass fabricators, designers and builders

There are many more. The systems and case studies in chapters 5 through 9 are organized with these types of enclosures, and therefore these groups.

Role

The exterior enclosure subcontractor's role is to provide the materials and labor necessary for the enclo-sure type and for their systems' interface with adjacent construction systems. Materials and labor bracket the basics for construction. A wider range of responsibilities is as follows:

RESPONSIBILITIES

1. Design consultation
2. System design
3. Detailed enclosure document preparation
4. Engineering
5. Material procurement
6. Fabrication
7. Assembly
8. Installation
9. Testing
10. Final Review

Whether the exterior enclosure is for a small- or large-scale project, or whether it is standard or custom, it is advantageous for the architect and the exterior enclosure contractor to fully understand each other and to offer and listen to advice. The architect can and should explain the design intent and performance criteria, and provide insights and background on the logic used to develop the enclosure contract documents. Conversely, with the design and detail logic explained, the exterior enclosure contractor can offer constructability, fabrication, and installation advice. Additionally, enclosure contractors may provide insights that can enhance the design and tailor it to the construction process. The following list presents four combination scenarios and the associated role of the exterior enclosure contractor.

- Standard enclosure during the design phases

    There are multiple manufacturers of standard exterior enclosures. In most cases, the cross-sectional sizes and properties and the performance capacities are very similar. As the architect collects this information, it is advisable to discuss the system and details with each manufacturer, to further understand the limitations and, equally important, the boundary conditions where the standard system will interface with structural support points or with adjacent systems. After establishing that a manufacturer's standard enclosure can fulfill the required performance criteria, established by the architect, further design and detailing can continue. After reviewing several manufacturers' system details and specifications, small differences among them will become apparent. The task of deciding which systems to proceed with as a basis of detailing involves establishing a lowest common denominator approach, so that each selected manufacturer's system used in the design and detailing effort—if awarded—can successfully meet the required performance and space limitation criteria.

    The level of detailing illustrated on the architectural drawings, within the system, is usually less when a standard system is selected. There is no need to show detail internal to a standard enclosure system. There is nothing to show that the manufacturer doesn't already know, and that the architect hasn't already understood through research. The important contract document detailing resides in any system modifications for either visual or performance reasons and in the connection methodology used for attachment to the structure or to adjacent enclosure systems. Interfaces with adjacent systems—enclosure and others—is critical. Most standard enclosures define the typical system details. If this is the only enclosure system, the interfaces are within itself. If there are other enclosure systems, terminations and interfaces require detailing by the architect. These modifications—if any—must be reviewed with the manufacturers' technical representatives.

- Standard enclosure during the construction phase

    Most manufacturers' standard systems are installed by exterior enclosure contractors who are approved by the manufacturers for installation. The shop drawing submittal volume for standard walls is usually smaller in quantity than for a custom wall. The typical details (head, jamb, sill, and corners) for opaque and vision areas vary slightly, if at all, from the details provided through the system manufacturers. Project-specific details combine the manufacturer's standard shapes, materials, and profiles with case-specific modifications to accommodate the project design and the interface with adjacent subcontractor trades. It is vital that the architect, contractor, and exterior contractor fully understand how to achieve performance continuity between the standard system details and adjacent subcontractors' work. Several items that the architect should pay close attention to are finishes, features, and, if glazing is included, the type, thickness, kind, and so forth, detailed and installed in vision and opaque areas.

- Custom enclosure during the design phase

    Custom enclosures require a more in-depth understanding and extent of documentation than standard enclosure assemblies. The physics and principles are the same or similar; however, because of design or performance requirements, it may be decided that a standard system does not fulfill the required design intent or performance requirements. A custom enclosure can vary in complexity from a masonry wall (brick or stone), which is assembled from more traditional materials, to a custom glass and metal wall. There are exterior enclosure contractors in locations in or near the project or remotely located who offer their expertise to architects during the design phase. The level of interaction that can be offered depends on the architect's knowledge and the project bidding requirements. Most exterior enclosure contractors with experience in custom-type work are very adept at providing consultation advice on details, system viability, cost range, and constructability. The architect should openly describe the project's delivery method requirements so all are informed and can provide commentary.

- Custom enclosure during construction phase

    This scenario is based on the architect and its consultants providing a set of exterior enclosure contract documents for the project. The exterior enclosure contractor (with the general contractor) is charged with taking the architect's documents and developing a system or systems that comply with the design and performance requirements. The custom enclosure proposed by the enclosure contractor typically utilizes technologies, materials, fabrication, and assembly procedures that have been previously employed by the contractor or are new and specifically developed for the project at hand. This can occur on small- and large-scale projects, but tends to occur more often on larger-scale projects or those with specialized performance requirements. It is advisable in this scenario to convene a review meeting prior to commencement of full shop drawing preparation. The review meeting allows the architect to explain the basis of design illustrated in the contract documents and gives the exterior enclosure contractor the opportunity to explain proposed typical system details

and other solutions to the design documents. After discussion of visual and performance parameters from each viewpoint, common and agreed-upon viewpoints can be established as a basis of moving into further detail. It is important to remember that a successful exterior enclosure is the result of each entity understanding the basis of design, performance, and constructability, and realizing that a team effort yields more positive results. After establishing the basic details that address design, performance, and constructability, the further development of atypical details and interface conditions can begin.

Summary

The realities of modern enclosure design and construction rely on a functional, committed, and experienced team of professionals who have a common goal: a successful project. Each participant has a primary role and multiple responsibilities. These are specifically defined for the project at hand. There is a shared obligation to listen, challenge, collaborate, coordinate, and, above all, communicate. All participants are responsible for fulfilling their tasks to the mutual benefit of other team members.

I have been involved on projects where this has occurred and on projects where there have been one or more weak links and the results were less than envisioned. These shortcomings are usually not due to inability, but rather to misaligned expectations. Understanding what is expected, when it is expected, who is expecting it, why they are expecting it, where it is expected, and how it will get done, within the context of the total project team, sets the stage for the next step—the design process for exterior enclosures.

Chapter 3
Design Process

STEP 1: Define and Establish Enclosure Goals

If you don't know where you are going, how do you expect to get there?

BASIL S. WALSH

Every journey has a beginning and an end. Enclosure design has a beginning—defining the project and the exterior enclosure goals—and an end: the final documents that illustrate how the enclosure will be built. The multiphase design process is the work in between. Exterior enclosure goals must be identified and established at the beginning of the design process to illuminate and guide the planning of the design and documentation efforts. Enclosure goals establish what the owner and project design team want to achieve, and why. This provides the project participants with a direction and a glimpse of where they and the design are going. The enclosure Design

Process Timeline with the goals step is presented in Figure 3.1.

ENCLOSURE GOALS ARE:
1. Big picture
2. Representing, in abstract, the design aspirations
3. Lofty, yet attainable
4. Providing a framework for further defining objectives and concepts, which are the "how"

The exterior building enclosure is the visible expression of the building design. Therefore, the goals that guide the enclosure design must embody the goals set for the building design.

Verbalizing goals in a brainstorming exercise at project inception is an invigorating and mentally stimulating starting point. These must be discussed, vetted with the project team participants, and documented. Stated and accepted enclosure design goals must include input from the owner and design team members. They cannot be established in isolation.

Goals are vitally important for the design team and the architect, who wants to know the "what" and

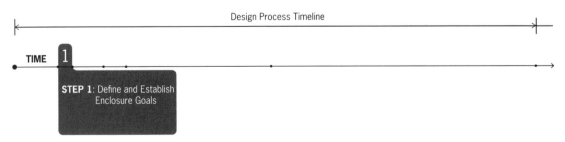

FIGURE 3.1 Goal definition is the initial step in the enclosure design process. Qualitative and quantitative goals for the enclosure are established.

the "why" of the design problem or opportunity at hand. Goals are more than words or a list on paper. There is no inspiration in a list. There should be inspiration in the goals. The architect should lead and facilitate this kick-off effort in collaboration with all project team participants. Each and every participant can find inspiration in the enclosure design goals. The set of goals in all design efforts, particularly in the design of the exterior building enclosure, should include qualitative and quantitative goals.

Qualitative goals are those that are felt; they range from aspiration to inspiration to "mom and apple pie." Inspirational goals that are too general or ambiguous are not particularly useful. No one can dispute the value of these goal types, but they can be somewhat difficult to clarify, which can make it difficult to ascertain if they are achievable. Who can argue with a goal of: "The exterior enclosure should project the spirit of the company"? This is highly inspirational and highly vague. A vague goal statement can lead to multiple interpretations by team participants, often in different directions. Restating this qualitative goal with more definition, such as: "The exterior enclosure should achieve maximum transparency to project the open spirit of the company" conveys a mental picture and more definitive direction for design team participants.

Quantitative goals are those that can be measured. Combining qualitative goals with quantitative goals that have metrics for evaluation helps enable the "whole-brain thinking" necessary for a complete design process. Some qualitative and quantitative enclosure goals using whole-brain thinking are illustrated in Figure 3.2. Quantitative goals should not be isolated to only pragmatic or practical goals. Qualitative and quantitative goals can both be practical (or impractical). A goal stated as: "The exterior enclosure must be the most energy-efficient ever designed" has little opportunity to be achieved. It is frankly too far-reaching and ambiguous. Restated as: "The enclosure must be 25 percent (or whatever percentage is lofty and achievable) more energy-efficient than an enclosure in a comparable building" provides a measureable target. Similarly, an ill-defined or overly lofty quantitative cost goal such as "The exterior enclosure should be the most cost-effective" can be further defined as: "The exterior enclosure must be X dollars per square foot at the time of contract award."

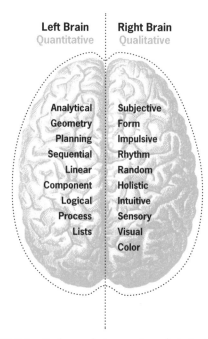

Left Brain Quantitative	Right Brain Qualitative
Analytical	Subjective
Geometry	Form
Planning	Impulsive
Sequential	Rhythm
Linear	Random
Component	Holistic
Logical	Intuitive
Process	Sensory
Lists	Visual
	Color

FIGURE 3.2 Enclosure design requires whole-brain thinking.

There should be a healthy mix of both qualitative and quantitative design goals for the project and the exterior enclosure. In addition to the enclosure, each of the project's building systems has design goals. All team participants will have their individual focus set on attaining their goals. The challenge lies in structuring, cultivating, and maintaining a team environment where the goals of each team participant become the goals of all. Once the exterior enclosure design goals are set, be persistent and flexible on the objectives and concepts developed, but stick to the goals. Don't change the ends (goals); change the means (objectives and concepts).

There are several groups of enclosure design goals. These are influenced by the type of project and set by the project team. As team participants are added during the enclosure design process, restate the project design and enclosure goals for the entire expanded project team. Some enclosure goal groups are:

Organizational goals: This goal type is usually owner-, client-, or user-influenced. These are usually qualitative types of goals. "How can the enclosure express or provide support to the purpose of the owner or the building use?" "How can the enclosure exemplify the organization's mission or vision statement?" "How can the enclosure portray the values of the organization?"

Visual goals: This goal type helps define the nature and appearance of the enclosure. These are qualitative types of goals. They may establish a potential design path for "blending" with adjacent building massing, materials, or other attributes of the surroundings. They may establish a path of visual independence from adjacent structures and their exterior expression. They may evoke a character of solidity or transparency. This type of goal delineates a character and attitude for the exterior enclosure expression.

Performance goals: This goal is a quantitative type that defines the level of enclosure structural performance, weather protection, energy efficiency, acoustics, security, or other measurable performance requirements. Performance goals are for the enclosure itself; its influence on the occupied interior environment and on other building systems; and its response to climate, the natural environment, and human-created surroundings.

Cost goals: This goal is a quantitative type that defines the cost parameters for the enclosure and the financial consequences for other building systems that are interdependent with the enclosure. Cost influences system alternatives for achieving the design and performance requirements, as well as the ability to design, document, produce, construct, and maintain the enclosure. Costs include the design and documentation efforts, which are "soft" costs, and "hard" costs, which are the enclosure fabrication and construction efforts. Soft and hard cost goals are easier to establish with enclosure systems that are known or slightly custom. Soft and hard costs for custom or first-time design efforts are difficult and time-consuming to establish. Custom enclosures require custom thinking and, to a certain degree, a leap of faith. Cost goals should include first, operational, and life-cycle costs.

Time goals: This goal type includes time goals for all project team participants. These are a quantitative type of goal. No matter the project delivery method or organization, the project team of the owner, architect and consulting disciplines will include, either initially or eventually, a team of builders, suppliers, fabricators, installers, and others in the construction phase. Time goals must include design, detailing, interdisciplinary collaboration and coordination, documentation, contractor review, pricing, fabrication, assembly testing, checking shop drawings, fabrication, construction installation, and commissioning time.

Defining goals is typically associated with the programming phase of the design process. Applying an enclosure goal definition step provides a framework to initiate the enclosure design process. Often, goals will enlarge the vision of the design team. Goals may indicate that a particular expertise needs to be added to the team to achieve a stated goal. Defining goals is more of an art than a science. No matter the unfamiliarity or difficulty, establishing appropriate enclosure goals is a vital step and must be done. The enclosure goals lead to concepts, the next step in the process, which are the means to achieve the project design goals.

STEP 2: Enclosure Concepts

Practice safe design: Use a concept.

PETRULA VRONTIKIS

Enclosure goals define the "what" and often the "why." Enclosure concepts are the "how" to initiate achieving the goals. Enclosure concepts are the means to achieve the enclosure goals. All design starts with an idea—the concept. This is the foundation of the design process. Everything and every step that follows inform and reinforce the concept. The Design Process Timeline with the concept step is illustrated in Fig. 3.3.

Concept design is the earliest phase of the design process and should be used to explore multiple options, using uninhibited thinking and far-ranging ideas. Ideas should be plausible, but they often set aside technical, material, or other expected considerations. Instead, concepts favor the abstract. Concept

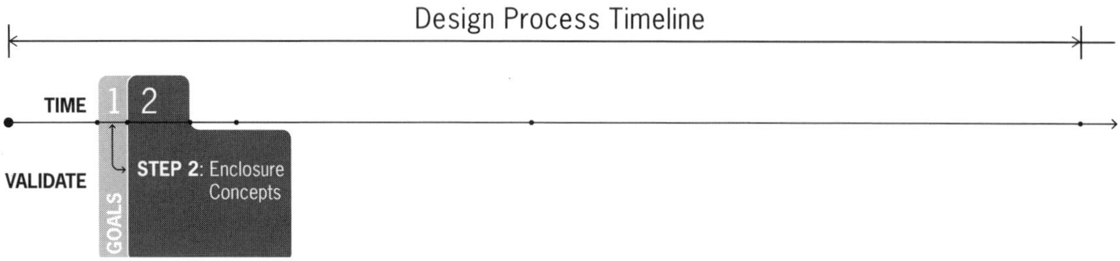

FIGURE 3.3 The concept step in the Design Process Timeline. Concepts provide the enclosure design foundation.

design is "blank paper or blank screen" design. It is an abstraction, which embodies conceptual content through imagery. An image, sketch, diagram, or other medium represents ideas generated to entice and challenge design team member participants to explore options that may not have been considered if a fresh approach is not proposed.

Concept design is invigorating and sometimes uncomfortable; since the design exploration is often "off the beaten path," the results usually vary from a more conventional solution. Concept design should be embraced. After all, every design team member is also challenging him- or herself with a look into the unknown.

The concept design phase does not require a long period of time. There are many who hold the opinion that concept design is frivolous and generates options that may not be, or appear not to be, directly applicable to the design problem. Some view this step as impractical and only as an opportunity for architects and engineers to "flex their design muscles" without regard to the "mountains" of work that remains to be done. An enclosure concept design phase should be encouraged. It serves as a catalyst for innovation. Other design fields such as automotive and fashion design develop concept cars and high-fashion haute couture to generate interest and elicit a wow factor (see Figure 3.4). Enclosure concept design should do the same.

Enclosure concept design can yield results that are powerfully persuasive. It also informs planning in subsequent steps in the design process. Enclosure concept design can apply the basics discussed in Chapter 1, "Basics," in a conceptual manner to ascer-

tain if the concept will allow further development in subsequent design phases. Possible actions and results in the concept design step are:

1. Enclosure concepts take a broad view of the design problem. Multiple concepts and options are generated to explore possibilities. These concept options can be studied in various media, such as physical models, computer-generated images and models, renderings, sketches, and so forth, with less expense than at higher levels of detail, in later steps of the process.
2. Enclosure concepts allow the architect and the project design team to frame a problem from a fresh viewpoint or perspective, in ways that make possible solutions more interesting.
3. Enclosure concepts and the resulting images and forms can offer rich visualization that evokes strong and passionate responses from the owner, design team, consultant team, and builders.
4. Enclosure concepts galvanize team members to form a common core understanding of the essence of the design. With an understanding shared by all, each subsequent step in the process builds on the concept as the foundation with more detail and definition.
5. Enclosure concepts allow exploration of multiple options in the search for the best possible and most unique option to capture the spirit and goals identified for the project. This minimizes the possibility that the architect—or even worse, the owner—will ask in later phases, or after the project is completed, "Did you take a look at this?" or, "Why didn't you design it this way?"

Automotive Concept Car   High Fashion / Haute Couture

FIGURE 3.4 Other creative industries and designers employ concepts to inspire.

Concepts for the building and the exterior enclosure can find inspiration in the natural environment or in response to the natural environment. They can express a response, through form or composition, to the building type, use, or the client's mission and goals. Concepts can express the diagrammatic nature of the building and its uses. Concepts can be abstractions using symbolic references. It is important to understand the parallels and differences between architectural concepts for the building as a whole and concepts for the exterior enclosure. This is difficult for some architects to wrap their head around. Each must reinforce the other. The architectural concept is an abstract idea or ideas intended to embody the client's goals, requirements, and intentions, without necessarily defining the physical nature of the enclosure concepts. Enclosure concepts should acknowledge concept-level principles, forces, and elements in the composition. Some examples of architectural concepts and exterior concepts are:

- Architectural concept: Express solidity.
- Enclosure concept: opaque areas of masonry, concrete, or metal with minimal joinery
- Architectural concept: Maximize transparency.
- Enclosure concept: an enclosure with high quantities of vision glass
- Architectural concept: Express the building's functions with varied spatial experiences.

- Enclosure concept: private spaces—opaque enclosures; public spaces—clear transparent enclosures to maximize daylight and provide user orientation

These are a few examples, not from any particular projects, and are fairly common. Enclosure concepts are limited only to the imagination of the project participants. Some are deliberate and obvious. Some may appear obtuse until viewed in conjunction with the project's goals.

Enclosure concept design, like concept design in other design fields, should embody an idea through a distinct and memorable statement and image. The concept may be thematic. It may propose to use distinct materials. The concept may propose use of materials in an innovative way. In any case, the concept sets the tone and challenges of the project for subsequent design phases. See Figure 3.5 for an example of a design concept and the associated enclosure concept sketch.

Tools used by the architect and design team to illustrate the concept should be easy to use. The goal is to describe the idea quickly and effectively. Owners and architects recognize a good idea. It does not require elaborate documentation or embellishment. The concept is the core of the schematic design to follow that becomes a powerful communication tool to define and inspire the direction for the subsequent steps, leading to a more complete project solution.

The enclosure concept is discussed with the design team member participants, to achieve "buy-in" that the concept can be developed and advanced in subsequent design phases.

The goal of the concept step is to stimulate thinking. The result of the concept phase is a product that identifies the best concept, or, if the design opportunity requires, multiple alternative concepts. Enclosure concept design can occur at either the concept design phase or the schematic design phase. Today's building enclosure design is at a significant transition point, given the way enclosures must respond to increasing performance requirements, environmental issues, and energy consumption reductions. Fresh and innovative responses that address climate, incorporate new technologies, and work in concert with other building systems necessitate the interdependence of multiple design and construction participants at the concept phase.

STEP 3: Research, Collection, and Analysis

If we knew what it was we were doing, it would not be called research, would it?

ALBERT EINSTEIN

Research is what I'm doing when I don't know what I'm doing.

WERNHER VON BRAUN

There were so many applicable quotes for this step, by some influential people, that two were included. Research, collection, and analysis are performed concurrently with concept and schematic design. This step consists of assembling what you know, identifying what you don't know, and performing information gathering. This step in the process is more heavily weighted in the initial design process. It does, however, continue throughout the design development and construction process. Concept and schematic design requires supporting information gained

FIGURE 3.5 Enclosure concept example.

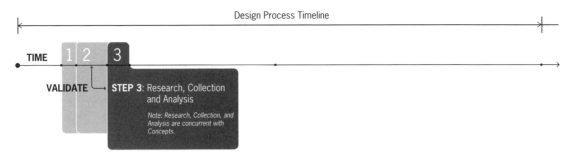

FIGURE 3.6 Enclosure design requires research, collection, and analysis. This step informs concepts and subsequent steps in the design process.

in this parallel step to inform the viability of the concept in order to achieve the visual and performance goals, as well as to establish the necessary regulatory and jurisdictional requirements. The Design Process Timeline with the Research, Collection, and Analysis step is shown in Figure 3.6.

There is a massive amount of information available out there. With today's easier access to information, there is as much (or more) un-useful as useful information. In the early design phases, develop a general plan of what and how to research, the extent of information to collect, and a process to analyze what is collected. Without a plan, you won't know where to start, and you sure won't know when you have enough to say you are to a "level of done." Design is not linear, so the term "level of done" is more applicable than a definitive statement of done. A building contractor once explained to me the concept of the seven "P's": "Proper prior planning prevents partial or poor performance." An enclosure design process without the requisite research, collection, and analysis is doomed to piss-poor performance.

Identifying enclosure research topics and the depth of research is similar to planning a trip to the grocery store. Make a checklist. Without a list you will forget something, or in most cases, several things. The checklist should identify required topics and topics to be considered, with a space for topics that are identified or discovered during research and collection. A systematic research, collection, and analysis method allows architects and design team participants to cover the basics and fine-tune select research topics for project case specifics.

RESEARCH

Whether you have experience designing an exterior enclosure or this is your first effort, do not get overwhelmed in concepts or research—and never stop asking questions. Research is a search for knowledge and understanding in a systematic way, so as to eventually establish facts. Research will basically fall into two types. One is research on information readily available. Examples are building codes, local regulations, site and climate data (for most areas), industry standards, similar project examples or enclosure strategies, and material particulars and standards. The other type of research is for information that either does not exist, is unknown at the time, or exists in a form not easily accessed. Examples are user specifics, operational issues, new materials, climate history (for certain areas), unknown similar project enclosure examples, strategies, and performance criteria. Note that preliminary performance criteria can be identified to initiate research, but it must be validated in later steps in the process.

Enclosure goals identified in Step 1 inform the type of information for research. State what the research topics are to team participants. Research can be conducted in a variety of subheaders per topic, including technology, behavior studies, environment, and history. Enclosure research topics and subheaders should be fine-tuned per project. Most will also apply to all enclosure designs. A sample and nonexhaustive list of categories and topics for research is shown in Figure 3.7.

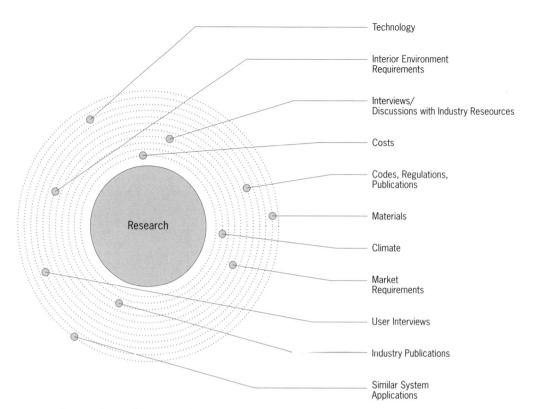

Technology

Interior Environment
Requirements

Interviews/
Discussions with Industry Reseources

Costs

Codes, Regulations,
Publications

Materials

Climate

Market
Requirements

User Interviews

Industry Publications

Similar System
Applications

Research

FIGURE 3.7 Some enclosure design research topics.

There are several methods of searching and identifying relevant information per topic. These include literature searches, discussions with regulatory authorities having jurisdiction, discussions with design team participants/consultants and industry contacts, Internet searches, user surveys, and interviews. Research, like design, is a layering process. Research is peeling back layers to reveal needed information, whereas design is applying layers of definition.

Literature research involves a review of readily available material. This includes the applicable code(s) and regulations, trade publications, online information, manufacturers' product data, white papers, magazines, and other published material. The majority of this is easily accessible and can be obtained quickly. Finding more detailed information will require more time and effort, depending on the specificity you are seeking. This information should be gathered quickly. After checking that the literature is the most current (codes and standards in particular), distill the necessary information from the literature into a format that

can be used by the entire design team. Information is useful only when it is distributed to all and becomes an integral part of the problem-solving process. Keep in mind that research is supportive to the concept or schematic, so efficiency and expedience are paramount.

After a preliminary content review of the gathered literature, discussions with people who have specific knowledge of the topics are very helpful for gaining additional insights into the content. This also provides a check to determine if you have identified an adequate level of gathering and researching material.

Discussions with those in the profession, or an applicable industry, who are engaged in enclosure design and execution with experienced professionals, can lead to information that is not publicly available, or that is too new to be found in the printed literature. On a cautionary note: Although discussions are valuable, they can and might yield subjective information and opinions. Discussions are more helpful when you have performed a preliminary review of the material. The quality and depth of discussion points and the questions asked during discussions will be better informed when you have a basic understanding of the topics and the materials. Often these discussions will yield access to sources of information that may have been overlooked or simply unknown during the initial research.

Obtaining information through interviews can be done in a group setting or on an individual basis. This method is usually more time-consuming, so preparing and providing a questionnaire in advance assists in expediting thoroughly prepared responses. The depth and quality of the responses are dependent on the knowledge of the interviewee, the specificity needed, and the amount of time available and required for the interviewee to prepare responses.

COLLECTION

Once the sources and types of information have been identified through research, the collection process begins. Not all research leads to collection. There can be a large quantity of information identified and researched, so collect judiciously. Related information collected should be generally defined. Don't get hung up on being too specific. Collect information that is close to what you are proposing to do. It should be current, relevant, and applicable. The information that does not make the "to do" or collection "stack" should be retained if it is deemed potentially useful during preliminary analysis. Collection organization is illustrated in Figure 3.8. Most architects and engineers maintain some form of repository for codes and standards. It sounds fundamental, but verifying that the collected information is current—or will be current when the enclosure design is documented for release—is critical. After collection, there should be a preliminary presentation of what has been collected. Informal presentations allow an initial level of organization of what is collected that begins to reveal how it is or will be relevant to the design opportunity.

Collected enclosure performance information should be organized into categories. Categories include:

1. Material or component performance
2. System performance
3. Interior environment performance

Performance requirements or standards can be organized into a preliminary outline matrix, with the information source(s) identified. This is a helpful tool for discussions with consulting engineers and design team participants. Performance topics, by categories, can be compiled from trade journals, outline specifications, and industry standards. The performance topics can be enhanced by reviewing the base matrix with the goals identified in earlier steps. Another helpful organizing guide is to arrange the performance information into groups. One group will be enclosure-specific, and other groups are the performance requirements and standards of related building system concepts defined by participant consultants. Climate, weather, and meteorological information are available through multiple sources, including several governmental websites, such as the U.S. Department of Energy, NASA, NOAA, and others. Local climate and weather data can be obtained through local agencies and weather observation stations and airports. Building services engineers, particularly mechanical and plumbing engineers, are well-informed resources for climate and weather information.

Collection Check-Sheet

There is a fine balance between collection and overstimulation. The goal is to collect applicable information, not for the collection process to burden the design team or process. The check-sheets, or whichever tracking device is used, should be simple. Most simply identify the topic and assign due dates. Collection of quantitative data can be streamlined by defining the unknowns in a graphic template format. This can be a graph, pie chart, spreadsheet, or other graphic organization. Examples are climate data for solar, rainfall, winds, and other information. The template identifies the information to collect, specifies who collects it, and sets up the following analysis steps.

User and operational information collected through questionnaires, surveys, and interviews will begin to yield groups of responses with similarities and differences. The responses and the source of responses should be grouped in topic headers. Those that influence the enclosure designs should be noted.

Case study comparisons are particularly helpful when the building typology or enclosure concept(s) contemplated for possible use are outside of the architect's or participant's previous experience. Often a comparative case study of other examples, executed

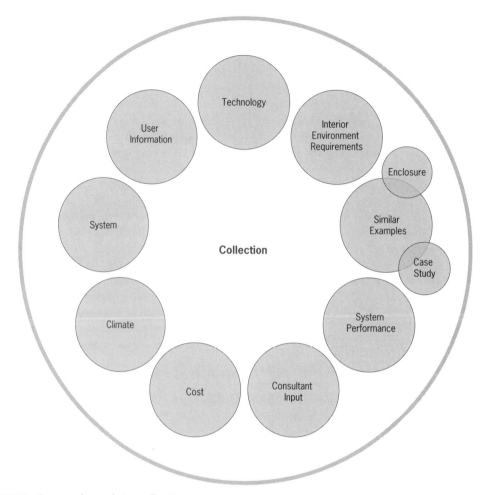

FIGURE 3.8   Some enclosure design collection topics.

or proposed, offers information in scale, performance, materials, and design strategies.

The collection of information initially identified by the design team and identified in the research and collection process will yield qualitative and quantitative data. Quantitative information will result in more specifics. This can range from the highest recorded wind speeds to the lowest and highest temperature extremes. Qualitative research information collected will usually produce a range of results that often require further definition or a second round of discussions to gain more insights and a better understanding. These range from user information (wants or needs) to quantity of glass, interior temperature and humidity controls, materials, or other items that

the exterior enclosure concept or schematic design must address. Qualitative data collection is rarely as linear a process as collecting quantitative information and data. It is iterative and progressive. It encourages thinking and questioning by the design team. Research tasks make the unseen visible, hidden or internal processes external, and private items public. This is basically turning over as many rocks as possible during research.

ANALYSIS

After analysis, relevant information becomes facts. Collect relevant information. Relevant information is only important to the design process if it is appropriate

Exterior Building Enclosures

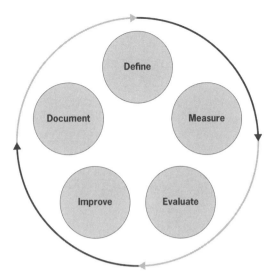

FIGURE 3.9 Analysis is a process of evaluation and improving.

Analysis goes beyond sifting and sorting. With topics researched and collected, it is time to think. You need to make sense out of the information. Patterns and relationships begin to emerge. In-depth questioning becomes second nature. Analysis can be achieved through thoughtful deliberation, or it may require assistance through graphs, charts, and computer programs. Once there is a fundamental or basic level of understanding, then schematic enclosure design can begin.

STEP 4: Schematic Design/Design Development: Enclosure System Development

Design is a plan for arranging elements in such a way as best to accomplish a particular purpose.

CHARLES EAMES

The design process, at its best, integrates the aspirations of art, science and culture.

JEFF SMITH

and timely. Extracting the information required for exterior enclosure design requires evaluation and editing. This is not a one-time effort. The collected information, organized by topic, is initially analyzed to inform the development of enclosure system concepts or schematics. The larger body of information should be organized and, where applicable, cross-referenced for more detailed analysis during subsequent design development and construction documentation steps.

The design process is iterative, and so is the depth of analysis of the information researched and collected. Analysis is defining, measuring, evaluating, improving, and then documenting. This is illustrated in Figure 3.9. Analysis offers guidelines to inform the "big idea." Topics requiring initial analysis range from geographic to climatic to jurisdictional items. Initial analysis should result in a preliminary code analysis, preliminary performance requirement checklist, and relevant user requirements and climate information. Analysis is the examination and evaluation of relevant information to inform the appropriate course of action to develop the enclosure system concept or schematic. At the enclosure system concept or schematic level, don't get too hung up on details. Developing system definition and details occurs in the schematic and design development phases, respectively.

Schematic design and design development are the primary design phases. These should be distinct, separate, and successive. The enclosure system concept is typically identified in the schematic design phase. Exterior enclosure concepts may be developed in the concept design phase, but this is more the exception than the norm. Design never stops; however, the enclosure system construct and typical system(s) details are established, developed, refined, and documented in these two phases. Documentation of the enclosure design and details for atypical conditions occurs in the construction document phase. The Design Process Timeline with the Schematic Design and Design Development steps is shown in Figure 3.10.

Schematic design and design development are the traditional phase names. Project delivery methods vary and are constantly changing and evolving.

TIME

VALIDATE

Step 4: Schematic Design
Design Development

Note: Research, Collection, and Analysis are concurrent with Schematic Design and Design Development.

GOALS

CONCEPTS

RESEARCH COLLECTION ANALYSIS

FIGURE 3.10 Schematic design and design development are the design phases in the traditional Design Process Timeline.

New names are assigned to traditional phases. No matter what delivery method is used or how design services and deliverables are packaged, the end result, prior to construction documents, remains the same: a developed enclosure system design illustrating layout, materials, typical system(s) details, and interfaces with adjacent building systems.

Schematic Design

SCHEMATIC DESIGN: COMPOSITION, EXTENTS, PROFILES, AND FINISHES

Schematic design for the exterior enclosure is not a singular discipline or one individual's effort. It is collaboration. Design is a team sport and, as in team sports, every team needs a leader. The architect leads the enclosure design team. Complete enclosure design addresses and responds to visual, performance, and interdisciplinary collaboration and coordination items. Developing enclosure system schematics is the initial synthesis of the goals, analysis, and building concept design steps. It appears to be an obvious statement that the enclosure composition takes inspiration from the building design concept. However, many enclosure design presentations (verbal and graphic) and written descriptions differ, in both subtle and obvious ways, from what is required to adequately achieve the fundamental goal of supporting and reinforcing the building design concept. Worse is when the exterior enclosure concept is not directly linked to the building concept.

Enclosure schematic design is where form is given to the concept. It is the visible and outward physical appearance of the building that is seen by the public. Its success is dependent on careful planning and quality execution. Tenacity and adaptability are just as important as creativity. Enclosure composition is the architectural features and primary materials in plan, elevation, and section. Enclosure materials and system diagrams are initially selected and composed. Profiles and finishes are evaluated for visual and performance considerations. The schematic design efforts of each collaborating discipline—structural, mechanical, electrical, energy, acoustic, and others—are discussed, designed, and incorporated into the enclosure system and its interrelated components and connections.

The building shape, massing, and orientation, in conjunction with the enclosure schematic design, are composed to respond to basic performance principles, natural forces and elements, functional requirements, regulatory requirements, and other considerations identified in the enclosure goals and analysis steps.

SCHEMATIC DESIGN: CONSIDERATIONS AND COLLABORATION

Enclosure schematics address the basic performance requirements and functions of:

- Enclosure system structure
- Enclosure system weathertightness capability
- Enclosure system energy performance

- Enclosure system movement/joinery
- Enclosure system function and longevity

These are evaluated for their respective ability to accommodate elements and forces acting independently and often simultaneously. The natural and human-created forces evaluated at a schematic level are:

- Wind
- Precipitation
- Temperature
- Sunlight
- Noise (acoustic)
- Seismic (if applicable)
- Blast (if applicable)

There is no prescribed order for the design to accommodate forces, since each design opportunity will influence the order of importance.

FUNCTIONAL REQUIREMENTS INCLUDE, BUT ARE NOT LIMITED TO:
- Building use
- Program
- Owner/user specifics
- Weathertightness
- Energy efficiency
- Durability

REGULATORY REQUIREMENTS INCLUDE, BUT ARE NOT LIMITED TO:
- Setbacks
- Separations
- Fire resistance
- Minimum code-required performance standards

Three-dimensional enclosure system schematic design exploration involves studying the building design massing through plan, section, and elevation drawings, isometrics, concept diagrams, and computer or physical study models. The goal is to establish a thorough overview of the enclosure and its relationship to other building system schematics.

Plan extent (x- and y-axis) of opaque and transparent areas is defined to a massing and a dimensional level. Plan dimensional definition includes typical spacing, corners, and defining geometry.

Elevations, sections, and isometrics define the volumetric (z-axis) extent of opaque and transparent

areas to an equivalent massing, dimensional, and geometric definition level. Opaque and transparent zones and their physical relationship to the structure, floor-to-floor heights, building services systems, and other finish systems are defined. Primary horizontal floor datum levels of top of structure (or top of finish, if they are different) to a corresponding enclosure horizontal datum or work-point are defined. Enclosure horizontal datum points are system- and material-dependent. These can be centerlines or top of materials. There are pros and cons of each, which should be finalized in the design development step.

Digital and/or physical models are helpful tools for the design team and those outside the design team, allowing them to visualize enclosure design intent in three dimensions. Schematic design models clarify the typical areas for definition in design development and identify areas of future study for atypical conditions in construction documents.

Collaboration in schematic design can be a bit of a "chicken or egg" situation. Each design team participant is a contributor to others, but each is also responsible for the design of his or her system as well. So who goes first? Conducting an initial kick-off schematic workshop with all collaborating participants allows for an open forum for enclosure ideas and design baseline discussion. This sets the tone for discussion and dialogue that continue with more detail as schematic design progresses and in subsequent phases. An initial enclosure plan, section, and elevation allow each discipline to verbalize options and sketch interface conditions. All input is interdependent and concurrent. Although there is no prescribed order for functional schematic evaluation, the enclosure structure is a tangible and familiar starting point for most architects.

The enclosure system structural schematic may be inherently strong enough to support itself and accommodate the applied forces, or in some design cases it may require a separate substructure support system. Enclosure systems structure may be homogenous solid (concrete), component solid (masonry), component framing members with cladding (masonry stone, window wall, curtain wall, cable systems, etc.), or combinations of some or all. The schematic design usually provides initial evidence for vertical spanning solids or framing members (floor to floor or to intermediate horizontal supports), horizontal spanning solids or framing (column to column, wall to wall, or intermediate vertical supports), diagonal, or other geometries. Examples of schematic enclosure structural diagrams are shown in Figure 3.11. The enclosure system supporting structural concept begins to identify efficiencies and a framework, both figuratively and literally. The goal is to schematically test and validate the initial enclosure system structural concept that allows the enclosure to span, accept, and transfer forces through the system to either the primary building structure or an intermediate substructure. This exercise is performed with the constant reminder that the structure of the enclosure must reinforce the stated visual and performance design goals. As noted in the goals step, if the design does not address the stated goal(s), the design is altered—not the goal.

Layered on the enclosure system structural concept diagram are the natural and human-created forces. The preliminary magnitude of the forces should have been identified in Step 3: Research, Collection, and Analysis. If there are no preliminary force values identified, you have gotten ahead of yourself, so pause the design for a bit and establish these to a schematic level. Schematic design solutions are only partial when the design problem is not adequately defined.

Staying with developing the enclosure structural system concept, materials are the next consideration. Every material has its own unique properties of strength, weight, availability, and so forth. Applying materials to the enclosure structural diagram defines an initial range of sizes in width and depth. Both are important. Keep depth in mind, since it factors heavily into a later discussion on weathertightness concepts in the design development step. With the enclosure structural concept in its infancy, establish a preliminary spacing, size, and material selection. Infill or cladding, whether opaque (stone, metal, etc.) or transparent (glass, plastics, films, etc.), between framing supports or out of plane of the framing supports, will also have its own unique span capabilities and ability to accommodate and transfer loads.

The enclosure system structural schematic will require a corresponding attachment and anchorage concept. Cladding attachments transfer loads and forces to enclosure framing or planar surfaces. Anchorages transfer forces from the enclosure framing to the primary building structure. The exterior enclosure schematic defines a load path diagram transferring exterior forces through cladding attachments to framing and framing anchorages to the primary building structure. Most primary building structural systems are very definitive as to where exterior enclosure loads can and cannot be accommodated by the structure. This collaborative exercise is usually an enlightening experience for both the architect and the structural engineer. Load path diagrams for anchorage and attachments are shown in Figure 3.12. The location of enclosure system anchorage connections and the load path should be identified to allow the structural engineer to anticipate and develop the corresponding structural schematic to accommodate the enclosure loads into the primary building structural concept.

In schematic design, it is helpful to stick to basics and diagrams. Defining structural to architectural adjacency interfaces sets out architectural and structural edges and boundaries in all three dimensions. This adjacency also sets the wall assembly zone (WAZ) for the enclosure. WAZ components include the cladding, enclosure structural components, and anchorage areas. A wall assembly zone diagram is shown in Figure 3.13. When the structure is exposed either fully or partially to the exterior of the enclosure, there are defining boundary adjacencies in plan, section, and elevation. When the structure is the interior side of the enclosure, there are defining boundary adjacencies predominately in plan. Primary building structural movement diagrams are superimposed to determine the influences of the primary building structure on the enclosure to a schematic level.

THE GOAL OF THE STRUCTURAL/ARCHITECTURAL COLLABORATION IN THE SCHEMATIC PHASE IS TO ESTABLISH:

1. Building geometry
2. Wall assembly zone depth by wall zone components
3. Enclosure load path diagram to structure
4. Architectural to structural adjacencies
5. Structural movements

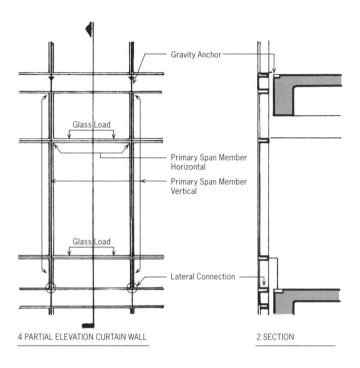

Gravity Anchor

Glass Load

Primary Span Member Horizontal

Primary Span Member Vertical

Glass Load

Lateral Connection

4 PARTIAL ELEVATION CURTAIN WALL

2 SECTION

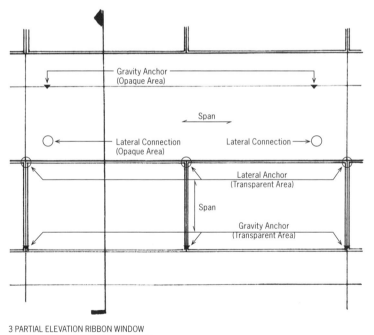

Gravity Anchor (Opaque Area)

Span

Lateral Connection (Opaque Area)

Lateral Connection

Lateral Anchor (Transparent Area)

Span

Gravity Anchor (Transparent Area)

3 PARTIAL ELEVATION RIBBON WINDOW

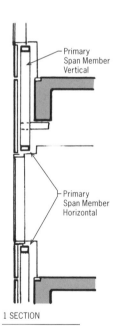

Primary Span Member Vertical

Primary Span Member Horizontal

1 SECTION

FIGURE 3.11 Examples of enclosure system structure logic.

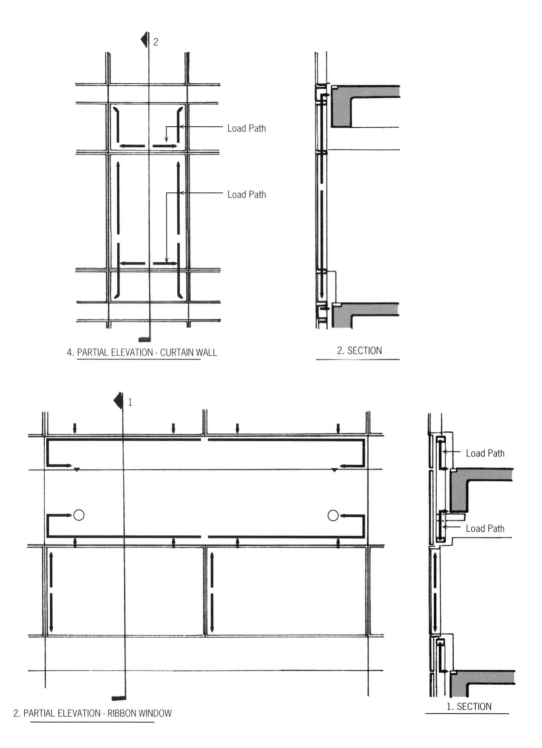

Load Path

Load Path

4. PARTIAL ELEVATION - CURTAIN WALL

2. SECTION

Load Path

Load Path

2. PARTIAL ELEVATION - RIBBON WINDOW

1. SECTION

FIGURE 3.12 Examples of enclosure system structure load paths. Loads are transferred through the exterior enclosure to the primary building structure.

Exterior Building Enclosures

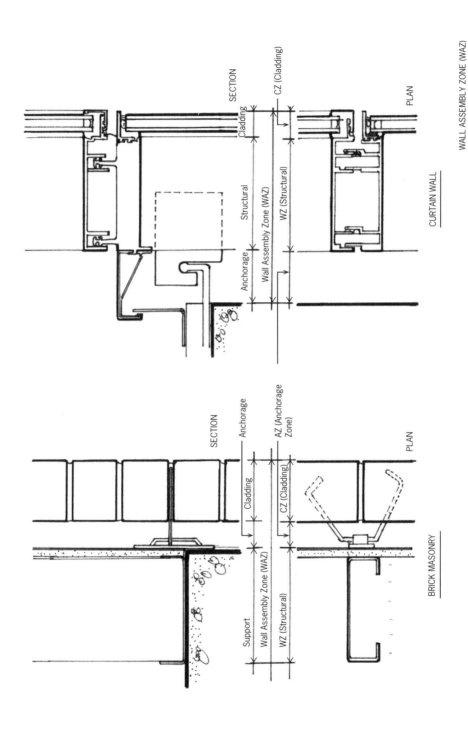

FIGURE 3.13 Examples of enclosure wall assembly zones (WAZ).

The architect and structural engineer should have the same level of understanding of each item, for their system and the influence of their collaborator's system.

Concurrent with structural collaboration is the initial collaborative effort between the architect; building services engineers; the mechanical engineer, in particular, and the energy consultant, if applicable. Generally, the architectural enclosure schematic design will illustrate the extent of opaque and transparent areas for the exterior enclosure. The enclosure is inextricably linked to the project's energy performance. A design team brainstorming workshop sets the strategy to determine the preliminary mechanical plant sizing requirements, mechanical distribution, and energy efficiency basis of design for the enclosure.

The enclosure schematic design sets the "foundation" for the building mechanical system and equipment sizing. A combination of code requirements and the project energy performance goals, set out in the goals step, guides the selection and sizing of the mechanical equipment and the annual energy consumption. The enclosure and the mechanical system/equipment design are mutually inclusive and should be performed concurrently.

A design workshop including the architect and mechanical engineer, similar to the structural engineering work session, is invaluable. The goal is to define the performance expectation of the enclosure and its implications for the mechanical equipment quantity, its size, and the resulting energy consumption and efficiency. There are big picture enclosure and mechanical design decisions to be made, such as building orientation, massing, overhangs, glass selection/performance criteria, vision glass areas, insulating opaque areas, daylighting strategies, and others. This workshop usually results in an initial establishment of vision glass areas, performance requirements, the insulation quantity, and insulation type. The resulting R-value for the opaque areas and U-values and shading coefficient performance ranges of glass are dependent on the local climate, solar orientation, and building use. Each is project-specific and has a direct influence on the enclosure's visual appearance and energy efficiency. Macro- and microclimates and building orientation and massing directly influence the enclosure composition and the level of energy efficiency and related mechanical equipment sizing. In the schematic design phase, the goal is to establish a holistic energy strategy. The enclosure is a key component of this strategy and should be responsive and not predetermined. Enclosure composition decisions establish the foundation to build upon in subsequent phases without altering the fundamental layout, material selections, and orientation.

In any climate, enclosure design that has all elevations the same uses a lowest common denominator design approach. The building's exterior enclosure composition and appearance should be governed by the more onerous orientation and exposure. The other and more responsive end of the enclosure design spectrum is that each elevation's design is tuned to the specific orientation, solar gain, and subsequent influences. This approach can and usually does influence the cost of the enclosure, typically resulting in moderate to high costs. Achieving a schematic enclosure design that addresses and responds to energy efficiency and occupant comfort, while providing elegant proportions with cost effectiveness, is where "design with a capital D" is accomplished. Energy efficiency is one of multiple design considerations for ascertaining that each performance parameter is considered in the most advantageous composition. The completed enclosure schematic design must integrate each parameter and reinforce the stated building and enclosure design intent goals.

The mechanical engineer, energy consultant, and other design team participants are collaborators, not "fixers." Appropriate design tools must be utilized at the appropriate time in schematics to support and validate the direction of the enclosure schematic. The architect must question, process, analyze, understand, and incorporate the recommendations by design team participants in the enclosure composition and design.

ITEMS TO DEFINE IN COLLABORATION WITH THE MECHANICAL ENGINEER/ENERGY CONSULTANT INCLUDE, BUT ARE NOT LIMITED TO:

1. Enclosure interfaces with the mechanical/electrical/plumbing systems
2. Influence of building services on the enclosure, and vice versa
3. Floor-to-floor heights

4. Enclosure extent of glass
5. Enclosure glass performance criteria
6. Enclosure extent of opaque areas
7. Enclosure R-value of opaque areas
8. Extent of overhead, underfloor, or other distribution system and the interface with the enclosure and other systems

There are acoustical, fire/life safety, and other collaborators who, depending on the project requirements, will have input on and should be involved in the schematic design of the enclosure. The extent of this collaboration is dependent on the building use.

In collaboration with the design team participants, the architect graphically defines the plan, section, elevations, and models or 3D drawings of the enclosure. Each graphic includes material identifications. With this three-dimensional view, the enclosure system schematic can be "tested" to define the most appropriate enclosure system.

SCHEMATIC DESIGN: DELIVERY PRODUCT

The resulting schematic design for the exterior enclosure includes at a minimum:

GRAPHICS
1. Building plan(s) at appropriate scale (typically ⅛″ = 1′0″ min. or 1:100). These are sometimes at a smaller scale for very large building footprints.
   a. Extent of opaque and transparent materials
   b. Dimensional definition (see Figures 3.14a and b)
   c. Material identification
2. Elevation (preferably at same scale as plan)
   a. Extent of opaque and transparent materials
   b. Dimensional definition (see Figure 3.14b)
   c. Material identification
   d. Geometric definition
3. Section (preferably at same scale as elevation)
   a. Extent of opaque and transparent materials (see Figure 3.14c)
   b. Relationship of structure
   c. Relationship of mechanical requirements
      1. Ceiling heights/plenum
      2. Underfloor, if applicable

4. Isometrics
   a. Extent of opaque and transparent materials (see Figure 3.15)
   b. Relationship of structure
   c. Relationship of mechanical requirements
      1. Ceiling heights/plenum
      2. Underfloor, if applicable

TEXT
1. Enclosure narrative description
   a. Establish initial wall assembly zone
   b. Material identification
2. Schematic basis of design
   a. Loads/pressures
   b. Design temperature ranges
   c. Interior temperature/humidity ranges
   d. Other project-specific requirements

MODELS
1. Overall massing models (see Figure 3.16)
2. Other models as needed to explain the enclosure schematic

This assembly of drawings, text, and models is the building enclosure schematic. Other design discipline drawings and text must be developed to a similar graphic and narrative development. Schematics are the foundation for the follow-on phases of enclosure system development and documentation.

Design Development

Design development is exactly what the name states. The approved schematic design is further developed and refined by adding and defining additional layers of information and detail. Detail definition ranges from overall enclosure organization to actual detail drawings. As an example, the enclosure may utilize very few system details, but the organization has multiple elevations and plan conditions. This will require more development of plans, elevations, and sections. A building enclosure with a regular shape with multiple enclosures requires more details to clarify system interfaces.

Design development is the least understood and utilized phase of the design process. The American Institute of Architects' (AIA) initial paragraph

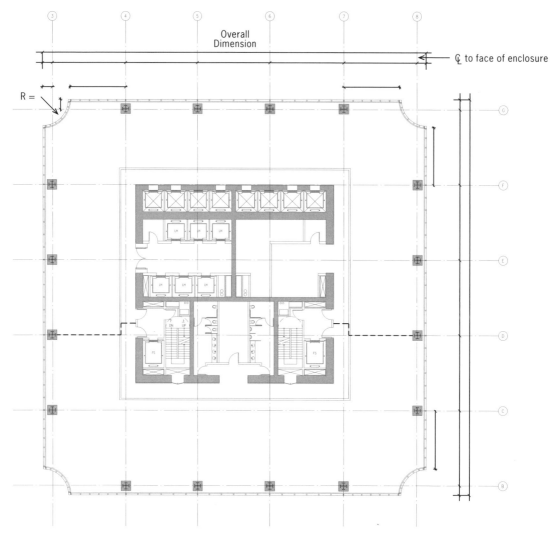

FIGURE 3.14a Schematic design plan illustrating location, extent, and overall dimensions. *Skidmore, Owings & Merrill LLP*

describing the architect's responsibilities in the design development phase states:

> Based on the Owner's approval of the Schematic Design Documents and on the Owner's authorization of any adjustments in the Project's requirements and the budget for the Cost of the work, the Architect shall prepare Design Development Documents for the Owner's approval. The Design Development Documents shall illustrate and describe the development of the approved Schematic Design Documents and shall consist of drawings, and other documents including plans, sections, elevations, typical construction details and diagrammatic layouts of the building systems to fix and describe the size and character of the Project as to the architectural, structural, mechanical and electrical systems, and such elements as may be appropriate. The Design Development Documents shall also include outline specifications that identify major

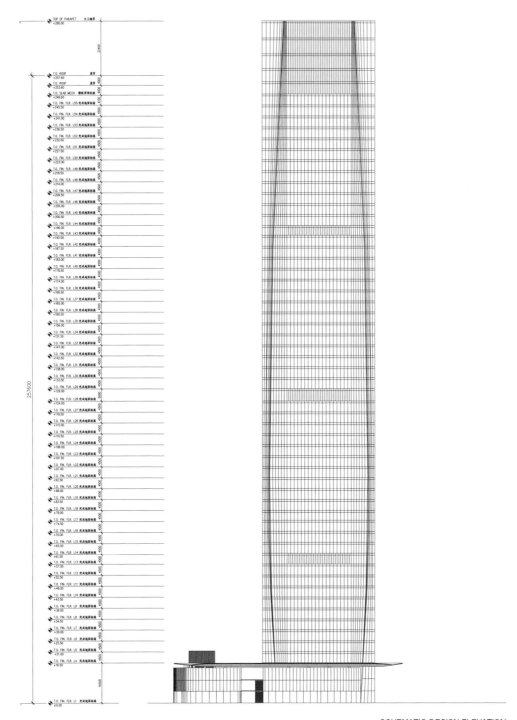

SCHEMATIC DESIGN ELEVATION

FIGURE 3.14b Schematic design elevation illustrating extent of enclosure systems, materials, and composition. *Skidmore, Owings & Merrill LLP*

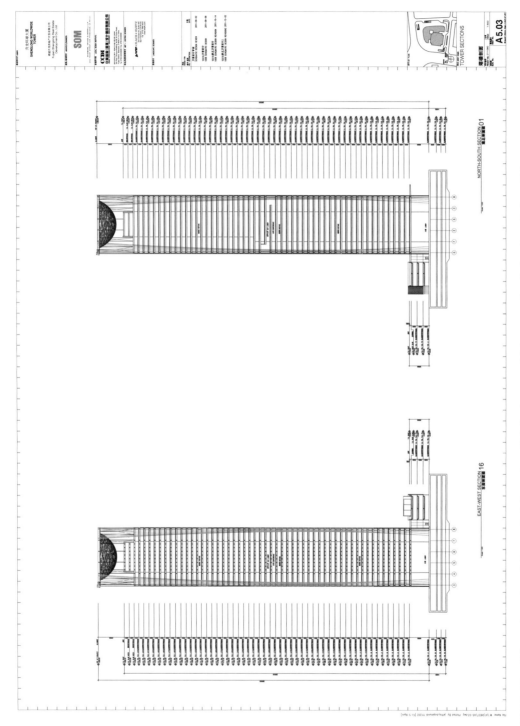

FIGURE 3.14c Schematic sections define vertical dimensions. This begins to establish extent of typical and atypical conditions.

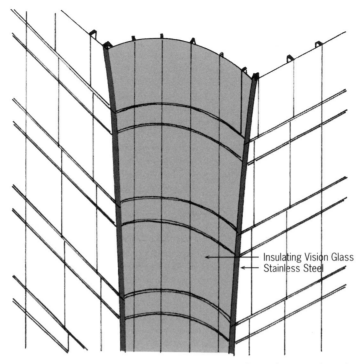

FIGURE 3.15 Schematic design isometric is a quick method to illustrate the enclosure in three dimensions.

materials and systems and establish in general their quality levels (AIA A201).

DESIGN DEVELOPMENT: SYSTEM SELECTION

The enclosure composition and materials were studied and selected in schematic design. The preliminary wall assembly zone has also been initially established in the schematic phase. Design development requires study of representative typical system details at a larger scale. This is not mysterious or daunting. Head, sill, and jamb details for typical and corner conditions are developed at a large scale (the larger the scale, the better), with appropriate and accurate material indications. This increased scale exploration provides opportunities for further definition of the enclosure system structural performance, weather protection, energy efficiency, acoustics, fire and life safety, and other performance-related issues. Usually, several detail studies are conducted to test visual profiles, system depths, materials, and relationships/

interfaces with adjacent systems. Enclosure system exploration is a series of evolutionary details. Details should be studied in two- and three-dimensional drawings and models.

Exploration at a larger scale in design development offers opportunities to study and evaluate visual relationships of materials and joinery concurrent with the integration of the performance functions. Interdisciplinary collaboration initiated in the schematic design phase continues with further integration of engineering disciplines specifics merged into the enclosure development.

DESIGN DEVELOPMENT: WEATHER PROTECTION

An informative first step in detail exploration and study is to apply weather protection principles. The enclosure design development profiles, materials, system depth, and initial detail studies offer clues as to whether a single line of air and water defense (such as a barrier or mass principle) or a dual line of water

FIGURE 3.16 Schematic design enclosure model. *Skidmore, Owings & Merrill LLP*

defense (such as a rain screen or rain screen/pressure-equalized principle) may be more applicable. A starting point in "testing" which weather barrier principle to apply is to select a line of primary defense for air within the enclosure assembly. Remembering the Basics from Chapter 1, there can be one line of air defense with additional methods for water reduction, management, collection, and removal from within the enclosure. For example, a glass wall is a candidate for a barrier system if the glass-to-glass panel joints are sealed and the glass is either self-supporting or supported by a support system in a separate and distinct plane from the glass. The air and water barrier is (1) the glass itself, which is impervious to air and water infiltration, and (2) the sealant, which, when applied continuously and correctly, is also impervious to air and water infiltration. An example of this system is shown in Figure 3.17.

Precast or architectural concrete with the concrete finish exposed to the exterior is a candidate for a mass

weather barrier principle. Insulation in these types of enclosure systems is either located internally or installed on the interior spaces or surfaces. This principle requires defining a primary air/water defense utilizing either material thickness/density or application of a waterproof or water-resistant material on the interior side of the enclosure. Interior space and occupant requirements should be carefully considered when this type of weather barrier principle is utilized. Additional design and detail strategies may be required in tandem with a single-line-of-defense approach. The mass principle is applicable to the opaque material areas. The joinery in between the opaque-to-opaque or opaque-to-transparent materials may be a barrier type or a dual-line-of-weather-protection strategy, which is discussed later in this section.

Masonry walls such as brick, stone, or other modular units supported on a substructure support system are candidates for a rain screen or a pressure-equalized principle. Examples of the differences and similarities of these are shown in Figure 3.18. This is an abstract that is not from any specific project to illustrate: 1) the principle and 2) areas of study.

Window walls, storefronts, stone masonry, and curtain walls are candidates for a rain screen or rain screen/pressure-equalized principle. The defining characteristic for the pressure-equalized principle is the ability to incorporate a delimiter in the rain screen zone. This delimiter forms a pressure-equalized chamber or zone between the primary inner line of weather protection and the outer secondary line of weather protection. The depth and extent of the pressure-equalization chamber vary by system types. These range from a shallow pressure-equalized chamber in a stick-built assembly to the opportunity for a deeper pressure-equalization chamber in unitized assemblies. Some metal and masonry enclosures can be pressure-equalized, depending on the ability to introduce a delimiter in the design.

As noted in the "Schematic Design" section of Step 4, the enclosure system depth provides the available space to implement the type of weather protection principle. The enclosure system depth is also checked against the structural requirements. Each informs the other, and they must coexist. Depending on the system design, the depth requirement to achieve structural performance is a key factor, and

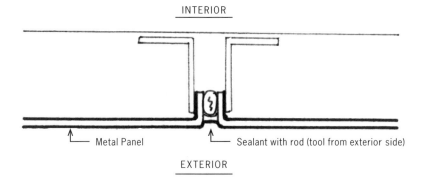

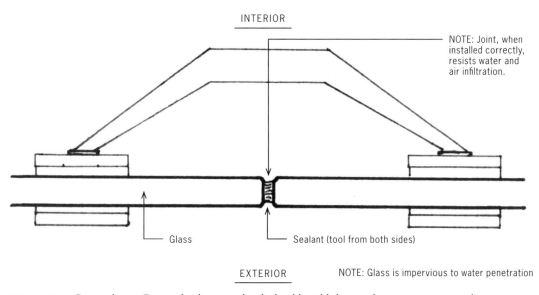

FIGURE 3.17 Barrier design. Design development details should establish a weather protection principle.

the weather protection principle is adapted to this depth. Each enclosure design will have its unique requirements, so the two functions of structure and weather protection should be evaluated in tandem.

The common design objective in the four weather barrier principles noted previously is to establish a location of the primary air/water line, often referred to as the primary line of defense. This line must be continuous in each principle. A good design validation test is to place your pen or curser on the proposed primary air/water defense line and

"track" this from sill to jamb to head and around corners in three dimensions, without picking up the pen or cursor. Examples are given in the series of diagrams shown in Figures 3.19a–c. In rain screen and pressure-equalized principles, there are opportunities for an outer line of water protection. This is the secondary defense line and is achieved with baffles and/or openings in the joint or joint material to allow drainage from the rain screen cavity or pressure-equalization chamber. This outer water deflector is the secondary line of water defense.

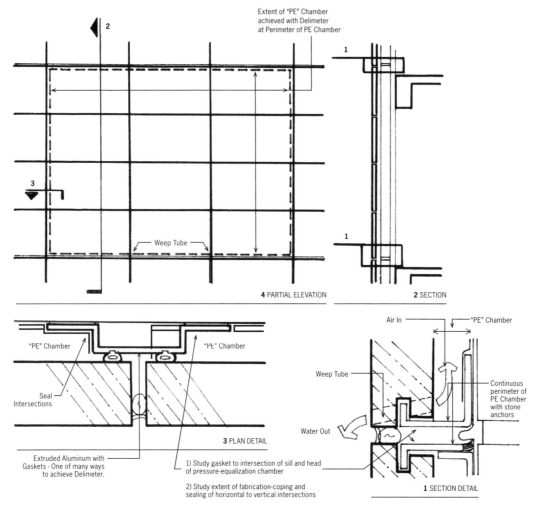

Extent of "PE" Chamber
achieved with Delimeter
at Perimeter of PE Chamber

Weep Tube

4 PARTIAL ELEVATION

Air In   "PE" Chamber

Weep Tube

Water Out

Continuous
perimeter of
PE Chamber
with stone
anchors

1 SECTION DETAIL

2 SECTION

"PE" Chamber   "PE" Chamber

Seal
Intersections

Extruded Aluminum with
Gaskets - One of many ways
to achieve Delimeter.

1) Study gasket to intersection of sill and head
of pressure-equalization chamber

2) Study extent of fabrication-coping and
sealing of horizontal to vertical intersections

3 PLAN DETAIL

FIGURE 3.18   Pressure-equalization diagram. Design development details should establish a weather protection principle.

DESIGN DEVELOPMENT: ENCLOSURE STRUCTURE

The enclosure system structural logic was outlined in the schematic design step. The final structural approach and solution for the system and the cladding attachments is defined in design development. Structural and architectural enclosure design development collaboration efforts are performed for the typical conditions with an eye towards inside and outside corners, base (starter), coping conditions, and openings/

recesses. The results are questioned and discussed between the architect and structural engineer to achieve a common level of understanding and expectations. Tolerances of the architectural systems and structural components and systems are layered over the adjacency and interface studies to a schematic level. Because the design development defines the enclosure system details, tolerances are salient and should be included in system details. The big idea is to acknowledge tolerances early to determine how they

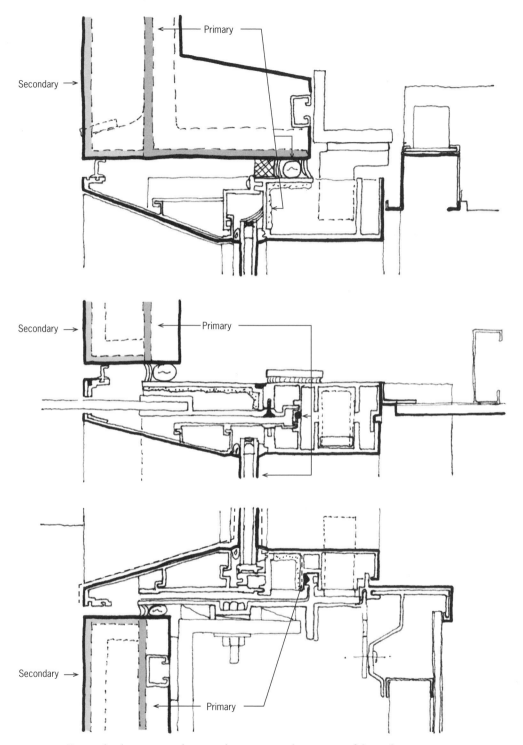

FIGURE 3.19a Design development: tracking weather protection lines in one of the enclosure systems.

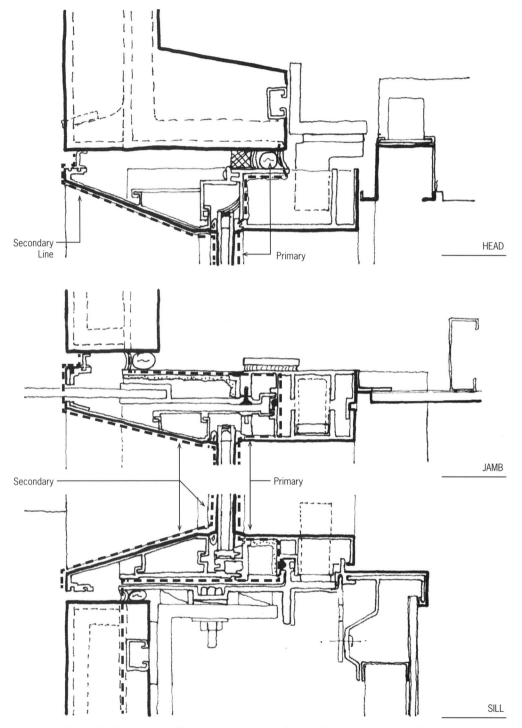

Secondary
Line

Primary

HEAD

Secondary

Primary

JAMB

SILL

FIGURE 3.19b Design development: tracking weather protection lines in the window enclosure system.

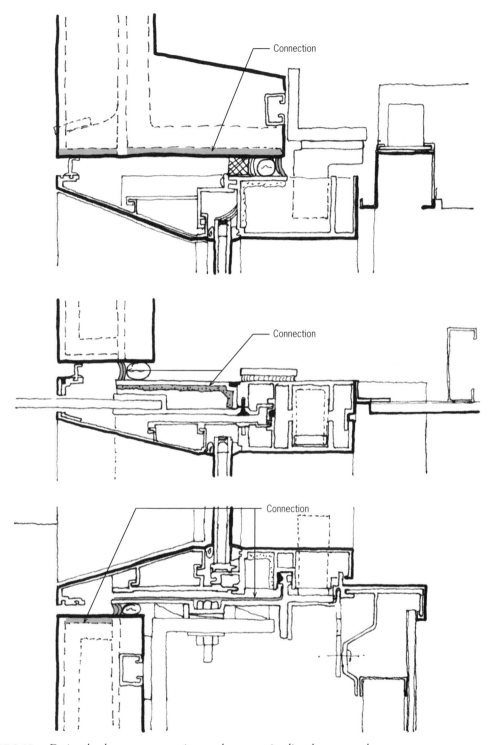

FIGURE 3.19c Design development: connecting weather protection lines between enclosure systems.

will or will not enhance or impede future design development. Tolerances can be derived through industry standards, previous experiences, and discussions with team members or those in the construction industry.

The enclosure system anchorage can be designed by the architect/structural engineer or by the contractor, with performance criteria defined by the architect. The responsibility is dependent on the project delivery method or the experience of the architect and design team.

DESIGN DEVELOPMENT: MATERIAL RESEARCH AND SELECTION

Gathering project-specific material samples contemplated for use in the enclosure provides a tactile and hands-on appreciation for their attributes and limitations. Collecting, reading, and evaluating material product data provides a more in-depth knowledge of the quality standards and manufacturing process, which will inform the enclosure details. Actual material samples, which can be held and examined, bridge the gap between visualization and reality for the architect and owner.

Specifications, whether in outline form or full format, must be developed with the full involvement of the architect. These are not developed by a mysterious guru in the back room, or by a remote participant in the design process. As stated earlier, the architect cannot know everything, but he or she definitely needs to be actively engaged in the specification development. Material fabricators and their supply source are excellent resources for specifics to evaluate and include in enclosure system detail development and specification preparation.

DESIGN DEVELOPMENT: INPUT AND CRITIQUE

With system design development details (either in progress or to a level of done) of the typical systems, intersections of typical systems, the layout and composition of the enclosure design, and the in-progress specifications, it is time to solicit additional input and critique. This can be obtained from a variety of sources. Informal discussions and presentations with other team participants will promote the consistency of the overall building design. Details from the enclosure systems inform other building systems in design development, and vice versa. Input from material suppliers and manufacturers provides the opportunity to fine-tune the application of materials and the compatibility of materials contained in the details. Input from builders or system designers who make their living constructing or designing enclosures provides insights on constructability, cost implications, and construction logistics implied in the design development system and details.

With this input, the enclosure design and system details can be composed into a design development set of documents. The resulting enclosure design development set can include, at a minimum, the materials outlined in the following section.

DESIGN DEVELOPMENT: DELIVERY PRODUCT

Graphics

1. Building plan(s) at appropriate scale (typically ⅛″ = 1′0″ min. or ¼″ = 1′0″)
   a. Extent of opaque and transparent material areas
   b. Further dimensional definition (see Figure 3.20)
   c. Relationship of structure
2. Elevations at same scale as plan
   a. Extent of opaque and transparent materials
   b. Material identification
   c. Possible system identification
   d. Relationship of structure
   e. Dimensional definition (see Figure 3.21a)
3. Section at same scale as elevation
   a. Extent of opaque and transparent materials
   b. Relationship of structure
   c. Relationship of mechanical requirements
   d. Dimensional definition (see Figure 3.21b)
4. Isometrics (see Figure 3.22)
5. Details of each enclosure system head, jamb, sill, and other conditions as appropriate @ large scale 1½″ (1:10), 3″ = 1′0″ (1:5) or larger (see Figure 3.23)
6. System interface details on projects with multiple enclosure systems @ 1½″ (1:10), 3″ = 1′0″ (1:5) or larger

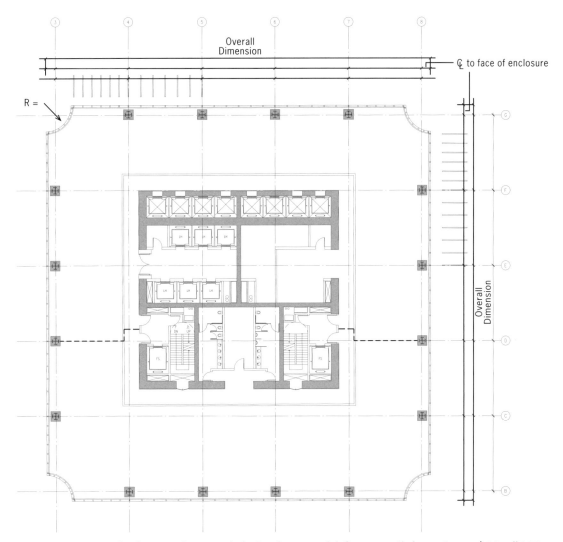

FIGURE 3.20 Design development plans provide further dimensional definition.   *Skidmore, Owings & Merrill LLP*

TEXT: SPECIFICATIONS

1. Enclosure outline or full format specifications
2. Finalized basis of design
   a. Movement
   b. Loads/pressures
   c. Design temperature ranges
   d. Interior temperature/humidity ranges

MATERIALS

1. Product-specific material selections and samples
2. Product data
3. Model (if applicable)

This assembly of drawings, written text, and material review and selection is the building enclosure design development. Other design discipline drawings and text must be developed to a similar graphic and narrative level of development.

STEP 5: Construction Documents

God is in the details.

LUDWIG MIES VAN DER ROHE

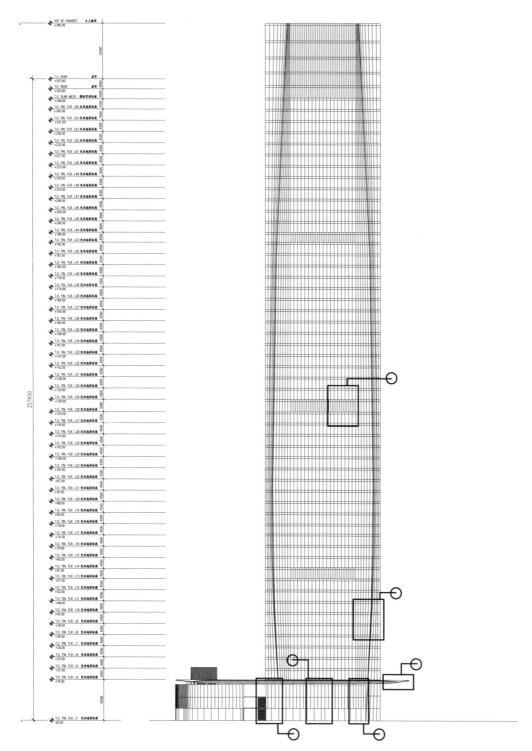

FIGURE 3.21a Design development elevations provide further material and detail definition. *Skidmore, Owings & Merrill LLP*

Exterior Building Enclosures

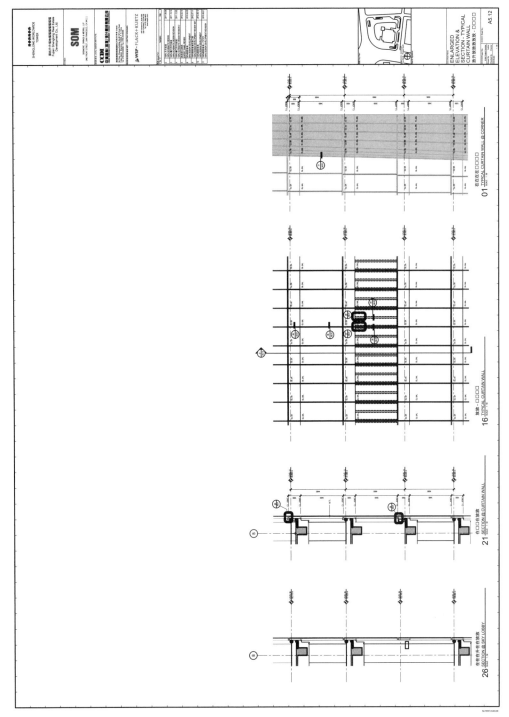

FIGURE 3.21b Design development elevations and sections further define vertical dimensions and extents of opaque and transparent areas and materials.

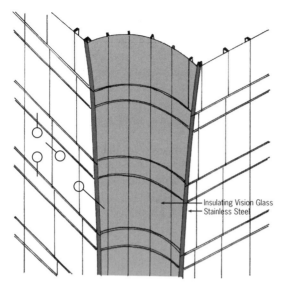

FIGURE 3.22 Design development isometrics provide further enclosure system details.

Insulating Vision Glass
Stainless Steel

Construction documents are the final phase of the traditional enclosure design process. Typical enclosure system (or systems) design is developed and documented in design development. The intersections of multiple exterior systems are also initially defined and documented in design development. As noted in Step 4's "Design Development" section, design never stops. Design continues in construction documents. However, the enclosure design efforts are more focused on finalizing intersections and atypical details. The team dynamics and relationships with other participants shift from collaboration to coordination. The Design Process Timeline with the Construction Documents step is shown in Figure 3.24.

Enclosure construction documents consist of the drawings and technical specifications. The drawings are the graphics, illustrating the enclosure plans, elevations, and sections with large-scale details. These details define the visual requirements of the enclosure system, materials, interfaces with other enclosure system(s), and interfaces with other building systems, the functions, and performance principles. The drawings define the enclosure extent and details. The specifications are the written instructions and define the quality standards, materials, fabrication, and installation specifics. The drawings and specifications are mutually

complementary. They should always be developed concurrently. The completed set of enclosure construction documents translates the owner's stated needs and goals into a coordinated set of drawings and specifications that can be understood within the construction industry. This construction document description is known and familiar to most in the design and construction industry. Construction document unknowns usually reside in how much documentation is required. The construction document phase is also an opportunity to tune the enclosure design. In the two design phases (schematic and design development), visual design is the lead, and design details are the support. In construction documents, the enclosure system details lead and assist in streamlining the design. Each atypical condition should not require a distinct and completely new type of detail. Rather, there is a suite of details for the systems with simple and direct modifications to address the atypical details. When (and if) you get to this actuality, the enclosure design and documentation finish line is visible.

GOAL OF CONSTRUCTION DOCUMENTS

The goal of the construction documents is a thorough set of drawings and specifications that are clear and coordinated. Construction documents are used by contractors (general and exterior enclosure) to review, price, bid, fabricate, and construct. This objective should be stated at the onset of every project construction document phase, as a reminder to all team participants. The construction documents prepared by the design team can be used directly for construction (e.g., certain masonry brick enclosures) or by specialty contractors in preparation of shop drawings (e.g., a custom enclosure). In either case, the design team construction documents are the instructions to the contractor(s) on how the project should be constructed to comply with the visual and performance design requirements. Construction documents for exterior enclosures need to "speak construction language." They are similar to assembly instructions for other manufactured items. Anyone who has assembled a bicycle late on Christmas Eve can appreciate a set of assembly instructions that are legible, concise, coordinated, complete, and understandable.

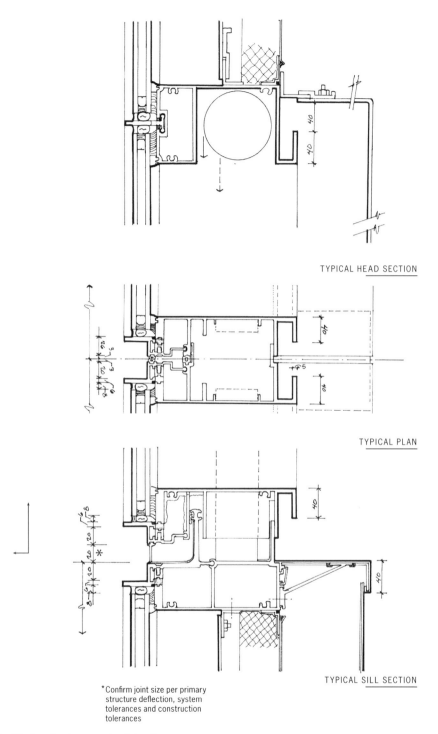

TYPICAL HEAD SECTION

TYPICAL PLAN

TYPICAL SILL SECTION

*Confirm joint size per primary
 structure deflection, system
 tolerances and construction
 tolerances

FIGURE 3.23 Design development level details.

CONSTRUCTION DOCUMENT ORGANIZATION

THE TYPICAL QUESTIONS REGARDING EXTERIOR ENCLOSURE CONSTRUCTION DOCUMENTS ARE:

- How much drawing and detailing is required?
- What scale should this be drawn?
- How much should be shown on details? This is usually related to the inner workings of systems.
- Do you have to draw everything?

The list of questions is endless, but they are centered along the same train of thought. The design, enclosure system type, and project delivery method determine the scale, level of detail, and quantity of drawings and details required.

With the understanding that the construction documents are for the eventual use of the contractor(s), document clarity and organization are primary considerations. Enclosures should be illustrated with particular detail of adjacent systems and finishes integrated into the documents set. The drawing set should be organized with a roadmap to define the drawings' location, use, and hierarchy. Each drawing is important. Some illustrate the big picture (location or key plans and elevations), and some show layout and composition (plans and elevations). Some point the way (detail references), some show how a particular enclosure system is built (details), and some show intersections and interfaces (details) with other systems. An example of a drawing roadmap for exterior enclosures is illustrated in Figure 3.25. The roadmap shown is a "one-way flow" drawing set. In the "one-way flow" approach, the plans, elevations, and sections lead to larger-scale drawings and the large-scale details. Some owners, agencies, and contractors will request that the details, which are the destination in a one-way flow set, can be back-referenced to where they occur. This may be possible for very simple and repetitive enclosures. However, it is very difficult to implement this type of roadmap for many complex or large-scale projects with multiple enclosure system types and details.

The cartoon set described earlier is an excellent organizer to guide the development of the enclosure roadmap. The cartoon set identifies the logistics of the drawings, scale, and location in the documents. An example of selected cartoon sheets for: (1) exterior enclosure elevations, (2) enlarged elevations, (3) enlarged details, and (4) detail placement is shown in Figures 3.26a–c. The cartoon set is the first three P's (proper, prior, planning) of the seven P's described earlier in this chapter. The cartoon set can be done one time for smaller-scale or simple exterior enclosures. More complicated designs and buildings with multiple enclosure systems may require that plans, elevations, and sections be cartooned and drawn initially, and that a follow-up cartoon set for details be developed once the enclosure layout drawing sheets have been sufficiently developed. The quantity of enclosure details, the detail scale, and the level of detail are dependent on the following items:

1. Project delivery method
2. Complexity of enclosure (is the system a manufacturer's standard or custom?)
3. Team expectations
4. System(s) interfaces

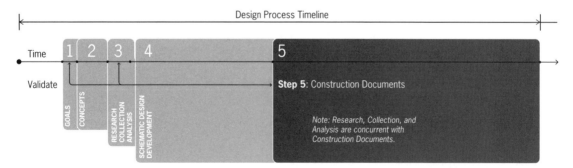

FIGURE 3.24 Construction Documents step in the Design Process Timeline. Enclosure design continues, but the focus is on documentation and final coordination of design disciplines.

PROJECT DELIVERY METHODS

There are multiple project delivery methods. The selection of the project delivery method is typically made at the project inception. It is mentioned here because it usually determines the level of detail in the construction documents and often in the design development phase. Each delivery method has its associated level of expectations of detail specificity for team member participants initially engaged and those who will eventually join the project team. Enclosure system details can be grouped into two categories:

1. "A way"
2. "The way"

In each of the delivery methods it is advisable for the architect to illustrate "a way" for the enclosure system(s) construction to achieve the design and performance requirements. The final method, after contractor review and input with architectural agreement, becomes "the way" that the enclosure will be fabricated and constructed. These may be the same, but there are distinctive traits that enclosure trades and contractors prefer. The architect who has thoughtfully considered visual, materials, and performance considerations in the document development will be able to highlight which portions of a contractor's proposed construction method comply and which are not acceptable.

The design-bid-build project delivery usually requires the architect and design team to provide a higher level of detail for the enclosure system(s). Depending on the architect's expertise, this work can be performed by the architect or by the architect with assistance from specialty enclosure consultants. The drawings should illustrate details with "a way" for construction that convey the visual and performance design intent and requirements. The specifications define the basis of design and expected and required performance requirements.

The design-build project delivery has many definitions. There are design-build team organizations where the architect/engineer/builder is a combined team. There are design-build delivery methods whereby the architect establishes overall profiles with performance specifications for the eventual selected contractor or contractors to develop in more detail after selection in shop drawings. The quantity of enclosure drawings is not necessarily any less in design-build than in design-bid-build. However, the level of detail on the architectural drawings is usually lower in design-build. The level of detail is further developed by the selected design-build contractors with input from the architect.

The design-assist delivery method incorporates preselected contractors and enclosure contractors to provide consultation to the architect in the system

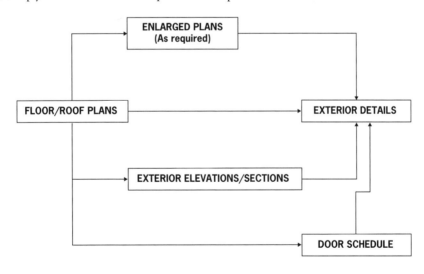

FIGURE 3.25 A drawing "flow path" to navigate the enclosure documents.

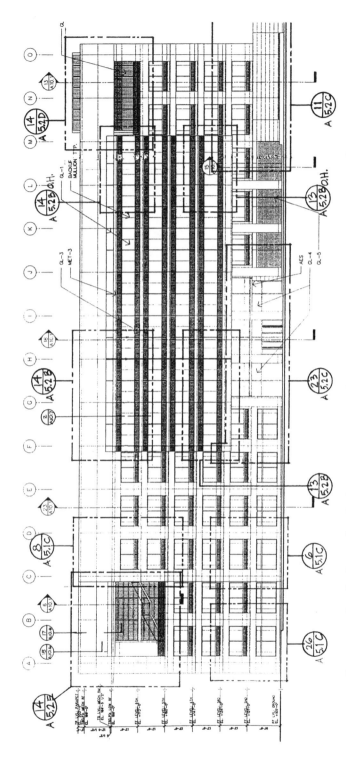

FIGURE 3.26a Cartoon sets identify what needs to be drawn. A construction document example is shown. *Skidmore, Owings & Merrill LLP*

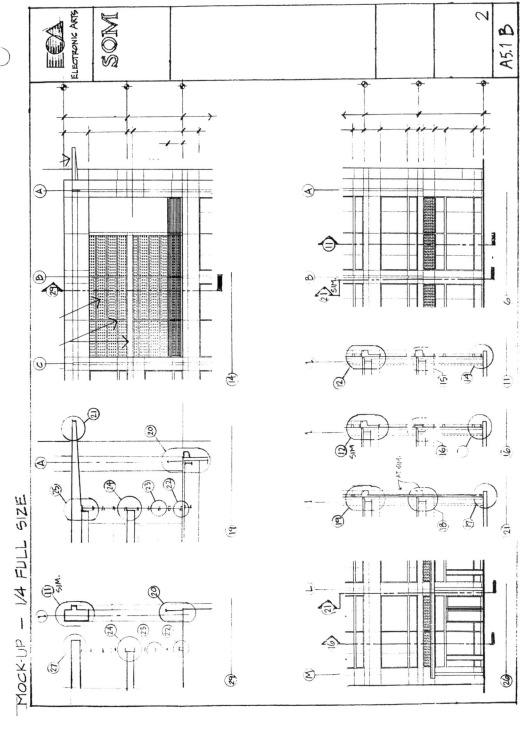

FIGURE 3.26b Cartoon set identifies enlarged elevations and sections with details to be drawn noted. *Skidmore, Owings & Merrill LLP*

125

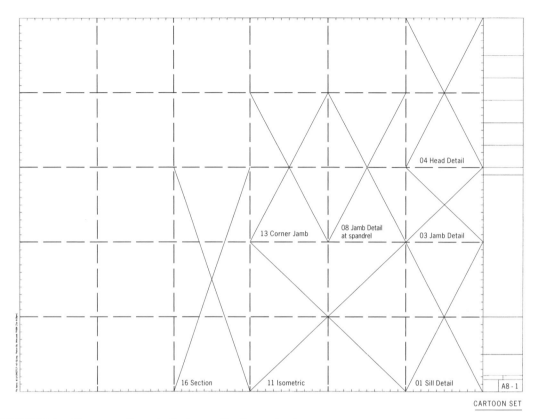

04 Head Detail

13 Corner Jamb

08 Jamb Detail
at spandrel

03 Jamb Detail

16 Section

11 Isometric

01 Sill Detail

A8 - 1

CARTOON SET

FIGURE 3.26c   Cartoon set "mapping" a layout of enclosure details.

detail development and in the interfaces between systems. The extent of documentation—either by architect or contractor—is project-specific, depending on who draws what.

In the delivery methods noted, the level of detail in the construction documents will vary. The constant that will not vary between methods is the need for team participants to establish and agree on expectations of each and the level of detail to be included in the construction documents. A hypothetical example of the level of detail for a custom exterior enclosure detail, in each of the three delivery methods, is illustrated in Figure 3.27.

COMPLEXITY OF ENCLOSURE: STANDARD TO CUSTOM

The variety of exterior enclosure systems has no limits. Complex enclosure designs may require the architect

to fully detail each component of the system, or this may be done through profiles and performance specifications. The design development exploration and system development details will define whether the enclosure goals can be accomplished by either a manufacturer's standard system, customization of a manufacturer's standard, or a fully custom system.

FOR MANUFACTURER'S STANDARD SYSTEMS, THE EXTENT OF DESIGN AND DESIGN DETAIL IS PRIMARILY:

1. Show composition and layout.
2. Illustrate anchorage location to the structure.
3. Illustrate interfaces with adjacent systems.
4. Define materials and finishes.

Since the system is a manufacturer's standard, there is no need to detail the inner workings of frames or other items. This is pre-engineered and, because it is standard, any internal detailing by the architect is

126

redrawing what is already known. The prime considerations are material and finish identification and interfaces with adjacent systems.

FOR A CUSTOMIZED MANUFACTURER'S STANDARD, THE EXTENT OF DESIGN AND DESIGN DETAIL IS PRIMARILY:

1. Show composition and layout.
2. Illustrate anchorage location to the structure.
3. Illustrate interfaces with adjacent systems.
4. Define materials and finishes.
5. Illustrate the level of customization on the drawings and in the specifications.

The level of detail of customizing a standard should illustrate the "base" system with minimal graphics, and illustrate the necessary material notations, dimensions, finishes, and other particulars to convey the design intent and performance requirements for the customization.

For custom enclosures, the extent of design and design detail is more involved. Custom enclosures have unique visual and/or performance requirements. Custom enclosures are typically utilized for high-visibility, high-performance, large-scale projects or for other case-specific reasons. Custom enclosures are utilized on smaller-scale enclosures as well.

THE EXTENT OF DESIGN AND DETAIL FOR CUSTOM ENCLOSURES IS PRIMARILY:

1. Show composition and layout.
2. Define the system visual requirements (profiles, materials, finishes, etc.).
3. Illustrate interfaces with other systems.
4. Illustrate anchorage connection location to structure.
5. Define materials and finishes.
6. Depending on delivery system expectations, illustrate a level of internal working parts.

Custom enclosure system item six (6) is often debated between architects, owners, contractors, and consultants. This is the "how much to draw" question. There is no standard answer or silver bullet. In custom masonry enclosures, the architect may be expected to detail every component. In some cases, the contractor may prefer to do the detailing and expect the architect to define the layout, pattern, and finish materials, and define the performance requirements. In other cases, using the example of a custom curtain wall, for example, the architect may be expected to define the profiles, finishes, weathertightness details, and many others. In many cases, the contractor will realize that different curtain wall contractors utilize slightly different approaches for the inner workings, so a high level of architectural detailing is often not helpful. This goes back to expectations from all team members and defining for future team members what is provided by the architect and what is expected of the contractors and subcontractors. In a custom enclosure, the extent of architectural detailing should define the system composition, materials, and "a way" that the enclosure could achieve the visual and performance requirements.

TEAM EXPECTATIONS

This has been discussed briefly in previous sections. The level of detail to be included in the construction documents is a topic that must be discussed and agreed upon by all participants at the initial phases of the project. In this discussion, a picture is worth a million words. Early in the process, whether at design development or the beginning of construction document, providing examples of enclosure drawings and details that identify the expected level of detail, to elicit a discussion and to reach an agreement, can preclude misunderstandings during the construction document process, when the project timeline can least afford rework.

ENCLOSURE SYSTEM INTERFACES

This is an area where the architect must take the lead. Properly connecting two enclosure systems requires design intent for the visual profiles, finishes, materials, and joinery, and technical design for weathertight continuity, system structural integrity, thermal continuity, and other issues. This is where the details define "a way." This also influences the level of detail necessary in the "base" systems to properly document the performance functions where systems interface. Practicing what is being preached, Figure 3.28 illustrates some system interface examples.

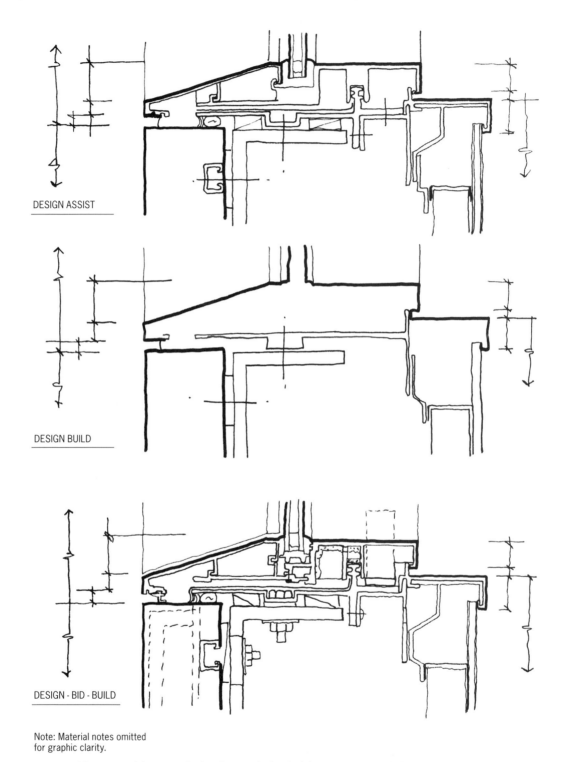

DESIGN ASSIST

DESIGN BUILD

DESIGN - BID - BUILD

Note: Material notes omitted
for graphic clarity.

FIGURE 3.27 The project delivery methods influence the level of documentation and detail to be defined by the architect and design team.

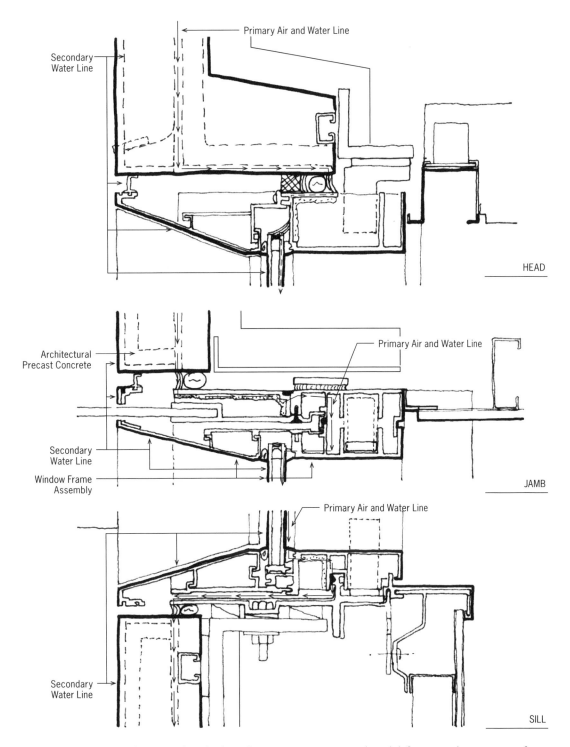

FIGURE 3.28 Exterior enclosures with multiple enclosure systems require study and definition at the system interface conditions.

Where an enclosure system interfaces with another system, the architectural construction documents must illustrate this intersection with a sufficient level of detail to define the visual requirements and performance continuity between the two systems. A detail is by definition where two or more materials or two or more systems come together. This intersection definition—the detail—is applicable for standard, customized standard, and custom systems. The question: "How much should be shown on the details?" often centers on intersections. This is why there are details. I often hear from architects that these intersections are the contractor's responsibility. This is incorrect. The design detail from the architect illustrates "a way" for multiple systems to interface visually and to achieve the necessary performance features. The contractor coordinates the installation and sequence of work between multiple contractors with an understanding of the drawing and specification requirements.

ARCHITECTURAL CHECKING AND COORDINATION

Interdisciplinary coordination with engineers and consultants is more productive if the architectural work is coordinated. Each system and each drawing should be reviewed prior to and in coordination with other disciplines. Coordination is a two-way street. Coordination between discipline participants can occur when the work of each discipline is internally coordinated. This starts with architects who are actively involved with design and detail development checking their own work, and it is enhanced through independent checks by other team members or by architects outside the team. A hands-on way to achieve a coordinated detail set is for team members to present their work to others. This allows a real-time check and back check by the "author" of the work. Quality is the responsibility of every team participant; no matter the level of experience.

The collaboration effort among design team participants in schematic design and design development shifts more towards coordination in construction documents. Each design team discipline continues to further develop their respective

systems with details and specifications. Coordination is a multistep process of checking and back checking. Hard copy and electronic media may be used for this coordination. Face-to-face review meetings should be held between disciplines to discuss coordination findings and sign-offs. Coordination must include the typical and the atypical conditions and details.

KEY COORDINATION ITEMS BETWEEN THE ARCHITECTURAL AND STRUCTURAL ENGINEER TEAM MEMBERS ARE:
- Finalizing the enclosure connection points to the structure
- Finalizing enclosure gravity load and lateral load paths to the structure
- Finalizing the enclosure assembly weights for structural dead load basis of design

KEY ENCLOSURE COORDINATION ITEMS BETWEEN THE ARCHITECTURAL AND MECHANICAL ENGINEER TEAM MEMBERS ARE:
- Finalizing material insulation requirements
- Finalizing details for thermal control (heat loss or heat gain and condensation review)
- Coordinating final material selections and properties

KEY ENCLOSURE COORDINATION ITEMS BETWEEN THE ARCHITECTURAL AND OTHER SPECIALTY ENGINEERS OR CONSULTANT TEAM MEMBERS ARE:
- Finalizing performance requirements
- Finalizing details to achieve these requirements
- Coordinating final material selections and properties
- Coordinating the work referenced from each discipline's drawings and specifications

DRAWING AND SPECIFICATION COORDINATION

The enclosure drawings and the specifications must work together. An exterior enclosure contractor once mentioned to me, after an exterior enclosure bid proposal review: "Your drawings are good, but your specifications are better. I am not accustomed to an architect actually knowing what is in the specification and how to use it." The exterior enclosure drawings illustrate multiple items such as profiles, finishes, materials, and more, which convey the visual and performance design intent. The specifications provide the level of quality for the materials, specialized fabrication requirements, and specifics for installation. The specifications provide the expected performance parameters and basis of design that the enclosure system must meet. The drawings must graphically support this. Achieving a coordinated drawing and specification package is a team effort. An individual alone cannot make this happen. In order to demystify an enclosure specification, team members should not only read it, but also understand its meaning. Specifications are a meal best enjoyed and "digested" in small bites. The Part 2, "products," section of the specifications identifies the materials for the enclosure. For most projects, the products section is populated as the design team finalizes material research, collection, analysis, and selection. The exact material nomenclature used in the spec should be listed on the drawings. To get this point across to team members involved in the development of the enclosure documents, I have stated: "If it is misspelled on the drawings, misspell it in the specs." Now obviously this is taking things to the extreme, to make the point that the drawing language and specification language must be one and the same. As design team members' specification familiarity increases with Part 2 of the specs, "products," Part 1, "references, standards, and performance levels," and Part 3, "execution of the work," as well as other portions of Part 2 for special fabrication, will become a little less foreign and obtuse.

Exterior enclosure specifications are not boilerplate. They are also not written by a mysterious person in the corner and delivered like Moses with the Ten Commandments. The specifications—like the drawings—are a team effort. The team performs the ongoing back check and quality assurance and quality control (QA/QC) by developing the drawings and the specifications concurrently. Each informs the other. Developing and completing a high quality set of enclosure construction documents is a professional necessity and includes coordinated drawings and specifications. There is no in between.

INPUT/REVIEW

Construction documents for the project and the enclosure systems result in the largest portion of the architect's services and the largest set of documents produced in the design phases. Construction documents for larger projects can be hundreds of sheets with thousands of specification pages. Every line and every word has meaning. It is advisable to perform periodic enclosure construction document reviews with others outside the project team. This is a helpful in-progress check to see if those not involved in the daily development can interpret and understand the language of the documents.

Many enclosure designers and contractors are happy to assist and will oblige in providing review, commentary, and suggestions on the enclosure construction documents. Input, critique, and advice—from those who develop and build enclosures for a living—are invaluable. These groups can bring a fresh view to the design and details. The review results are usually more in the form of "tweaks" than "throw it out and start over" suggestions. This type of review is excellent practice for the design team to see if the work can be understood by those in the construction industry.

CONSTRUCTION DOCUMENT: DELIVERY PRODUCT

The resulting enclosure construction documents can include at a minimum:

GRAPHICS: DRAWINGS

1. Building plan(s) at appropriate scale (typically $\frac{1}{8}'' = 1'0''$ min. or $\frac{1}{4}'' = 1'0''$)
   a. Extent of opaque and transparent areas
   b. Dimensional definition (see Figure 3.29)
2. Elevations at same scale as plan, and enlarged elevations as appropriate
   a. Extent of opaque and transparent
   b. Relationship of structure
   c. Dimensional definition (see Figure 3.30)
3. Section at same scale as elevation, and enlarged sections as appropriate
   a. Extent of opaque and transparent (see Figure 3.31)
   b. Relationship of structure
   c. Relationship of mechanical requirements
4. Isometrics
5. Details of each system head, jamb, sill, starter, coping, and other conditions as appropriate @ large scale 1½″ (1:10), 3″ = 1′0″ (1:5), or larger

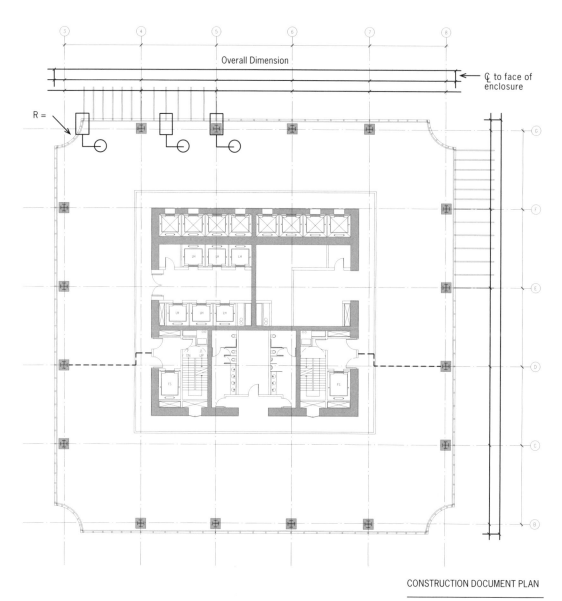

CONSTRUCTION DOCUMENT PLAN

FIGURE 3.29 Construction document plan identifies dimensions and detail locations. *Skidmore, Owings & Merrill LLP*

6. System interface details on projects with multiple enclosure systems @ large scale 1½″ (1:10), 3″ = 1′0″ (1:5), or larger
7. Atypical detail intersections @ large scale 1½″ (1:10), 3″ = 1′0″ (1:5), or larger

a. Movement
b. Loads/pressure
c. Design temperature ranges
d. Interior temperature/humidity ranges

TEXT: SPECIFICATIONS
1. Full format specifications
2. Finalized basis of design

MATERIALS
1. Actual material selections and samples
2. Product data

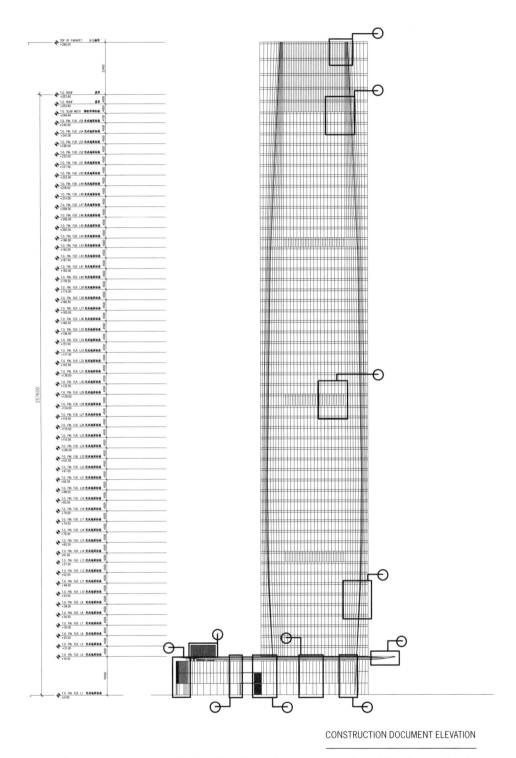

CONSTRUCTION DOCUMENT ELEVATION

FIGURE 3.30 Construction document elevation identifies enclosure systems, enlarged elevations, and section locations. *Skidmore, Owings & Merrill LLP*

Construction documents for exterior enclosures are more about quality and less about quantity. An economy of detail where each line of each drawing has meaning, coupled with an appropriate scale tailored to the needs of conveying a clear definition of the visual and performance criteria, sets a positive path for the upcoming construction phase. Details, when properly defined and organized, convey a clear and deliberate approach to the enclosure design. Examples of Construction Document details are intentionally not shown here. There are case specific details illustrated in chapters 5-9.

Summary

At the completion of the construction document phase, there will be a set of documents (drawings and specifications) commensurate to the level defined for the project delivery method. These documents include: What are the enclosure systems? What are the visual requirements? Where the enclosures occur? What and where are the interfaces with other systems? What are the performance requirements? How can it be built? These documents set the foundation to proceed to the next step–Construction.

Chapter 4

Construction

All things are difficult before they are easy.

THOMAS FULLER

STEP 6: Construction Process

THE ENCLOSURE CONSTRUCTION PROCESS CONSISTS OF TWO STAGES:

1. "Paper stage"
2. "Bricks and mortar" stage

In the construction stages, the architect's role gradually shifts from enclosure design leader to co-leadership with the contractor and enclosure contractor(s) in an active review and support role, as the project team participant ranks expand. This transition can be daunting for some architects. The architect and design team participants have nurtured the enclosure design, development, detail, and documentation. It is similar to taking your child to her or his first day of school. No matter how good a job you have done in preparation (of the design or child), it is difficult to let go. As with any change, success is measured in how well and quickly you can assume and master the new responsibilities of shepherding and guiding the enclosure in its evolution from paper to reality.

No matter the project size and enclosure design and requirements, the construction timeline is typically as long as, and often longer than, the design and documentation phases. The enclosure timeline with the full construction phase is presented in Figure 4.1. The project delivery method, defined at the onset of the project, does determine the level of enclosure documentation illustrated in the contract documents. To set the stage for the impending enclosure construction phase, the following sections give brief descriptions of delivery methods in relation to the particulars of the exterior enclosure construction process.

DESIGN-BID-BUILD

Design-bid-build is the more traditional project delivery system. In this delivery method, the expectations of the enclosure documents are typically a full set of drawings, with specific details and specifications

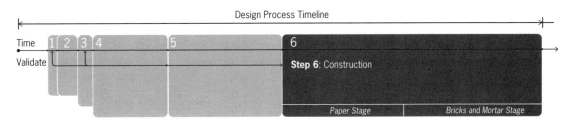

FIGURE 4.1 The construction process timeline in relation to the design phases. The Construction step includes a paper stage and a "bricks and mortar" stage.

to a high level of definition. In the bidding phase associated with this delivery method, the architect may have the opportunity, prior to award, to review the contractor's proposed enclosure system(s) and details for conformance to the design intent and performance requirements identified in the construction documents. Contractors' proposed details are their interpretation of the enclosure system(s).

At this point, the architect still has the more in-depth understanding of the enclosure requirements. The initial step is to review and seek any clarification from the bidders. The primary goal is to comment, educate, and reach a mutual understanding of the proposed enclosure bid/proposal between the design team and the construction team. Once this is achieved the architect provides design and technical commentary and, jointly with the owner, can discuss the suitability of the bid proposals. With this input, the owner makes the financial decisions.

There are many ways to evaluate bid/tender proposals and rank contractor submissions. Words can assist in this communication, but the "great communication" tool is graphics. There is a lot of truth in the old saying "a picture is worth a thousand words." A careful review by the architect of the bid /tender proposal(s), with graphic commentary in the form of sketches and diagrams directly on the proposal details, is invaluable for all participants. These graphic review comments should identify design and performance issues based on the design team's understanding of the proposal. This is the initial and pivotal step of establishing communication between the design team and the construction team in the "midwife" phase between the design process and construction process.

DESIGN-ASSIST

In a design-assist delivery system, the architect, builder, and enclosure builder have mutually developed the enclosure system during the design phases. Subcontractors and material suppliers get involved early or become participants at some stage of the design process.

The design-assist delivery model is predicated on an integrated design and construction team. The enclosure system design and details, construction methods, and costs have been developed

concurrently as the design has progressed. The enclosure system details and award of the work occur during the project development, in contrast to the award in a design-bid-build delivery method. The paper stage of construction still occurs and is typically earlier than the traditional design–bid–build delivery due to early builder involvement during the design phases.

NEGOTIATED

The negotiated delivery method can consist of the general contractor and possibly the enclosure contractor(s) being selected through negotiations at some period in the design phases. The general contractor and/or enclosure contractor participate in the design enclosure system and detail development to provide construction and cost-related input and assistance based on a negotiated price structure. Bids from subcontractors, sub-subcontractors, or material suppliers are negotiated by the general contractor and enclosure contractor(s) at stages in the design timeline. The architect provides design and technical documents, with design and cost consultation from the builder and enclosure contractor. The enclosure contractor still provides shop drawings for the design team participants' review.

DESIGN-BUILD

The term design-build has multiple definitions as related to enclosure delivery and design. One definition applies to the delivery method and one to the type of documentation.

Design-build is a project delivery method in which the design and construction services consist of one team assembled at the onset of the project. The entity is referred to as the design builder. The architect's client is the contractor. The client or owner has one contract with the contractor-led design-build team, consisting of the contractor, architect, engineering disciplines, and subcontractors. Enclosure documentation is developed in collaboration with builder team members to the level of definition defined by the project for the contractor and enclosure contractor to implement.

Another definition used for design-build relates to the type of enclosure documentation. In design-build documents, the architect provides drawings to a layout and profile level with defined performance requirements. The internal system parts and details are detailed, engineered, fabricated, assembled, and installed by the respective enclosure contractor(s) to comply with the architectural profiles and performance requirements.

These are a few examples of project delivery methods. There are others. The point is to define, discuss, and understand participants' responsibilities to provide the appropriate level of enclosure documentation for the requirements of the delivery method.

Bidding or Tender: The Step In-Between

In traditional project delivery methods such as design-bid-build, completed building and enclosure system(s) construction documents are made available to qualified builders. Qualification standards for general and enclosure contractors are defined in the project specifications and bid forms prepared by the owner and architect led design team. The bidding or tender phase is a process for a builder (contractor), enclosure contractors, and material suppliers to submit a proposal to undertake the work. The bid or tender proposal typically consists of a technical and financial offer identifying project specifics, construction processes, qualifications, and other items, for submission to the owner for review and selection. The bidding process is typically associated with delivery methods whereby the architect and engineers prepare documents for contractor bids. The terms "bidding" and "tender," while different, do have similar characteristics and for discussion purposes will be combined.

IN-BETWEEN

The bidding phase, when required, is the step "in-between" enclosure document completion and construction. The bidding phase may occur in the latter stages of the design phase or paper stage of construction, but it doesn't fit neatly into either one, so it is referred to as the "step in-between." This phase is indicated in the project timeline in Figure 4.2. This phase often allows enclosure bidding contractors the opportunity to review the documents and ask clarification questions. The bidding phase has characteristic types. These are:

1. Blind: The bidding enclosure contractor receives drawings, specifications, and bid instructions with no presentation or explanation from the author. Questions, clarifications, and dialogue during the bid process are not permitted.
2. Presented: The bidding enclosure contractor receives drawings, specifications, and bid instructions. After a brief period to gain a level of familiarity with the documents, a presentation of the design and documents is provided by the author.
3. Preceding: The bidding enclosure contractor receives in-progress drawings, specifications, and bid instructions during development. There are multiple opportunities to request and obtain clarifications from the author.

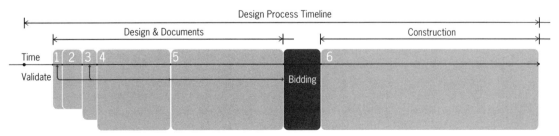

FIGURE 4.2 The bidding (or tender) phase is "in-between" the design and construction process. The diagram shown is a traditional delivery method. Other delivery methods have similar steps with various precedent steps.

Even with the multiple project delivery methods, there are projects in which the architect is not involved with the enclosure contractor/builder selection, no matter which bidding/tender process is utilized. This occurrence is rarely discussed, but it does happen. The "in-between" time period is not as vague as it sounds. There are projects where there is a significant time period between the completion of the enclosure construction documents and the commencement of construction. This occurs for multiple reasons such as approvals, funding, size of the project and many others. As with any of the other delivery methods, the construction documents and the architect and design team's ability to communicate the design intent and performance requirements to those who construct are critical. This communication dialogue and knowledge exchange is usually welcomed by the enclosure builder(s).

Owner preferences and certain contracting regulations usually govern the type of bidding/tender phase implemented. As with most design and construction efforts, the quality of bidding benefits from concise communication. Questions can be written, graphic, oral, or a combination of some or all of these. Prior to the final enclosure bid submission, there should be an opportunity for the enclosure contractor to provide typical system details to the owner and architect for review and comment. Some will debate that this submission and review should occur after award; however, after award is too late. The bid price is deemed as final, so if the enclosure system(s) is not acceptable, how can the construction process initiate successfully? It is this opportunity to review typical system details, prior to bid, that leads to system validation.

SYSTEM VALIDATION

Whether performed during the bid stage (traditional design-bid-build), during the document development stage (design-assist), during the document detail stage (design-build), or in the paper stage of construction, the enclosure construction stage foundation is system validation. Enclosure system validation should be performed with a select handful of details that represent the base system, or if the project has multiple enclosures, the base systems.

The base system can usually be defined with a jamb, head, sill (starter and typical), intermediate horizontals, and corners. An example of system validation details is shown in Figure 4.3. The details must be at full (1:1) scale, supplemented with key plans, elevations, and sections. The plans, sections, and elevations must indicate interface conditions with adjacent trades (structural, mechanical, plumbing, electrical, etc.) for review with the corresponding engineering discipline documents. Agreements made on the base enclosure system details provide a solid foundation for preparation of full enclosure contractor submittals.

THERE ARE MULTIPLE ITEMS FOR THE ARCHITECT TO REVIEW IN THE SYSTEM VALIDATION EFFORT. AT A MINIMUM, THESE ARE:

1. Composition
   a. Spacing: in plan (x and y), elevation (z), and section (z)
   b. Joinery: static and dynamic, including materials
   c. Material location
2. Materials
   a. Location of each
   b. Finishes of each
   c. Intersections
3. Performance
   a. System structural logic
   b. Weathertightness
   c. Design performance principle application
   d. Thermal
   e. Movement characteristics and capabilities
   f. Others per project requirements

The architect's review of the proposed enclosure system(s) should be deliberate and methodical. It should emulate the thought and development process utilized in the preparation of the architectural enclosure documentation. It should be cross-checked with the architectural drawings and specifications. The system validation review is the crossing where the enclosure system lead responsibility shifts from the architectural documentation to enclosure contractor documentation. Some readers will debate this point. They will say that, no matter what, the architectural contract documents will govern. They do. However, the contractor's proposed enclosure system documents—as reviewed, commented on, marked up, discussed, modified, and agreed upon—are the enclosure construction system documents utilized for fabrication and construction.

During the system validation, it must be determined that the proposed system, when constructed properly, can achieve the architectural visual and performance requirements. All of the team participants are making a joint commitment to the base system details of the enclosure system(s).

ENLARGE THE TEAM

The agreed-upon commitment to the enclosure system(s) and details along with acceptance of financial terms between the owner and contractor/enclosure contractor brings the project enclosure team participant level to full strength. The contractor and enclosure contractor are full-time participants. This may occur after bidding and award, or in earlier phases, in other project delivery methods. They assume enclosure team co-leadership with the owner and architect. With the full team complement, the process of knowledge transfer between architect and enclosure contractor continues. In a positive project environment, the architect, contractor, and enclosure contractor are working to gain each other's respect and confidence.

As Good or Better?

In most projects, enclosure system contractors provide shop drawings that identify their proposed systems. The enclosure contractor's system interpretation of the architect's enclosure system documents must respect the profiles, materials, finishes, composition, and performance requirements provided in the contract documents. The enclosure contractor's system should not be anything less. The architect's review of the contractor's proposed enclosure system should not be treated as an opportunity to redesign or overly embellish the enclosure beyond what is indicated in the documents. Working in tandem there are often mutually beneficial topics that will provide the owner with an enclosure system or systems that, at a minimum, meets the visual and performance

requirements of the enclosure construction documents and optimally provides enhancements within the established project construction budget. When this "sweet spot" is achieved, the enclosure system to be built is as good or better.

Paper Stage of Construction

Like the enclosure design and documentation process performed by the design team, the enclosure construction process requires planning by the general contractor, the enclosure contractor(s), their subcontractors, and materials suppliers, prior to execution of the work. This is the construction paper stage and consists of submittals from the contractor and subcontractor to the architect. The process most often associated with the paper stage of enclosure construction is shop drawing preparation and review. Enclosure shop drawings are required for many enclosures, even when the architectural drawings are very detailed. Materials and systems that require shop or select field fabrication and installation will entail shop drawings.

ENCLOSURE SHOP DRAWINGS ARE:
1. A drawing or set of drawings produced by the contractor, enclosure contractor, specialty enclosure fabricator, or specialty enclosure vendor
2. Prepared for shop-fabricated components and assemblies
3. Prepared for select field-fabricated or -installed components and assemblies
4. Drawn and detailed to illustrate fabrication specifics
5. Drawn and detailed to illustrate installation specifics

SHOP DRAWINGS ARE NOT:
1. Drawings prepared by an architect or engineer
2. Drawings to make design modifications

Shop drawings are the full complement of enclosure fabrication and installation drawings. These should follow the accepted enclosure system validation drawings previously described. Shop drawings address the exterior enclosure appearance and

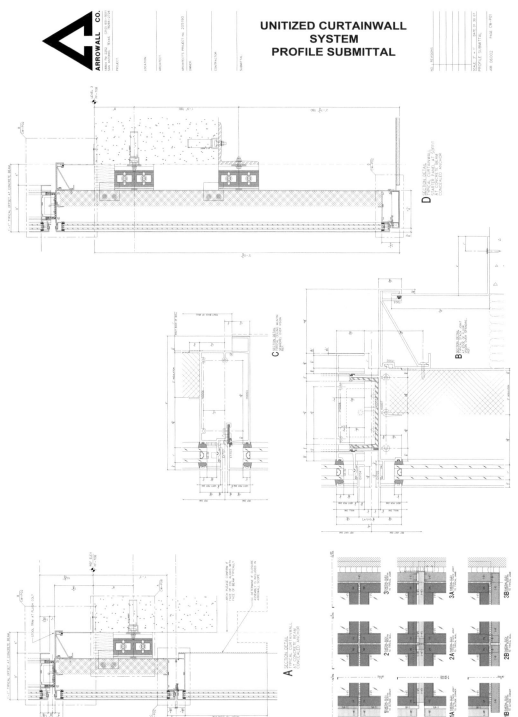

FIGURE 4.3 System validation drawings are the step between the contract documents and the full shop drawing submittals. *Arrowall*

ARROWALL CO.
16884 sw 2252
SAN ANTONIO, TEXAS
(210) 651-3011
78245-2728

PROJECT:

LOCATION:

ARCHITECT:

ARCHITECT'S PROJECT No. 205190

OWNER

CONTRACTOR

SUBMITTAL

UNITIZED CURTAINWALL
SYSTEM
PROFILE SUBMITTAL

NO. REVISIONS

SCALE 3" = 1'
DATE 01-30-07
PROFILE SUBMITTAL
PAGE CW-P01
JOB 06002

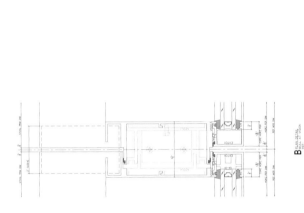

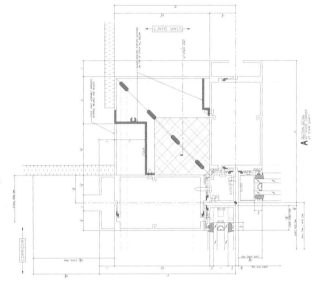

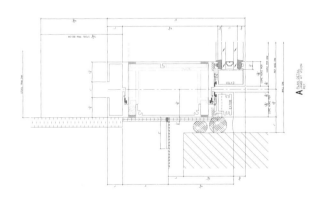

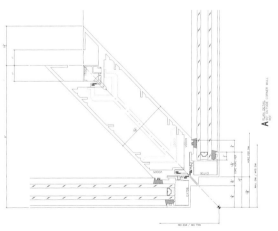

FIGURE 4.3 Continued

performance items. They represent the enclosure contractor's version of the architectural enclosure drawings and specifications.

Architectural review of shop drawings is a learned art. It must be taught. Architects are not taught to completely design exterior enclosures in school. There is usually not an opportunity in a school or classroom environment to teach the nuances of shop drawing review. This must be done in an office environment under a competent mentor.

Shop drawing review is time-consuming when done properly. Review and comments noted on submittals are usually performed under tight time constraints. Shop-fabricated items cannot be started without approved shop drawings, so the shop drawing submittal turnaround time, with clear graphic and written notations by the architect, is extremely important. As with any endeavor, there are multiple approaches to properly accomplishing this task. Shop drawings are assembly and fabrication instructions. One approach to shop drawing review is to "take it apart" and "put it back together" on paper. Shop drawings represent the means and methods of exterior enclosure construction. When an architect has reviewed a shop drawing and achieves a fundamental understanding of how the enclosure system is fabricated, assembled, and installed, then perceived inconsistencies in visual and performance design issues can be highlighted for discussion and resolution with all involved in the review and the construction. A possible reminder or mantra is: If the architect has a good set of tools, has he or she achieved the requisite level of understanding of the contractor's enclosure system in order to comment intelligently on how the enclosure is fabricated, assembled, and installed if they had to perform the work?

This is not the architect crossing the line to say how to build it. It is the architect questioning and commenting directly on the shop drawing submittal—preferably through graphics—with a high level of care and attention to detail. The key is graphic notations. The meaning of words and phrases can be misinterpreted. In review of shop drawings with multiple languages, graphics are understood by all. It is the architect learning the enclosure construction language of the project. Each enclosure system has its own "language dialect." Even similar enclosure systems will vary from project to project. Learn to speak the language of *this* enclosure system(s) of *this* project by taking the time and expending the effort to understand it as well as the originating author.

The quantity and type of submittals are directly influenced by the enclosure design and detailing. Some examples are included in the following sections.

Enclosures Detailed Primarily by the Architect

As noted in the previous sections, there are many types of custom exterior enclosures that are delineated to a high level of detail on the architectural documents. Many of these are explained in more detail in the systems and case studies in following chapters, ranging from brick or stone masonry to custom curtain walls.

Custom enclosures such as brick or stone masonry, while detailed on the architectural documents (and sometimes including the structural drawings), will require submittals from suppliers, manufacturer's material product data, installation literature, and samples. Enclosures with a high level of detail on the architectural drawings may require specific engineering by the contractor or a specialty engineer hired by the contractor or enclosure contractor. Depending on the level of layout and dimensioning illustrated on the architectural drawings, layout drawings may also be an enclosure contractor submittal requirement. The manufacturer's product data is reviewed by the architect, the contractor, and the enclosure subcontractor(s). The architect's review of product data for enclosure systems, such as brick masonry, is for comparison with the project specifications, to address conformance to the quality level, specific material, performance criteria, finish, color, and other specified requirements. Manufacturer material product data should include the manufacturer, product name, model type (if applicable), quality level, and other particulars. There are often test reports to validate that the materials have been tested for performance, durability, fire resistance, and many other standards. Systems requiring multiple product data submissions by multiple contractors are a telltale sign for intensive site coordination at material intersections.

Material review by both the contractor and the architect is another quality assurance/quality control step in the overall enclosure construction process.

ENCLOSURES REQUIRING SHOP DRAWINGS

Standard systems, customized standard, and custom enclosure systems such as stone masonry, curtain walls, all glass, and other enclosures usually require a high quantity of shop drawing submittals with a high level of detail. Whether the enclosure is a standard, customized standard, or custom is typically delineated in more detail on the shop drawings than the architectural drawings.

There are hundreds of comparison points that can illustrate the similarities and differences between the architectural construction documents (drawings and specifications) and the enclosure contractor shop drawings. Whether similar or dramatically different, a key point is: The architectural construction documents illustrate the visual design and performance design requirements with "a way" to construct the enclosure. The enclosure contractor submittal delineates the contractor's interpretation of the visual design and performance design requirements, with a proposal for "the way" the enclosure is to be constructed. The architect must review the submittal for conformance with the design intent and to determine how the specified performance requirements can be achieved when the enclosure contractor's proposed submittal is properly fabricated, assembled, and installed. The architect must understand the contractor's proposed system. As described previously, this involves figuratively taking the enclosure system apart and putting it back together. The architect provides review sketches, comments, and questions to gain an understanding of the contractor's proposed system submittal's positives and negatives. When this level of understanding and review is reached, the shop drawing review process is demystified.

There are lines of contractual responsibility that must be maintained. The architect's enclosure documents illustrate the design, details, and specified materials and performance. The contractor and enclosure contractor(s) detail and build. They often

will be required to design and engineer. This is defined per project and should be established for the best possible outcome considering the enclosure's complexity and the participants' talents and experience. No matter what the project is, the ultimate goal is to deliver a high-quality exterior enclosure. All team members should review, critique, question, discuss, debate, and agree on the best possible enclosure solution. To quote an enclosure contractor comment during a shop drawing review meeting, "It is only paper. Comments, questions, sketches, only help in making sure that everyone has considered how to accomplish the work. We can revise drawings easier than modify fabricated assemblies or make changes during construction." This comment personifies a team approach to achieve a high-quality product. Architectural drawings and shop drawings are tools to achieve the maximum level of understanding prior to fabrication and assembly. Some shop drawings are easy to review and will have few, if any, comments. Some shop drawings will look as if they have been dipped in a sea of red ink. In the end, it is in the interest of all involved with the building and the enclosure to vet as much as possible while in the paper stage of construction.

SAMPLES

Samples are another primary submittal component in the paper stage of construction. If a drawing is worth a thousand words, imagine the clarity of the actual sample. In the paper stage, samples are typically of individual materials and components of a size that allows the material qualities to be reviewed and approved by the architect. Independent of the project and enclosure size, samples should be required in the submittal process. Sample submittal should be defined and required to include natural materials, such as stone, and human-made materials, such as brick, metals, sealants, and others. The architect's review is for color, finish, and other visual items. The samples should be the type, thickness, finish, and color of the actual material to be used for the project. Fabricated samples are a more elaborate material assembly's submittal process, which is discussed in the following "Bricks and Mortar" stage of construction.

"Bricks and Mortar" Stage

The bricks and mortar stage of construction is the physical construction of the enclosure. For larger-scale enclosure projects, there is often an overlap between the paper stage and the bricks and mortar stage. Construction occurs in stages. The goal in enclosure design and construction is to complete the necessary paper reviews and achieve an agreed-upon submittal in sufficient time to fabricate items for installation on site.

WHAT IS DONE TO DATE IN CONSTRUCTION

The paper stage of enclosure construction occupies a distinct time frame. As the paper stage moves along its timeline path of preparation, review, and approval, on-site construction work has usually started. On large-scale or custom enclosure projects, the paper stage of construction can be many months long. The building superstructure can proceed at a quick pace while the enclosure paper stage is proceeding. The paper stage process must acknowledge—and vice versa, the bricks and mortar stage must acknowledge—each stage's time requirements. The primary building superstructure will require preparation for enclosure anchorages and attachments.

LAYOUT AND EMBEDDED ENCLOSURE COMPONENTS

Almost all, if not all, enclosure systems will require some type of item to be embedded into the primary structure. The embedded items, depending on the type and design, are either very specifically located or "oversized" to accommodate more flexibility and forgiveness in the next layer of enclosure attachment or anchorage. An example of an enclosure embed is illustrated in Figure 4.4. Just as enclosure design is a layering process towards completion, so is construction. In enclosure construction, embeds for anchorages precede finish anchorage materials to the project site. This is where the typical enclosure system validation and acceptance can assist. If the base enclosure system details are accepted by the team participants, the base enclosure system embedded components and assemblies and their relationship to the base enclosure system can be reviewed with a familiarity

FIGURE 4.4 Enclosure embed, system anchor, and enclosure system under construction.

with the typical enclosure system details. Shop drawing submittal layouts for embedded items will often precede the full enclosure system submittal. Having a preview of the typical system details is invaluable for review of embedded anchorage items.

FABRICATED SAMPLES AND MOCK-UPS

Parallel and often concurrent with the construction of embedded items, layout, and installation are fabricated samples and mock-ups.

Fabricated samples consist of full assemblies in sufficient size, including cladding, supports, attachments, anchors, and the like. These are usually required for specific assemblies, to verify construction quality at a relatively small scale prior to full fabrication and assembly. Fabricated samples are assemblies of sections of the enclosure fabricated and submitted for the architect's review prior to construction. The extent of fabricated samples must be identified by the architect on the drawings and in the specifications. For enclosures that are composed of factory-manufactured modular units, such as brick masonry, the fabricated samples are often constructed at the project site. An example of an on-site fabricated sample is shown in Figure 4.5. Shop-fabricated and -assembled enclosure assemblies can be constructed and submitted either to the architect's office for smaller samples or at the project site for larger samples. An example of a shop-fabricated sample is shown in Figure 4.6. The fabricated samples should be reviewed for visual design compliance and for fit, finish, and quality of construction. Actual project materials must be used, to accurately reflect the contractor's ability to achieve the requisite level of quality. Fabricated samples typically occur either concurrent with or just subsequent to the shop drawing review and approval process.

Mock-ups are fabricated assemblies at a much larger scale. The purpose of mock-ups, when specified and provided, is twofold:

1. To achieve visual approval
2. To physically test for performance requirements

It is helpful and advisable to have the contractor and enclosure contractor(s) provide fabricated samples

FIGURE 4.5 On-site fabricated sample. Samples vary in size and complexity.

FIGURE 4.6 Shop-fabricated samples illustrate joinery, finishes, and expected and agreed-upon level of quality.

and mock-ups prior to on-site enclosure construction, regardless of the size of the enclosure. This is the final opportunity to review and identify issues prior to on-site construction.

On larger-scale projects, full-scale mock-ups should be identified in the construction documents. Full-scale mock-ups are usually one to two floors tall and several typical unit or plan widths. If possible, identify mock-ups to include typical and corner conditions. Mock-ups can be for visual review, performance testing, and preferably both. An example of a full-scale mock-up is illustrated in Figure 4.7a and Figure 4.7b.

FIGURE 4.7a   Full-scale mock-ups can be used for visual review, performance testing, or both.

FIGURE 4.7b   Full scale visual mock-up constructed on site.

The goal with mock-ups is to evaluate and reach agreement on the quality of construction, and for performance mock-ups to identify any visual, craft, or performance problems in the enclosure system prior to on-site construction. For this and other reasons, performance mock-ups are constructed by the responsible contractors at an independent testing laboratory. Performance mock-ups are valuable for single-system and multiple-system enclosures. Enclosure "weak points" usually occur at joinery and transition conditions. Even the most thorough shop drawing review by members of the construction and design team can miss system "holes." The value of testing is: "You can't fool Mother Nature." Visual and performance mock-ups provide the opportunity for the project team to:

1. Verify that the details function in accordance with the specified requirements.
2. Verify and confirm an acceptable quality level for fit and finish.
3. Determine that the enclosure contractors possess the required skill level necessary for assembly and installation.
4. Provide the opportunity for each contractor involved to develop "hands-on" experience in installation, sequence, and interface conditions.
5. Provide the project team with the opportunity to identify and resolve potential problem or conflict areas prior to construction.

Mock-ups are a confirmation and learning tool. Design continues in a more direct manner even during mock-ups. It is not design by revision or changes; it is design as collaboration between contractor(s) and architect. Successful mock-ups go beyond passing the battery of tests. When true collaboration kicks in, contractors responsible for the mock-up exhibit the same pride of authorship in the finish work as the design originator has in the enclosure composition and documentation.

"The Valley"

For most architects there is a period of time that occurs during construction that is referred to as the "valley." Other "low point" monikers can also be applied to the time when little if anything happens.

One exterior enclosure contractor compared it to "it is darkest before dawn." The construction site is a flurry of activity for superstructure work, embeds, and other rough-ins. Soon the "valley" stage subsides as anchorage installation for the enclosure begins.

First Glimpse

There is nothing in enclosure design as exhilarating as the first glimpse of the fabricated enclosure installed on the building. Months' or years' worth of planning, design, redesign, detailing, and checking are all summed up on the first glimpse. With the first glimpse, the architect continues to shepherd the enclosure through observations during installation. Each person performing the construction of the enclosure has a specific task he or she is responsible for implementing. The architect has the overall knowledge, having designed, detailed, checked shop drawings, and reviewed samples and mock-ups. The architect has the institutional knowledge of the enclosure gained by leading, co-leading, and participating in the entire gestation of the enclosure design and construction process to date. The architect must observe the installation of each component and assembly carefully. Continuity of the design in construction for both visual and technical performance requires monitoring and reiterating the intricacies of the enclosure design.

Installation Stages: Layering

Each enclosure system is fabricated and installed in layers. The enclosure system wall assembly zone (WAZ) described in Chapter 3, "Design Process," as anchorage zone, enclosure zone, and infill zone, occurs either in fabrication, assembly, or construction as layers. Systems such as hand-set, stone masonry install all three zones on-site. Prefabricated, shop-assembled enclosures such as unitized curtain walls may have the enclosure zone and infill zone assembled in a shop and installed to the anchorage, located in the anchorage zone, on the construction site. Each zone or layer has sequential steps to follow that have been defined either in the construction documents or in shop drawings. An example of stages of enclosure installation with multiple exterior enclosure systems is illustrated in Figure 4.8. When this process is understood by all

FIGURE 4.8 Stages of exterior enclosure construction. *Maurice Hamilton Jr.*

participants, construction is like a symphony with each instrument blending in harmoniously. When the layering process is not understood or is deviated, it is like a symphony orchestra warming up. The components are there, but the results are not pleasant.

OBSERVATION

Each team participant in the enclosure has an observation responsibility.

THE ARCHITECT:
1. Reviews at regular intervals
2. Comments, verbally and in writing, to the owner and contractor on visual and construction compliance, deviations, and concerns

THE OWNER:
1. Reviews at regular intervals
2. Requires that the other participants are observing and commenting on their respective area of responsibility

THE CONTRACTOR:
1. Reviews at regular intervals
2. Coordinates the sequence of the enclosure with other building trades' installation

3. Protects installed work
4. Verifies that the installation meets the requirements of the shop drawings and construction documents

THE ENCLOSURE CONTRACTOR:
1. Installs the work in compliance with the contract documents and the shop drawings
2. Reviews at regular intervals
3. Coordinates the sequence of the enclosure with other building trades' installation
4. Protects installed work
5. Verifies that the installation meets the requirements of the shop drawings and construction documents

Quality Control

The contractor and enclosure contractor are the lead participants in the fabrication, assembly, and installation of the enclosure. Enclosure quality control is the responsibility of these contractors. Enclosure work that is not to the accepted quality levels established with all participants will require rework or removal, refabrication, and reinstallation. The prefix "re-" is time-consuming and costly. The less "re-," the better.

Field-Testing

Close to or at enclosure completion, the enclosure must be field-tested. Field-testing should be required by the contract documents and performed, no matter the extent of testing performed in the previously described full-scale mock-ups. The quantity and types of testing must be identified in the contract documents. Enclosures that look good, but don't perform as specified and/or tested, require rework. Again, the less use of the prefix "re-," the better.

Completion

Enclosure completion is not a "level of done." It is the dictionary definition of done. When the building and enclosure are complete and ready for the owner's use, the enclosure has been reviewed by contractor, enclosure contractor, and architect. Punch lists and remedial corrections have been completed and checked.

Many tests of exterior enclosures are commissioned by independent testing agencies to determine that the enclosure as constructed meets the performance requirements. These are independent checks and tests that must be identified in the contract documents by either the owner or the architect. This work is performed by a commissioning agent. The commissioning entity will prepare a compendium of documents that are used to train the on-site engineering and maintenance staff on the maintenance methods for the enclosure. It includes the closeout documents such as warranties, materials used, supplier information, and other topics necessary for ongoing use and maintenance. This provides the owner's staff with guidance for areas, components, and assemblies that may require outside vendors' assistance for care, service, and maintenance during the enclosure's service life.

Summary

This and the preceding chapters have discussed enclosure basics, the participants, the enclosure design process, and now the enclosure construction process. Where applicable, enclosure particulars have been identified. In many cases, the discussions have been global in nature, in order to be applicable more to the process than to specifics. As noted several times, each enclosure will have its own project-specific visual and performance criteria and requirements.

The following five chapters are devoted to particular enclosure system types, with supporting case studies. The case studies identify the system visual design and performance design strategies implemented. There are examples of different project delivery systems and their influence on who provided what in each enclosure, and how. Very few project case studies are a single enclosure system. The final chapter addresses putting it all together, which is the integration of multiple project enclosures into an overall exterior composition.

Chapter 5

Brick Masonry

Architecture starts when you carefully put two bricks together. There it begins.

LUDWIG MIES VAN DER ROHE

Overview

Masonry is the broad category of enclosure design and construction systems composed of individual units, typically constructed on-site and bound together by mortar and reinforcing. Masonry is also the term for the units themselves. Brick is a type of masonry unit that has been implemented in design and construction of buildings for thousands of years. Brick masonry cavity wall load-bearing and non-load-bearing assemblies have been implemented for exterior enclosures for hundreds of years.

Enclosure design considerations and case studies presented here are non-load-bearing cavity wall assemblies consisting of an exterior wythe of brick masonry, a cavity space, and an inner supporting wall. "Wythe" is the brick masonry unit of thickness in plan and section. Exterior brick wythe veneer material options are concrete masonry units (CMU), clay tile, terra cotta, brick, or other human-made masonry units. Cavity spaces range from 2″ (50 mm) to 4 ½″ (½ mm) in depth and, depending on the climate, enclosure and design response, may contain insulation. The inner supporting wall consists of an interior wythe of concrete masonry units, concrete wall, or heavy gage steel stud and exterior sheathing assemblies. A diagram of an exterior brick cavity wall with zones and materials is shown in Figure 5.1.

Design

Brick masonry cavity wall enclosures are generally custom-designed assemblies composed of multiple components. The custom classification is due to each project's design having different brick types, bonds, coursing, patterns, colors, textures, massing, anchors, cavity thickness, inner wall supports, or other project specifics required to achieve the design intent and performance requirements. However, the basic performance principles are consistent in most designs. Visible layouts and patterns in brick are referred to as "bonds." There are unlimited design options that can be achieved by bond pattern, varying brick placement, projecting or recessing brick in the enclosure plane, brick color, brick texture, and combining multiple brick types, joint types, joint sizes, and joint colors. Examples of brick bonds are illustrated in Figure 5.2.

Mortar provides detail at the joints by creating flush, shadow, or color lines. Mortar joint sizes can be varied to create additional design patterns. Mortar joints serve multiple functions. Mortar bonds brick masonry together and makes up for the dimensional variations in the individual brick units. Mortar bonds to the lateral anchors and reinforcing in the brick. Mortar joints can be troweled or tooled. Trowel joints are struck and finished with a trowel. For tooled joints, a tool is used to compress mortar into shapes within the joint. Examples of mortar joint types are illustrated in Figure 5.3.

Brick has been used in enclosures to evoke an image of strength and permanence. Brick, used as the primary visible exterior envelope material, can be used to achieve many design styles. These include, but are not limited to, Tudor, Jeffersonian, Georgian, Prairie

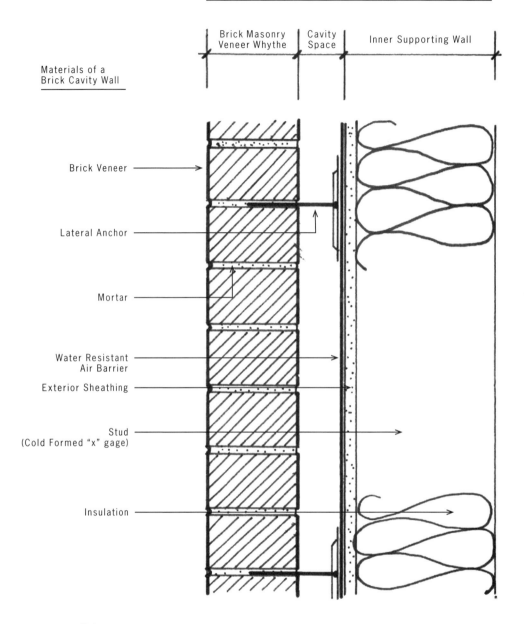

Materials of a
Brick Cavity Wall

Brick Veneer

Lateral Anchor

Mortar

Water Resistant
Air Barrier

Exterior Sheathing

Stud
(Cold Formed "x" gage)

Insulation

Note:
1. Flashing is not shown in this diagram. Flashing is
required at openings and movement joints to drain water
to the exterior.

2. Insulation is illustrated in the inner supporting wall
assembly. Insulation may be located in the cavity space
when required for a specific design.

FIGURE 5.1 Masonry brick cavity exterior enclosure walls consist of three primary zones. These are the: (1) inner supporting wall, (2) cavity space, and (3) outer brick masonry veneer.

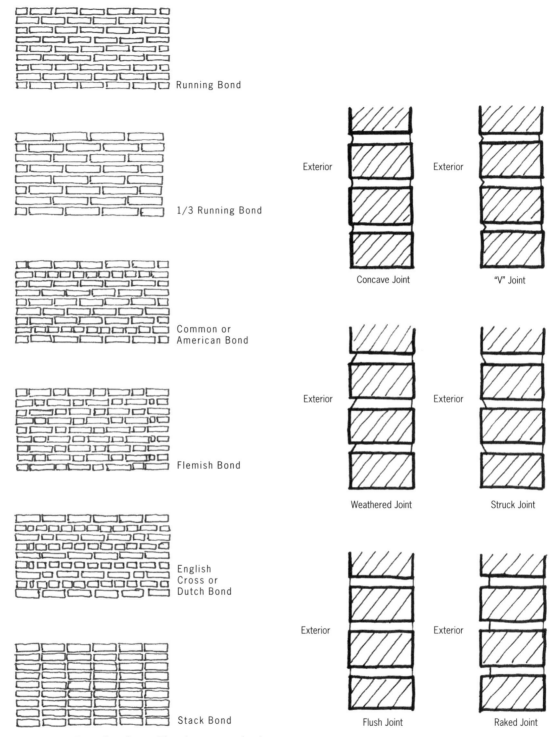

FIGURE 5.2 Examples of typical bond patterns in brick masonry.

Running Bond

1/3 Running Bond

Common or American Bond

Flemish Bond

English Cross or Dutch Bond

Stack Bond

FIGURE 5.3 Mortar joints can be struck or tooled in a variety of profiles. Joint configurations have distinct visual and performance implications.

Exterior — Concave Joint

Exterior — "V" Joint

Exterior — Weathered Joint

Exterior — Struck Joint

Exterior — Flush Joint

Exterior — Raked Joint

Style, Gothic, Modern, and many others building design styles. Examples of brick buildings in a variety of architectural styles are illustrated in Figures 5.4a–e.

Enclosure Structural Considerations

Brick masonry cavity walls can be load-bearing or non-load-bearing. Load-bearing masonry brick is exactly what the name implies. The interior reinforced concrete masonry unit or brick wythe supports the dead structural floor system and building loads. The outer brick wythe serves as the exterior facing and cladding. Load-bearing masonry is typically designed as a series of floor-by-floor assemblies, one on top of the other. This type of enclosure design requires close collaboration with the project structural engineer for design and documentation responsibilities. The design process and considerations noted herein with case studies are non-load-bearing enclosures. Non-load-bearing masonry brick cavity wall enclosures are designed to accommodate and transfer lateral loads such as wind, seismic, and the like, to the primary building structure or the interior supporting wall, which then transfers loads to the primary building structure. The structural design considerations for this type of enclosure assembly are:

1. The brick masonry itself
2. The influence of the building structural system on the brick masonry enclosure and the joinery

BRICK MASONRY STRUCTURAL CONSIDERATIONS

Brick masonry self-load, or dead load, is supported either by the building structure or by shelf supports. Shelf supports are typically steel; however, some designs will utilize exposed concrete. The height, width, and associated weight of the brick determine the design of the supporting steel shelf size, thickness, and spacing frequency. This is typically an angle or combination of steel shapes with a horizontal surface for placing the brick. The shelf should be engineered by a structural engineer. Anchorage for the shelf must be designed for deflection between support connections and for rotation of the shelf

supporting the brick. The shelf assembly is in a wet environment; therefore, material choice, preparation, and method of connection to the structure must be selected for long-term durability in "wet" conditions. The wet cavity space area is discussed in the "Weather Protection" section later in this chapter.

In addition to the brick masonry self-weight, the design of the brick cladding accommodates and transfers lateral loads acting perpendicular and parallel on the exterior brick cladding to the building structure or inner wall through lateral anchors. Those lateral anchors are selected and designed to transfer the lateral loads and also accommodate the construction tolerances of the structure, the inner lateral supporting wall, and the outer brick cladding. Design of the lateral anchors can be performed by the architect, structural engineer, or contractor, depending on the contract requirements and project delivery method. The frequency and spacing—horizontally and vertically—of the lateral anchors will depend on the lateral anchor size and type. The design of the lateral anchorage must address the area and cavity depth openings, inside and outside corners, base or "starter" conditions, and parapet conditions. Design guidance for the lateral anchors can be found in model codes such as the International Building Code (IBC), which references the Masonry Standard Joint Committee's TMS 402/ACI 530/ASCE 5.

There are two methods to design the brick and the inner wall. These are: (1) the prescriptive method, and (2) the rational method.

Prescriptive Method

The prescriptive method requires the inner wall to be designed to resist the entire lateral wind load. This method provides thickness, lateral anchor tie spacing, and tributary areas for the brick veneer. A high percentage of brick masonry cavity walls utilize the prescriptive method. Brick enclosure design parameters and the basis of design should be researched in the schematic design phase and established either in the schematic design phase or early in the design development phase. Brick masonry cavity walls are classified as noncomposite walls. In noncomposite action each wythe, or wall plane, is designed to accommodate and resist the effects of the imposed

Jeffersonian Style

Prairie Style

Romanesque Style

Gothic Style

FIGURE 5.4 Masonry brick, used as the primary visible exterior enclosure material, can be utilized to create multiple design styles.

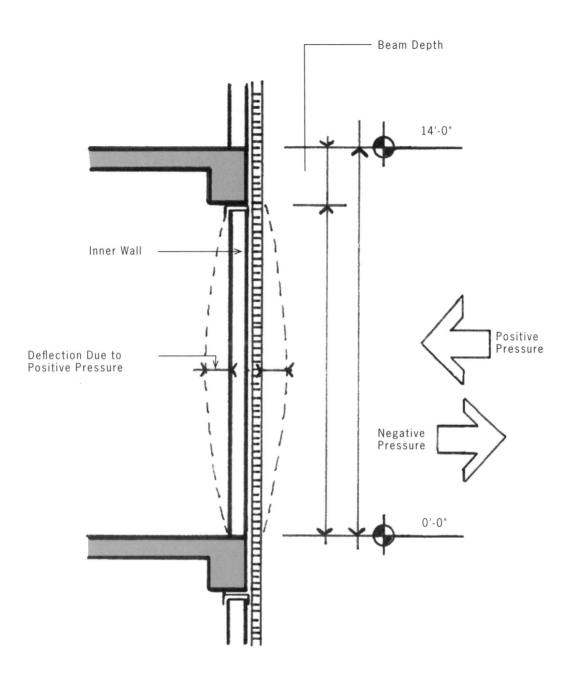

Floor to Floor height = 14'-0"
Beam Depth = 2'-0"
Resulting inner wall span: 12'-0" = "L"
12'-0" × 12" = 144"
144"/600 = 124 or 1/4"

FIGURE 5.5   Masonry brick cavity wall design employs "stiff" deflection criteria limits.

lateral wind loads. Exposed exterior brick masonry deflects only a small amount when lateral wind loads are applied. The exterior brick is anchored to the inner wall and will therefore act in kind to the deflection of the inner wall. The inner wall design is deflection-based and is designed to fully resist the full wind load. Industry standards, such as those of the Brick Industry Association, recommend an inner wall design of the span height (L) over 600 (L/600). A deflection diagram is shown in Figure 5.5.

Rational Method

The rational method is used when the project brick enclosure design has a cavity width in excess of 4 ½″ (112 mm) or the exterior wind design speed exceeds 130 mph (209 kph). The rational method distributes the forces applied to the exterior veneer using principles of mechanics. This method is more time-consuming to design, and because of its specialized design, it should be reviewed with authorities having jurisdiction (AHJ) and with a structural or specialty structural engineer.

BUILDING STRUCTURE INFLUENCE ON BRICK MASONRY

The primary building structure (columns, beams, slabs, etc.) and its associated movement characteristics under loading will influence the joinery design of the masonry brick enclosure. Brick masonry self-load supports typically attach to the perimeter structural framing members or slab either directly or through a supporting framework to the building structure. Deflection, due to the brick cladding self-load, must be accounted for in the structural design for deflection. Primary building structural frame dead load deflection is typically achieved prior to the installation of the masonry brick. If this is not done, the structural dead load deflection must be added to the imposed dead load of the masonry brick. Primary building structure live load deflection, in addition to the dead loads already noted, must be accounted for in the masonry joinery design. Locations where primary joinery materials or building structure deflections are accommodated require soft

joinery materials. This is usually sealant and a compressible backer. If other design approaches are utilized, the same considerations will apply. The joint systems and material(s) movement capacity characteristics include durability, compression, extension or elongation, bonding of the joint material to the brick, and compatibility with adjacent masonry and other materials. Soft joints are also referred to as movement joints. Structural deflections and installation tolerances added to the movement capacity of the joint material will determine the total movement joint size. A movement diagram and the associated joint size are indicated in Figure 5.6. Joinery must be sized and designed for the typical brick cavity wall, openings, inside and outside corners, cantilevers, and parapet conditions. Movement joint sizes are visible, so movement joint size in relation to the mortar joint size is an important design consideration.

Brick masonry cavity walls behave as panels or planes. This basically means that while the outer wythe and inner wall are made of components, the final assemblies of exterior brick, mortar, lateral ties, inner supporting wall of steel studs, and sheathing or CMU configurations, are panels that remain in their geometric configuration in a static or dynamic state. Consequently, the panels and the surrounding panel joinery must allow for lateral movement, or "drift." Lateral movement of the primary building structural frame is referred to as drift. Drift is induced by wind pressure and/or seismic forces. When a building structural frame drifts, the floors displace in relation to each other, and columns bend. A structural frame drift diagram is shown in Figure 5.7. Structural frame drift occurs parallel and perpendicular to the brick masonry cavity wall assembly. Joinery design at the top, bottom, and at vertical intervals in the brick must accommodate the structural frame drift. Drift parallel to the brick enclosure plane creates a sliding edge condition at the top of the masonry plane and a bearing edge condition at the base or sill of the masonry. Brick masonry bearing at the base of the enclosure slides in kind with the supporting element. The top of the brick enclosure plane slides in relation to the supporting elements above. The enclosure design and joinery must allow the panels to remain rectangular while the

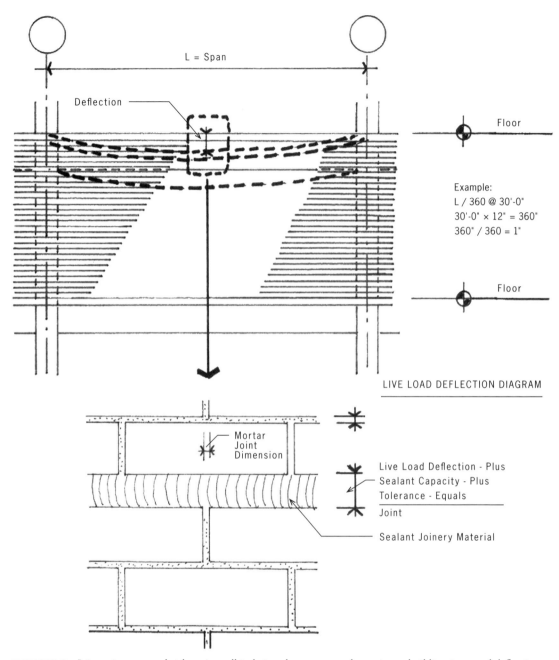

L = Span

Deflection

Floor

Example:
L / 360 @ 30'-0"
30'-0" × 12" = 360"
360" / 360 = 1"

Floor

LIVE LOAD DEFLECTION DIAGRAM

Mortar
Joint
Dimension

Live Load Deflection - Plus
Sealant Capacity - Plus
Tolerance - Equals
Joint

Sealant Joinery Material

FIGURE 5.6 Joinery in masonry brick cavity wall is designed to accommodate primary building structural deflection. This is often expressed in the brick joinery. Primary building structure deflection of 1″ combined with a sealant joint movement capacity of +/−50% results in a 2″ nominal joint. Enclosure design is influenced by and dependent on systems designed by other design disciplines.

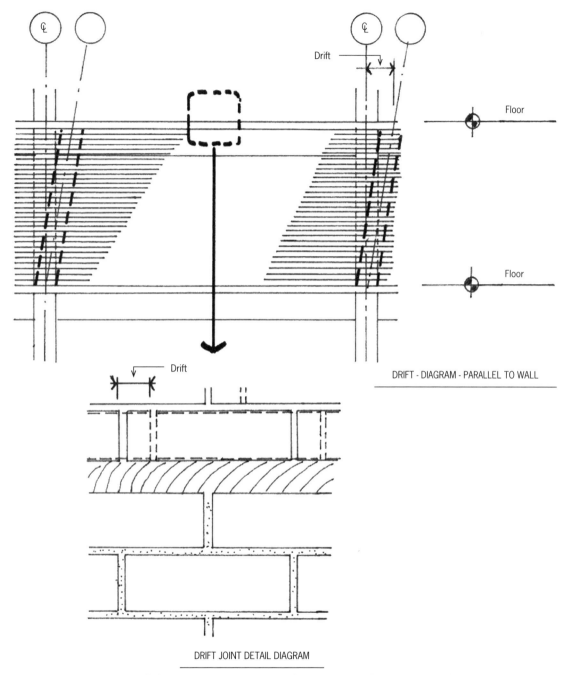

Drift

Floor

Floor

DRIFT - DIAGRAM - PARALLEL TO WALL

Drift

DRIFT JOINT DETAIL DIAGRAM

FIGURE 5.7 Brick cavity wall design joinery must accommodate primary building structural drift. This is often expressed in the brick joinery.

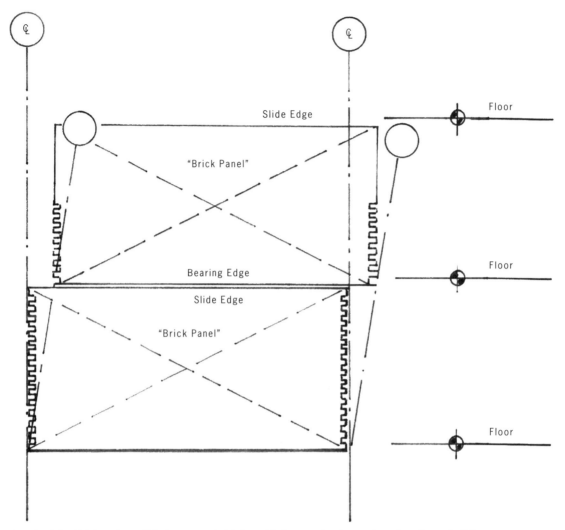

FIGURE 5.8 Brick cavity wall design creates brick "panels" that remain planar when the primary building structure experiences drift.

structural frame drift movement results in a parallelogram configuration. A diagram of one floor displacing above the brick "panels" of a lower floor is shown in Figure 5.8. Drift occurring perpendicular to the brick enclosure will induce a tipping effect as one floor moves relative to the floor above or below. The enclosure plane will rotate about the movement joint and must be designed to remain as a panel while tipping in and out. Drift perpendicular to the enclosure plane is illustrated in Figure 5.9. Primary building structure parallel and perpendicular movement creates corner conditions when both movements occur. Examples of corner conditions are illustrated in Figure 5.10 and the following case studies in this section.

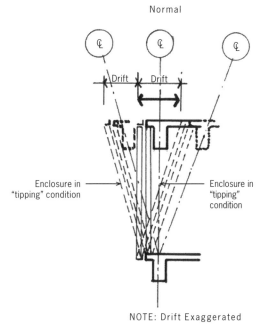

Normal

Drift | Drift

Enclosure in "tipping" condition

Enclosure in "tipping" condition

NOTE: Drift Exaggerated

FIGURE 5.9 Primary building structural drift perpendicular to the enclosure will create "leaning" or "tipping" in the brick enclosure. Brick masonry reinforcing and the inner supporting wall must maintain the masonry as a continuous plane.

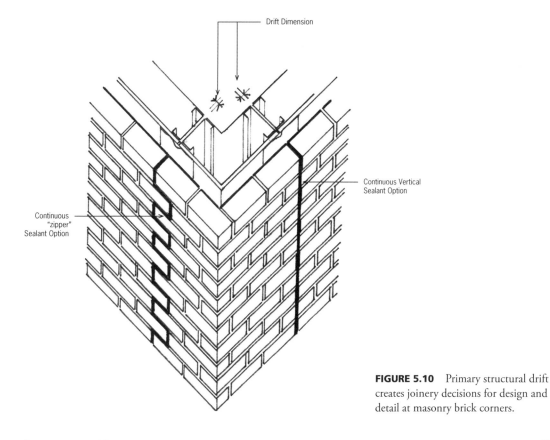

Drift Dimension

Continuous Vertical Sealant Option

Continuous "zipper" Sealant Option

FIGURE 5.10 Primary structural drift creates joinery decisions for design and detail at masonry brick corners.

Weather Protection

The primary weather protection concern, or big idea, is to control and manage air filtration and water. Brick masonry cavity wall assemblies with waterproofing as an air or a vapor barrier typically employ a rain screen approach for protection against air and water infiltration to interior occupied spaces. If the design can accommodate a method to compartmentalize the cavity, a pressure-equalized rain screen assembly can be achieved.

A rain screen and pressure-equalized rain screen assembly have a primary line of protection and a secondary line of protection. The exterior face of the inner wall is typically the primary line of air and water infiltration protection. Whether concrete masonry units, concrete, or a heavy gage steel stud and sheathing assembly, the inner wall assemblies with an applied material provide a continuous air and water barrier. The local climate will determine the placement of the air barrier in the enclosure assembly. The applied air/water barrier, in concert with the flashings at joints, openings, and intersections, is required for a complete weather protection application. The types of applied materials are climate design-dependent on whether the inner wall is an air barrier, vapor barrier, or vapor retarder. The specifics/nuances of these terms require project based research.

The air cavity space between the inner wall and outer brick wythe varies in depth depending on whether it is an insulated or uninsulated cavity. The cavity space must be kept clear of obstructions, which can trap water. Flashing must also be kept clear of construction debris, mortar droppings, and other materials, to allow proper drainage to the exterior and ventilation of the cavity to promote drying. Flashings must be visualized, designed, and detailed in three dimensions. Some flashings are continuous lengths and some have end terminations at openings and adjacent enclosure systems. Flashing materials are not fabricated in infinite lengths, so laps and seams must be detailed and specified. Flashings are typically three-sided at openings or terminations in the brick masonry, with an upturned back and ends to provide an end dam to direct water through the openings, or "weeps," in the outer brick wythe to the exterior. End dams are upturned containment areas to contain, manage, and direct the water to the desired exterior location. These typically occur at jambs and intersections/interfaces with the inner wall or other materials at enclosure plane changes or system transitions. The exterior leg of the flashing typically projects through and beyond the "wet" cavity space to the outside face of the exterior brick, or slightly beyond the brick face. Flashings in this wet area are noncorrosive sheet metal and/or membrane materials selected for longterm durability. Inside and outside corner conditions usually require custom-fabricated flashing assemblies to accommodate the corner geometry.

The exterior brick wythe is the rain screen layer. The brick and mortar form the outer second weather barrier for water control. Brick is not a waterproof material. It has a high moisture retention capacity and can be wet on the exterior and through the brick to the interior face of the cavity. Water can and will enter through the brick and mortar to the air cavity and to the exterior face of the inner wall. Provisions must be designed to allow water to drain out of the air cavity and allow air to move in the cavity, allowing venting and drying. For masonry brick veneer, this is usually accomplished by either omitting the vertical mortar between bricks at the bottom and top course at the horizontal support boundaries, or by wicking material at regular intervals. The openings and materials are referred to as "weeps." Weeps also occur at windows, openings, and other similar areas.

Thermal Design/Vapor Control/ Condensation

THERMAL DESIGN

To achieve a high-performance brick masonry enclosure, you need insulation. The questions are usually:

1. What type of insulation?
2. How much insulation?
3. Where is the insulation located in the cavity wall assembly?

Insulation is one of the components in the brick cavity of a wall assembly. Each type of insulation has specific qualities and values. Designing a high-performance cavity wall is not that difficult, once the project's thermal goals are defined. In consultation with the mechanical engineer, determine the necessary R-value for the enclosure. The codes enforced for the project may dictate the level of thermal design. The thermal performance goals established for the design may dictate an increased level of insulation beyond the code-prescribed minimums. Once an R-value is established, add up the R-values of each material layer in the assembly. R-value by layer is illustrated in Figures 5.11 and 5.12. The two examples illustrate options for insulation placement and type. Climate determines if the insulation is on the "wet" (exterior side) of the primary air and water protection line or the "dry" or (interior) side of the primary weather protection line.

It is obvious that insulation in the air cavity has more opportunities for insulation continuity. Insulation in the "dry" area of the stud and sheathing inner wall assembly must account for the discontinuity of the insulation at the stud locations. Note that there is an R-value reduction for the insulated inner wall because of the stud/insulation detail interface. Whether the insulation is in the dry or wet location, the goal is to design and detail the insulation in a manner that is as continuous as possible. This is easier to achieve in some designs than in others. A discontinuity in the thermal line is referred to as a "thermal bridge." This thermal bridge should be reviewed for potential condensation per climate conditions. The design and detail of the cavity wall should make every effort to minimize or eliminate thermal bridges.

VAPOR CONTROL/CONDENSATION

Other thermal considerations are the placement and location of the insulation and the influence on vapor drive and dew point. This is where those physics classes, consultation with mechanical engineers, and—if necessary—computer software come in handy.

Type and location of water-resistant or waterproof barriers, air barriers, vapor barriers, vapor retarders, and insulation influence the transmission

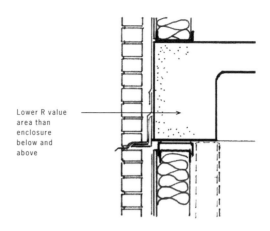

Lower R value area than enclosure below and above

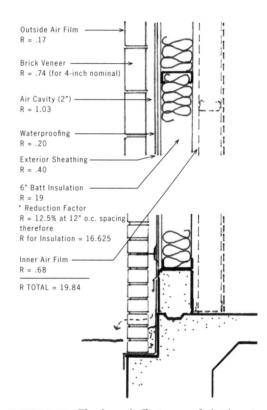

Outside Air Film
R = .17

Brick Veneer
R = .74 (for 4-inch nominal)

Air Cavity (2")
R = 1.03

Waterproofing
R = .20

Exterior Sheathing
R = .40

6" Batt Insulation
R = 19
* Reduction Factor
R = 12.5% at 12" o.c. spacing
therefore
R for Insulation = 16.625

Inner Air Film
R = .68
_____
R TOTAL = 19.84

FIGURE 5.11 The thermal effectiveness of a brick cavity wall is determined by adding the R-values of the multiple enclosure materials. Each has its own thermal resistance (R) contribution. The example shown has insulation layer interrupted by the inner wall vertical stud supports, so the R-value is reduced.

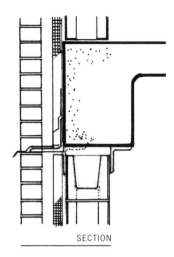

SECTION

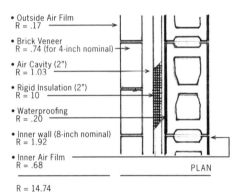

- Outside Air Film
  R = .17
- Brick Veneer
  R = .74 (for 4-inch nominal)
- Air Cavity (2")
  R = 1.03
- Rigid Insulation (2")
  R = 10
- Waterproofing
  R = .20
- Inner wall (8-inch nominal)
  R = 1.92
- Inner Air Film
  R = .68

R = 14.74

PLAN

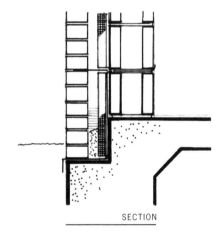

SECTION

FIGURE 5.12 Continuous insulation is illustrated in the cavity. R-values for the example shown could be increased with an insulated interior partition.

of air, which contains water, and the temperature at the barrier location in the cavity. These materials and their location, when considered with the exterior and interior temperature and humidity, determine the temperature gradient, dew point, and location of insulation and the air barrier within the enclosure assembly. The type of barrier or retarder and its location within the enclosure assembly are climate-dependent. What works in one situation usually is not appropriate for another. Each material, assembly, and layering of materials must be designed on a case-by-case basis, incorporating climate, interior temperature and humidity, the air barrier, and insulation placement.

Air and vapor barriers are continuous membranes that block and prohibit air and moisture transmission through the material. For this to occur, the material selection and the design and detail methods for sealing penetrations are key design considerations. Continuity of the barrier is a prime consideration.

The exterior surface of the inner wall is typically a continuous air and water barrier. The exterior side of the cavity is allowed to dry toward the exterior. The materials in the cavity are designed for use and durability in the wet environment. The interior side of the air/water barrier of the inner wall should be allowed to dry toward the interior. This is of particular importance where the insulation is located on the interior side of the inner wall. Interior finishes, including paint, should be reviewed to determine if they are required to be vapor permeable, allowing drying toward the interior. Remember the basics: Temperature moves from warm to cold, and air carries water; a heating-predominant interior (cold climate) or a cooling-predominant interior (hot climate) or mixed climate with both heating and cooling determines vapor drive direction.

No matter the climate, it is advisable to check the enclosure assembly for vapor drive and dew point/condensation location. This will require setting summer and winter design temperatures and defining the interior temperature and humidity basis of design. An example of a dew point/condensation analysis review is shown in Figures 5.13a and b. Because of the custom nature of this type of enclosure design and the specifics of the climate

Exterior Building Enclosures

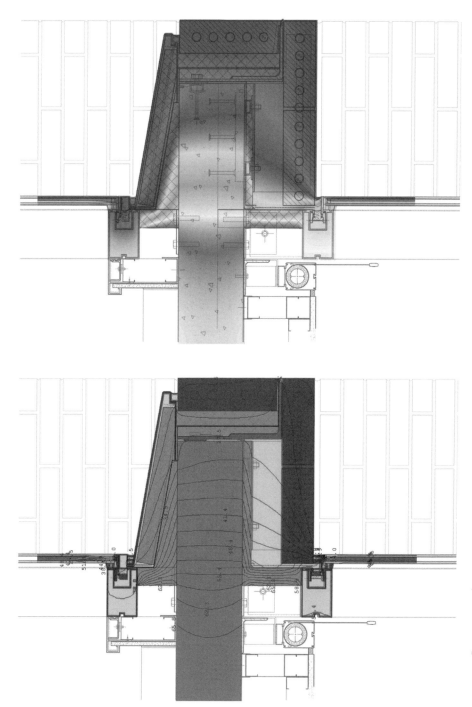

FIGURE 5.13a Computer analysis is helpful in the design phase to determine condensation/dew point winter condition parameters for the local climate, building use, and interior temperature and humidity conditions. This design tool assists the architect to select materials, determine appropriate material properties, and place materials in the enclosure assembly detailing. The example shown is a winter condition. *Skidmore, Owings & Merrill LLP*

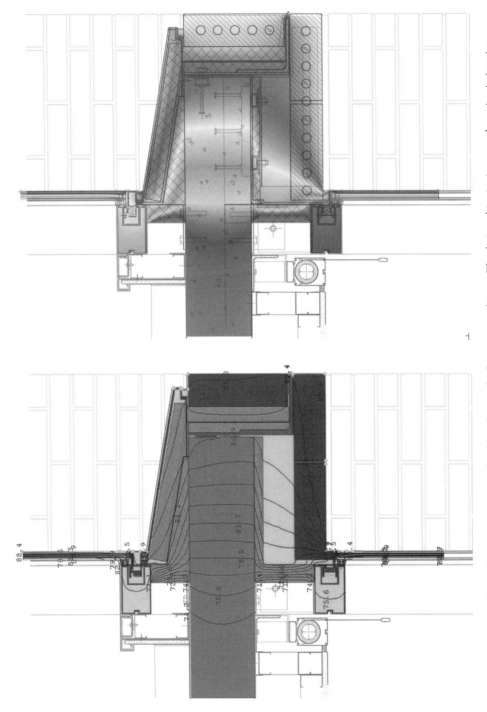

FIGURE 5.13b Summer analysis. Condensation review should analyze multiple season conditions. The design objective is no condensation in interior environments or within materials in the enclosure assembly. *Skidmore, Owings & Merrill LLP*

and interior temperature and humidity, a condensation analysis should be performed. Sample condensation analyses are included in the Harvard University Northwest Science Building case study in this chapter.

Fire Resistance/Life Safety

Brick masonry, by its natural properties, is fire resistant. The brick cavity wall fire resistance required by the applicable code enforced for the project will depend on the type of construction use, occupancy, type of building, and the location of the enclosure wall in relationship to the property line or adjacent buildings. After determination of the required fire-resistant construction, there are several methods to determine the masonry brick non-load-bearing cavity wall fire resistance. These are:

1. Building code requirements
2. Recognized testing laboratories, such as Underwriters Laboratories (UL)
3. Calculated fire resistance

BUILDING CODE REQUIREMENTS

The International Building Code provides fire resistance ratings for masonry brick and certain wall assemblies. The tables contained in the IBC provide prescriptive ratings.

Testing Laboratories

Independent testing laboratories, such as Underwriters Laboratories and others, provide testing results for many masonry brick wall assemblies. Independent testing lab results are typically accepted by authorities having jurisdiction (AHJ). Laboratory tests are conducted on the basis of ASTM E119 or other recognized laboratory tests. Enclosure design assembly should be compared with the tested assembly to verify that the components and layers

within the design assembly match the previously tested assembly.

Calculated Fire Resistance

Fire resistance rating of a brick masonry cavity wall is a function of the wall's mass or thickness. The calculation of a brick cavity wall's fire resistance period is described in NBS BMS-92, "Fire Resistance Classification of Building Construction."

The appropriate method to calculate brick cavity wall fire-resistance hourly rating will be project-dependent. The method and results should be discussed with the AHJ to validate concurrence and acceptance.

Summary

Brick masonry design considerations have been described herein with a focus on the non-load-bearing brick cavity wall exterior enclosure. Most building designs that utilize this type of design and construction also include window, door, louver, and other openings within the masonry brick. These interface areas require a high level of attention and care in design and detail. There is abundant information on design, detail, and materials available to the architect. Because of the familiarity of the material and its custom-design opportunities, a higher level of enclosure detail is often expected of the architect's documents. Openings in brick masonry enclosures require close attention to the structural supports of the brick and the openings themselves, along with the influence of the building structure on the opening area. Weatherproofing concepts of primary and secondary lines of defense for air and water infiltration must transfer from the masonry brick cavity wall to the design and detail of the assemblies in the openings. Thermal and vapor lines must also follow a clear design approach for materials and location and the all-important detail transitions within the brick and other enclosure systems for windows, louvers, and other openings and adjacent enclosure systems. Examples for each of these are illustrated in the following case studies.

Masonry – Brick

Harvard University Northwest Science Building

Location:
Cambridge, MA, USA
Building Type:
Campus Laboratory and Office

PARTICIPANTS
Owner:
Harvard Faculty of Arts and Sciences – Cambridge, MA
Architect:
Skidmore, Owings & Merrill LLP – San Francisco, CA
Structural Engineer:
Skidmore, Owings & Merrill LLP – San Francisco, CA
Mechanical Engineer:
Bard, Rao + Athanas Consulting Engineers, LLC – Watertown, MA
Contractor:
Bond Brothers – Everett, MA
Masonry Contractor:
Pizzotti Brothers, Inc. – Everett, MA
Curtain Wall Contractor:
Ipswich Bay Glass Co., Inc. – Rowley, MA

Project Description

The Harvard University Northwest Science Building is a multidiscipline research facility housing faculty members and their research groups, totaling approximately 400 people. The building is 530,000 sq. ft. with four stories above grade and four stories below grade, and includes faculty and students from a wide array of disciplines: neurosciences, bioengineering, systems biology, and computational analysis. The building defines a new campus yard on the north edge of the campus, creating an important link between Harvard and the adjacent Cambridge community. The above-grade building features include administrative spaces, faculty offices, amenity spaces, conference rooms, and wet and computational laboratories.

Laboratories are located along the northern and western half of the above-grade floors facing the campus. Labs are designed and organized to be flexible, with bench areas free of columns and vertical penetrations. A central spine containing mechanical, electrical, plumbing, and laboratory service infrastructure supports the north- and west-facing labs and the south- and east-facing office and administration areas on each floor. A site plan illustrating the building organization and location on the Harvard campus is shown in Figure 5C1.1.

The project delivery method was a negotiated general contractor selection. After contractor selection, several masonry and curtain wall contractors reviewed the construction documents and provided bid pricing and constructability comments. The owner, contractor, and architect team reviewed the qualifications of the subcontractors. Final masonry subcontractor selection by the contractor and owner was qualifications-based.

Enclosure System Types

The laboratory spaces are enclosed by an insulated masonry brick rain screen cavity wall. The brick is a Norman size brick (depth = 3 5/8″ [92 mm], height = 2 1/4″ [57 mm], length = 11 5/8″ [295 mm]) in a running bond pattern covering the spandrel, column covers, pier, and wall areas. The laboratory floor-to-floor heights are 14′-0″ (4.267 m) typical and 16′-8″ (5.08 m) from level 1 to level 2. The masonry brick west and north elevation is illustrated in Figure 5C1.2. Brick is gravity supported at each floor on galvanized steel shelf angles and laterally supported by 8 inch (203 mm) deep cold formed metal framing at 12 inches (305 mm) on center with exterior sheathing. The cavity space contains rigid insulation and continuous waterproofing membrane adhered to the sheathing serving as the air and water barrier.

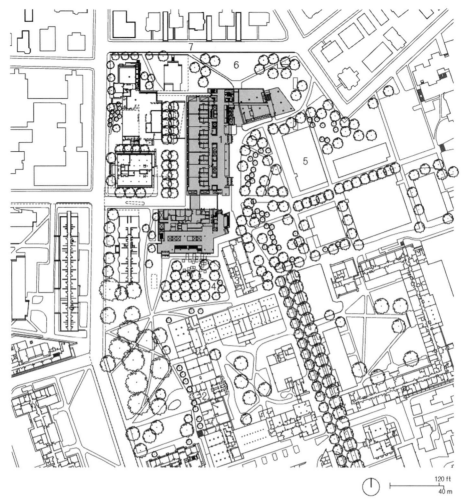

FIGURE 5C1.1 Harvard Northwest Science Building site plan. The building is located on the northern edge of the Harvard campus. *Skidmore, Owings & Merrill LLP*

Corner control joints are organized in a "zipper" configuration following the running bond pattern. Zipper joints are filled with silicone sealant and "dusted" with mortar to visually match the finish of adjacent mortar joints. Dusting the joints is achieved by broadcasting mortar on the sealant during installation prior to the sealant curing, to achieve a mortar appearance. Control joints in the brick wall areas occur in the soldier, row lock, and running bond courses. Control joints in spandrel areas are dusted sealant joints in the vertical joints of the soldier brick course adjacent to the window openings. Windows located in the brick cavity wall openings are high-performance, thermally improved, fixed and operable extruded aluminum frames with low-E insulating glass.

The office and administrative areas are enclosed with a customized standard unitized aluminum curtain wall composed of low-E insulating glass in the vision areas and thermally improved aluminum frames. Spandrel areas are clear insulating glass and wood panel shadow box assemblies.

Exterior Building Enclosures

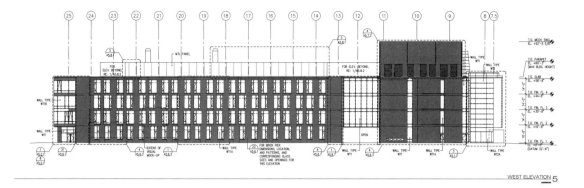

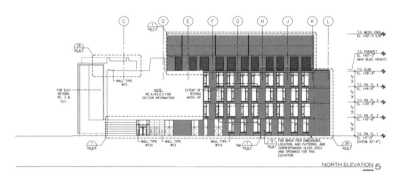

FIGURE 5C1.2 The north and west elevations, which house the lab spaces, are enclosed in an insulated brick cavity wall with "punched" window openings. *Skidmore, Owings & Merrill LLP*

Enclosure System Goals

The Norman brick masonry cavity wall massing, color, texture, and bond pattern harmonize with and respect the color and character of the adjacent brick masonry university structures. Special angular brick jamb returns of the masonry column covers at window openings are factory fabricated to achieve the syncopated enclosure geometry.

The laboratory spaces had high thermal insulation and vapor control requirements due to the climate and the building use. The laboratory brick cavity wall was designed and detailed with rigid insulation in the cavity to achieve a continuous thermal envelope. Tall "punched' aluminum framed openings in the brick masonry are organized and arranged at the lab work spaces to allow natural daylight deep into the lab work areas.

The office areas front a residential neighborhood consisting of houses with wood siding. Spandrel areas of the customized standard curtain wall have wood shadow box panels installed behind clear insulating glass harmonizing with the adjacent residential neighborhood. Each glass opening is "captured" by exterior glazing trim mitered at each corner to achieve a continuous reveal joinery pattern.

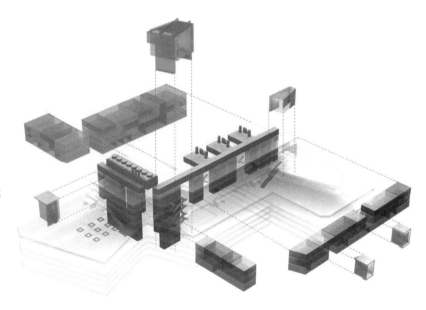

FIGURE 5C1.3 The building organization was defined in the schematic design phase. The four floors above grade are illustrated in the exploded isometric diagram. *Skidmore, Owings & Merrill LLP*

Enclosure System Design Process

SCHEMATIC DESIGN

The building organization consists of four distinct plan zones. These are:

1. Laboratory spaces
2. Central utility/service spine
3. Office administration
4. Public functions

Interconnecting multi-height public and collaboration spaces are integrated into key locations to promote casual interaction among the faculty and research students. The building organization diagram is illustrated in Figure 5C1.3.

Design Development

To achieve the client-stated performance criteria, the brick cavity wall enclosure assembly required a high R-value with minimal discontinuities in the insulation, to respond to the cold Cambridge, Massachusetts, winters and the building use. Multiple alternative detail studies were conducted at large scale (1:2) to evaluate the masonry cavity enclosure, masonry support materials and system, and insulation continuity. Plan and section detail studies of the masonry cavity wall at openings are illustrated in Figures 5C1.4 and 5C1.5, respectively. Material selection and placement define the primary and secondary weather protection lines of the cavity wall, and continuity and interface with window openings. The primary air and water weather line is located at the back of the cavity. The secondary weather line for water is located at the exterior brick face. Lines of weather protection are illustrated in Figures 5C1.6 and 5C1.7. Continuity of the thermal enclosure is illustrated in plan in Figure 5C1.8, and in section in Figure 5C1.9.

Exterior Building Enclosures

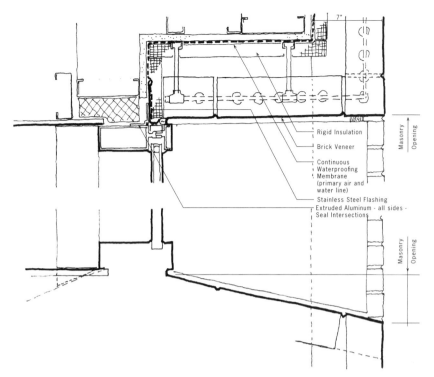

FIGURE 5C1.4 Plan details of the masonry opening illustrate the materials of the brick cavity wall. The brick masonry and anchor/cavity zones of the wall assembly required a 7″ dimension. The interface of masonry brick and window frame enclosure was defined in design development.

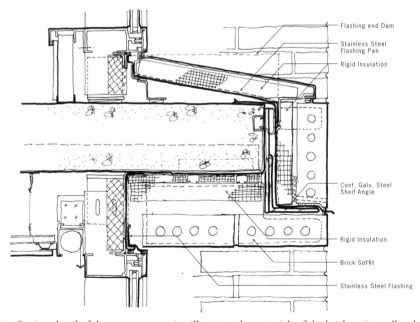

FIGURE 5C1.5 Section detail of the masonry opening illustrates the materials of the brick cavity wall and the interface with the window frame enclosure.

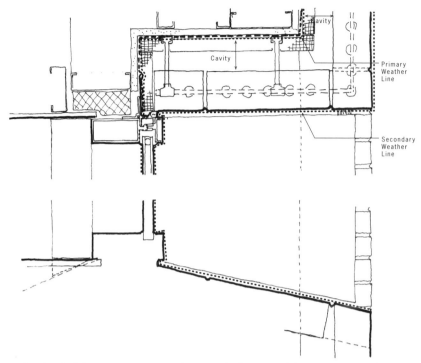

FIGURE 5C1.6   Plan detail of the masonry opening illustrates the location of the primary air and water protection line and the secondary line of water protection. The intersection and continuity of the weather lines were studied at the brick-to-window-enclosure interface.

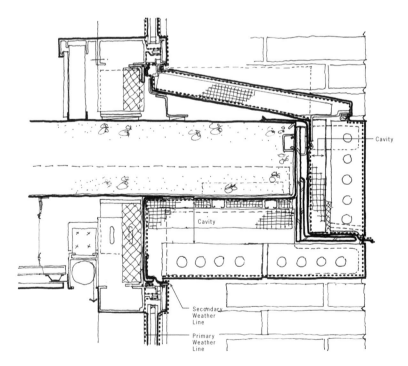

FIGURE 5C1.7   Section detail of the masonry opening at the laboratory areas with window openings above and below illustrates the location of the primary air and water weather protection line and the secondary line of water protection. Discussions were held with the builder and enclosure contractors on the construction sequence for brick supports and interface with the aluminum frame enclosures.

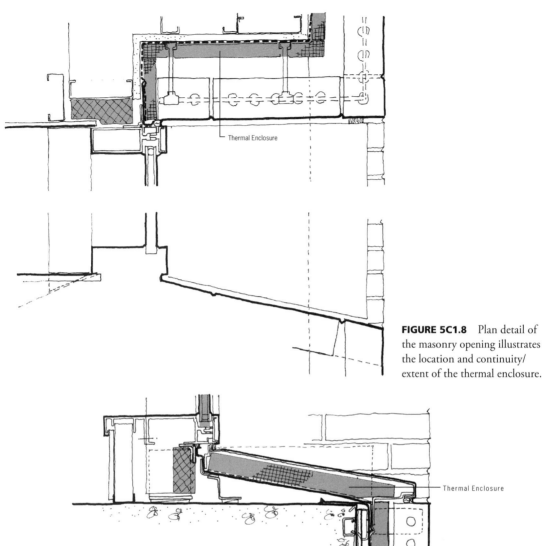

Thermal Enclosure

FIGURE 5C1.8 Plan detail of the masonry opening illustrates the location and continuity/extent of the thermal enclosure.

Thermal Enclosure

FIGURE 5C1.9 Section details of the masonry opening illustrate the location and continuity/extent of the thermal enclosure.

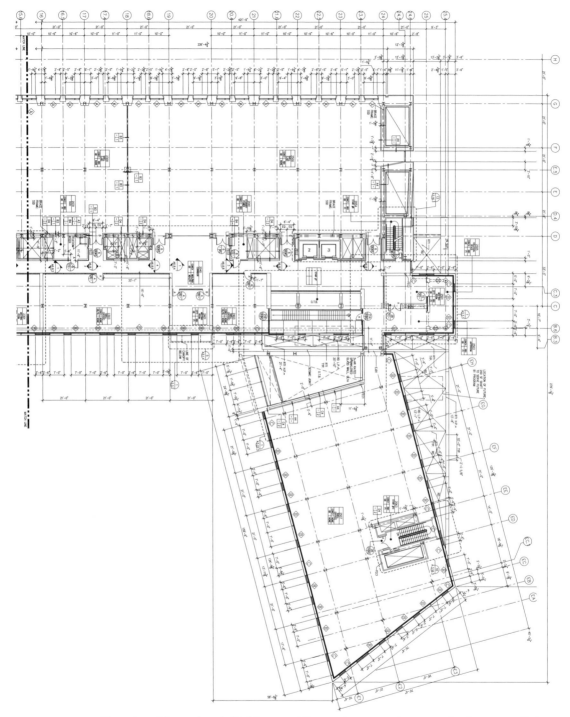

FIGURE 5C1.10 Floor plan of the northern half of the second floor, with masonry dimensions for the piers. *Skidmore, Owings & Merrill LLP*

Construction Documents

Masonry cavity wall coursing and masonry openings were meticulously organized utilizing the Norman brick modular dimensions. Plan dimensional organization is illustrated in Figures 5C1.10 and 5C1.11. Each masonry opening was dimensioned and detailed to facilitate the typical brick module and special brick shape

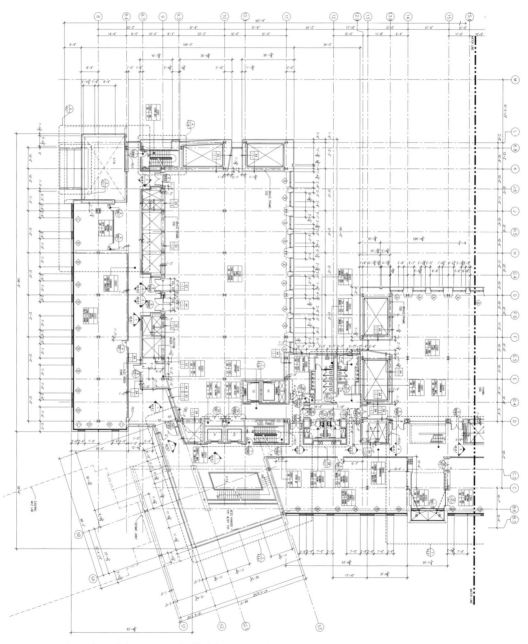

FIGURE 5C1.11 Floor plan of the southern half of the second floor, with masonry dimensions for the piers and full-height exterior enclosure walls. *Skidmore, Owings & Merrill LLP*

requirements. This is illustrated in the brick pier layout details shown on Figure 5C1.12. Partial building elevation and sections in Figure 5C1.13, and a partial building elevation in Figure 5C1.14, illustrate example extents of brick masonry details and the "zipper" control joint at masonry corners. Brick pier and glazing modules were defined per elevation. An opening, with pier and window reference elevation, is illustrated in Figure 5C1.15. Plan and section details for the masonry to window frames are illustrated in Figures 5C1.16 and 5C1.17. Considerable collaboration and coordination of the cantilevered structural slab edge was required between the architect and the structural engineer to achieve the narrow spandrel profile.

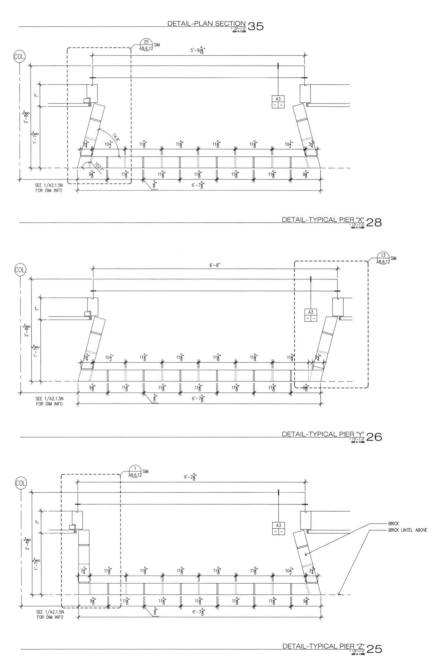

FIGURE 5C1.12 Pier layouts with corner geometry to define standard and custom shape Norman brick masonry sizes. *Skidmore, Owings & Merrill LLP*

Exterior Building Enclosures

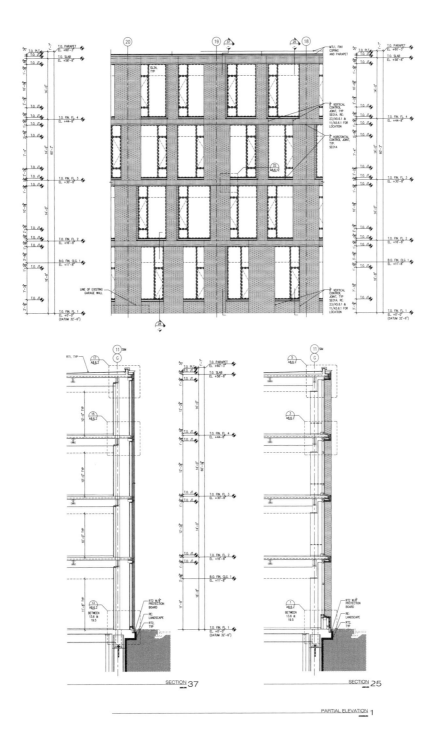

FIGURE 5C1.13 Partial building exterior elevation and sections at the west façade define extent of masonry and the relationship with the primary building structure. *Skidmore, Owings & Merrill LLP*

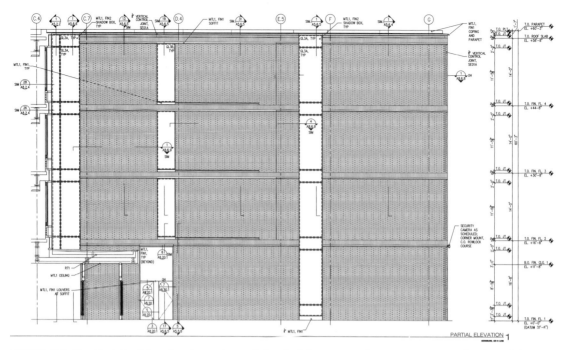

FIGURE 5C1.14 Partial building elevation at the north façade defines extent of masonry, openings, details, and the corner "zipper" control joint. *Skidmore, Owings & Merrill LLP*

Construction

A one-floor-high by three-openings-wide on-site mock-up of the brick cavity wall and window assemblies was constructed to achieve team consensus for quality of brick coursing, acceptable brick color variations, mortar joinery, control joints, and interfaces with adjacent materials and construction. The brick visual mock-up is illustrated is Figure 5C1.18. An image of the brick at the lintel with the rebate to accept the galvanized steel support angle is illustrated in Figure 5C1.19.

Concurrent visual mock-ups were constructed for the unitized curtain wall assembly. A floor-to-floor by one-unit-width curtain wall unit panel is shown in Figure 5C1.20.

Enclosure Challenges

Window openings were designed and detailed to align with the modular brick dimensions of the rowlock and soldier course. The angled plan openings and masonry brick returns are custom-fabricated brick masonry units. The soffit material at the "punch" windows was designed with one option for brick masonry and another alternative option for an aluminum soffit assembly. The aluminum soffit material was selected during the construction process. Multiple detail options for the soffits were developed for visual, weatherproofing continuity, installation sequence, and construction review. Completed brick masonry openings and pier organization with the aluminum soffit assemblies are illustrated.

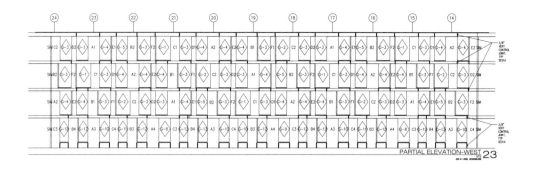

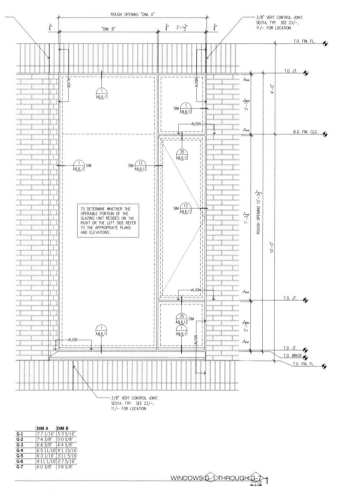

	DIM A	DIM B
G-1	7'-7 1/16"	5'-3 5/16"
G-2	7'-4 3/8"	5'-0 5/8"
G-3	6'-8 3/8"	4'-4 5/8"
G-4	6'-5 11/16"	4'-1 15/16"
G-5	6'-3 1/16"	3'-11 5/16"
G-6	4'-11 1/16"	2'-7 5/16"
G-7	6'-0 3/8"	3'-8 5/8"

WINDOWS G-1 THROUGH G-7

FIGURE 5C1.15   Window openings in the masonry piers define the masonry opening to window enclosure and detail references.   *Skidmore, Owings & Merrill LLP*

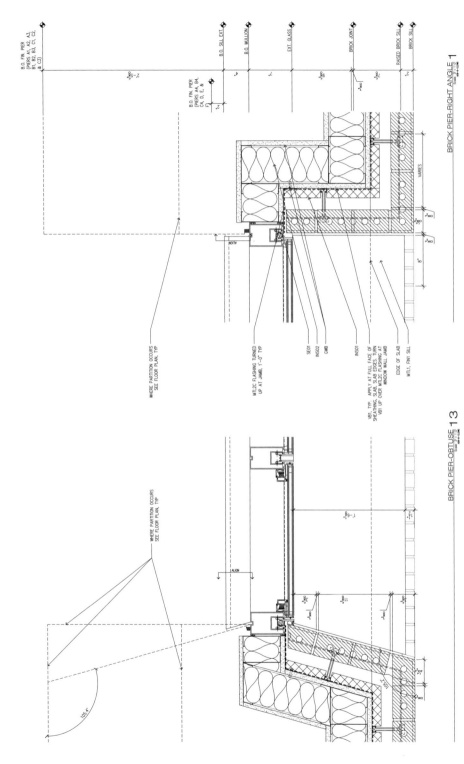

BRICK PIER-RIGHT ANGLE 1

Skidmore, Owings & Merrill LLP

BRICK PIER-OBTUSE 13

FIGURE 5C1.16 Construction document plan details of the brick cavity wall at the window openings with material notes.

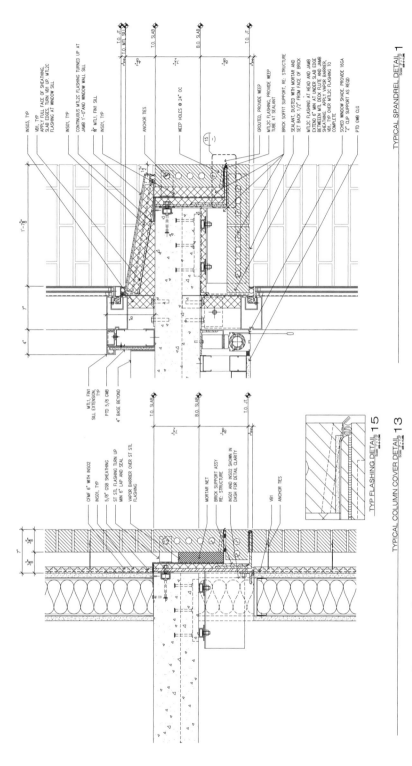

FIGURE 5C1.17 Construction document section details at the masonry openings for windows and planar masonry walls with material notes. *Skidmore, Owings & Merrill LLP*

183

FIGURE 5C1.18   A one-floor-high by three-window/four-pier-wide visual mock-up was constructed on-site prior to masonry installation, to review brick construction and weather protection interfaces with aluminum windows, soffits, and sills.   *David J. Frey AIA*

FIGURE 5C1.19   Special shape lintel bricks allow installation of the galvanized steel lintel angle.   *David J. Frey AIA*

FIGURE 5C1.21 Completed west elevation of masonry brick cavity wall with "punch" and recessed window openings. *Anton Grassi*

FIGURE 5C1.20 The custom unitized curtain wall enclosure visual mock-up panel with wood shadow box. *David J. Frey AIA*

SUMMARY

The completed brick masonry utilizes the predominate campus material in a modern composition. The deliberate and collaborative team environment created a high performance masonry enclosure with traditional materials. See Figure 5C1.21 for completed masonry.

Masonry – Brick

Rice University BioScience Research Collaborative

Location:
Houston, TX, USA
Building Type:
University Campus Laboratory and Office

Rice University BRC

PARTICIPANTS
Owner:
Rice University
Architect:
Skidmore, Owings & Merrill LLP – San Francisco, CA

Structural Engineer:
Haynes Whaley – Houston, TX
Mechanical Engineer:
Bard, Rao + Athanas Consulting Engineers, LLC – Watertown, MA
Contractor:
Linbeck Group, LLC – Houston, TX
Masonry Contractor:
W.W. Bartlett Masonry, Inc. – Houston, TX
Curtain Wall Contractor:
Arrowall Co. – San Antonio, TX

PROJECT TIME FRAME
Concept Design:
February 2006–March 2006
Schematic Design:
May 2006–July 2006
Design Development:
August 2006–November 2006
Construction Documents:
November 2006–May 2007
Construction:
April 2007–June 2010

Project Description

The Rice University BioScience Research Collaborative (Rice BRC) in Houston, Texas, is a multi-institutional facility fostering collaboration between researchers of different scientific disciplines from Rice University and various institutes at the adjacent Texas Medical Center. The center is designed to support the interdisciplinary dialogue necessary for research in the Information Age. It enables researchers and physicians from the world's largest medical center to team up with Rice University scientists and engineers on bioscience and biotechnology research capabilities and speed the transfer from bench to practice.

The 477,000-GSF building is strategically located to bridge between the two adjacent campuses, bringing the inside of Rice University out, engaging Texas Medical Center, and welcoming the City of Houston. A site plan is illustrated in Figure 5C2.1. At the heart of the Rice BRC is a central "collaborative hub." This cylindrical core, expressed in the building's form, serves as the center of intellectual and social exchange in the building. These two-story interaction areas bring together students working for different principal investigators, to mix in this open-plan workspace connected by double-height lounges accessed by open staircases, to further promote interaction. The "scientific marketplace" at the two-story brick masonry base of the building brings scientists from all floors together in shared core facilities, including imaging, vivarium, microscopy, classrooms, and an auditorium, plus amenities such as retail, an outdoor plaza, and cafés.

A brick cavity wall exterior enclosure for the laboratory uses is organized in a 12-story tower massing oriented along the southern portion of the building, facing Main Street and the adjacent Texas Medical Center. A schematic design rendering of the tower and scientific marketplace base is illustrated in Figure 5C2.2.

The Rice BRC project team—owner, architect, engineers, and contractor—were assembled at the project inception. The contractor provided cost and constructability input in each design phase.

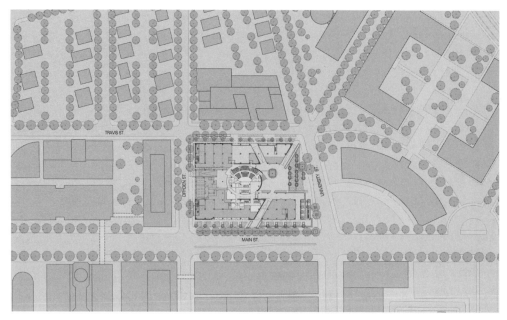

FIGURE 5C2.1 The Rice University BRC site plan with the laboratory tower footprint, collaboration hub, scientific marketplace, and classrooms. The Texas Medical Center is across Main Street. Rice University is to the east, across University Street. *Skidmore, Owings & Merrill LLP*

FIGURE 5C2.2 Schematic design rendering from Main Street. *Skidmore, Owings & Merrill LLP*

Enclosure System Types

The laboratory building volume and the scientific marketplace base of the building are enclosed in a brick masonry rain screen cavity wall. The Rice campus standard brick is a "handmade" brick, in a rose color, organized with 1″ (25 mm) high mortar joints, flush struck; and ⅜″ (10 mm) wide flush struck vertical mortar joints in a running bond pattern. The Rice BRC is designed with brick and brick coursing to match the brick and bond coursing pattern prevalent on the Rice campus. Floor-to-floor heights are 15′4″ (4.67 m) on floors 3–10, with a 20′0″ (6.10 m) tall floor-to-floor from level 1 to level 2, and a 24′0″ (7.315 m) tall floor-to-floor from level 2 to level 3. South and west building elevations are illustrated in Figure 5C2.3. Brick is gravity-supported on galvanized steel shelf angles on the typical floors and by a suspended galvanized steel strong-back at level 2. The brick cavity wall is laterally supported for the high Houston wind loads by 8″ (315 mm) deep cold-formed metal framing at 12″ (305 mm) on center, with exterior sheathing. Sheathing is covered by a continuous air and water barrier membrane to address vapor drive in the hot/humid climate, with stainless steel flashing at the masonry cavity wall to custom-design window frame openings. Unfaced batt insulation is installed within the cold-formed metal framing. Horizontal movement joints at each floor and vertical control joints are organized about the jamb and sill openings to accommodate building movement, expansion/contraction, and mortar crack control.

Windows in the brick openings are custom-designed extruded aluminum frames with insulating low-E glazing. The window frame head, jambs, and sill incorporate continuous perimeter aluminum flanges with joints sealed to receive flashing transitions, to maintain the primary air and water protection line between the brick cavity wall and the window frame assemblies. The masonry enclosure continues two floors above the enclosed occupied spaces on level 10, to visually screen mechanical and laboratory equipment.

Enclosure System Goals and Criteria

The brick color and texture were selected to visually continue the character of the masonry on the existing campus. Movement and control joint locations were placed to continue the "window" pattern on the south, east, and west laboratory enclosure. Vertical control joints are placed in the larger masonry expanses of the building base to create a secondary joinery pattern within the brick bond.

Houston's hot, humid climate and high rain quantity resulted in particular attention in design and detail of the cavity wall. The brick cavity wall is vented at the "top" and drained through weeps with baffles at the floor sill conditions of each floor.

Enclosure System Design Process

SCHEMATIC DESIGN

The location of the punch windows was carefully organized to provide natural light for the interior laboratory spaces and align with full masonry modules and coursing. The custom aluminum and glass window assemblies are recessed from the primary masonry plane for solar heat gain reduction. One of the masonry jambs and the head are masonry brick returns. The opposite jamb is a ³⁄₁₆″ (5 mm) thick custom-formed aluminum plate projecting 4″ (100 mm) from the primary masonry plane to emphasize the visual opening depth and provide increased solar shading at lower sun angles. The building organization and the exterior tower masonry enclosing the laboratory spaces and building enclosure of the base are illustrated in Figure 5C2.4. The laboratory tower plan organization of the window and masonry opening pattern is illustrated in Figure 5C2.5. The south masonry brick facade along Main Street is illustrated in Figure 5C2.6.

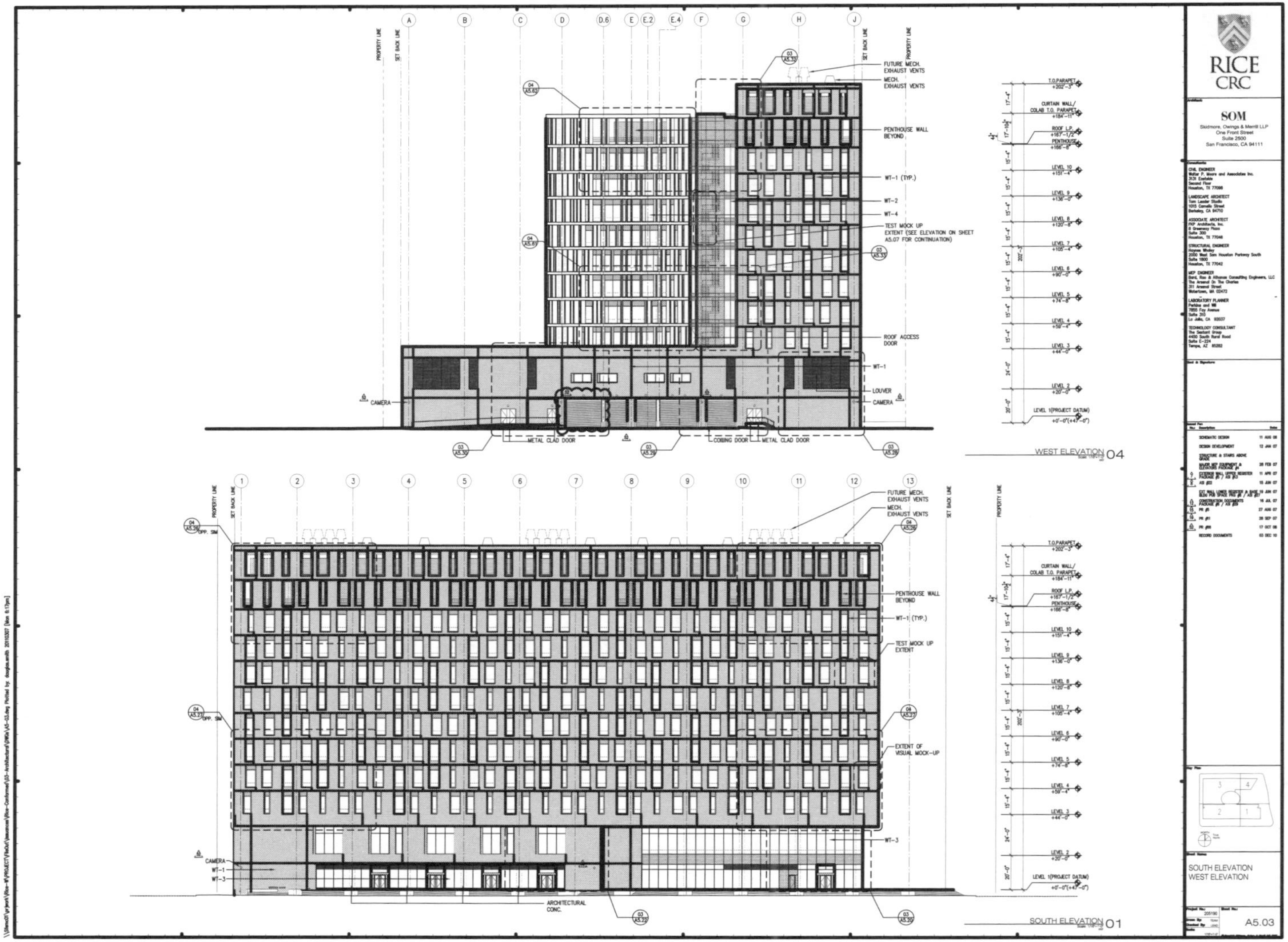

FIGURE 5C2.3 The south and west elevations identify floor-to-floor heights, brick masonry extent, and window opening locations. *Skidmore, Owings & Merrill LLP*

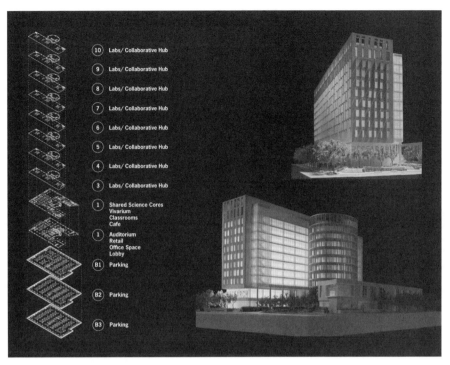

FIGURE 5C2.4 "Exploded" building organization isometric identifies uses by floor. The laboratory spaces are enclosed in the rectangular "bar." Model photos illustrate the enclosure composition of brick masonry enclosing the laboratory uses and curtain wall at offices. *Skidmore, Owings & Merrill LLP*

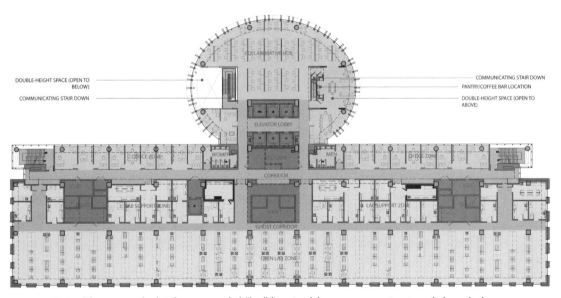

FIGURE 5C2.5 The rectangular brick masonry clad "bar" housing laboratory spaces is oriented along the long east-to-west axis of the site. Punch windows are recessed for shading the laboratory spaces on the south, east, and west elevations. *Skidmore, Owings & Merrill LLP*

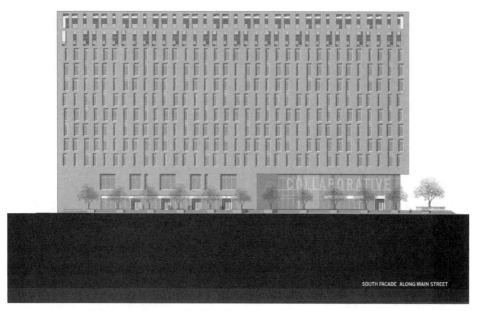

FIGURE 5C2.6 Rendered elevations define brick masonry color and composition of window openings. *Skidmore, Owings & Merrill LLP*

Design Development

Plans, sections, and elevations were developed for each enclosure system. A bay study of the brick cavity wall is illustrated in Figure 5C2.7. Typical masonry brick enclosure system details and system interfaces with the custom window assemblies were studied at full scale. This allowed the project team (architect and contractor) to further refine the building enclosure openings, primary building structure deflection criteria, enclosure system deflection requirements, weatherproofing interfaces, and masonry joinery dimensional requirements. The design development typical head, sill, and two jamb conditions are illustrated in Figure 5C2.8.

Construction Documents

The spacing and pattern for the masonry and the openings were dimensionally defined along the entire length of each building face in plan and section. As a result of dimensional inconsistencies in handmade brick, masonry "piers" and openings were dimensioned in plan per panel and referenced to each gridline to prevent dimensional creep. This is illustrated in Figures. 5C2.9 and 5C2.10.

The 1″-high horizontal joints required dimensional references to each floor datum work point. This is illustrated in Figures 5C2.11 and 5C2.12. Steel shelf angles were designed and detailed by the project structural engineer and detailed on the architectural drawings to illustrate interface with other materials in the brick enclosure system. Horizontal sills are ³⁄₁₆″-thick formed aluminum plates to provide a water-impervious surface at the recessed window openings. Details at the primary masonry plane and recessed two-story areas are illustrated in Figures 5C2.13, 5C2.14, and 5C2.15.

Construction

The Rice BRC was designed and constructed under a fast-track delivery method. The custom masonry brick and curtain wall enclosures were designed, detailed, tested, and fabricated to allow fabrication to commence

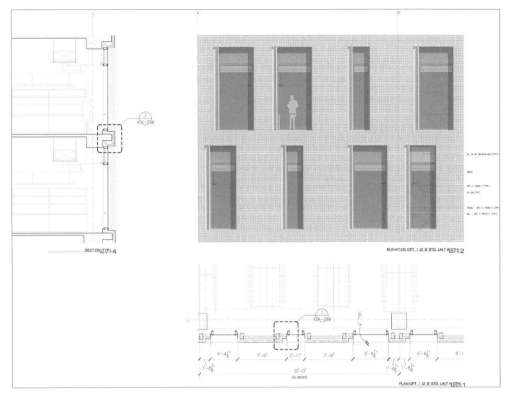

FIGURE 5C2.7 Design development typical bay study was developed to organize the enclosure system composition and details. *Skidmore, Owings & Merrill LLP*

early in the construction process. Masonry cavity wall construction involves multiple construction trades. Typical details and the critical intersections with the building structure curtain wall and window wall required multiple mock-ups to refine the most applicable and direct construction techniques. Visual mock-ups were constructed to review brick color, blending, and the joinery size and pattern. An image of a brick mock-up panel for color and joinery review is illustrated in Figure 5C2.16. The brick soffits provided the project team with distinct challenges. The architectural drawings detail a proprietary brick soffit support system. The contractor and brick masonry contractor proposed and constructed three alternative procedures and mock-ups. The final brick soffit and lintel detail mock-up is illustrated in Figure 5C2.17. Reviews by the owner, architect, contractor, and subcontractor team discussed the pros and cons of each approach. The selected system satisfied the visual and performance goals and additionally accelerated the construction installation.

A full-size mock-up of the brick masonry cavity wall and custom aluminum-framed windows was constructed for visual review and performance testing. Note the open vertical joint in the brick masonry at the base and above the brick lintel/window head of the mock-up. The performance mock-up is illustrated in Figure 5C2.18. Construction progress of the brick masonry cavity enclosure is illustrated in Figures 5C2.19, 5C2.20, 5C2.21, and 5C2.22. Flashing in the masonry wall cavity extends 1″ (25 mm) beyond the exterior face of the brick masonry.

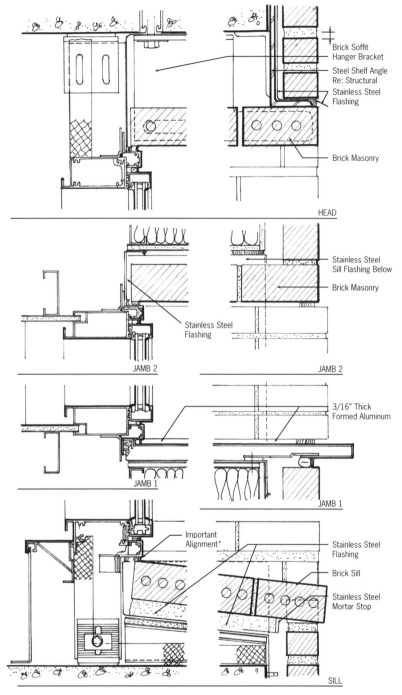

FIGURE 5C2.8 Typical head, jamb, and sill details were developed early in the design development phase to illustrate the material and system interfaces between the brick masonry cavity wall enclosure and the custom window enclosure system.

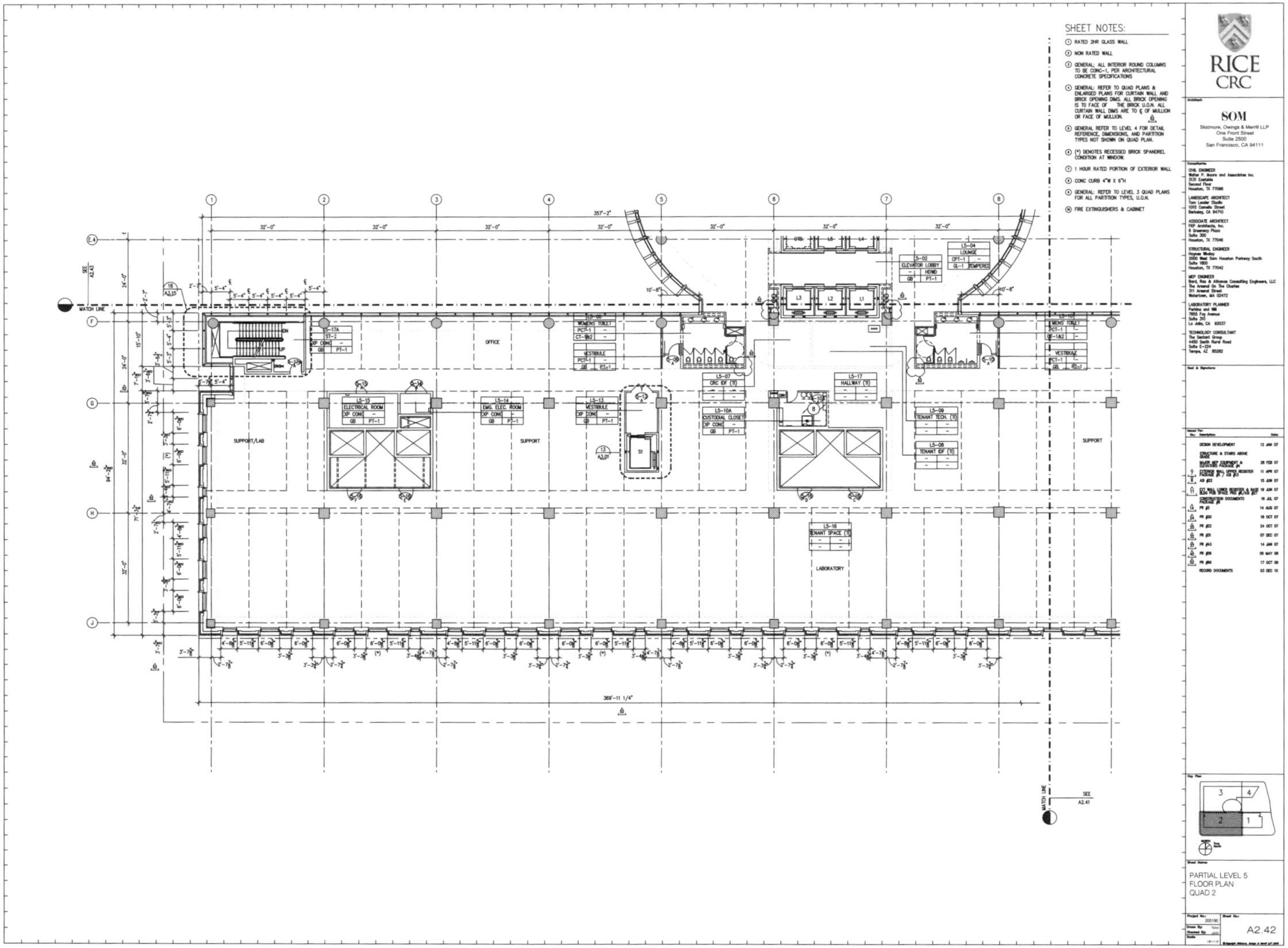

FIGURE 5C2.9 Construction document floor plans have extensive brick dimensions and work points tied to each column grid line. *Skidmore, Owings & Merrill LLP*

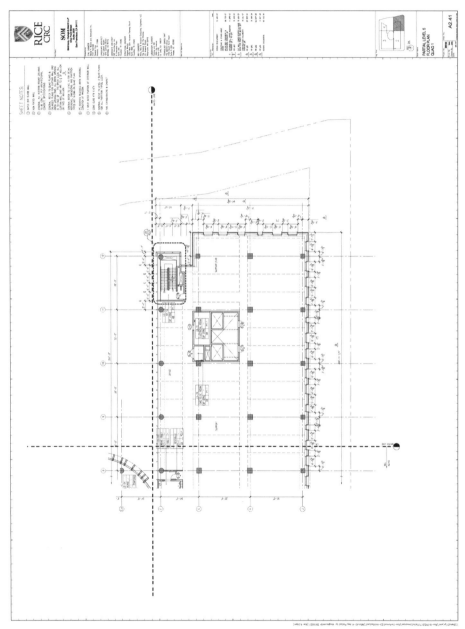

FIGURE 5C2.10 Construction document floor plans have extensive brick dimensions and work-points tied to each column grid line. *Skidmore, Owings & Merrill LLP*

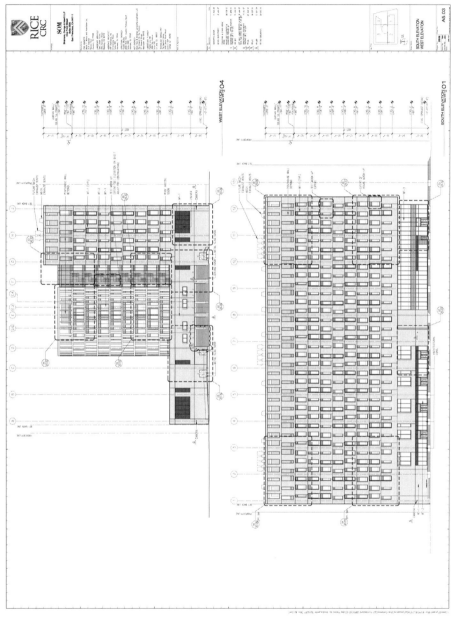

FIGURE 5C2.11 Construction document south and west elevations indicate the floor-to-floor heights and the extent of brick masonry and window opening locations. *Skidmore, Owings & Merrill LLP*

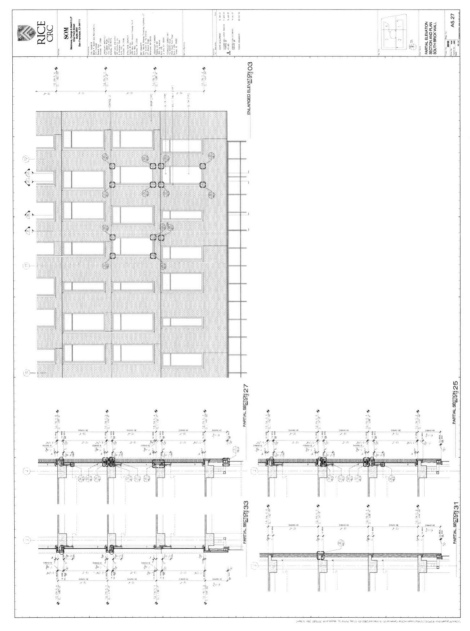

FIGURE 5C2.12 Partial building elevations and sections define vertical brick coursing and detail references. *Skidmore, Owings & Merrill LLP*

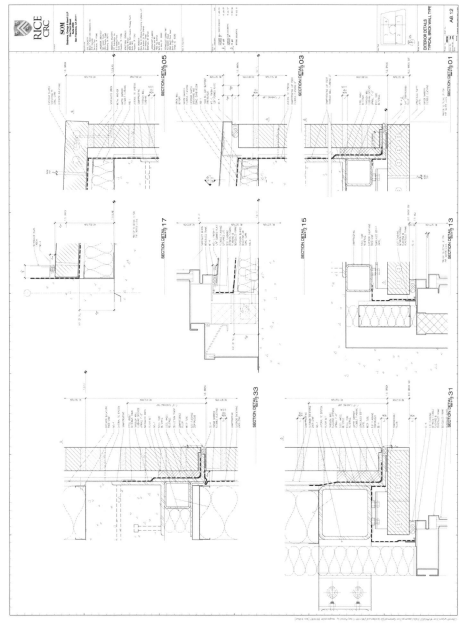

FIGURE 5C2.13 Construction document half-full-scale details illustrate the brick masonry cavity wall details and interfaces with the custom window enclosure assemblies. The "inner workings" of the aluminum frames are left blank on the architectural drawings and were developed in a design-build delivery method by the curtain wall contractor. *Skidmore, Owings & Merrill LLP*

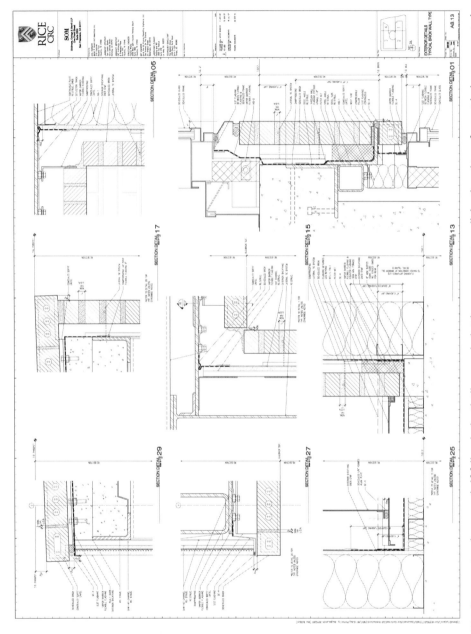

FIGURE 5C2.14 Construction document half-full-scale details illustrate the brick masonry cavity wall details and interfaces with the custom window enclosure assemblies. The "inner workings" of the aluminum frames are left blank on the architectural drawings and were developed in a design-build delivery method by the curtain wall contractor. *Skidmore, Owings & Merrill LLP*

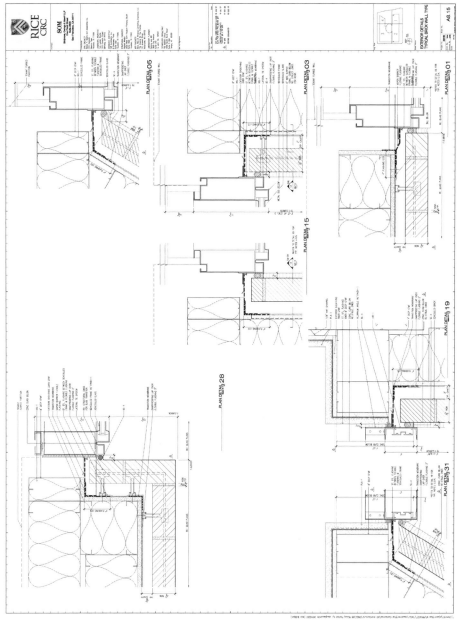

FIGURE 5C2.15 Construction document half-full-scale details illustrate the brick masonry cavity wall details and interfaces with the custom window enclosure assemblies. The "inner workings" of the aluminum frames are left blank on the architectural drawings and were developed in a design-build delivery method by the curtain wall contractor. *Skidmore, Owings & Merrill LLP*

201

FIGURE 5C2.18 Full-scale performance test mock-up. *Maurice Hamilton Jr.*

FIGURE 5C2.16 Brick masonry mock-ups for color and joinery review and approval by all participants. *Maurice Hamilton Jr.*

FIGURE 5C2.17 Brick masonry lintel and soffit mock-up. *Maurice Hamilton Jr.*

FIGURE 5C2.19 Brick masonry enclosure stages of construction progress. Note the sheathing on upper floors, primary air and water protection line below scaffold floors, and masonry on the lower floor. *Maurice Hamilton Jr.*

FIGURE 5C2.20 Brick masonry soffit construction progress. The brick soffit assembly was prefabricated and lifted into place in sections. *Maurice Hamilton Jr.*

FIGURE 5C2.21 Brick masonry lintel angle, brick masonry gravity support, and flashing construction progress. *Maurice Hamilton Jr.*

FIGURE 5C2.22 In-progress construction of masonry cavity enclosure. *Maurice Hamilton Jr.*

FIGURE 5C2.23 Completed brick cavity wall enclosure. © *Cesar Rubio Photography*

Enclosure Challenge

The typical handmade brick typically utilized on the campus was not available in the quantity and time frame for the project, because of damage at the brick plant from the previous hurricane season. Extensive research for an acceptable match was performed by the architectural and construction team. An excellent match in a wire-cut brick was custom-fabricated by a regional Texas brick kiln to match the surface texture and color for the project. The completed masonry cavity wall and custom window wall is shown in Figure 5C2.23.

Masonry – Brick

UCLA Anderson School of Management

Location:
Los Angeles, CA, USA
Building Type:
Academic Building

The Anderson School is a six-building campus within the larger UCLA campus. *Pei Cobb Freed*

PARTICIPANTS
Owner:
University of California Regents
Architect:
Pei Cobb Freed & Partners Architects LLP
Associate Architect:
Leidenfrost/Horowitz & Associates – Glendale, CA
Structural Engineer:
CBM Engineers Inc. – Houston, TX
Mechanical Engineer:
Hayakawa and Associates – West Hollywood, CA
Contractor:
PCL Construction Services, Inc. – Los Angeles

Brick Manufacturer:
Pacific Clay Products – Lake Elsinore, CA
Mason:
R & R Masonry INC. – North Hollywood, CA

PROJECT TIME FRAME
Schematic Design:
Planning commenced November 1987
Design Development:
Early 1990–Fall 1990
Construction Documents:
Fall 1990–Spring 1990
Construction, Building Occupancy, and Project Close-Out:
September 1991–April 1995 (includes the University of California Capital Planning occupancy review
    period)

Project Description

The UCLA Anderson School of Management (The Anderson School) on the University of California, Los Angeles (UCLA) campus, is a 284,753-sq.-ft. (2,646 sq. m) academic facility. The UCLA Anderson School complex is a campus in a campus comprising six interconnected buildings housing state-of-the-art instructional facilities and computer technologies. Functionally integrated, each of the six building components focuses on a specific aspect of graduate management.

The building's scale, materials, and siting are informed by the nearby campus core quadrangle and the steeply sloping site connecting the upper and lower UCLA compounds. The original predominant campus architectural style is Romanesque Revival, utilizing brick, terra-cotta, limestone, and limestone-colored precast architectural concrete as primary exterior materials. The five-story complex is designed as a permeable organization, each story distinct yet linked on certain levels to function as a whole. At the center is an outdoor plaza that encourages interaction and emphasizes circulation. The UCLA Anderson School maximizes its sloped site with access to the mild Southern California weather via exterior terraces on four of its five levels. A site plan of the Anderson School, adjacent to the original campus is shown in Figure 5C3.1.

Enclosure System Materials and Type

The UCLA architectural campus standards define exterior building materials standards to maintain consistency with the original campus architecture. The primary materials for new construction typically include UCLA-blend brick and buff color stone, terra-cotta, or concrete. These components are allowed to be applied in a variety of architectural styles and languages responding to the function of particular buildings and their sites.

The UCLA Anderson School exterior enclosure utilizes the basic material element of the UCLA campus—the UCLA brick. The brick is a Norman size (11 ½″ [292 mm] × 2 ¼″ [57 mm] × 3 ½″ [89 mm]) in a unique four-color blend. The brick is manufactured by the same company that provided brick for the original campus buildings. The four-color blend is defined in the campus architectural guidelines as 24 percent, 16 percent, 20 percent, and 40 percent proportions of rose, light rose, tan, and imperial peach, respectively. Brick is composed in a ⅓ running bond pattern. The face texture is a "ruffle" finish on all exposed sides. Mortar joints are required to match the campus color and tooled slightly concave. An elevation of the Collins Center, one of the six buildings at The UCLA Anderson School, is illustrated in Figure 5C3.2.

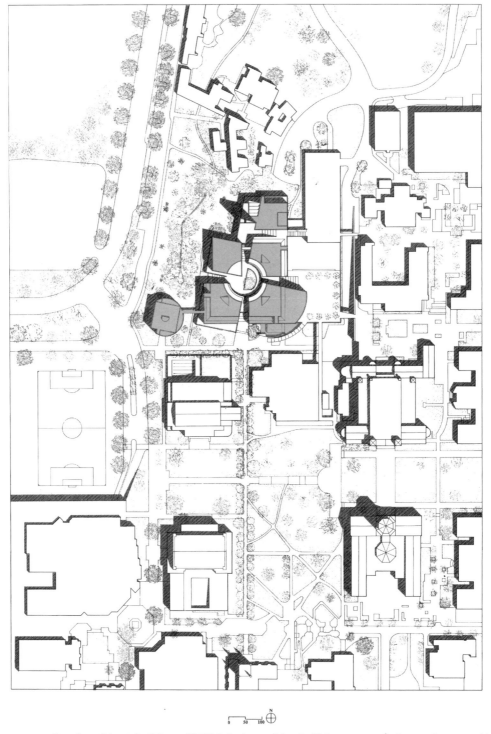

FIGURE 5C3.1   Site plan of the six buildings of UCLA Anderson School of Management, with central courtyard located west of the main campus core.   *Pei Cobb Freed & Partners*

FIGURE 5C3.2 A four-inch (4″) offset results in a ⅓ running bond brick coursing with UCLA-blend brick. Limestone color architectural precast concrete banding occurs at floors. Architectural precast frequency increases at the ground floor.

FIGURE 5C3.3 Horizontal precast banding defines sills and intermediate transoms/ lintels at openings and at the coping terminations.

Brick cavity walls are accentuated at soffits and copings with horizontal accents of limestone-colored architectural precast concrete. Horizontal architectural precast concrete banding is designed between larger expanses of brick masonry expressing floor datum lines. Greater quantities of architectural precast concrete horizontal profiles are located at the lower floors. Smaller precast horizontal profiles define transoms and lintels at window openings. The precast banding and brick enclosure is illustrated in Figure 5C3.3. The brick is designed as a cavity wall with brick gravity loads supported above the architectural precast concrete floor coursing.

Project and Enclosure System Goals

The management complex design is a modern interpretation of the Romanesque style of central Italy associated with UCLA's traditional buildings. The academic village, connected with a series of pathways and bridges, was

FIGURE 5C3.4   The brick enclosures define an open courtyard with preserved coral tree.

patterned after an Italian hillside community, to take advantage of the 40-foot difference in elevation between the southern and northern ends of the complex.

The brick enclosure façade was inspired by a neighboring structure, Royce Hall, one of the four original UCLA structures and a campus landmark. The mixture of UCLA-blend brick and limestone-color architectural precast concrete follow the campus building material standard that express a quality of permanence and durability. The four-color blend has been developed in an approximation of the colors of the original buildings, and has been used successfully on a number of newer buildings on the UCLA campus such as The UCLA Anderson School.

UCLA Physical Design Framework July 2009

A design goal of UCLA Anderson is to provide a pedestrian link to the upper and lower campus, as well as to capture exterior spaces for students and faculty. Outdoor brick terraces and public functions such as lounges, conference rooms, and dining spaces focus on a coral tree preserved from the original site. A view of the courtyard with coral tree is shown in Figure 5C3.4.

Enclosure System Design Process

SCHEMATIC DESIGN

The project's outline program, scope, and budget were prepared in a project planning guide. This early design phase identified detailed analysis of the site conditions and several possible architectural solutions. The schematic design floor plans validated program uses for each of the six building components. The massing, scale,

FIGURE 5C3.5   Schematic design elevation of brick and architectural precast with 40′0″ site elevation difference from upper to lower campus.   *Pei Cobb Freed & Partners*

character, and exterior enclosure materials were developed to respond to the program, the larger master plan context, and the steeply sloping site. A schematic design elevation is illustrated in Figure 5C3.5.

The prescribed campus standard ⅓ running bond brick coursing is employed for the majority of the opaque enclosure surfaces. Multiple design options studied the extent of limestone-color architectural precast at the ground level to anchor the façade to the earth, and copings to trim the brick façade against the sky. Within the body of the elevations of each of the six buildings, architectural precast is incorporated to further visually punctuate window openings and lintels at entrances in the brick masonry cavity walls.

DESIGN DEVELOPMENT

The campus standard brick expansion joint is a "zipper" type joint. Zipper joints are located three courses away from each building corner. Architectural precast concrete corners fabricated in an "L" shape in plan align with the brick zipper joints, further reinforcing the stated goal of permanence and solidity. Corner composition is illustrated in Figure 5C3.6. Final building geometry was confirmed in the design development phase utilizing the corner composition.

The UCLA campus is located in an area of high seismicity. This results in design performance criteria of multiple inches of drift per floor. The brick cavity wall was developed as a vertical cantilever "truss" at each floor. The inner wall zone and architectural precast concrete are anchored to the floor primary structure. The inner wall zone is designed to cantilever vertically without lateral connections to the enclosure at the floor above. This concept allows each floor-high enclosure section to move in a seismic event with respect to the support floor superstructure. A wall section and detail are illustrated in Figure 5C3.7.

Enlarged elevations to illustrate brick and limestone composition were studied for the opaque wall areas, corners, and window openings. Details of brick masonry and window interfaces were reviewed with the campus architect. A detail image of the brick masonry and architectural precast concrete at window openings is illustrated in Figure 5C3.8.

The schematic and design development phases are referred to as "Preliminary Design" by the UCLA Capital Improvement Process. At the completion of design development, the project was reviewed and approved by the Board of Regents and the Chancellor.

CONSTRUCTION DOCUMENTS

Multiple building sections were developed to define brick masonry, gravity, and lateral supports. Seismic drift criteria were finalized in conjunction with corner control zipper joints in the multiple brick corner geometries. The composition and color range of the UCLA-blend brick are illustrated in Figure 5C3.9.

FIGURE 5C3.6 Brick and precast building corners. The brick control joints are composed in the campus standard "zipper" corner joint and precast form "L" shapes at each building corner, to accommodate seismic movement. Architectural precast joints center on zipper joint.

Details of the cantilever brick cavity wall, sizes of the components of the inner wall zone, and masonry anchorage were finalized and documented in the construction documents. Wind load, seismic drift, and deflection limits were established to provide the basis of design used to develop the details. These were identified in the project specifications.

The Los Angeles area climate is predominantly dry; however, winter months do have periods of consecutively rainy days. Flashing details at window openings, lintels, and copings were further developed, with openings at window heads flashed to divert water to the cavity zone of the brick cavity wall. Weep tubes are placed within the architectural precast vertical joints at the floor lines to drain water penetrating the brick and vent the cavity for drying. Weep tubes within the brick and precast enclosure are illustrated in Figure 5C3.10. Architectural precast concrete sills are fabricated with a sloping surface in the opening area to drain water to the exterior, and flat at the jambs to align with the brick coursing.

Construction

The delivery method for the UCLA Anderson School follows the competitive bidding policy utilized by the University of California Capital Planning project procurement procedures. The project was bid to multiple, prescreened construction contractors. Following review and acceptance of the construction bid, budget, and schedule, a notice to proceed for construction was issued.

Brick samples of the UCLA four-color blend were provided to the project team for review and acceptance. Limestone-color precast samples were also submitted to verify a harmonious color and finish blend with existing campus finishes. A two-story "L"-shaped corner mock-up was constructed at an independent testing laboratory

Exterior Building Enclosures

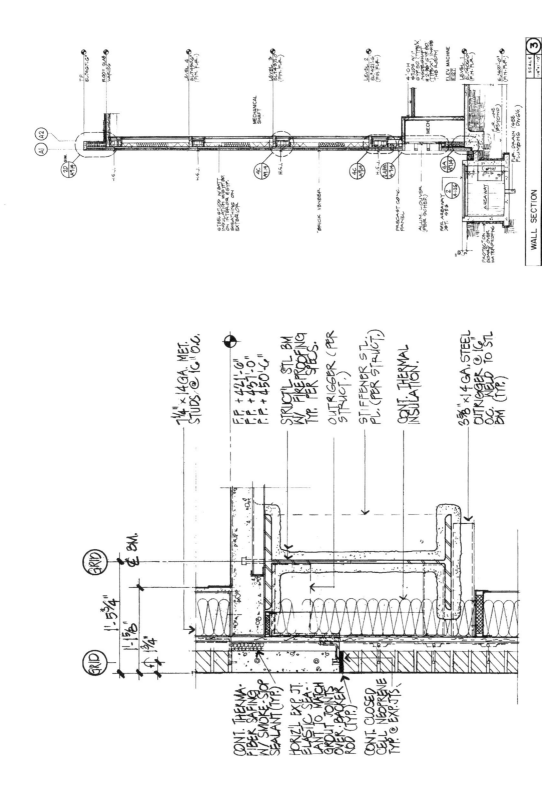

FIGURE 5C3.7   The wall section defines edge of the structure, brick, lime stones, color precast, and the wall supports.   *Pei Cobb Freed & Partners*

213

FIGURE 5C3.8 Shaped architectural precast serves as a window sill and transom. The precast is sculpted to align with brick coursing and allow water drainage.

FIGURE 5C3.10 Weep tubes in the vertical precast joints drain the brick cavity wall enclosure.

FIGURE 5C3.9 UCLA-blend brick, with color range and ruffle face texture, is a campus standard.

FIGURE 5C3.11 Brick and architectural precast enclosures are composed in a stepped massing to create exterior arcades and terraces.

for air infiltration, water infiltration, wind load (enclosure system structural), and seismic drift performance tests. Following successful testing for air, water, and wind loads, the masonry brick, precast, and window assembly was tested for seismic drift parallel and perpendicular to the enclosure plane. Particular attention was paid to the slender precast spandrel and the "L"-shaped masonry corner assembly. The brick masonry assembly passed the seismic testing with minor sealant shear at the horizontal movement joint.

Masonry brick installation was observed on a regular basis by the contractor, with periodic observation by the design team, with a focus on spacing of lateral seismic anchorages and clearances within the masonry cavity. Brick masonry and architectural precast installation required close coordination for sequence anchorages to properly accommodate the exterior cladding to gravity load path.

Summary

The UCLA Anderson School exterior enclosure brick masonry language, materials, and scale form a modern interpretation of the Romanesque campus architecture style. Masonry brick materials, coursing, bond, and mortar joinery, coupled with the interconnected multi-building hill-town organization, respond to the multiple program components and reinforce the academic village concept. The Anderson School serves as a pivotal crossroads extending UCLA's consistent and rich exterior enclosure architectural traditions.

Chapter 6

Natural Stone Masonry

Every block of stone has a statue inside it and it is the task of the sculptor to discover it.

MICHELANGELO

Overview

Natural stone has been used in design and construction of buildings since early civilization. Natural stone is a popular material choice for structures of civic importance. The wide range of color, finish, and fabricated shape options, coupled with the recognition of stability, durability, and permanence, has long made stone a popular exterior material choice. Stone species widely used for exterior enclosures include granite and limestone. Travertine and marble are also employed, depending on strength, density, and the local climate. Other stone species are used, but to a lesser extent. Stone enclosures designed and constructed in the 1700s, 1800s, and early 1900s were solid, multi-wythe, load-bearing assemblies utilizing one or multiple combinations of natural stones installed with very tight tolerances on masonry supporting walls. Technological advances in the early twentieth century in building structural systems, particularly the skeletal frame, allowed stone exterior enclosure systems to evolve to non-load-bearing assemblies. Technological advances in stone fabrication techniques allowed quarried blocks of stone to be cut in thinner slabs. These thinner stone slabs, fabricated into panels, new cladding anchorage methods, and curtain wall systems, expanded the use of natural stone to cladding in exterior enclosures.

Stone enclosure design considerations and the case studies presented are non-load-bearing exterior enclosure assemblies consisting of stone cladding, anchors and attachments, cavity space, and a supporting backup system or structure. Stone cladding panel thicknesses range from 1-3/16 (30 mm) to cubic stone in larger thicknesses. Cubic stone is defined as thicker cross sections of stone fabricated to custom shapes. The supporting backup systems may include reinforced concrete masonry units (CMU), reinforced concrete, heavy gage, steel studs and sheathing, steel strong backs, or aluminum frames. Methods and types of stone anchorage are dependent on the stone proportion, supporting system, preparation (to receive anchors), and the method of load transfer from stone cladding to the primary structure. A section and plan diagram of a stone cladding assembly is shown in Figure 6.1.

Natural stone is formed by process of nature, unlike manufactured masonry such as brick. Visual and physical traits and characteristics range from consistent to highly variable. Each type is unique. As an Italian stone fabricator once stated, "Stone is a material made by nature. Architects need to develop a 'feel' for the material and an understanding of the fabrication process from the quarry, through production to installation." A poetic statement—especially in an Italian accent—and true. At the other end of the spectrum, a stone mason, present at the same time, stated, "You are hanging rocks on the building, nothing more, nothing less." A deliberately, less poetic and more pragmatic yet also true, statement. Both statements, while dramatically different, highlight the unique nature of stone and the range of

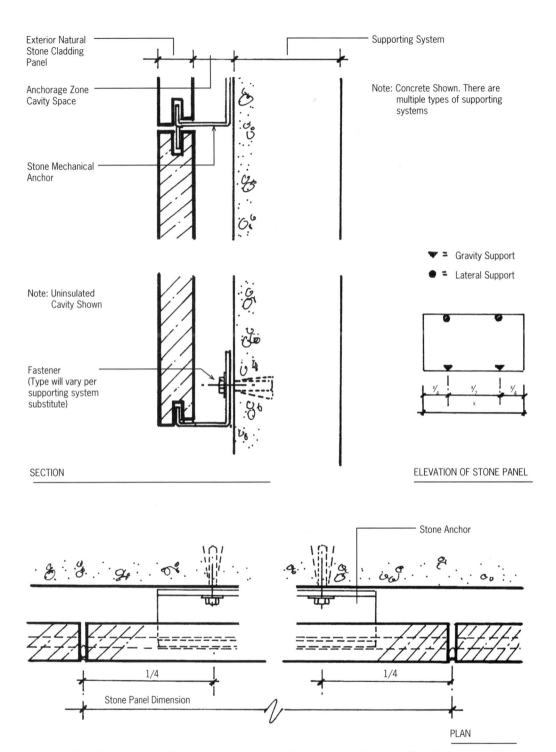

FIGURE 6.1 The plan and section illustrate the three principal masonry natural stone wall enclosure zones. These are: (1) exterior natural stone cladding panel, (2) anchorage zone/cavity space, and (3) supporting system.

Exterior Building Enclosures

considerations when using natural stone for exterior building enclosures.

Natural stones have distinct geological characteristics and are categorized by their geology, mineral, and chemical composition. Characteristics vary between different categories and between stone of the same categories. The following is a brief summary of stone categories:

Igneous: Granite is the result of volcanic activity and the consolidation of molten rock magma. Granite contains quartz, mica, feldspar, and other minerals in a relatively uniform crystalline structure.

Sedimentary: Limestone and travertine are the result of deposits of sediment materials in prehistoric river and lake beds. The sediment is the result of erosion of other rocks and decomposition of rocks, minerals, and organic material bonded together through compaction and naturally created cementitious matrix.

Metamorphic: Marble is the result of heat and pressure over millions of years and is formed when limestone is subjected to prolonged exposure to heat in a confined environment. The resulting marble is a recrystallization of preexisting stone.

Because of its grain structure, marble is susceptible to a phenomenon referred to as hysteresis, which occurs when marble expands and contracts as a result of multiple factors, including, but not limited to, moisture, temperature, sun, and other environmental factors during its service life. Consequently, the grain structure of marble does not always return to its original position. Thinner panel cross sections result in a noticeable bow in marble panels. This phenomenon should be considered when determining the use, environment, panel thickness, and anchorage. Much has been written on hysteresis, and it is not a focus or discussion point here.

Since each stone category and types within categories have particular and varied visual characters and strength properties, research and selection should include visual attributes, physical properties, bedding, excavation, fabrication, and weathering particulars. These must also be researched and understood by the architect during design.

Design

Stone exterior enclosures are typically custom-designed assemblies. Patterns, stone types, finishes, profiles, and layouts offer unlimited design options. Performance design principles applied in design are contingent on the stone type; therefore, design for stone requires a basic understanding of the material. Following the sage advice that "it's always best to start at the beginning," initiate research with the original stone source—the quarry supply. Research how and in what size stone blocks can be quarried. Where is the quarry located? Is there a sufficient quantity of stone in the quarry? These and the other basic questions provide insights into the stone and the available sizes, thickness, quality, strength, and other useful preliminary design information. Some stones are boulders, which are not quarried from large deposits of stone—but that is a whole treatise in itself, so the focus will remain on quarried stone blocks. In the early research stage, obtain information on the basics from the source. Input from dealers, vendors, brokers, and the like can be obtained in later design phases.

Concurrent with research on the stone source, find out if the stone under consideration has been used previously in an exterior environment, and in what manner. Historical precedents, physical data on the stone, and previous experience are invaluable sources for design guidance. This information is available from stone fabricators, stonemasons, and installations. Obtain finish samples from the stone quarry source or the fabricator. Samples must be of sufficient size and the actual thickness contemplated for use. These preliminary samples begin to define the range of color, grain, and other natural variations in the stone, and how long it takes to get the material. Remember, stone is a natural material, so there is always a range of color, grain, consistency and other visual and physical characteristics,—will the variations satisfy the design intent? Natural stone has long been associated with the craft of building. Newer stone fabrication and anchorage technology has augmented this industry and to a certain extent replaced traditional craftspeople. Stone is more than slabs and panels. Design and execution in the hands of architects, quarry sources, fabricators, and builders who understand and exalt stone's inherent qualities and characteristics can lead to dramatic and fantastic results.

Further design enrichment and detail can be achieved through details such as stone finishes, sculpting, shaping, and treatment of the joinery. Finishes add color contrast, even when using the same stone. Wide varieties of finishing and tooling applications are employed by stone fabricators. These include, but are not limited to:

- Polished: Yields a reflective finish where the stone color is more vivid and distinct. The finish surface is smooth.
- Honed: Yields a nonreflective finish where the stone color is visible but muted. The finish surface is smooth.
- Sawn: Yields a nonreflective finish where the stone color is very muted. The finish surface is semi-smooth.
- Sand-blasted: Yields a nonreflective finish where the stone color is muted and the impact of the finishing process often results in a lighter color. The finish surface is rough.
- Flamed: Yields a nonreflective finish where the stone color is muted and usually lighter. The finish surface is rough.
- Chiseled/Cleft: Yields a nonreflective finish where the stone color is distinctive and muted. The surface is rough and irregular.

These finishes and tooling descriptions are industry standard words only, which allow the participants—owner, architect, quarry, supplier, fabricator, mason, contractor, etc.—to generally speak the same language. There are regional or other fabricator specific particulars, even in the definitions. This is where actual samples with actual finishes further define the desired/required stone and finish.

The finishes described are dependent on the stone's geology. Granite, because of its uniform crystalline structure, can be polished, honed, sawn, sandblasted, and chiseled/cleft. Marble, because of its composition, can be polished, honed, and textured by mechanical processes. Travertine can be polished, honed, sandblasted, and textured by mechanical processes. Limestone, depending on its source location and structure, can be sawn, textured, and in certain species honed and polished.

Examples of stone finishes by types are illustrated in Figure 6.2.

Enclosure Structural Considerations

Stone exterior enclosure cladding assembly components consist of: exterior stone veneer cladding, mechanical anchors and attachments in the cavity space, and the supporting wall or framework. Each has its own load transfer responsibilities.

EXTERIOR STONE VENEER CLADDING

Stone veneer is the visible exterior cladding. Stone panel sizes and thicknesses are the result of the stone's strength and properties, joinery and intersections, aspect ratio (length and width), shapes and profiles, and type of anchor. The stone panel accommodates and transfers self (or dead load) and lateral loads, such as wind and seismic, through the stone to the anchor attachments to a backup supporting system. Most stones have available historical data on strength, material composition, and other specifics. This is helpful in concept and schematic design. However, stone is a natural material and has variations. The actual properties are defined and confirmed at several stages in the design and construction process. Granite produced for a project is as good as the volcano that produced it; limestone, travertine, and marble are as good as the layering of the sedimentary materials that occurred millions of years ago. Stone's strength is determined by physical testing of multiple representative project samples. Since stone has variable strength, safety factors are applied to the tested strength results from material sampling. Safety factors vary between stone categories, species, and types. The safety factors are used to accommodate variations in the material grain, aging, load variations, and defects, using statistical probabilities. The higher the variation in the physical stone properties, the higher the safety factor. Industry standards from organizations such as ASTM, Natural Building Granite Quarries Association (NBGQA), Marble Institute of America (MIA), and others, should be consulted during material research.

FIGURE 6.2 Masonry natural stone can have many types of applied finishes. Each finish and stone species yields a distinct color and texture. *Campolonghi SPA*

MECHANICAL ANCHORS AND ATTACHMENTS

Stone anchorage carries the stone's dead (or self-) weight and transfers the self-weight and applied lateral loads to the supporting framework or structure. Types of stone anchorage are highly dependent on the intended type of installation. There are two primary categories for installation. These are hand-set and panelized.

Hand-set method: Each stone panel is individually set, usually on the construction site, on anchors supported by a backup or support system. Depending on the design and performance requirements, each stone panel can be independently supported, or a "starter stone" can be gravity-supported to the supporting

backup system, with additional stone panels set or stabilized on top of the starter stone via anchors. The gravity load of the stacked stone is carried down to the starter stone. The lateral load of each of the stacked stone panels is transferred laterally by anchors to the backup system. Each hand-set approach comes with its pros and cons. There are design implications for the stone, the backup system, and the building structural system, which supports the exterior stone assembly. A section diagram of these two hand-set methods, showing load paths, is presented in Figure 6.3.

Panelized stone: stone is supported by anchors to a supporting metal frame, precast, or other panelized supporting assembly. The panelized system assembly typically attaches directly to the building's primary structural system. In some designs, the

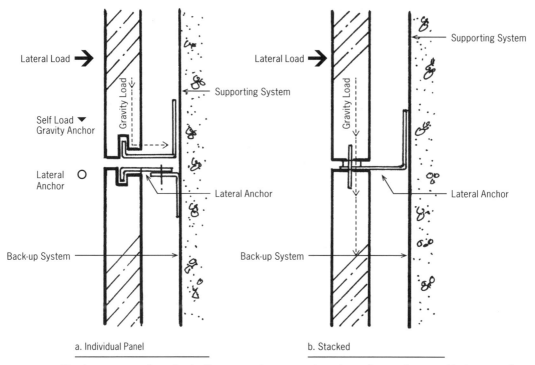

Lateral Load ➡

Gravity Load

Self Load ▼
Gravity Anchor

Lateral Anchor ○

Supporting System

Lateral Anchor

Back-up System

a. Individual Panel

Lateral Load ➡

Gravity Load

Supporting System

Lateral Anchor

Back-up System

b. Stacked

FIGURE 6.3   Hand-set stone can be individually supported stone panels to the anchor, as shown in (a). Stone can be stacked on other stone for gravity support to a starter stone, as shown in (b). In the stacked (b) condition, each stone is laterally supported to the support system.

panels may attach to a secondary support backup system. A diagram of one type of panelized stone is shown in Figure 6.4.

In either of these systems, stone panels are mechanically attached to the backup system, primary building structure or panels. Anchorage materials are typically non-corrosive metals such as stainless steel or coated aluminum. Anchorage design approaches and the general system is an architectural design responsibility. Final design, detailing and engineering responsibility is typically performed by the Contractor, a specialty engineer, specialty consultant, or stone mason depending on the project complexity, contract requirements and project delivery method. Attachments (fasteners) of the stone anchor to the supporting back-up system is dependent on the back-up system material (i.e. bolts for concrete, threaded fasteners for steel, welding etc.) Stone fabricators typically have the primary responsibility for conducting stone physical testing and anchorage testing of the

stone panels. There are multiple types of stone anchors. Some examples of stone anchors for gravity loads (self-load) and the type of stone preparation to receive the anchors are illustrated in Figure 6.5.

SUPPORTING BACKUP SYSTEM

The supporting backup system for stone veneer cladding enclosures can be reinforced concrete masonry units (CMU), reinforced concrete, heavy gage steel stud and sheathed assembly, precast concrete, heavy-gauge aluminum frame, or a steel framed assembly. The backup system type is dependent on the stone installation method, pattern, and joinery, and on the performance requirements for the project. The supporting backup system accepts the loads from the exterior stone and anchors and transfers these loads to the primary building structure. Stone cladding design is deflection-based. Stone veneer reacts in kind with the deflection characteristics of the backup system.

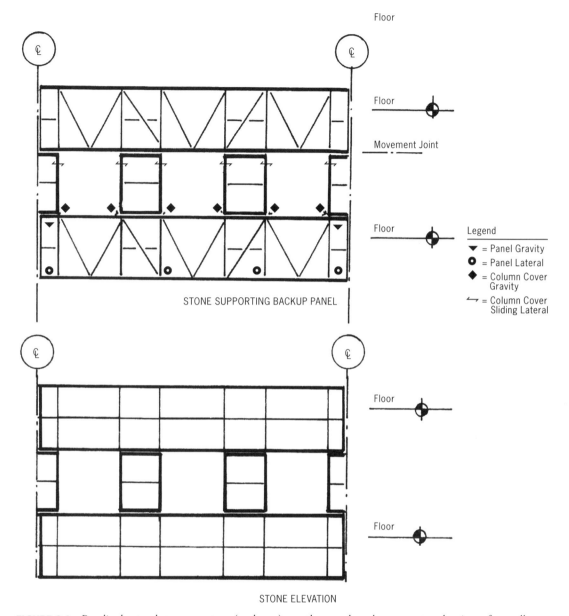

Floor

Floor

Movement Joint

Floor

STONE SUPPORTING BACKUP PANEL

Legend

▼ = Panel Gravity
● = Panel Lateral
◆ = Column Cover Gravity
↰ = Column Cover Sliding Lateral

Floor

Floor

STONE ELEVATION

FIGURE 6.4 Panelized natural stone on a truss (as shown), or other panels such as precast or aluminum frame allow off-site fabrication.

There are no established standards, only guidelines, for stone enclosure deflection design. However, most industry opinions recommend stiff-deflection criteria ranging from L/720 to L/1000. The "L" is the clear span of the supporting system, usually expressed in inches or mm. As with all design, guidelines and standards need review in context with the project's design conditions, locale, and performance requirements. A short span of 10'-0"@ L/720 is: 10'-0" × 12"/H = 120"/720 = ⅛" deflection. Most buildings have taller span conditions. For comparison, a 20'-0" span @ L/720 is: 20 × 12 = 240/720 = 5/16"

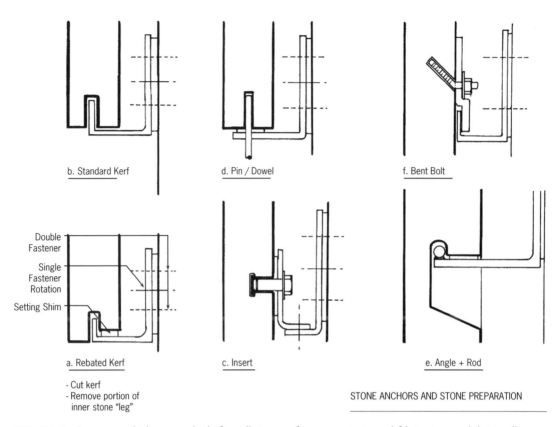

b. Standard Kerf

d. Pin / Dowel

f. Bent Bolt

Double Fastener

Single Fastener Rotation

Setting Shim

a. Rebated Kerf

- Cut kerf
- Remove portion of inner stone "leg"

c. Insert

e. Angle + Rod

STONE ANCHORS AND STONE PREPARATION

FIGURE 6.5 Stone type, thickness, method of installation, performance criteria, and fabrication capabilities will influence the method of stone anchorage.

deflection. In designs with multiple stone panels, as opposed to a design with fewer stone panels per span, the size and quantity of joints have a direct influence on the ability of the stone veneer to accommodate the supporting backup system deflection. Deflections should be reviewed and criteria selected using a span to allow deflection based design (L/number), with a maximum deflection limit established that will allow each stone panel, anchor, and stone-to-stone joint to perform properly. A diagram of a stone wall system at 14′-0″ (4.27 m) floor-to-floor with deflection criteria is presented in Figure 6.6.

BUILDING STRUCTURE INFLUENCE ON THE STONE ENCLOSURES

Primary building structure (columns, beams, slabs, etc.) and associated movement characteristics, under loading, influence the joinery design, size, and material,

along with anchorage of the stone enclosure. The primary structural frame dead load and deflection due to the stone cladding assembly self-load must be accounted for in the primary structural system design. Primary building structure live load and dead load deflections must be accounted for in the stone and support system joinery design. Locations where building structure deflections are accommodated require soft joinery materials. This is usually sealant with a compressible backer, or gasket joinery in instances of a curtain wall with stone veneer. These joints are referred to as movement joints. Structural deflections, when added to the joint material movement capacity characteristics, determine the final movement joint size. A live load movement diagram and the associated joint size are indicated in Figure 6.7. Joinery must be sized and designed for the typical stone enclosure, openings, inside and outside corners, cantilevers, and parapet conditions.

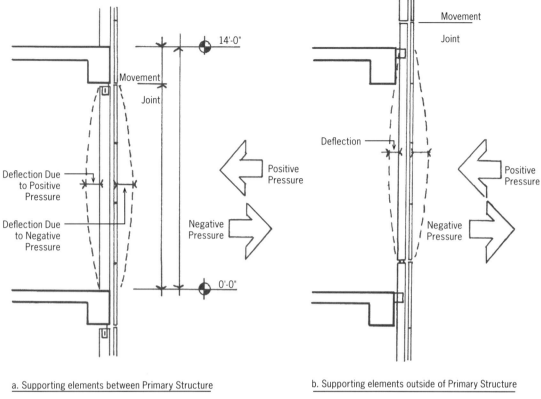

14'-0"

Movement
Joint

Deflection Due
to Positive
Pressure

Deflection Due
to Negative
Pressure

Positive
Pressure

Negative
Pressure

0'-0"

Movement

Joint

Deflection

Positive
Pressure

Negative
Pressure

a. Supporting elements between Primary Structure

Floor to Floor height = 14'-0"
Beam Depth = 2'-0"
Resulting inner wall span: 12'-0" = L
12'-0" × 12" = 144"
144" / 700 = .20 = $\frac{3}{16}$"

b. Supporting elements outside of Primary Structure

Floor to Floor height = 14'-0"
Beam Depth = N/A
Resulting inner wall span: 14'-0" = L
14'-0" × 12" = 168"
168" / 700 = .24 = $\frac{1}{4}$"

NOTE: Movement Joints

FIGURE 6.6 Natural stone enclosure design is deflection-based design. The deflection occurs between connection points.

Individual hand-set stones behave as individual stone panels reacting to the movement characteristics of the supporting backup system. Stacked hand-set stone enclosures behave as a plane the height of the stone panels. Behavior of panelized stone enclosures is inherent to the stiffness of the supporting panel frame configuration. Stone enclosure joinery design at the top, bottom, and vertical intervals must accommodate the primary structural frame drift. Drift parallel to the plane of the stone enclosure is evaluated as one floor shifting, with the floor above or below remaining in place. This creates a horizontal displacement at the top and bottom of each stone panel. In a panelized stone assembly, panels either slide or tip and rotate. Enclosure movement is dependent on the panel assembly and stiffness, how the stone is anchored to the panel, how the panel is attached to the primary building structure, and the weight of the panelized assembly. Stone panels remain rectangular, while the structural frame drift results in a parallelogram configuration.

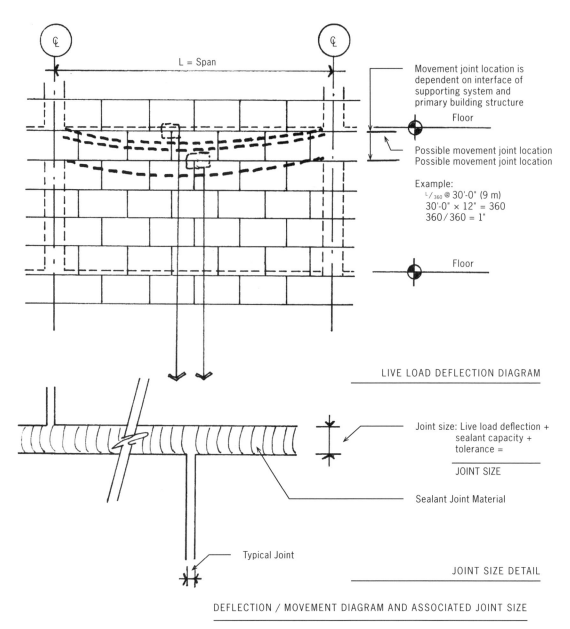

L = Span

Movement joint location is dependent on interface of supporting system and primary building structure

Floor

Possible movement joint location
Possible movement joint location

Example:
$L/_{360}$ @ 30'-0" (9 m)
30'-0" × 12" = 360
360 / 360 = 1"

Floor

LIVE LOAD DEFLECTION DIAGRAM

Joint size: Live load deflection + sealant capacity + tolerance =

JOINT SIZE

Sealant Joint Material

Typical Joint

JOINT SIZE DETAIL

DEFLECTION / MOVEMENT DIAGRAM AND ASSOCIATED JOINT SIZE

FIGURE 6.7 Natural stone veneer enclosures must accommodate the primary building structure movements. The location of the movement joint occurs where the movement is accepted by the stone support system. The size of the movement joint is dependent on the beam deflection.

Diagrams of primary structural frame drift with several types of stone enclosure supporting systems are shown in Figures 6.8, 6.9, and 6.10. Drift perpendicular to the plane of the stone enclosure will induce a tipping effect. The enclosure rotates at the movement joint or panel joint and must be designed to remain in place during tipping in and out. A diagram of drift perpendicular to the stone enclosure is shown in Figure 6.11. Primary building structure parallel and perpendicular movement creates corner conditions that must address both movements concurrently. Examples of corner drift movement conditions are

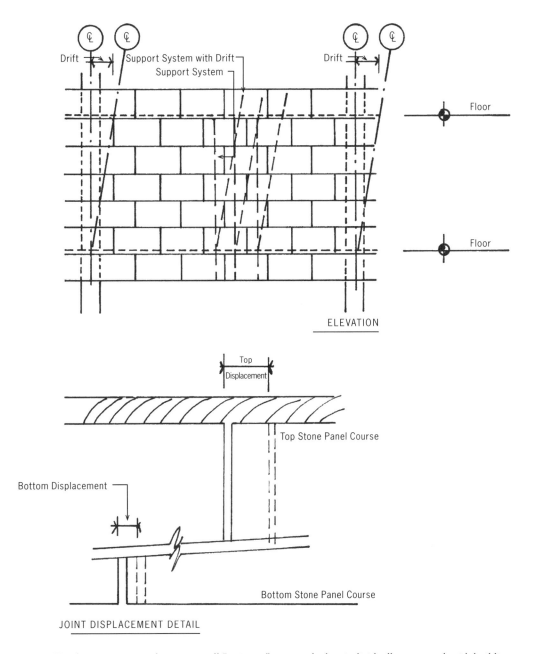

Drift

Support System with Drift

Support System

Drift

Floor

Floor

ELEVATION

Top Displacement

Top Stone Panel Course

Bottom Displacement

Bottom Stone Panel Course

JOINT DISPLACEMENT DETAIL

FIGURE 6.8 Hand-set stone on steel supports will "stair step" per panel when individually supported, with building drift such as wind or seismic movement parallel to the plane of the enclosure.

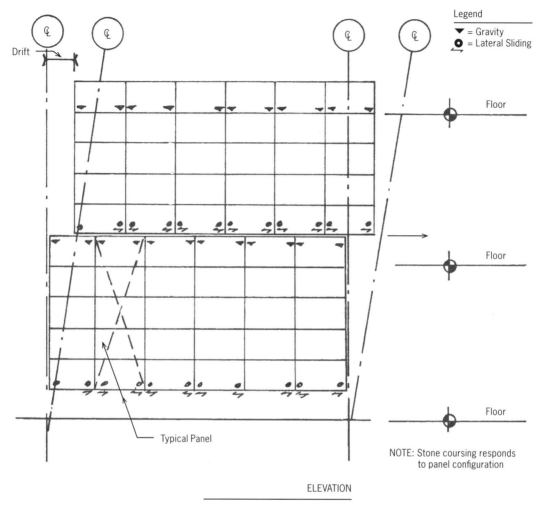

Legend
▼ = Gravity
⊙ = Lateral Sliding

Drift

Floor

Floor

Floor

Typical Panel

NOTE: Stone coursing responds to panel configuration

ELEVATION

FIGURE 6.9 The panelized stone shown slides as a floor-to-floor panel in building drift. The panel-to-panel horizontal joint allows for sliding parallel to the wall plane.

illustrated in Figures 6.12 and 6.13, and in the following case studies in this section.

Weather Protection

Stone veneer enclosure designs of cladding, anchorage, and the supporting backup structure or panel can employ a barrier, mass, rain screen, or pressure-equalized weather protection principle. Stone densities vary by stone type. Some are very dense. Some

are very porous. However, stone is a water-resistant material; it is not a waterproof material.

BARRIER DESIGN

In a barrier design, the stone and the joinery material are the only lines of protection for air and water infiltration. This weather protection approach has been used on exterior cladding. Barrier design relies on perfectly sealed joinery and various (minimal to very heavy) amounts of water (rain) incident on the stone.

Exterior Building Enclosures

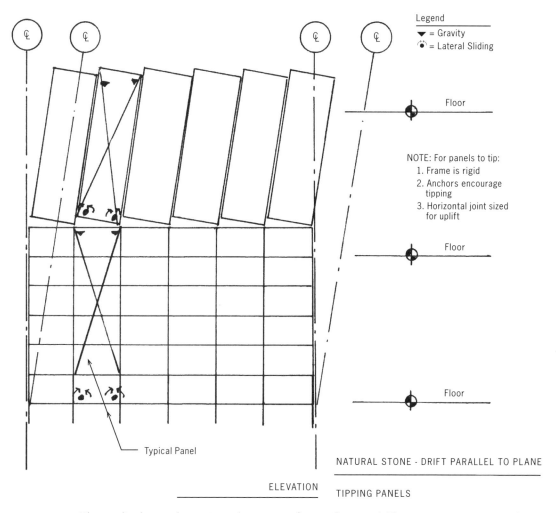

Floor

NOTE: For panels to tip:
1. Frame is rigid
2. Anchors encourage tipping
3. Horizontal joint sized for uplift

Floor

Floor

Typical Panel

NATURAL STONE - DRIFT PARALLEL TO PLANE

ELEVATION   TIPPING PANELS

FIGURE 6.10 The panelized stone shown tips and rotates as a floor-to-floor panel. The stone support system and anchorage design must encourage the tipping.

In a barrier design approach, specific provisions for other moisture control (collection and removal) behind the stone should be implemented. A diagram of a barrier design is shown in plan in Figure 6.14. The flashing indicated in the section collects water and drains back to the exterior.

RAIN SCREEN AND PRESSURE-EQUALIZED RAIN SCREEN DESIGN

The rain screen and pressure-equalized rain screen design approach relies on a primary air and water

barrier attached to the supporting system. This primary protection line can be accomplished with continuous flashing, waterproofing, or other continuous weatherproof materials. The exterior stone veneer is the rain screen and the secondary water barrier/deflector. Figure 6.15 shows a plan and section of a rain screen design approach.

Depending on density, stone has moisture retention capacity and can be wet on the exterior, through the stone in varying depths, or all the way through the stone to the interior face of the cavity. Some water will enter through the stone or the joint material to

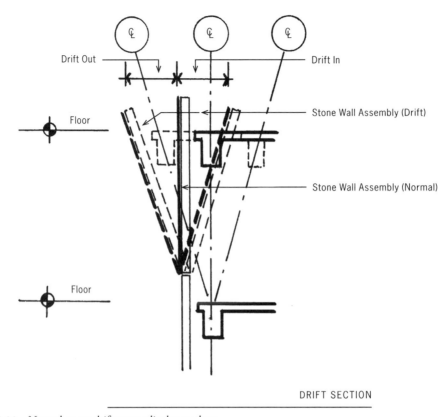

Drift Out

Drift In

Floor

Stone Wall Assembly (Drift)

Stone Wall Assembly (Normal)

Floor

DRIFT SECTION

FIGURE 6.11   Natural stone: drift perpendicular to plane

the cavity and the exterior face of the inner wall. Provisions must be incorporated into the design to allow water to drain out of the air cavity and to allow air in the cavity, promoting venting and drying. For stone veneer, this is usually accomplished by detailing openings, referred to as weeps, between the stone at the bottom joinery and at the top course at horizontal support boundaries at regular intervals. Weeps work in concert with either flashing or other methods to collect and water in the cavity and drain it to the exterior. An example of a weep in a stone enclosure utilizing a gutter and a rainscreen principle with a gutter is illustrated in Figures 6.14 and 6.15 respectively. A section and elevation diagram of a weep with internal "plumbing" at a continuous extruded aluminum stone anchor in a stone enclosure is shown in Figure 6.16.

The cavity between the stone cladding veneer and the backup system varies in depth, depending on whether it is an insulated or uninsulated cavity. To allow proper drainage to the exterior, the cavity and flashings must be kept clear of obstructions and debris, which can trap water. Flashings in a hand-set method are typically three-sided with an upturned back and ends, to contain water and direct it through the weeps in the outer stone veneer to the exterior. Flashings occur in wet areas and are noncorrosive sheet metal and/or membrane materials. Inside and outside corner conditions usually require custom-fabricated flashing assemblies to accommodate the corner geometry.

The inner backup system is the primary line of protection against air and water infiltration in rain screen and pressure-equalized assemblies. The inner wall of the enclosure assembly can employ applied flashing or waterproof materials, which provide a continuous air- and water-resistant barrier. The types of applied materials are design-dependent on whether the inner wall is a vapor barrier or vapor retarder.

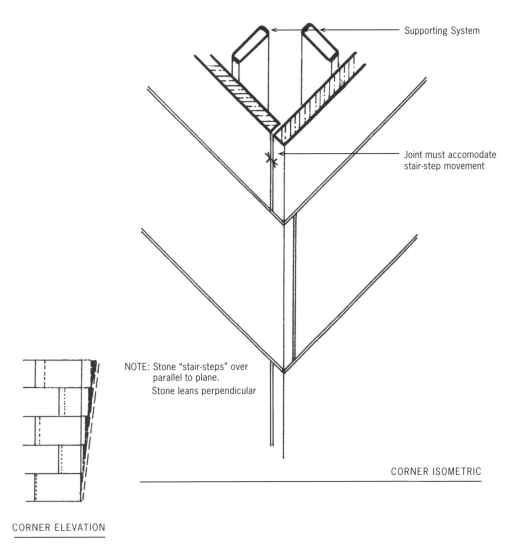

Supporting System

Joint must accomodate
stair-step movement

NOTE: Stone "stair-steps" over
parallel to plane.
Stone leans perpendicular

CORNER ISOMETRIC

CORNER ELEVATION

FIGURE 6.12 Drift parallel on one enclosure plane and perpendicular on another meets at corners. Corner supports and joinery must be designed, located, and sized to accept drift movement.

THERMAL DESIGN

To achieve a high-performance stone enclosure, insulation is required. The climate thermal design criteria and approach determine if the insulation is on the "wet," or exterior, side, or the "dry," or interior, side of the primary weather protection line. In either location, the design goal is insulation that is as continuous as possible, with minimal discontinuities in the insulation. This is easier to achieve in some designs than others. Primary thermal considerations

are the placement and location of the insulation and the influence on thermal gradient through the enclosure, vapor drive and dew point.

Stone enclosure walls are assemblies of many different components. Each has insulation qualities and values. Designing a high-performance stone enclosure for thermal is not that difficult, once the thermal goal is established. In consultation with the mechanical engineer, determine the necessary R-value for the enclosure. Examples of R-value by layer are illustrated in Figures 6.17 and 6.18. The two examples illustrate

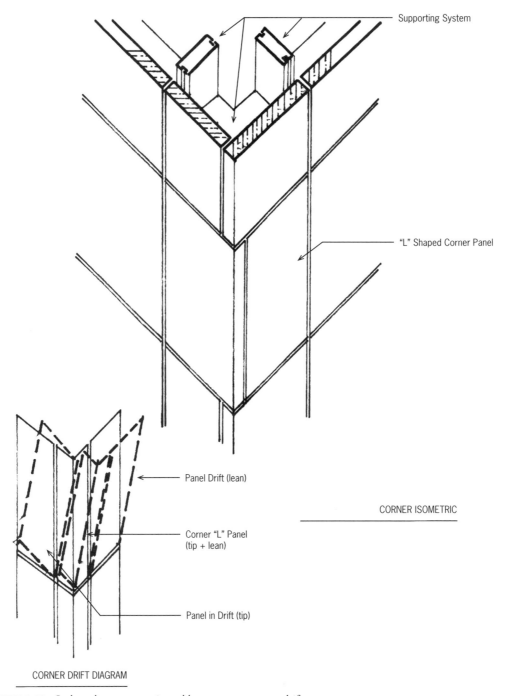

Supporting System

"L" Shaped Corner Panel

CORNER ISOMETRIC

Panel Drift (lean)

Corner "L" Panel
(tip + lean)

Panel in Drift (tip)

CORNER DRIFT DIAGRAM

FIGURE 6.13   L-shaped corners can tip and lean to accept corner drift movement.

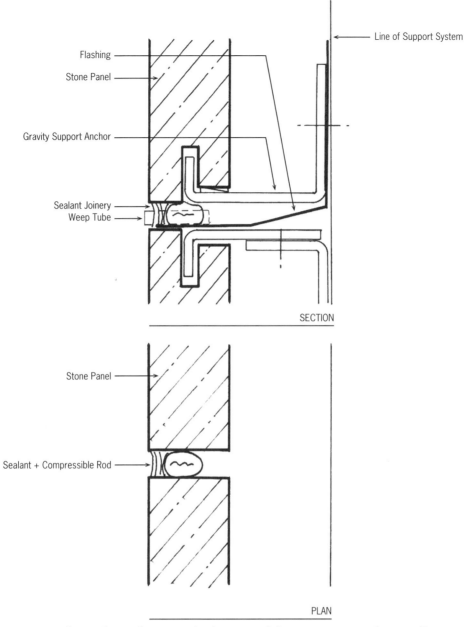

Flashing

Stone Panel

Gravity Support Anchor

Sealant Joinery
Weep Tube

Line of Support System

SECTION

Stone Panel

Sealant + Compressible Rod

PLAN

FIGURE 6.14 Barrier design relies on the stone and sealant material alone to prevent air and water infiltration. Provisions to collect water that may penetrate the single line of defense should occur at regular intervals.

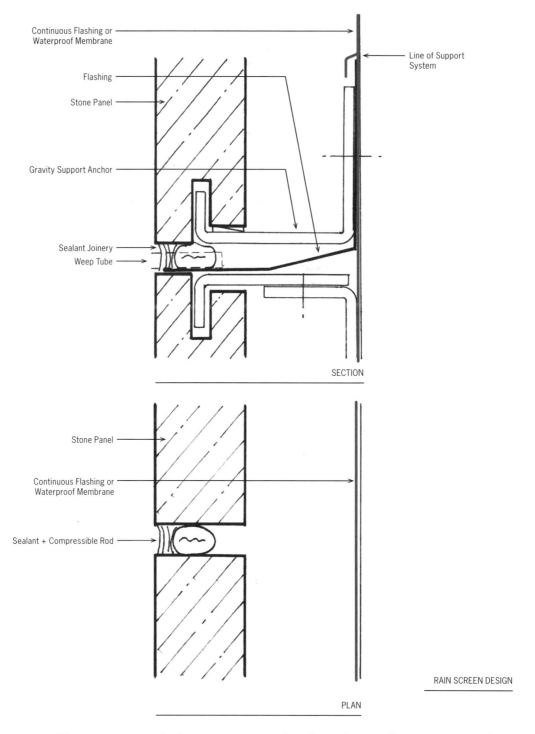

Continuous Flashing or
Waterproof Membrane

Line of Support
System

Flashing

Stone Panel

Gravity Support Anchor

Sealant Joinery

Weep Tube

SECTION

Stone Panel

Continuous Flashing or
Waterproof Membrane

Sealant + Compressible Rod

RAIN SCREEN DESIGN

PLAN

FIGURE 6.15 The rain screen principle relies on a primary inner line of air and water infiltration protection. The stone and sealant are the rain screen.

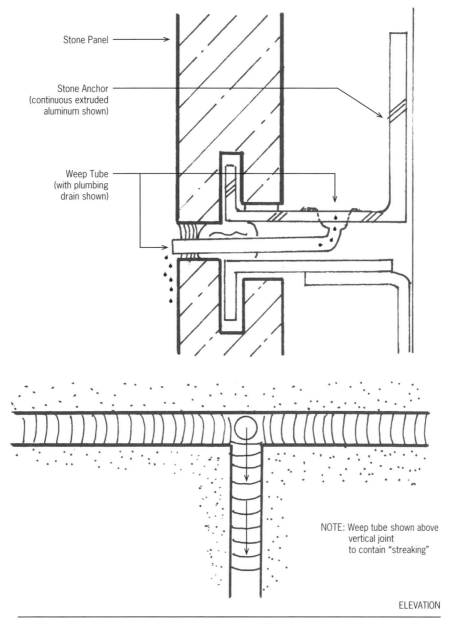

Stone Panel

Stone Anchor
(continuous extruded
aluminum shown)

Weep Tube
(with plumbing
drain shown)

NOTE: Weep tube shown above
vertical joint
to contain "streaking"

ELEVATION

FIGURE 6.16   There are several methods in design to remove water from the cavity zone. A weep tube connected to a drain attached to a continuous stone anchor is one method.

options for insulation placement and type. Insulation in the cavity has more opportunities for insulation continuity. Insulation material selection for a wet cavity should consider both material properties and acceptance of the insulation material by local jurisdictions. Insulation in the "dry" area of the assembly must account for the discontinuity of the insulation at the supporting inner wall supports. It is advisable to check the assembly for vapor drive and dew point location. This will require setting summer and winter design temperatures based on the local climate and defining the interior temperature and humidity basis of design.

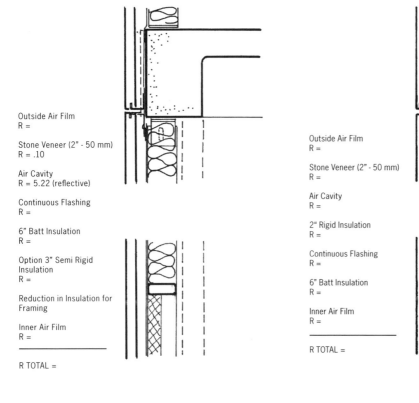

Outside Air Film
R =

Stone Veneer (2" - 50 mm)
R = .10

Air Cavity
R = 5.22 (reflective)

Continuous Flashing
R =

6" Batt Insulation
R =

Option 3" Semi Rigid
Insulation
R =

Reduction in Insulation for
Framing

Inner Air Film
R =

_____

R TOTAL =

Outside Air Film
R =

Stone Veneer (2" - 50 mm)
R =

Air Cavity
R =

2" Rigid Insulation
R =

Continuous Flashing
R =

6" Batt Insulation
R =

Inner Air Film
R =

_____

R TOTAL =

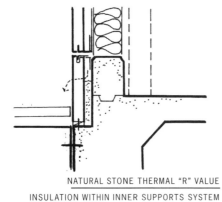

NATURAL STONE THERMAL "R" VALUE

INSULATION WITHIN INNER SUPPORTS SYSTEM

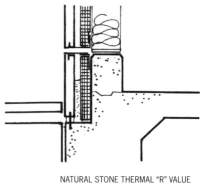

NATURAL STONE THERMAL "R" VALUE

INSULATION IN CAVITY

FIGURE 6.17 A total R-value is achieved by adding the "R" of each material in the assembly. Adjustments (reductions) to the insulation address the thermal discontinuity at supports.

FIGURE 6.18 R-value of a natural stone enclosure with continuous insulation in the cavity.

Miscellaneous

Stone Mock-Ups

There are many types of stone mock-ups. The mock-up quantity and extent should be tailored to the project needs and requirements. Mock-up types include:

- Stone range: color, grain, consistency, etc.
- Visual mock-up assemblies
- Performance mock-ups

Stone Range

Final selection of the acceptable range of color, grain, and other natural characteristics must be done with multiple slabs of stone from multiple blocks. It cannot be accomplished through one or a few small sample pieces. It is more effective to perform this review at the place of fabrication. This is where the work is done. It is the place where fabrication packaging and shipping is preformed. A stone range review with large slabs of stone is illustrated in Figure 6.19a. Subsequent to the review of the range of color, grain, vein, and other characteristics in slabs, smaller stone panels are cut from these to represent the full range for final review. Smaller panels cut from the larger slabs at the same range review are illustrated in Figure 6.19b.

Visual Mock-Ups

After final range selection, a fabricated visual mock-up of the stone enclosure is very helpful for joinery composition, range inclusion, and other design-related items. Visual mock-ups are for evaluation and fine-tuning design and detail issues. They are not intended for major design modifications. It is advisable to conduct these at the stone fabricator's location. A visual mock-up is illustrated in Figure 6.20.

Performance Mock-Ups

Projects with large quantities of stone or with particular performance criteria should include a performance mock-up. The extent of testing usually includes wind loading, seismic (if applicable), air and water infiltration, and other case-specific loading and pass/fail criteria. A performance mock-up is illustrated in Figure 6.21.

FIGURE 6.19a Natural stone has distinct color, grain, and inclusions characteristics. A range review of slabs cut from multiple stone blocks allows selection of acceptable variations to an agreed-upon acceptable range.

FIGURE 6.19b Final stone range review identifies the acceptable color, grain, inclusions, and other natural characteristics.

FIGURE 6.20 A visual mock-up example of the same stone species with multiple finishes.

FIGURE 6.21 Natural stone in an exterior enclosure performance mock-up.

Maintenance and Repair

Stone is inherently a durable material. The surface finish greatly influences its ability to resist dirt, stains, and the like. Smoother surfaces usually require less maintenance than textured. The density of the stone directly affects its ability to resist abuse, stains, and scratches.

Installed stone enclosures should be reviewed on a regular basis to check for structural, weatherproofing, and other wear-and-tear issues.

Summary

Stone veneer design considerations have been described in this chapter with a focus on non-load-bearing natural stone cladding wall exterior enclosure. Most building designs that utilize this type of design and construction also include window, door, louver, and other openings within the stone. These interface areas require a high level of attention and care in design and detail. Weatherproofing concepts of primary and secondary lines of defense for air and water infiltration must transfer from the stone veneer enclosure wall to the design and detail of the assemblies in the openings. Thermal and vapor lines must also follow a clear design and detail transition. Examples for each of these design and detail considerations are illustrated in the following case studies.

Masonry – Natural Stone

The Gas Company Tower

Location:
Los Angeles, CA, USA
Building Type:
High-Rise Office Building with Retail and Multilevel Lobby

The Gas Company tower crown. *Skidmore, Owings & Merrill LLP*

Owner:
Maguire Thomas Partners – Los Angeles, CA
Architect:
Skidmore, Owings & Merrill LLP – Los Angeles, CA
Structural Engineer:
CBM Engineers – Houston, TX
Mechanical Engineer:
James A. Knowles & Associates – Los Angeles, CA

Contractor:
Turner Construction – Los Angeles, CA
Exterior Stone Fabricator:
Campolonghi SPA – Montignoso, Italy
Stonemason, Lower Register:
DBM Hatch – El Monte, CA
Curtain Wall Contractor, Tower:
Enclos Corporation (formerly Harmon Contract Glazing Inc.) – Walnut, CA, and Minneapolis, MN

PROJECT TIME FRAME
Schematic Design:
March 1988–early May 1988
Design Development:
Mid-May 1988–July 1988
Construction Documents:
July 1988– March 1989
Construction:
1989–June 1992

Project Description

The Gas Company Tower personifies the Southern California Gas Company's image in a 754'-0" (228 m) tall, 52-story tower with 1,200,000 sq. ft. (111,484 sq. m) of office and retail space. Rising from the blue and gray granite shaft is an elliptical blue glass volume, whose shape symbolizes a gas flame. The design reduces the mass toward the top, responding to the dramatically sloping site conditions and adjacent downtown high-rise buildings. The tower's central shaft is rectangular in form like the neighboring Arco Plaza and City National Bank Tower complex, enclosed in a blue/gray granite clad custom unitized aluminum curtain wall. The side volumes of the granite shaft are wrapped in a polished gray granite clad custom unitized aluminum curtain wall enclosure, in response to a neighboring metal-clad high-rise building. A site plan and tower isometric is shown in Figure 6C1.1.

The base of the tower is referred to as the lower register. Its massing responds to the Central Library and Pershing Square, two important urban places in downtown Los Angeles. The Pershing Square building entrance is proportioned to relate to the openness of the adjacent park and to the historic Biltmore Hotel directly across Fifth Street. The four-story

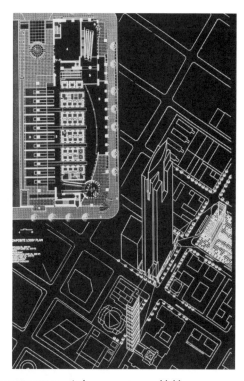

FIGURE 6C1.1 A three-story terraced lobby accommodates the 50-foot elevation site slope. The isometric identifies the Central Library and Pershing Square lobby entrances. *Skidmore, Owings & Merrill LLP*

stone base facing Pershing Square is cut to correspond to the height of the limestone façade of the neighboring hotel. The tower lower register at Pershing Square is illustrated in Figure 6C1.2.

An important design consideration was a 50-foot-high site elevation difference from the northwest Bunker Hill to the southeast corner at Pershing Square. A three-story lobby incorporates the building's two primary entrances, retail spaces, and restaurants linking together the three sides of the site at different grade levels. A six-story floor-to-floor glazed element rises from a cantilevered granite corner marking the entrance facing the Central Library. The Central Library corner entrance is illustrated in Figure 6C1.3.

The project delivery method utilized a fast-track process. Schematic design was completed in a very compressed time frame with particular focus on the tower office floor plan efficiencies and tenant layout test planning. The tower form and imagery were developed to promote the tenant's identity through the building form and color. At the completion of the schematic design phase, a series of staged drawing "packages" were developed to a design development level, for review with the owner and contractor. The contractor was an integral member of the project team, beginning at project inception. Design development drawing packages consisted of plans, sections, and elevations with a series of typical details and sketches to establish the design and detail systems for the granite-clad unitized curtain wall for the tower levels 2–50 and the hand-set stone-clad lower register. Construction documents (drawings, specifications, and bid instructions) were developed by the owner, architect, and contractor team for the tower curtain wall from level 2 through the top parapet. Construction documents were issued when the lower register base was in the early design development phase. Approximately 10 months after the tower granite curtain wall documents were issued, the lower register construction drawings, specifications, and bid instructions were issued.

Enclosure System Types

TOWER

The tower enclosure from level 2 to the tower crown is a custom-designed, unitized, granite-clad curtain wall utilizing the pressure-equalized rain screen design principle. The central shaft is clad in 1-$\frac{3}{16}$" (3 cm) thick polished blue Lanhelin granite with flame-finished accents and "punched" windows with silver metallic reflective 1" (25 mm) insulating glass. The north and south side volumes of the curtain wall enclosures are clad in

FIGURE 6C1.2 The stone lower register includes hand-set Blue Lanhelin granite at the building cantilever over the Pershing Square entrance. Verde Nuevo green and Absolute Black granite define the lower register exterior enclosure along Fifth Street.

FIGURE 6C1.3 Polished Blue Lanhelin granite with flamed granite accent defines the central tower shaft. Polished Barre Gray with custom gray aluminum panels defines the side volume curtain wall. Cantilevered Lanhelin granite forms the fascia and soffit for the Central Library entrance at Fifth Street and Grand Avenue.

FIGURE 6C1.4 Three curtain wall expressions; two with granite and one in all glass utilize the same curtain wall system.

1³⁄₁₆″ (3 cm) thick polished Barre Gray granite and fluoropolymer resinous coated aluminum plate horizontal bands and silver metallic reflective insulating glass. The elliptical shaped glass curtain wall is a 1″ (25 mm) insulating blue, titanium coating, reflective glass beginning at level 35 on the south and 42 on the north rising to the top of the tower. The three curtain wall expressions, while visually quite different, utilize a consistent custom-designed aluminum framing system. Multiple aluminum extrusion adapters connect to the curtain wall framing to accommodate the exterior cladding / infill materials and details. The tower curtain wall composition with the blue and gray granite enclosure expressions are illustrated in Figure 6C1.4. Granite-clad curtain wall partial elevation and details for the blue and gray granite enclosure are shown in Figures 6C1.5a–d. Aluminum curtain wall frames are gravity-supported on preset embeds at the floor slab. Lateral loads are transferred from the stone to the aluminum frame via extruded aluminum stone anchors. Lateral wind and seismic loads are transferred through shear transfer bar inserts at the vertical mullions between unit frames at the curtainwall stack joint located at each floor.

Los Angeles is an area of high seismicity. The granite-clad unitized frames are designed to remain rectangular in a seismic event and tip parallel to the plane of the enclosure and tilt inward or outward perpendicular to the plane of the enclosure. The corner curtain wall units have an "L" shape and either tilt or tip, similar to an open book tipping or tilting about its binding. A unit and movement diagram is shown in Figure 6C1.6. The aluminum frames are floor-to-floor height by typically 5′-0″ (1.52 m) or 7′-9″ (2.36 m) wide. The floor-to-floor heights are 13′-9″ (4.19 m) at floors 2–29 and 13′-2″ (4 m) at floors 30–52. Floors 2–29 include an additional 7″ (180 mm) additional raised floor for the primary tenant electrical requirements.

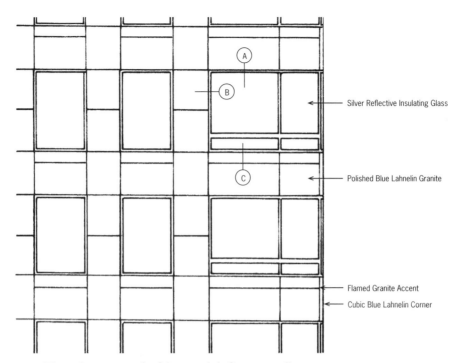

FIGURE 6C1.5a The enclosure materials of the central shaft curtain wall.

Silver Reflective Insulating Glass

Polished Blue Lahnelin Granite

Flamed Granite Accent
Cubic Blue Lahnelin Corner

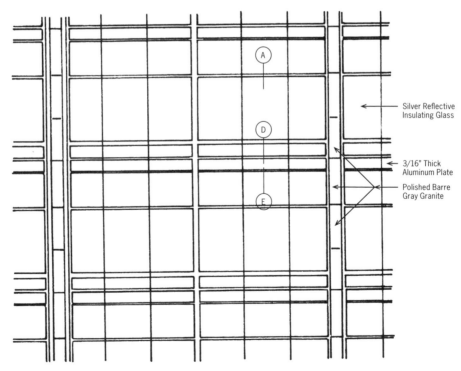

FIGURE 6C1.5b The enclosure materials of the side volume curtain wall.

Silver Reflective
Insulating Glass

3/16" Thick
Aluminum Plate

Polished Barre
Gray Granite

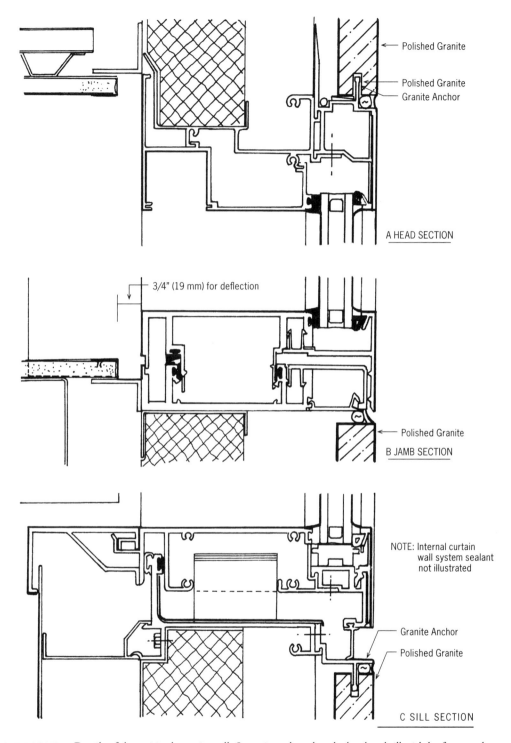

Polished Granite

Polished Granite
Granite Anchor

A HEAD SECTION

3/4" (19 mm) for deflection

Polished Granite

B JAMB SECTION

NOTE: Internal curtain
wall system sealant
not illustrated

Granite Anchor

Polished Granite

C SILL SECTION

FIGURE 6C1.5c Details of the unitized curtain wall. Stone is anchored at the head and sill with kerf cuts and extruded aluminum anchors integral with the curtain wall system.

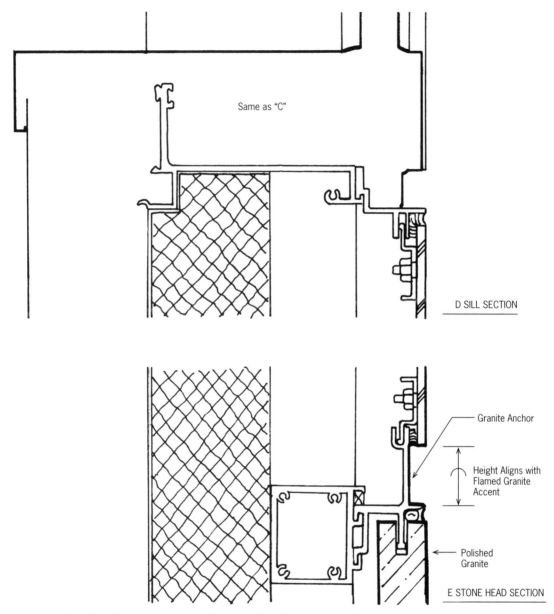

Same as "C"

D SILL SECTION

Granite Anchor

Height Aligns with
Flamed Granite
Accent

Polished
Granite

E STONE HEAD SECTION

FIGURE 6C1.5d The side volume curtain wall details utilize the same extruded aluminum stone anchors.

LOWER REGISTER

The lower register base incorporates three species of granite, each with a distinct design approach. Tower columns extend to grade at the north elevation and the two corner entrances with hand-set blue or gray granite corresponding to the tower granite enclosure above. Polished Absolute Black granite is the base course. Cubic 6″ (152 mm) granite sections Absolute Black stone corners reinforce the solidity at the stone base course. A corner detail is illustrated in Figure 6C1.7. Two-inch (50 mm) thick Verde Nuevo green granite with horizontally

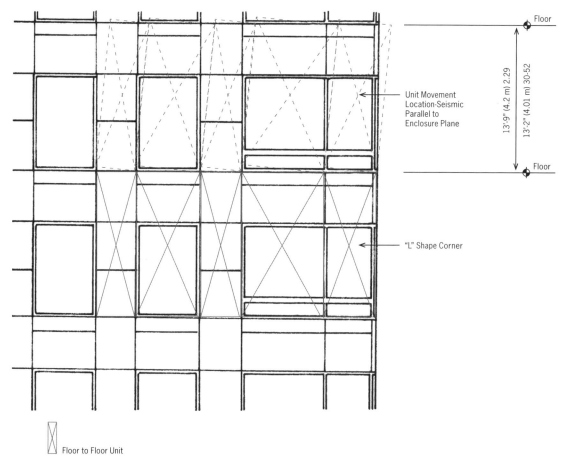

Floor to Floor Unit

FIGURE 6C1.6 Unitized floor-to-floor curtain wall units with natural stone cladding are designed to remain rectangular and tip parallel to the enclosure plane.

beveled notches emphasizes the slope of the site on the south Fifth Street elevation. The lower register granite composition at Fifth Street is illustrated in Figure 6C1.8. A detail image of the Fifth Street stone detail is illustrated in Figure 6C1.9.

Enclosure System Goals

The granite and glass clad tower curtain wall enclosure's visual design goals are: (1) to symbolize the company's iconic blue gas flame in the building color and form, without the need for exterior signage, and (2) to recognize the neighboring urban towers in color, massing, and form. The tower massing steps down from north to south, reflecting the steep Grand Avenue and Fifth Street hillside site location. The central elliptical curtain wall enclosure shape, when viewed from the pedestrian level and distant skyline views, is the abstract form of the primary occupant tenant's gas flame logo. The polished gray granite curtain wall enclosure achieved the owner's goal of achieving the visual solidity of stone and acknowledging the metallic quality of neighboring towers.

The lower register goal is to accommodate the steep site slope and introduce large glass openings at building entry and retail locations. Stone surfaces are polished to minimize maintenance and to capture and reflect daylight in the dense urban building and street environment.

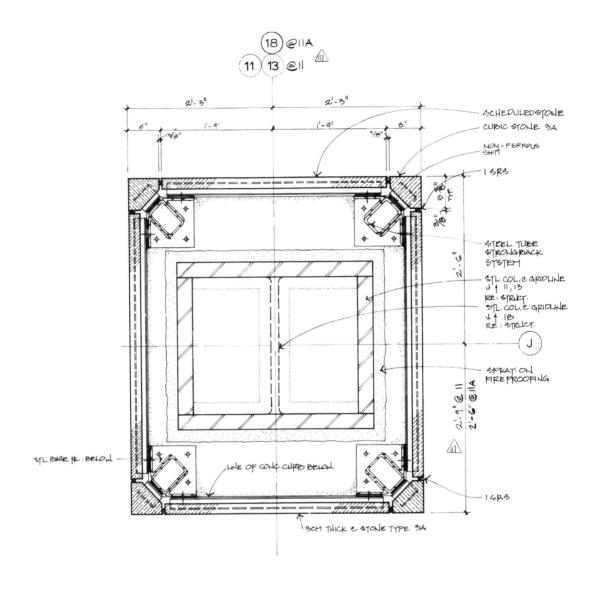

11 COLUMN PLAN at FIFTH STREET RETAIL BAY
SCALE : 1 1/2 "= 1'- 0"
11A

FIGURE 6C1.7 Lower register stone corners are 6″ cubic shapes. *Skidmore, Owings & Merrill LLP*

FIGURE 6C1.8 Fifth Street lower register enclosures with three stone species. *Skidmore, Owings & Merrill LLP*

FIGURE 6C1.9 Two-inch-thick (50 mm) polished Verde Nuevo natural stone is beveled to emphasize a horizontal datum. Polished Absolute Black granite wainscot visually anchors the tower to the sloping ground plane.

The tower curtain wall and lower register enclosure were required to exceed the high performance standards established by California's Title 24 Energy Code. The design strategy established in schematic design set the extent of glazing to 50 percent vision glass. The opaque granite-clad column and spandrel zones are designed to achieve the required R-value (11 or higher) established to conform with project energy requirements.

Enclosure System Design Process

SCHEMATIC DESIGN

Floor plan sizes and shapes from floor 2 to floor 29 respond to the floor area requirements for the primary tenant. The tower form and massing respond to the corporate image of the major tenant's "blue flame" logo. An isometric of the tower is illustrated in Figure 6C1.10a. Upper floors from floor 30 to floor 50 reduce in size to further emphasize the tower's three massing elements and offer various-size floor plates for other tenants. Floor plans of the low- and mid-rise floors (2–29) for the primary tenant and the high-rise floors (30–52) for other tenants are shown in Figure 6C1.10b.

The lower register design responds to the steeply sloping site with entrances at the two corners. The primary lobby is located one floor above the southwest entrance and two floors above the southeast entrance, creating a dynamic three-story lobby/public space. The design of the three granite façade enclosures at the lower register is distinct to their role. The west elevation lower register, illustrated in Figure 6C1.11, is a continuation of the central tower shaft to the steep grade at Grand Avenue. The south elevation lower register, illustrated in Figure 6C1.12, is horizontally organized to emphasize the site slope along Fifth Street and continue the horizontal orientation of the tower enclosure above, as well as to address the multiple lobby entrances and program functions. The east elevation, illustrated in Figure 6C1.13, is composed of green and blue granite to address neighboring Pershing Square and continue the Fifth Street granite design composition.

Design Development

System pricing packages were developed for the tower curtain wall and lower register enclosure systems. Three-dimensional isometric drawings and typical system details were reviewed with the owner and contractor for budget pricing and construction review prior to construction document preparation. Three stone types for the blue and gray granite were identified for budget pricing. A half-full-size mock-up was constructed with each of the three granite options for owner and architect review and material selection.

The lower register systems pricing document package included plans, sections, elevations, and isometrics of the multiple project and site conditions. Details at $3'' = 1'0''$ (1:5) of the typical head, jamb, and sill for each condition with an outline specification were prepared, to identify materials, systems, and project performance requirements.

Construction Documents

Following budget pricing by the contractor and approval of the design development packages by the owner, separate bid sets of full construction documents were developed for the tower and lower register within the fast-track schedule.

The tower stone curtain wall system was designed to express the granite color and finish. Particular attention and study were given to the corners. A cubic stone section with a re-entrant aluminum corner was eventually developed to allow the stone material to turn the corner without the need for either a corner joint or a joint very close to the corner. Seismic movement is incorporated at the typical unit-to-unit corner joinery. The corner detail is illustrated in Figure 6C1.14. The final cubic corner granite shape is illustrated in Figure 6C1.15. The completed stone curtain wall cubic corner is illustrated in Figure 6C1.16.

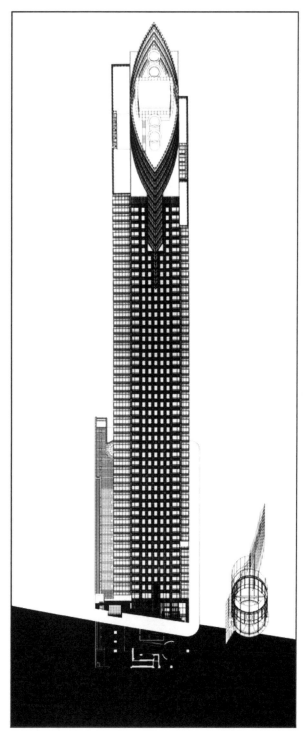

FIGURE 6C1.10a Tower isometric defines the tower massing and iconic "gas flame" building crown. *Skidmore, Owings & Merrill LLP*

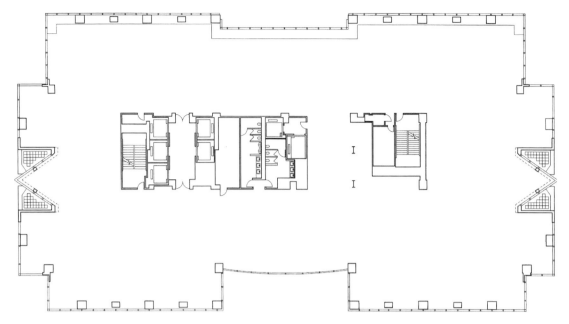

Plan, high-rise floor.

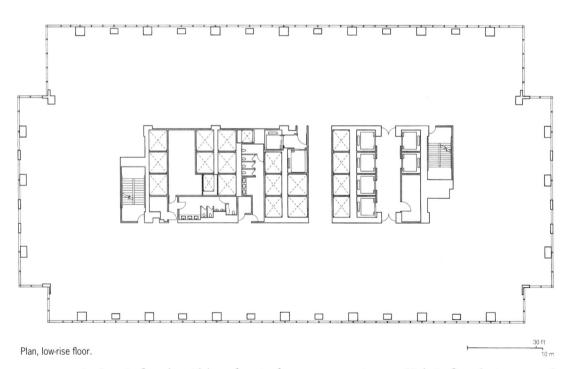

Plan, low-rise floor.

30 ft
10 m

FIGURE 6C1.10b Low-rise floor plan with larger footprint for tenant area requirements. High-rise floor plan is punctuated with recesses for reduced floor area and building enclosure massing definition. *Skidmore, Owings & Merrill LLP*

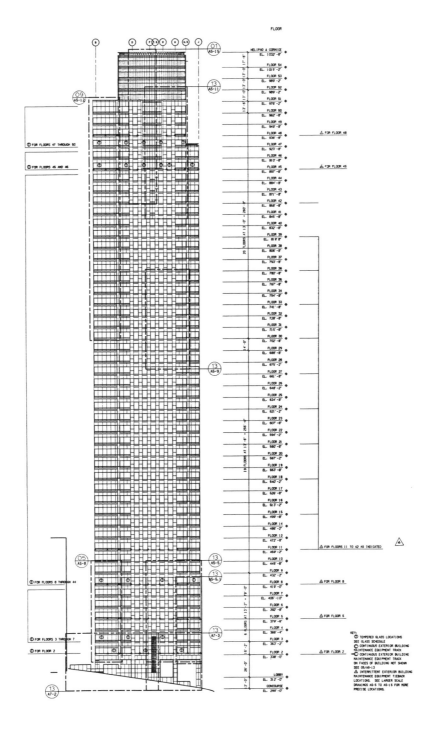

01 WEST ELEVATION

FIGURE 6C1.11 West elevation construction document identifies natural stone exterior enclosures. *Skidmore, Owings & Merrill LLP*

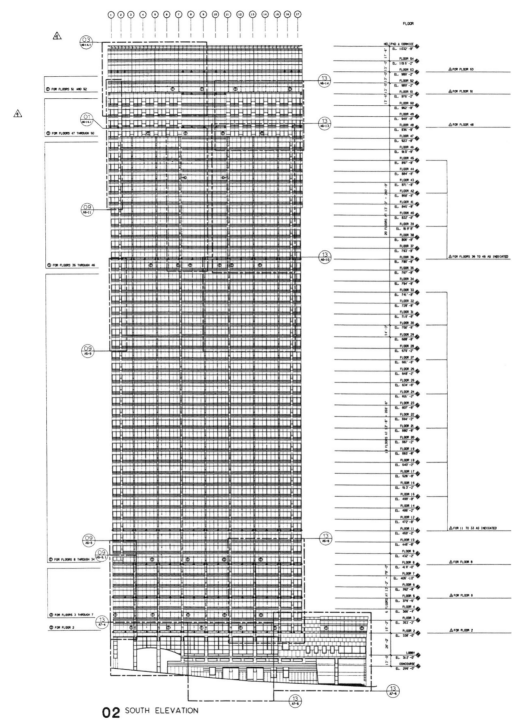

02 SOUTH ELEVATION

FIGURE 6C1.12 South elevation construction document identifies natural stone exterior enclosures for tower and lower register. *Skidmore, Owings & Merrill LLP*

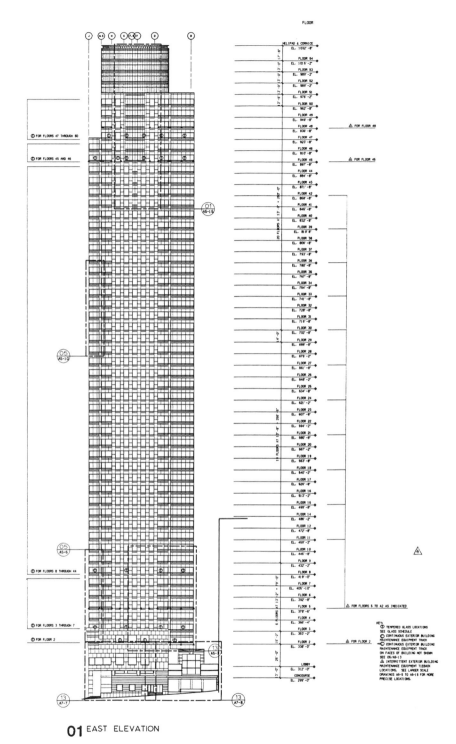

01 EAST ELEVATION

FIGURE 6C1.13 East elevation construction document identifies natural stone exterior enclosures for tower and lower register. *Skidmore, Owings & Merrill LLP*

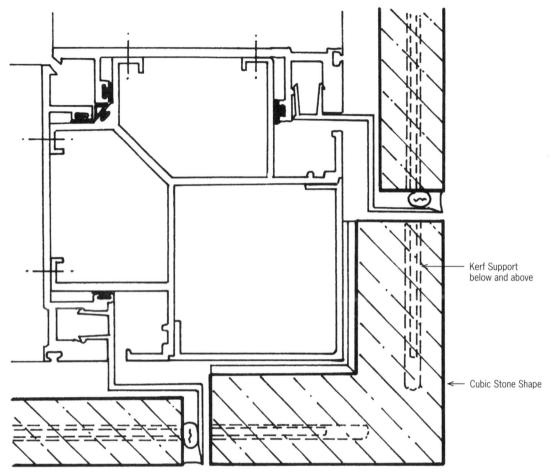

FIGURE 6C1.14   Cubic stone corner in unitized curtain wall. The cubic shape is anchored at the sill and head with kerf cuts and extruded aluminum anchors.

Kerf Support
below and above

Cubic Stone Shape

FIGURE 6C1.15   Cubic stone corner sample.

FIGURE 6C1.16 Detail image of cubic stone corner and re-entrant aluminum corner frame.

Site conditions at the lower register slope 15 degrees along the west Grand Avenue elevation and 8–10 degrees on the south Fifth Street elevation. The west elevation is illustrated in Figure 6C1.17. The south lower register construction document elevation and completed installation are illustrated in Figures 6C1.18a and 6C1.18b. Hand-set granite was detailed, with each stone panel individually supported on extruded aluminum anchors. The black granite base course is hand-set to a continuous concrete curb for durability at the street level. Supporting structures for the green granite are steel tube "goal posts" spanning between the primary building structure with infill of exterior sheathed cold-formed metal framing. The steel tube framing sizes and connections were engineered by the structural engineer, with locations established and coordinated by the architectural team. Lower register stone sections and details are illustrated in Figures 6C1.19a and 6C1.19b. The lower register weather protection is a rain screen design principle. The exterior face of the supporting substructure is the primary air and water protection line. The stone and sealant joinery between stone panels is the rain screen secondary water protection line. The cavity between stone and supporting substructure is weeped at the stone course sill of each floor line stone course.

FIGURE 6C1.17   Lower register natural stone enclosure meets 14 percent slope along Grand Avenue.

Construction

The tower granite curtain wall has two distinct granite clad expressions, while using the same system. Full-size performance tests for the tower granite and glass curtain wall units were conducted at an independent testing facility. Tower granite-clad curtain wall units of 13'-9" (4.2 m) tall by either 5'-0" (1.52 m) wide or 7'-9" (2.36 m) wide were tested to validate performance criteria. The performance mock-up is illustrated in Figure 6C1.20. The curtain wall system passed all tests successfully. Stone-clad factory-assembled curtain wall units were installed on the tower at the rate of one full floor every three days. In-progress tower construction is illustrated in Figure 6C1.21.

The exterior lower register stone of individual hand-set granite on a steel subframe with an infill of exterior sheathing and cold-formed framing allowed stone setting sequence and installation of the multiple custom glass enclosures and flashing interfaces. A detail of the lower register stone supports with adjacent openings is illustrated in Figure 6C1.22.

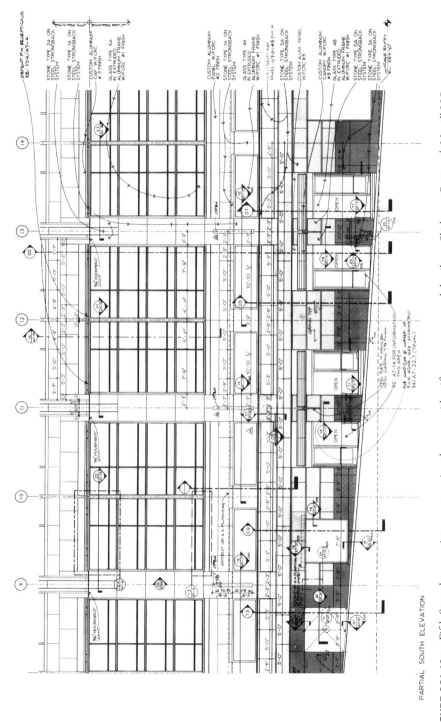

FIGURE 6C1.18a Fifth Street lower register construction document identifies stone types and details. *Skidmore, Owings & Merrill LLP*

PARTIAL SOUTH ELEVATION

259

FIGURE 6C1.18b Fifth Street lower register from Grand Avenue to Pershing Square.

Summary

The completed tower enclosure promotes the tenant's identity through form and color. The stone-clad lower register responds to the dramatic sloped site condition on each of the three street frontages. The multiple exterior materials and appearance are achieved through an economical use of consistent supporting systems. Weather protection and seismic design criteria were incorporated in each of the enclosure systems and their interface areas. The combined owner, architect, engineering, contractor, and subcontractors collectively collaborated and coordinated throughout the design, documentation, and construction phases. The completed Gas Company Tower is illustrated in Figure 6C1.23.

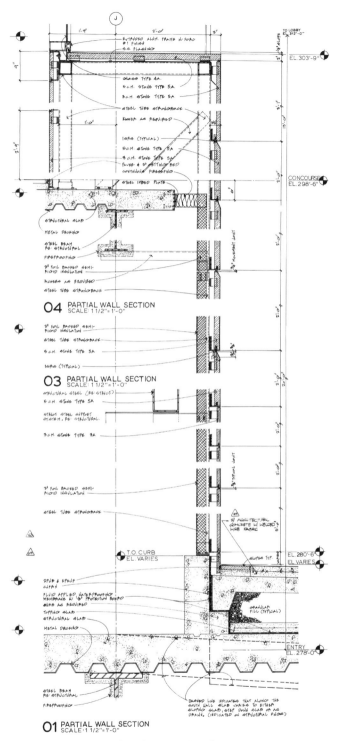

FIGURE 6C1.19a Construction document partial wall section identifies stone, stone anchorage, and stone inner wall supports. *Skidmore, Owings & Merrill LLP*

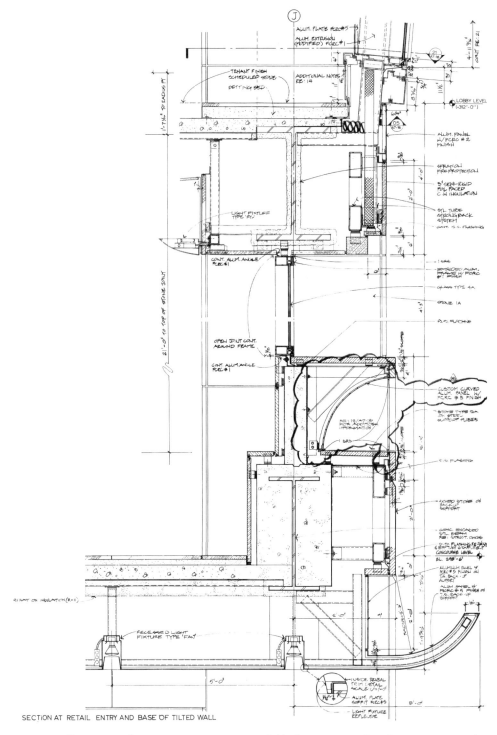

SECTION AT RETAIL ENTRY AND BASE OF TILTED WALL

FIGURE 6C1.19b Construction document section at concourse lobby lower register identifies stone, stone anchorage, and stone supports. *Skidmore, Owings & Merrill LLP*

FIGURE 6C1.20   Natural stone enclosure performance mock-up.

FIGURE 6C1.21   Unitized stone curtain wall under construction.

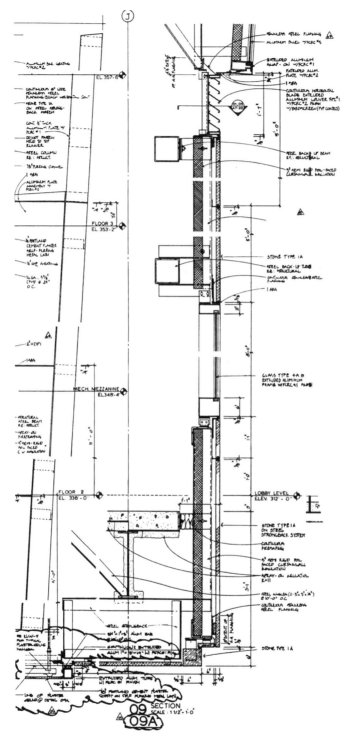

FIGURE 6C1.22 Construction document wall section at Pershing Square lower register with window, louver openings, and stone supports. *Skidmore, Owings & Merrill LLP*

264

FIGURE 6C1.23   The completed tower on the downtown Los Angeles skyline.   *Nick Merrick ©Hedrich Blessing*

Masonry – Natural Stone

ARCO Tower One

Location:
Dallas, TX, USA
Building Type:
Corporate Headquarters Office Building with Retail and Parking

ARCO Tower.

PARTICIPANTS
Owner:
ARCO Oil and Gas Company – Dallas, TX
Architect:
I.M. Pei & Partners (now Pei Cobb Freed & Partners Architects LLP) – New York, NY
Structural Engineer:
Weiskopf & Pickworth – New York, NY
Mechanical Engineer:
Cosentini Associates LLP – New York, NY

Contractor:
J W Bateson Construction – Dallas, TX
Exterior Stone Fabricator:
Campolonghi SPA – Montignoso, Italy
Stone Masonry Contractor:
Blaesing Granite Company – Beaverton, OR
Dee Brown Masonry – Dallas, TX
Metal-Framed and Glass Assemblies:
Benson Industries LLC – Portland, OR

PROJECT TIME FRAME
Schematic Design:
August 1978–January 1979
Design Development:
February 1979–August 1979
Construction Documents:
September 1979–May 1980
Construction:
May 1980–August 1983

Project Description

ARCO Tower is a 49-story corporate office building headquarters. Rising from a trapezoid-shaped site created by two intersecting city grids, the tower is a series of three 30–60 degree triangles connected in plan. A site plan and tower plan diagram with floor heights per triangular plan component is shown in Figure 6C2.1.

The first triangle in the tower composition is six stories tall, and forms the tower base and street elevation along Billington Street and Bryan Street. The remaining two triangles form an equilateral triangular plan for the tower. A 30 degree vertical angular notch on the northwest side of the triangular floor plan further dramatizes the building's angular geometry. The triangular notch in the tower is illustrated in Figure 6C2.2. The final 30–60 degree triangle in the tower composition rises to the 49th floor. A tower massing isometric diagram is shown in Figure 6C2.3.

The tower rises to 630 ft. (192 m) with 1,200,000 sq. ft. (111,484 sq. m) of offices. The remaining site area not occupied by the tower is a 30–60 degree triangular plaza. Granite paving is configured in isosceles triangles, following the tower's triangular planning/design grid module.

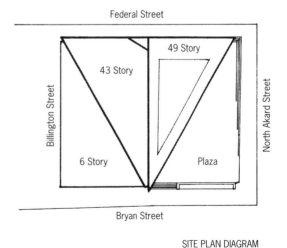

SITE PLAN DIAGRAM

FIGURE 6C2.1 The tower plan is composed of three 30/60/90 degree triangles.

FIGURE 6C2.2 A vertical notch in the stone enclosure composition emphasizes the tower's angular geometry.

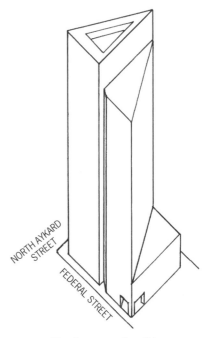

FIGURE 6C2.3 The three triangles of the tower terminate at different heights to define the three-triangle exterior composition.

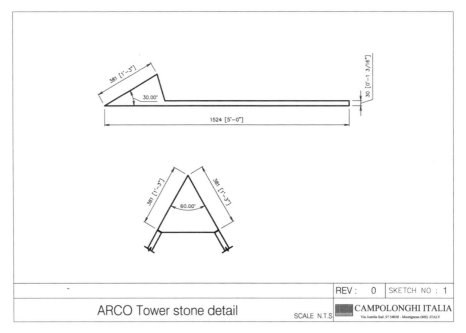

FIGURE 6C2.4 Cubic stone fabrication details of the 60 degree cubic granite corner: Each of the three sides are 1″–3″ (381 mm) The 30 degree cubic corner section is integral with the 5′-0″ (1.52 m) long spandrel. *Campolonghi SPA*

Enclosure System Types

ARCO Tower is clad in polished Regal Barre Gray granite mounted to an insulated steel truss. The stone was quarried in Barre, Vermont, in blocks and shipped to Italy for fabrication. Each stone is individually gravity-supported on kerf anchors at the sill and laterally connected at the head of each stone. Stone panels in the 30′-0″ (9.15 m) wide column bays consist of a lower course of 5′-0″ (1.52 m) × 5′-0″ (1.52 m) × 1-3⁄16″ (30 mm) thick panels and a top course 2′-6″ (762 mm) high × 10′-0″ (3.05 m) × 1-3⁄16″ (30 mm) thick. Stone corners (30/60 and 60/60) of the tower and tower base are cubic stone sections to reinforce the crisp angular geometry by turning the corner with the stone material in lieu of a joint at the corner. Stone fabrication drawings of the cubic corners are presented in Figure 6C2.4.

A vertical extruded aluminum continuous window washing restraint track is located at each column, with a horizontal extruded aluminum accent in the stone spandrel providing a subtle subgrid tracery over the stone exterior envelope. Unitized window frames, each measuring 5′-0″ (1.5 m) high × 5′-0″ (1.5 m) wide are #8 mirror-polished stainless steel with clear reflective monolithic glass. The stainless steel exterior glazing covers are welded at the jamb-to-head and jamb-to-sill intersections and polished after fabrication. The welded exterior frames are permanently attached to the window frames in the assembly shop. Removable interior glazing frames allow glass replacement if required. A #8 mirror-polished stainless steel column cover in the vision area with a diagonal return to a 90 degree flanker return window provides visual "punctuation" at the column locations. A typical bay column-to-spandrel composition is illustrated in Figure 6C2.5. An isometric of the granite-faced truss, stainless steel column cover, window washing track, and ribbon unitized window assembly is illustrated in Figure 6C2.6.

The spandrel zone weather protection principle is a pressure-equalized rain screen principle. Continuous flashing on the outboard face of the steel truss and seals at the vertical window washing track define the pressure-equalization chamber in the spandrel zone. The sealed stone joints are weeped above the window heads to introduce pressure-equalization to the spandrel assembly. A section diagram through the stone on truss is presented in Figure 6C2.7.

Enclosure System Goals

The enclosure materials and composition were envisioned to promote dignity and permanence. Minimalist details belie a high level of attention to exquisite design details at typical intersections—particularly at the corners.

The Dallas climate is very hot in the summer and cold in the winter. The building owner, an energy company, stated the exterior enclosure is the building's public statement of energy efficiency. At the time of design, the design community was acutely aware of the need to maximize the enclosure's energy reduction, in the wake of the mid-1970s oil embargo. The ratio of vision glass to insulated opaque stone and stainless steel is under 40 percent, resulting in a high-performance enclosure many years ahead of its time.

FIGURE 6C2.5 Typical enclosure bay composition at column.

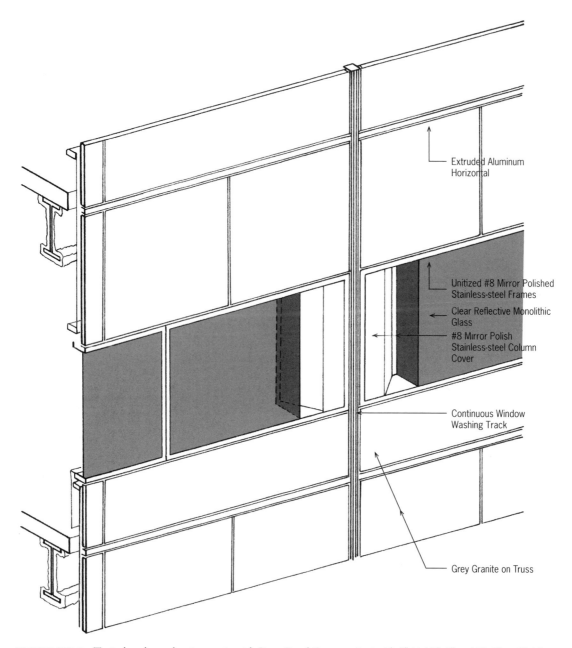

FIGURE 6C2.6 Typical enclosure bay isometric with Barre Regal Gray granite in 2'-6" × 10'-0" and 5'-0" × 5'-0" panels with mirror-polished stainless steel detail at window openings.

The labels in the figure read:

Extruded Aluminum Horizontal

Unitized #8 Mirror Polished Stainless-steel Frames

Clear Reflective Monolithic Glass

#8 Mirror Polish Stainless-steel Column Cover

Continuous Window Washing Track

Grey Granite on Truss

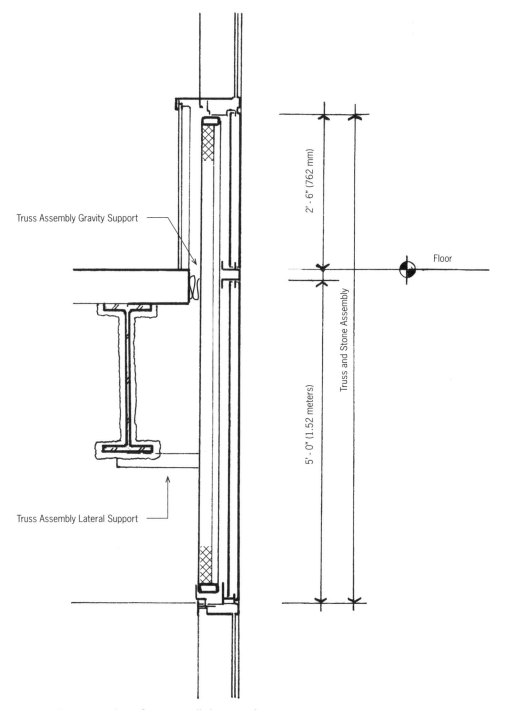

Truss Assembly Gravity Support

Truss Assembly Lateral Support

2' - 6" (762 mm)

5' - 0" (1.52 meters)

Truss and Stone Assembly

Floor

FIGURE 6C2.7 Granite panels are factory-installed on a steel truss.

Enclosure System Design Process

SCHEMATIC DESIGN

The organizing triangular tower plan geometry of the 60 degree equilateral triangle with subdivisions into 30–60 degree triangles was developed for the building and site. Floor-to-floor height studies were conducted to ascertain the extent of glazing and the relationship of sill and head heights to the interior tenant's use.

DESIGN DEVELOPMENT

Initial detail studies of the typical bay (column-to-column and floor-to-floor), with large-scale details, were developed to study intersections and design continuity of line.

The typical column cover evolved from a reflective glass enclosure to the final stainless steel configuration following a visual mock-up. The glass visual mock-up revealed the reflective glass column cover to be a play of reflections rather than one that offered shadows deemed necessary to visually articulate the column. Mirror-polished stainless steel was selected so that all exterior surface materials would be reflective. Multiple corner studies of 2" (51 mm) thick expressed stone and cubic corners were developed for cost comparison studies.

Multiple drawing and model studies were prepared to study how the stone material properties could best reinforce the overall tower triangular geometry. Panelized stone spandrel gravity and lateral anchorage connections were established between the Architect and Structural Engineer. Stone slabs with 2" (51 mm) exposed edges cut and polished at angles in conjunction with pinned and epoxied stone corners were reviewed with the owner team for design evaluation. Head and sill sections of the stone truss to window frame assemblies are illustrated in Figure 6C2.8.

Construction Documents

Final stone material selections were determined for the stone species. Regal Barre Gray was selected for its color consistency and strength characteristics. Visual mock-ups were constructed at the stone fabricator's yard in Italy. The panelized stone spandrel mock-up at the stone fabricator's plant is illustrated in Figures 6C2.9 and 6C2.10. Most granites exhibit a grain pattern with various grain directions. Regal Barre Gray, which has a very consistent grain, is no exception. A subtle directional pattern was noted in the panel sections. The stone blocks were slabbed to accentuate the grain in a horizontal orientation at the 10'-0" (3.05 m)-long spandrel panels. The 5'-0" × 5'-0" (1.525 × 1.525 m) lower spandrel stone panels have the grain oriented 45 degrees from horizontal. Following the visual mock-up, the typical tower stone corners were revised and further refined. This stone fabricator suggested solid cubic stone corners over the detail of pinned and epoxied stone corners for ease of fabrication and in-service longevity.

Summary

If an exterior building enclosure can be compared to finely tailored clothing, then ARCO is that enclosure. The attention to the rigorous bay composition and intersections of high-quality materials in the overall composition show masterful design and execution. Many of the exterior photographs shown in the figures were taken in spring 2011. The typical bay image in Figure 9C2.11 and the corner image in Figure 9C2.12 were also photographed in spring 2011. The stone enclosure is a testament that time and effort in the design phases, collaboration with fabricators, careful installation in the construction phase, and an appropriate budget for high-quality materials that can stand the test of time are investments that pay returns.

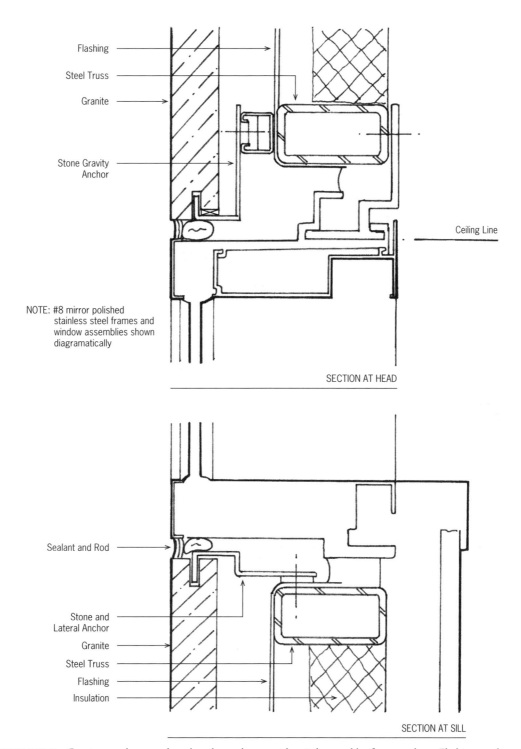

Flashing

Steel Truss

Granite

Stone Gravity
Anchor

Ceiling Line

NOTE: #8 mirror polished
stainless steel frames and
window assemblies shown
diagramatically

SECTION AT HEAD

Sealant and Rod

Stone and
Lateral Anchor

Granite

Steel Truss

Flashing

Insulation

SECTION AT SILL

FIGURE 6C2.8   Granite panels are anchored to the steel truss with stainless steel kerf-type anchors. Flashing on the exterior truss face provides a pressure-equalized cavity.

FIGURE 6C2.9 Visual mock-up at the stone fabricator's plant for stone grain direction selection. *Campolonghi SPA*

FIGURE 6C2.11 Typical bay at tower base 29 years after completion.

FIGURE 6C2.10 Visual mock-up at the stone fabricator's plant for 30 degree stone corner in 30-mm thickness. The mock-up review gave the project participants the opportunity to consider cubic stone for longevity of the enclosure. *Campolonghi SPA*

FIGURE 6C2.12 Completed image of 30 degree cubic granite corner.

Masonry – Natural Stone

The New Beijing Poly Plaza

Location:
Beijing, People's Republic of China
Building Type:
Speculative Office Building on Lower Tower Floors, Corporate Headquarters on Upper Floors, and Cultural Museum

The New Beijing Poly Plaza with hand set and panelized travertine enclosures.   *Photo © Tim Griffith*

Owner:
China Poly Group Corporation – Beijing, China
Design Architect:
Skidmore, Owings & Merrill LLP – San Francisco, CA
Local Design Institute Architect (LDI)
Beijing Special Engineering Design and Research Institute – Beijing, China

Design Structural Engineer:
Skidmore, Owings & Merrill LLP – San Francisco, CA
Local Design Institute Structural Engineer (LDI)
Beijing Special Engineering Design and Research Institute – Beijing, China
Design Mechanical Engineer:
Flack & Kurtz – San Francisco, CA
Contractor:
China State Construction – Beijing, China
Stone Source:
Poggi SPA – Tivoli, Italy
Frateli Pascucci SRL – Tivoli, Italy
Stone Fabricator:
KangLi Stone Company – Shenzen, China
Curtain Wall Contractor:
Shenzen Zhongjin Lingnam Nonfemet Limited

PROJECT TIME FRAME
Competition:
January 2003
Schematic Design:
March 2003–June 2003
Design Development:
July 2003–December 2003
Construction Documents:
January 2004–July 2004
Construction:
August 2004–December 2006

Project Description

The New Beijing Poly Plaza is sited adjacent to the existing Poly complex and highly visible from the heavily traveled Second Ring Road. The plan organization of this iconic building is two rectangular office "bars" in an "L" shape configuration facing an interior 24-story-high atrium. Façades of floor-to-floor custom-unitized window walls and Italian travertine brise soleil form a strong presence in the area and set a tone of architectural excellence for future developments south of the site. A site plan is shown in Figure 6C3.1.

The office space in the tower is primarily speculative lease space. The client's design brief required maximizing leasable floor area. The design responds with lease spans that optimize efficient office layouts, while maintaining maximum access to natural light. Travertine-clad vertical and horizontal sunshades on the southeast and southwest elevations provide passive solar shading solutions for climate control. An office floor plan illustrates the L-shaped office organization and atrium in Figure 6C3.2.

In addition to 624,300 sq. ft. (58,000 sq. m) of Class-A offices, The New Beijing Poly Plaza contains an eight-cinema multiplex, 86,110 sq. ft. (8,000 sq. m) of supporting retail space, and an eight-story cultural museum. The Poly Art Museum was founded to develop and display traditional national culture and retrieve and

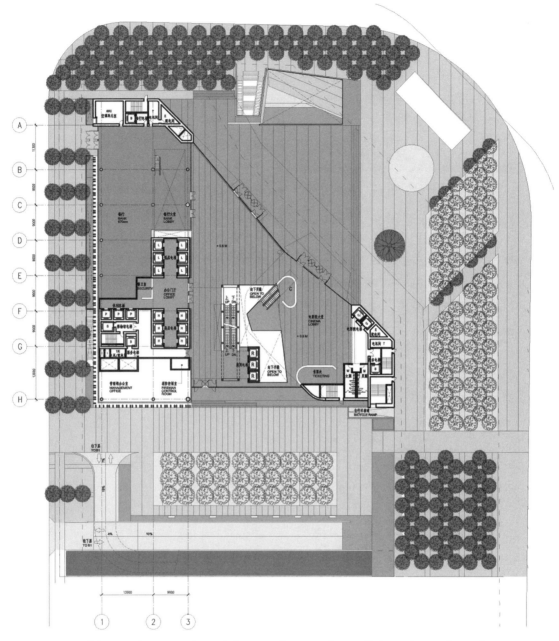

FIGURE 6C3.1 Schematic design site plan with the triangular tower plan. *Skidmore, Owings & Merrill LLP*

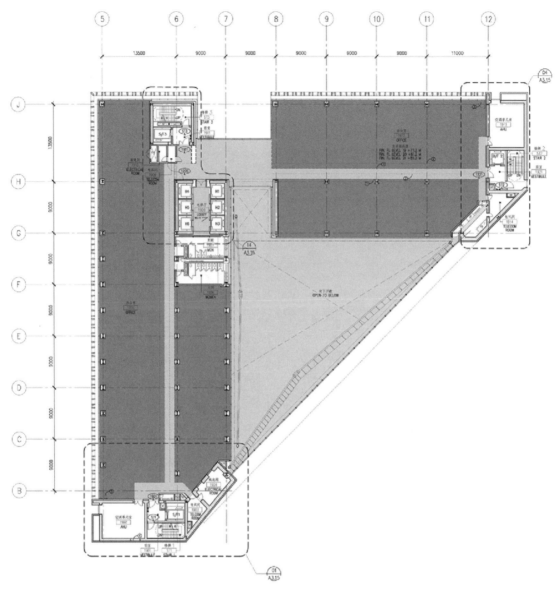

FIGURE 6C3.2 Office spaces are organized in rectangular "bars." The office space exterior enclosure is a unitized window wall with travertine brise soleil on the southeast and southwest enclosures. *Skidmore, Owings & Merrill LLP*

protect Chinese cultural relics from abroad. The majority of the exhibits are bronze antiquities that present the development of China's ancient Bronze Age civilization.

Enclosure System Types

The New Beijing Poly Plaza includes two types of travertine exterior enclosure systems. The planar travertine surfaces adjacent to the signature 22-story-high cable net wall cable net all-glass enclosure (discussed in Chapter 9 case study) and stair enclosures are panelized travertine on a steel truss. The southeast and southwest elevations, forming the brise soleil for the enclosure window walls, are hand-set travertine on hot-dipped galvanized steel subframes. The travertine panels are cross-cut perpendicular to the stone bedding plane, yielding a distinctive mottled color and grain pattern.

Planar travertine surfaces are designed to accentuate the building plan form, and to border the glass expanses and travertine brise soleil areas on two of the three primary elevations. The southeast corner is illustrated in Figure 6C3.3. Filled and honed travertine panels are mounted to galvanized steel trusses in one-floor-high prefabricated panels. Floor-to-floor panelized travertine-clad panels are attached to steel frames anchored to cast-in-place structural concrete walls. Shop-assembled travertine panels under construction are illustrated in Figure 6C3.4. To facilitate construction sequence and structural concrete tolerances, a zinc-chromate-coated steel ledger frame is mounted to the concrete superstructure. Galvanized steel flashing 1.5 mm (¹⁄₁₆″) thick is field-installed spanning between steel ledgers at each floor and at 5′-0″ (1.5 m) spaced steel vertical members. Joints in the flashing are sealed. Insulation is installed continuously behind the flashing directly to the concrete substrate. The flashing constitutes the primary air and water protection line and is weeped at each horizontal joint. Travertine-to-travertine joints within shop-fabricated panels are recessed ¼″ (6 mm) from the exterior face and factory-sealed. Panel-to-panel joints are field-sealed with recessed sealant joinery to match the typical stone-to-stone joinery. A completed elevation of a panelized travertine area is illustrated in Figure 6C3.5.

The travertine brise soleil enclosure consists of hand-set travertine stone panels on steel subframes at each floor. A building elevation indicating the travertine brise soleil composition is illustrated in Figure 6C3.6. The 1′-5¾″) (450 mm) deep brise soleil cantilevers 3′-5⅜″ (1.05 m) from the primary building enclosure line.

FIGURE 6C3.3 The brise soleil and large planar expanses are rift-cut travertine. The travertine composition expresses the building's interior functions. *Photo © Tim Griffith*

FIGURE 6C3.4 Travertine is panelized on steel-framed panels and installed in one-floor heights on preset anchors.

FIGURE 6C3.5 Travertine pattern is accentuated by rift-cut stone and ¼″ (6 mm) wide recessed sealant joinery.

Two-inch (50 mm) thick and tapered cubic travertine shapes are hand-set on stainless steel kerf clips. The steel subframe is galvanized steel with bolted connections at vertical to horizontals. Stone-to-stone joinery is field-sealed with joints recessed ¼″ (6 mm). A plan and section at the brise soleil is shown in Figure 6C3.7. The brise soleil employs a barrier weather protection design principle. The unitized glass and aluminum window wall employing a pressure-equalized rain screen principle, 1.05 meters (3′ – 5-⅜″) inboard of the travertine, is the weather and thermal separation line between the exterior elements and interior occupied spaces.

Enclosure System Goals

The owner expressed the goal that The New Beijing Poly Plaza have its own unique identity while respecting the existing adjacent Poly complex across the street. Travertine was selected for color compatibility with the existing complex. A parallel design goal was expressing the color and grain character of travertine at close and long-distance views. Cross-cut travertine, exhibiting a wider range of color and tone variation, was selected to address this design goal. Additional detail in the travertine was achieved by recessing the sealant joinery material with defining shadow lines to accentuate the stone coursing and pattern.

Performance goals included maximizing natural light to office spaces and minimizing heat gain. The office spaces are organized in rectangular floor plates, with one elevation facing the enclosed interior atrium, and the exterior elevation clad with the travertine-clad brise soleil.

Enclosure System Design Process

SCHEMATIC DESIGN

Office floor plan and office massing were organized in the L-shape plan. A 4′-11″ (1.5 m) plan module was established for the office and window frame spacing. Alternate spacing patterns for the travertine brise soleil

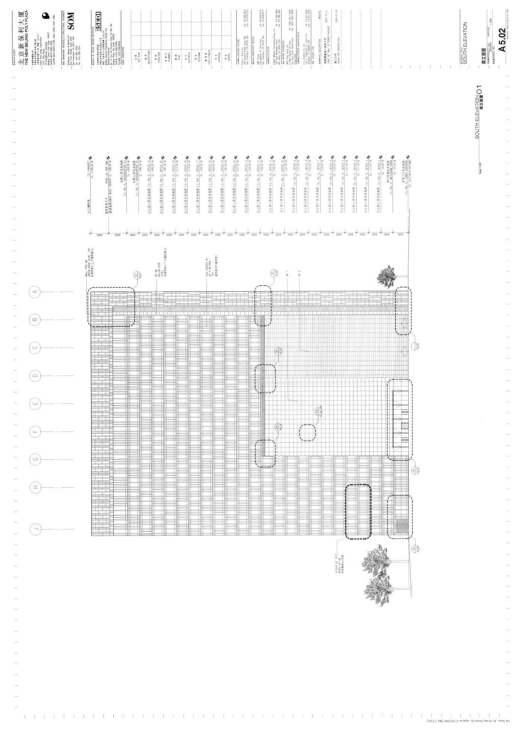

FIGURE 6C3.6 Travertine brise soleil are composed in a staggered pattern providing solar shading.   *Skidmore, Owings & Merrill LLP*

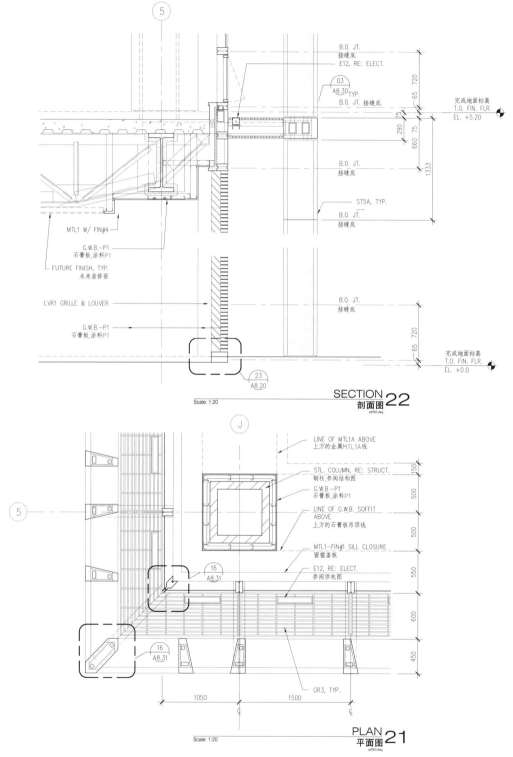

SECTION 剖面图 22
Scale: 1:20

PLAN 平面图 21
Scale: 1:20

FIGURE 6C3.7 Tender document plan and section details of the travertine brise soleil. *Skidmore, Owings & Merrill LLP*

were studied. Stone samples with color ranges from cream to yellow were gathered for review, including local Chinese stones and Italian travertine. Material sources, quarry location, block sizes, yield, and historical strength data was compiled for the stone types under consideration.

Design Development

One of the primary building uses of The New Poly Plaza is the eight-story cultural museum. The museum features Chinese bronze cultural artifacts and antiquities repatriated from other countires and within China. An alternate exterior enclosure design scheme for the brise soleil was studied utilizing bronze cladding. The bronze option is illustrated in Figure 6C3.8. Comparison exterior elevation studies were presented to the owner for

FIGURE 6C3.8 An alternative bronze enclosure option was developed for owner review along with the travertine enclosure option. *Skidmore, Owings & Merrill LLP*

travertine and bronze. The extent of bronze cladding was selected for the museum floors, further reinforcing the bronze dialogue between the building enclosure and the museum's exhibit mission statement. Travertine was the selected stone exterior enclosure material for the office functions.

Typical details of the panelized travertine and the hand-set travertine were developed and reviewed with stone fabricators. The primary goal of the design development details was to establish the stone thickness and suggested stone anchoring methods. Stone setting dimensions were established and enclosure system depths finalized to allow structural and architectural coordination. Thermal criteria and requirements were finalized for opaque stone enclosure extents and final glass selection and spandrel insulation requirements.

Construction Documents

Anchorage details were further studied and finalized for the panelized and hand-set travertine. The brise soleil vertical and horizontal stone panels employ a kerf cut in the head and sill of each stone panel. Each travertine panel is individually supported. Steel support members sizes were designed in collaboration with the project structural engineer. Corner travertine is fabricated in a "home plate" shape to emphasize the continuous stone wrap of the brise soleil enclosure. Details of the hand-set travertine are illustrated in Figure 6C3.9.

The panelized travertine system employs a plug-type anchor inserted into the back face of travertine and anchored with a threaded bolt and angle to the steel panel frame. The plug anchorage system was suggested by the travertine fabricator. This attachment method allows adjustment and final fixing prior to handling and shipment of the panels. Details of the travertine panels are illustrated in Figure 6C3.10.

Historical stone test data for Italian travertine was reviewed to establish safety factors for the stone panel anchorage in the project specifications. Prior to issuance of the stone construction documents/tender set, a full-size visual mock-up was constructed in Italy of the brise soleil and planar wall expanse, for owner review and approval. The travertine mock-up is illustrated in Figure 6C3.11.

Construction

The travertine was procured directly by the owner from two separate quarry suppliers and provided to the local stone fabricator. One source yielded a lighter color range, and the second source yielded a wider color and grain range.

Blocks of travertine from two stone quarries in Italy were shipped to China. The stone blocks were slabbed to the required thickness and were organized in two separate areas at the fabrication plant. A color and finish range review was conducted utilizing multiple slabs of travertine from multiple blocks of each source to establish the final acceptable color and grain range. The travertine color and grain range review is illustrated in Figures 6C3.12 and 6C3.13. To express the natural character of the travertine, the wider color range stone was applied to the panelized wall expanses, and the narrow color and grain range travertine was applied to finer-grain vertical and horizontal brise soleil sunshades. This approach of two stone sources is highly unusual and is not the normal procedure.

An on-site mock-up was constructed to review stone installation methods. The on-site mock-up is illustrated in Figure 6C3.14. Construction progress of the travertine brise soleil is illustrated in Figures 6C3.15 and 6C3.16.

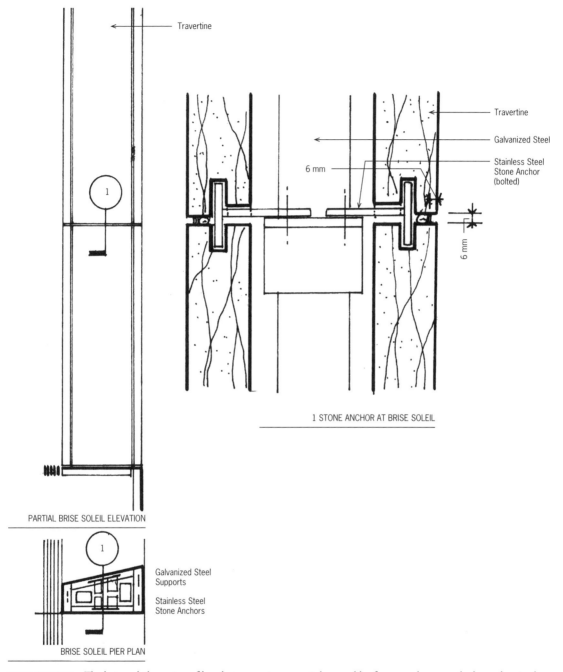

Travertine

Travertine

Galvanized Steel

Stainless Steel
Stone Anchor
(bolted)

6 mm

6 mm

1 STONE ANCHOR AT BRISE SOLEIL

1

PARTIAL BRISE SOLEIL ELEVATION

1

Galvanized Steel
Supports

Stainless Steel
Stone Anchors

BRISE SOLEIL PIER PLAN

FIGURE 6C3.9 The brise soleil consists of handset travertine on stainless steel kerf type anchors attached to galvanized steel supports.

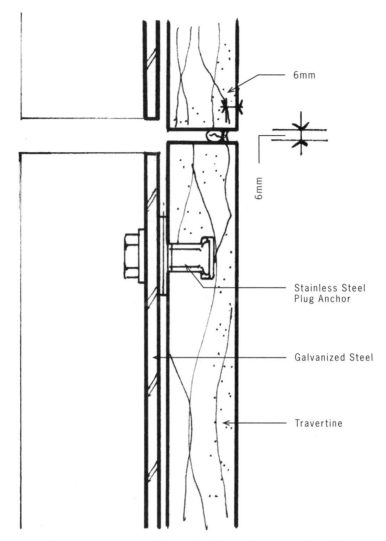

6mm

6mm

Stainless Steel
Plug Anchor

Galvanized Steel

Travertine

FIGURE 6C3.10 Panelized travertine is set on stainless steel anchors and a galvanized steel frame in an off-site assembly plant.

Summary

The New Poly Plaza creates a landmark structure in its form and execution. The color and grain characteristics of travertine are uncommon for exterior materials typically implemented in China. The vision by the client was to create a unique landmark structure that would proudly display an open appearance to the public, herald the unique qualities of the company and the museum, and emphasize the prominence of the building and its location. The travertine enclosure during the day and night is illustrated in Figures 6C3.17 and 6C3.18.

FIGURE 6C3.11 A full-scale visual mock-up of planar and brise soleil travertine was constructed in Italy to evaluate rift-cut stone color, finish, and pattern. *Primo Mariotti*

FIGURE 6C3.12 Final stone range selection was performed at the fabrication plant in China.

FIGURE 6C3.13 Panelized travertine color and range review with owner, stone fabricator, installer, and architect in China.

FIGURE 6C3.14 A two-story on-site mock-up was constructed to confirm acceptable stone installation quality.

FIGURE 6C3.15   Construction progress of hand-set travertine brise soleil.

FIGURE 6C3.16   In-progress construction of the brise soleil travertine assembly.

FIGURE 6C3.17 Completed travertine brise soleil during the day viewed from the Second Ring Road. *Photo © Tim Griffith*

FIGURE 6C3.18 The completed travertine brise soleil at night. The maintenance walkway space between the unitized window wall and travertine is internally lit at each floor. *Photo © Tim Griffith*

Masonry – Natural Stone

Ronald Reagan Building and International Trade Center

Location:
Washington, DC, USA
Building Type:
Multiuse Government, Public, and Private Office Building and Trade Center

Ronald Reagan Building and International Trade Center.

PARTICIPANTS
Owner:
Pennsylvania Avenue Development Corp. (lead agency until 1995),
United States General Services Administration, and
International Cultural and Trade Center Commission (terminated 1992)
Developer Team:
Federal Triangle Corporation
Zeckendorf Company – New York, NY
Silverstein Properties – New York, NY
The Hapsmith Company – Beverly Hills, CA

Mendelsohn Associates – San Francisco, CA
Owner's Representative:
Tishman Construction
Design Architect:
Pei Cobb Freed & Partners Architects LLP – New York, NY
Associate Architect:
Ellerbe Becket Architects and Engineers, PC – Washington, DC
Structural Engineer:
Weiskopf & Pickworth – New York, NY
Mechanical Engineer:
Cosentini Associates LLP – New York, NY
Ellerbe Becket Inc. – Washington, DC
Construction Manager:
Perini Corporation – Framingham, MA
Stone Fabricator:
Indiana Limestone Company – Bedford, IN
Trade Contractors:
Harmon Contract Glazing, Inc.
Chas. M. Thompkins Builders/Cathedral Stone Works/Miller Druck Specialty Contracting, Inc. Joint Venture
Specialty Engineer for Stone Shop Drawings and Engineering:
Curtainwall Design & Consulting, Inc. – Dallas, TX
Curtain Wall:
Midwest Curtainwalls, Inc. – Cleveland, OH

PROJECT TIME FRAME
Design Competition:
Begun October 1989
Schematic Design:
Begun Spring 1990
Design Development, Exterior Enclosure:
Completed January 1992
Construction Documents:
Completed March 1993
Construction:
December 1990–May 1998

Project Description

The Federal Triangle is an area in Washington, DC, formed by 15th St. NW, Constitution Ave., Pennsylvania Ave., and 6th Street NW. The 70-acre triangle development began in 1926 with much of the construction complete by 1931. Building construction for the majority of the Triangle was completed and occupied in 1938. Full implementation of the master plan was not completed because of the lack of funds created by the Great Depression.

A 1926 plan for the Federal Triangle proposed a Great Plaza, which is the current site for the Ronald Reagan Building and International Trade Center. The Great Plaza was never developed. This remaining undeveloped site was a large parking lot until the U.S. Congress passed the "International Cultural and Trade Center" bill in August 1987 to provide office space for both the Justice and State Departments. The plan called for the U.S. government to finance the property and for private developers to construct it.

The Ronald Reagan Building and International Trade Center occupied the last open site and completes the building development of the Federal Triangle. The Reagan Building is a 2.8 million sq. ft. (260,128.5 sq. m) facility consisting of 1.6 million sq. ft. (148,645 sq. m) of office space and trade center, atrium, retail, conference center, dining, and exhibition/reception halls. A site diagram of the Federal Triangle, with the Reagan Building identified, is presented in Figure 6C4.1. The project's size is the second-largest United States federal building ever undertaken, second only to the Pentagon.

Enclosure System Types

The nine-story (eight occupied) Reagan building is 127'-7" (38.9 m) tall. Indiana limestone was selected as the predominant exterior material, for compatibility with the surrounding historic buildings. Four-inch thick (102 mm) limestone in a full color blend of four grades (select, standard, rustic, and variegated) of Indiana limestone is designed in 4" layered planes. Each elevation presents an architectural language with modern detailing, while the massing is organized to harmonize with the adjacent existing historic structures. The Pennsylvania Avenue building elevation is illustrated in Figure 6C4.2.

The three-story base consists of hand-set Indiana limestone on a steel truss substructure supporting frame. Limestone surfaces at the base are rusticated with a vertical hand-tooled finish with smooth surfaces at the borders. The limestone base rests above a hand-set granite base course.

Floor four through the eighth-floor roof level and the set-back ninth floor are clad in a variety of shaped, flat, curved, and sculpted full-color blend limestone. Full-color blend limestone is a composition of buff to light gray shades with subtle veining. Buff color limestone is used for trim and transition stone sections. Limestone panels for these floors were set in an off-site assembly shop on factory-fabricated steel trusses. There are approximately 2,700 limestone-clad trusses for the enclosure. The limestone is anchored to the steel truss with a "Kone" plug-type anchor. Threaded stainless steel bolts are inserted into the plug anchors and fastened to angles welded to the trusses. Anchor preparation in the stone was performed at the limestone fabrication shop in Indiana. Trusses and stone were assembled in Baltimore, Maryland, and shipped to the site in downtown Washington, DC, for installation. All totaled, over 42,000 limestone slabs, each measuring 8'-0" (2.44 m) by 5'-0" (1.52 m) by 3'-0" (914 mm), were fabricated from blocks, cut and finished to panels with each piece numbered and signed by the fabricator.

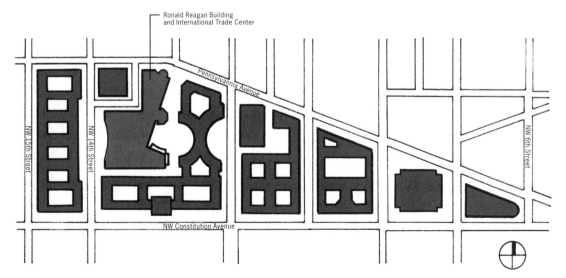

FIGURE 6C4.1 Site plan diagram of the buildings of the Federal Triangle, with The Ronald Reagan Building and International Trade Center identified.

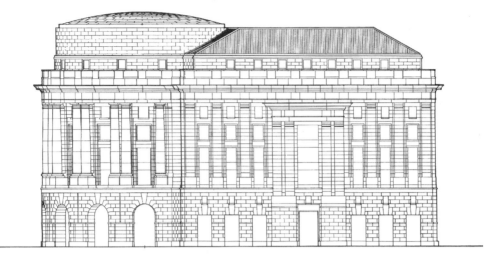

FIGURE 6C4.2   The Pennsylvania Avenue elevation with stone coursing pattern.   *Pei Cobb Freed & Partners*

Limestone covers approximately 70 percent of the enclosure area. Limestone panel edges at the head, jamb, and sill are recessed to create a capillary break if water penetrates the exterior seal. Two distinct lines of silicone sealant were installed between limestone panels in the shop. Truss-to-truss limestone panel assemblies were sealed with two lines of sealant at the project site. The weather design principle combines pressure-equalization, created by the dual seal lines, and mass density of the stone panel surfaces. Custom-designed "punched" and two-story vertical strip window areas are recessed from the primary enclosure plane stone facing.

Enclosure System Goals

The genesis of the Reagan Building was the Federal Triangle Development Act, which authorized a federal building complex and international cultural and trade center to complete the development of Pennsylvania Avenue. The Act specified the project goal that the building "reflect the symbolic importance and historical character of Pennsylvania Avenue and the nation's capital and represent the dignity and stability of the Federal Government."

The design architect noted that:

> It was clear from the outset that the building would be granite and/or limestone and that the overall proportion of the windows to walls would have to be carefully balanced. If one even marginally adopts some aspects of the classical language, or in any way assumes it proportionally, the ratio of glass to masonry is about 1:3. For every three modules of opaque surface, one is transparent. With much more than that, the surface weight of classical building is lost; it becomes too glassy.[1]

Enclosure System Design Process

DESIGN COMPETITION

The Reagan Building at the Federal Triangle is the result of a design competition. In 1989 seven teams composed of architects, engineers, developers, and contractors responded to a request for proposal (RFP) issued by the Pennsylvania Avenue Development Corporation (PADC) to design, finance, and construct the complex. The building massing, site organization, and general character visible in the completed building are evident in the competition model. Competition model images are shown in Figures 6C4.3a and 6C4.3b.

---

[1]James Ingo Freed. *The Ronald Reagan Building and International Trade Center*. Washington, DC: The National Building Museum, 1998.

FIGURE 6C4.3a Model images from the design competition. *Nathaniel Lieberman*

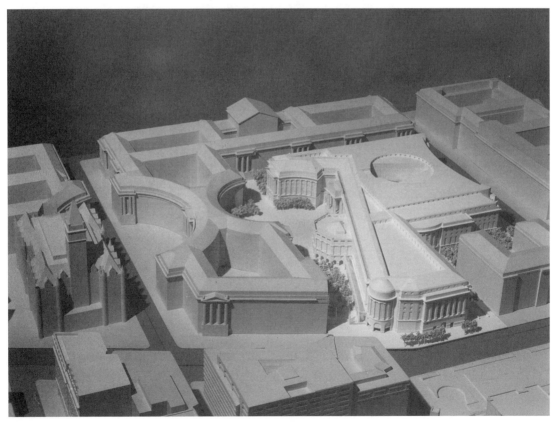

FIGURE 6C4.3b Model images from the design competition. *Nathaniel Lieberman*

The site is an "L"-shaped 11-acre parcel two blocks from the White House. Unlike the surrounding government buildings, which require strict security, the trade center consists of many public uses and requires a more open and welcoming presence. The design required resolving circulation for the mix of federal, trade, and public uses from adjacent buildings and from the street and the Mall. The resulting design orients the plaza open space and the exterior enclosure 90 degrees to Pennsylvania Avenue. This creates a symbolic Federal Triangle at right angles to Pennsylvania Avenue itself. A site plan/ground floor plan is shown in Figure 6C4.4.

Schematic Design

Limestone was chosen as the major enclosure material, for harmony with the existing structures on the Federal Triangle. The building was described by James Ingo Freed of Pei Cobb Freed as a "hybrid building." The massing and proportions respect the existing adjacent structures, but do not mimic the details or existing architectural styles.

The Indiana limestone maintains the scale and massing of neighboring buildings, in what Freed described as an "aclassical" way."

> A virtual classicism was developed by designing the limestone in layers of flat slabs, one plane on top of the other. There are no pilasters, in the strict definition, only flat stone standing upright in layers.

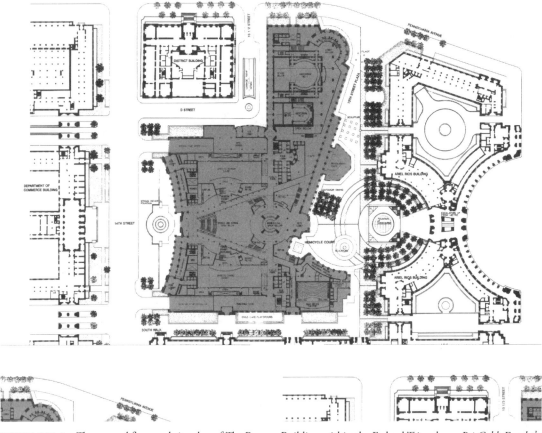

FIGURE 6C4.4   The ground floor and site plan of The Reagan Building within the Federal Triangle.   *Pei Cobb Freed & Partners*

There is no podium in the strict definition, rather a rusticated base designed to capture light and shadow. The exterior of the building consists not of solids, but of layered planes and screens, screens on top of screens; and at one point or another, the screens all peel away. The most important and visible of these layered façades is on 14th Street opposite the massive Commerce Building.[2]

The Reagan Building was sited back from the street and also curved so as not to be overwhelmed by the bulk of the neighboring Commerce Building. The 14th Street elevation is illustrated in Figure 6C4.5.

Design Development

The project utilized a fast-track project delivery method with a construction manager. In this delivery method, there are multiple trade contractors managed by a construction manager, as compared to subcontractors whose work is coordinated by a general contractor in a conventional design-bid-build project delivery method. The design development of the exterior stonework is defined in three broad horizontal zones. These are:

1. A lower register, or base, from the ground floor to the third floor
2. The upper register from the third floor to the parapet at level eight
3. The setback area from the eighth floor to the top of the parapet or Rotunda Dome

The design development drawings consist of approximately 200 architectural sheets of drawings. Key plans provide an overview "road map" for multiple sheets of building elevations. Each elevation is designed and documented at $\frac{1}{16}''$ (1:200) scale for overall context. Beginning at the Pennsylvania Avenue façade and moving clockwise around the building, all exterior wall areas from grade to the eighth floor are elevated at $\frac{1}{4}'' = 1'0''$ (1:50) scale. The $\frac{1}{4}''$ scale drawings provide the limestone panel coursing, plan dimensions, joinery types, changes in plane, and panelization boundaries. A $\frac{1}{16}$th scale building elevation with key plan is illustrated in Figure 6C4.6. A $\frac{1}{4}''$ scale partial building elevation is illustrated in Figure 6C4.7.

The deliberate clockwise documentation strategy is continued for the upper set-back floor. Each building return and elevation relief is included in the elevations to define the extent of stone as well as typical and atypical corners and interfaces. Each $\frac{1}{4}''$ scale elevation defines the stone coursing levels from the granite base: course 1 through the parapet, course 42, or 48 depending on the location.

Exterior building sections define the limestone panels and projecting layers, cornices, and pilasters. The concrete building superstructure is maintained in a relatively constant plane from column to column. Exterior profiles and relief are achieved by varying-depth trusses supporting the limestone slabs and cubic limestone shapes. The trusses that support limestone are not detailed in the design development documents. A truss zone is established for each of the panelization areas with performance criteria and designated anchorage block-outs in the superstructure.

The thermal envelope consists of 2" (50 mm) rigid insulation applied to the concrete columns and spandrel beams. Insulated interior partitions spanning from the floor slab to the underside of the insulated structure complete the thermal envelope. A building section of the rusticated base is illustrated in Figure 6C4.8a, levels 3–5 in Figure 6C4.8b, and levels 6–8th floor parapet in Figure 6C4.8c.

To achieve the design and proportion compatibility with the adjacent buildings in the Federal Triangle, the Ronald Reagan Building employs many of the principal characteristics of beaux arts architecture. The hand-set rusticated limestone base system rises from a hand-set granite base. The limestone base course 2 through 13 terminates at the belt course. The base section is illustrated in Figure 6C4.9. The primary elevation from stone course 15 through stone course 42 includes a plinth base, plinth, pilaster base, pilaster, pilaster capital, architrave, frieze, cornice, and balustrade. A section with these zones is illustrated in Figure 6C4.10.

---

[2]James I. Freed from the exhibit at The National Building Museum "Completing the Federal Triangle."

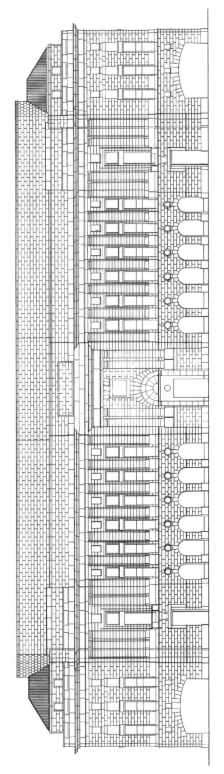

FIGURE 6C4.5 The 14th Street elevation stone coursing pattern. *Pei Cobb Freed & Partners*

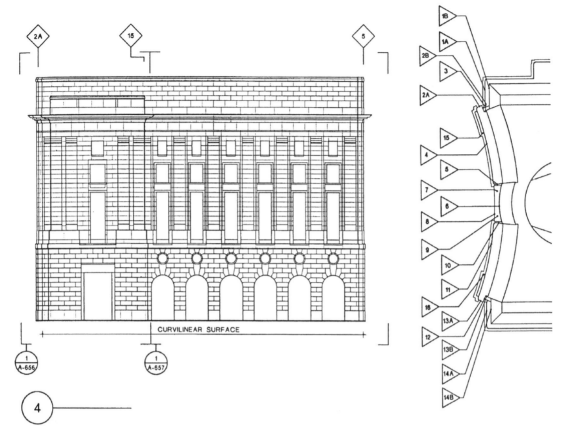

FIGURE 6C4.6 Design development "key" plan identifies each exterior building face, primary and return elevation, for documentation. One of the elevations is illustrated. *Bradford C. Cary*

The truss design approach allowed architectural and structural interdisciplinary collaboration of the enclosure connection points to the concrete primary building structure for gravity and lateral loading, while the final design of the individual stonework panels proceeded. To accommodate the fast-track construction, primary gravity and lateral load connection points for the enclosure stone-clad trusses were detailed, which allowed these primary connection points to be included in the early structure package release. This provided the necessary time for further design of the joinery and the resulting stone connections.

Construction Documents

Early construction documentation packages of drawings were released to facilitate excavation and primary building superstructure work. The construction documents for the exterior enclosure were released in March 1993, many months after the primary building superstructure documents were released for construction.

The limestone enclosure construction document drawings are organized in a similar manner as the design development documents. A key plan establishes all building elevation targets and detail keys. The construction document key plan is shown in Figure 6C4.11. Building elevations for each area of the exterior enclosure at ¼″ = 1′-0″ (1:50) identify the stone layout, coursing, and dimensions.

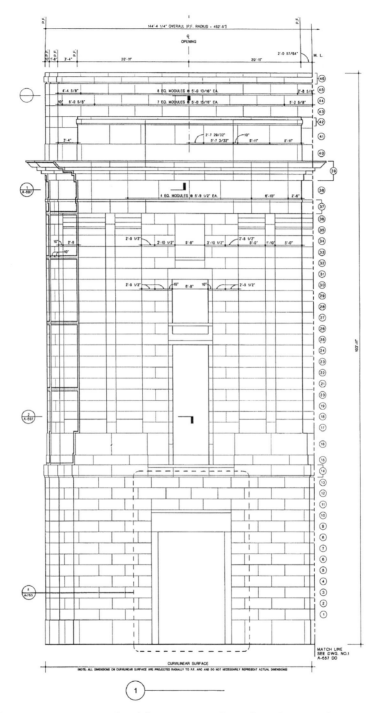

FIGURE 6C4.7 Limestone coursing is numbered from course number 1 above the granite base course to the parapet. *Bradford C. Cary*

Exterior Building Enclosures

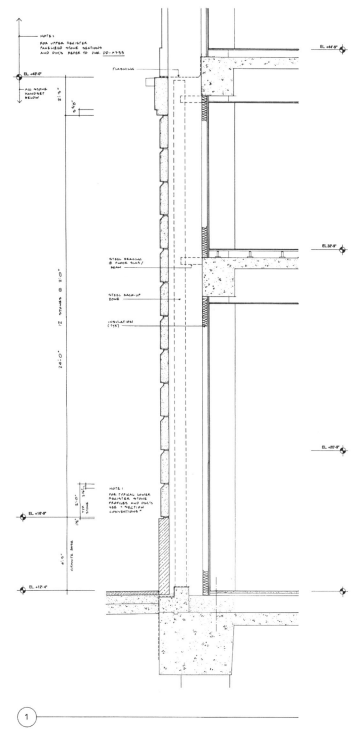

FIGURE 6C4.8a Design development lower register section defines stone coursing height, thickness, and relationship to stone supports and building superstructure. Wall assembly zones were defined to collaborate and coordinate with the primary building structure. *Bradford C. Cary*

Chapter 6   Natural Stone Masonry

301

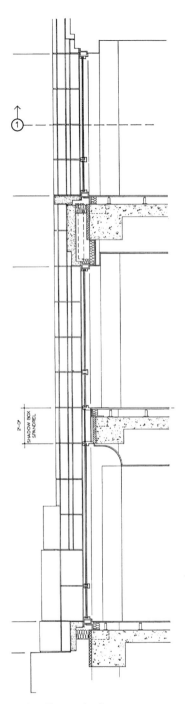

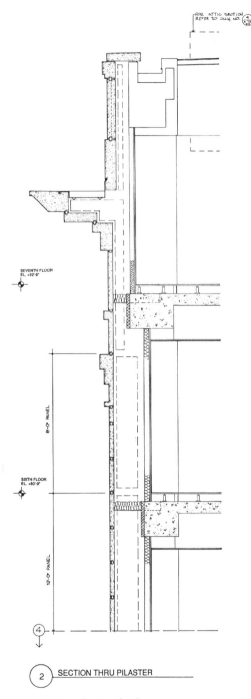

FIGURE 6C4.8b Design development upper register building section at multi-floor window opening heights in stone masonry enclosure. *Bradford C. Cary*

FIGURE 6C4.8c Design development upper register section defines stone panels, stone support zones, and cornice profiles. *Bradford C. Cary*

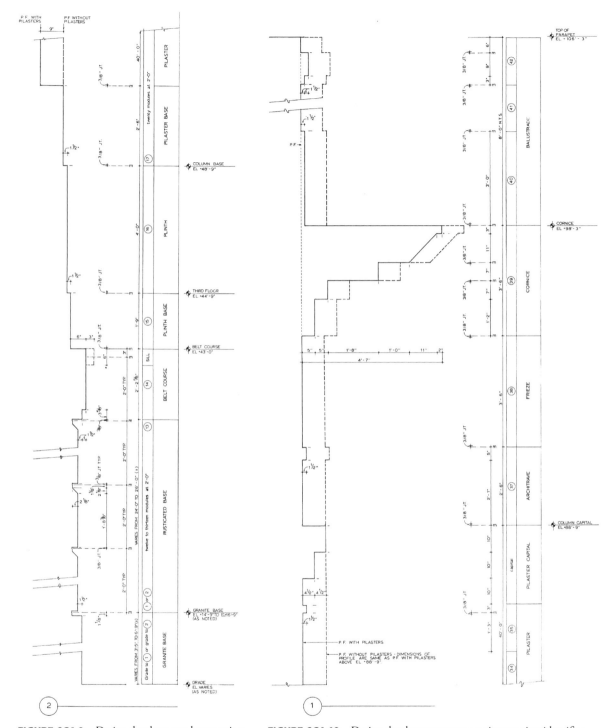

FIGURE 6C4.9 Design development base section identifies stone design zones. *Bradford C. Cary*

FIGURE 6C4.10 Design development upper register section identifies stone design zones. *Bradford C. Cary*

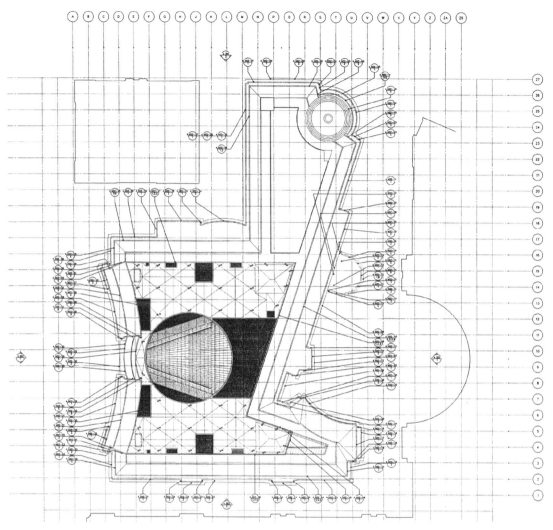

FIGURE 6C4.11 Construction document key plan identifies drawing organization for exterior elevations. *Bradford C. Cary*

Lower register sections and details provide further detail for the steel substructure for the stone support. The location of stone anchors for each hand-set stone panel is identified. A construction document elevation is shown in Figure 6C4.12.

Each limestone panel is individually gravity-supported on stainless steel anchors; either kerf-cut or back-anchored with a bent bolt "plug" type anchor into the limestone. Lateral support is accomplished by the anchor at the top of the stone panel. A section detail is illustrated in Figure 6C4.13. The granite base course is hand-set, flashed, and grouted with weeps at the vertical joints to drain any moisture in the cavity. A detail is illustrated in Figure 6C4.14. Limestone panels from the granite base to the belt course have a single line of sealant and employ a barrier and mass weather protection principle design. Stainless steel gutters are provided as a secondary

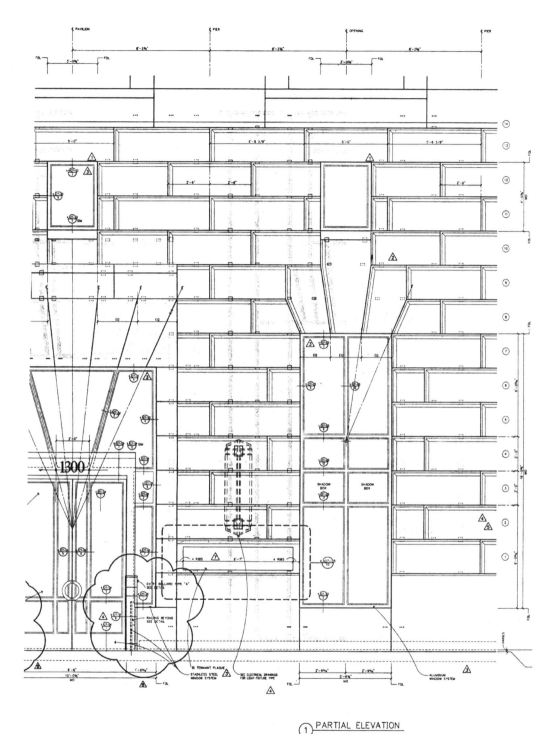

FIGURE 6C4.12 Construction document partial elevation identifies stone anchor placement for each stone panel. *Bradford C. Cary*

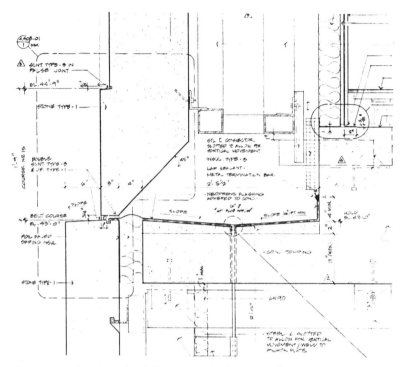

FIGURE 6C4.13 Construction document detail illustrates multiple stone anchor types, supporting system, insulation, and structure. *Bradford C. Cary*

weather protection line for water infiltration collection and removal. The gutter assembly is illustrated in Figures 6C4.15a and 6C4.15b.

The upper register elevations further define the limestone panelization. Anchor types are indicated for each panel. Limestone panelization and anchors are illustrated in Figure 6C4.16. Cubic limestone panels the depth of the stone and the truss assembly turn the corner to reinforce the solidity of the design. Limestone corners are illustrated in Figure 6C4.16a. Construction document exterior wall sections are illustrated in Figure 6C4.16b, 6C4.16c, and 6C4.16d. Stone panels receive an exterior and interior line of sealant. The head of each stone panel is recessed to collect any water, if the exterior seal is compromised, and drain to the vertical cavity created by the two lines of sealant. Stone on truss panel-to-panel joinery also receives the dual sealant lines. Panels were organized in the design development layout to accommodate access from the interior for this weather protection system approach. Limestone truss assembly panel joints do not occur at column or beam locations. Details of the dual sealant are illustrated in Figs. 6C4.17a and 6C4.17b. Weeps are discretely integrated where the channel groove in the stone drains to the vertical joint.

The lower to upper register transition is compartmentalized with a continuous flashing. The weather protection approach of each system identified here is contained in each respective area. Stone anchorage details were developed in each area to indicate gravity and lateral connections with performance specifications.

Construction

The large size of the Reagan Building required an equally large construction team of fabricators, engineers, and specialty contractors. Multiple builder entities formed joint ventures to design, engineer, and fabricate the steel trusses for the upper register and steel substructure for the lower register, as well as assemble and erect the limestone

306

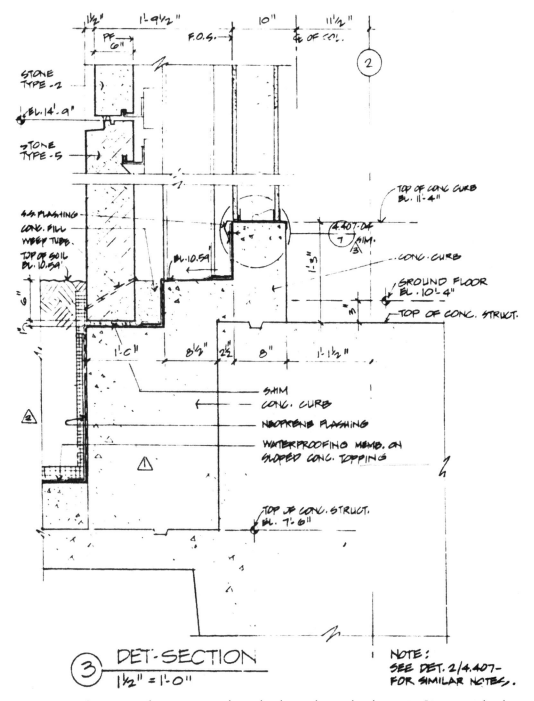

FIGURE 6C4.14 Construction document granite base is hand-set and weeped to the exterior. Limestone is hand-set and anchored to an engineered steel support system. *Bradford C. Cary*

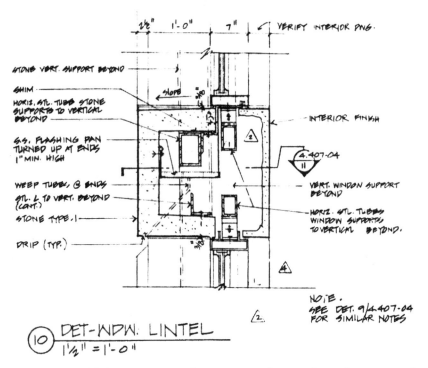

FIGURE 6C4.15a Stainless steel flashing occurs at window openings with weep tubes to drain water to the exterior. *Bradford C. Cary*

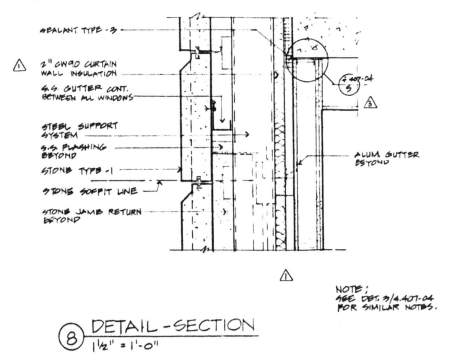

FIGURE 6C4.15b Stainless steel gutters collect water behind the stone if the sealant barrier or stone mass allows water penetration at determined heights. Weep tubes are located and routed to the exterior at vertical stone joints. *Bradford C. Cary*

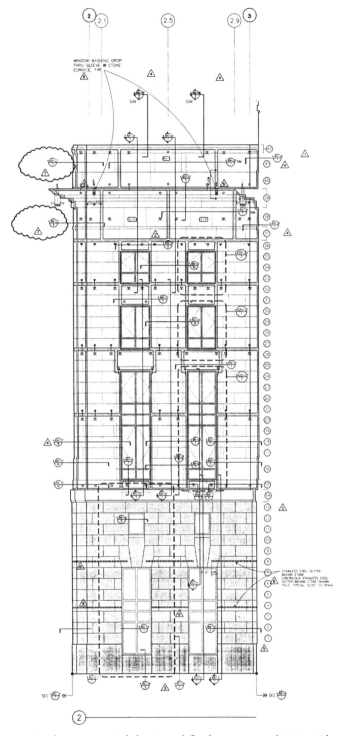

FIGURE 6C4.16a Construction document partial elevations define limestone panelization with gravity and lateral anchor locations. *Bradford C. Cary*

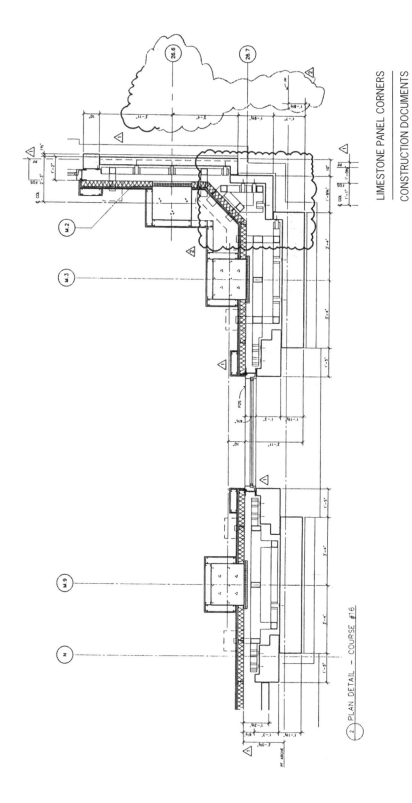

FIGURE 6C4.16b Construction document enlarged plan defines cubic L-shaped limestone corners. *Bradford C. Cary*

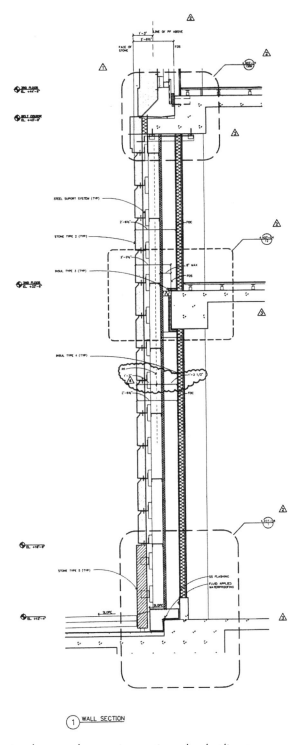

① WALL SECTION

FIGURE 6C4.16c   Construction document lower register section at handset limestone.

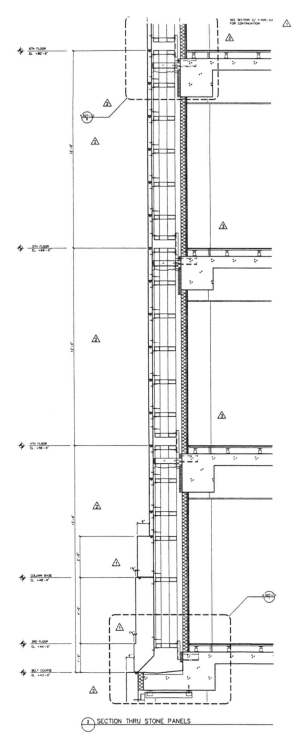

FIGURE 6C4.16d Construction document limestone panels on steel truss are floor-to-floor height assemblies. *Bradford C. Cary*

Exterior Building Enclosures

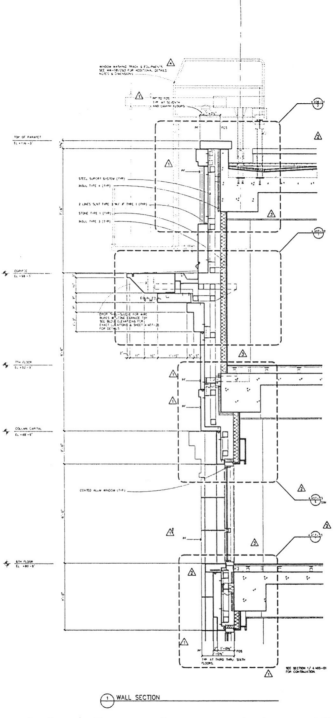

FIGURE 6C4.16e Construction document limestone cornice truss construction documents define limestone panels, prefabricated sections, depths, profiles, and anchorage locations. *Bradford C. Cary*

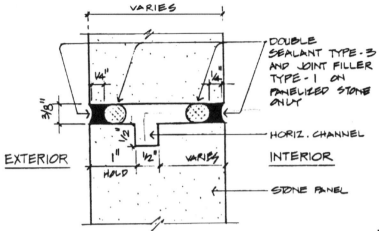

DETAIL - HORIZ. JOINT
FULL SIZE SCALE

FIGURE 6C4.17a Each limestone panel-to-panel joint is sealed on the exterior and interior. A horizontal channel is fabricated in each stone head section to divert water to the vertical joint. *Bradford C. Cary*

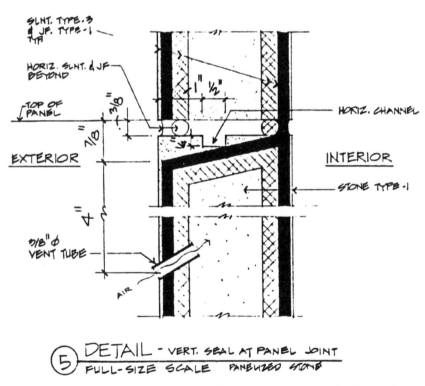

DETAIL - VERT. SEAL AT PANEL JOINT
FULL-SIZE SCALE PANELIZED STONE

FIGURE 6C4.17b Dual sealant lines at each panel are joined front to back at the top of each panel for weather seal continuity. *Bradford C. Cary*

on the prefabricated trusses. Stone shop drawings were prepared by a specialty engineering company. Stone shop drawings indicating size, thickness, finish, and anchor preparation were developed and submitted to the architectural team for review and approval. After approval, individual cutting tickets for each panel of stone were prepared, identifying the size, shape, anchor preparation, finishes, and grain orientation. These stone shop tickets were provided to the stone fabricator for production of each stone panel.

From the stone cutting tickets, Indiana limestone blocks, which were quarried ahead of shop drawing development, were cut to slabs to the required thickness. Individual limestone panels and shapes were fabricated, and the preparation for the stone anchors was performed by the stone fabricator in Indiana. A detail image of the installed base rustication is shown in Figure 6C4.18a. Application of rusticated finish of the lower register limestone by stonemasons in Indiana is illustrated in Figure 6C4.18b.

Finished limestone panels were numbered with "piece marks," crated, and shipped to the assembly warehouse in Baltimore, Maryland. Approximately 2,700 truss panels were assembled at the Baltimore warehouse, utilizing overhead cranes. The limestone assembled on a truss at the assembly facility is illustrated in Figure 6C4.19. The large cubic limestone shapes for the cornice and frieze, described in the earlier design development phase, were also shop-assembled into panels. A cornice panel at the assembly facility is illustrated in Figure 6C4.20. The stone-to-stone panel joinery was sealed in a shop controlled environment and shipped to the project site for erection.

A visual mock-up was constructed at the project site. The extent of the mock-up is illustrated in Figure 6C4.21, including sections of the rusticated base, level 4–7 enclosure, and the cornice, frieze, and balustrade.

FIGURE 6C4.18a Detail of rusticated limestone finish at lower register.

FIGURE 6C4.18b Applied rusticated finish application in stone fabrication plant. *Bradford C. Cary*

FIGURE 6C4.19 Limestone on panels in assembly plant. *Bradford C. Cary*

FIGURE 6C4.20 Limestone cornice panel at assembly plant. *Bradford C. Cary*

FIGURE 6C4.21 On-site limestone visual mock-up. Note the variegated color range within stone panels. *Bradford C. Cary*

FIGURE 6C4.22 Limestone and window enclosure system performance mock-up. *Bradford C. Cary*

The full color blend, of gray and buff, is visible in several limestone panels on the mock-up. The visual mock-up served as the quality benchmark for the stone enclosure construction.

Performance tests were performed on the stone and custom window assemblies. The extent of performance mock-up is illustrated in Figure 6C4.22. The mock-up was tested for air infiltration, static water infiltration, dynamic water infiltration (via aircraft engine, to simulate buffeting wind), and wind load, for system deflection. The mock-up successfully passed all tests.

Views of the limestone enclosure construction at the 14th Street elevation are illustrated in Figures 6C4.22 and 6C4.23. Note the steel substructure for the lower register and the block-outs in the concrete superstructure at floors 3–7 to receive the limestone on truss gravity anchors.

Summary

The sheer size and geometric complexity of the Ronald Reagan Building were designed and documented in a very deliberate and methodical manner. Dimensional organization coupled with definitive system details for

FIGURE 6C4.23   14th Street construction progress. Note steel backup system support for limestone.   *Alan E. Tiu/ Architect/Photographer*

FIGURE 6C4.24   14th Street construction progress. Note block-outs in concrete structure to receive steel supports for limestone.   *Alan E. Tiu/Architect/Photographer*

FIGURE 6C4.25   14th Street completed elevation and entry.

the lower and upper register, along with interfaces at the custom window assemblies, established a consistent detail and construction methodology. What was referred to for many years as the "plague spot" is today referred to as the "Crown Jewel" in the Federal Triangle. The completed limestone exterior enclosure fulfills its requirements for visual compatibility with its predecessor neighboring structures and, through its high-quality design and execution, it promotes the dignity and stability required for such a prestigious location. The Fourteenth Street elevation and entry is shown in Figure 6C4.25.

Chapter 7

Architectural Concrete

If you don't have time to do it right the first time; when will you have time to do it over?

OLD SAYING

Overview

Concrete is a composite material consisting of measured amounts of Portland cement, coarse aggregate, fine aggregate, water, admixtures, and other cementitious replacement materials. When water is added, it reacts with the cement and bonds the aggregates and admixtures together, resulting in a stone-like finished material. Exposed concrete can be broadly classified as either visually exposed structural concrete or architectural concrete. Visually exposed structural concrete has no particular consideration of finishes, joinery, or color. The modifier term "architectural" in "architectural concrete" refers to concrete that is exposed to view and finished to project-specific requirements for uniform color mix, texture, joinery, minimal surface defects, surface flatness, precise tolerances, and alignment of surfaces. Concrete elements and finished surfaces utilized in exterior enclosures are the result of the concrete mix, reinforcing, and formwork.

Architectural concrete is a complex finished product achieved by developing and tailoring the design and details to fit the construction process. There are few, if any, definitive architectural concrete standards. Finishes, standards, materials, details, and particularly the construction process, must be understood and well defined during the design process and diligently executed in the construction process, to achieve a successful finished product. This is particularly important for an architectural concrete exterior enclosure. Once architectural concrete is placed, it is very difficult and time-consuming to successfully perform large-scale remedial repairs—therefore, "Do it right the first time." Initiating design using architectural concrete requires a basic understanding of the concrete mix raw materials, the physical and chemical reactions created by the concrete curing process, formwork framing, and formwork facing. Each has a role in final architectural concrete composition.

Architectural concrete is a moldable material well suited for achieving sculptural exterior enclosure forms in a wide variety of shapes, patterns, finishes, surface textures, and colors.

Design

Architectural concrete enclosures are specifically designed per project and are therefore custom-designed assemblies. The design effort requires close collaboration between the architect and structural engineer to develop the visual and performance goals. While both disciplines are very involved in the design of architectural concrete, each has distinct primary and support responsibilities regarding who designs what. It is also important to define where the work and information of each discipline reside in the documents.

Architectural concrete is moldable, making it a popular material suited to sculptural shapes, patterns, finishes, surface textures, and color. Architectural

321

concrete is a "plastic" material, taking on the shape, finish, and texture of the formwork. Anyone who has built sand castles with plastic cups and buckets has, in an abstract way, worked with formwork. Concrete itself is not modular. However, the formwork should be designed with modular repetition in mind. The formwork is the module, and the finished architectural concrete is the resulting product of the formwork.

Important architectural concrete enclosure design considerations are:

1. Mix
2. Reinforcing
3. Formwork
4. Joints and patterns
5. Surface finish and texture
6. Color

MIX

The concrete mix is a definitive recipe of ingredients with many minute details, and like most recipes, it is seasoned with a specific result in mind. The concrete mix consists of raw materials in measured amounts, including Portland cement, coarse aggregate (such as gravel, crushed rock, granite, and limestone), fine aggregate (sand), admixtures, cementitious replacement materials (such as fly ash and slag), and water. The base mix ingredient is Portland cement. Portland cement is manufactured by heating a limestone and clay mixture to very high temperatures. This material mix begins to melt at the edges, which results in a lumpy product referred to as "clinker." The clinker is ground and mixed with gypsum or other sulfates to make cement. Cement colors are typically shades of gray and white. Other color hues can be obtained through adjusting the heating or reheating the clinker. The cement color is the base pigment color, similar to the base pigment color in paint. Architectural concrete that utilizes gray cement will result in a grayish color no matter the color of the aggregate, exposure of the aggregate, or quantity of color admixture additives. White cement as the base pigment allows for both a lighter and/or whiter finish and a more accurate final color when color admixtures are incorporated in the mix.

There are two basic types of aggregates: coarse and fine. Coarse aggregates include crushed gravel, granite, and other dense materials. These should be strong and hard, not gravel that crumbles or flakes. Aggregates should be clean and free of dirt and clay, or the bond created with the cement will be weak. The aggregates should be graded in size so they fit together well in the mix. Rounded aggregates yield a more workable mix, and angular aggregates yield a mix harder to place and compact, but they can often make concrete stronger. Fine aggregates include sand. Silica sand, the result of quartz, is typically used because of its chemical inertness and hardness. The composition of sand is highly variable, depending on the source. Colors range from very white to black, and each type of sand has distinct geological properties and color. Each aggregate in the mix directly affects the strength and visual appearance of the architectural concrete.

There are a wide range of admixtures. These include air-entraining admixtures, water reducers/superplasticizers, retarders, accelerators, and supplemental cementitious replacement materials such as fly ash, slag, silica fume, and metakaolin. The use of admixtures, if required or needed, is very particular to the specific conditions and should be discussed with multiple sources to provide technical advice during the design and documentation phases.

Water is a key component in the concrete mix. It must be clean and free of deleterious materials and mixed in the correct quantity. Concrete hardens after mixing with water and placement in a chemical hydration process. Water, combined with Portland cement (or cementitious replacement materials), forms a cement paste that bonds coarse and fine aggregate together. The quantity of water influences the compressive strength, density, flow, and workability of concrete.

Mix design for architectural concrete is a joint design effort between architect and structural engineer, with technical input from concrete product manufacturers who are knowledgeable about the local availability of the raw concrete mix materials.

REINFORCING

Reinforcing provides tensile strength in concrete to complement the natural compressive strength. Reinforcing for architectural concrete is typically steel reinforcing bars with a deformed surface. Reinforcing is designed by the structural engineer of record. On some architectural concrete enclosures, the architectural concrete may not be the primary structure. Reinforcing in the concrete is still a structural engineering responsibility, provided by either the structural engineer of record or a specialty structural engineer.

FORMWORK

Formwork is the mold into which the concrete mix and reinforcing are placed. There are many types of formwork, and even though it is a method of construction, architects who design with architectural concrete must understand the construction method, in order to achieve a successful final product. Formwork consists of framing and facing materials.

Formwork framing can be wood or heavy timber, steel, or aluminum framing. On large-scale projects with repetition, custom forms fabricated with facings of steel, aluminum, or fiberglass can yield large concrete panels. Smaller-scale projects or small architectural concrete areas tend to use wood formwork framing and plywood form facing. Designs with plywood form facing need to recognize the size of plywood sheets and the resulting panel-to-panel joinery. Formwork framing is engineered, usually by specialty engineers, to provide the necessary strength and deflection limits required for the facing material and the hydrostatic pressure created during concrete placement. Wood-framed formwork is illustrated in Figure 7.1. Steel-framed formwork is illustrated in Figure 7.2.

Formwork facing materials provide the "off form" finish surface. Off form concrete is left exposed, after form removal, with no further finishing. The combined stiffness of the formwork facing material and formwork framing determines the finish concrete surface flatness. Formwork facings are usually classified as absorbent and nonabsorbent. Facing materials include plywood (in various face grades), plywood with overlay materials, steel, aluminum, and fiberglass-reinforced plastics.

JOINTS AND PATTERNS

Joinery patterns provide visual breaks to minimize variations that occur between consecutive concrete

FIGURE 7.1 Wood-framed formwork is often constructed on-site. Note formwork support frequency at the lower portion, to resist pressure during concrete placement. *Michael Fukutome*

FIGURE 7.2   Steel-framed formwork is typically fabricated off-site and used for repetitive concrete placements.

placements. Whether repetitive or irregular, joinery serves as a scaling device to further express the design intent. For discussion purposes, there are three types of architectural concrete joinery. These are:

1. Construction joints
2. Rustication joints
3. Unwanted joints

Construction Joints

Construction joints are either recessed "reveal" joints or "cold" joints defined by the extent of concrete placement. There are many terms used for the physical construction activity of concrete construction, often associated with the type of equipment utilized, ranging from pouring to pumping, and others. These terms are often slang and technically incorrect. Concrete is placed. Architectural concrete can be placed in small, medium, or large areas. It requires continuous placement and relatively fast pour rates to achieve a high level of finish and color consistency, and to prevent differential set, concentrations of cement paste, and "bleed" from water in the concrete, which can result in

inconsistent and unwanted lines and surface color variations. Reasonable concrete placement extents are usually related to the number of concrete trucks required and available. Concrete placement creates "end conditions" at the top, the bottom, and side. These end conditions result in construction joints.

A distinct recessed reveal type of joint can visually mask the construction joint between new and existing architectural concrete. A "cold joint" type of construction joint results in an often irregular line with adjacent surfaces of new and existing concrete that may or may not be in plane. The reveal type of construction joint addresses the "stop" of the concrete placement and the "start" of the adjacent placement above or beside the completed extent of architectural concrete. An architectural concrete construction joint is illustrated in Figure 7.3.

Rustication Joints

Rustication joints are either recessed or project from the concrete surface. Rustication joint shapes and sizes are developed and located to suit the design. Recessed

Exterior Building Enclosures

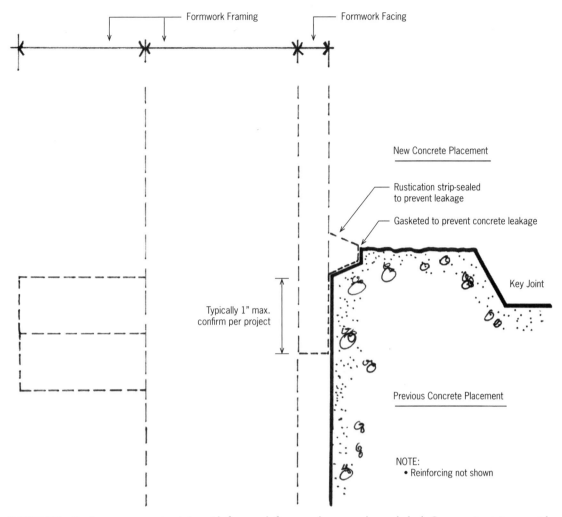

FIGURE 7.3 Section at construction joint with formwork for next placement shown dashed. Construction joints provide visual relief to conceal starts and stops in concrete placement.

rustication joints are sometimes referred to as "control joints." Rustication joints are illustrated in Figures 7.4a and 7.4b. Rustication joints can be used to create additional joinery and pattern in addition to the required construction joints. Rustication joints can also be used to visually mask joints between formwork faces when smaller formwork facing materials such as plywood are used. As an example, typical plywood sheet sizes are $4'-0''$ (1.22 m) $\times$ $8'-0''$ (2.49 m). There are larger plywood sheets; however, while it is likely they can be used as forms, it is atypical to employ this size of plywood material. The end-to-end condition at plywood sheets in formwork creates joints. These joints are often (and usually) out of alignment because of the strength of the formwork or inconsistencies in the edges of the plywood. These joints may be desired or acceptable in the design, or they may fall into the next joint category: unwanted joints.

FIGURE 7.4a Recessed rustication joint provides locations to visually conceal formwork panel joinery locations. Rustication joints can be added to provide pattern, shadow, and finish transitions. *Michael Fukutome*

FIGURE 7.4b Projecting rustication joint requires a "negative" recess in the concrete form and very careful formwork removal. *Tim Waters*

Unwanted Joints

Unwanted joints can be due to factors including, but not limited to: inconsistencies in the concrete placement, cold joints, formwork facing material section joints, or discontinuities in concrete placement. The bottom line is that these joints can occur in locations not intended and detract from the design intent when expressed in the finished architectural concrete surfaces. When there is a time lag in placing concrete during a pour, the material placed begins to set. Adjacent concrete placed next to the set concrete will cause an irregular pour line or cold joint. The moisture content in discontinuous pours may also result in an uneven color, which further highlights the cold joint.

Creating a pattern of construction joints and rustication joints that addresses (1) concrete placement starts and stops, (2) formwork facing joinery, and (3) the particulars of placing concrete is one of several design, detail, and construction process considerations for architectural concrete enclosures. The big idea is to have joints where the design requires them and to avoid unintended and unwanted joints.

SURFACE FINISH, TEXTURE, AND FLATNESS

Architectural concrete is a "plastic" material that takes the shape and finish of the formwork material used. There are numerous formwork materials, and each imparts its own unique finish to the architectural concrete surface.

Off-form concrete surface finish resulting directly from formwork facing ranges from mirror smooth to smooth, rough, pattern, texture, and many others. The construction documents, drawings, and specifications must identify appropriate formwork and formwork facing material to achieve the intended surface finish. An example of an off-form concrete finish is illustrated in Figure 7.5.

As an alternative to surface finish and texture achieved by the formwork facing alone, there are applied finishes. These are achieved after the concrete is placed and formwork is removed. Applied architectural concrete surface textures can be sandblasted, picked, bush-hammered, etched, or multiple other applied textures which are achieved by working the concrete after placement, curing, and formwork removal. Applied finishes have a window of time for application after placement. Heavy finishing is usually done in two to three days, while light finishing can occur in five or more days after concrete placement. Other applied finishes include tints and paints. These are applied finishes with a shorter life span and require reapplication at intervals depending on many

FIGURE 7.5 Off-form board finish architectural concrete. *Michael Fukutome*

factors such as applied finish, material quality, exposure to sunlight, absorption into concrete and the like. Examples of applied architectural concrete finishes are illustrated in Figures 7.6a, 7.6b, and 7.6c.

Completed concrete shapes, surface finishes, and the previously mentioned joinery patterns are the result of the formwork. Concrete surface flatness is the result of the type of formwork, and its ability to resist bowing due to the hydrostatic pressure of the concrete and the dynamic pressure of concrete placement, vibration, and other construction activities. Surface flatness variations can be more visible with changes in the angle and amount of light on the finished concrete surface. There are industry standard guidelines for allowable bow (in and out) in the formwork and therefore in the finish concrete work. These should be carefully evaluated and established to ascertain if industry standards will achieve the desired flatness results, or if project-specific flatness criteria are required.

Architectural concrete may develop cracks. These are often very fine cracks referred to as "microcracks." The length, width, depth, and size of the crack are

FIGURE 7.6a Heavily textured concrete finish achieved by bush hammer to placed and cured concrete.

FIGURE 7.6b Project visual mock-up of smooth and applied texture finish. *Michael Fukutome*

FIGURE 7.6c Applied concrete tint to placed architectural concrete. *Michael Fukutome*

dependent on how the concrete is placed and how it cures. The inevitable fact is that most concrete does have a tendency to crack. Typically, the bigger the concrete surfaces between joints, the higher the likelihood of cracks. Where there are cracks, there is the opportunity for water infiltration. Determining the depth that moisture will penetrate the concrete is only possible afterwards, through measurements. Waterproofing materials can be applied to interior concrete surfaces in a negative side water protection approach, to resist infiltration. Each project should have a design detail strategy to address potential concrete cracking.

No matter which form framing or facing material is used, there are size limitations. The design should acknowledge the formwork surface facing material, or a "butt" joint or seam will be visible. If this is the design intent—OK. If not, the design must address the form facing panel joint with a deliberate and designed alignment detail or joint profile. Once concrete is placed and has achieved an initial set, forms are removed or stripped. Stripping formwork is a construction effort. Joinery, particularly at corners and openings, must allow form removal with preferably no damage, or at least with minimal chipping. Examples of concrete corners are illustrated in Figures 7.7a and 7.7b.

COLOR

A prime visual element of architectural concrete is the color. Each ingredient in the concrete mix recipe will have an influence on the color. Color additives are pigments either mined from the ground or manufactured in plants. The dose of color additives in the mix is based on the cement content. Architectural concrete that utilizes gray cement will have a grayish color, either warmer or cooler depending on the actual cement color, even with pigment additives. If gray is not the intended final tint, then the mix should include white cement.

Architectural concrete color and finish will age under the effects of weather and environmental considerations such as dust, pollution, and the like, and the natural tendency of concrete is to gradate towards a warmer shade as it ages. Aging effects and long-term appearance must be deliberated and considered in the design process.

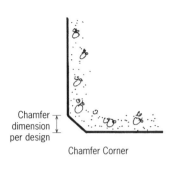

Chamfer
dimension
per design

Chamfer Corner

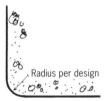

Radius per design

Round Corner

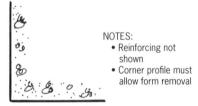

NOTES:
• Reinforcing not
  shown
• Corner profile must
  allow form removal

Square Corner

FIGURE 7.7a Examples of concrete corners. Corner details must allow form removal with minimal damage.

FIGURE 7.7b Square architectural concrete corner. *Michael Fukutome*

Structural Considerations

The term "architectural concrete" refers to the color, finish, joinery, and other visible aspects of the finished product. Design and detail are developed and documented in very close collaboration with the structural engineer. Since many architectural concrete enclosures are also the primary building structure, dimensioning, reinforcing, and joinery (construction joints, rustication joints, and form joints) must be indicated to a construction level on the structural drawings. Collaboration in design development and coordination between the architectural and structural drawings must be aligned very deliberately during the construction documents phase.

Cement, aggregates, and water provide the compression strength in concrete. Concrete is strong in compression. This is due to the cement and water mix bonding with the aggregates to transfer compression loads. Reinforcing steel and/or fiber provides the tensile strength and carries the tension loads in concrete. Reinforcing steel is designed by the structural engineer. Reinforcing steel requires concrete coverage to develop the composite strength and to protect the steel reinforcing from exterior elements.

Location of construction and rustication joints should be indicated on both structural and architectural drawings. Tops of wall enclosures to the floor-supporting structure of either slabs or beams usually determine stops and starts of concrete pours and formwork lifts and, therefore, joints. Finished shapes and profiles of construction and rustication joints can occur on either document set, but usually reside in the architectural drawings.

Concrete formwork typically requires methods of securing and supporting two sides of forms together.

This is commonly accomplished with form ties, which connect through the architectural concrete and tie the interior and exterior formwork together. These ties result in form tie holes, which are visible even when filled, and impart a definitive pattern to the concrete. The required spacing of tie holes and the size of the ties require research and consultation advice from builders to establish size and spacing "rules of the game." These are based on the strength and stability of the formwork spans between the tie hole locations. With an understanding of the spacing and size requirements, patterns can be developed to support the desired visual results. Form tie holes can be minimized and sometimes avoided with the use of steel forms. This has cost implications, so the type of formwork design and specification is an important area of focus in design. Images of architectural concrete form ties and the resulting visible pattern are shown in Figures 7.8a, 7.8b, and 7.8c.

Architectural concrete is a load-bearing exterior enclosure designed to carry gravity, dead load, live load, lateral wind, and if applicable, seismic loads. Openings in the architectural concrete enclosure for windows, louvers, and doors are treated as finished—not rough—openings, and must coordinate with the architectural interface details. Embedded items such as window- or louver-supporting embeds, conduits for electrical and lighting items, openings and inserts for mechanical and related items (required by other design team member disciplines) must be integrated and illustrated on the structural drawings.

Structural considerations that have an impact on architectural concrete design and detail are:

1. Required thickness
2. Reinforcing at openings and embedded item interfaces

REQUIRED THICKNESS

Structural design is typically based on the effective thickness of a wall, beam, or slab. If the 12″ (305 mm) thick architectural concrete wall has a ¾″ (19 mm) to 1″ (25 mm) deep rustication joint on the exterior side, the effective thickness is 11″ (12″ − 1″ deep joint). There must be a mutual understanding between architect and engineer on where concrete thickness is measured. Cost of architectural concrete, like many other exterior enclosure materials, is heavily

FIGURE 7.8a Form tie pattern in completed architectural concrete. Form ties are visible in various degrees in the completed architectural concrete.

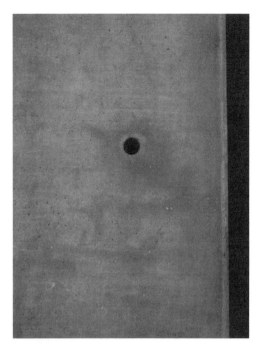

FIGURE 7.8b Form tie hole from formwork left unfilled.

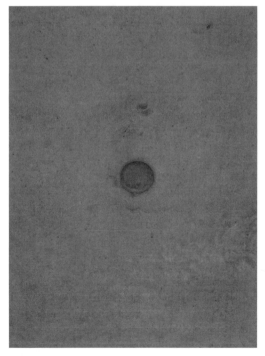

FIGURE 7.8c Form tie from formwork filled. Fill materials vary.

dependent on quantities. If the engineer's understanding of wall thickness is 12″, non-inclusive of the reveal, an additional 1″ of material thickness to achieve the rustication joint results in an 8 percent thickness and material increase.

REINFORCING AT OPENINGS AND INTERFACES

Openings in architectural concrete require particular reinforcing bar design and details, and embeddings and other items inserted to accept other enclosure attachments into the concrete opening edges. These are competing interests for the same real estate. Good design and detail practice is to illustrate items embedded in concrete on the structural drawings. For this to occur, the structural engineer needs to know specifically what types of items are required. This is where collaboration in design development and coordination in construction documents is a must.

Weather Protection

Architectural concrete relies on thickness, density, and mass for weather protection between exterior elements and occupied interior spaces. Applied exterior weather-resistant coatings can be utilized; however, the durability of applied exterior coatings has a distinct life span and will alter the finished exterior appearance. Waterproofing materials applied on the interior result in a negative-side water protection approach. Water infiltration prevention is a particular area of focus and concern. Architectural concrete is as water resistant as the density, thickness, and cracks. It is not, strictly speaking, a waterproof material. Mix design and density will create some wetting of the concrete surfaces into the body of the architectural concrete enclosure. Reinforcing steel materials should be evaluated and selected on the basis of local climate and rainfall. Horizontal surfaces such as sills and copings should be carefully contemplated in design, material selection, and detail. Materials that are waterproof, such as metals or a secondary top concrete surface material with waterproofing applied on the architectural concrete below, should be evaluated and considered for water infiltration protection.

Openings in architectural concrete are potential weak spots for air and water infiltration protection. Deliberate design, detailing, and care should be exercised at seals and flashings to provide weather protection continuity between the architectural concrete and the other exterior enclosure assemblies in the openings. Often this is accomplished with two distinct lines of sealant, as illustrated in Figure 7.9, or by flashings with a single line of sealant, as illustrated in Figure 7.10. A key performance design objective is to evaluate the possibility that water can infiltrate through the concrete and "around" the weatherproofing interfaces of the openings.

THERMAL DESIGN/VAPOR CONTROL/ CONDENSATION

Insulation for architectural concrete typically occurs on the interior side. Achieving a continuous thermal envelope is usually difficult, if not impossible, because of the structural floor slab and beam interface and connections with the exterior architectural concrete. A section with insulation in an independent insulated interior partition wall is illustrated in Figure 7.11. The envelope's thermal design should consider the density and mass at the "uninsulated" areas for heat gain, heat loss, and diurnal thermal lag. Interior insulation can be applied via furring attachment clips to the interior concrete faces, or with freestanding interior insulated partitions. In either approach, the terminations at openings, top of floor slab, and underside of structure must have a developed suite of details to address insulation continuity.

Architectural concrete can incorporate internal insulation. This usually requires staggered or separate pours. The two planes of concrete will need to be structurally connected by concrete and reinforcing. This introduces thermal discontinuities at the connecting concrete sections between the two wall planes. A detail of internally insulated concrete is illustrated in Figure 7.12.

VAPOR CONTROL

Architectural concrete should be designed and detailed to allow drying towards the exterior and interior faces. Exterior wetting dries towards the exterior. Interior surfaces should provide an air cavity separating the insulation from the concrete surface. This can be achieved through a separate insulated interior partition or furring strips for insulation attachment with an air space between the concrete and the insulation.

Concrete thickness, profile, quantity of shrinkage, cracking, and exterior climate and interior temperature and humidity conditions will influence design for moisture and vapor transmission and control.

Detailing and Specifications

Design, detailing, and specifying architectural concrete properly will push the experience limits of most architects and structural engineers. Architects and engineers must adopt a "How would I build it?" mentality. Architectural concrete enclosure design includes multiple interrelated steps. These are:

1. Diligent material and construction process research
2. Builder and contractor discussion and input
3. Thorough details
4. Project-specific specifications for materials and the execution requirements

Even when the architect and project team have experience in this type of work, seek out advice and consultation from a specialty consultant or builder who has a "hands-on" understanding and experience in architectural concrete construction in the project location. Project specifications should include an Architectural Concrete specification section separate from the Structural Concrete section. Part 3 of the specification, "execution of the work" (see Chapter 3, "Design Process"), should have definitive language for actions required beyond the standard structural practices. This is often written with the "How would I build it?" mentality. Thorough and coordinated details and specifications are critical components for achieving high-quality architectural concrete.

The construction process usually allows only one chance to get it right. Very few, if any, projects will remove or significantly alter architectural concrete other than for patching. There are essential

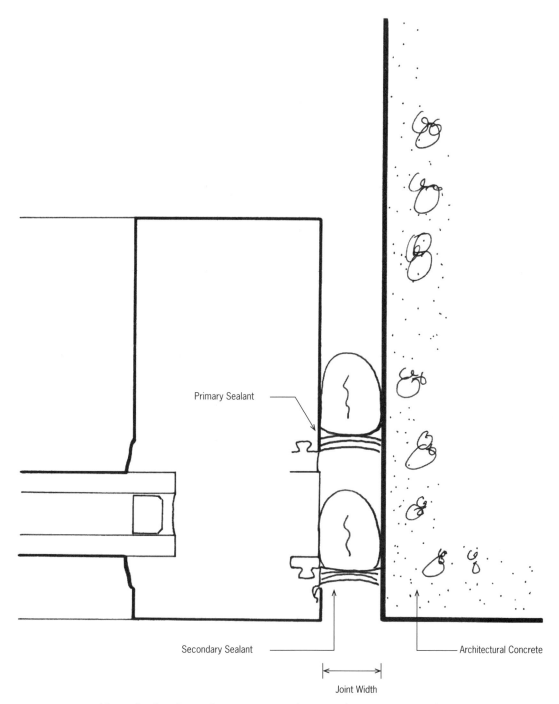

FIGURE 7.9 Dual lines of sealant for weather protection at adjacent enclosure systems in architectural concrete openings.

Primary Sealant

Secondary Sealant

Architectural Concrete

Joint Width

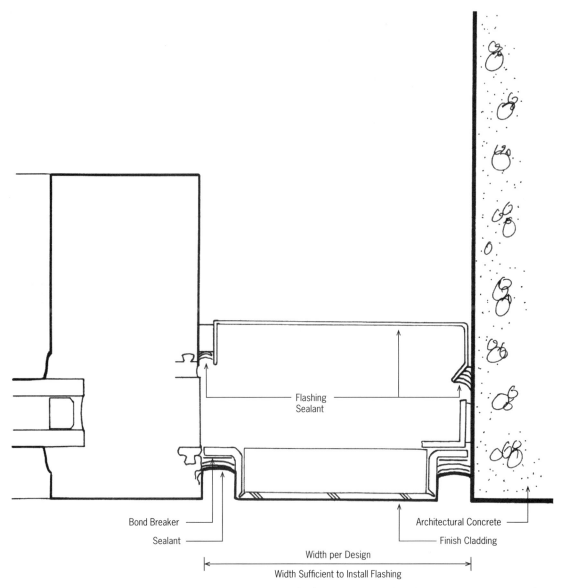

FIGURE 7.10 Flashing may be used in a concealed location and a finish material with sealant to achieve two lines of weather protection between adjacent enclosure systems and openings in architectural concrete. Adequate dimensions should be provided for installation of flashing and sealant.

intermediate construction steps between the documents and actual on-site architectural concrete placement. These are:

1. Color and finish samples
2. Mock-up(s)

COLOR AND FINISH SAMPLES

Obtaining color and finish samples in the design and preliminary detail execution of architectural concrete is essential, not optional. Builders who "self-perform" concrete work can provide samples and construction

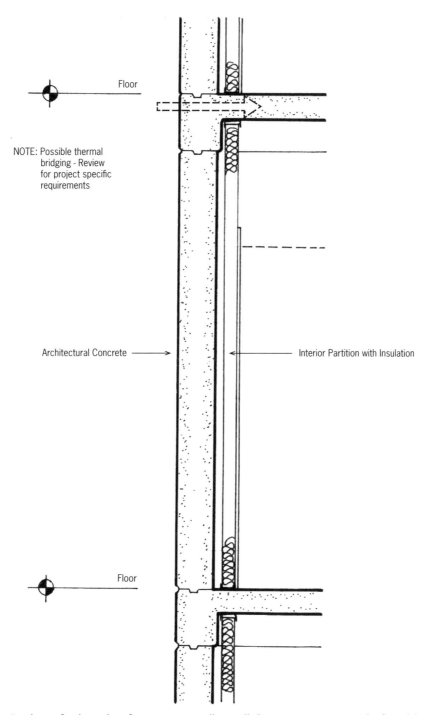

Floor

NOTE: Possible thermal
bridging - Review
for project specific
requirements

Architectural Concrete ——→   ←—— Interior Partition with Insulation

Floor

FIGURE 7.11 Insulation for thermal performance is typically installed in interior partitions. The floor slab or perimeter beam conditions should be reviewed per project for thermal bridging, energy performance, and a drying profile between the interior and exterior.

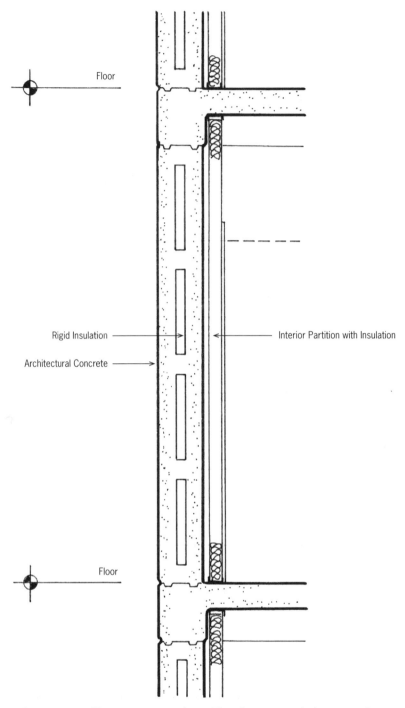

Floor

Rigid Insulation ──────────→

Architectural Concrete ──────→

Interior Partition with Insulation

Floor

FIGURE 7.12 Insulation contained between concrete planes. This often requires dual concrete placement. Continuous insulation is difficult to achieve, so an interior insulated partition is typically required.

guidance on how to achieve the intended color and finish. Architectural concrete precasters are also an excellent design phase resource to discuss colors and finishes. These companies have a wide range of experience in how to obtain the intended color and finish through use of cement, color additives, admixtures, and aggregate. They can also offer helpful advice on ingredients for the mix design.

Physical samples of architectural concrete need to be clearly specified. They must be obtained, reviewed, discussed, and agreed upon prior to construction. The method of fabricating the samples must be the same as intended for construction. Joinery and finishes of the same size and method of construction should be incorporated into the samples. After establishing a mix design, small samples of approximately 2'-0" (600 mm) × 2'-0" (600 mm) in full thickness should be developed and cast by the contractor in the manner used to create the architectural concrete. Once an agreeable color and finish are achieved through small samples, the next step is a larger-scale mock-up, or more often a series of mock-ups.

MOCK-UP(S)

Site mock-ups of project conditions are invaluable and essential in establishing standards that are mutually acceptable to the owner, architect, and builder. Mock-ups should include typical surfaces, corners, joinery, and openings. As noted with the samples, the method of constructing the mock-up should be the same as used in construction. The size of the mock-up is dependent on the extent of architectural concrete on the project, the complexity, and the budget. Mock-ups are an item to be included when developing the project budget and should not be reduced or eliminated. They more than pay for themselves.

Mock-ups should be oriented in the same direction in which the project conditions occur. If all cardinal directions (north, south, east, and west) are architectural concrete, it is advisable to orient the mock-up toward the maximum amount of sunlight. Timing of the mock-up with the construction schedule is very important. Every participant team member will learn from the mock-up. There must be enough time to incorporate lessons learned from the mock-up into the construction process.

After the mock-up is constructed, it should be used to test patching, sealers, and any other processes or products applied after concrete is placed. Concrete will experience levels of damage in construction, so testing how to achieve an acceptable patch is advisable and should be mandatory. The final mock-up serves as the acceptable project quality standard. The mock-up should exhibit the final and agreed-upon color, texture, finish, joinery, and level of craft.

Summary

Architectural concrete is a popular choice for exterior enclosure designs because of its ability to achieve unique shapes, multiple finishes, textures, colors, and joinery patterns. As an enclosure system, architectural concrete can have limitations for water protection and thermal envelope continuity. These limitations should be evaluated and understood by all participants.

Architectural concrete is extremely durable and relatively easy to maintain. Samples and mock-ups are definitely advised to achieve a project benchmark for acceptance. Achieving high-quality architectural concrete requires "How would I build it?" documents coupled with the experience and skill of the builder. The following case studies are examples of architectural concrete enclosures that highlight the positive attributes of this type of enclosure.

Architectural Concrete

United States Embassy Beijing

Location:

Beijing, People's Republic of China Building Type:

Government Office Buildings, Consulate Building, Marine Guard Quarters, Recreational Building, Parking Garage, and Entry Pavilions

Architectural concrete for the new U.S. Embassy in Beijing is crafted to match limestone to promote permanence and dignity.   *Credit: Tim Hursley*

PARTICIPANTS

Owner:

United States Government, United States Department of State

Architect:

Skidmore, Owings, & Merrill LLP – San Francisco, CA

Structural Engineer:

Skidmore, Owings, & Merrill LLP – San Francisco, CA

Mechanical Engineer:

Skidmore, Owings, & Merrill LLP – Chicago, IL

Contractor:

Zachry Caddell Joint Venture

    Zachry Construction Corporation – San Antonio, TX

    Caddell Construction Company – Montgomery, AL

Project Description

The new United States Embassy Complex in Beijing is the second-largest embassy compound ever undertaken by the United States government. The new embassy consolidates and co-locates staff and personnel from multiple disparate locations into a single compound. Eight buildings constitute the 10-acre site, which includes two office buildings, a consular services building, marine guard quarters and recreational facility, a parking garage with workshops, and perimeter entry pavilions.

The design is a fusion of Eastern and Western influences, drawing from the regional vernacular for materials and color palettes, as well as building massing and siting.

The Embassy compound is organized into three "neighborhoods": a social neighborhood with guard quarters and recreation spaces, a professional neighborhood with office space, and a consular neighborhood. This site and building organization was imperative for the creation of a design aesthetic and for serving functional needs uncompromised by mission constraints. A site plan is shown in Figure 7C1.1. A model of the embassy compound is shown in Figure 7C1.2.

The buildings are designed to maximize the qualities of natural light on a modest material palette of local granite and site batched and placed architectural concrete.

Enclosure System Types

Primary exterior elevations are architectural concrete. The limestone color with multiple finishes and profiles in the architectural concrete is achieved through steel formwork and form liners. Expressing the plastic qualities of architectural concrete, surface finishes, patterns, and textures in the facades are grouped by the character of the compound neighborhoods. The Consular entry with the United States Seal smooth finish concrete is illustrated in Fig 7C1.3.

Buildings located in the professional neighborhood consist of two sizes of shiplap profile concrete. The office building elevation with shiplap pattern is illustrated in Figure 7C1.4. Joinery in the concrete wall expanses is designed in a modular pattern to facilitate form reuse and construction sequence. Window patterns are arranged horizontally with extended aluminum sills to reflect and harvest natural daylight. The aluminum sills perform multiple functions: reflecting sunlight to the interior ceiling, reducing the use of artificial lighting, and providing enhanced weather protection for horizontal architectural concrete surfaces. Vertically oriented windows are organized at office circulation zones. Architectural concrete parapets extend to visually screen mechanical equipment.

Buildings located in the social neighborhood are board-formed architectural concrete enclosures. Formwork boards are sized in a modular pattern to align with the shiplap spacing. An elevation of board-formed concrete of the gymnasium is illustrated in Figure 7C1.5.

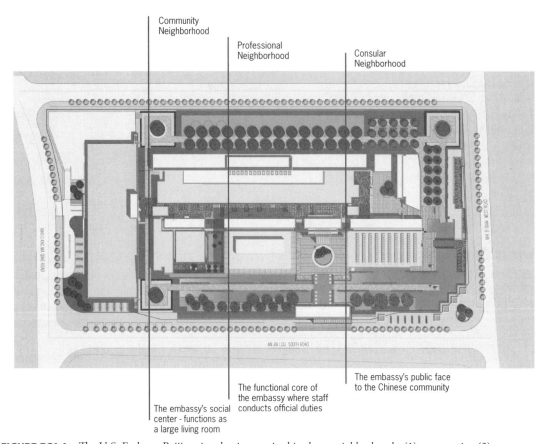

Community
Neighborhood

Professional
Neighborhood

Consular
Neighborhood

The functional core of
the embassy where staff
conducts official duties

The embassy's public face
to the Chinese community

The embassy's social
center - functions as
a large living room

FIGURE 7C1.1 The U.S. Embassy Beijing site plan is organized in three neighborhoods: (1) community, (2) professional, and (3) consular. *Skidmore, Owings & Merrill LLP*

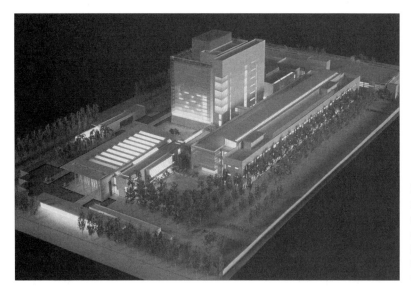

FIGURE 7C1.2 Presentation model of Embassy buildings and compound. The view is from the north, and is composed primarily of architectural concrete enclosures. *Skidmore, Owings & Merrill LLP*

FIGURE 7C1.3 The United States Great Seal is mounted to smooth architectural concrete at the Consular main entry and "front porch." ©*Timothy Hursley*

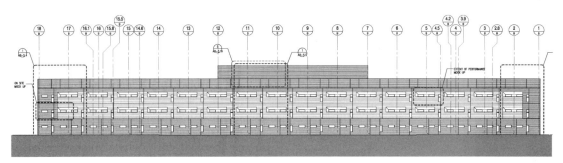

FIGURE 7C1.4 Architectural concrete enclosures for the professional neighborhood buildings are designed in an off-form finish shiplap profile. *Skidmore, Owings & Merrill LLP*

The consular neighborhood buildings are smooth off-form finish architectural concrete with a mirror-like finish and minimal construction and rustication joints. An elevation and image of the smooth finish concrete are illustrated in Figures 7C1.6a and 7C1.6b.

Enclosure System Goals

The U.S. Embassy Beijing included multiple visual and functional enclosure system performance goals. The client group's mission statement required this and other U.S. buildings to represent the best of modern American architecture in a campus of buildings that embodied a safe, secure, and functional state-of-the-art facility. Exterior materials required a variable scale design modulator for the long enclosure expanses. Color, inherent in the material, was selected to convey the timeless quality and stability of traditional limestone-clad federal buildings.

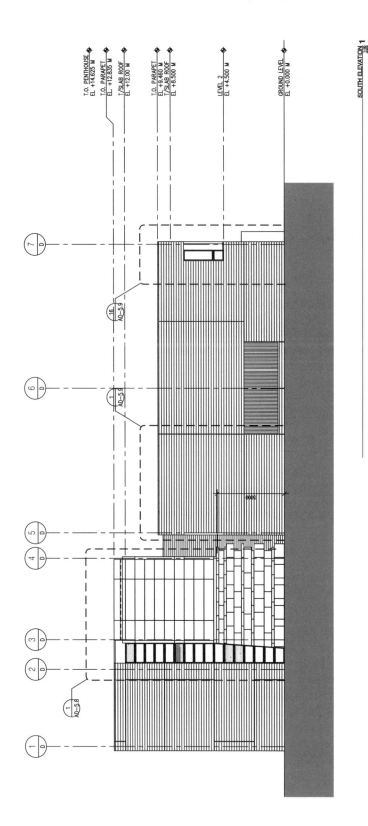

FIGURE 7C1.5 Architectural concrete enclosures for the community neighborhood buildings are designed in an off-form finish board-form concrete. The form facing board height used in the formwork matches the height of the shiplap profile utilized in the professional neighborhood architectural concrete. *Skidmore, Owings & Merrill LLP*

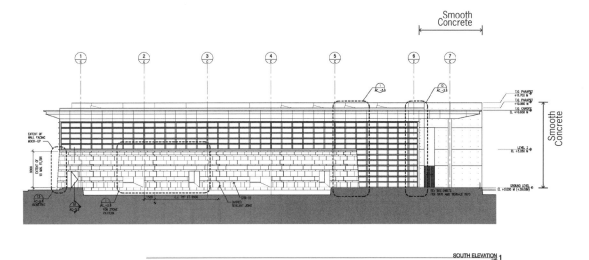

FIGURE 7C1.6a Architectural concrete enclosures for the consular neighborhood building are a smooth finish concrete with minimal rustication joinery. *Skidmore, Owings & Merrill LLP*

FIGURE 7C1.6b A view of the smooth finish architectural concrete at the consular entrance. *©Timothy Hursley*

Functional and performance requirements included low maintenance, low life-cycle costs, security, and energy performance. The enclosure design required materials that could be locally and site fabricated and yield high quality. Additionally, the exterior opaque enclosure material was required to provide thermal inertia to address the Beijing climate.

After review of multiple enclosure material options, architectural concrete with an integral limestone color was selected as a primary enclosure material and system to achieve the visual and performance goals set by the owner/architect team.

Enclosure System Design Process

SCHEMATIC DESIGN

Building organization diagrams and interior program spaces and adjacencies were tested and verified. A comprehensive repetitive plan module was defined for the site organization and each building. The plan module included a primary 29′-6-⅜″ (9 m) structural bay module with subdivisions of 4′-11″ (1.5 m) for typical modular spacing and a 1′-2-¾″ (375 mm)—a 1/4 module—for corners. A parallel study of vertical module pattern was developed for floor-to-floor heights, primary shiplap profile, and secondary (½ primary height) shiplap profiles. The board form concrete modularity matches the plan and vertical shiplap design modularity. Renderings of the office building schematic elevations are shown in Figure 7C1.7.

DESIGN DEVELOPMENT

Typical concrete-to-concrete and concrete opening detail requirements were developed by architectural and structural engineer team members. The extent of information to be illustrated by each design discipline drawing

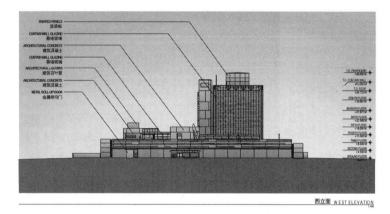

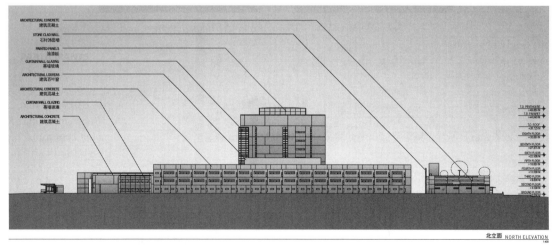

FIGURE 7C1.7　Schematic design phase building elevation renderings identify the color and primary joinery pattern of the architectural concrete.　*Skidmore, Owings & Merrill LLP*

was defined. Floor-to-floor pour heights and suggested pour lengths were evaluated for concrete placement and quantities that could be placed in a continuous pour sequence.

Diagrammatic construction joinery patterns were developed to test the concrete pour extent areas. Using the agreed-upon joint locations, rustication joinery was judiciously added, to further develop the elevation character. Outline specifications were developed for formwork, formwork facing, concrete mix design, and reinforcing.

Construction Documents

Enlarged building elevations and sections with pattern, joinery, and extent of details were developed for each bay condition per building. Examples of partial exterior bay elevations are illustrated in Figures 7C1.8, 7C1.9, and 7C1.10. A building section through the three-story architectural concrete enclosure is illustrated in Figure 7C1.11.

Details of typical and atypical concrete joinery finish and profiles were developed. Details are illustrated in Figure 7C2.12. The final concrete mix specification was developed to include a white Portland cement and color admixture to simulate Indiana limestone select buff as the final color and finish. Small sample blocks of the mix were cast to test the mix quantities and finish results. The control sample developed in the construction document phase is illustrated in Figure 7C1.13. To achieve the design profiles and develop the project specifications, form liner fabricators were consulted to determine materials, thicknesses, and suppliers. Specification submittal requirements define sample submittals for form liners.

Construction

The project delivery process for the U.S. Embassy in Beijing was design-bid-build. A presentation of the concrete drawings was conducted by the owner/architect team with the selected contractor, to explain the architectural concrete design and detail logic and document organization.

Following the submittal requirements identified in the construction documents, a series of progressive samples and mock-ups were constructed on-site, utilizing the contractor's staff personnel who were responsible for the concrete placement and execution. Concrete placement was self-performed by the contractor. Sample 4″ (100 mm) cubes were cast to achieve approval of the color rendition of the mix design. Following color and finish approval, a series of 2′-0″ × 2′-0″ (600 mm × 600 mm) sample test panels were constructed on-site with multiple form liners, to test the flow of concrete and to determine methods to minimize air pockets and surface "pockmarks." Photos of the test panel samples are shown in Figure 7C1.14. Following approval of the test panel samples, a large-scale one-floor-high × 45′-0″ (12 m) long section was cast on-site in an area adjacent to the construction, to review quality and color consistency. The mock-up was also utilized to test concrete placement methods, form tie profiles and spacing, reinforcing, interfaces at shiplap edges, and profile terminations at window openings. Images of the large-scale mock-up are shown in Figures 7C1.15 and 7C1.16.

Architectural concrete walls were constructed with custom-fabricated form liner attached to steel formwork. The form liner face sheet prior to concrete placement for the visual mock-up is illustrated in Figures 7C1.17 and 7C1.18. Construction formwork is illustrated in Figure 7C1.19. Architectural concrete at various stages of construction is illustrated in Figures 7C1.20 and 7C1.21.

The city of Beijing was in the midst of a tremendous amount of construction in preparation for the 2008 Summer Olympic Games. To monitor quality and to maximize control of the schedule, the contractor erected a concrete batch plant on-site to produce the material for the architectural concrete. The concrete mix materials were stockpiled on-site and cast in a floor-by-floor sequence.

Summary

The completed architectural concrete work represents the diligence of the owner and project team to achieve the stated project goals with a high degree of quality. The limestone-color concrete, in each of the three finishes,

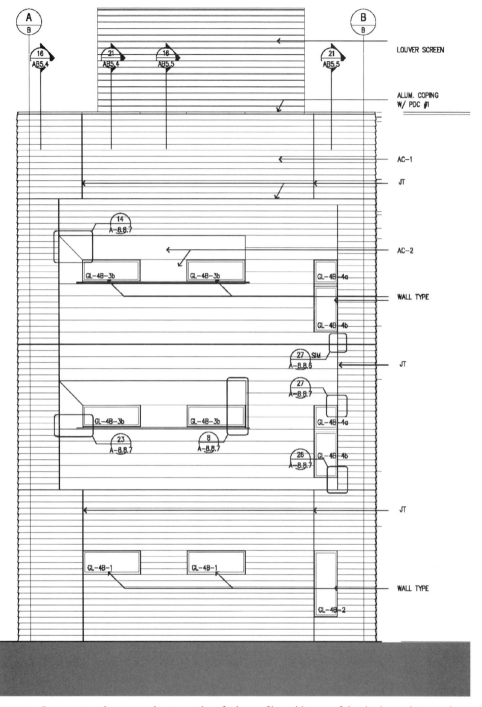

Labels on the drawing:

A / B
B

16 / AB5.4
21 / AB5.4
16 / AB5.5
21 / AB5.5

B / B

LOUVER SCREEN

ALUM. COPING W/ PDC #1

AC-1

JT

14 / A-8.8.7

AC-2

GL-4B-3b
GL-4B-3b
GL-4B-4a

WALL TYPE

GL-4B-4b

27 SIM / A-8.8.6

JT

27 / A-8.8.7

GL-4B-3b
GL-4B-3b
GL-4B-4a

23 / A-8.8.7
8 / A-8.8.7

26 / A-8.8.7
GL-4B-4b

JT

GL-4B-1
GL-4B-1

WALL TYPE

GL-4B-2

FIGURE 7C1.8 Construction document elevations identify the profile and layout of the shiplap architectural concrete and the location of the construction joinery. *Skidmore, Owings & Merrill LLP*

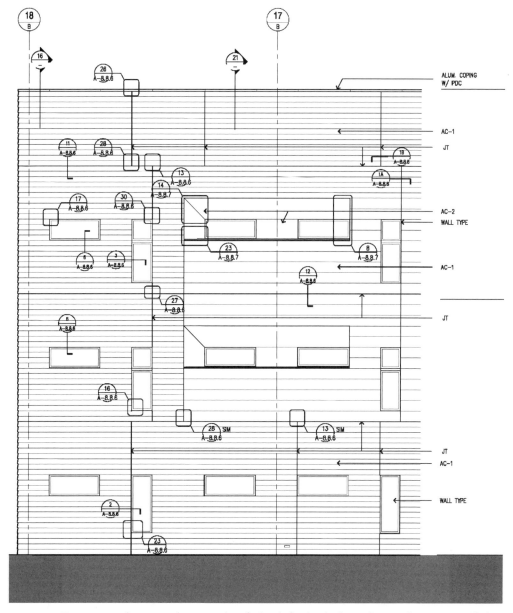

FIGURE 7C1.9 Construction document elevations identify details for the shiplap architectural concrete. *Skidmore, Owings & Merrill LLP*

results in an enclosure that provides a high level of durability. The design objective for a color range consistent with limestone coupled with a level of detail joinery and shadow was achieved through a deliberate and methodical process of detail design, knowledge transfer to the contractor, and follow-through by the owner, architect, and contractor team. Completed architectural concrete is illustrated in Figures 7C1.22, 7C1.23, and 7C1.24.

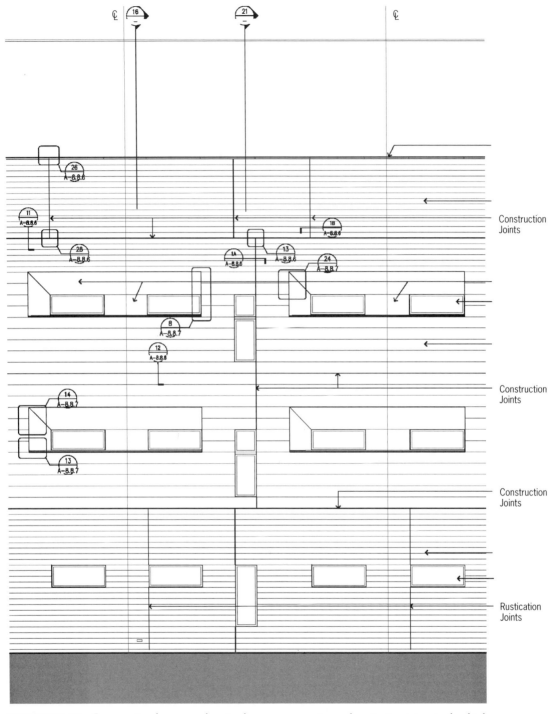

FIGURE 7C1.10   Construction document elevation locates construction and rustication joints in the shiplap architectural concrete.   *Skidmore, Owings & Merrill LLP*

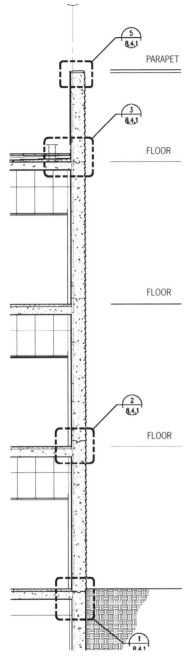

FIGURE 7C1.11 Construction document building sections identify architectural concrete placement lifts (construction joints) and shiplap profile. The architectural concrete enclosure is insulated via an interior insulated partition to achieve the project's required R-value. *Skidmore, Owings & Merrill LLP*

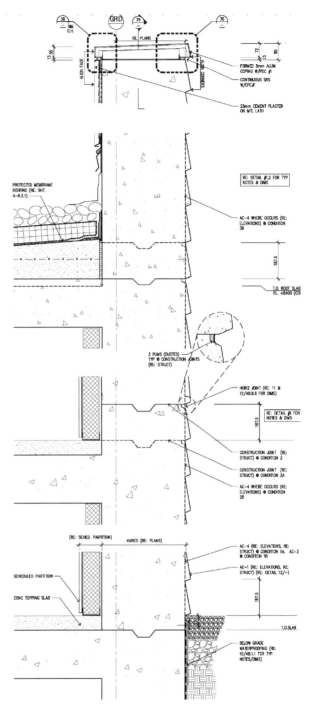

FIGURE 7C1.12 Construction document architectural concrete details illustrate profiles, placement joints (construction joints), weather protection, and thermal envelope design. *Skidmore, Owings & Merrill LLP*

FIGURE 7C1.13   Small architectural concrete samples were cast to achieve the final architectural concrete color.

FIGURE 7C1.14   Test panel samples were cast to achieve agreement on color, surface quality, and texture prior to larger architectural concrete mock-ups. Concrete sample panels were reviewed by the owner, architect, and contractor.

FIGURE 7C1.15 Full-scale, one floor high × 45'-0" (12 m) long, architectural concrete mock-ups were site-cast. The mock-up includes multiple project conditions.

FIGURE 7C1.16 View of large-scale mock-up. Note shiplap form liner adjacent to mock-up.

FIGURE 7C1.17   Architectural concrete shiplap form liner.

FIGURE 7C1.18   View inside formwork for the visual mock-up with form liner and reinforcing steel.

FIGURE 7C1.19   Architectural concrete formwork with reusable modular steel forms custom-fabricated for the project.

FIGURE 7C1.20   Construction of architectural shiplap concrete. Note formwork being removed with form liner and rustication joints.

FIGURE 7C1.21   In-progress architectural concrete construction prior to window enclosure installation.

FIGURE 7C1.22   Completed architectural shiplap concrete. The aluminum coping at the roof transition is formed in a profile to match the architectural concrete shiplap profile. Recessed horizontal surfaces at the window enclosures are formed aluminum with a high-performance coating.   *©Timothy Hursley*

FIGURE 7C1.23 Completed shiplap architectural concrete in the community neighborhood. ©*Timothy Hursley*

FIGURE 7C1.24 Completed board form architectural concrete in the community neighborhood. ©*Timothy Hursley*

Architectural Concrete

Dallas City Hall

Location:
Dallas, TX, USA
Building Type:
Municipal City Center, Plaza, Fountain, and a 1,325-Car Underground Parking Garage

PARTICIPANTS
Owner:
The City of Dallas – Dallas, TX
Design Architect:
I. M. Pei & Partners (now Pei Cobb Freed & Partners Architects LLP)
Associate Architect:
Harper & Kemp – Dallas, TX
Structural Engineer:
Terry-Rosenlund and Company – Dallas, TX
Mechanical Engineer:
Gaynor and Sirmen – Dallas, TX
Contractor:
Robert E. McKee, Inc. – Dallas, TX

Project Description

Design of the Dallas City Hall, originally called the Municipal Administration Center, involved more than just the building. When planning began in 1966, the area around the site located in the northeast area of downtown Dallas was sparsely developed. The city of Dallas civic leadership envisioned a symbolic building to define the quality and character of a new civic center. The new City Hall required an iconic building and an open and inviting civic space. The original 7-acre site was expanded by 10 acres, creating a combination of building, park, and fountain. Dallas City Hall, at 560'-0" long (170.7 m), is a horizontal skyscraper, creating an iconic civic presence, contributing open space, and serving as a catalyst for development in the surrounding area. A ground-floor site plan is presented in Figure 7C2.1.

The building is a mix of an expressive exterior material and innovative engineering and construction. The 113'-0" (34.44 m) tall architectural concrete structure cantilevers and slopes at a 34 degree angle along the northern elevation facing the plaza and fountain. Each floor is 9'-4" (2.844 m) wider than the one below. Dallas City Hall is 126'-0" (38.4 m) wide at the ground floor and 200'-0" (61 m) wide at the uppermost floor. The sloping north elevation is illustrated in Figure 7C2.2. The building is seven floors above grade, housing 775,000 sq. ft. (72,000 sq. m) of office and city administration, and two floors below grade, with parking and support functions. The building form has symbolic and functional logic. The sloping architectural concrete enclosure serves as a "front porch" welcoming approaching pedestrians, providing shelter from rain and the intense Texas sun. A transverse section through the building, Figure 7C2.3, illustrates the sloped north face. East and west elevations also cantilever in an inverted stairstep configuration. The west cantilever is illustrated in Figure 7C2.4.

The cantilevered floors of the sloping northern façade are supported by 14 bearing walls, each 18" (460 mm) thick, organized in seven pairs. There are two groups of paired concrete walls. One group flanks the three stair towers, and the second group of four pairs is 14'-0" (4.27 m) outside to outside face. The building plan module is 4'-8" (1.42 m)—thus the additional 9'-6" cantilever width per floor (2 modules of 4'-8"). Long-span post-tensioned architectural concrete spans 65'-4" (19.91 m) between the four pairs of concrete walls. Architectural concrete is the finish material employed for the exterior enclosure and in the interiors as exposed walls and coffered concrete ceilings.

Enclosure System Types

Dallas City Hall is site-placed architectural concrete. Multiple shapes and finished composition respond to the intended function.

Large wall expanses of architectural concrete are used to express the 34 degree slope on the east and west elevation and the stairstep cantilevered floors of the southwest and southeast corners. The west stairstep cantilever

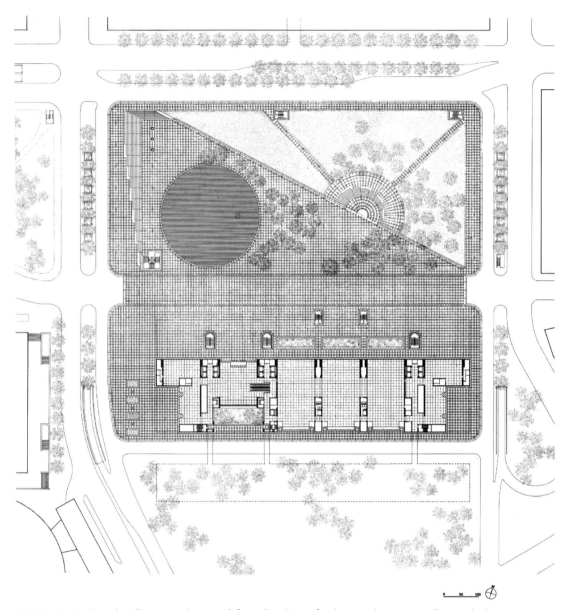

FIGURE 7C2.1 Site plan illustrating the ground-floor plan. Pairs of architectural concrete walls provide the primary building structure and elevator enclosures. *Pei Cobb Freed & Partners*

and south wall expanse are illustrated in Figure 7C2.5. Subtle architectural concrete formwork joints and form ties are visible in the concrete wall surfaces. These joints are organized horizontally at the floor beam level and vertically spanning between the beam levels at floors.

Long-span architectural concrete beams span 65'-4" (19.91 m) between the pairs of walls on the north elevation and between large wall expanses on the east, west, and south. Form joints are carefully concealed in the visible beam profiles, enhancing the monolithic long-span function. An image of the sloping beam profile and sloping window wall detail is shown in Figure 7C2.6.

Exterior Building Enclosures

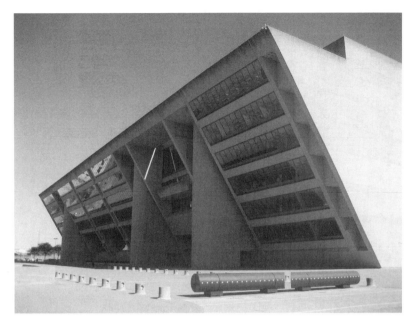

FIGURE 7C2.2 The north elevation slopes out at 34 degrees from vertical. Each ascending floor is 9'-6" (two 4'-8" modules) larger than the floor below.

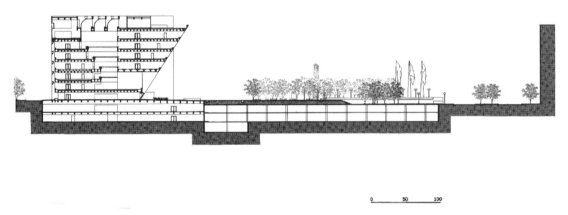

FIGURE 7C2.3 Transverse section (view from east) of the sloping north face and brise soleil sunshades on the south elevation. *Pei Cobb Freed & Partners*

Cast-in-place architectural concrete sunscreens are suspended from the beams on the upper floor of the east and west façade and on floors 3–7 of the south façade. Sunscreens and recessed windows provide solar shading for the majority of the day while preserving unobstructed occupant views. The south sunscreen is illustrated in Figure 7C2.7.

Construction joints between pours are located at the top and bottom of beams expressing the construction sequence logistics. Long-span beams are monolithic concrete, spanning from primary concrete transverse walls. Openings in the concrete enclosure are recessed on the east, west, and south from the primary building face, providing punctuation on the façade and solar shading. The sloping metal-framed and glass assemblies on the north elevation span from concrete spandrel beam to spandrel beam.

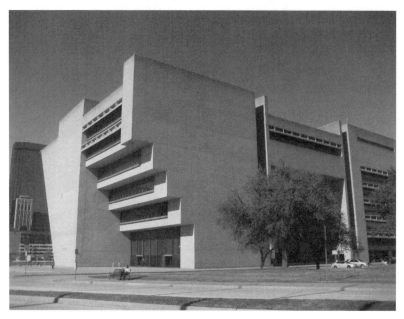

FIGURE 7C2.4 The southwest corner cantilevers in a stairstep profile at floor structure and concrete placement locations. Note the subtle formwork joinery.

FIGURE 7C2.5 The inverted stairstep cantilever on the west elevation provides solar shading for the window enclosure system at each floor.

FIGURE 7C2.6 The long-span concrete beam is sloped at 34 degrees, matching the sloping elevation profile. Window frames are recessed at the sill, providing shadow line and additional detail.

FIGURE 7C2.7 The south elevation windows are recessed with cantilevered architectural concrete brise soleil.

Enclosure System Goals

Then mayor of Dallas, Eric Jonsson, created the "Goals for Dallas" program to transform the city's tarnished image in the wake of the 1964 Kennedy assassination. He stated, "We demand a city of beauty and functional fitness that embraces the quality of life for all its people." This client and civic goal was the impetus to build a new city hall to replace the outdated and outgrown existing structure.

Monumental geometric gestures coupled with monumental quality were essential to the design. I. M. Pei has been quoted that he wanted the building to feel like an organic product of North Texas. This goal was achieved by the buff-colored concrete that recalls the local Dallas earth tones. Architectural concrete's durability to withstand high use with little maintenance, the inherent diurnal heat lag, and the "plastic" capability to achieve the building's forms and long spans are qualities that led to the material selection for the exterior enclosure and the majority of exposed interior walls and ceiling.

Enclosure System Design Process

SCHEMATIC DESIGN

The building plan and section organization is the result of space plan requirements of city government departments. Dallas City Hall is a building open to the public. Public interface functions yielded smaller floor area requirements at the ground levels and larger office space floor needs on the floors above. This led to a planning diagram with smaller floors at grade and increasing floor areas high up, to house government offices. Occupant program and stacking studies in plan and section revealed the smaller-to-larger floor plan requirements and the resulting cantilevered building forms.

Architectural concrete was contemplated for the primary structural and architectural enclosure material because it was the only material the city could afford that met the design criteria. In response to the visual top-heavy sloped and cantilevered north face, three cylindrical concrete volumes containing stairwells originally hidden within the building were relocated to the exterior, to provide visual support. These stairwells, illustrated in Figure 7C2.8, do not actually bear the load of the cantilever surfaces. A design sketch of the exterior form is shown in Figure 7C2.9.

DESIGN DEVELOPMENT

A design philosophy of the architectural team is "honesty of materials." The use of solid materials that are homogenous and not veneered led to the selection of architectural concrete. Exposed concrete wall surfaces were originally designed as board form finish, which would produce a finished texture, as illustrated in Figure 7C2.10. To accommodate project cost parameters, board forming was revised to 14-ply phenolic resin plywood for the form facing. The phenolic plywood form resulted in a smooth concrete finish. An additional benefit is the ability to reuse the plywood-faced forms. Formwork design development details were developed in parallel with the various shapes, planes, and building geometries. Board form finish was utilized in site walls and select interior areas.

Construction Documents

The consistency of the architectural concrete color range is evident in the finished work. Concrete color was a primary focus in the design and documentation phases. At the time of design and construction (1972–1977), integral admixtures to achieve colored concrete, which are available in the construction market today, were not available. It is typical to use white Portland cement and color admixtures. The buff color achieved at Dallas City Hall resulted from the use of buff-colored Portland cement. This Portland cement was made by oxidizing the clinker in the kiln. Other variables in the mix, such as cement and aggregate properties, water to cement ratios, variations from ready-mix batches, and curing processes, were researched, discussed, documented, and agreed upon.

FIGURE 7C2.8 The stair towers are enclosed in cylindrical architectural concrete enclosures.

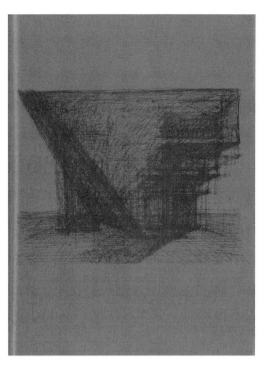

FIGURE 7C2.9 A design hand-sketch of the building form and profile. *Pei Cobb Freed & Partners*

FIGURE 7C2.10 The original design for architectural concrete of the Dallas City Hall was board form concrete. As a result of cost reductions, it was revised to a smooth off-form finish. The board form finish was retained for architectural concrete site walls.

FIGURE 7C2.11   View of the north wall, sculpture, and reflecting pool. The photo was taken 31 years after project completion.

Construction

Mock-ups were constructed to familiarize the construction, design, and owner team with construction practices and the expected final product. A freestanding mock-up, 14'-0" (4.3 m) wide, 23'-4" (7.11 m) long, and one story high, included the sloped window and frame assemblies and nine ceiling coffers.[1] Concrete mix, placing, and curing procedures were reviewed after the mock-up. Modifications to enhance the finished product from lessons learned in the mock-up were implemented prior to concrete placement in the building.

In addition to the valuable lessons learned from the mock-up, the placement of architectural concrete in the basement levels provided on-site locations to further adjust and refine the mix and placement. Forms were left in place for longer time frames and covered with wet mats to cure the architectural concrete.

Challenges

In addition to the color and formwork considerations noted, an important issue, both visually and structurally, was to minimize shrinkage cracking in the concrete. The design engineering and construction team toured areas of Texas observing large cast-in-place concrete buildings, paying attention to cracking characteristics. Different aggregates and mix designs were tested through multiple sample panel castings, but none was entirely satisfactory.

The project structural engineer had previous experience with shrinkage–compensating concrete, which would provide the needed control of drying-shrinkage cracking and reduce loss of post-tensioning force due to drying shrinkage.[2] A local cement producer was a licensee of the patent for Type K cement, used to make shrinkage-compensating concrete. For the Dallas City Hall, a specific buff-colored Type K cement was developed.[3]

Summary

The photos included in the case study were taken in March 2011. This is 34 years after completion. The concrete surfaces and finishes have aged gracefully and are in remarkable visual condition. The current visible condition of the architectural concrete exterior is a testament to the perseverance and quality demanded and practiced by the owner, architect, structural engineer, and construction team. A view of the north architectural concrete elevation with fountain and floating sculpture in the foreground is illustrated in Figure 7C2.11.

---

[1]Steven Miller. "Engineering a Pei Cantilever," *Architecture Week*, August 2009.

[2]Jack E. Rosenlund. "Use of Shrinkage-Compensating Cement Concrete in the Dallas Municipal Center." American Concrete Institute, Special Publication 64, July 1980.

[3]Steven Miller. "Engineering a Pei Cantilever," *Architecture Week*, August 2009.

Chapter 8

Metal Framing and Glass

The building is like a book. Its architecture is the binding; its text is in the glass and sculpture.

MALCOLM MILLER

Overview

Metal framing and glass is a broad category of exterior enclosure systems that includes storefront, window wall, and curtain wall systems. The metal framing components are primarily aluminum, but also include stainless steel, bronze, or other architectural quality metals. Infill supported by or within the framing includes transparent or opaque materials. Transparent infill materials include insulating, laminated, or monolithic glass; polycarbonates; and thermoplastics. Opaque infill materials include architectural metals such as aluminum, stainless steel, or bronze; natural stone; fiber reinforced panels; terra cotta; or louvers.

Metal framed and glass enclosures, particularly curtain walls with aluminum framing, date from the early twentieth century. This design and construction technology developed rapidly after World War II, when the supply of aluminum was more available for nonmilitary use.[1]

There are subtle yet specific differences in the definitions of the metal framing and glass systems noted above. For this chapter and the associated case studies, system definitions are:

Storefront: A floor-to-floor or floor-to-underside-of-structure enclosure, either one or multiple stories high, located at the base of a building. Plan extents vary, including column-to-column, multicolumn width, or completely enclosing a floor area.

Window wall: Floor-to-floor, floor-to-ceiling, or floor-to-underside-of-enclosure supported within the building structure at the sill and head. Plan extents vary, including column-to-column, wall-to-wall, or enclosing on itself expanse of framing and glass. Window walls include fixed and operable window openings.

Curtain wall: A metal framing and glass (or other infill material) enclosure supported from and outboard of the building structure.

Diagrams of the three systems noted above shown in Figures 8.1, 8.2, and 8.3. These systems are further classified by their design construction fabrication and installation methods, as:

1. Stick: A stick system is composed of vertical and horizontal framing members with infill of glass, aluminum, stone, or other materials. Framing members are usually extruded aluminum, but can be other architectural-quality metals, shop-fabricated to size with shop-applied finishes and assembled on-site to the designed framing configuration. Infill materials, infill attachments, system anchorages, sealants, and gaskets are installed at the project site.

2. Unitized: A unitized system is composed of shop-fabricated and assembled frames with glass or other infill materials. The shop-fabricated

---

[1]Whole Building Design Guide – Curtain Walls www.wbdg.org/design/env_fenestration_cw.php

365

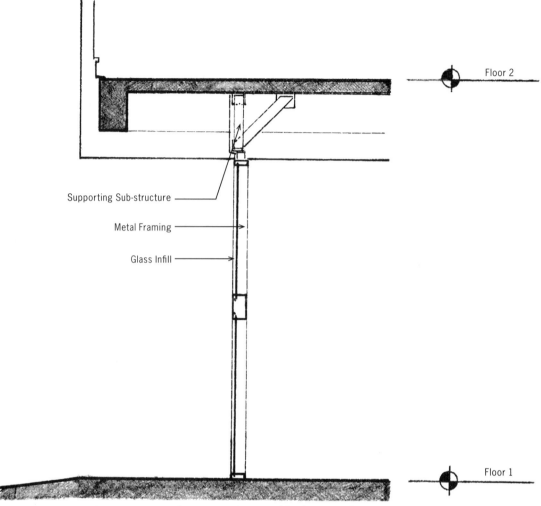

Supporting Sub-structure

Metal Framing

Glass Infill

Floor 2

Floor 1

FIGURE 8.1 A storefront system typically occurs at the ground level or base of a structure. The storefront is one or multiple floors high and often includes entrances. The supporting substructure may be steel, aluminum, or other framing. An air barrier should be designed with the substructure.

"unit" assemblies are shipped to the project site and installed on system anchors preset onto the structure or substructure. Units mate together with adjacent units along the jamb (vertical), head (top), and sill (bottom) edges. Shop fabrication for unitized assemblies typically allows for higher quality because the fabrication and assembly occur in a controlled shop or factory environment, in lieu of the construction site.

3. Unitized on a stick: A unit on a stick system is composed of vertical or horizontal framing members—the sticks—of either aluminum or

steel. Sticks are attached to the building structure or substructure with preset anchors. Units are shop-assembled. Sticks are erected and attached to the building structure, and units are installed on system anchors on the sticks at the project site. The primary difference between this and a unitized system is the addition of a more robust "stick" to accommodate higher lateral loading, taller floor-to-floor areas, or multiple unit frames within a floor-to-floor area.

4. Column cover/spandrel panel: A column cover/ spandrel panel system is composed of panelized

Exterior Building Enclosures

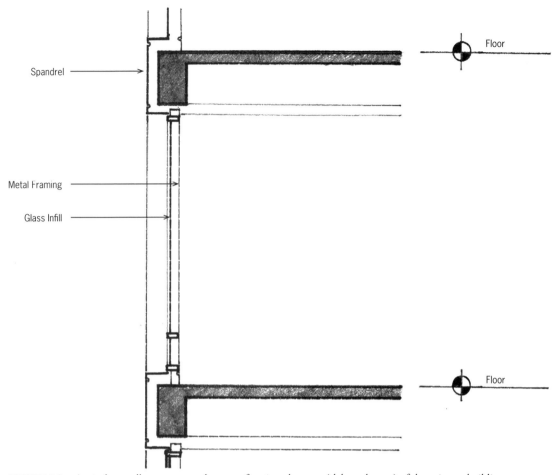

Spandrel →

Metal Framing ————→

Glass Infill ————————→

Floor

Floor

FIGURE 8.2   A window wall system spans between framing elements (slabs or beams) of the primary building structure.

column covers and/or panelized spandrels. Infill areas between column covers and spandrels consist of stick or unitized framing with glass or other infill materials. Systems with only spandrels and continuous lengths of metal-framed and glass infill are often referred to as "ribbon windows."

Diagrams of system classifications are shown in Figures 8.4 (stick), 8.5 (unitized), 8.6 (unitized on a stick), and 8.7 (column cover/spandrel panel).

Design

Metal framed and glass systems can be manufacturer's standard, customized standard, or custom design.

Unlimited design options are achieved by framing patterns, infill materials, metal types, infill attachment methods, colors, and finishes. Performance principles and levels vary between system classification types. System type and weather protection concept inherent with each system influence the design joinery. This is discussed in the "Weather Protection" section of this chapter and in the case studies presented.

STANDARD ENCLOSURES

Many manufacturers offer standard metal-framed systems. These systems typically have been tested and have defined span lengths. Weather protection options, structural performance, and thermal performance

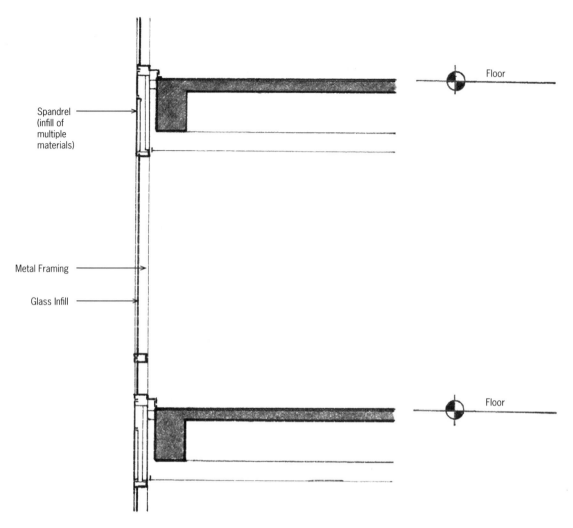

Spandrel
(infill of
multiple
materials)

Metal Framing

Glass Infill

Floor

Floor

FIGURE 8.3 A curtain wall system spans outboard of the primary building structure.

design data are available for standard enclosures. Architects implementing standard systems should verify that the selected standard system can perform to the design configuration and performance requirements established for the project.

CUSTOMIZED STANDARD

Many manufacturers of standard systems can accommodate a level of customization. Visual customization includes exterior profiles for attaching glass or other infill, which can be custom-fabricated to suit the design profiles. A wide variety of finishes

and colors can be customized per project requirements. Structural performance can be enhanced and "customized" with additional interior reinforcing to accommodate increased span distances or higher lateral loads. System structural customization should be discussed and verified between the architect and the system manufacturer. Weather protection performance criteria for air and water control are determined by the manufacturer's tests or calculations. Customizing enhanced air and water control should also be discussed with the manufacturer to determine what, if any, enhancements are achievable.

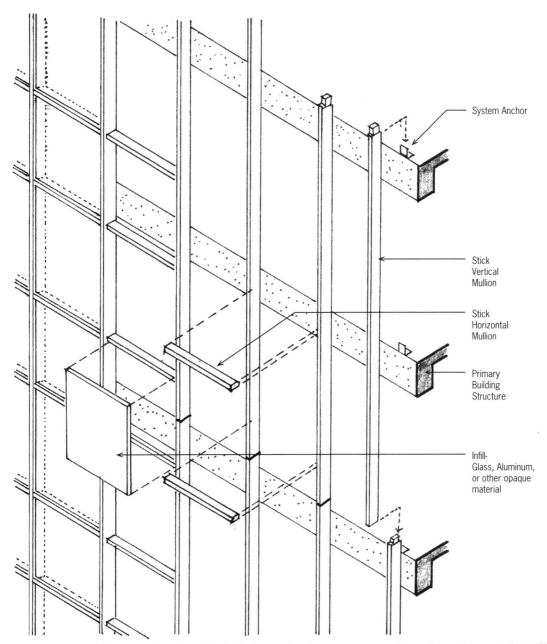

FIGURE 8.4 Metal framing referred to as "sticks." Along with other components such as sealants, glass, and other infill, these components are shop-fabricated and field-installed in a stick system. Sticks can be one or multiple floors tall.

CUSTOM

Custom designs are usually implemented on large-scale or highly design-specific projects. Custom design can be performed by the architect and design team, or in collaboration between the architect/design team and an enclosure company. Enclosure companies are typically a contractor that has design, engineering, fabrication, assembly, and construction expertise and personnel. Custom designs include specific performance requirements, including, but

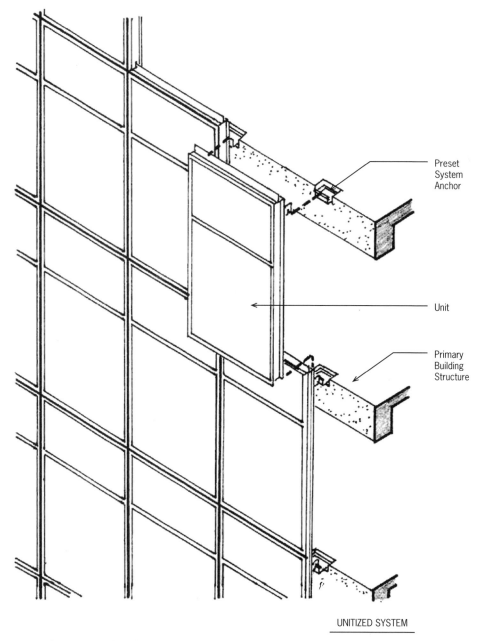

Preset System Anchor

Unit

Primary Building Structure

UNITIZED SYSTEM

FIGURE 8.5 Unitized systems are shop-fabricated and shop-assembled as completed units, with infill materials such as glass, aluminum, and other infill materials. Units are typically one floor tall and field-installed on preset system anchors.

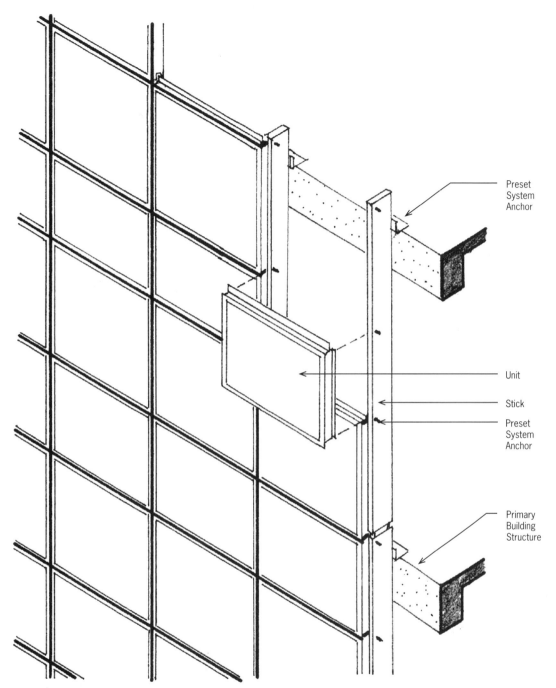

Preset
System
Anchor

Unit

Stick

Preset
System
Anchor

Primary
Building
Structure

FIGURE 8.6   In a unit on a stick system, stick framing is shop-fabricated and anchored to preset system anchors. Shop-fabricated and shop-assembled "units" are installed on the sticks at the project site.

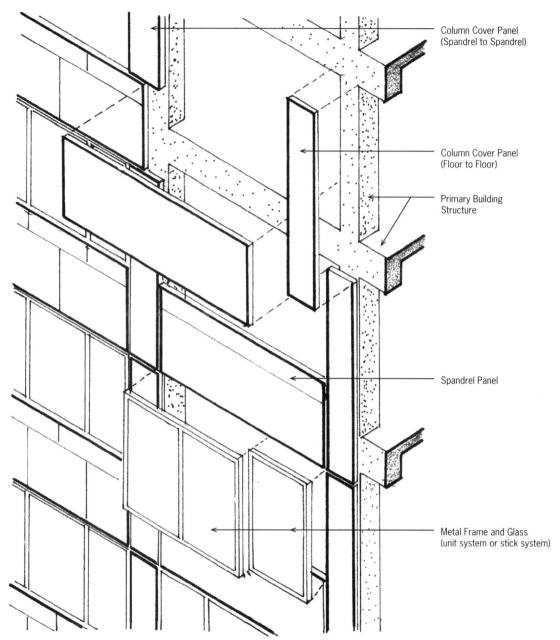

Column Cover Panel
(Spandrel to Spandrel)

Column Cover Panel
(Floor to Floor)

Primary Building
Structure

Spandrel Panel

Metal Frame and Glass
(unit system or stick system)

FIGURE 8.7 Column cover panels and/or spandrel panels are shop-fabricated and -assembled and installed on the primary building structure. The openings created by the column cover and spandrel panels are stick-built or unitized framing and glass or other infill.

Exterior Building Enclosures

not limited to, structural, weather protection, occupant comfort, acoustics, daylighting, thermal, blast, integration of other building systems and often special materials, profiles, configurations, finishes, and other design-related items.

Enclosure Structural Considerations

Metal framed and glass enclosures are typically non-load-bearing. The infill material and framing are designed to accommodate lateral loads, such as wind and seismic, and transfer them to the primary building structure or a backup framing system. Structural considerations are:

1. The framing, infill or cladding, cladding anchorage, and system anchorage systems
2. The influence of the building structural system on the enclosure and enclosure joinery

FRAMING, INFILL, AND SYSTEM ANCHORAGE

METAL FRAMED AND GLASS SYSTEMS HAVE FOUR PRIMARY ZONES:

1. Framing
2. Infill or cladding materials
3. Infill or cladding anchorage
4. System anchorage

A diagram of the zones, using a unitized curtain wall as an example, is shown in Figure 8.8. Other systems are similar.

Framing

The span (height or width) of framing members and the tributary area between framing members determine the depth, thickness, and geometry of the framing members. A tributary area diagram for a framing system is shown in Figure 8.9. The framing considered is aluminum or steel. Steel framing members are selected by the grade, shape, and size required to achieve the necessary strength and deflection criteria. Aluminum framing is typically extruded in shapes, profiles, and thickness to accommodate structural

and weather protection performance requirements. Extrusions can be designed in a wide variety of profiles and thicknesses to accommodate the span, the infill or cladding attachment method, and system anchorage. System framing is deflection-based design. Industry standards for deflection perpendicular to the plane of the enclosure are typically L (the span)/175 or ¾" maximum deflection for spans up to 13'-6" (4,115 mm) or L/240 + ¼" (6 mm) for taller vertical spans up to 40'-0".[2] Framing member vertical deflection is dependent on what function the horizontal member is performing and the infill. Horizontal members supporting glass and other infill will typically be limited to ⅛" (3 mm) deflection vertically. Horizontal framing members spanning openings for doors or other should be defined in a project case-by-case for the design and layout configuration.

Infill

The infill's size and thickness are determined by its ability to accommodate and transfer lateral loads to the framing system. There are multiple infill attachment methods. Glass infill is typically either captured, adhered with structural silicone, or attached with combinations of the two. "Captured glass" is held with aluminum framing and gaskets. Captured glass infill attachments include glazing clips, pressure plates, or glazing adapters. Adhered glass is attached to the metal framing with silicone adhesive.

Designs for climates requiring thermal breaks introduce material other than metal to transfer the glass dead load and wind load to the framing members and reduce direct thermal transmission from exterior to interior. The thermal break material occurs between the enclosure structural framing and the infill attachment. Special care in design and detail drawing review should be exercised for the structural capacity and weatherproofing continuity of thermal break materials.

Examples of glass infill attachment methods are illustrated in Figures 8.10a and 8.10b. Each infill attachment method has its pros and cons for visual and performance issues. Attachment methods influence

---

[2]American Architectural Manufacturers Association, TIR A-11: 2004, "Maximum Allowable Deflection Of Framing Systems For Building Cladding Components At Design Winds Loads."

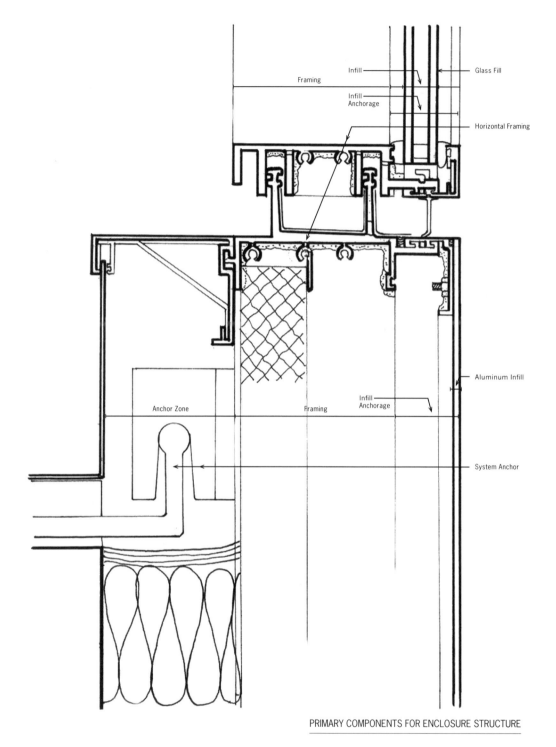

Infill
Glass Fill
Framing
Infill
Anchorage
Horizontal Framing

Aluminum Infill

Anchor Zone
Framing
Infill
Anchorage

System Anchor

PRIMARY COMPONENTS FOR ENCLOSURE STRUCTURE

FIGURE 8.8 The four primary zones of framing depth, anchor zone, infill anchorage, and infill for the vision glass and opaque area of a curtain wall.

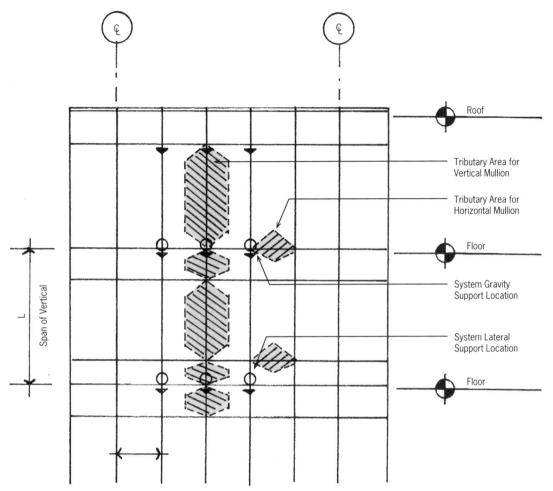

FIGURE 8.9 The infill materials (glass, aluminum, or other) transfer lateral loads to the system framing. The framing tributary area and the magnitude of the load influence the size, thickness, and design of the framing members and profiles.

profiles and joinery, and also define whether the glass is installed from the exterior or interior. This is an important design and performance consideration for the initial installation, reglazing, and long-term maintenance. Reglazing options are illustrated in Figure 8.10c.

Infill Attachment

Infill attachment can be in the same zone or plane as the infill, or in a separate zone between infill and the framing. Stone or metal panels, such as aluminum held

with concealed infill attachments, often require a larger dimension than the glazing adapters used for glass.

Methods of infill attachment to the framing must be understood by the architect for visual and performance issues, and are typically shown schematically by the architect. Final design of adapters and infill anchors and attachments is typically performed by the enclosure contractor to fulfill visual and performance requirements. Horizontal to vertical intersections of all infill attachments require close study for visual composition, structural capacity, and weather protection continuity.

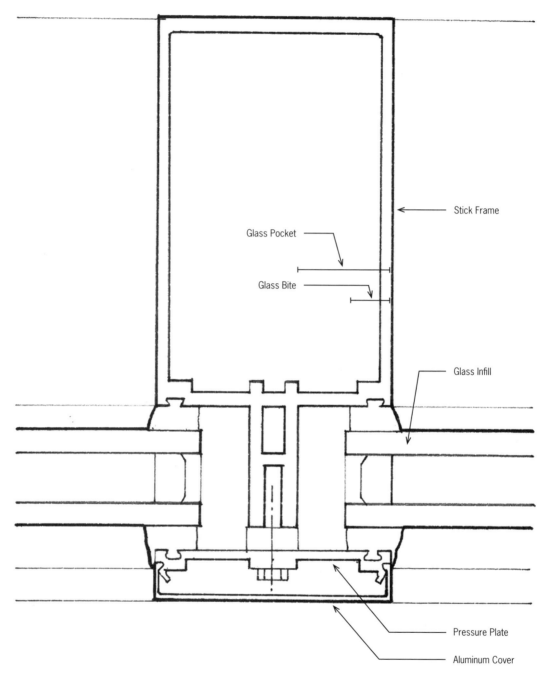

Stick Frame

Glass Pocket

Glass Bite

Glass Infill

Pressure Plate

Aluminum Cover

Note: Stick system vertical
mullion illustrated.

FIGURE 8.10a Glass infill is "captured" between the stick framing and the pressure plate. A stick wall vertical mullion is shown for example.

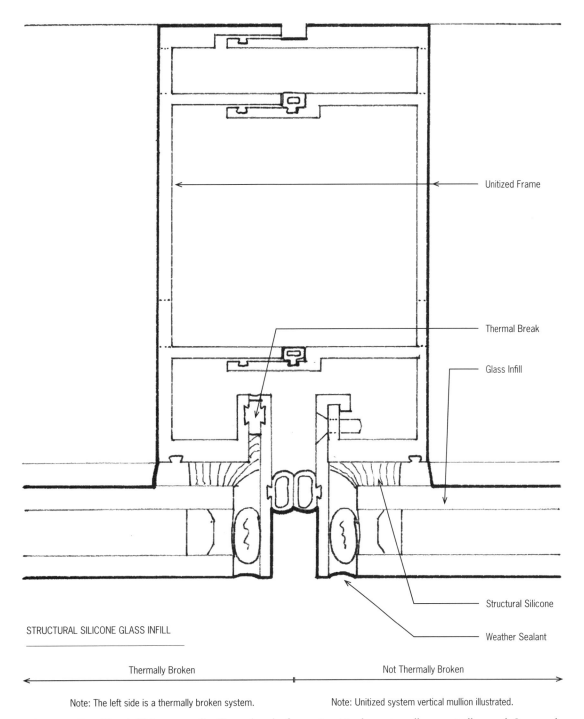

STRUCTURAL SILICONE GLASS INFILL

Unitized Frame

Thermal Break

Glass Infill

Structural Silicone

Weather Sealant

Thermally Broken | Not Thermally Broken

Note: The left side is a thermally broken system. Note: Unitized system vertical mullion illustrated.

FIGURE 8.10b Glass infill is structurally siliconed to the frame. A unitized curtain wall system is illustrated. Structural silicone adhesion requires careful preparation and installation to achieve proper adhesion of glass infill to framing.

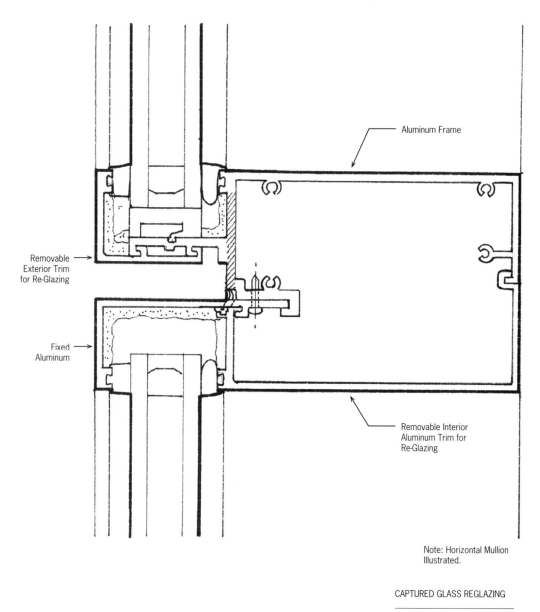

Aluminum Frame

Removable
Exterior Trim
for Re-Glazing

Fixed
Aluminum

Removable Interior
Aluminum Trim for
Re-Glazing

Note: Horizontal Mullion
Illustrated.

CAPTURED GLASS REGLAZING

FIGURE 8.10c   Glass infill is "captured" between fixed aluminum and a removable aluminum section. The upper piece of glass shown can be removed from the exterior. The lower piece of glass shown can be removed from the interior. Removal is achieved by removing gaskets to release the interlocking hooks of the aluminum.

System Anchorage

System anchorage is the device that attaches the metal framing to the primary building structure. The primary building structure typically has either embedded anchors, plates, or other assemblies to attach the system anchorage. These can occur at slabs, beams, columns, or combinations of these. The space required in design for the system anchorage is dependent on the metal frame system classification (stick, unit, etc.), performance criteria, and whether the system anchors attach to the face or the top of the primary building structure. The architect should

378

define the system anchor location and layout in the design and detail phases. This allows the structural engineer to include enclosure reactions, location of reactions, and load path of the enclosure forces in the primary building structural design and detailing. Additionally, the architect should dimensionally define the anchorage zone, which is the clear dimension inclusive of construction tolerances allocated for the system anchor. The system anchorage accommodates structural system and enclosure installation tolerances. The architectural design and detail is a schematic of the system anchor that illustrates enclosure attachment and basis of design for the enclosure movement characteristics for lateral loads. Actual system anchor design is by the contractor or enclosure contractor. The system anchor location must be designed with an eye toward insulation, fire safety continuity, and slab-edge closures.

BUILDING STRUCTURE INFLUENCE ON METAL FRAMED AND GLASS ENCLOSURES

Primary building structure (columns, beams, slabs, etc.) and associated movement characteristics under loading influence the joinery of the metal framed and glass enclosure. Metal framing and infill system dead load typically attach to the perimeter structural framing members or slab via the enclosure system anchor. Structural frame dead load deflection should be verified if already achieved prior to the installation of the system. In some instances, if the enclosure installation begins prior to structural completion, consult with the structural engineer for dead load deflection and/or column shortening values. Deflection due to the enclosure self-load must be accounted for in the primary building structural design for deflection.

The primary building structure live load deflection must be accounted for in the metal-framed system joinery design. Joint locations where the primary building structure deflections are accommodated require either:

1. Soft joinery materials, usually sealant with a compressible backer
2. Gasket joinery, either visible or concealed

Both of these approaches result in movement joints.

Live load deflections, system thermal expansion, and tolerances when added, typically determine the size of the movement joint. In buildings with large amounts of drift, the drift movement may determine the movement joint size. Joint material movement capacity characteristics in conjunction with the movement values, determine the final movement joint size. Sealant joinery design and sizing require a review and understanding of the primary structural system deflection and the movement capacity of the joint material. Joinery utilizing gaskets in either a visible or concealed arrangement requires continuous contact between gaskets and metal surfaces. The joint size with visible or concealed gaskets will require enough space for movement and for installation. A live load deflection diagram and the resultant sealant or gasket joint size is indicated in Figure 8.11. Joinery must be sized and designed for the typical metal framing and glass infill enclosure wall, openings, inside and outside corners, cantilevers, and parapet conditions.

Metal framed and glass infill enclosure systems behave as panels retaining the original geometric shape or deforming frames. The shape of the framed system will behave according to the system framing connections (jamb-to-head and jamb-to-sill), the infill and infill attachment method, and the schematic of the system anchorage. Lateral movement of the primary building structural frame, induced by wind pressure and seismic forces, is referred to as "drift." When the structural frame drifts, floors displace in relation to each other, and columns bend parallel and perpendicular to the enclosure. Enclosure joinery and the infill attachment method must accommodate structural drift. Drift parallel to a metal framed and glass infill enclosure creates joinery design conditions at the head, jamb, sill, and corners. Metal framed and glass infill can tip and rotate, slide, or deform to a parallelogram. Enclosure diagrams of the three movement conditions created by structural drift parallel to the enclosure plane are shown in Figures 8.12, 8.13, and 8.14. Each of the three movements will require design for the typical condition within the system, corner conditions, and interfaces with other systems or adjacent materials. Drift perpendicular to the metal framed and glass infill enclosure induces a tipping effect. The enclosure rotates about the movement joint during floor displacement. Primary building structure movement parallel and perpendicular results in corner conditions that must address both movements concurrently. Examples of

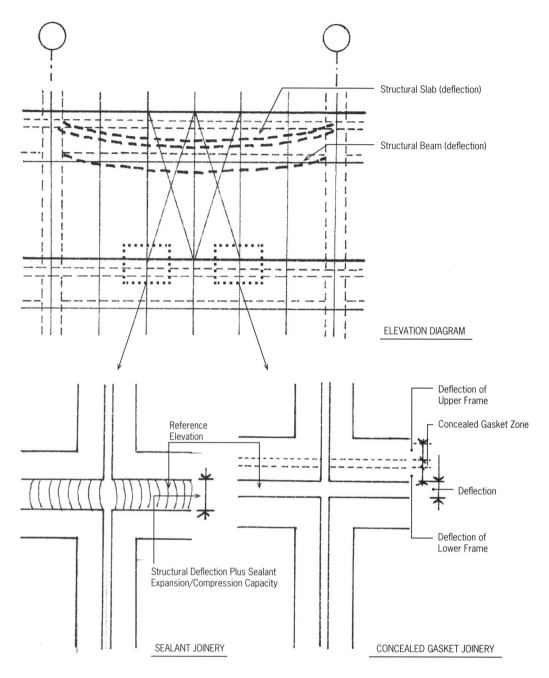

Structural Slab (deflection)

Structural Beam (deflection)

ELEVATION DIAGRAM

Deflection of
Upper Frame

Concealed Gasket Zone

Reference
Elevation

Deflection

Deflection of
Lower Frame

Structural Deflection Plus Sealant
Expansion/Compression Capacity

SEALANT JOINERY

CONCEALED GASKET JOINERY

FIGURE 8.11 Live load deflection can be accommodated by the enclosure in several ways. The sealant joinery results in a joint size typically two times the movement. The concealed gasket joinery has an exterior joint smaller than the sealant type, but a larger metal profile to accommodate the concealed gasket.

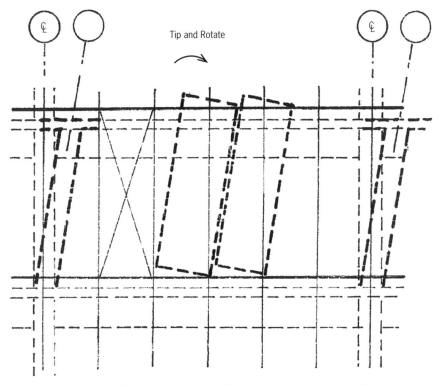

Tip and Rotate

FIGURE 8.12 Building structural drift can be accommodated in the enclosure in multiple design approaches. For frames that remain rectangular with glass infill, this system can tip and rotate parallel to the enclosure plane.

corner conditions are illustrated in the case studies in this chapter.

Weather Protection

Storefront, window wall, and curtain wall enclosure systems can employ a barrier, rain screen, or rain screen/pressure-equalized approach for protection from air and water infiltration to the interior occupied spaces. The rain screen and pressure-equalization chamber varies in joinery and depth, depending on the system. A rain screen pressure-equalized concept in an aluminum and glass enclosure is very similar to other types of enclosures. However, the level of attention to detail, the materials used, and their intersections are typically more complicated. The complication should not deter or alarm the architect. It is a mindset. A basic knowledge of "how to" goes a long way toward demystifying the complexity. When explaining the weather protection basics, pictures are

worth thousands of words. The following paragraphs describe the weather protection concepts utilized in each of the system classification types.

Stick wall: The stick framing is the structural portion of the enclosure. Infill material (glass, aluminum, or stone) is set into the frame and mechanically attached and/or captured. The "pocket" created between the outside face of the framing, the back edge of the infill, and the infill attachment forms the pressure-equalization chamber. The pressure-equalization chamber is the sill, jamb, and head "pocket." This is illustrated in Fig. 8.15. A stick wall that utilizes structural silicone as the infill attachment typically does not have a pocket. Therefore, there is no pressure-equalization chamber. The weather protection approach in this case is a barrier design. This is illustrated in Figure 8.16.

Rain screen/pressure-equalized assemblies have a primary air and water line of protection and a secondary water line of protection. To create the

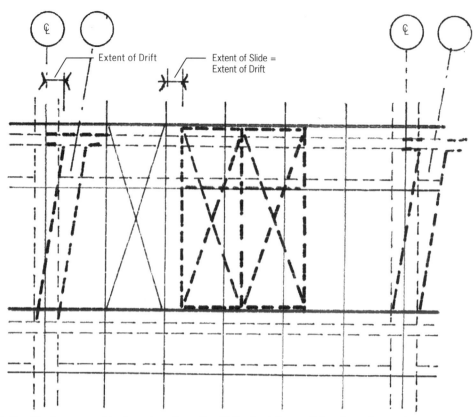

Extent of Drift

Extent of Slide =
Extent of Drift

FIGURE 8.13 The frames can slide about the split mullion/deflection joint parallel to the enclosure plane.

pressure-equalization chamber, a continuous primary air and water seal line is necessary. The depth of the pressure-equalization chamber influences the air and water control capacity of the system.

Unitized wall: "Unitized" has been defined several ways in multiple publications. The definition used here is a shop-fabricated and -assembled aluminum framing, sealant, gaskets, and infill (glass or other infill) "unit." Unit sizes are typically one floor tall by a prescribed unit width from unit jamb to unit jamb. Unitized systems employ a rain screen pressure-equalized air and water control system, usually with the opportunity for a larger pressure-equalization chamber than a stick wall, achieved by including the vertical framing member cavity width and depth in the pressure-equalized chamber. A plan and section of a unitized system with the pressure-equalized chamber identified is shown in Figure 8.17. A key to maintaining the primary and

continuous protection line occurs at the intersections of the horizontal and vertical members, within each unit and unit-to-unit.

Unit on a stick: The unit on a stick system typically employs a rain screen pressure-equalized air and water protection approach. The same level of detail attention discussed for the unitized system applies to unit on a stick system.

Column cover and/or spandrel panel: The column cover and/or spandrel panel with unit or stick infill weather protection approach can employ either the barrier, rain screen, or pressure-equalized approach, or combination of any of the two. Key study items for design and weather performance are the intersections of the spandrel panel and column cover panels to the metal frames and glass infill. The primary and secondary lines must be continuous. The locations of the primary line between column cover/spandrel and the metal framed with glass infill often

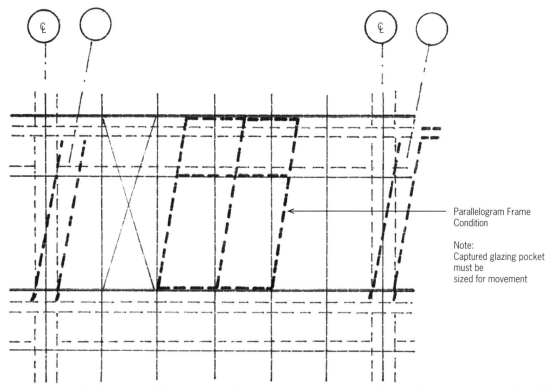

Parallelogram Frame Condition

Note:
Captured glazing pocket must be sized for movement

FIGURE 8.14 The frames can deform into a parallelogram shape to accommodate floor-to-floor drift. Note that the infill is a panel, and the method of attachment of infill to frame must allow for the frame displacement with no infill damage.

occur at dimensionally different depths from the exterior, but in every case must be connected.

In the system classifications described in this section, continuity of the primary weather line for air and water is essential. Designing weatherproofing continuity during the design phase is the responsibility of the architect. Weather continuity in the shop drawings "paper" phase of construction is the responsibility of the contractor, with architectural review. Continuity in the "bricks and mortar" phase of construction is the responsibility of the contractor.

Thermal Design/Vapor Control/ Condensation

THERMAL DESIGN

Thermal design and performance in a metal framed and glass enclosure require review of the infill material, framing, insulation behind opaque materials,

insulation at framing members in the opaque areas, infill connection details, and the glass type. Metal, such as aluminum, has a very high thermal conductivity. To decouple direct thermal transfer between exterior and interior, materials of low thermal conductivity can be introduced in the metal framing. These materials and their methods of fabrication are referred to as "thermal breaks." Thermal break materials such as polyurethane, polyester-reinforced nylon, neoprene, or polyvinyl chloride (PVC) are introduced between the infill attachment and the framing. A thermal break is illustrated in Figure 8.18.

Opaque infill areas are composed of multiple materials, usually with a layer of air space and insulation attached to the framing. Opaque infill and insulation material, with the air spaces, will provide an R-value for this area. It is important in design and detail to include insulation at interior faces of the horizontal and vertical framing members in opaque areas. Insulation should be continuous, or as continuous in application of materials and thickness

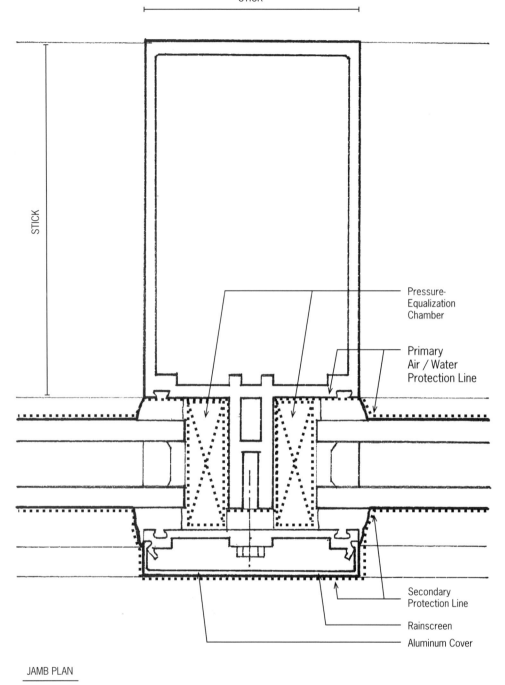

STICK

STICK

Pressure-Equalization Chamber

Primary Air / Water Protection Line

Secondary Protection Line

Rainscreen

Aluminum Cover

JAMB PLAN

FIGURE 8.15 The primary line of air and water protection is indicated at the interior face of the glass, through the glazing pocket to the adjacent interior face of glass, for a continuous weather line. The pressure-equalization chambers (compartments) are the glazing pockets. The pressure-equalization chamber includes the head and sill glazing pockets.

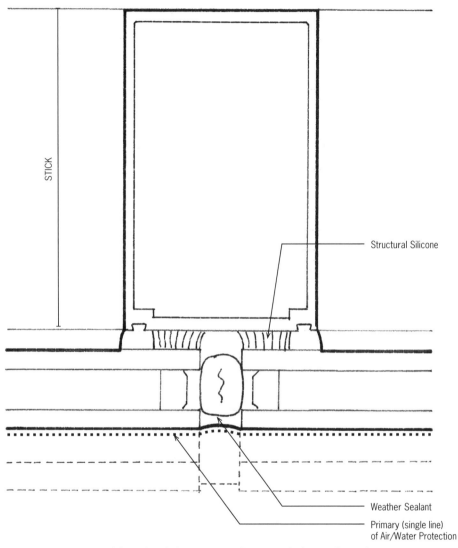

STICK

STICK

Structural Silicone

Weather Sealant

Primary (single line)
of Air/Water Protection

FIGURE 8.16 A stick-type metal framed and glass system with structural silicone glazing has no space to create a rain screen or pressure-equalization chamber. This system is a candidate for a barrier system.

as possible. Careful attention is required for condensation prevention or control in spandrel areas.

Transparent vision areas with glass infill have insulating qualities based on the glass type, coating, and glass assembly. Glass can be monolithic, laminated, or insulated. As a result of stricter energy codes and regulations, the majority of glass in metal-framed enclosures is insulating glass with high-performance coatings. Insulating glass, even with high-performance coatings, does not have high insulation values. The R-value for insulating glass is typically about R = 2. There are some triple-pane insulating glass types with gas fill and special edge spacers that achieve an R = 4 value. The extent of vision glass in

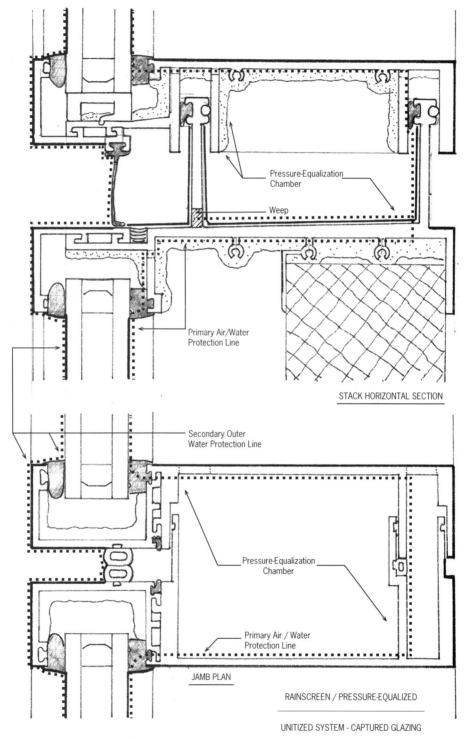

Pressure-Equalization
Chamber

Weep

Primary Air/Water
Protection Line

STACK HORIZONTAL SECTION

Secondary Outer
Water Protection Line

Pressure-Equalization
Chamber

Primary Air / Water
Protection Line

JAMB PLAN

RAINSCREEN / PRESSURE-EQUALIZED

UNITIZED SYSTEM - CAPTURED GLAZING

FIGURE 8.17 A unitized type metal framed and glass system allows for a larger rain screen/pressure-equalized chamber. Intersections of jamb to horizontals (stack and static) require careful detail and execution to maintain weather protection continuity.

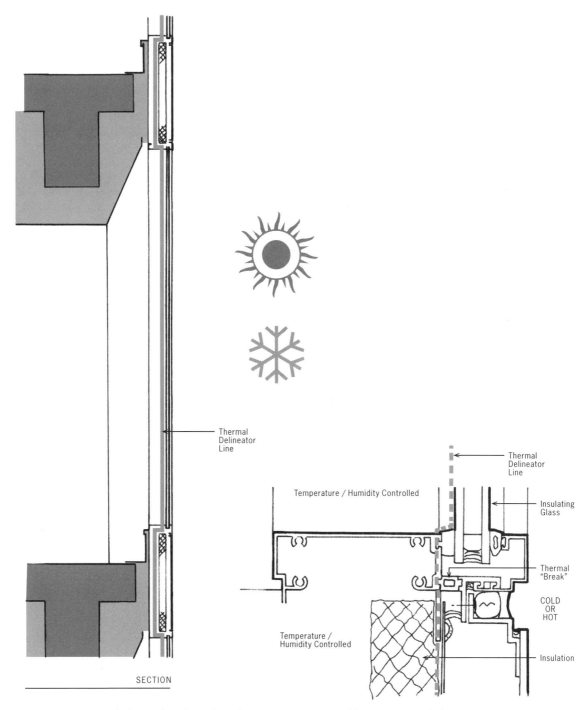

SECTION

FIGURE 8.18 Materials that are low thermal conductivity are incorporated between materials that are exposed to exterior temperatures and the controlled interior temperature and humidity environment.

conjunction with the extent of high R-values in opaque areas determines the insulation capability of the enclosure.

VAPOR CONTROL/CONDENSATION

Water in the form of water vapor or humidity migrates from higher water vapor pressure to lower pressure. This movement is not a problem unless the water vapor condenses on a material surface. The metal framing, typically aluminum, and glass are impermeable, so water vapor does not flow through them. However, the climate and the interior space temperature and humidity conditions must be reviewed on a case-by-case basis to verify that condensation does not occur on the material surfaces. This is relatively easy to check in the visible areas.

The opaque spandrel, column cover, and/or vertical opaque areas require more design and detail study. These areas are typically where the highest R-values can be achieved through insulation and air spaces. The location of the primary line of weather protection will influence the location and type of insulation, which in turn determines the vapor profile of the opaque area. The insulation should be allowed to vent and dry.

Fire Safety

Materials inherent in metal framed and glass infill enclosures predominantly result in noncombustible system assemblies. There are distinct differences in noncombustible and fire-resistant systems. Noncombustible materials and assemblies are defined by their tested flame spread and smoke developed material characteristics. Fire resistant assemblies have been specifically tested to designated hourly ratings. Building codes define the extent, if required, of fire resistance for a metal framed and infill enclosure, based on building type, occupancy type, location to property line, and other criteria. There are two primary focus areas for design and detailing:

1. Noncombustible or fire-resistant requirements for the enclosure

2. Continuity of the floor and floor structure rating and floor-to-floor separation to the interior face of the enclosure

NONCOMBUSTIBLE OR FIRE-RESISTANT REQUIREMENTS FOR THE ENCLOSURE

Most metal framed and infill enclosures are noncombustible as a result of their material component characteristics. Glass in aluminum frames is noncombustible. It is not tested as fire-resistant. Most building codes provide limits on the extent of glass in openings with specific fire-resistive or fire rating requirements. In many designs, there are code-required fire rating requirements for the opaque areas with prescribed limitations on the extent of unprotected glazed openings in the vision areas. There are fire-tested assemblies for opaque areas that utilize noncombustible interior insulation materials in combination with the other enclosure materials. Each tested assembly is very specific. The design—whether custom, customized standard, or standard system—must comply with the material assemblies and size requirements that have been tested by independent testing agencies to be used as fire-resistant. Assemblies without approved fire resistance tests must be reviewed with the appropriate authority having jurisdiction at the earliest design phases, to ascertain if the proposed design assembly is acceptable or what tests or simulations are required for verification of acceptability.

CONTINUITY OF THE FLOOR RATING AND FLOOR-TO-FLOOR SEPARATION TO THE INTERIOR FACE OF THE ENCLOSURE

Metal framed and infill enclosures such as window walls utilize the primary building structural system as the floor-to-floor fire separation. This is illustrated in Figure 8.19. Systems such as curtain walls, which are suspended on the exterior of the structure, require tested fire-rated assemblies to extend the primary structural floor rating to the interior face of the noncombustible or fire-rated opaque enclosure assemblies. These floor fire-rated closure assemblies prevent fire (heat) and smoke (gases) from passing from one

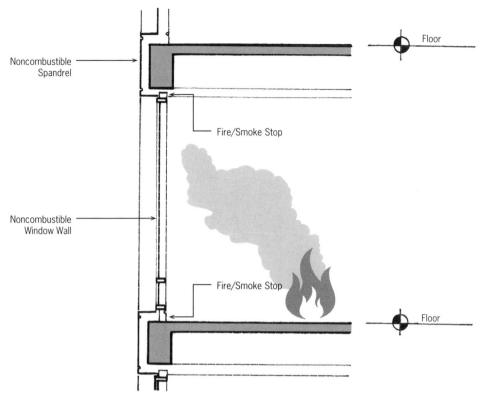

FIGURE 8.19 Fire and smoke containment on a floor can be accomplished via the structure and the enclosure spanning between the structure slabs and beams.

floor to another with a fire rating equivalent to the structural floor assembly. Design and details for these assemblies require interface with the enclosure, the enclosure system anchorage, and the structural system details. Examples of fire-rated floor separation diagrams are shown in Figure 8.20.

Additional Design Requirements

MAINTENANCE

All enclosures require maintenance to maximize their service life—ranging from cleaning the glass and metal surfaces to repair/replacement of joinery materials or replacement of glass or other infill. Sealant joinery has a service life in the range of 10 to 15 years. Each sealant type performs with its own unique characteristics. Removal and replacement of exposed

joinery material is direct and requires careful and meticulous preparation and application. Sealants within the enclosure are often not accessible. Detailing, material selection, and installation must acknowledge that concealed sealants need to perform for very long periods of time.

Glass and glazing seals and gaskets require periodic maintenance and inspection. The method of glazing, whether from the interior or exterior will determine how it can be re-glazed. This should be discussed with the owner to determine which offers the most direct and convenient method for long-term maintenance and reglazing.

BLAST

Explosions and threats are design considerations for specialized building types and uses. Exterior enclosures

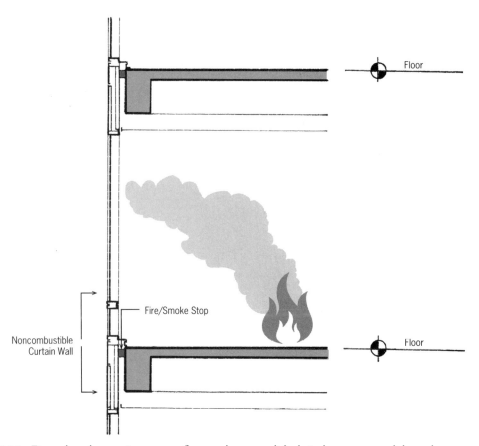

FIGURE 8.20 Fire and smoke containment on a floor can be accomplished via the structure and the enclosure spanning outboard of the structure with fire- and smoke-resistant infill materials.

are the membrane that separates occupants from the force, pressure, and debris resulting from an explosion. Other than the separation distance from the blast source, the enclosure is the primary line of defense to protect occupants.

Blast loads result in high loads for short durations. The pressures are hundreds of times higher in magnitude than lateral wind loads. Lateral load wind pressures are measured in lbs./sq. ft. Blast loads are measured in lbs./sq. in. To provide an example to illustrate the magnitude of the difference: an enclosure in a hurricane zone may have an exterior pressure of 85 psf; a building in the non-hurricane area may have a blast pressure of 4 psi. The equivalent pressure in psf is 576 psf. Blast load durations and impulses are measured in milliseconds. The duration, which is the time effect of the load of a blast, is in milliseconds in lieu of 3-second wind gust.

The load path for exterior blast loading is similar to that of wind loads. The infill must accommodate the load and transfer it to the frames. The frames transfer the load to the system anchors into the primary building structure. Glass infill for blast design is typically laminated assemblies with glass/interlayer/glass, or for higher blast loads, multiple glass/interlayer/polycarbonate/glass assemblies. Glass infill attachment is typically structural silicone, often within a captured frame. Blast loads create very high positive pressures (exterior to interior direction) and very high negative pressures and rebound (interior to exterior direction). Both directions must be considered in design. Metal framing typically requires additional depth and thickness, as well as internal reinforcing, to accommodate the higher loads. System anchors are more robust than conventional anchors for transferring the enclosure loads into the primary structure.

Exterior Building Enclosures

The enclosure design objective for blast is to protect occupants from pressures and airborne projectiles and debris. The enclosure is expected to return to normal service after resisting lateral wind or seismic loads from a small or moderate seismic event, but blast-resistant enclosures often sustain damage. The extent of acceptable damage is a case-by-case decision. In all blast design, the infill material—glass or other materials—may break, but it will not evacuate the opening or separate from the framing.

TESTING

Manufacturers' standard metal framed and glass enclosures typically have been tested and offer defined levels of structural and weather protection performance. Custom metal framed and glass infill enclosures are tested with multiple performance tests. These tests are conducted by independent testing agencies. Customary tests include air infiltration, water infiltration under static and dynamic loads, and structural tests simulating lateral wind loads. Additional tests for seismic, thermal cycling/thermal performance, acoustics, and others can also be performed to the specified project requirements.

Summary

Metal framed enclosures with infill of glass and other materials include multiple system types and system classifications. Structural design and detail considerations can be applied to all systems, system classifications, and designs. Weatherproofing approaches for primary lines of defense against air and water infiltration and secondary water protection are dependent on the system and the design. Because of the multiple materials involved, architects must pay particular attention to the material strengths and weaknesses and the complex and intricate details, particularly at intersections and corners. Examples of each of these systems are illustrated in the following case studies.

Metal Framed and Glass

San Francisco International Airport

Location:
San Francisco, CA, USA
Building Type:
Airport Terminal

San Francisco International Airport terminal.   ©*Timothy Hursley*

PARTICIPANTS
Owner:
City and County of San Francisco
San Francisco Airport Bureau of Design and Construction
The Joint Venture Architects:
Skidmore, Owings & Merrill LLP/Del Campo & Maru/Michael Willis and Associates – San Francisco, CA
Structural Engineer:
Skidmore, Owings & Merrill LLP/OLMM Consulting Engineers/Faye Bernstein & Associates – San Francisco, CA
Mechanical Engineer:
Ajmani & Pamidi Inc. – San Francisco, CA
Contractor:
Tutor-Saliba Corporation/Perini Corporation/Buckley Joint Venture – Sylmar, CA

Curtain Wall Contractor:

Enclos Corporation (formerly Harmon Contract Glazing) – Walnut, CA and Minneapolis, MN, Bruce Wall Systems Corporation – Tucker, GA

Architectural Glass and Aluminum (fifth floor, Shoulder Building)- Oakland, CA

PROJECT TIME FRAME
Design Competition:
Spring 1994
Schematic Validation Design:
July 1994–November 1994
Design Development:
December 1994–September 1995
Construction Documents:
September 1995–October 1996
Construction:
November 1996–January 2000

Project Description

The International Terminal at San Francisco International Airport (SFIA) is the centerpiece of the airport's $2.6 billion expansion and modernization program. The SFIA master plan expansion consists of five major projects and multiple other smaller-scale projects. The five major projects are: (1) the International Terminal, (2) Boarding Area A, (3) Boarding Area G, (4) two parking garages, and (5) the rental car facility. The master plan completion, presented in Figure 8C1.1, greatly increases the airport's efficiency and capacity with 26 new gates, and maintains San Francisco's standing as America's gateway to the Pacific Rim. The International Terminal roof structure and main façade are visible from approaching roadways and the air, providing a visual cohesiveness and an iconic sense of identity. The International Terminal's (IT) five-story vertical organization presents a model for other urban airports with limited buildable land. The IT spans the inbound and outboard roadway, and its location with respect to other terminals is illustrated in Figure 8C1.2. The IT exterior enclosure and structure are designed to the highest seismic safety requirements ever imposed on an American airport terminal, in order to remain operational in the event of a major earthquake.

Enclosure System Types

There are three metal framed and glass enclosure system classifications designed and implemented on the San Francisco International Terminal:

1. Custom unitized curtain wall system
2. Custom unitized curtain wall on a stick system
3. Custom stick system

Custom Unitized Curtain Wall System

The main departure hall is enclosed by a 705′-0″ (215 m) long by 235′-0″ (71.6 m) wide by 115′-0″ (35 m) tall custom pressure-equalized rain screen unitized curtain wall, located beneath the long-span roof

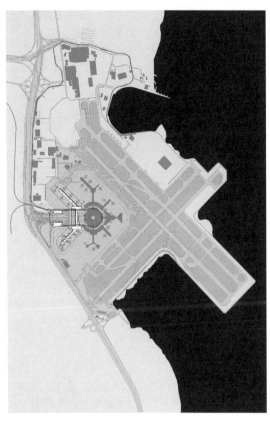

FIGURE 8C1.1 The master plan for the San Francisco International Airport identifies the major projects. These are: (1) Boarding Area A, (2) Boarding Area G, (3) two parking garages, and (4) the International Terminal. *Skidmore, Owings & Merrill LLP*

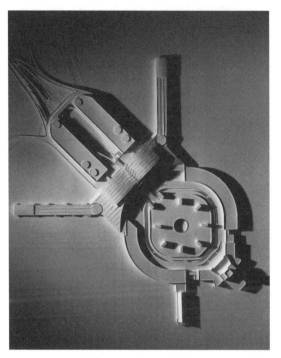

FIGURE 8C1.2 Schematic design validation site model of the International Terminal. The terminal spans over the inbound and outbound roadways. *Skidmore, Owings & Merrill LLP*

structure. Each curtain wall unit is typically 9'-0" (2.74 m) high by 20'-0" (6.1 m) long. Corner units are 9'-0" (2.74 m) high by 2'-6" (.762 m) long on each side in an "L"-shaped configuration. Curtain wall units are supported on custom-designed, visually exposed, extruded aluminum anchors bolted to an architectural steel backup system. Curtain wall units in the middle third of the primary west elevation and the north, south, and east elevation are composed of 1-5/16" (33 mm) thick insulated/laminated glass infill captured in extruded aluminum frames. Glass has a low-E coating on the #2 surface and a custom ceramic frit on the #3 surface. Curtain wall units on two-thirds of the west exterior are composed of extruded aluminum frames with 3/16" (5 mm) thick exterior aluminum plate with 3/16" (5 mm) thick interior perforated aluminum plate and thermal/acoustic insulation. Vision glass in this wall composition is 1-5/16" (33 mm) thick insulated/laminated/fritted glass infill captured in extruded aluminum frames.

Curtain wall units are a female/female jamb frame system to facilitate a discontinuous construction installation sequence. The typical 9' × 20' enclosure units are designed to remain rectangular and, given their unit geometry and weight, to slide under seismic movement parallel to the enclosure plane. Units tip and lean perpendicular to the enclosure plane under seismic movement. The 2'-6"-wide corner units

Exterior Building Enclosures

remain rectangular as an "L"- shaped corner and tip or lean, depending on the seismic drift direction of the primary building superstructure. The unitized curtain wall composition is illustrated in Figures 8C1.3 and 8C1.4.

Custom Unitized Curtain Wall on a Stick System

The side "shoulder" buildings, connecting the International Terminal to Boarding Area A and Boarding Area G and the central office building on the east side of the International Terminal, are enclosed with a custom unitized curtain wall on a stick system. This system employs a pressure-equalized rain screen weather protection principle. Floor-to-floor span heights are 24'-0" (7.3 m) on level one, 20'-0" (6.1 m) on level 2, and 17'-0" (5.2 m) floor-to-floor for levels 3 through 5. To accommodate the taller floors and resulting enclosure spans, a steel tube "stick" is anchored at 10'-0" (3.04 m) plan spacing. Individual custom-designed female/female jamb frame units of 10'-0" (3.04 m) wide by 5'-0" (1.52 m) high are installed on the sticks. The units have 1-5/16" (33 mm) thick insulated/laminated vision or spandrel glass, aluminum plate, or louver infill. Steel sticks are clad in the vision glass areas with unitized extruded aluminum frames. The curtain wall unit on a stick composition with each type of unit infill configuration is illustrated in Figure 8C1.5.

Custom Stick System

The entry areas on level 1 and 2 west elevation of the International Terminal and the lower 17'-0" (5.2 m) portion of the level 3 departure hall are enclosed with a custom stick system. Twelve-inch (300 mm) deep custom vertical extrusions—"sticks"—are spaced at 10'-0" (3 m) on center with intermediate 7" (178 mm) deep extruded aluminum vertical sticks; align on the 5'-0" building design module. A transom glass lite, 10'-0" (3.04 m) wide by 5'-0" (1.52 m) high completes the framing composition. The stick system is a pressure-equalized rain screen weather protection approach. The composition is illustrated in Figure 8C1.6.

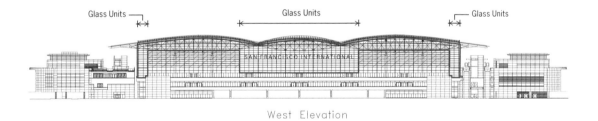

West Elevation

East Elevation

FIGURE 8C1.3 A custom all-glass unitized curtain wall enclosure system encloses a large portion of the primary west elevation and the upper extent of the east elevation. *Skidmore, Owings & Merrill LLP*

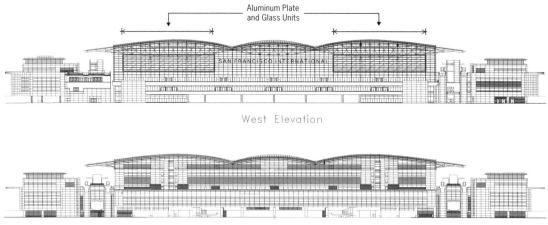

FIGURE 8C1.4 A custom glass and aluminum plate unitized curtain wall enclosure system is located on the west elevation to provide design composition and sun shading.   *Skidmore, Owings & Merrill LLP*

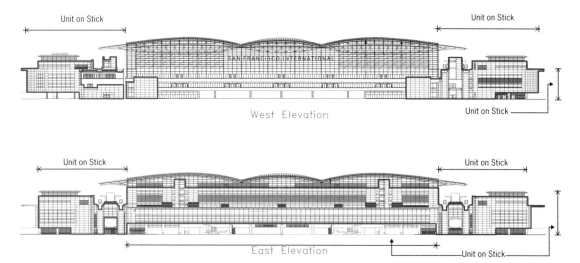

FIGURE 8C1.5 A custom unit on a stick unitized curtain wall enclosure system encloses the "shoulder buildings" and a large extent of the east terminal elevation.   *Skidmore, Owings & Merrill LLP*

All curtain wall enclosure systems have a fluoropolymer resinous coating on the exposed aluminum surfaces. The aluminum color of the International Terminal is custom metallic silver, and the curtain wall on a stick is a custom white. Laminated insulated glass provides acoustic noise reduction from adjacent roadway and airfield noise, as well as blast resistance. The insulated/laminated glass in the all-glass unitized curtain wall has a low-E coating on the #2 surface and a custom frit pattern of alternating ⅛" (3 mm) translucent lines and ⅛" (3 mm) clear areas for glare protection on the #3 glass surface. The "San Francisco International" letter graphic is fabricated into the glass in a three-color custom integral frit on the primary west facing elevation. The graphic glass is illustrated in Figure 8C1.7.

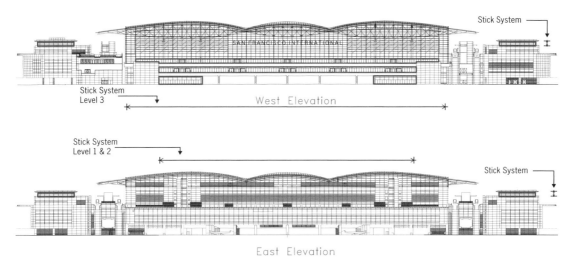

FIGURE 8C1.6 A custom stick system enclosure is located at the terminal storefront on levels 1, 2, and 3, and on the 5th floor of the "shoulder buildings." *Skidmore, Owings & Merrill LLP*

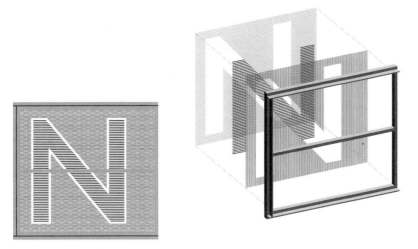

FIGURE 8C1.7 The "SAN FRANCISCO INTERNATIONAL" graphic is a custom frit pattern integral in the insulated and laminated exterior glass. The letter "N" and the composition in the aluminum curtain wall frame are illustrated. *Skidmore, Owings & Merrill LLP*

ENCLOSURE SYSTEM GOALS

The enclosure design goals are:

1. Maximize natural daylight/high energy performance
2. Acoustic noise reduction from aircraft and adjacent roadways
3. Blast protection

Maximize Natural Daylight/Energy Performance

To create the natural-light-filled public space, it was necessary to achieve a balance of glare control and energy performance. The mild San Francisco climate and direct western exposure offered design opportunities for large quantities of vision glass and daylight, which reduced the quantity of interior light fixtures. The line frit pattern diffuses daylight and minimizes glare from the low afternoon sun angles for the terminal passengers and ticket agents. The insulated/laminated low-E glass provided high energy performance, which reduced cooling loads.

ACOUSTICS

Asymmetrical laminated glass lay-up composition of 2 plies of ¼″ (6 mm) thick glass with a 1.52 mil thick PVB interlayer, ½″ (13 mm) air space, and a layer of ¼″ (6 mm) exterior glass lite assembly provides enhanced acoustic separation for air field and roadway noise. The "unbalanced" glass assembly adds mass and multiple layers of glass thickness to reduce sound transmission. The unitized curtain wall assembly on two-thirds of the west elevation is perforated aluminum plate on the interior opaque areas with sound absorption insulation to reduce interior sound reverberation.

BLAST

A ⁹⁄₁₆″ thick laminated component of the 1-⁵⁄₁₆″ thick insulating/laminated glass assembly is located towards the occupied interior spaces for blast protection. Aluminum curtain wall frames are internally reinforced to resist roadway blast threats.

Enclosure System Design Process

COMPETITION AND SCHEMATIC VALIDATION

The San Francisco International Airport Terminal and Complex was a design competition. Among several other items, the airport competition brief required each competing design team to define the exterior image and the spatial quality of public spaces. The signature roof structure evokes the image of flight. The long-span roof structure was developed to span over the existing inbound and outbound roadway network. The exterior enclosures were designed to provide large expanses of glass to maximize harvested natural daylight. Images from the design competition are shown in Figures 8C1.8 and 8C1.9.

During the schematic validation phase, the design team refined the plan and elevation layout with airport staff and the airlines. Site placement and adjacencies with the boarding areas and the roadway system were developed for final site placement and vertical floor-to-floors heights. Floor-to-floor heights were established to accommodate the design aircraft threshold heights, roadway clearances, baggage system conveyor heights and layouts, and exterior enclosure schematic design requirements.

DESIGN DEVELOPMENT

Multiple enclosure design options were studied for the departure hall. The restricted site available for construction at an operational airport, and continued operation of the incoming/outgoing airport roadway system through the IT site, meant that off-site prefabrication was a primary design and detail consideration for the enclosure systems. The broad expanse of the unitized curtain wall along the west elevation yielded a modular panelization of 20′-0″ (6.1 m) long, with a 10′-0″/5′-0″/2′-6″ (3.04 m/1.52 m/.762 m) submodule plan length. The selected enclosure design option is illustrated in Figure 8C1.10. A comprehensive vertical dimensional organization and corner design/detail approach were developed to apply to each of the exterior enclosure and interior systems and building components.

The design of each metal framed and glass system was developed to respond to the uses of each of the International Terminal's five main building components. These five components are: (1) Main International Terminal, (2) South Shoulder Building, (3) North Shoulder Building, (4) South Light Rail Enclosure, and (5) North Light Rail Enclosure. They are illustrated in the isometric in Figure 8C1.11. Largescale models of the

FIGURE 8C1.8 The design competition exterior view of the International Terminal. The design competition required each competing team to illustrate their design solution from the same view. *SOM/Doug Jameson*

FIGURE 8C1.9 The design competition interior view of the International Terminal. The design competition required each competing team to illustrate their design solution from the same view. *SOM/Doug Jameson*

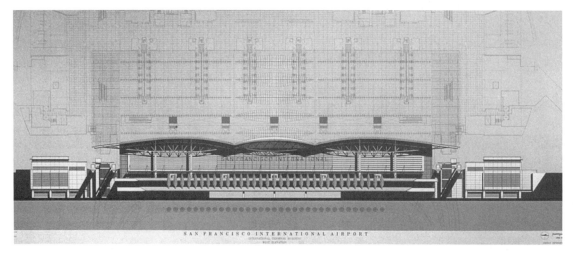

FIGURE 8C1.10 Design development rendered west elevation. Multiple design options were studied before selecting a composition with fritted glass and aluminum plate in a custom curtain wall. *Skidmore, Owings & Merrill LLP*

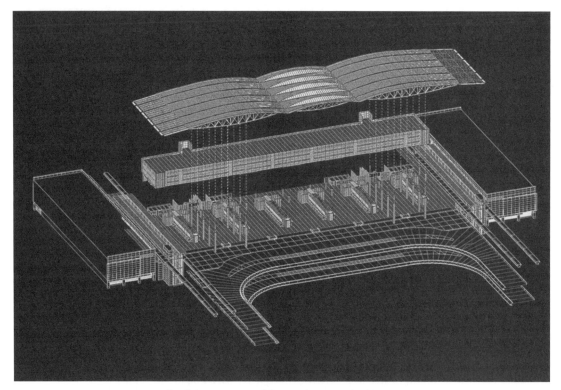

FIGURE 8C1.11 An isometric study of the International Terminal primary building components. *Skidmore, Owings & Merrill LLP*

west elevation of the International Terminal were built to study the unitized and stick enclosure systems' intersections, as well as the intersections of the curtain wall back-up support steel and the long-span roof structure. A design development model image is illustrated in Figure 8C1.12.

Construction Documents

The three enclosure system typical head, jamb, and sill details were developed between the end of design development and early stages of construction documents. System profiles were defined on small- and medium-scale drawings with further system definition on large-scale (3″ = 1′0″ and larger) details. The system type and representative detail sections for the enclosure systems are:

1. Custom unitized system: Framed aluminum and glass infill and the aluminum plate with smaller height glass infill. Elevations, with the corresponding details for each, are illustrated in Figures 8C1.13, 8C1.14, 8C1.15, and 8C1.16.

2. Custom unitized curtain wall on a stick system: The "shoulder buildings" connecting the boarding gates and the central office building house airline lounges, offices, and mechanical spaces. The enclosure design and detail solution allows unit infill of vision glass, spandrel glass, aluminum panels, or louvers supported on the stick subframe. Elevations with the corresponding unit on a stick type are illustrated in Figures 8C1.17, 8C1.18, and 8C1.19.

3. Custom stick system: The first, second, and third levels of the International Terminal accommodate passenger services. Each custom stick "storefront" spans 24′0″, 20′0″, and 17′9″ respectively. The stick system design respects the 10′0″ design plan module with 12″-deep verticals at 10′-0″ spacing and intermediate 7″-deep verticals on a 5′0″ planning submodule. Transom glass is 10′0″ (3.05 m) wide × 5′0″ (1.52 m)

FIGURE 8C1.12 A design development model of the primary west elevation illustrates the relationship of curtain wall system, stick system, cantilevered canopy with skylight, and long-span roof structure. *Skidmore, Owings & Merrill LLP*

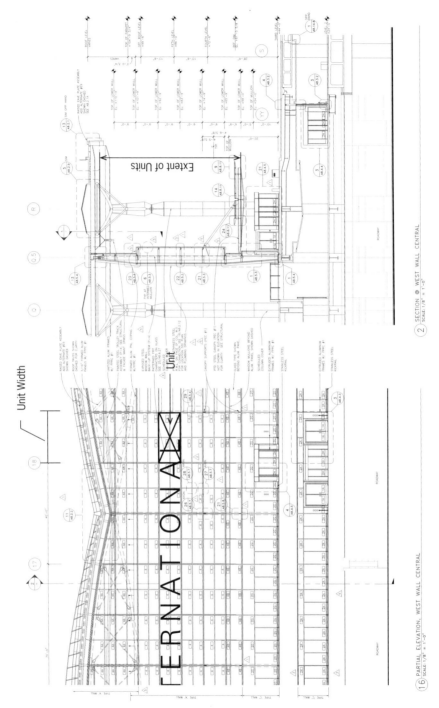

FIGURE 8C1.13 Construction document partial elevations and section of the custom all-glass and metal-framed unitized curtain wall. Custom-designed unitized curtain wall frames are typically 9'-0" high × 20'-0" long. The design composition of the custom stick system at levels 3 and 2 is organized in a 10'-0" spacing with intermediate 5'-0" vertical sticks and a 10'-0" wide transom lite. *Skidmore, Owings & Merrill LLP*

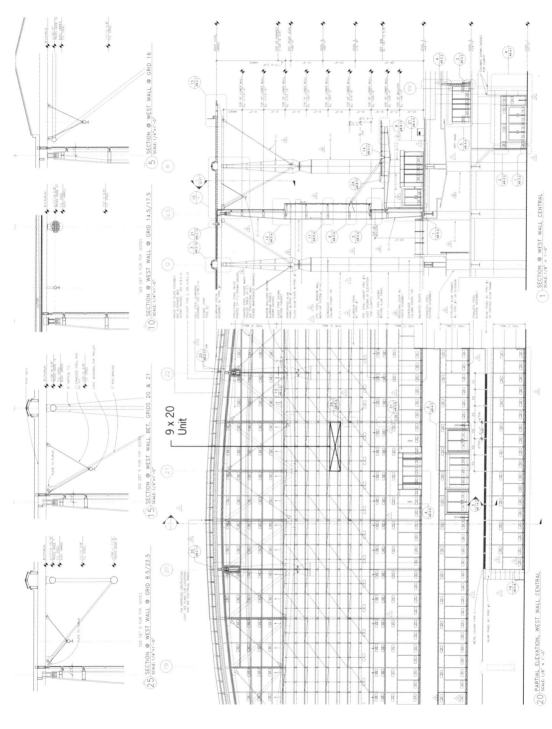

FIGURE 8C1.14 Construction document partial elevations and section of the custom glass and aluminum plate metal-framed unitized curtain wall. Custom-designed unitized curtain wall frames are typically 9'-0" high × 20'-0" long. The design composition of the custom stick system at levels 3, 2, and 1 is organized in a 10'-0" spacing with intermediate 5'-0" vertical sticks and a 10'-0" wide transom lite. *Skidmore, Owings & Merrill LLP*

403

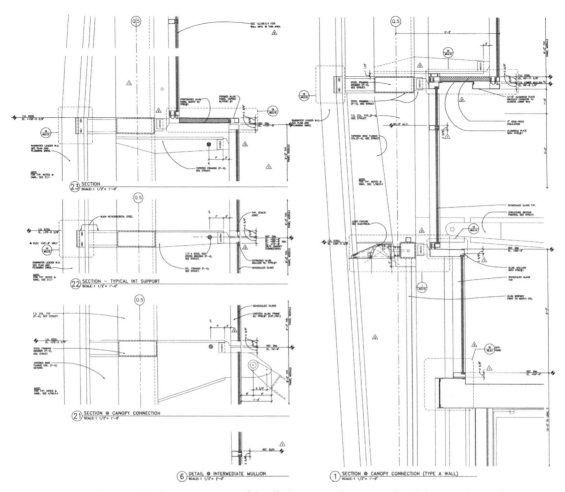

FIGURE 8C1.15 Construction document section of the all-glass unitized curtain wall and the transition to the custom stick storefront system.   *Skidmore, Owings & Merrill LLP*

tall. Openings in the storefront are framed by steel surrounds to accept balanced swing doors and 16′0″ (4.88 m) diameter revolving doors. Steel frame surrounds with a metallic, high-performance automotive paint coating were selected for durability, to resist baggage and pedestrian traffic damage. Elevations with the corresponding details are illustrated in Figures 8C1.20 and 8C1.21.

Construction

The San Francisco International Airport project delivery process was design-bid-build. After a competitive public bidding process, the selected general contractor and enclosure contractor submitted typical system details for each system for review and comment. Final details for the unitized enclosure are illustrated in Figures 8C1.22a and 8C1.22b. Final details for the unit on a stick are illustrated in Figures 8C1.23a and 8C1.23b. Final details for the stick are illustrated in Figure 8C1.24.

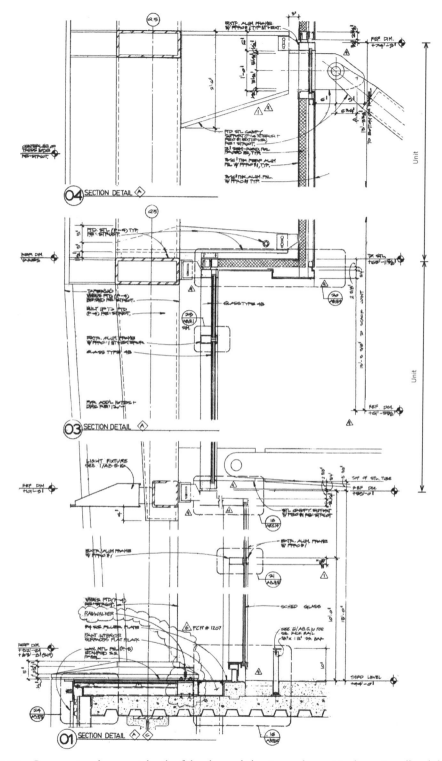

FIGURE 8C1.16 Construction document details of the glass and aluminum plate unitized curtain wall and the transition to the custom stick storefront system. *Skidmore, Owings & Merrill LLP*

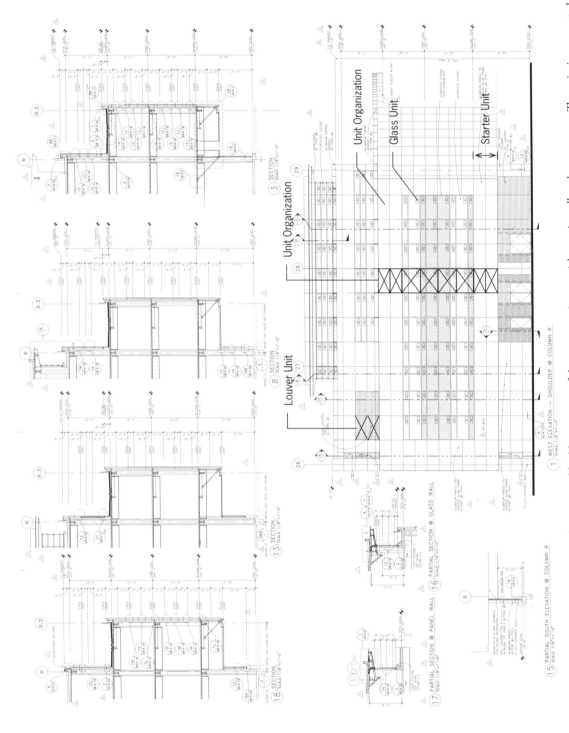

FIGURE 8C1.17 Construction document elevations and building sections of the custom unit on a stick curtain wall enclosure system. The unit sizes are noted with an "X." Units have either insulated laminated glass or aluminum plate infill cladding. *Skidmore, Owings & Merrill LLP*

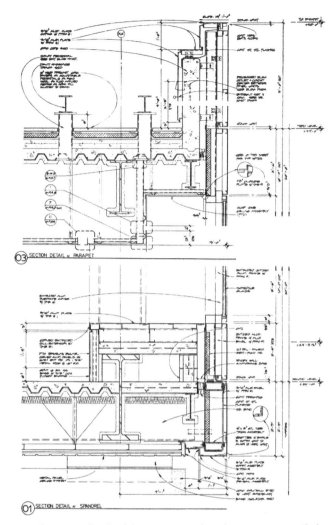

FIGURE 8C1.18   Construction document details of the unit on a stick enclosure system.   *Skidmore, Owings & Merrill LLP*

Curtain wall design review meetings between the enclosure contractor, general contractor, and architect were conducted to agree on the primary system details. Following agreement on each system, shop drawings were developed and reviewed in multiple packages to coincide with the construction stages. Fabricated samples were constructed to validate the system finishes, quality of construction, and joinery. Images of the fabricated samples for the unitized, unit on a stick, and stick systems are shown in Figures 8C1.25, 8C1.26, and 8C1.27. The International Terminal enclosure has multiple plane transitions and interfaces with adjacent materials and systems. The enclosure system module work-point of the typical details defines the relationship

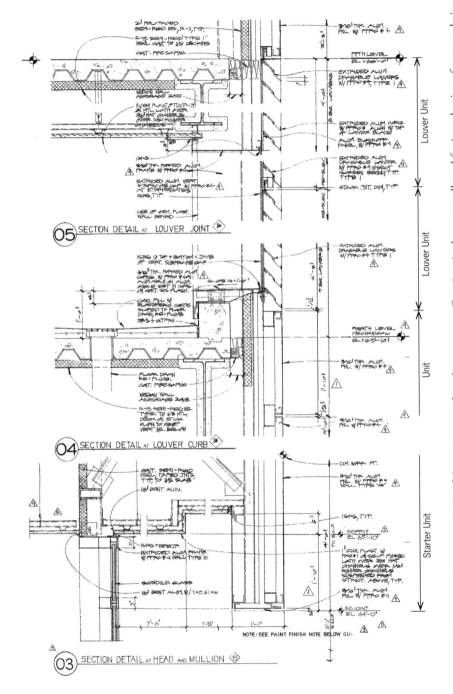

05 SECTION DETAIL at LOUVER JOINT

04 SECTION DETAIL at LOUVER CURB

03 SECTION DETAIL at HEAD and MULLION

NOTE: SEE PAINT FINISH NOTE BELOW 01/-

FIGURE 8C1.19 Construction document details of the unit on a stick enclosure system. Openings in the system allowed for introduction of custom-designed louvers within the enclosure system. *Skidmore, Owings & Merrill LLP*

408

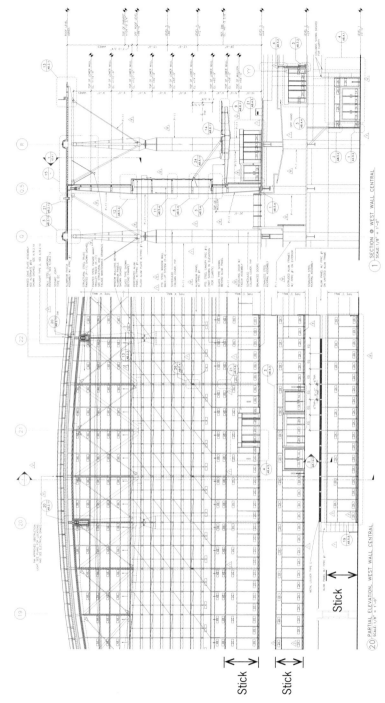

FIGURE 8C1.20 Construction document elevations and sections of the custom stick storefront system. *Skidmore, Owings & Merrill LLP*

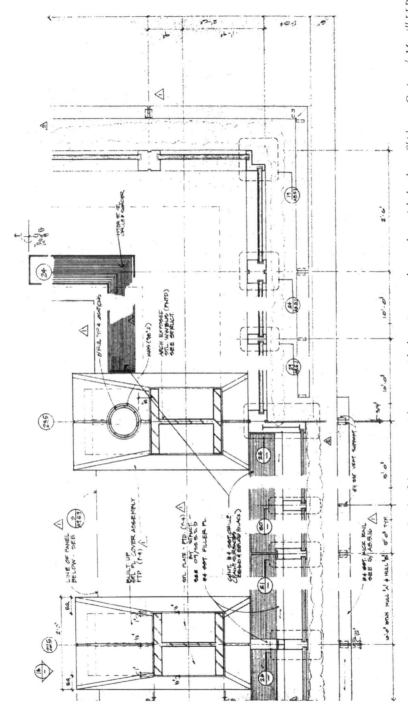

FIGURE 8C1.21 Construction document details of the custom stick system with the primary and secondary stick depth.   *Skidmore, Owings & Merrill LLP*

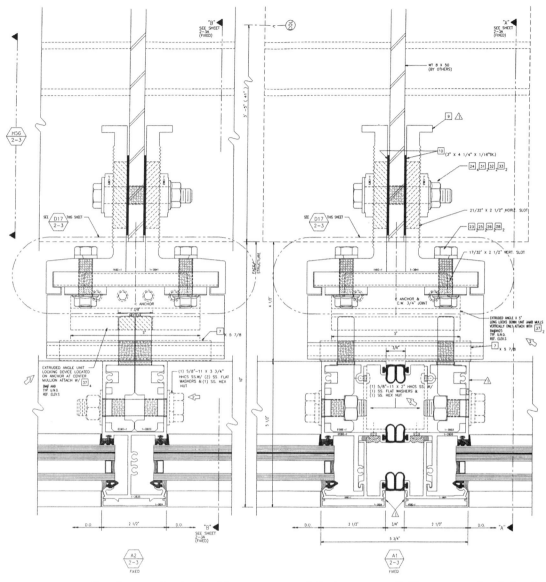

FIGURE 8C1.22a Shop drawing plan details of the custom unitized all-glass curtain wall. The system is a female/female unit system. *Bruce Wall Systems Corporation*

to the inside and outside corner module and face of enclosure. The goal for the design and the construction team was to develop a consistent set of dimensional ground rules that would conform to the construction documents and maintain constant system detail joinery at unit-to-unit in plane locations and at inside and outside corners. To achieve this goal, the plan work-point of the building enclosure face is set ½ of the unit joint inboard. This allows the inside and outside corner joinery and units to each have a full unit-to-unit joint. Dimensional face of the enclosure from the grid was modified (reduced) by ⅜″ (9 mm), which is half of a joint width.

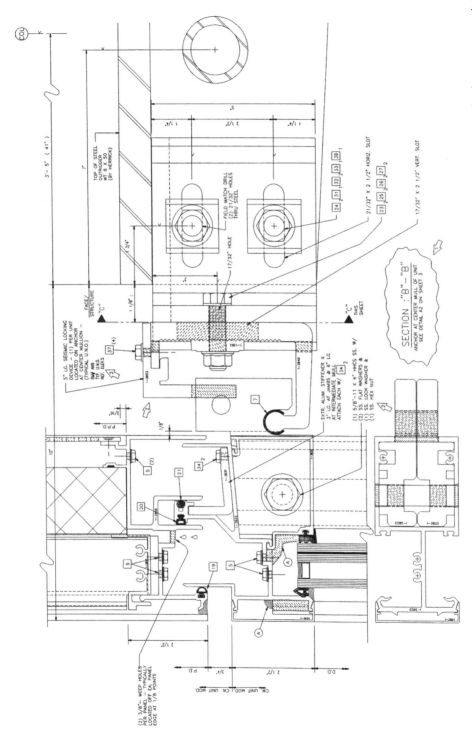

FIGURE 8C1.22b Shop drawing section details of the custom unitized all-glass curtain wall at the unit-to-unit stack joint. The system utilized a custom extruded aluminum anchor in a visually exposed location. *Bruce Wall Systems Corporation*

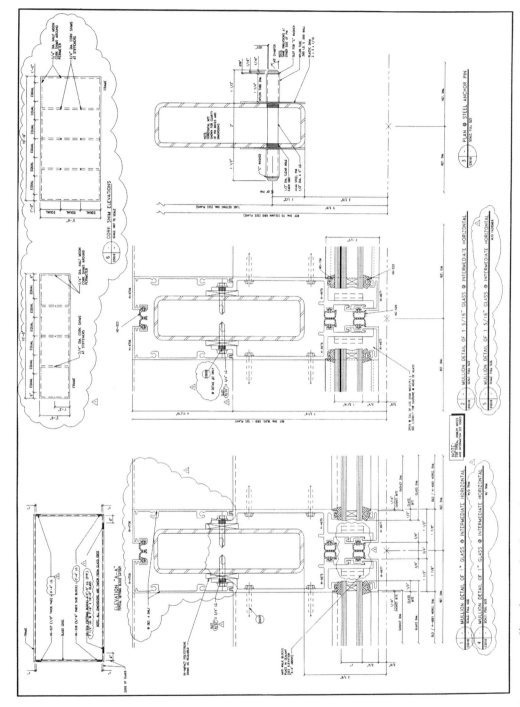

FIGURE 8C1.23a Shop drawing plan details of the custom unit on a stick enclosure system. The stick is a steel tube with preset anchors to receive the units. *Enclos Corp.*

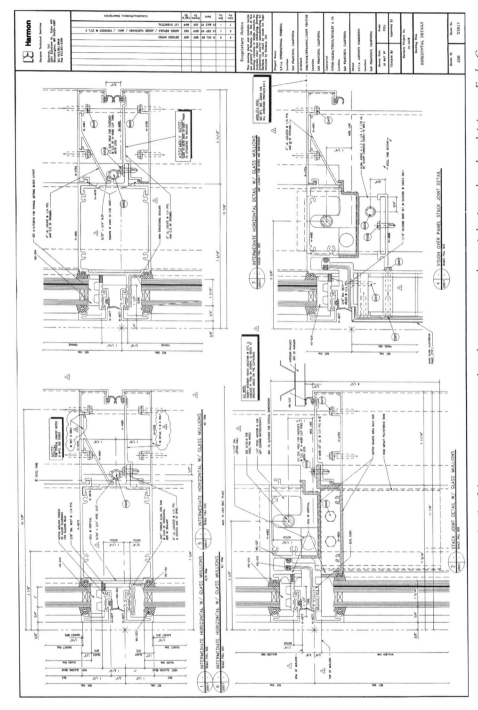

FIGURE 8C1.23b Shop drawing section details of the custom unit on a stick enclosure system at the static horizontals and stack joints. *Enclos Corp*

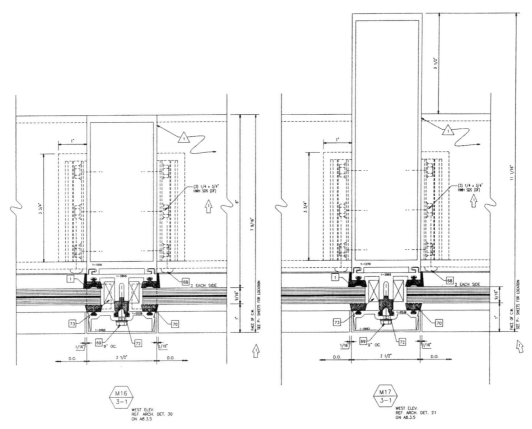

FIGURE 8C1.24 Shop drawing plan details of the custom stick enclosure system. The stick at 10′-0″ center is 12″ deep, and the intermediate stick at 5′-0″ center is 7″ deep.   *Bruce Wall Systems Corporation*

Full-scale performance mock-ups were conducted to evaluate fit, finish, joinery, and performance testing. The performance mock-up for the unitized and unit on a stick systems is illustrated in Figures 8C1.28 and 8C1.29.

The curtain wall units arrived on-site, via truck, fully fabricated. Unit anchors were preset and adjusted to final location through an extruded aluminum anchor with 3-way adjustment. Units were hoisted directly from truck to the installed anchors. Field installation consisted of unit placement and installation of a silicone sleeve at the unit-to-unit panel connections prior to placement of the unit above. Construction images of the unitized curtain wall enclosure system are shown in Figures 8C1.30 and 8C1.31. The unit on a stick vertical tube with receiver pins was installed on preset system anchors. The units arrived on-site fully fabricated and were hoisted directly onto the preset stainless steel pins factory-installed in the zinc primed tube steel sticks. Glass and louver units utilized the same framing system. Construction images of the unit on a stick system are shown in Figures 8C1.32 and 8C1.33.

FIGURE 8C1.25   A fabricated sample of the all-glass unitized curtain wall.

FIGURE 8C1.29   The custom unit on a stick curtain wall performance mock-up test specimen.   *Philip Kaeffer*

FIGURE 8C1.26   A fabricated sample of the unit on a stick unitized curtain wall.

FIGURE 8C1.30   Unitized curtain wall panels were fabricated off-site and delivered ready for installation on the preset anchors.   *Kirit S. Sedani*

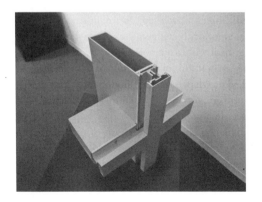

FIGURE 8C1.27   A fabricated sample of the custom stick storefront vertical and horizontal mullion.

FIGURE 8C1.28   The custom unitized curtain wall performance mock-up test specimen.

FIGURE 8C1.31   Unitized curtain wall construction.   *Kirit S. Sedani*

FIGURE 8C1.32   Unit on a stick curtain wall construction. Note the steel sticks and the aluminum framed glass unit.   *Kirit S. Sedani*

FIGURE 8C1.33   Unit on a stick curtain wall construction. Note the louver panel installation on the steel sticks.   *Kirit S. Sedani*

Summary

The San Francisco International Airport International Terminal custom exterior enclosures were fully fabricated off-site. This allowed system testing and curtain wall fabrication, finishing, and assembly to occur concurrent with the primary building superstructure installation. Large curtain wall units were received on-site and installed on the same day, easing congestion on the construction site and minimizing damage to the system and finishes. The rigorous design and detail dimensioning order organized the enclosure layout in design and created repetitive units. This resulted in economies in design, detail, and construction. Final images of the multiple enclosures are shown in Figures 8C1.34 and 8C1.35.

FIGURE 8C1.34   Completed unit on a stick curtain wall.   *©Timothy Hursley*

FIGURE 8C1.35   Completed unit installation of the all-glass and the glass and aluminum plate units from the interior.   *©Timothy Hursley*

Metal Framed and Glass

Jinta Tower

Location:
Tianjin, People's Republic of China Building Type:
High-Rise Office Building

Jinta Tower at dusk.

PARTICIPANTS
Owner:
Tianjin Finance Group
Design Architect:
Skidmore, Owings & Merrill LLP – San Francisco, CA
Local Design Institute (LDI)
East China Architecture and Design Institute (ECADI) – Tianjin, China
Design Structural Engineer:
Skidmore, Owings & Merrill LLP – San Francisco, CA

Local Design Institute (LDI)
East China Architecture and Design Institute (ECADI) – Tianjin, China
Design Mechanical Engineer:
Flack & Kurtz – San Francisco, CA
Contractor:
China State Construction
Curtain Wall Contractor:
Beijing Jianghe Curtain Wall Co. Ltd. Beijing, China

PROJECT TIME FRAME
Concept Design:
March–June 2005
Schematic Design:
January 2006–May 2006
Design Development:
June 2006–December 2006
Construction Documents:
January 2007–August 2007
Construction:
September 2007–March 2011

Project Description

Jinta Tower is sited in the historic heart of Tianjin. The 1,105'- 8″ (337 m) tall tower marks the city center and provides a visual point of reference for visitors and residents alike.

The pleated metal framed and glass curtain wall cladding that encloses the tower recalls the structure and lightness of Chinese paper arts. Jinta contains 2,583,339 sq. ft (240,000 sq. m) of Class-A office space and a banking hall, while an observation deck and sky restaurant at the upper floors provide public access to 360 degree views of the city. At the base of the tower, an all-glass storefront encloses the tower lobby entrance overlooking the Haihe River.

Jinta Tower is one component of a multi-building complex including three residential towers, a hotel, and retail. A site isometric is shown in Figure 8C2.1. The office tower has a unique oval-shape floor plate with projecting bay windows defining the pleats at each column bay. Typical floor plans of the ground-level, low-level, mid-level, and high-level office floors and a building section are presented in Figure 8C2.2.

Enclosure System Types

The tower enclosure from level 2 through the top of the tower penthouse is a custom unit on a stick curtain wall. Sticks occur at the valley and peak of each pleat. Curtain wall units are attached to the sticks with extruded aluminum anchors to preset anchor pins located in the stick. The curtain wall vision glass areas are insulating low-E vision glass from the 2'-7- ½″ (800 mm) high sill to the underside of the ceiling. Spandrel areas are custom ⅛″ (3 mm) thick aluminum plate shadow boxes mounted 4″ (100 mm) behind insulated low-E vision glass. Shadow box aluminum plates are detailed with the top fixed via concealed welded stud fasteners. The two sides and bottom of the shadow box aluminum plate are connected with a continuous concealed aluminum angle and aluminum clip in a "floating" configuration, to allow for thermal expansion and contraction, and the temperature inside the shadow box assembly. Projecting horizontal extruded aluminum mullions on aluminum

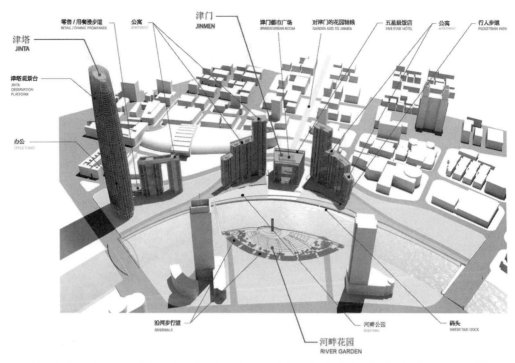

FIGURE 8C2.1 The site isometric identifies the Jinta Tower and the other buildings in the development. *Skidmore, Owings & Merrill LLP*

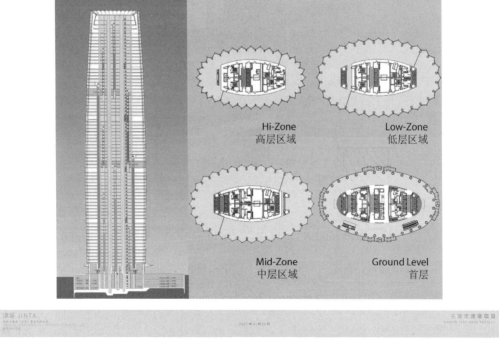

FIGURE 8C2.2 Schematic design low-rise, mid-rise, and high-rise floor plans illustrate the multiple floor plate sizes and enclosure geometry. The tower enclosure is the largest at the 26th floor. *Skidmore, Owings & Merrill LLP*

"stand-offs" provide solar shading. A partial plan, elevation, section, and isometric of the unit on a stick curtain wall enclosure are shown in Figure 8C2.3.

Enclosure System Goals

The tower's crystalline shape and curved silhouette are designed to change in color and reflectivity in different day-light and times of the day. Additional shadow and detail are achieved by the horizontal extruded aluminum sunshades. To maintain a consistent visual appearance, glass and aluminum plate shadowbox assemblies are designed to visually blend with the vision glass areas. To further maintain the all glass exterior appearance, tilted fixed glass panels with openings for intake and exhaust are employed in lieu of metal louvers at the multiple mechanical floors in four locations in the tower.

Enclosure System Design Process

SCHEMATIC DESIGN

Building plan and section geometry was refined at mid-schematics. The plan geometry is a series of intersecting circles with the radius of each of the two circles defining the oval plan enclosure. The tower plan geometry is illustrated in Figures 8C2.4 and in section in Figure 8C2.5. Projecting "bay windows" vary in angularity and

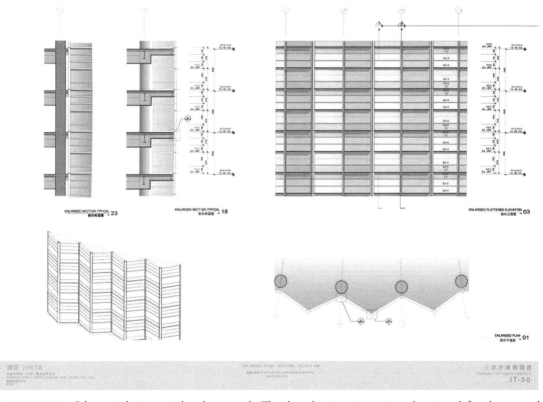

FIGURE 8C2.3 Schematic design typical enclosure study. The plan, elevation, isometric, and sections define the x, y, and z enclosure composition. The vision and shadow box glass is insulating low-E glass. Projecting horizontal mullions provide solar shading. *Skidmore, Owings & Merrill LLP*

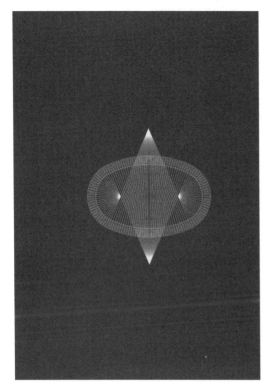

FIGURE 8C2.4 The tower plan enclosure geometry is defined by 4 radii of overlapping circles. *Skidmore, Owings & Merrill LLP*

FIGURE 8C2.5 The tower section illustrates the enclosure profile. The largest floor plan occurs at the 26th floor and tapers up and down from this floor. *Skidmore, Owings & Merrill LLP*

are dimensionally defined by the geometry of each floor. The broad side of the tower results in a wider angled bay window, and an acute angle bay occurs on the shorter ends of the plan. Bay window composition of the broad and shorter end bay configuration is illustrated in Figure 8C2.6. The tower elevation follows the principle of entasis by creating a slight convexity from level two to twenty six in the height of the tower to compensate for the illusion of concavity resulting if a straight taper was used. The entasis principle is illustrated in Figure 8C2.7. The section geometry results in a gentle curved form tapering up and down from the 24th floor.

DESIGN DEVELOPMENT

A three-dimensional computer model was generated to define work-points for the enclosure geometry. Each bay has a work-point in the x, y, and z point at each horizontal-to-vertical mullion intersection per floor. The computer model is illustrated in Figure 8C2.8. This defines the "valley" and "ridge" work-points. During the design development of the enclosure composition, a simple study model was made to study the tower and bay window proportions. The model shapes revealed that the glass surfaces were required to warp out of a flat plane to close the geometry from bay to bay and floor to floor. The two side planes of each projecting bay result in a parallelogram when viewed in a "developed" or flattened elevation. The parallelogram, when bent in three dimensions, defines the curved plan and section enclosure geometry.

Research was initiated to investigate methods to bend insulating glass and to determine what standards for glass bending existed to provide technical, detailing, and specification guidance. Research revealed that

Exterior Building Enclosures

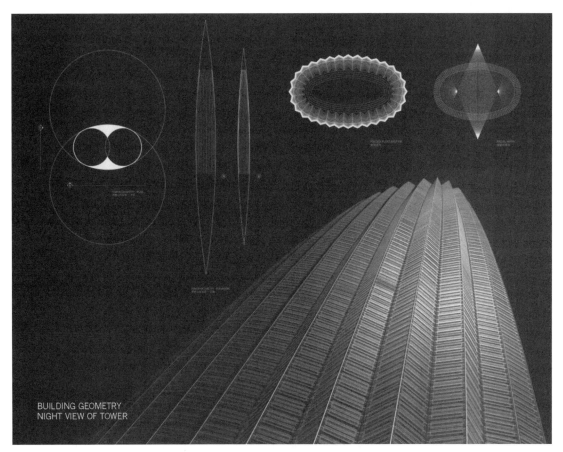

BUILDING GEOMETRY
NIGHT VIEW OF TOWER

FIGURE 8C2.6 The tower enclosure has two sets of bay window geometries per floor. As the floor plate sizes reduce, the plan and section angularity of the bay windows changes to accommodate the floor plate geometry.   *Skidmore, Owings & Merrill LLP*

standards did not exist. Cold-bent glass has been implemented on smaller-scale projects, but not to this large scale. Computer finite element analyses were performed to quantify embedded stresses in the glass and the stresses resulting from positive and negative wind loads. Reduction factors were applied to address strength reduction due to glass aging. Detail options for the valley and the peak were developed to illustrate the profiles necessary to accommodate the changing geometry for each floor. Design development vertical peak and valley details are illustrated in Figures 8C2.9 and 8C2.10.

Construction Document/Tender Documents

The tower geometry and enclosure system was reviewed with two local Chinese exterior enclosure contractors. The tender documents consisted of tower floor plans, elevations, bay window composition, the three-dimensional computer model, typical system profiles, and a performance specification. The system profiles and details included a combination of captured and structural silicone glass attachment to the unit frames. Concurrent with the document development, the design team contacted local glass manufacturers to perform glass cold-bending tests. Bending tests were conducted using the project insulating glass size and materials. Bending was conducted in ⅞" (20 mm) increments. The glass was bent to three times the amount of the maximum

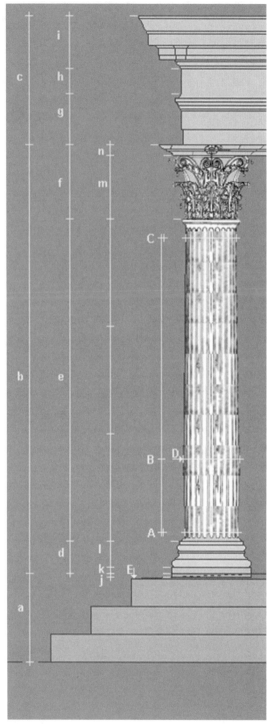

FIGURE 8C2.7   The principle of entasis was employed by the design team to develop the curved tower plan and enclosure shape.   *Skidmore, Owings & Merrill LLP*

Harvard Northwest Science Building site plan. Cambridge, MA, USA.   *Skidmore, Owings & Merrill LLP*

Rice University BioScience Research Collaborative. Houston, TX, USA

UCLA Anderson School of Management. Los Angeles, CA, USA

The Gas Company tower crown. Los Angeles, CA, USA.   *Skidmore, Owings & Merrill LLP*

The New Beijing Poly Plaza. Beijing, People's Republic of China. *Photo © Tim Griffith*

Ronald Reagan Building and International Trade Center. Washington, DC, USA

ARCO Tower One. Dallas, TX, USA.

U.S. Embassy Building. Beijing, People's Republic of China.   ©*Timothy Hursley*

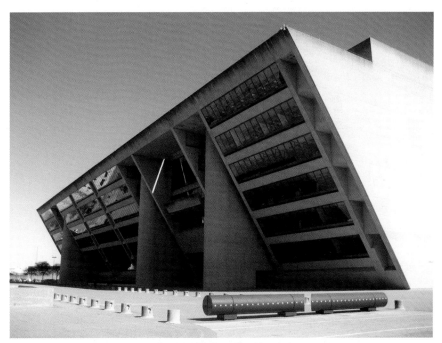

Dallas City Hall. Dallas, TX, USA

San Francisco International Airport terminal. San Francisco, CA, USA. ©*Timothy Hursley*

Jinta Tower. Tianjin, People's Republic of China

Shanghai Huawei Technologies Corporate Campus. Shanghai, People's Republic of China

Fountain Place Tower. Dallas, TX, USA

The New Beijing Poly Plaza. Beijing, People's Republic of China

Lenovo/Raycom Building C Entry Pavilion. Beijing, People's Republic of China

Howard Hughes Medical Institute Janelia Farm Research Campus. Ashburn, Virginia, USA.   *Paul Fetters*

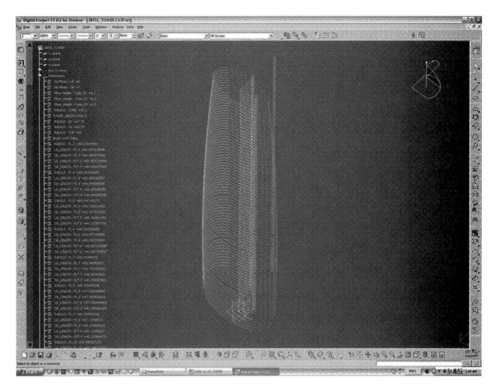

FIGURE 8C2.8   The tower enclosure was modeled in three dimensions using BIM software. A companion spreadsheet document to the architectural drawings defines the x, y, and z work-point coordinates of each bay at the mullions for the peak, valley, and stack joints.   *Skidmore, Owings & Merrill LLP*

calculated required bending, with no glass or insulating edge seal damage. Images of cold-bent glass in the actual glass size are shown in Figure 8C2.11.

The performance specification enclosure system description was developed to allow options for either a unitized or unit on a stick system. Site constraints necessitated that the exterior enclosure construction fabrication and assembly occur off-site. Tender proposals were developed by the two enclosure contractors for review by the design team.

Construction

A unit on a stick was selected to address construction sequence and installing shop-assembled units with cold-bending the glass and frames on-site. The stick anchors are set to the work-point geometries defined on the layout drawings. Sticks are installed between the anchors and surveyed for layout. Curtain wall units are half-floor high with a unit-to-unit stack joint at the 2′-7- ½″ (800 mm) sill height and at an intermediate vision head horizontal mullion. The sequence of enclosure installation is illustrated in Figures 8C2.12a and 8C2.12b.

A full-size visual mock-up was constructed for owner and architect review of the profiles and joinery. The visual mock-up served to test unit installation and reglazing of the system. Images of the visual mock-up are shown in Figure 8C2.13.

A separate full-size performance mock-up was constructed and tested to Chinese national curtain wall requirements and international curtain wall testing standards. Tests included air infiltration, water infiltration, enclosure structural (positive and negative wind load), small seismic (Delta S), as well as retests for water

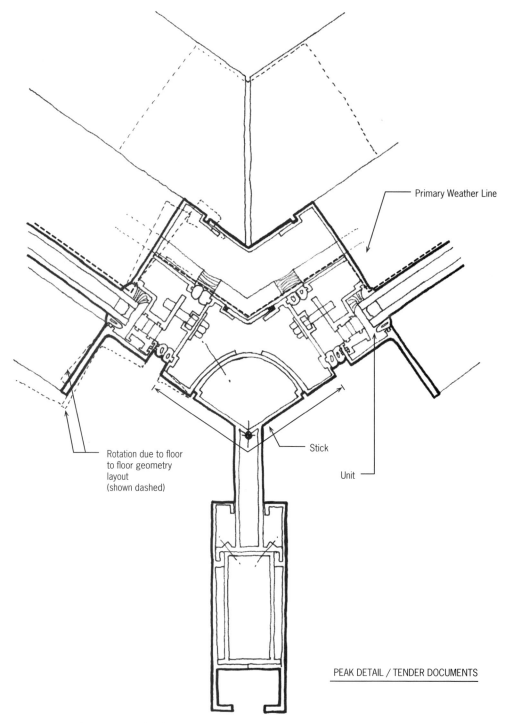

Primary Weather Line

Rotation due to floor
to floor geometry
layout
(shown dashed)

Stick

Unit

PEAK DETAIL / TENDER DOCUMENTS

FIGURE 8C2.9 Enclosure system details were studied and finalized in the tender document phase to address the constructability of warped planes and flat glass cold-bent in the field. A unit on a stick was selected to provide repetition of prefabricated aluminum system components. The peak detail is shown. The peak "stick" extrusion was modified in 7-floor intervals to maintain alignment between the peak stick and the adjacent units for alignment.

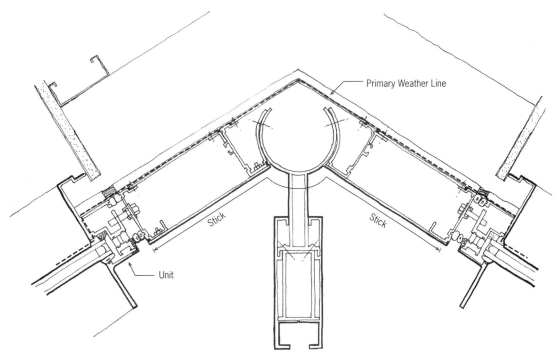

FIGURE 8C2.10 Enclosure system details were studied and finalized in the tender document phase to address the constructability of warped planes and cold-bent glass in the field. A unit on a stick was selected to provide repetition of prefabricated aluminum system components. The valley detail is shown. Primary and secondary weather protection lines were defined.

FIGURE 8C2.11 Project-size physical samples of the insulated glass were bent in a test frame at the glass fabricator's plant. The test evaluated the glass bending and the influence of cold-bending on the insulating glass edge seals. The amount of glass bending was measured during the test. The glass was bent to the maximum required for the project and then bent to three times the project requirements for study. *Skidmore, Owings & Merrill LLP*

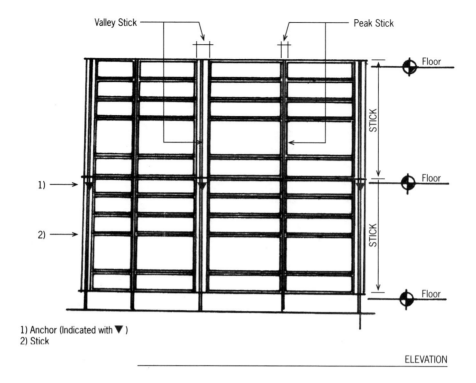

Valley Stick

Peak Stick

STICK

Floor

Floor

STICK

Floor

1) →

2) →

1) Anchor (Indicated with ▼)
2) Stick

ELEVATION

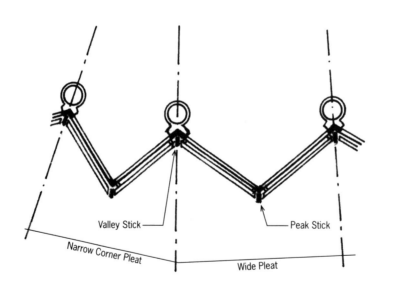

Valley Stick

Peak Stick

Narrow Corner Pleat

Wide Pleat

PLAN

FIGURE 8C2.12a The installation sequence for the enclosure system was defined. The sequence is: (1) anchors, (2) sticks, (3) lower units, (4) silicone sleeve at unit to unit, (5) upper unit, (6) silicone sleeve, and then repeat per floor. Floor-to-floor sticks are installed at the valley and the ridge. Half-floor-height units are installed in the floor-to-floor sticks. *Skidmore, Owings & Merrill LLP*

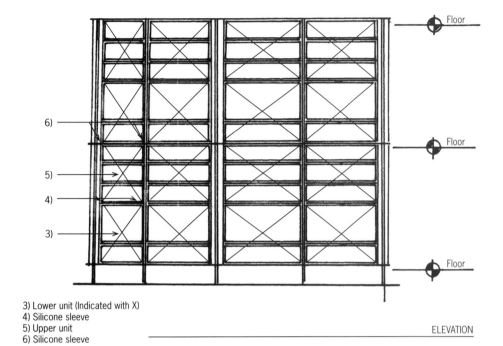

6)
5)
4)
3)

Floor
Floor
Floor

3) Lower unit (Indicated with X)
4) Silicone sleeve
5) Upper unit
6) Silicone sleeve

ELEVATION

PLAN

FIGURE 8C2.12b Unit installation sequence. *Skidmore, Owings & Merrill LLP*

FIGURE 8C2.13 A two-bay by two-floor-high visual mock-up using actual project extrusions was conducted at the curtain wall contractor's assembly plant for owner, architect, and curtain wall contractor review.

infiltration, large seismic movement (Delta M), and 1.5 times wind load for enclosure system structural safety factor. The performance test revealed that the stack joint gasket exhibited air leakage that exceeded the specified limits. A revised gasket intersection joinery method was developed in collaboration with the design team, curtain wall contractor, and curtain wall contractor's design consultant. The new intersection was installed and passed all tests. The performance mock-up is illustrated in Figure 8C2.14.

Construction progress images of the unit on a stick enclosure are shown in Figures 8C2.15, 8C2.16, and 8C2.17.

Summary

The tower geometry created unique enclosure design detail challenges. The building superstructure achieved the geometry through the use of sticks, columns, and beams. Early attempts in the schematic and design development phases to implement a unitized system revealed that the unit-to-unit closure at the peak and valley relied on exact anchor placement with no "geometry guidelines" for the curtain wall installation. A "backbone" aluminum stick provided the geometric guides from floor to floor in plan, section, and elevation. The resulting cold-bent unit on a stick curtain wall enclosure achieves the complex geometric enclosure and the design goal of a crystalline, pleated glass curtain wall. A view of the tower on the Tianjin skyline is illustrated in Figure 8C2.18. A detail image of the curtain wall is shown in Figure 8C2.19.

FIGURE 8C2.14   A full-size performance mock-up was tested to Chinese and international curtain wall testing standards.

FIGURE 8C2.15   Construction progress of 2nd floor sticks with units at starter condition.

FIGURE 8C2.16 Construction installation of 1st unit.

FIGURE 8C2.18 Tower form on Tianjin skyline. *Michael Duncan*

FIGURE 8C2.17 Construction progress on skyline.

FIGURE 8C2.19 Detail image of the tower unit on a stick completed bay window.

Exterior Building Enclosures

Metal Framed and Glass

Fountain Place (formerly Allied Bank Tower)

Location:
Dallas, TX, USA
Building Type:
High-Rise Investment Office Building and Banking Hall with Public Water Gardens

PARTICIPANTS
Owner:
Criswell Development Ltd. – Dallas, TX
Architect:
Pei Cobb Freed & Partners Architects LLP (formerly I. M. Pei and Partners) – New York NY
Associate Architect:
Architectural Consulting Services Inc. – Dallas, TX
Structural Engineer:

CBM Engineers, Inc. – Houston, TX
Mechanical Engineer:
Cosentini Associates LLP – New York, NY
Contractor:
The Beck Group Construction – Dallas, TX
Curtain Wall Contractor:
Flour City Architectural Metals – Glen Cove, NY

PROJECT TIME FRAME
Schematic Design:
June 1982–November 1982
Design Development:
January 1983–June 1983
Construction Documents:
July 1983–February 1984
Construction:
March 1984–September 1986

Project Description

Fountain Place is a 60-story, 720'-0" (230 m) tall, 1.3 million sq. ft. (120,744 sq. m) office tower. It is the first phase of a mixed-use multiphase development. Subsequent phases were planned to include an identical second office tower rotated 90 degrees to the phase 1 tower. Phase 1 completed construction in 1986. The second-phase tower was never constructed; however, the full site development of fountains and landscape was completed.

Fountain Place occupies a 5.5-acre full city block on the northern edge of Dallas's central business district. The building volume is recessed at the tower base to a height of 54'-0" (16.45 m). A parallelogram-shaped plan encloses the tower lobby, office elevator lobbies, and banking hall. Lobby spaces are surrounded by a terraced water garden and fountains, which provide the building's name and identity. An early schematic design site plan with tower one and tower two is presented in Figure 8C3.1. The typical tower office floor plan with the two-tower design is shown in Figure 8C3.1b.

The tower is a 10-sided prismatic volume of sloped and vertical custom metal-framed unitized curtain wall. Its slanted sides and sloping enclosure create different building profiles when viewed from different directions. The three-dimensional form is the result of sculpting a 192'-0" (58.5 m) × 192'-0" (58.5 m) square floor plan to a parallelogram. The green-tinted and reflective glass curtain wall volume takes on the form of a glazed prism. The tower massing elevation is illustrated in Figure 8C3.2.

Tower floor plate sizes and configurations range from 36,864 sq. ft. (3968 sq. m) square at floors 6 through 13, to "interlocking" squares with reducing floor areas due to the opposing side sloping planes from floor 14 to 40, and a parallelogram-shaped floor plate from floor 45 to the 63rd floor. Parallelogram floor plates reduce in size with each succeeding floor, culminating at the peak of the tower geometry. The last occupied office floor is 1,500 sq. ft. (139.4 sq. m) at floor 62. Typical office floors average 21,000 sq. ft. (1,950 sq. m). Multiple tower floor plan configurations are illustrated in Figure 8C3.3.

The tower is organized on a 6'-0" (1.8 m) plan module. Maintaining the precise triangular geometry and exterior mullion alignment between orthogonal and angled curtain wall planes creates 6'-8½" (2.044 m) wide

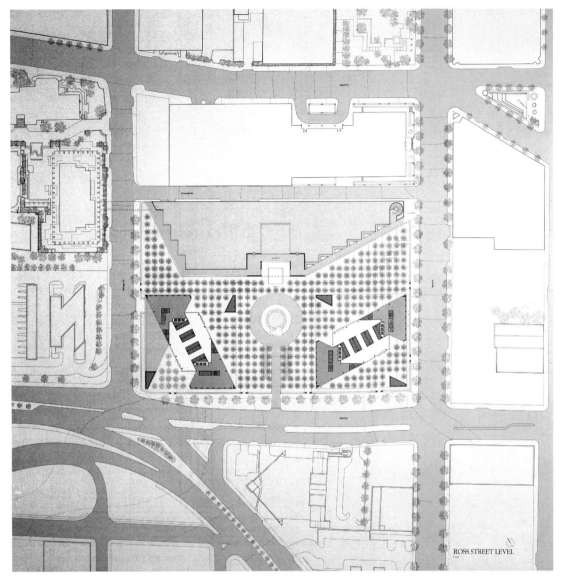

FIGURE 8C3.1a Site plan of Fountain Place with two towers. Tower 1 was constructed. *Pei Cobb Freed & Partners*

curtain wall units at the hypotenuse intersection of the 116.56 degree obtuse plan angle and the 63.44 degree acute plan angle vertical wall planes to the sloping curtain wall planes. A geometry plan diagram is shown in Figure 8C3.4. The sloped curtain wall areas enclose 32 floors and slopes at 26.56 degrees from vertical.

Enclosure System Types

The tower is clad in a floor-to-floor custom unitized curtain wall. The rigorous tower plan and vertical geometry and mullion alignments result in "families" of unit widths depending on the floor configuration. Curtain

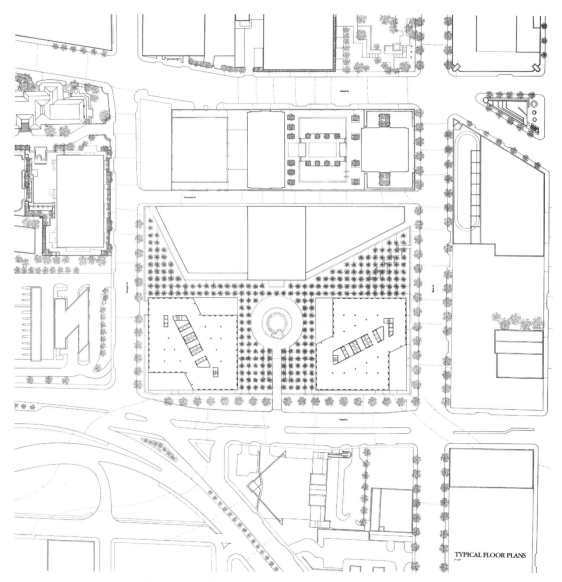

FIGURE 8C3.1b Schematic design low-rise floor plan. *Pei Cobb Freed & Partners*

wall unit plan dimensions are 6'-0" (1.8 m) wide on the "outside square" plan location. The diagonal wall unit mullions align in plan with the 6'-0" typical unit spacing, which results in 6'-8½" (2.044 m) wide units. Typical floor-to-floor heights are 12'-0" (3.6 m) with the unit stack joint sill at 2'-4½" (724 mm) above finish floor. Vision glass is 6'-0" (1.828 m) high. The unitized curtain wall is also employed on the sloping enclosure of the north and south façade. The vertical to sloping curtain wall transition occurs at a half-height unit location achieved with a "folded" unit configuration. This allows the fold to be achieved with shop-fabricated angular units instead of unit-to-unit or field-jointed assemblies, maintaining the crisp tower geometry. A partial plan, elevation, and floor-to-floor sections of the vertical and sloping curtain wall are presented in Figure 8C3.5.

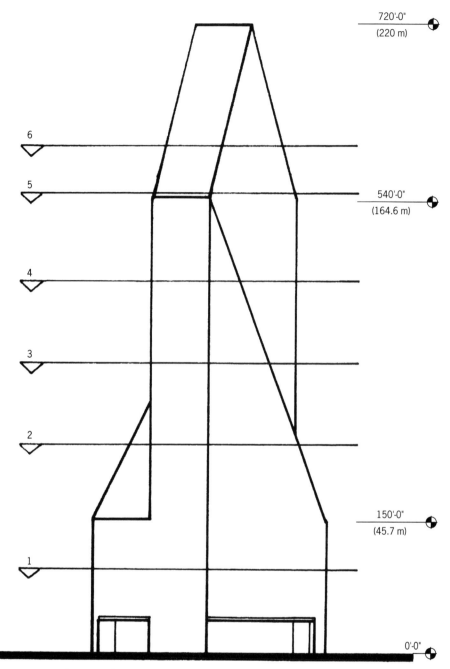

FIGURE 8C3.2 Massing elevation of Fountain Place tower 1. Floor plan configuration and enclosure geometry varies per floor.

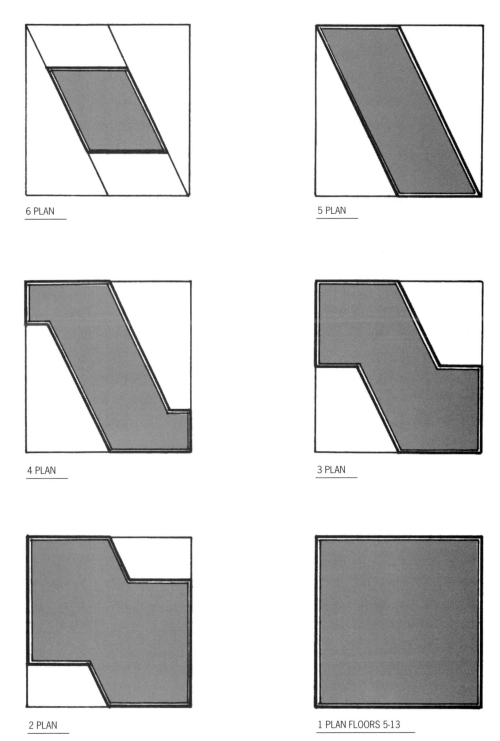

6 PLAN

5 PLAN

4 PLAN

3 PLAN

2 PLAN

1 PLAN FLOORS 5-13

FIGURE 8C3.3   Floor plan enclosure follows tower form and geometry.

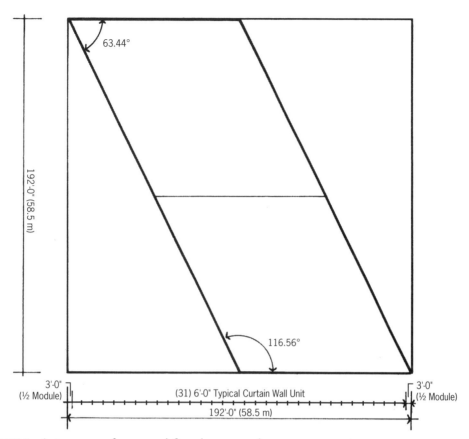

FIGURE 8C3.4 A rigorous set of geometry defines the tower enclosure.

Each curtain wall unit is framed by a 3″ (76 mm) wide split vertical male/female mullion. The narrow mullion exterior face profile is achieved by securing the glass with structural silicone to aluminum glazing "legs" of the extruded mullions extending from the interior surface of the split mullion profile. A plan detail at the unitized curtain wall unit-to-unit joint split vertical mullion is illustrated in Figure 8C3.6. The metal finish at the unit-to-unit joints is clear anodized aluminum, resulting in the silver grid. Each curtain wall unit is subdivided vertically and horizontally by a 1-½″ (38 mm) wide extruded aluminum mullion finish in dark green fluoropolymer coating, creating a subtle secondary frame. A plan detail of the secondary frame is illustrated in Figure 8C3.7. The curtain wall corner is illustrated in Figure 8C3.8, the stack joint in Figure 8C3.9, and the vertical curtain wall head frame in Figure 8C3.10. The sloped curtain wall shown in Fig. 8C3.11 utilizes the same system with laminated glass attached to the frame with structural silicone. The unitized curtain wall employs a pressure-equalized rain screen weather protection principle. The primary and secondary curtain wall unit pattern is illustrated in Figure 8C3.12.

Vision and spandrel glass in the vertical curtain wall is ¼″ (6 mm) thick green-tinted reflective glass. Vision and spandrel glass in the sloped curtain wall is 9/16″ (14.5 mm) thick green-tinted laminated reflective glass.

The unitized curtain wall for the tower enclosure begins at the plaza/grade level. The namesake fountains are held approximately 6″ (150 mm) from the curtain wall to reinforce the design intent of a tower in the waterscape. An image of the curtain wall to fountain interface is shown in Figure 8C3.13.

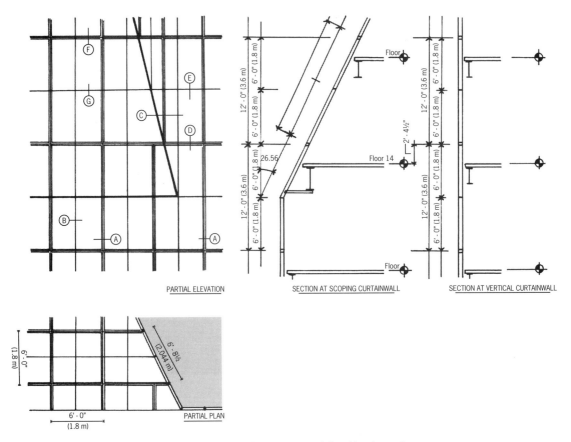

FIGURE 8C3.5   Partial plan, elevation, and sections dimensions are defined by the enclosure geometry.

The lobby entrance is a 28'-0" (8,534 m) tall clear glass mullion and clear monolithic glass storefront. A 2'-0" (6 m) high aluminum-clad transom provides 8'-0" (2.44 m) floor-to-transom silicone sealed mono-lithic clear glass from grade to the underside of the aluminum-clad transom. The storefront from the top of the transom to the aluminum surround is clear tempered glass gravity-supported at the transom with clear tempered glass mullions for lateral wind load resistance. The lobby enclosure glass-to-glass joints in the storefront is sealed with silicone and utilizes a barrier design weather protection design principle. The lobby entrance storefront composition is illustrated in Figure 8C3.14.

Enclosure System Project Design Goals

The owner defined two project and enclosure goals:

1. Create an inviting public presence at street level
2. Establish a unique identity on the skyline

The majority of the 5.5-acre site consists of terraced fountains and cascading waterfalls in multiple levels from the Ross Avenue address to the lobby level. Embedded in the fountains are planters with Texas cypress

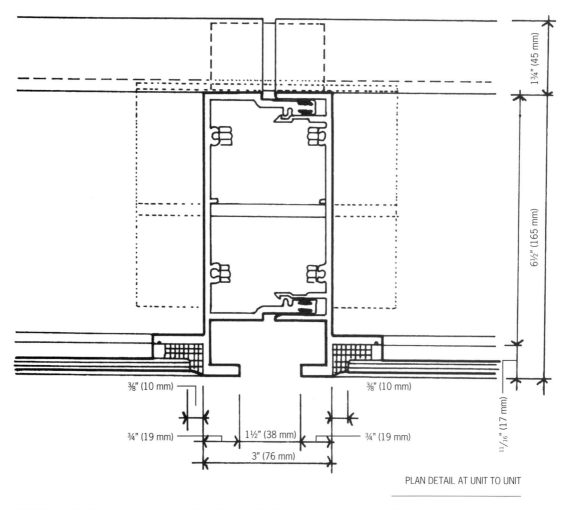

Dimensions shown on figure: 1¾" (45 mm), 6½" (165 mm), 1¹/₁₆" (17 mm), ⅜" (10 mm), ⅜" (10 mm), ¾" (19 mm), 1½" (38 mm), ¾" (19 mm), 3" (76 mm)

PLAN DETAIL AT UNIT TO UNIT

FIGURE 8C3.6 The unitized curtain wall mullion at 6'-0" center-to-center spacing. The exterior aluminum profile provides the primary exterior grid. Monolithic glass cladding is structurally silicone attached.

trees organized in the grid pattern of the tower. The fountains and tower curtain wall enclosure meet at all areas except the lobby entrances. The tower is literally sited in the fountains.

The tower's green-tinted reflective glass curtain wall and geometric massing present ever changing silhouettes and reflections, depending on the time of day and sky conditions. The clarity of the tower form and geometry is made possible by the flush metal framing and structurally glazed curtain wall.

Enclosure System Design Process

SCHEMATIC DESIGN

The original project included two identical towers. The sizes, placement, and tower and site geometry were developed early in schematic design. Design architect Henry Cobb summarized the design as "geometry pursued with rigor."

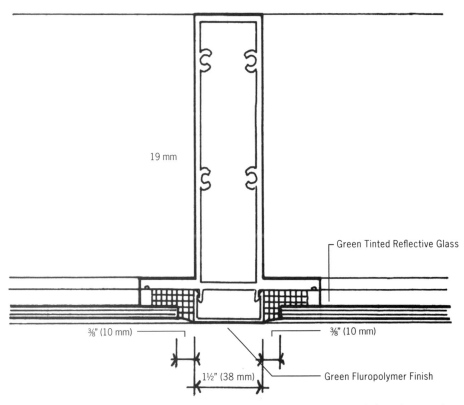

FIGURE 8C3.7 The intermediate vertical unit mullion at 3′-0″ center-to-center spacing defines the secondary grid. The green color exterior aluminum profile is achieved with a high-performance coating.

DESIGN DEVELOPMENT

Curtain wall elevations and sections were developed to determine the unit stack joint vertical datum. The 50 percent vision glass (6′-0″ vision and 6′-0″ (1.82 by 1.82 m) spandrel) was evaluated for solar heat gain to determine the necessary glass performance requirements and extent of vision and spandrel (opaque) glass with insulation. Monolithic green-tinted and reflective coated glass was selected to provide the required solar shading and visible light transmittance.

Construction Documents

System profiles and in-progress details were reviewed with curtain wall fabricators. Fountain Place is one of the earliest large-scale applications of structural silicone glazing. Details for sealant adhesion and reflective coating compatibility were reviewed with glass and curtain wall manufacturers. System details were developed for visual profile, weather protection, and surface areas requirements for application of structural silicone.

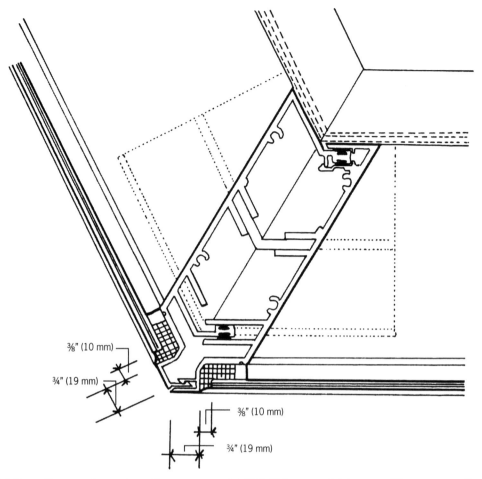

FIGURE 8C3.8 Corner unit-to-unit mullion occurs on a 3′-0″ (half-design module) spacing. The exterior profile matches the intermediate vertical mullion profile.

Summary

Fountain Place is a dramatic image on the Dallas skyline. The clarity of the prismatic geometry is achieved through flush glass and metal alignment utilizing the then-new technology of structural silicone glazing on a monumental scale. The use of high-performance glass with 50 percent vision and 50 percent insulated spandrels achieved a high level of energy performance without compromising the exterior enclosure design goals. Fountain Place Tower gracefully sits in the water garden, providing shelter below the tower and an urban oasis in the Central Business District. The tower on the skyline is illustrated in Figure 8C3.15.

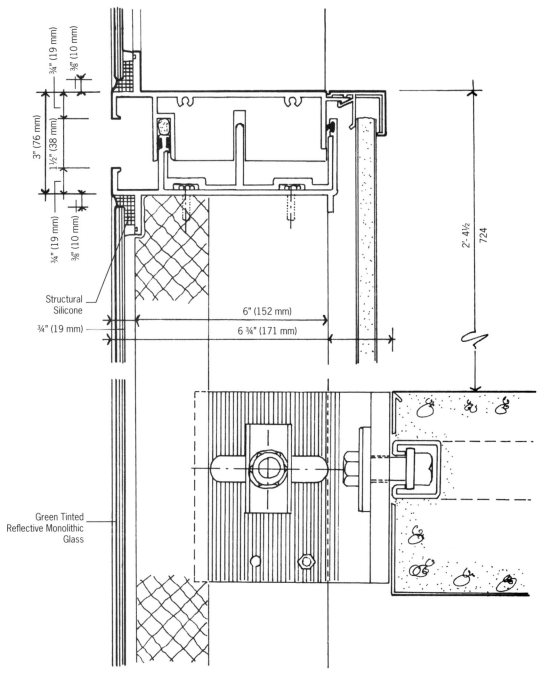

FIGURE 8C3.9 Unit-to-unit joinery at vertical curtain wall stack joint. The exterior horizontal aluminum profile completes the primary exterior grid. Monolithic vision and spandrel glass cladding is structurally silicone attached.

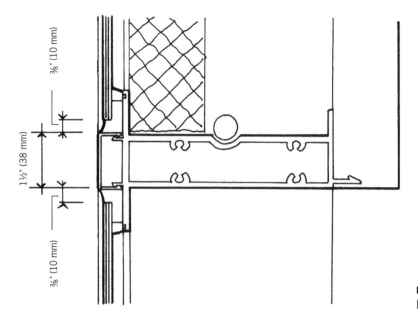

FIGURE 8C3.10 Curtain wall head detail at vision to spandrel.

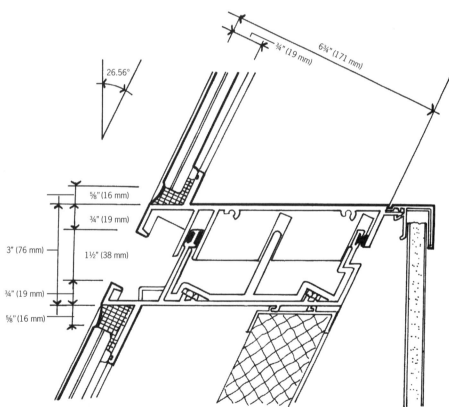

FIGURE 8C3.11 Unit-to-unit joinery at sloped curtain wall stack joint. The exterior horizontal aluminum profile is designed to the same exterior face expression as the vertical curtain wall. Laminated vision and spandrel glass cladding is structurally silicone attached.

FIGURE 8C3.12 Unitized curtain wall with primary grid expression at unit-to-unit joinery. The secondary grid is static horizontal and vertical mullions.

FIGURE 8C3.13 The unitized curtain wall begins at the plaza and fountain level. The unitized curtain wall is revealed at the fountain weir interface.

FIGURE 8C3.14 The lobby entrance storefront is a glass mullion system. The aluminum panel surround of the storefront provides the detail and enclosure system transition to the unitized curtain wall.

FIGURE 8C3.15 The prismatic form of Fountain Place Tower on the Dallas skyline.

Metal Framed and Glass

Shanghai Huawei Technologies Corporate Campus

Location:
Shanghai, People's Republic of China Building Type:
Research Development Campus and User-Specific Office Building

PARTICIPANTS
Owner:
Shanghai Huawei Technology Co. Ltd.
Design Architect/Exterior Enclosure Design:
Skidmore, Owings & Merrill LLP – San Francisco, CA
Local Design Institute Architect (LDIA):
Shanghai Institute of Architectural Design & Research (SIADR) – Shanghai, China
Design Structural Engineer:
Skidmore, Owings & Merrill LLP – San Francisco, CA
Local Design Institute Structural Engineer (LDISE):
Shanghai Institute of Architectural Design & Research (SIADR) – Shanghai, China
Mechanical Engineer:
Flack & Kurtz – San Francisco, CA
Local Design Institute Mechanical Engineer (LDIME):
Shanghai Institute of Mechanical Design and Research (SIMDR) – Shanghai, China
Contractor:
China State Construction Company #8 – Shanghai, China

Curtain Wall Contractors:
Jianghe Curtain Wall Co. Ltd. – Shanghai, China
Yuanda China – Shenyang and Shanghai, China

PROJECT TIME FRAME
Concept Design:
March 2005
Schematic Design:
August 2005–December 2005
Design Development:
January 2006–May 2006
Construction Tender Documents:
February 2007–August 2007
Construction:
January 2008–Oct0ber 2010

Project Description

Huawei Technologies completed construction on a vast research and development (R&D) campus in late 2010 in Shanghai's emerging Pudong District international community. Designed to accommodate 7,500 employees, the Huawei campus encompasses 3,222,000 occupied sq. ft. (299,333 sq. m), in a single building five stories above grade with two levels below grade, and a length of 2523′-0″(769 m) linked through a continuous skylit atrium. At the heart of the campus are two long five-story R&D building sections, the interiors of which are divided into open-office work plans and closed laboratories. A ground floor plan/site plan is illustrated in Figure 8C4.1.

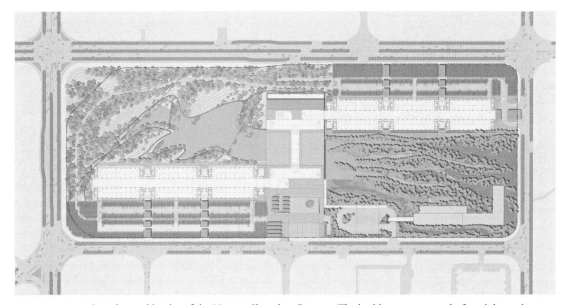

FIGURE 8C4.1   Site plan and level 1 of the Huawei Shanghai Campus. The building is composed of modules each 305′-1½″ (93 m), long for a building length of approximately half a mile.   *Skidmore, Owings & Merrill LLP*

The various departments that occupy building modules are linked through a continuous skylit atrium. To maximize flexibility and anticipate future change in research and technology, the building floor plates are designed as a series of modules, 305′-1½″ (93 m) long by 59′-0″ (18 m) wide, with repetitive structural bays 59′-0″ (18 m)wide by 29′-0″ (9 m) long. Each floor plate building module is connected by 34′-5 ⅜″ (10.5 m) wide elevator lobbies on the western façade and toilet facilities on the eastern façade. An R&D module floor plan is illustrated in Figure 8C4.2. This department plan organization amplifies interior exposure to natural light and exterior views with one long elevation towards the exterior and the other long elevation toward the interior skylit atrium.

The siting of the R&D buildings allows a continuous landscape to traverse the length of the site, and also connects the two buildings to the cafeteria and other amenities at grade. To the east is a forest, which contrasts with a public park to the west. A schematic design phase model illustrating the siting of the building within the campus landscape is shown in Figure 8C4.3.

Enclosure System Types

There are three primary exterior enclosure systems designed and implemented on Huawei Shanghai Technologies Campus:

1. Custom unitized system
2. Custom unit on a stick subframe system
3. Custom stick skylight over the interior atriums

CUSTOM UNITIZED

A six-story high atrium entry serves as the campus's "front door" and is enclosed with a custom unitized shop-fabricated curtain wall. Each curtain wall unit is typically one-floor high − 14′-9″ (4.5 m) × 4′-11″ (1.5 m) wide. Corner units are 14′-9″ (4.5 m) high × 2′-5½″ (.75 m) wide. The unitized system employs a pressure-equalized rain screen weather protection principle. Each unit is suspended from custom-designed extruded aluminum curtain wall system anchors attached to embedded inserts within the exposed architectural concrete superstructure. The curtain wall unit is a slender 6″ (150 mm) deep aluminum extrusion, inclusive of the glass. Glass infill is secured to the unitized frames with four-sided structural shop-installed silicone glazing. An exterior view of the entry curtain wall is illustrated in Figure 8C4.4.

The east façade R&D building modules are modulated by 34′5 ⅜″ (10.5 m) wide unitized glass curtain walls, which enclose toilet facilities. Custom unitized curtain wall units, 14′9″ (4.5 m) high × 4′11″ (1.5 m) wide, are combined with an interior floor-to-ceiling operable frosted laminated glass privacy wall at the toilet facilities on each floor. Curtain wall spandrel zones are 1 ³⁄₁₆″ (30 mm) thick insulating low-E vision glass with ³⁄₁₆″ (5 mm) thick aluminum plate shadow boxes and 2″ (50 mm) semi-rigid insulation. An exterior view of the toilet room curtain wall enclosure is illustrated in Figure 8C4.5. An interior view of the curtain wall with the operable frosted glass panels is illustrated in Figure 8C4.6.

A custom double wall façade encloses the east and west building module elevations of the office and R&D areas. The exterior layer of the double wall is a unitized window wall supported by a concealed galvanized steel subframe. The inner layer of the double wall is a unitized window wall with operable windows. Between the inner and outer layer is a wood veneer aluminum motorized blade sunscreen. The sunscreen motors are linked to the building management system to open and close at preset light levels, to modulate daylight to the interior spaces. An exterior view of the double wall is illustrated in Figure 8C4.7. Interior views of the double wall in the work spaces and circulation are illustrated in Figure 8C4.8a and 8C4.8b

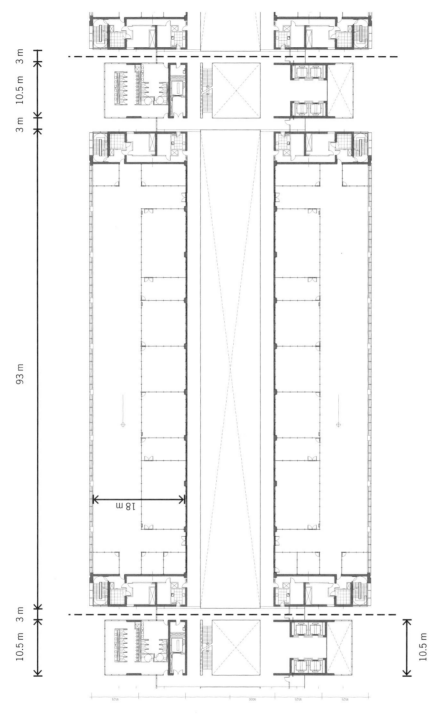

FIGURE 8C4.2 Building plan for 1 module. Each module is 305'-1½" (93 m) long and connected with 34'-5 ⅜" (10.5 m) wide elevator and toilet facility modules. Multiple metal framed and glass enclosure systems are designed per interior uses. *Skidmore, Owings & Merrill LLP*

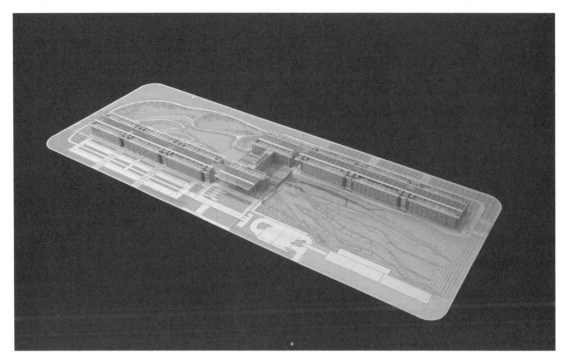

FIGURE 8C4.3   Schematic design model of the campus.   *Skidmore, Owings & Merrill LLP*

FIGURE 8C4.4   Public spaces such as the building entry are enclosed with a custom unitized curtain wall.   *Photo ©*
Tim Griffith

FIGURE 8C4.5 Toilet facility modules are enclosed with a custom unitized curtain wall and an interior frosted glass privacy screen. *Michael Fukutome*

FIGURE 8C4.6 Toilet facility interior. The frosted glass privacy screen is to the left. *Michael Fukotome*

FIGURE 8C4.7 Office and research areas are enclosed with custom double unitized vented window wall systems. The cavity space between window walls houses a motorized horizontal sunscreen linked to the building management system for sun-shading. *Photo © Tim Griffith*

FIGURE 8C4.8a Interior view of double window wall with horizontal sunscreens in R & D work areas. *Photo © Tim Griffith*

FIGURE 8C4.8b Detail image of double wall in circulation zone.

CUSTOM UNITIZED ON A STICK SUBFRAME SYSTEM

The east and west façades of the north and south building modules are modulated by 34′-5 ⅜″ (10.5 m) wide elevator lobbies on each floor. The elevator lobby at level 1 is one story tall with a floor-to-floor height of 14′-9″ (4.5 m). The elevator lobbies at floors 2 to 3 and 4 to 5 are two stories high—29′-6″ (9 m)—to allow natural light deep into the 59′-0″ (18 m) deep lobby spaces. Field-erected, two-story-tall steel tube "sticks" are clad with custom-prefinished aluminum extrusions. Curtain wall units 14′-9″ (4.5 m) high are installed on the sticks with custom-designed exposed anchors. An exterior view of the elevator lobby section is illustrated in Figure 8C4.9. An interior view of the unit on a stick system in the two-story-high elevator lobby is illustrated in Figure 8C4.10.

Exit stairs are located at the ends of each R&D building module along the east and west façades. The exit stairs are located adjacent to the exterior building face and enclosed with a custom unit on a stick system. An exposed steel tube subframe stick, prefinished to architectural steel surface quality and painted with a polyvinylidene fluoride (PVDF) finish, are attached to the cast-in-place concrete stair structure with custom-designed steel plate anchors. Units are installed on the steel sticks via custom extruded aluminum anchors. An exterior view of the exit stair unit on a stick curtain wall enclosure is illustrated in Figure 8C4.11.

FIGURE 8C4.9 Two-story elevator lobby areas are enclosed with a custom unit on a stick curtain wall system. *Tim Griffith*

FIGURE 8C4.10 Interior view of elevator lobby with unit on a stick curtain wall enclosure.

FIGURE 8C4.11 Egress stairs are enclosed by unit on an exposed steel stick curtain wall system. *Photo © Tim Griffith*

CUSTOM STICK SKYLIGHT SYSTEM

A continuous skylight runs the full length of the campus, creating the enclosed atrium between R&D building modules. Interior views through the atrium are illustrated in Figure 8C4.12. The skylight is a custom stick system utilizing a barrier weather protection approach. Extruded aluminum plates extend up from the skylight rafter mullions at 10′-0″ (3 m) spacing for window-washing support tie-offs and the attachment of the lightning protection grounding system. Aluminum expansion skylight rafters are spaced at 29′-6″ (9 m) spacing to accommodate thermal expansion and contraction. Condensation gutters are detailed into the rafters and purlins to collect potential moisture from vapor condensation at the top of the atrium. The gutters are continuous profiles integral with each frame. Concealed flashing provides weathertight continuity from the inside face of skylight glass and aluminum assembly at the base of the skylight system to the continuous aluminum fascia bordering the building roof.

FIGURE 8C4.12 Atriums are located the full length of the office and research modules. A custom stick system skylight with a suspended fritted and laminated glass lay-light sunscreen encloses the atrium spaces. Atrium view toward the elevator lobby. *Photo © Tim Griffith*

To provide additional solar control in the atrium, a "lay-light" glass panel is suspended from and below each skylight frame. The lay-light consists of two tempered glass lites of ⅝" (15 mm) laminated with a 1.5 mil thick polyvinyl butyral interlayer. A custom ceramic frit diffuses natural light to the bamboo-planted atrium.

Enclosure System Goals

The system design goals are:

1. Economy and quality through repetition
2. Maximized daylight in public areas, filtered daylight in workspaces
3. Visually delicate frames

ECONOMY AND QUALITY THROUGH REPETITION

Consistent design profiles were developed and applied to the unitized and unit on a stick curtain wall systems. The custom unitized enclosure details and frames repeat for both the unitized and unitized on a steel stick subframe systems. Additional span heights at stairs and two-story spaces are achieved through the introduction of the stick to achieve the specified system deflection performance requirements. The stick for the unit on the stick system is clad with extruded aluminum in public space locations that require higher finishes, such as the elevator lobbies. Architectural exposed steel tubes, prefinished with a PVDF finish, are utilized in the more utilitarian stairways.

MAXIMIZED DAYLIGHT IN PUBLIC AREAS, FILTERED DAYLIGHT IN WORKSPACES

Floor-to-ceiling glass in the public spaces, such as the elevator lobby, stairwells, and toilet facilities, provide abundant natural daylight into the interior spaces. The R&D workspaces require flexibility to filter the quantity of daylight, depending on the task. Low-E glass was designed for the exterior with operable louvers between the double wall planes to modulate daylight.

VISUALLY DELICATE FRAMES

The unitized curtain wall unit assemblies are 6" (150 mm) deep. The aluminum frame depth is 4'-11⁄16" (120 mm), supporting 1-5⁄16" (30 mm) thick insulating low-E glass. The aluminum extrusion wall thicknesses vary from 3⁄16" (5 mm) to ¼" (7 mm) thick. The system profile frame width is 3" (75 mm). Each unit frame is 1" (25 mm) wide at each unit glazing opening, with a 1" (25 mm) wide continuous reveal between aluminum frames. The frames were CNC milled with compound cuts and postfabrication painted aluminum to maintain the reveal continuity at horizontal to vertical intersections. An interior view detail of the mullion intersection is illustrated in Figure 8C4.13. An isometric of the interior unit-to-unit frame intersection is illustrated in Figure 8C4.14.

Collaborative work sessions were conducted between the design architect and design structural engineer to determine the sizes of internal steel shapes to support the double wall and the sizes of the steel tube stick spans and deflection. Steel member sizes were defined on the documents to accommodate the specified deflections.

Enclosure System Design Process

SCHEMATIC DESIGN

A repetitive plan and vertical dimensional strategy were developed to achieve a design consistency for the immense quantity of enclosure. Each enclosure system is typically 4'-11½" (1.5 m) wide by one floor high. Corners are typically ½ typical unitized widths: 2'-5½" (750 mm) on one or both curtain wall elevations to maintain the repetitive plan dimension.

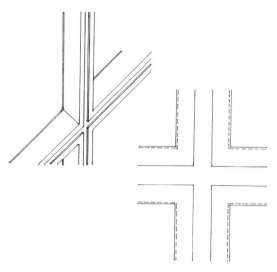

FIGURE 8C4.14 Isometric and interior elevation of curtain wall reveal frame joinery. The design goal was to create a visually delicate frame profile through minimal metal and shadow.

FIGURE 8C4.13 The interior curtain wall profile is a 1 inch (25 mm) continuous reveal between each vertical and horizontal frame.

Floor-to-floor height studies yielded a 14'-9" (4.5 m) height for office and R&D spaces. Common datum lines for sills and ceiling heights were determined for intersection of the exterior enclosure to the interior finishes and building systems. An exterior rendering of the building context, enclosures, and landscape viewed from the garden is illustrated in Figure 8C4.15.

DESIGN DEVELOPMENT

Curtain wall systems and typical details were developed for the unitized curtain wall and the unitized double-wall window wall system. The unitized curtain wall system section at the six-story entrance lobby is illustrated in Figure 8C4.16. The unitized curtain wall system section at the toilet room areas is illustrated in Figure 8C4.17. The head, jamb, sill, and corner details are illustrated in Figures 8C4.18, 8C4.19, 8C4.20, and 8C4.21. A section through the unit on a stick system at the elevator lobby is illustrated in Figure 8C4.22. A section through the exit stair unit on a steel stick system is illustrated in Figure 8C4.23. The north and south façades are enclosed with a custom unitized curtain wall. Units are 14'-9" (4.5 m) high × 4'-11" (1.5 m) wide, combined with a vertical operable louvered sunshade and interior floor-to-ceiling operable clear laminated glass wall at the ends of the atrium on each floor. The operable interior glass wall panels allow maintenance access for cleaning from each floor of the atrium bridges. A section through the double curtain wall at the atriums on the north and south elevation is illustrated in Figure 8C4.24.

The double unitized window wall with the exposed architectural concrete superstructure at the R&D modules is illustrated in Figure 8C4.25. The head, jamb, and sill details are illustrated in Figures 8C4.26,

FIGURE 8C4.15   Schematic design rendering of campus from the landscape garden.   *Skidmore, Owings & Merrill LLP*

8C4.27, and 8C4.28. System joinery, resulting from the enclosure wall sections and the typical detail development, was applied to enlarged-scale building elevations of each area, to further refine alignments and intersections with the exposed architectural concrete superstructure.

Construction/Tender Documents

Enlarged building elevations identified the basis of design location for each curtain wall system's gravity connections and lateral load locations. This was done as a diagram for each system in each location, for coordination with the structural engineers, and the enclosure load path diagrams. A partial elevation of the elevator lobby is illustrated in Figure 8C4.29. The system details are illustrated in Figure 8C4.30. A partial elevation of the R&D double wall is illustrated in Figure 8C4.31. Construction document system details for the double wall are illustrated in Figure 8C4.32. Final construction documentation, including atypical enclosure details were finalized for interfaces with the architectural concrete and canopies, entries, skylight intersections, and concrete flashing/sealant intersections. Project specifications were updated from the design development stage to include Chinese and international curtain wall standards.

Construction

Because of the size and quantity of enclosure systems, the project was tendered to nine enclosure contractors based in China. Proposed typical system details were provided to the design architect for design and technical

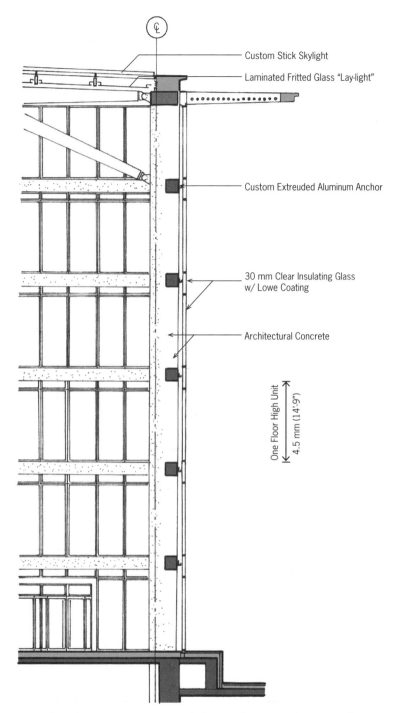

Custom Stick Skylight

Laminated Fritted Glass "Lay-light"

Custom Extreuded Aluminum Anchor

30 mm Clear Insulating Glass
w/ Lowe Coating

Architectural Concrete

One Floor High Unit
4.5 mm (14'-9")

FIGURE 8C4.16 Section through six-story entry areas with floor-to-floor unitized curtain wall enclosure. The skylight is a custom stick system with a laminated fritted glass "lay-light" suspended below for glare control.

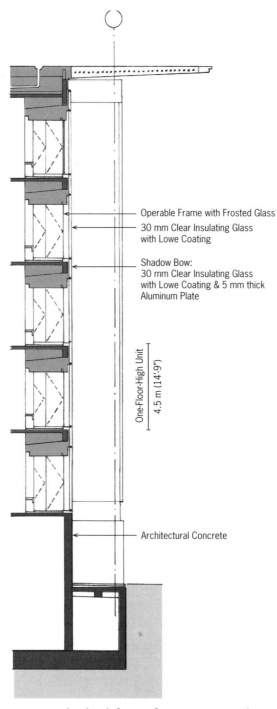

Operable Frame with Frosted Glass

30 mm Clear Insulating Glass
with Lowe Coating

Shadow Bow:
30 mm Clear Insulating Glass
with Lowe Coating & 5 mm thick
Aluminum Plate

One-Floor-High Unit
4.5 m (14'-9")

Architectural Concrete

FIGURE 8C4.17 Toilet room areas are enclosed with floor-to-floor custom unitized curtain walls. The spandrel areas are designed with aluminum plate behind vision glass in a shadow box construction. An interior frosted glass privacy screen is operable for maintenance.

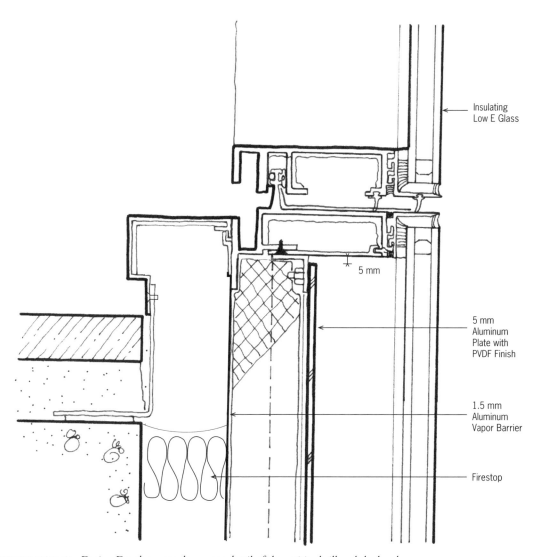

FIGURE 8C4.18   Design Development document detail of the unitized sill and shadow box.

evaluation in two phases. In Phase 1, representative shop drawing details of each of the systems were reviewed, including profile, alignments, finishes, materials, and other visual items. Technical performance review consisted of air and water continuity, attachments, materials, interface with the primary building structure, and other performance items. All nine sets were reviewed with detail red mark graphic sketches and mark-ups and then discussed with each contractor over multiday review sessions. Each contractor was given two weeks to make tender drawing revisions with material samples for final review. A technical evaluation was prepared by the architectural review team and provided to the owner with recommendations for selection. Two enclosure contractors were selected by the owner as a result of the large quantity of enclosures.

The primary building structure is exposed architectural concrete. The architectural concrete provided separations between curtain wall areas and delineation of the building modules, stairs, elevator lobbies, and public

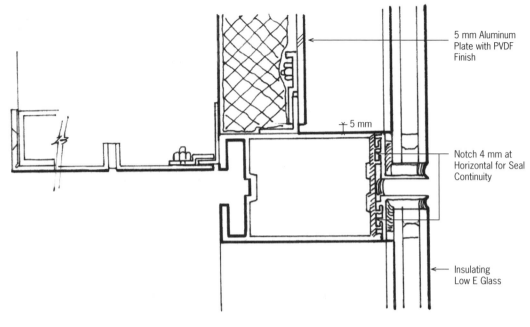

5 mm Aluminum Plate with PVDF Finish

5 mm

Notch 4 mm at Horizontal for Seal Continuity

Insulating Low E Glass

Shadow Box Head

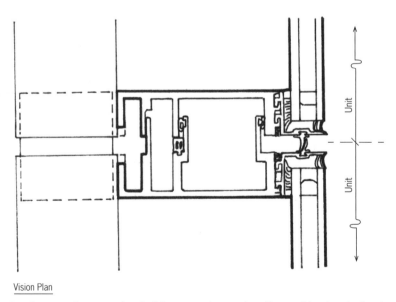

Unit

Unit

Vision Plan

FIGURE 8C4.19   Design Development document detail of the unitized vertical mullion and head at shadow box.

Exterior Building Enclosures

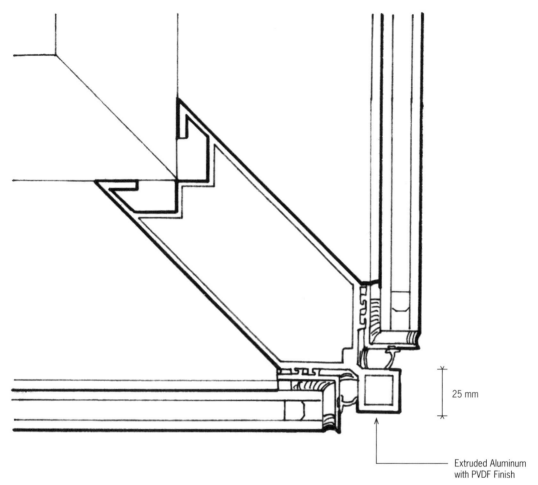

25 mm

Extruded Aluminum
with PVDF Finish

FIGURE 8C4.20 Design Development document detail of the unitized corner mullion. Corners were designed as an "L" shape with static vertical mullions.

space entry areas. This allowed the two contractors to mobilize multiple installation teams concurrently within the areas defined by the concrete. Each building module and enclosure system was under installation concurrently, with multiple crews working two 10-hour shifts. An image of the exterior enclosure during construction is shown in Figure 8C4.33.

Challenges

The size of the project, coupled with an aggressive construction schedule, resulted in the selection of two curtain wall contractors. Each contractor was responsible for engineering, fabrication, assembly, and installation of each of the vertical curtain wall and window wall systems. Both enclosure contractors provided a unitized and a unit on a stick system. A challenge for the architectural design team was to maintain matching profiles, finishes, color matches, and performance requirements. Each contractor was required to follow the visual and performance requirements of the tender documents, with no deviations.

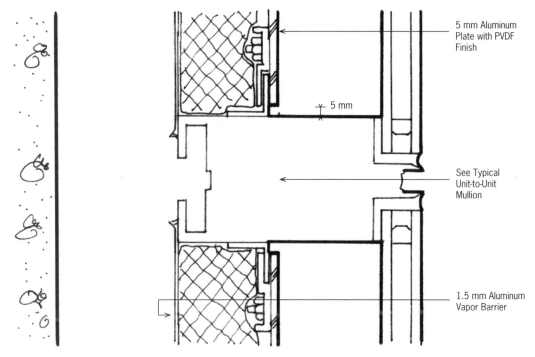

5 mm Aluminum
Plate with PVDF
Finish

5 mm

See Typical
Unit-to-Unit
Mullion

1.5 mm Aluminum
Vapor Barrier

FIGURE 8C4.21   Design Development document detail of the unitized vertical mullion at the shadow box spandrel.

Performance mock-ups of each system were required by the project tender specifications. Because two contractors had been selected, seven full-size performance mock-up tests were conducted. There were two each for the unitized system, unitized on a stick system, and the double window wall at the R&D module, and one for the skylight.

Enclosure Success

To validate final visual approval of each of the two selected enclosure contractors' systems, a mock-up was constructed, two stories high by one bay of 9 × 18 m (29'-6 ⅜" × 59'-⅝"), with a full atrium width. Following the initial review of each subcontractor's shop drawings, and each of the enclosure systems passing the performance mock-up testing, areas of the two-story mock-up were clad with each system by both contractors, for owner and architect team visual review. Images of the visual mock-up are illustrated in Figure 8C4.34, 8C4.35, and 8C4.36.

Summary

The quantity of exterior enclosure for the Huawei Shanghai campus is larger than that of many high-rise buildings. The volume of shop drawing, coordination meetings, reviews, and performance mock-ups was doubled as a result of the selection of two contractors. The final building enclosure exhibits a high quality of materials and joinery. Final images of the exterior are illustrated in Figures 8C4.37, 8C4.38, and 8C4.39.

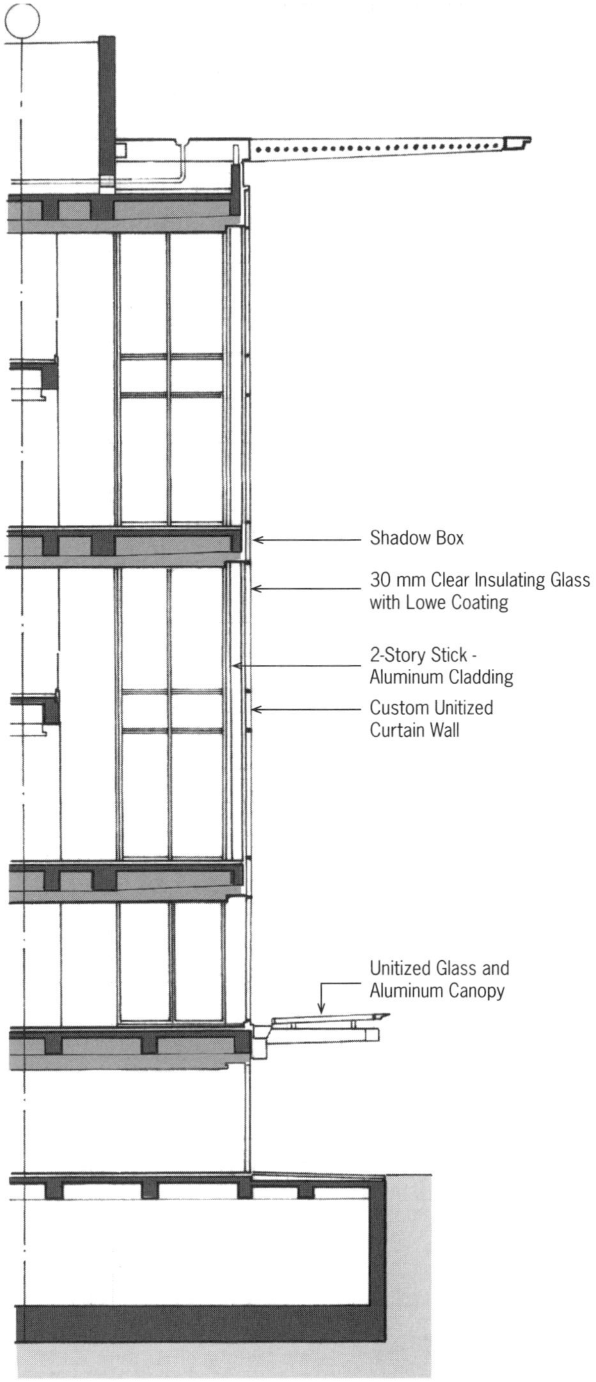
Shadow Box
30 mm Clear Insulating Glass
with Lowe Coating
2-Story Stick -
Aluminum Cladding
Custom Unitized
Curtain Wall
Unitized Glass and
Aluminum Canopy

FIGURE 8C4.22 Section at the two-story elevator lobby. The enclosure is a unit on a stick. The stick is a steel tube with extruded aluminum cladding. Floor-to-floor units are installed on the preset sticks.

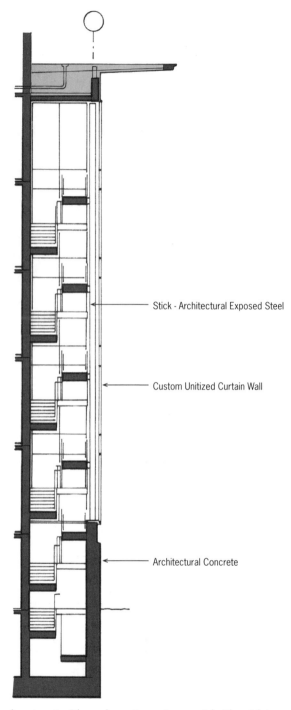

Stick - Architectural Exposed Steel

Custom Unitized Curtain Wall

Architectural Concrete

FIGURE 8C4.23 Section at the exit stairs. The enclosure is a unit on a stick. The stick is a steel tube with an architectural finish and high-performance coating. Floor-to-floor units are installed on the preset sticks.

Exterior Building Enclosures

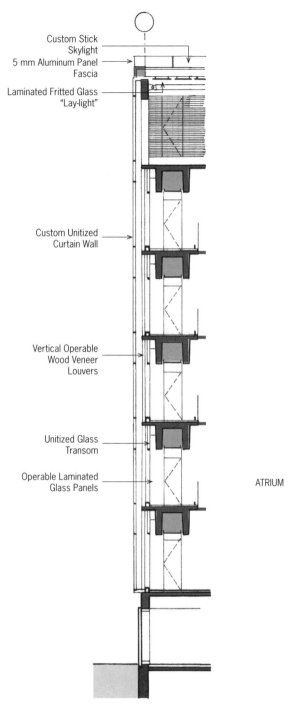

Custom Stick Skylight

5 mm Aluminum Panel Fascia

Laminated Fritted Glass "Lay-light"

Custom Unitized Curtain Wall

Vertical Operable Wood Veneer Louvers

Unitized Glass Transom

Operable Laminated Glass Panels

ATRIUM

FIGURE 8C4.24 Section at the ends of the atriums. The enclosure is a floor-to-floor unitized curtain wall. An interior operable glass wall completes a double-wall system for solar control and acoustic separation from exterior noise. Vertical operable sunshades are controlled by the energy management system.

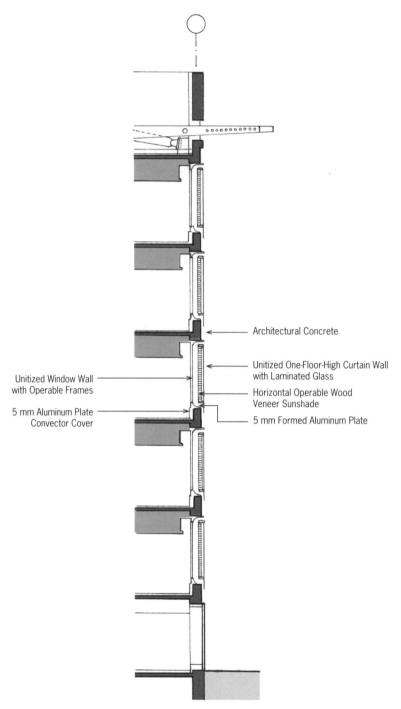

Architectural Concrete

Unitized One-Floor-High Curtain Wall
with Laminated Glass

Unitized Window Wall
with Operable Frames

Horizontal Operable Wood
Veneer Sunshade

5 mm Aluminum Plate
Convector Cover

5 mm Formed Aluminum Plate

FIGURE 8C4.25 Office and research areas are enclosed by a unitized double window wall. The cavity between the two window wall systems is open to the exterior for natural ventilation. Interior window frames are operable for natural ventilation and maintenance. Horizontal sunscreens provide shading.

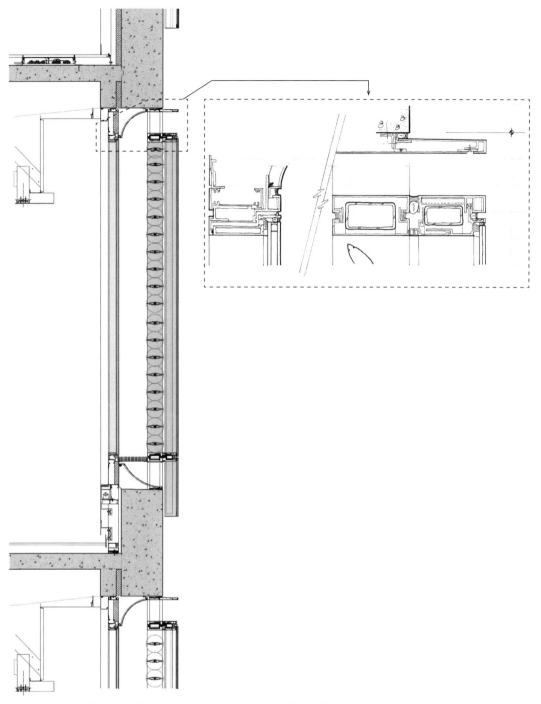

FIGURE 8C4.26 Head details at the interior and exterior window walls.

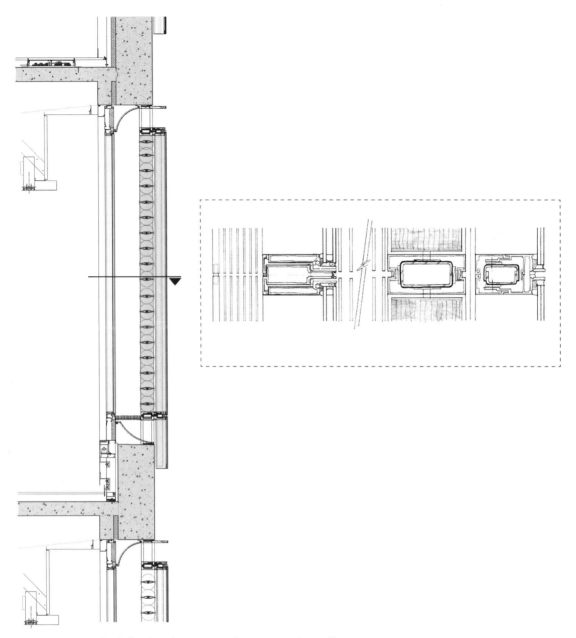

FIGURE 8C4.27 Jamb details at the interior and exterior window walls.

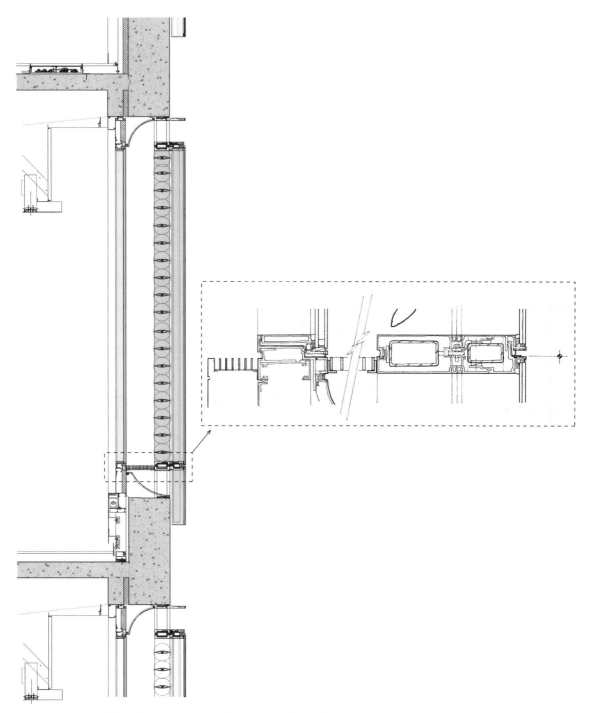

FIGURE 8C4.28 Sill details at the interior and exterior window walls.

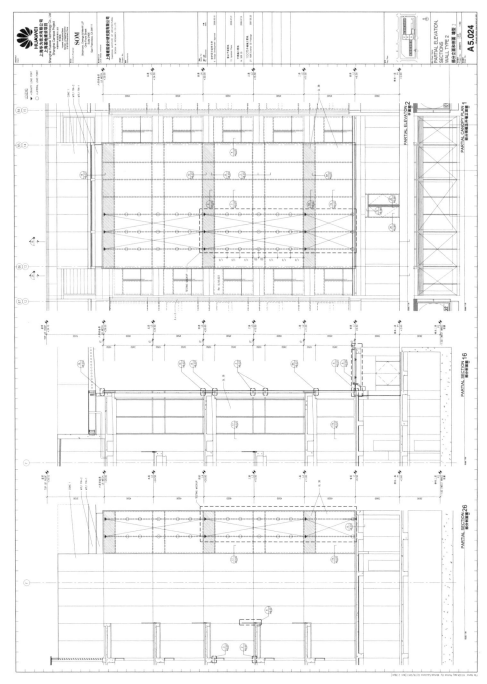

FIGURE 8C4.29 Partial elevation of the elevator lobby with curtain wall unit delineation and load support points.

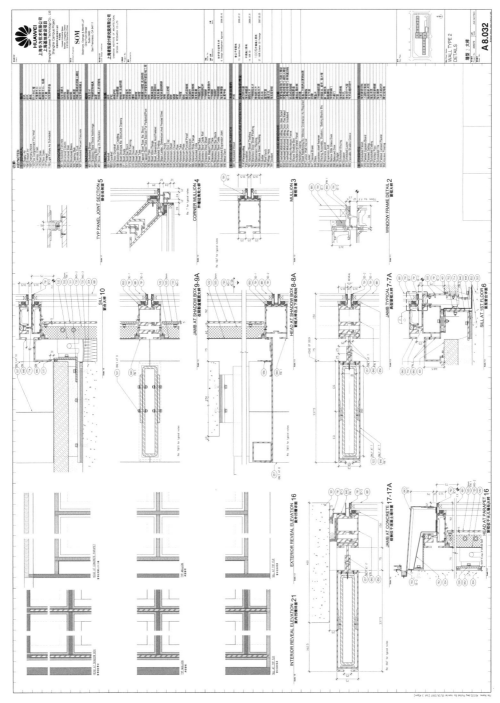

FIGURE 8C4.30 Tender document details for the custom unitized curtain wall. *Skidmore, Owings & Merrill LLP*

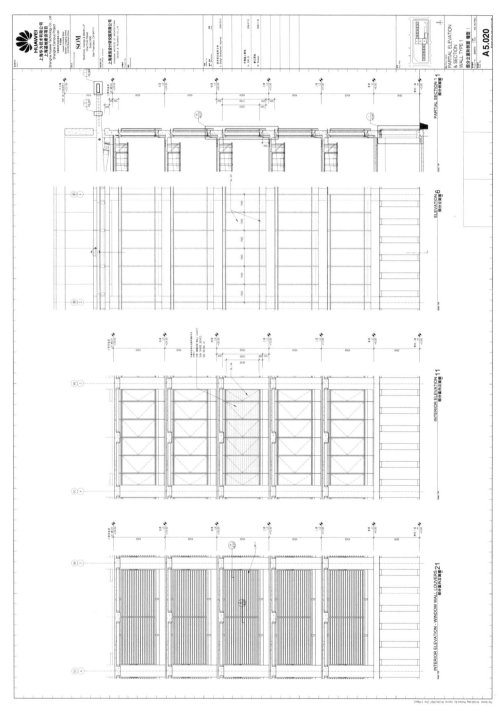

FIGURE 8C4.31 Tender document elevations and section of the multiple layers of the double window wall system. *Skidmore, Owings & Merrill LLP*

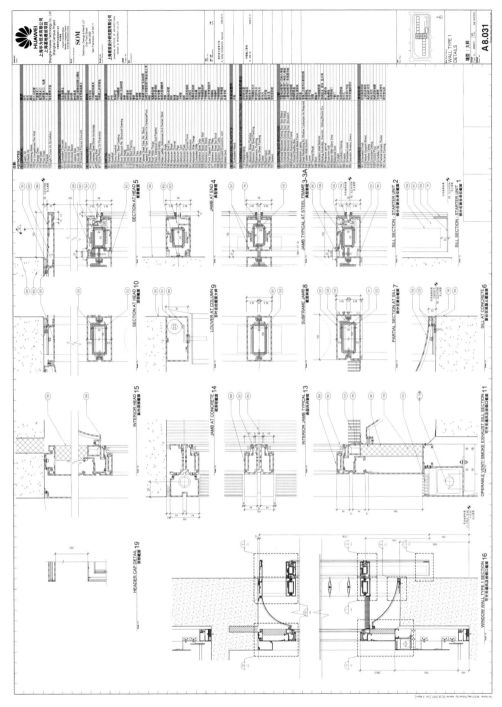

FIGURE 8C4.32 Tender document details for the double window wall system. *Skidmore, Owings & Merrill LLP*

479

FIGURE 8C4.33 Construction of unitized curtain wall at building entry.

FIGURE 8C4.34 Visual mock-up of double curtain wall with vertical sunscreen system. *Michael Fukutome*

FIGURE 8C4.35 Visual mock-up of the double window wall with motorized sunscreens. *Michael Fukutome*

FIGURE 8C4.36 Visual mock-up of unit on a stick egress stair enclosure system. *Michael Fukutome*

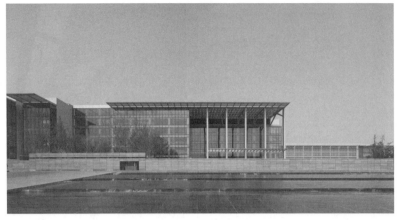

FIGURE 8C4.37 Image of completed unitized curtain wall at building entrance. *Photo © Tim Griffith*

FIGURE 8C4.38 Image of completed double window wall system. *Photo © Tim Griffith*

FIGURE 8C4.39 Image of completed unit on a stick elevator lobby enclosure system. *Photo © Tim Griffith*

Chapter 9

All-Glass Enclosures

It's really complex to make something simple.

JACK DORSEY

The details are not the details. They make the design.

CHARLES EAMES

Overview

The all-glass enclosure is a specialty category of exterior enclosure systems that includes glass as the primary cladding material attached to glass, cables, trusses, or other specialty-designed supporting systems with visually minimal connections. Other titles used for these types of enclosures are structural glass façades, total vision systems, frameless glass, point supported, glass fins, suspended glass, and others. "All-glass" further classifies these types of maximum transparency enclosures separately from metal-framed curtain walls or window walls discussed in the previous chapter. The design objective in all-glass enclosure systems is maximum transparency. There is an emphasis on the tectonics of each component expressing its unique function(s). All-glass enclosures are typically implemented on important public spaces and civic buildings. Maximum transparency can be achieved in a multitude of ways. One is to maximize the glass cladding size, resulting in reduced

joinery and intersections. Another lies in fine crafting and engineering components to minimal sizes used for the supporting system. The support system components discussed here and in the subsequent case studies are glass, steel cables, trusses, and other visually lightweight support systems. Transparent cladding materials include monolithic, laminated, insulating, and insulating/laminated glass.

All-glass enclosures date from the 1960s. There were earlier attempts, but material, analytical tools, and fabrication methods limited the amount of maximum transparency achievable without today's technology. Enclosure systems of this type require specialized design and engineering expertise by architects, engineers, specialty engineers, specialty consultants, and enclosure contractors. These enclosure types also require highly specialized fabrication of materials and components, usually by specialty fabricators, vendors, and sub-sub-contractors. There are books and publications that solely feature these types of enclosures. The focus here is on the basics of this enclosure system, the design process, specialty design and engineering participants involved, and examples of all-glass systems with various support system components and assemblies.

There are distinguishing features in all-glass enclosures that define types and encourage further subsystem definitions. The defining characteristics usually revolve around the supporting system and glass attachment method. All-glass system zones and components are:

1. Support systems
   a. Glass supports
   b. Cable supports (one-way and cable net)
   c. Truss supports

2. Glass attachment method
    a. Through glass
    b. Clamped
    c. Adhered

Design

All-glass enclosures are sometimes customized standard systems; however, most are custom-designed. These systems are characterized by unique designs created by innovative applications of glass cladding, glass attachment methods, support system materials and geometries, metal types, and finishes. There is a smaller quantity of built examples of all-glass enclosures, as compared with curtain walls, so fewer architects and engineers have actual hands-on design and implementation experience. As with most specialty designed systems, specialty engineers, fabricators, and builders have developed a practice with this type of enclosure design and construction.

All-glass design is performed with a mindset of successful performance in a worst-case failure mode. Performance criteria levels vary per support system and the building design performance criteria. All-glass enclosures often become a research and development project unto themselves and trend toward unique and one-of-a-kind design solutions. As a result of their desire for maximum transparency, these systems incorporate clear or decorative glass and celebrate lightness of materials by incorporating highly efficient supporting structures with a minimum of materials and connections.

Design complexities, coupled with the unique and atypical nature of these systems, benefit immensely from the involvement of specialty fabricators and builders in the early design phases. A design-assist project delivery method offers opportunities to engage specialty designers, fabricators, and installers with specific expertise as project design team participants in the early development of the enclosure documentation. This delivery method approach is also beneficial for development of interface details with the surrounding primary structure and weather protection performance design principles and details for continuity to adjacent enclosure systems.

The organization of this chapter generally follows the design consideration logic used in previous chapters. However, because of their unique qualities, a few of the headings are consolidated for applicability to the nature of all-glass enclosures.

All-Glass Enclosure Structural Considerations

All-glass enclosures described herein are non-load-bearing. There are executed load-bearing all-glass enclosures that are extremely case-specific and further elevate the level of custom design. In the non-load-bearing cases, the glass, glass attachments, and the supporting system are designed to accommodate and transfer self-loads and lateral loads, such as wind and seismic, to the boundary head, jamb, and sill conditions. From the boundary edges, the loads are transferred to either a secondary supporting backup framing system or to the primary building structure. Structural considerations by layer or zone are:

1. Type and kind of glass cladding
2. Glass attachment method
3. Support system: materials and geometry
4. Influence of the building structural system on the all-glass enclosure joinery, support system, and connections

This order begins at the exterior. Items 1, 2, and 3 define the three primary zones of an all-glass system. The supporting system can be designed and installed on the exterior if climate conditions, thermal expansion/contraction, and security issues allow. A diagram of the three zones in an all-glass enclosure wall assembly is shown in Figures 9.1a and 9.1b.

All-glass enclosures are deflection-based design. There are no published deflection criteria standards; however, this type of system is relatively more flexible than enclosures discussed in previous chapters. The supporting material will influence the deflection criteria. A glass "fin" support system will deflect less than a cable. The support system deflection also influences the glass cladding panel sizes, joinery dimensions at glass cladding panels, and the type of glass attachment.

TYPE AND KIND OF GLASS CLADDING

Beginning at the exterior enclosure face, the glass panel is the primary exterior cladding material. Sealant

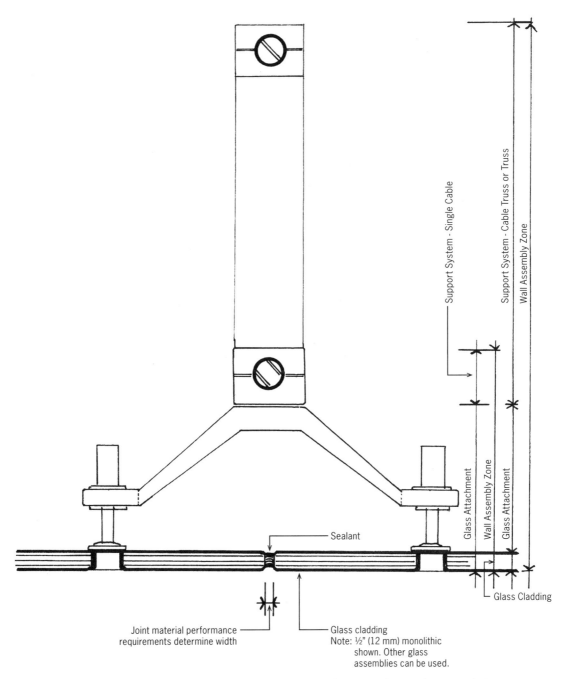

FIGURE 9.1a All-glass enclosure wall zones include: (1) glass panel cladding, (2) glass attachment, and (3) support system. These zones may overlap; however, the design goal is to establish a depth for the system for design and collaboration with design team member disciplines. Support zones shown include single cable and cable truss and the wall assembly zone for each.

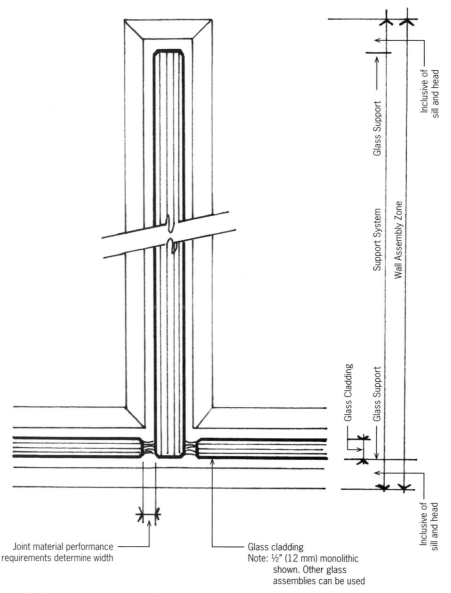

Glass Support

Support System

Wall Assembly Zone

Inclusive of sill and head

Glass Cladding

Glass Support

Inclusive of sill and head

Joint material performance requirements determine width

Glass cladding
Note: ½" (12 mm) monolithic shown. Other glass assemblies can be used

FIGURE 9.1b All-glass enclosure wall zones for glass fins are typically governed by the support system depth.

at glass-to-glass joinery and the glass attachment components complete the remaining visible exterior components. All-glass enclosures utilize glass as more than an infill material that is either captured or adhered to a framing system. An understanding of the basics of the manufacturing process and the physical properties of glass is extremely informative in order to optimize glass use within the material's structural limits.

It is amazing what you think you know and what you don't know about glass. There are many definitions for glass, depending on the source of research. The ASTM (1945) definition for glass states: "Glass is an inorganic product of fusion which has been cooled to a rigid condition without crystallization." Glass is generally considered to be a hard transparent material with a high softening point, substantially insoluble in water and organic solvents, and nonflammable in the usual sense. Architects or engineers engaged in design of all-glass enclosures must research the physical characteristics and mineral composition of glass to understand the material's inherent structure. Glass behaves in unique ways, differently than metal, wood, concrete, or other materials. Understanding the specifics of glass is required, because methods of glass attachment create loads and stresses on glass in a different manner than framed or adhering glass cladding in a metal-framed enclosure.

Architectural glass used in an all-glass enclosure is typically referred to as "flat glass." The majority of flat glass is manufactured by the float process. Flat glass can be curved and shaped by secondary glass processing techniques, but it begins as a flat sheet. Float glass is a process whereby raw mix materials of silicon dioxide (silica) in the form of pure quartz sand, soda, lime, dolomite, and aluminum oxide are batched (mixed) and melted in a glass furnace at high temperatures to produce soda lime glass. Soda lime clear glass will have a slight green tint due to iron oxides in the raw material mix. Several glass manufacturers produce a more optically clear and color-neutral clear glass by using raw mix materials with reduced iron content. This type is referred to as "ultra-clear." Glass manufacturers have various trade names to further delineate ultra-clear from clear glass.

Glass is the primary exterior facing material and often the supporting system in these types of enclosures. Raw materials are batched to their percentages in the mix and fed into the glass furnace. Molten glass is distributed over and floats on a layer of tin. The rate at which the molten glass is fed onto the tin produces the resulting thickness. Flat glass is manufactured in thicknesses ranging from ⅛″ (3 mm) to ¾″ (19 mm). The glass is moved along the fabrication line, where it is cooled on a device known as an annealing lehr. Glass continues along the fabrication line in continuous sheets, hundreds of feet long, which are cut to very long lengths at the end of the fabrication line. From these long sheets, glass is cut to project-specific size. A glass-manufacturing line diagram is illustrated in Figure 9.2.

Glass is manufactured in monolithic (single) thicknesses and can be further fabricated and assembled in secondary processes into laminated, insulated, and insulated laminated assemblies with preparations for fasteners and attachments. The assembly defines glass into types. Float glass is referred to as annealed glass. Annealed glass is cut to project-specific sizes and can be further processed with techniques to increase strength. The strength of basic clear float annealed glass is increased by heating the glass in a controlled process and then applying controlled convective high-pressure cooling known as quenching to create heat-strengthened or tempered glass. The type of heat treatment further defines glass into kinds. Basic glass kinds include: (1) annealed, (2) heat-strengthened, and (3) tempered. Tempered glass has an external envelope of compressive stress encapsulating balancing tensile stresses.

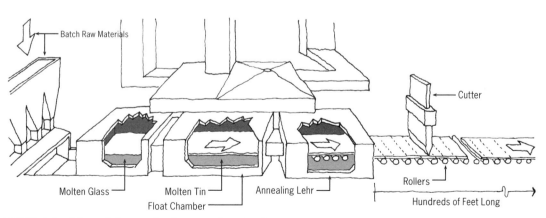

FIGURE 9.2 Schematic layout of a glass-manufacturing line.

The depth of the compressive layer is about 20 percent of the glass thickness. The basic process of heat-treating glass is briefly summarized as follows: Glass is first cut into the size and shape for the final product. It is then placed on a special conveyor that transfers the glass panel either horizontally or vertically into a heating chamber, where it is uniformly heated to approximately 620°C. Once the glass panel has reached a uniform temperature of approximately 620°C (1148°F), it is mechanically transferred into a quenching chamber. Here the glass is cooled (quenched) with ambient air blown through special nozzles that are arranged in a specific pattern to provide uniform heat exchange during the quenching process. The quenching causes the glass surfaces to be cooled more quickly than the center layer of the glass. The cooling of the molecules of the glass at the two surfaces locks them into position relative to the central areas of the glass panel. As the cooling process continues, the central areas of the glass panel will gradually cool and so cause these molecules to come closer together. Generally, when any material is heated it will expand, and consequently, when a heated material is cooled it will contract. This, in turn, will drag the surface molecules even closer together. This results in a compressive stress being developed in the two surfaces of the glass panel. The compressive stresses on the two surfaces are equal and balanced. For the glass panel to stay in equilibrium, there must be a corresponding tensile (pulling) stress developed in the central region of the glass thickness. The magnitude of the surface compression in tempered glass is twice the magnitude of the tensile stress encapsulated in the glass.

This process increases the glass strength. Tempered glass is referred to as "toughened" in some parts of the world. These processes improve the load resistance and affect the fracture behavior of the glass. After heat treatment, the monolithic glass panels can be further assembled into laminated, insulating, or insulating/laminated glass type assemblies. Remember that glass has been cut to size and any special preparations for cuts and holes have been performed prior to heat treatment. Heat-treated glass sizes are dependent on the furnace size and quenching equipment. Glass fabricators must be consulted in the design phases to ascertain heat-treated glass size availability.

Each kind of glass (annealed, heat-strengthened, and tempered) has distinctive performance characteristics. Glass naturally has innumerable microcracks in the surface known as Griffith flaws. These microcracks gradually widen as glass in placed in tension. The coexistence of compression and tension in the glass panel is what makes tempered glass shatter into small pieces. When the outer compression layer is penetrated deep enough to reach the inner layer, the tension layer will instantly pull the glass apart. When glass is under stress, moisture in the atmosphere will cause a chemical reaction and result in crack growth. This crack growth will ultimately result in glass fracture. This is also referred to as "static fatigue." Understanding the limits of glass as a brittle material is important when defining the glass composition, deflection criteria, and method of glass attachment.

Glass deflects under exterior loads, which are typically wind or drift induced. Wind load–induced stress may also propagate to surface imperfections in the glass. When stress reaches a level that exceeds a critical value, the glass will break. Glass, unlike steel or aluminum, does not yield; it breaks at a high speed and fails. Therefore, in addition to selecting a type of glass for visual design requirements, selecting the appropriate type and kind of glass for exterior cladding requires material research, engineering analysis, and careful design and selection of both the glass and the glass attachment method. Glass panels in "all-glass" enclosures are selected by the architect and specifically designed by either a specialty designer or glass contractor, using computer analysis methods. An example of a finite element computer analysis model utilizing laminated glass and a clamp-type support is illustrated in Figure 9.3.

GLASS ATTACHMENTS

Attachments connect glass panels to the supporting system. Glass attachment techniques are grouped as either mechanically attached or adhered. Mechanical glass attachment techniques include:

1. Through glass fittings (sometimes referred to as point supports or spiders)
2. Embedded glass fittings (typically embedded in between multiple layers of laminated glass)
3. Clamps

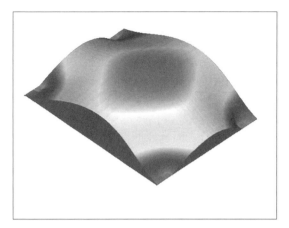

FIGURE 9.3 Finite element model screenshot of a laminated glass panel under wind load deflection. Finite models determine deflection and stress locations to inform the glass design and engineering process.   *Dr. Leon Jacob*

FIGURE 9.4a Installed example of through glass connectors.

FIGURE 9.4b Through-glass connector sample.

Adhered glass attachments include structural silicone.

Glass can also be captured in a frame similar to a curtain wall, which does not fit neatly into the definition used for all-glass enclosure discussion, but it is a design option.

Glass attachment devices can be fabricated from materials ranging from metals (stainless steel, aluminum, titanium, and others) to structural plastics. Metal clamps, bolts, brackets, and other device configurations provide mechanical connection of the glass to the supporting structure. Some terms used internationally include "fittings," "fixings," and others. Examples of project-specific mechanical glass attachments are illustrated in the case study section. Structural silicone, as a glass attachment method, provides an adhered connection of the glass to the glass attachment device or supporting structure. Adhered connections require very clean surfaces and a high level of craft, care, and execution to provide adequate and consistent adhesion. Examples of glass attachments are illustrated in Figures 9.4 a–d.

Glass attachment methods and devices influence the loading pattern on the glass and the load path transfer of wind or seismic loads through the glass attachment to the boundary conditions and supporting structure. The design of the fitting device is a combined engineering and sculptural design process. Initial profiles can be developed by the architect. Specific designs of clamps, armatures, bolts sizes, and the like, are best executed in collaboration with a specialty engineer or a

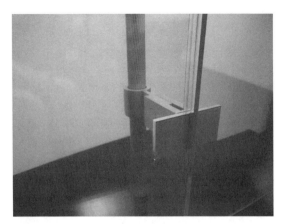

FIGURE 9.4c Design study model of embedded glass connector.

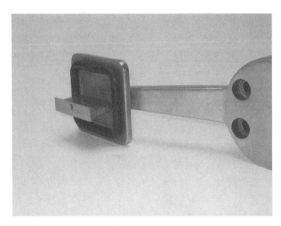

FIGURE 9.4d Glass clamp sample.

fabricator with in-house engineering capabilities and experience. Achieving the desired lightweight visual results requires specialized engineering design for an efficient minimal profile in the proper material to meet the necessary load requirements and capacity of the glass attachment. Specialty fabricators are an excellent resource in the early design phases to assist in developing profiles and material specifications. Final design is much more precise and requires specialized expertise as the design and details progress in development. Computational tools and technology have greatly elevated all-glass design. The finite models should be calibrated, questioned, and reviewed by those knowledgeable in the field of glass engineering

and fabrication. The old saying of "garbage in, garbage out" should be followed.

GLASS SUPPORT SYSTEMS: HORIZONTAL AND VERTICAL

One of the more distinguishing elements in an all-glass system is the supporting system. With the exception of an all-glass storefront, most all-glass enclosures are large enclosure areas often employing long-span supporting systems. The term "all-glass" is realized where the glass support system "framing" is provided in unexpectedly slender profiles and structurally expressive geometries. Visually lightweight supporting systems further maximize the transparent qualities of the glass cladding and overall enclosure assembly. Supporting systems include, but are not limited to:

1. Glass supports in horizontal or vertical configurations
2. One-way cables
3. Cable nets
4. Trusses

Glass Supports

Vertical glass supports are often referred to as "glass fins." This approach has been in use for several decades to provide stiffeners or stabilizers to transfer wind loads from glass cladding to the glass fins and the building primary structure. Fins can be gravity-supported at the sill spanning to a head condition with provisions for movement at the head. Fins are typically suspended. Glass self-loads and tributary wind load is transferred up to the primary building structure above. Movement of the fin stabilizers is provided at the sill. Diagrams for these supports and load paths are shown in Figure 9.5. Some images of tall glass fin enclosures are shown in Figure 9.6.

Horizontal glass fins are often referred to as "glass beams." These are customarily used in floor, roof, and canopy structures. Glass beams experience loading and load path transfer similarly to other commonly used beam support materials. However, the brittle nature of glass and building code

Exterior Building Enclosures

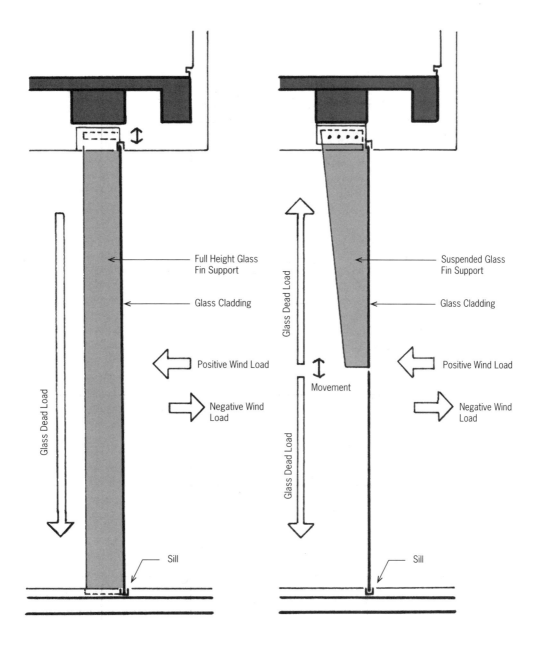

Glass fin and glass cladding dead load can also be
suspended from above. Movement provisions would
be required at the sill.

FIGURE 9.5 Glass fins can be the full height of the enclosure or suspended. The connection location determines movement joinery locations.

FIGURE 9.6 Example of tall glass fin-supported enclosure.

requirements often dictate that glass used as beams be laminated in multiple layers or plies for redundancy. Laminated glass assembled with an interlayer between each pair of glass sheets is typically used to address the potential occurrence for a glass beam that is damaged, or breaks, to remain in place, without evacuating the support location. This further reinforces the all-glass design philosophy of designing for worst-case failure. Glass structural capacity is greatly reduced or completely eliminated when glass breaks and requires immediate replacement. Glass beams can be simple spans, cantilevers, spliced beams with mechanical connections between glass beam sections, and other configurations. An example of a spliced glass beam enclosure under construction is illustrated in Figures 9.7a and b.

Cable Supports

Cables used as the supporting system can be configured in one-way vertical, one-way horizontal, and cable net configurations. The support system geometry is determined per all-glass enclosure size, span, movement characteristics, loading requirements, end conditions, and other case-specific design requirements. Cables are typically stainless steel or galvanized steel. As with any exterior enclosure material, material quality is paramount. Cable materials, method of manufacture, material source, and the handling method during manufacture and installation to prevent damage are critical design and detail considerations, requiring material research, specialty design, specialty engineering, source quality, and exacting specification.

FIGURES 9.7a and 9.7b Glass beam construction.

Cable support systems can be engineered by certain structural engineers of record (SER). All-glass enclosure cable systems are typically engineered by specialty structural engineers (SSE). Specialty engineers can be participant members of the design team or builder team. Cable system behavior under loads and deflections directly influences the design of the glass attachment, and therefore the glass cladding. A very high level of collaboration between architect, structural engineer, and specialty engineer are required to fully understand each component's performance and its associated influence on the other components in the all-glass system.

Trusses

Trusses used in all-glass enclosures can consist of steel, aluminum, wood, cables and compression posts, and combinations of each. Truss configurations range from one-way to two-way, mast-type, cable chords with compression struts, and many others. Trusses for all-glass enclosures are typically engineered by certain structural engineers of record and more often by specialty structural engineers. Deflection limits are based on horizontal or vertical application, size of glass cladding panels, methods of glass attachment, and the connection of the truss to the primary building structure via support system attachments. Deflection-based design should consider the material strength under deflection and the psychological influence of the glass and enclosure deflection on the occupants.

SUPPORT SYSTEM ATTACHMENTS

Support system attachments for all-glass enclosures have similar performance responsibilities as anchorage assemblies in other enclosure types, including transferring the enclosure loads to the primary building structure and accommodating primary building structural system deflections and movements. However, the complexity of all-glass systems often requires a higher level of scrutiny and specialty design at the support system attachment to the primary building structure. Complexity ranges from simple attachments such as angles with bolted and slotted connections for truss-type supports to more material-dependent attachments for glass fins and cables. Support system attachments, such as those used in fins or beams, must recognize the brittle nature of glass. These systems require separator materials to distribute friction over the surface of the glass and distribute concentrated stresses at connections to the glass supports. Components for glass supports include bushings, separators, fasteners, and materials that distribute loads over the glass and do not scratch or damage the glass surfaces or edges. Surface damage is more than a visual concern. As noted earlier in this chapter, glass surface imperfections or damage to either the compression layer of heat-treated glass or to edges of glass "attracts" stresses and can accelerate breakage or failure.

One-way cable and cable net systems require two groups of support system connections. One is a "dead head" and the other is an adjustable connection. "Dead head" is a slang term and is defined as a connection that accepts and transfers loads from the system into a nonadjustable connection. These types of connections may be fixed or pinned to allow rotation, but for most designs they are located and installed prior to the installation of the cable connection. An adjustable connection accepts and transfers loads from the all-glass system, allowing flexing and the ability to "tune" the tension in the cable support system to pre-specified forces. Cable and cable net support system attachments are similar to a guitar or a piano. To maximize and achieve the highest performance quality requires fine-tuning. Cable and cable net system deflections are accommodated by the cable flexing and rotation at the connection without weakening the end connections. There is some stretching of the cable. The design goal is to minimize the stretching and accept elongation of the system due to deflection through a spring, tensioner, or other device, to minimize the stretching of the cable. An example of a "dead head" cable connection is illustrated in Figure 9.8. An example of an adjustable/compression/elongation connection is illustrated in Figure 9.9. These are two examples from previous project experiences. Connections are specifically designed per project on a case-by-case basis.

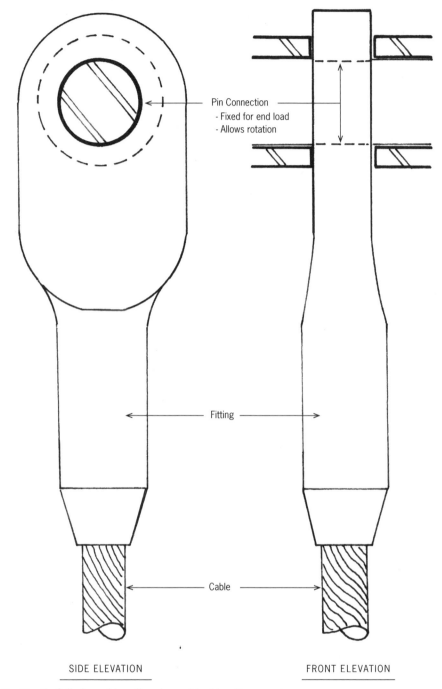

Pin Connection
- Fixed for end load
- Allows rotation

Fitting

Cable

SIDE ELEVATION

FRONT ELEVATION

FIGURE 9.8 Detail of all-glass cable wall enclosure "dead head" connection.

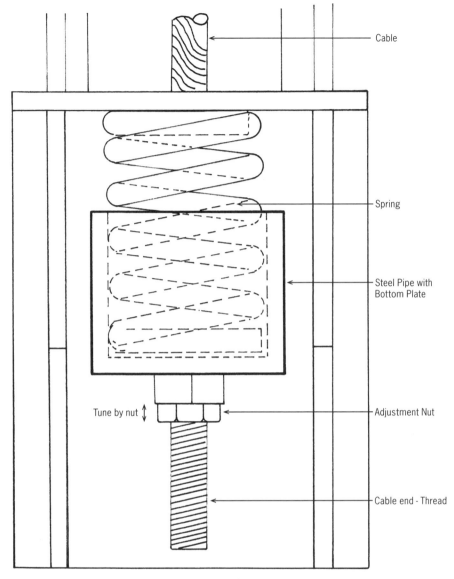

Cable

Spring

Steel Pipe with
Bottom Plate

Tune by nut ↕   Adjustment Nut

Cable end - Thread

FIGURE 9.9   Detail of all-glass cable wall enclosure "adjustable" connection.

BUILDING STRUCTURE INFLUENCE ON ALL-GLASS SYSTEMS

The primary building structure (columns, beams, slabs, etc.) and associated movement characteristics under loading will influence the movement and joinery of an all-glass enclosure. Conversely, the forces of the all-glass system and the supporting system influence the size of the boundary conditions in the primary structure. The glass and glass attachment devices' or fittings' self-load or dead load is typically secured to the glass supporting system members. The supporting system is secured to the primary building structure via the supporting system attachments. The primary building structural frame dead load deflection is typically already achieved prior to the installation of the all-glass system and should be verified with the SER. Deflection of the primary building structure due to the all-glass system self-load must be accounted for in the structural design for deflection. The primary building structure live load deflection must be accounted for in the all-glass system joinery design. Joint locations where the primary building structure deflections are accommodated require either:

1. Compensating head, sill, or jamb assembly (if the all-glass wall has no "internal" movement capabilities)
2. Soft joinery materials (usually sealant with or without a compressible backer)
3. Gasket joinery, either visible or concealed

These design approaches and their configurations are referred to as "movement joints."

Live load deflection of the surrounding primary building structure, drift, deflection of the all-glass enclosure, thermal expansion, and tolerances when added, typically determine the size of the clear movement for the movement joint. All-glass systems may have higher deflections than other enclosure systems, because of their longer spans, surface area expanses, and wind load, which may contribute to the movement joint size.

In buildings with large amounts of wind- or seismic-induced drift, the drift movement may dictate the movement joint size. The joint material movement capacity characteristics, in conjunction with the clear movement, will determine the final movement joint size. As with metal and glass enclosures, sealant joinery design and sizing require a review and understanding of the primary structural system deflection, the movement of the all-glass enclosure system, and the movement capacity of the joint material. Joinery, like most elements in all-glass enclosures, has a focus on minimizing, so joinery sizes are important design considerations.

Joinery utilizing gaskets in either a visible or concealed arrangement requires continuous contact between gaskets and metal surfaces. The visible joint size, with visible or concealed gaskets, will require

enough space for movement and for installation. These conditions can occur in all-glass enclosures at boundary edge conditions at the head, jamb, and/or sill, as well as internally depending on the method of glass attachment. A live load deflection diagram and the associated movement joint determination are indicated in Figure 9.10. Joinery must be sized and designed for the all-glass enclosure wall and, if applicable, for openings for doors and entrances, inside and outside corners, cantilevers, and parapet conditions.

Exterior glass cladding typically behaves like panels, remaining in its original geometric shape when viewed perpendicular to the plane of the glass. Glass will deflect perpendicular to the glass plane under wind loading, and when designed and installed properly will return to its "flat" state when the wind load is removed. Glass attachments should be designed to allow the glass cladding to retain its original geometry, no matter what the magnitude or direction of the movement is. Therefore, the fine details for the glass attachments, supporting system movement characteristics, and supporting system attachments must be carefully developed and detailed during the enclosure design phases.

Primary building structural system drift, which is induced by wind pressure and, if applicable, seismic forces, can be a little more complicated to incorporate in all-glass enclosure design. All-glass enclosures are often utilized in larger expanses than a single floor span. Therefore, the resulting design and detail strategy to accommodate the drift capacity can have design implications. The design must address drift parallel and perpendicular to the enclosure plane. The supporting system and the glass attachment method must accommodate the primary building structural drift. The connection points of the enclosure system to primary building structure are designed to accommodate rotation so that the glass configuration can remain without distributing stress into the glass cladding. Drift parallel to the all-glass enclosure creates movement conditions at the glass attachment and the boundary head, jamb, sill, and, if applicable, the corners. Diagrams of an all-glass enclosure with movement conditions created by primary building structural drift parallel to the enclosure plane are shown in Figure. 9.11. The glass in this

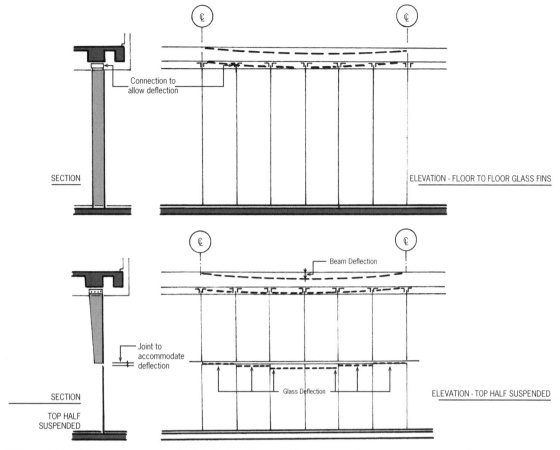

Connection to allow deflection

SECTION

ELEVATION - FLOOR TO FLOOR GLASS FINS

Beam Deflection

Joint to accommodate deflection

Glass Deflection

ELEVATION - TOP HALF SUSPENDED

SECTION

TOP HALF SUSPENDED

FIGURE 9.10 Primary structure live load deflection diagram. The top example accepts movement at the enclosure system head. The lower example requires movement at the intermediate horizontal joint within the all-glass enclosure.

case is designed like the scales on a fish. Each glass panel (fish scale) retains its original shape because of the glass attachment and joint size between glass panels. This diagram is for a hypothetical condition. Each project design must be analyzed on a case-specific basis. Each of the movements will require design for the typical conditions within the system, corner conditions, and interfaces with other systems or adjacent materials. Drift occurring perpendicular to the all-glass enclosure will induce a tipping effect. The enclosure will rotate about the movement joint or boundary edge condition during drift displacement. This occurs from one boundary or movement joint to the next, above or below. Parallel and perpendicular primary building structure movement must

be accommodated in the all-glass enclosure design. If corner conditions occur in the enclosure design, the corner details must accept each movement direction. This often becomes a geometry exercise to establish slotted connections or joint sizes between glass panels to accept each one's fractional component of the overall drift based on its size.

Weather Protection

The weather protection design approach in all-glass systems is typically a barrier design. Glass-to-glass joinery is typically sealed on-site with sealant or gasketed joints requiring a high level of skill and craft in

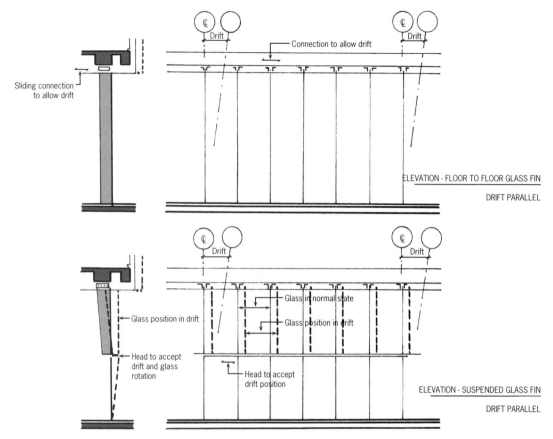

FIGURE 9.11 Primary structure drift diagram. The top example accepts sliding movement at the enclosure system head allowing the wall to remain in its original configuration. The lower example requires sliding movement at the intermediate horizontal joint within the all-glass enclosure.

on-site execution. Although the weather protection design of the all-glass enclosure proper is direct, there are design and detail challenges and opportunities at intersections with adjacent systems, copings, roof, and boundary edge terminations. Methods for weather protection are further discussed in the case studies. Glass-to-glass joinery is typically installed on-site and relies primarily on sealant, gaskets, or a combination of the two. Sealant joinery at glass-to-glass intersections requires tooling the joint from both sides. Where access is available, the detail is very direct and reliant on a high level of craft by on-site installation personnel. In all-glass enclosures without access on one side, a combination of gaskets and

sealant may be implemented. Diagrams of sealant and sealant with a gasket at glass-to-glass joints are shown in Figure 9.12.

Glass attachments require clever detailing and installation of weather protection depending on the attachment design. Flush through glass fittings typically employ high-density plastic bushings to separate the metal fastener from the glass surfaces and to distribute the load, preventing excessive load concentrations or surface damage at the holes in the glass panel. Either sealant is required between the plastic-to-glass and plastic-to-fastener intersection surfaces or a gasket that is soft enough to compress at the connection and distribute the load, preventing water

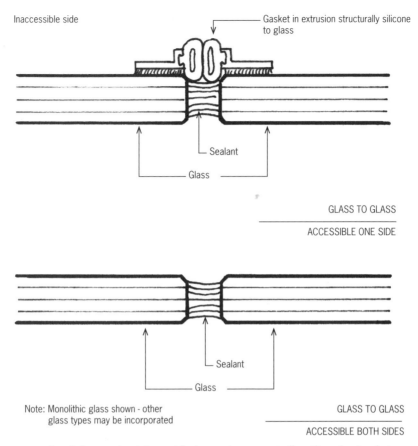

Inaccessible side

Gasket in extrusion structurally silicone to glass

Sealant

Glass

GLASS TO GLASS

ACCESSIBLE ONE SIDE

Sealant

Glass

Note: Monolithic glass shown - other glass types may be incorporated

GLASS TO GLASS

ACCESSIBLE BOTH SIDES

FIGURE 9.12 Some examples of glass-to-glass joinery. All-glass enclosures typically utilize a barrier-design weather protection principle. Access to each side of the joint will influence the joinery detail.

infiltration. Diagrams of sealant between fitting components and internal weather protection gasket are shown in Figure 9.13. Clamp-type fittings require sealant, gaskets, or combinations of both. There are many types of glass attachments, but the message is the same. Glass attachments typically require a seal on the exterior side of the glass to maintain weather protection. Glass attachments and the associated weather protection for glass fins are typically accomplished with a sealant that has structural and weather protection performance characteristics. An in-progress construction image of a clamp fitting with a continuous gasket providing weather protection is shown in Figure 9.14.

The perimeter boundary conditions of jamb, sill, and head also require clever detailing and precise installation of weather protection materials and seals. This may be accomplished with sealant, gaskets, or a combination. Perimeter boundary condition examples are illustrated in the case studies in this chapter.

In all-glass enclosure systems, sealant continuity is essential, since there is often a single weather line design approach. The seal intersection at glass-to-glass joinery is a straightforward design detail. The boundary edge conditions are more complicated for weather continuity and movement capability. Designing continuity in the system during the design phase is the responsibility of the architect. Designing

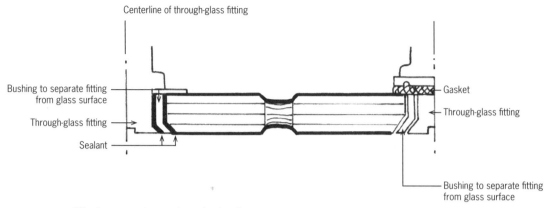

FIGURE 9.13   Weather protection at through-glass fittings.

Centerline of through-glass fitting

Bushing to separate fitting from glass surface

Through-glass fitting

Sealant

Gasket

Through-glass fitting

Bushing to separate fitting from glass surface

FIGURE 9.14   Weather protection at clamp fitting via gaskets at the glass connectors.

and reviewing weather continuity in the "paper" phase of construction—the shop drawings—is the responsibility of the contractor, with architectural input and review. Continuity in the "bricks and mortar" phase of construction is the responsibility of the contractor. Metal-to-metal continuity at perimeter conditions is a particular area of focus. "Tracking" and achieving weather continuity in metal requires sealant at the intersections and transitions to other systems or the primary structure.

THERMAL DESIGN/VAPOR CONTROL/ CONDENSATION

Thermal Design

Thermal design and performance in an all-glass enclosure is primarily governed by the glass type. Glass attachments have an influence; however, because of their small size, it is also very small. As noted in earlier chapters, glass has a low R-value in comparison to insulated assemblies. Transparent vision areas in all-glass enclosures have insulating qualities based on the glass type, high-performance coatings (if applicable in the design), and glass assembly. Glass can be monolithic, laminated, insulated, or insulated/laminated. Stricter energy codes and regulations may require the use of insulating glass with high-performance coatings. Insulating glass, even with high-performance coatings, does not have high insulation values. The R-value for insulating glass typically averages about R = 2.

Vapor Control/Condensation

Water, in the form of water vapor or humidity, forms when glass surface temperatures reach the dew point. When this occurs, water vapor condenses on the glass surface. Exterior climate design conditions and the interior space temperature and humidity conditions must be reviewed on a case-by-case basis to verify that condensation does not occur on glass surfaces. This is relatively easy to check in the visible areas. Providing air movement via mechanical systems or natural convective air currents can assist in reducing condensation on glass.

Additional Design Requirements

All-glass enclosure design is highly specialized. Performance criteria are typically defined by the design team. Often, the traditional design team of architect, structural engineer, and mechanical engineer is supplemented by a specialty engineer or glass designer, to assist in the design, development of performance criteria, and the development of system details. This team may be assembled during the design phases in a

design-build or design-assist approach, or engaged during the construction process. It is advisable to engage specialty engineers and designers in the early design phases if the traditional team participants' level of expertise does not include experience in all-glass enclosures. All-glass enclosures will typically require specialized interface, collaboration, and coordination of systems and details with building structural and mechanical systems, which must be defined in the design development and construction document phases.

MAINTENANCE

All-glass enclosures require maintenance to maximize the service life. Maintenance ranges from cleaning the glass to repair/replacement of joinery materials or replacement of glass. Sealant at the glass-to-glass joinery, when designed and installed properly, has a service life in the range of 10 to 15 years. Each sealant type performs with its own unique characteristics. Removal and replacement of joinery material exposed to the exterior requires careful and meticulous preparation and application. Sealants within the enclosure are often not easily accessible from a floor or other accessible vantage point. Glass and the exposed glazing seals require periodic maintenance and inspection. The method of glazing—interior or exterior glazed—should be discussed with the owner to determine which offers the most direct and convenient method for reglazing.

TESTING

All-glass enclosures are typically custom one-of-a-kind installations and merit performance testing to defined levels of structural and weather protection performance. The sealant joinery at glass-to-glass intersections and at glass attachments relies on craft; however, testing the overall system for wind load deflection and drift movement usually yields valuable insights that can be incorporated into the details and construction logistics. These tests are conducted by independent testing agencies. Tests for air infiltration and water infiltration under static and dynamic loads are customarily performed, as well as structural tests simulating lateral wind loads. Additional tests for

FIGURE 9.15 Performance mock-up specimen for an all-glass cable-supported enclosure.

seismic, acoustics, and other specialized areas can also be performed to the specified project requirements. An all-glass performance test sample is illustrated in Figure 9.15.

Summary

All-glass enclosures are often dramatic feats of architectural and engineering design. These highly transparent and visually light supporting systems are typically reserved for very specialized building uses or public space enclosures. Extensive research on materials and methods of installation is required to provide sufficient design detail on the fabrication, installation, and performance of each material and component of the total system.

All-Glass Enclosures

The New Beijing Poly Plaza

LOCATION:
Beijing, People's Republic of China Building Type
User-Specific Office Building and Cultural Museum

PARTICIPANTS
Owner:
China Poly Group Corporation (Poly) – Beijing, China .
Design Architect:
Skidmore, Owings & Merrill LLP (SOM) – San Francisco, CA
Local Design Institute Architect (LDI)
Beijing Special Engineering Design and Research Institute – Beijing, China
Design Structural Engineer:
Skidmore, Owings & Merrill LLP – San Francisco, CA
Local Design Institute Structural Engineer (LDI)
Beijing Special Engineering Design and Research – Beijing, China
Design Mechanical Engineer:
Flack & Kurtz – San Francisco, CA

Contractor:
China State Construction Co. – Beijing, China
Curtain Wall Contractor—Cable Net Enclosures:
Yuanda – Beijing and Shenyang, China
ASI, Consultant to Cable Net Contractor – Newport Beach, CA

PROJECT TIME FRAME
Competition:
January 2003
Schematic Design:
March 2003–June 2003
Design Development:
July 2003–December 2003
Construction Documents/Tender Documents:
January 2004–July 2004
Construction:
August 2004–December 2006

Project Description

China Poly Group requested a landmark building that would represent the company's disparate subsidiaries as a unified whole and present a transparent and open image of the company to the public and the world. The program defines a 100,000-square-meter (1,076,391 square foot) building, including a headquarters office, subsidiary offices, leasable office space, retail, restaurants, and the Poly Museum. The Poly Museum, established by one of the company's subsidiaries, has the unique purpose of repatriating China's cultural antiquities. The museum, an important physical and cultural feature, is located prominently as a "Museum Lantern" on floors two through eight, cantilevered from the concrete core and suspended by the primary cables supporting the 22-story cable-net-supported all-glass enclosure.

Located at a prominent intersection along Beijing's Second Ring Road, northeast of the Forbidden City, the building entry and main façade is a 22-story cable net glass wall oriented toward the roadway intersection and China Poly's existing headquarters. The schematic design rendering of the all-glass cable net enclosure is presented in Figure 9C1.1.

The building is a triangular form in plan, with its cable net wall hypotenuse addressing the roadway intersection. The two sides of the triangle result in an "L"-shaped office plan that cradles the atrium. The triangular shape minimizes the perimeter surface exposed to the elements, while a series of interior atriums gives office areas maximum access to daylight. The atrium is enclosed on the northeastern edge by the 22-story all-glass cable net wall and on the south by a 10-story all-glass cable net enclosure. The northeast orientation responds to the region's cold climate by providing greater access to direct natural daylight for the interior spaces. The schematic design site plan is shown in Figure 9C1.2.

Enclosure System Types

The exterior of the two atrium spaces is a cable-net-supported glass wall enclosure. On the south elevation, a 154'-0" (47 m) high × 79'-0" (24 m) wide rectangular cable net all-glass wall encloses the "sunset" atrium and extends from the ground floor to the underside of the 11th floor. A model of the 10-story cable net all-glass enclosure is illustrated in Figure 9C1.3. On the northeast elevation, a 295'-0" (90 m) high × 197'-0" (60 m)

FIGURE 9C1.1 Schematic design rendering of the 22-story all-glass cable net enclosure. *Skidmore, Owings & Merrill LLP*

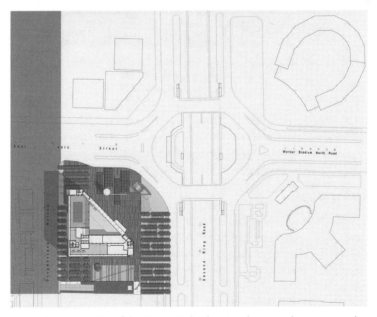

FIGURE 9C1.2 Schematic design site plan of the Beijing Poly Plaza in relation to the prominent location at the intersection of the Second Ring Road in Beijing. The 22-story cable net wall occurs on the broad elevation facing the ring road and expresses the design goal of an open and transparent company philosophy. *Skidmore, Owings & Merrill LLP*

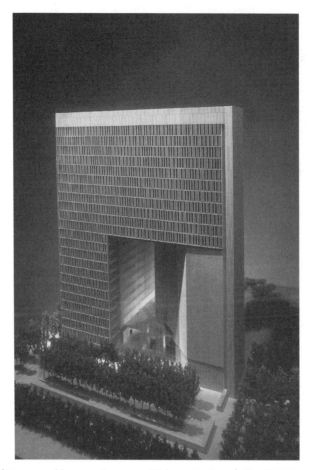

FIGURE 9C1.3 Model of 10-story cable net enclosure. *Skidmore, Owings & Merrill LLP*

wide cable glass net wall encloses the "all day" atrium with three distinct folded planes and extends from the ground floor to the underside of the 23rd floor. The exterior wall of each atrium is composed of clear laminated glass membranes supported on two-way galvanized steel cable nets. A building section illustrating the two atriums enclosed by the two cable-net-supported glass enclosures is shown in Figure 9C1.4.

Enclosure System Goals

To achieve a unified design for the 10-story and 22-story cable net wall, the building structure and architectural enclosure systems design and details were developed in a collaborative architectural and engineering design approach. For the 22-story cable net glass wall, a structural system composed of reinforced concrete shear walls provides the boundary at the end jamb conditions. These concrete walls support a three-story steel truss, which completes the head boundary of the 22-story-high cable net. The framing diagram is shown in Figure 9C1.5. For the 10-story cable net glass wall, steel columns in the southern "wing" do not continue below the 10th floor, creating a "bridge" between the cores and columns at the east and west ends. The "bridge" structure is supported by Vierendeel trusses over its entire height from level 10 to level 24. The sill boundary of the base of both the 10-story and 22-story net walls is steel with composite metal and concrete slabs.

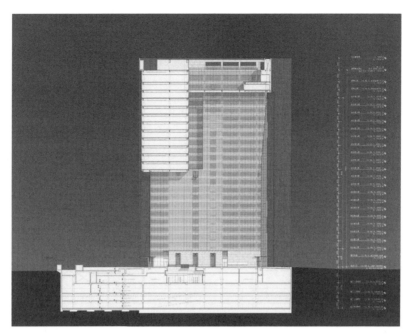

FIGURE 9C1.4 Building section with 22-story-high cable net enclosure to the right and 10-story cable net enclosure to the left. *Skidmore, Owings & Merrill LLP*

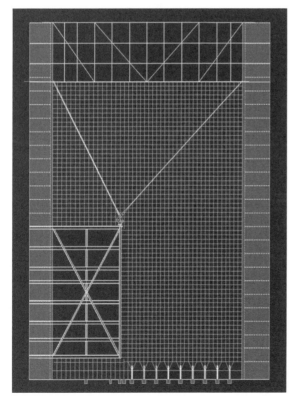

FIGURE 9C1.5 Elevation framing diagram of the 22-story cable net wall. The left and right edge boundary structures are cast on site concrete. The top boundary is a three-story truss. Diagonal cables suspend the cantilevered museum lantern. *Skidmore, Owings & Merrill LLP*

The Poly Museum lantern is suspended from the 23rd floor to the 10th floor from four primary bundled steel cables. The "lantern" is an eight-story-tall (starting at level 2) cross-braced steel frame that cantilevers 78'-9" (24 m) from the building core. With no columns underneath the lantern, the tip of the cantilevered frame is effectively propped by its connection to the primary diagonal cables, which serve as a counterweight for the cable net wall.

Clear laminated glass with a pyrolitic low-e coating on the #4 (inboard) surface was selected for each cable net enclosure to maximize visual transparency and natural light.

Enclosure System Design Process

SCHEMATIC DESIGN

The primary enclosure design elements of the two cable net walls were defined in the schematic design phase.

The primary elements of the 22-story (295' high × 197' wide [90 m high × 60 m wide]) cable net wall assembly are:

- boundary edge – top
- boundary edge – jamb
- pivoting stainless steel chained jamb
- boundary edge – sill and entry canopy
- main cables
- suspended lantern
- galvanized steel cable net
- stainless steel glass support fittings
- glass
- sealant

The primary elements of the 10-story (154' high × 79' wide [47 m high × 24 m wide]) cable net wall assembly are:

- boundary edge – top
- boundary edge – jamb
- boundary edge – sill
- galvanized steel cable net
- glass support fittings
- glass
- sealant

Design Development

The plan, section, and elevation layout of each cable net wall was dimensionally defined. Material, sources, specifications, and samples for the glazing, supporting cables, and cable hardware were researched to determine which were available locally in China and which were required to be imported. Typical details for the cable connections and access for tensioning were developed in order to integrate supports and openings in the steel and concrete primary building structure surrounding perimeter boundaries.

Boundary Edge – Top

Cable net main and vertical cables and attachment components and assemblies are anchored at floor 23 with springs and adjustable supports along the top of the 22-story cable net wall. Vertical cables are

1″ (26 mm) diameter galvanized steel. The cables are designed for position and tensioning in the initial installation in multiple stages. The four main cables supporting the lantern are anchored to the underside of the three-story truss.

The boundary edge or top perimeter condition for the glass is an extruded aluminum channel with stainless steel cladding. The channel is internally sealed at channel joints for weather protection continuity. Continuous flashing extends from the channel face to the flashing supported on steel subframing. A design development study section detail is illustrated in Figure 9C1.6.

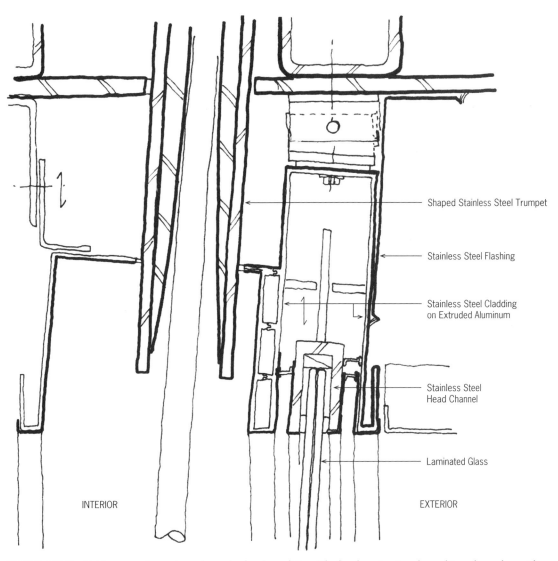

FIGURE 9C1.6 Cable net enclosure boundary edge head condition. The head section is a channel in a channel providing movement and primary and secondary weather protection gaskets.

Boundary Edge – Jamb

1'-5/16" (34 mm) diameter galvanized steel cables are designed to be inserted through sleeves in the concrete shear walls and anchored to embeds in concrete shear walls. The design of the stainless steel sleeve cast into the concrete shear wall is flared in a trumpet shape towards the cable net enclosure, to allow construction erection tolerance and to accommodate deflection due to wind load without binding or inducing bending fatigue to the cable over the service life of the building and enclosure. The glazing jamb consists of a channel to receive the glass nested in an outer gasketed channel receiver. This "jamb in a jamb" detail is pin-connected at each glass panel height to allow rotation of the jamb glazing, to accommodate deflection of the enclosure under wind loads. A design development study section at the hinged jamb is illustrated in Figure 9C1.7.

Boundary Edge – Sill

The sill for the 10- and 22-story cable nets has two sill detail conditions. In the first condition, the cable extends down through the slab and to the underside of the ground-floor steel supporting structure. The second condition occurs above the ground-floor entry vestibule composed of tapered steel plates supporting doors, side lites, and canopy glass. To mitigate cold air moving down the glass wall as a result of stack effect, over occupants entering or exiting the atrium, warm supply air is supplied at the top of the vestibule in a glass-enclosed air plenum to maintain human comfort.

Main Cable

The scale of the 295' tall × 197' wide (90 m tall × 60 m wide) cable net glass wall greatly exceeds anything that has been built before. This presented specific challenges, other than those of smaller-scale all-glass structure enclosure walls. Preliminary analysis showed that the cable net spans of the 22-story wall were too large to be economically achieved using a simple two-way cable net design. It was determined in design development that the cable net for a wall of this size could be achieved by subdividing the large cable net area into three smaller zones by folding the cable net into a faceted surface, and introducing a relatively stiff element along the fold lines. The faceted cable net solution allows the individual sections of the cable net to span to a virtual boundary condition at the fold line, effectively shortening the spans. Rather than introduce a major beam or truss element to stiffen the fold line, a large-diameter cable under significant pre-tension is used. The fold line represented a unique design detail challenge for the enclosure. The fold required the all-glass enclosure to flex under wind load and be field-adjustable for angularity. A hinged mullion at the "Y" intersection, illustrated in Figure 9C1.8, was developed.

The final design solution was achieved with the largest of the four primary cables 11" (275 mm) in diameter and consisting of a parallel strand bundle of 199 individual 5/8" (15.2 mm) diameter 1 × 7 type strands. Using the faceted design solution, the typical horizontal and vertical cables are limited in diameter to 1-3/8" (34 mm) and 1" (26 mm). Cables are spaced at 4'-4" (133.3 mm) horizontally and 4'-6" (137.5 mm) on center vertically.

Rocker Mechanism

Beijing is in an active seismic zone, so the primary building structure drifts under anticipated seismic loads. The cables will act as braces and attempt to resist the base building drift unless the force levels in the cables are limited in some manner. Designing the main diagonal cables to resist these brace forces while maintaining an appropriate factor of safety would have significantly increased the primary diagonal cable sizes that are employed in the final design solution. This would result in an initial level of pre-tension in the primary diagonal cables being in the lower portion of the cable breaking strength, to accommodate the additional brace demands. When cable systems are installed with only a nominal level of initial pre-tension, the tendency of that system to exhibit

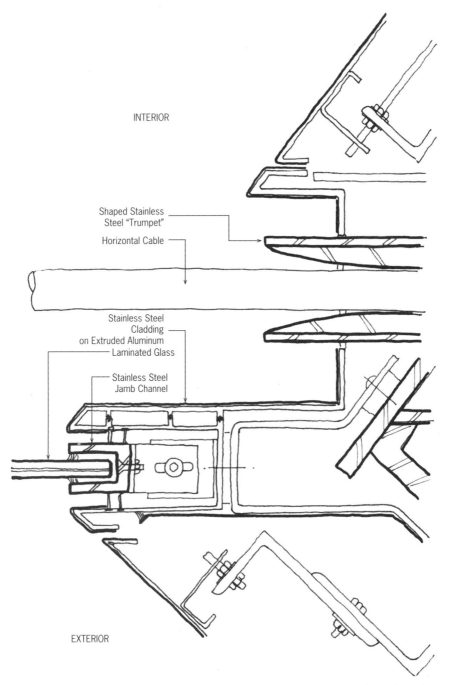

INTERIOR

Shaped Stainless
Steel "Trumpet"

Horizontal Cable

Stainless Steel
Cladding
on Extruded Aluminum
Laminated Glass

Stainless Steel
Jamb Channel

EXTERIOR

FIGURE 9C1.7 Cable net enclosure boundary edge jamb condition. The jamb section is a channel in a channel providing movement due to wind loads, seismic drift, and primary and secondary weather protection gaskets.

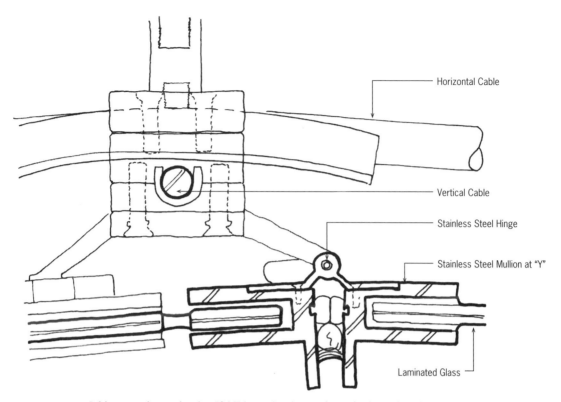

Horizontal Cable

Vertical Cable

Stainless Steel Hinge

Stainless Steel Mullion at "Y"

Laminated Glass

FIGURE 9C1.8 Cable net enclosure detail at "fold" line. The glazing channel is hinged to allow rotation due to the all-glass enclosure deflection. Enclosure system joinery is gaskets on the interior and sealed on the exterior.

significant deflections due to the self-weight of the cables is greatly increased. Therefore, it was determined that the design solution required that the primary diagonal cables (the only cables that may act as braces) be decoupled from the lateral system of the base building structure.

The final design development detail solution resulted in the decoupling mechanism nicknamed the "rocker," consisting of the equivalent of a pulley at the lower point of the "V" cables. A cast-steel "rocker mechanism" was designed to perform the equivalent function of the pulley. Crossing the cables and connecting to the rocker casting arms eliminated the need to provide curved pulley surfaces and curved sections of the main cable. To evaluate the effectiveness of the design solution prior to completing in-depth analysis of the system, a physical diagram model of the "rocker mechanism" was built, along with a model of a concept for reference comparison. The rocker concept model is illustrated in Figure 9C1.9. The physical model test demonstrated significant extension in the springs using the "link" model and negligible extension in the springs using the "rocker mechanism" model, highlighting the ability of this connection to decouple the main cables from the base building lateral system.

Cable Net

The three glass planes of the 22-story cable net wall and the single plane of the 10-story cable net are supported by a series of 1″ (26 mm) vertical cables and 1′-⅝″ (34 mm) horizontal cables. The cable net intersection points are connected with custom-designed stainless steel clamps and stainless steel glass fittings.

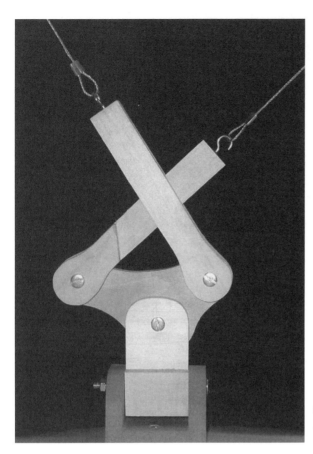

FIGURE 9C1.9 Cable net enclosure rocker mechanism concept study model. *Skidmore, Owings & Merrill LLP*

Stainless Steel Glass Fitting

During the design development phase, multiple sketches and foam model prototypes were developed to shape and refine the component profiles. Photos of the foam prototypes are shown in Figure 9C1.10. The expanse of the 10- and 22-story glass cable net walls offered the opportunity to amortize the cost for custom castings over several hundred intersection points. Design and cost control dictated that the fittings for both cable net glass walls be the same.

Piston-Shaped Stand-Off

The three planes of 22-story cable net wall attaching to the primary suspension cables result in a dimensional geometry that varies in depth between the constant fold line of the glass plane and the curving primary cable from the rocker at level 11 to the 23rd floor. A series of cast stainless steel support rods, nicknamed the "pistons," was developed in the design and each rod length specifically calculated to maintain the exterior all glass cable net enclosure geometry. The pistons are fabricated from machined stainless steel clamps and solid stainless steel rods, with a pivot device to accommodate rotation and construction tolerance.

Glass

Glass panel sizes were defined using a repetitive plan dimension, which is a subset of the building planning module. The vertical glass dimension is derived through a combination of wind loading deflection limits of

FIGURE 9C1.10 Design development study model of glass clamp connector. *Skidmore, Owings & Merrill LLP*

12 mm and subdividing the glass into the floor-to-floor height in three equal panels. The joinery size between the pieces of glass is defined by the height component of seismic drift.

Sealant

To provide a visually crisp edge at the glass intersections, black silicone sealant is detailed utilizing a barrier principle recessed to the back of the beveled and polished glass arris edge.

Construction Documents

Because of the specialized design and the client's direction for design and technical continuity, the design team developed the construction tender documents (drawings and specifications), working closely with the local design institutes (LDI) for interface and coordination. The LDI provided liaison with the local expert panel reviews to explain and achieve panel approval for the design of the components and the systems through the design and documentation process. To facilitate communication and collaboration in multiple languages, a keynote system for material notes was developed and implemented on the documents.

Boundary Edge – Top, Sill, and Jamb

The details at the boundary conditions were further defined in construction documents to interface with the primary weather lines of the surrounding enclosure systems. The detail of the jamb-in-a-jamb condition is illustrated in Figure 9C1.11.

Rocker Mechanism

The final design of the "rocker mechanism" included five large castings per connection. The main cable clevis castings are approximately 13″-2″ (4 m) in length. The clevis castings are designed to pass through each other to maintain concentric load paths through the connection. A detail of the rocker mechanism is illustrated in Figure 9C1.12.

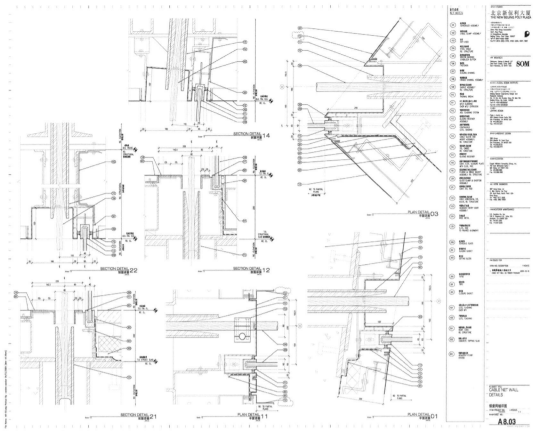

FIGURE 9C1.11 Tender document cable net boundary details. *Skidmore, Owings & Merrill LLP*

Cable Net

The cable net with the glass infill extends over a large surface area. The wind direction is predominantly from the north. The cable net is designed to deflect approximately 3′-3″ (1 m) in the positive and negative directions. Each glass lite accommodates a component of the wind-induced deflection. The wind deflection diagram of the cable net with glass is shown in Figure 9C1.13.

Stainless Steel Glass Fitting

The organization of the 22-story cable net wall in three planes to accommodate deflection and seismic drift required special detailing along the fold lines. Several design details were developed, with the final solution consisting of two glazing channels with a hinged intersection. The profile developed needed to provide a crisp visual delineation of planes from the exterior and adequate surface area to attach custom-designed hinges on the interior side of the glazing channel. Precise geometry alignment of horizontal to vertical cable placement and the resulting glass panels established the plane delineation to points that emanate from the intersection at the rocker. To provide a level of redundant weather protection of this flexible intersection, each hinged section contains a continuous bulb gasket as the primary weather line and a secondary weather sealant line. An elevation

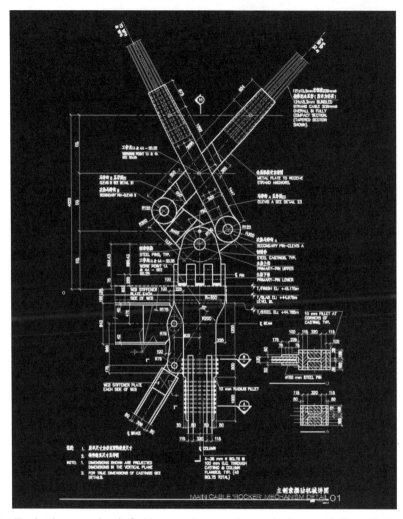

FIGURE 9C1.12 Tender document detail of cable net enclosure rocker mechanism. *Skidmore, Owings & Merrill LLP*

of the hinge joint intersection is illustrated in Figure 9C1.14. The detail of the hinged mullion is illustrated in Figure 9C1.15.

The design intent for both glass cable net walls is to achieve maximum transparency with minimal obstruction from cables or glass supports. To achieve glass fabrication with a minimum of edge or corner fabrication or prepping for holes, and to keep the glass plane unobstructed, the glass is supported at the sill and head of each glass lite through the glass-to-glass joint. The glass support interior armature is a cast stainless steel yoke in a horizontal orientation with an applied finish. The exterior cover is a stainless steel plate slotted to index to the interior yoke and bolted through the glass-to-glass joint to the interior yoke. The stainless steel armature required additional material strength to accommodate the flexing and to resist metal fatigue over the service life of the wall. The stainless steel is a duplex high-strength alloy, used to achieve these performance criteria. To integrate exterior building maintenance within the design profiles, an extended fitting at the fastener location provides for tie-backs for exterior building maintenance. A detail of the typical glass fitting is illustrated in Figure 9C1.16.

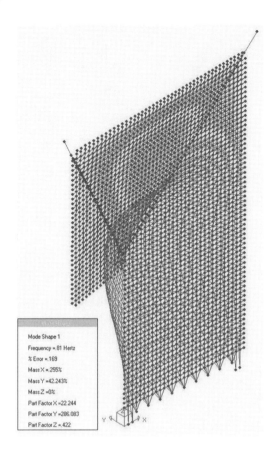

Mode Shape 1
Frequency =.81 Hertz
% Error =.169
Mass X =.255%
Mass Y =42.243%
Mass Z =0%
Part Factor X =22.244
Part Factor Y =286.083
Part Factor Z =.422

FIGURE 9C1.13 Finite element model of cable net deflection under lateral wind loading. *Skidmore, Owings & Merrill LLP*

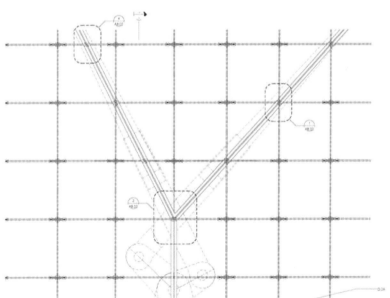

FIGURE 9C1.14 Elevation at "fold "in 22-story cable net enclosure. *Skidmore, Owings & Merrill LLP*

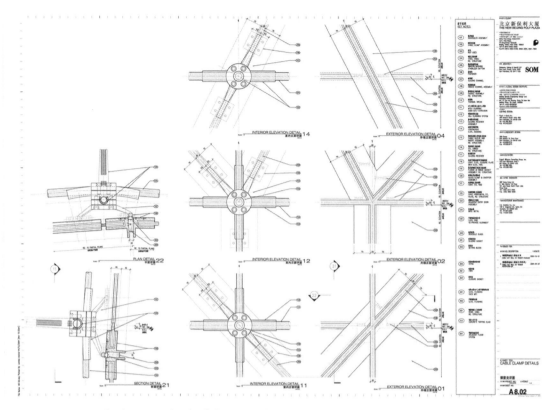

FIGURE 9C1.15   Tender document details of glass clamp fitting at fold in cable net enclosure.   *Skidmore, Owings &*
Merrill LLP

Glass

The expressed design intent for both cable net walls is maximum transparency. Coupled with this visual goal
are also performance goals for strength, minimum deflection, safety, and heat gain/heat loss criteria. Laminated
tempered glass was selected for multiple reasons. In the event of a glass break, laminated glass would remain in
the wall and not evacuate the stainless steel glass fitting support. The final glass specification was laminated clear
tempered glass with a pyrolitic low-E on the #4 surface. Extensive finite element analysis modeling was used
during the design phase to establish the glass thickness and kind. A finite element analysis model for glass
deflection is illustrated in Figure 9C1.17.

Construction

CONTRACTOR SELECTION AND WALL TESTING

Poly and SOM realized early in the design process that a project of this size and complexity would require
specialized contractors and material vendors who were accustomed to the rigorous demands of this type of
work. A list of preselected contractors/vendors was compiled and interviewed during the tender/bid phase.
Performance and experience qualifications were reviewed and discussed to select the most qualified team to
construct the project.

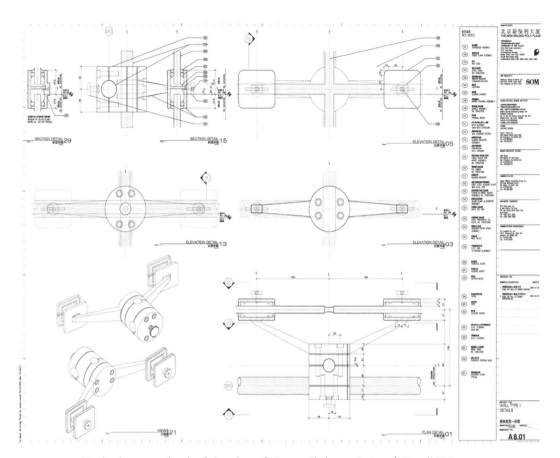

FIGURE 9C1.16 Tender document details of glass clamp fitting. *Skidmore, Owings & Merrill LLP*

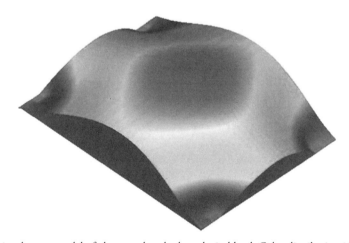

FIGURE 9C1.17 Finite element model of glass panel under lateral wind load. Color distribution identifies stress levels in glass. *Dr. Leon Jacob*

CONSTRUCTION OF THE CABLE NET

The selected cable net wall contractor provided a preliminary set of details for profile and structural capacity review. After agreement on the details, a series of prototype samples was fabricated with finishes, for joint review by client, architect, and contractor. Samples of the prototypes are illustrated in Figures 9C1.18a, 9C1.18b, and 9C1.18c. A performance test was conducted with particular attention to the jamb, hinged mullion, and sealant continuity at the gasketed glass clamp fittings. The performance testing mock-up is illustrated in Figure 9C1.19.

After the cables were initially installed and allowed to hang to remove slack, they were anchored at the sill condition and pre-tensioned by adjusting the top connection to pre-specified forces. The horizontal cables were draped behind the vertical cables to allow the cables to release slack. An image of the cable net installation process is shown in Figure 9C1.20. The cables are "dead head' connected at the sill on level 1 or along the top of the entry canopy steel. The dead head connection is a clevis connection that anchors one end of the cable yet still allows rotation. The cables are tensioned at the 23rd floor. The cable tensioning is illustrated in Figure 9C1.21. Glass clamp installation with the exterior neoprene weather-seal gasket is illustrated in Figure 9C1.22. A construction image of the hinge mullion cable clamp is shown in Figure 9C1.23.

Summary

The 22-story and 10-story cable net all-glass enclosures were accomplished thanks to a dedicated client and a collaborative working relationship between the design and construction team participants. The design goals of an open and transparent business image and maximizing natural daylight were achieved, creating an inviting work environment and significant public space at a bustling intersection in Beijing. Completed images from the interior of the two cable-net-supported all-glass enclosures are shown in Figures 9C1.24 and 9C1.25. The completed rocker assembly is illustrated in Figure 9C1.26. Completed images of the cable net components and enclosures are shown in Figures 9C1.27 and 9C1.28.

FIGURE 9C1.18a   Final constructed prototype of glass cable clamp with cable sections attached.   *Skidmore, Owings & Merrill LLP*

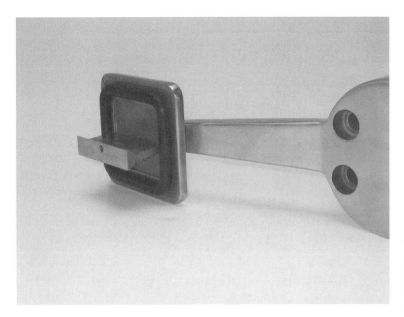

FIGURE 9C1.18b Detail of glass setting bar with interior gasket. The exterior face plate is removed. *Skidmore, Owings & Merrill LLP*

FIGURE 9C1.18c Final constructed prototype of piston-shaped stand-off. The stainless steel rod length is fabricated to specific lengths per location along the 22-story cable net enclosure fold line. *Skidmore, Owings & Merrill LLP*

FIGURE 9C1.19 Performance mock-up test specimen at Beijing construction testing laboratory.

FIGURE 9C1.20 Cable net under construction. Cables were installed loosely and allowed to "relax" prior to tuning the enclosure. *Skidmore, Owings & Merrill LLP*

FIGURE 9C1.21 Cable adjustment devices at the 23rd floor. Tension in the cables was monitored during tuning.

FIGURE 9C1.22   Glass installation progress prior to sealant installation at glass panel joinery.

FIGURE 9C1.23   Construction progress at hinged glazing channel at fold line intersection viewed from interior.

FIGURE 9C1.24   View of 22-story cable net glass enclosure from atrium interior.

Chapter 9   All-Glass Enclosures

523

FIGURE 9C1.25 View from atrium interior. The 22-story glass and cable net enclosure is on left, and the 10-story glass and cable net enclosure is on right.

FIGURE 9C1.26 Completed cable net at fold intersection and rocker mechanism.

FIGURE 9C1.27   Installed glass clamp fitting.

FIGURE 9C1.28   View from southeast. The 10-story cable net is bordered by travertine and bronze panel enclosures.   *Photo © Tim Griffith*

All-Glass Enclosures

Howard Hughes Medical Institute Janelia Farm Research Campus

Location:
Ashburn, Virginia, USA
Building Type:
Research, Master Planning, Laboratories (Computational, Electrophysiology, Open, Wet, Robotics),
Conference Center, Apartments, Auditorium, Hotel, Cafeteria, Lounge Areas, Meeting Rooms,
Private Offices, Vivarium)

Paul Fetters

PARTICIPANTS
Owner:
Howard Hughes Medical Institute (HHMI)
Architect:
Rafael Viñoly Architects – New York City, NY
Structural Engineer:
Thornton Tomasetti Engineers – Newark, NJ
Design Mechanical Engineer:
Burt, Hill Kosar Rittelmann – Washington DC

Project Description

ARCHITECTURAL GOALS:
1. Total transparency (no mullions)
2. Connection to exterior (both visual and physical)
3. Connection between labs and office pods
4. Total transparency to encourage and reinforce an open and interactive work environment

ENERGY PERFORMANCE GOALS:
1. Double wall construction in labs, with skylight as the only connection to the exterior

Enclosure System Description

SKYLIGHT SYSTEM

The Landscape Building is divided into three horizontal ribbons, as illustrated in the site plan in Figure 9C2.1. A north-facing glass corridor runs the length of the building on each floor, providing circulation, dividing the offices and labs, and allowing light to flow deep inside. The 8′-wide (2.44 m) glass corridor, illustrated in Figure 9C2.2, rims the exterior wall on all lab floors. It is composed of three pieces of glass, two vertical (one is the exterior window, the other is the divider between corridor and lab space), and one horizontal (the glass roof). The roof lites cantilever over the top of the interior partition, creating a skylight to the lab and transferring the loads to the concrete slab. The ribbons are bisected by two atriums. The centerpiece of each is a grand cantilevered staircase that accesses all three levels, provides egress to the meadow, and architecturally links the structural glass corridor with the ground-floor stainless steel frame system. A ground-floor plan is presented in Figure 9C2.3.

INNOVATIVE CURTAIN WALL APPLICATIONS

The project has two different curtain wall systems. One is an all structural glass system, illustrated in Figure 9C2.4, and the other is a stainless steel and aluminum frame system braced with glass, as illustrated in Figure 9C2.5. The

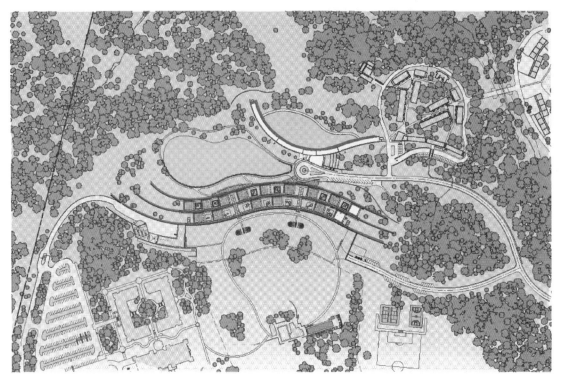

FIGURE 9C2.1 Site plan of the Howard Hughes Medical Institute. All-glass enclosures face north, providing natural daylight to public and research facilities.   ©*Rafael Viñoly Architects*

FIGURE 9C2.2 Two vertical glass panels and sloping glass roof comprise the all-glass enclosures that run the length of the north building face.   *Brad Feinknopf*

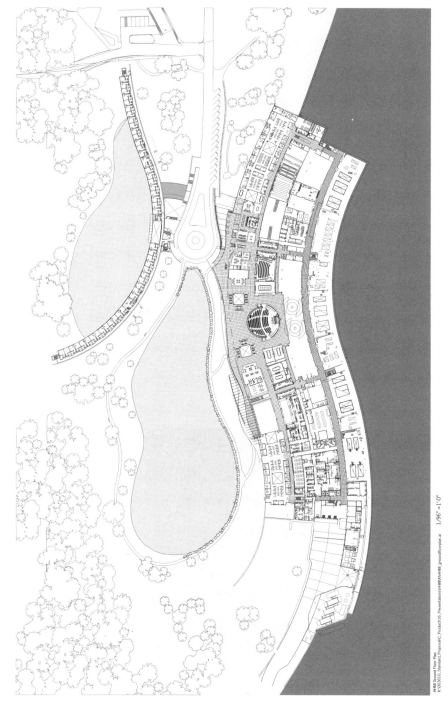

FIGURE 9C2.3 Ground-floor plan of the research building. The building is embedded into the earth with continuous glass enclosures facing north for natural daylight. ©*Rafael Viñoly Architects*

HHM Ground Floor Plan
K:\003610_Standard_ProposalAC_Product\16_Presentation\HMRA\HMI_groundfloorplan.ai   1/96" =1'-0"

FIGURE 9C2.4 Detail of one of the all-glass enclosures. The sloping glass is supported by the exterior glass wall, extruded aluminum receiver at the ceiling level, and the interior glass wall. The interior glass wall shown is at the glass portal opening. *Brad Feinknopf*

FIGURE 9C2.5 Detail of the aluminum and stainless steel glass enclosure. The glass braces system framing.
Jeff Goldberg

Exterior Building Enclosures

glass plays an important role in both systems. The curtain wall glass in the lab corridors is structural; wind, snow, and self-weight loads are transferred through the glass into the concrete slab. All the layers of glass, braced against each other, become a solid entity. The lobby or public floor of the facility is conceptually similar to the lab, except that the corridor now expands to form the lobby for the public spaces. The lobby, which varies in widths up to a maximum of 44′ (13.4 m), could not be economically structured with an all-glass structure. On this level, the main load-carrying elements are constructed of vertical stainless steel "T" and horizontal aluminum rafters. The glass becomes the lateral bracing element for the enclosure system.

INNOVATIVE COMMERCIAL DOOR OR DOOR COMPONENTS

The laboratories at the Janelia Farm Research Campus emphasize collaboration through flexibility and an incredible openness of the space. The glass corridor on each laboratory floor puts the researchers in view of their project leaders, principal investigators, fellow researchers, and visitors. Interior lab spaces are illustrated in Figure 9C2.6. To work with the unique glass structural walls, the doors had to be rethought to work with the adjacent walls. This resulted in minimizing a custom door frame to the absolute bare requirement to achieve the weather and acoustic seal, meet the thermal requirement, and take on all the normal operations of a door. Standard components, closers, pivot, and locking devices were incorporated with custom extrusions to a seamless transition from door to wall.

The interior glass partitions take on a unique role in the Landscape Building because they also serve as the structure for the skylight. For safety and strength, the glass had to be hefty. Interior walls are 1-⅝″ thick, made of three layers of laminate with PVB interlayers. The exterior glass has a total thickness of 1-¾″, including three layers of laminated, tempered glass, a high-performance low-E coating, and a 0.5″ air space. The low-E coating lends a shading coefficient that is in lieu of a ceramic frit. For clarity and to eliminate the green tint that comes with thick glass, low-iron "museum" glass was specified. To make an opening in the corridor, glass portal beams carry the weight over the openings, and the doors have glass headers.

FIGURE 9C2.6 Interior view of research lab with all-glass enclosures providing natural daylight. *Brad Feinknopf*

Enclosure System Goals

Presented with the exceptional research mandate of the Institute—which employs scientists directly and creates unique self-directed research clusters which are brought together for longer-term goals than the usual single projects model—it was clear that the design approach to founding a new medical research campus had to begin with the behaviors required to undertake and disseminate advanced biomedical research in the twenty-first century. The program for the site asked for three components to serve their needs: the research laboratory, a conference and hotel facility, and residential provision for short- and long-term visitors. An organization diagram is presented in Figure 9C2.7.

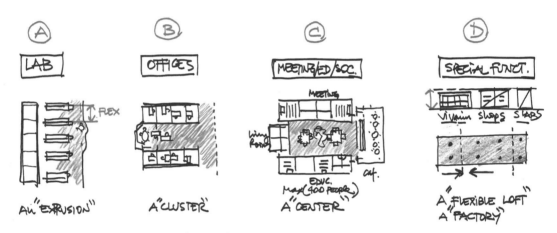

FIGURE 9C2.7　Organization program diagrams from the early design phase.　©*Rafael Viñoly Architects*

FIGURE 9C2.8　A design goal of integration and invisibility was accomplished by recessing the mass of the building into the landscape. The building terraces with landscape roofs and clear all-glass enclosures achieve the stated design goals.　*Paul Fetters*

Architecturally, the new site accommodating this endeavor has adopted a strategy of integration and invisibility: The research laboratory is a long, linear building following the contour of the land. An aerial view of the lab and circulation corridor in the landscape terraces is illustrated in Figure 9C2.8. It is built into the slope in the form of three ranks of descending planted terraces enclosing the three stories of interior spaces, which are amply daylit despite being nominally underground. A concept section sketch is shown in Figure 9C2.9. The terraced roofs illustrated in Figure 9C2.10 are the second largest in the U.S. and have carefully researched green

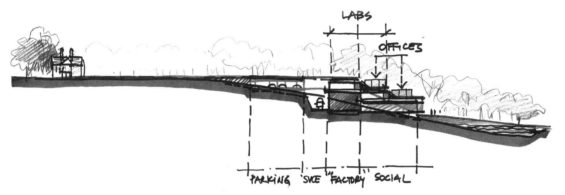

FIGURE 9C2.9   A concept sketch of the terraced building organization.   *©Rafael Viñoly Architects*

FIGURE 9C2.10   Green roofs provide outdoor habitable terraces and conceal the building mass.

roofs planted with meadow grasses or short grasses, which form habitable outdoor terraces. The building structure takes advantage of the technological advances of structural steel and glass curtain walls alongside traditional materials and finishes.

The internal organization of the laboratory building uses a logical long corridor to make the building legible internally, while naturally allowing for clustering and division of space for mechanical rooms, service corridors, support spaces, and laboratory benches. Office clusters organized around a conference room and shared support areas are placed regularly along the glass-walled circulation of the laboratories and are immediately accessible from them. The arrangement of these office clusters promotes interaction and exchange, which encourages development of communities of researchers from diverse disciplines sharing a common research goal and interacting with scientists not affiliated to their team.

The project's sustainability credentials are carried through more than its appearance. The green roof and environmental ponds affect the heating and cooling efficiency of the site and allow stormwater retention and small-scale improvements such as daylight sensors, which control interior lighting. One hundred percent of the trees removed on-site were used as interior floors, finishes, and veneers.

Enclosure System Design Process

Both the schedule and the uniqueness of the project drove requirements for design-assist and trade contractor input early on.

Four teams were interviewed and given preliminary drawings (Design Development drawings) of the building.

SCHEMATIC DESIGN

The scheme of the building was developed during the design competition phase. The schematic design phase was very short, fostering the exterior massing concept as a result of placement of the program on the site. For a building of such large size, the best location determined by site analysis was restricted by a view corridor building easement. This greatly hindered building in that location. Overcoming this restriction, the solution was to recess the lab building in the landscape, giving the building the name "The Landscape Building." From studying the site massing, geology, and water table, it was determined that the maximum number of stories that could be accommodated on-site was three. This also worked in conjunction with the philosophy of the institute, which wanted a building that would encourage interaction and collaboration, while restricting movement of people up and down to two stories. All labs were located on the highest two floors, and the administration and public functions on the lowest. This resulted in a long horizontal building, buried into the side of a small bluff.

This move defined the zones and requirements of the building, creating two distinct approaches to exterior systems: one of circulation, and the other of spaces or divisions between spaces. Both of these systems had the intention of focusing the program spaces into being a part of the landscape. Schematic design sketches are presented in Figure 9C2.11.

With the support spaces for the lab buried in the earth, the exterior enclosure became a volume for circulation between the labs in the earth and the primary investigators' office pods out in the terraced landscape. The goal was to create a feeling that all the primary workspaces were in, or directly connected to, the landscape. The glazed circulation volumes following the contours of the site are perpendicularly bisected with glazed volumes connecting all three levels. These volumes contain communicating stairs.

In the design approach on the lowest floor, the exterior systems become spaces and voids connecting and defining public space and administration zones. The ground-floor exterior system is conceptually similar to the

FIGURE 9C2.11 Interconnecting stairs are enclosed with stainless steel supported glass enclosures providing natural daylight from level 3 to level 1. *©Rafael Viñoly Architects*

glazed corridors of levels 2 and 3. The system either expands to become a foyer or pre-function space for the major public meeting rooms, or it becomes a courtyard dividing public and private spaces, and bringing natural light deeper into the building.

DESIGN DEVELOPMENT

To achieve maximum connection from the lab to the landscape, the components of the lab corridor became very minimum, paired down to only glass and the necessary connection system. Three planes of glass were used in order to form a self-supporting structure, bracing each other like a house of cards. The two vertical planes or walls cantilever from a fixed base, which is formed from a stainless-steel-clad aluminum extruded sill. The third plane, the roof, spans from the outer laminated plane of glass, over the inner laminated plane, connecting to the ceiling of the lab. This forms a skylight at the edge of the lab. The three different assemblies of low-iron glass are either structurally bonded or mechanically fixed together, forming a rigid tube that follows the contours of the green roof terraces.

The make-up of the insulated exterior wall and roof panel includes 5/16" (8 mm) of tempered glass with a high-performance solar control coating on the #2 surface, and a 5/8" (16-mm) air space and a 10 +10 heat-strengthened laminate with a PVB interlayer. The interior vertical wall is composed of three layers of laminate with a PVB interlayer. The thickness of the inner vertical glass is established in order to carry roof self-weight and snow, and also to perform as a transparent acoustical barrier between the lab and the corridor.

You enter the labs in an interstitial space between two labs, formed by replacing the inner glass plane with a planar glass portal frame. This portal frame consists of a four-layer laminated lap-jointed glass column and beam assembly. Depending on the curvature of the building, the span of the portal frame varies from 22' (6.7 m) to 26' (7.92 m). The geometry of the corridor is formed by a series of concentric arcs, alternately concave and convex, controlled by nine different center points along the length of the building. Each piece of glass is faceted

FIGURE 9C2.12 Interconnecting stairs are enclosed with stainless steel supported glass enclosures, providing natural daylight from level 3 to level 1. *Jeff Goldberg*

based on the layout of the lab benches and the maximum fabrication width of the solar coating. At approximately three points along the length, the corridor is interrupted with glass and a stainless steel stair enclosure that follows the slope of the hillside, connecting the labs with the green roof above and the public spaces below. The interconnecting stair is shown in Figures 9C2.12 and 9C2.13. The location of the stair opening also coincides with the expansion joints in the building, creating a natural break in its 1,000′ (305 m) length. The stainless steel portal frame is made with three hinged arches that articulate the spaces as the building expands and contracts, with no noticeable special joints in the systems.

CONSTRUCTION DOCUMENTS

Because of the unique design of the glass corridor, it was recommended to the client that the exterior package be put out to bid as a design-assist package with the design development documents.

Bringing a cladding contractor on board during the completion of the construction documents worked with the overall collaborative nature of the project. A project office was established next to the construction site,

FIGURE 9C2.13 A view from the upper interconnecting stair landing, with stainless steel supported glass enclosures. *Jeff Goldberg*

giving all parties workspace, promoting interaction and collaboration between the design team, the client, and the contractor, and implementing biweekly workshops. One of the advantages of getting the cladding contractor on board early was shortening the completion time of the contract document and the date when the building could be enclosed. Key shop drawings were developed simultaneously with the construction documents. With the building being primarily underground, the main structural frame was concrete. Having the cladding contractor on board early allowed for coordination of all concrete embeds before the completion of the cladding shop drawings. The two glass wall system shop drawing details are illustrated in Figures 9C2.14a, 9C2.14b, and 9C2.14c.

In addition to the design-assist contribution, having the cladding contractor on board early also was beneficial because of the additional performance test required to confirm the structural design of the structural glass corridor, over and above the normal curtain wall performance tests. Load destruction tests were performed on the glass portal frames, confirming design safety factors and the collapse mode of failure. In the end, every glass lite in the laminate glass construction make-up was broken, and the beam still was able to support its own weight.

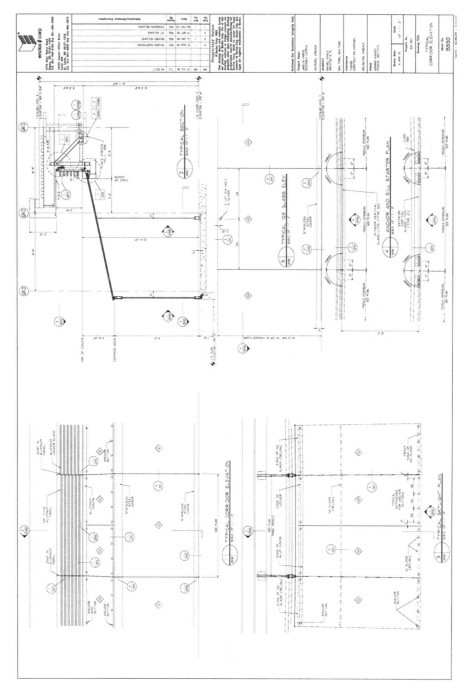

FIGURE 9C2.14a Plan, elevations, and sections through the all-glass corridor and sloped glass enclosure system. *Enclos Corp.*

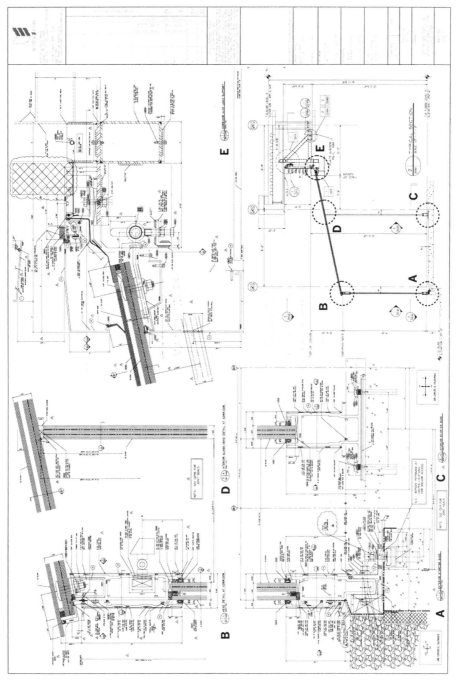

FIGURE 9C2.14b Details of the all-glass corridor and sloped glass enclosure. *Enclos Corp.*

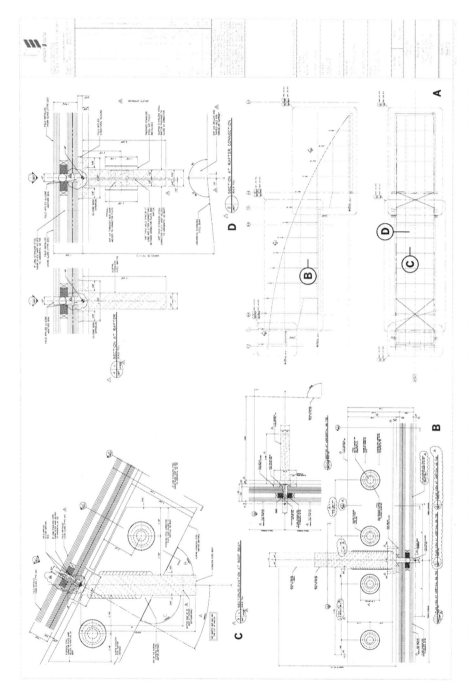

FIGURE 9C2.14c Plan, elevation, and details through the stainless steel and glass enclosure of the interconnecting stairways. *Enclos Corp.*

FIGURE 9C2.15 Night image of the building entry with internally illuminated all-glass enclosure system. *Brad Feinknopf*

Construction

The vision of an unprecedented degree of scientific collaboration and interaction was achieved through a process that was itself highly cooperative. The institute, the architect, and the builder established a project office at the site where all project meetings and major decisions occurred. All construction administration and management activities occurred in an integrated environment. The project's organizational structure has achieved the same level of integration and collaboration that the Institute envisioned for its new campus.

SCHEDULE

The initial design competition was held in 2001, and the building was completed in 2006, under a fast-track procurement schedule that took only four years from initial design to project completion.

Summary

The vision of an unprecedented degree of scientific collaboration and interaction was achieved through a process that was itself collaborative and interactive. All construction administration and management activities occurred in an integrated environment. The design team relocated to the site to manage the fast-track construction schedule, which allowed for continual contact with the construction manager and owner's representatives to review design issues and optimize costs. In order to avoid changes during construction and to expedite quality-control processes in the field through benchmarking, full-scale mock-ups of critical project elements were constructed and reviewed with the ultimate users. Furthermore, the enormous building site enabled significant economies of scale, with materials procured at a low unit cost and with great flexibility and ease in construction staging. The project was scheduled to open in the fall of 2006, and this deadline was met through a fast-track construction process. The primary building entry and illuminated interior spaces are illustrated in Figure 9C2.15.

All-Glass Enclosures

Lenovo/Raycom Building C Entry Pavilion

Location:
Beijing, People's Republic of China
Building Type:
Two Office Buildings and Cable/Truss-Supported All-Glass Entry Pavilion

Owner:
Legend Group Holdings Co.
Design Architect:
Skidmore, Owings & Merrill LLP – San Francisco, CA
Local Design Institute Architect (LDI)
Beijing Special Institute of Architecture and Design (BIAD) – Beijing, China
Design Structural Engineer:
Skidmore, Owings & Merrill LLP – San Francisco, CA
Local Design Institute Structural Engineer (LDI)
Beijing Special Institute of Architecture and Design (BIAD) – Beijing, China
Design Mechanical Engineer:
Flack & Kurtz – San Francisco, CA

Project Description

The Lenovo/Raycom Building C is the second development located in the Lenovo/Raycom InfoTech Park Campus. Building C consists of below-grade parking, below-grade retail and conference centers, retail, and two 17-story office towers linked by an all-glass entry pavilion. The entry pavilion is a column-free, all-glass structure with a cable and truss-supported glass roof and one-way cable-supported glass walls. The all-glass pavilion structure spans 203′-0″ (62 m) between the concrete core structures of the elevator lobbies located in the adjacent flanking office towers.

Following the completion of Building A, the first building to be built in the master plan, concept design began on the 968,752 sq. ft. (90,000 sq. m) Building C phase in spring 1999. The Building B parcel is left for future development. A lush landscape park setting provides a tranquil environment removed from the surrounding urbanized district. A site/master plan of the Lenovo/Raycom Info Tech Campus, showing Building C, is presented in Figure 9C3.1.

Enclosure System Types

The enclosure of the glass pavilion is defined by a series of four suspension cables anchored to the fourth floor of the concrete elevator core structure of the 17-story office towers. These cables support tapered steel plate trusses at 6-6 ¾″ (2 m) on center spacing with curved wind cable bracing. A roof plan diagram is shown in Figure 9C3.2. Insulated laminated glass enclosing the roof is supported by through-glass fittings on adjustable stainless steel rods attached to the steel trusses.

The two vertical glass enclosure walls are supported by stainless steel cables attached with a stainless steel clevis connection to the steel plate roof trusses. Spring-fitted end connections anchored below the ground-level primary building structure provide adjustment for tensioning the stainless steel cables. The west elevation is a continuous glass wall enclosure from the roof to grade. The east glass wall elevation is punctuated with a framed opening for entry doors and canopy. Insulated clear low-E glass is attached to the vertical cables with custom-designed cast and machined stainless steel fittings and flush through glass connections. A spherical joint in the fitting to the through glass fitting allows rotation to accept glass deflection under wind load conditions. An elevation of the vertical all-glass enclosure is illustrated in Figure 9C3.3. A section through the glass pavilion and office towers is illustrated in Figure 9C3.4.

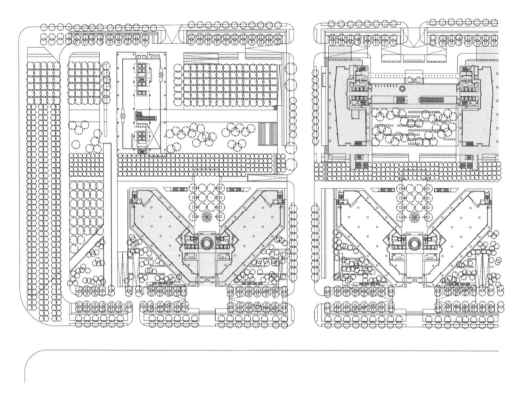

FIGURE 9C3.1   Site plan of the Lenovo Raycom Campus master plan, showing all-glass pavilion with adjoining supporting office towers. Building C is in the upper right hand corner of the site plan.   *Skidmore, Owings & Merrill LLP*

Enclosure System Goals

A ceremonial point of arrival for the new development was a requirement in the master plan. The glass entry pavilion is sited between the two office towers, recessed from the tower faces. A granite paved vehicular drop-off with water features over glass skylights and reflecting pools provides a distinguished arrival sequence for tenants of each office tower. A view from inside the south tower to the glass pavilion and vehicular drop-off below is illustrated in Figure 9C3.5. The glass pavilion design goals were to provide a climate-controlled entry lobby for each tower, with unobstructed views to the landscape garden to the west. The design goal of the pavilion was to visually connect the pavilion interior to the landscape. The pavilion is a transition lobby. A performance goal was to minimize energy consumption and reduce artificial lighting. Fritted laminated/insulating roof glazing filters natural light to the pavilion lobby and to the lower-level retail and conference centers. The glass entry pavilion exterior from the garden is illustrated in Figure 9C3.6.

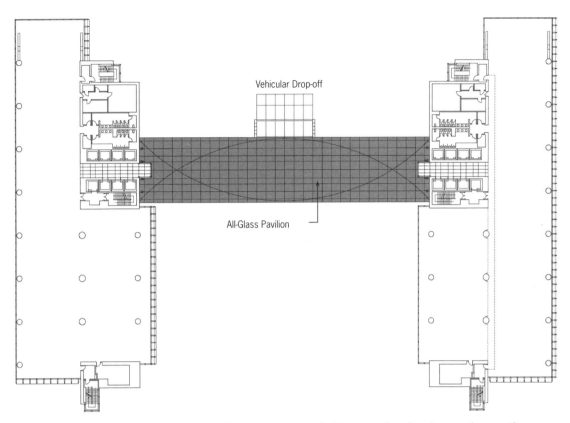

FIGURE 9C3.2 Roof plan of Lenovo glass pavilion. Supporting roof cables are anchored to the two adjacent office tower elevator core structures. The two curved cables provide lateral wind bracing. *Skidmore, Owings & Merrill LLP*

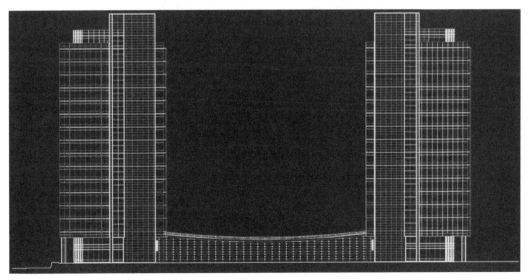

FIGURE 9C3.3 Elevation of Lenovo all-glass pavilion and adjacent office towers. *Skidmore, Owings & Merrill LLP*

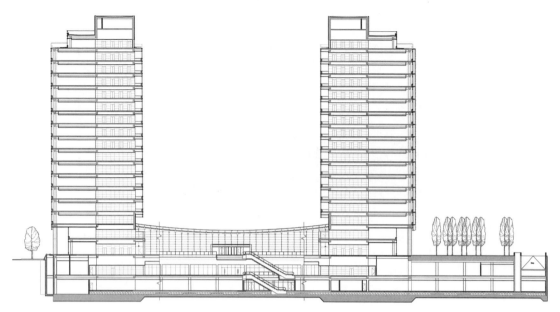

FIGURE 9C3.4 Section of glass pavilion and adjoining supporting office towers. The glass pavilion serves as the office lobby and admits natural daylight to the lower-level retail spaces. *Skidmore, Owings & Merrill LLP*

FIGURE 9C3.5 Pavilion glass roof viewed from south office tower elevator lobby.

Exterior Building Enclosures

FIGURE 9C3.6 Glass pavilion at dusk from landscape garden. *Photo © Tim Griffith*

FIGURE 9C3.7 Schematic design rendering of glass pavilion exterior. *Skidmore, Owings & Merrill LLP*

Enclosure System Design Process

SCHEMATIC DESIGN

The glass pavilion was envisioned in the early schematic design phases as a sheer and transparent arrival and meeting point. Design options were studied to provide a unified arrival point for the twin office towers. The pavilion is organized as the center point to the second phase of the development, to establish a primary point of entry while maintaining visual continuity to the landscape environment of the campus. A rendering of the entry pavilion exterior is presented in Figure 9C3.7. An interior rendering is shown in Figure 9C3.8.

FIGURE 9C3.8 Schematic design rendering of pavilion interior. *Skidmore, Owings & Merrill LLP*

DESIGN DEVELOPMENT

The plan organization was further refined in design development to organize office user and visitor circulation along the eastern edge of the pavilion. Openings to the lower level along the western garden edge provide direct access between the pavilion lobby and the retail/conference centers below grade. Exit stair enclosures and mechanical return plenums are housed in freestanding granite-clad enclosures at the two ends of the pavilion adjacent to each tower. A design development floor plan is shown in Figure 9C3.9. A 6′-6¾″ (2 m) plan module for the pavilion was finalized for proportions and to coordinate with the 29′-6″ (9 m) below-grade column spacing.

The Lenovo/Raycom Building C office towers and pavilion project was tendered with a detailed set of design development drawings and performance specifications. Details for the vertical-cable-supported glass and cable truss roof glazing enclosures were developed to illustrate the profiles, finishes, and dimensional organization.

ROOF ENCLOSURE

Insulated/laminated glass was selected for the roof enclosure to provide increased thermal performance and to minimize condensation between cold exterior temperatures and the conditioned interior environment. To assist in condensation mitigation, return air plenums at each end of the pavilion induce air movement across the interior surfaces of the roof glass. Adjustable stainless steel connections with rotating glass fittings were developed to accept installation tolerances between the steel cables and trusses and the glass roof enclosure. The water infiltration protection details at the connection utilize a stainless steel cap fitting with an integral gasket

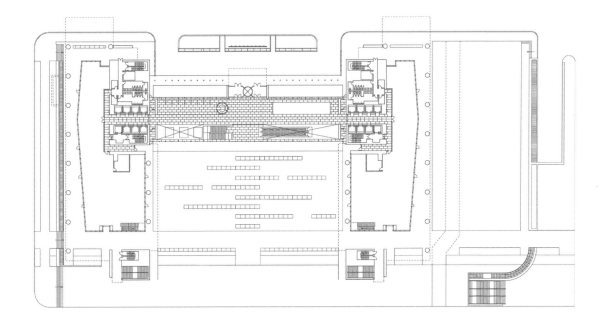

FIGURE 9C3.9 Design development floor plan of pavilion and office towers. Cable wall support locations and spacing were finalized and coordinated in the design development phase. *Skidmore, Owings & Merrill LLP*

to prevent water intrusion at the glass-to-fitting connection. A detail of the glass roof connection is illustrated in Figure 9C3.10.

Multiple detail options were reviewed for the leading edge of the glass roof to the vertical glass wall intersection. An earlier developed scheme of a formed aluminum coping with integral gutter and rainwater downspout was redesigned, at the owner's request, to a minimal glass-to-glass corner. A detail was developed with an aluminum extrusion structurally silicone attached to the projecting underside edge of the roof glass. The transition resulted in an edge with a minimal aluminum sight line profile. Vertical aluminum bars attached to the edges of the insulating/laminated roof glass divert water at each 6′-6¾″ (2 m) plan dimension to the projecting glass and aluminum drip edge. Rainwater is directed down the vertical sealant joint at each 6′-6¾″ (2 m) glass-to-glass joint. A section and isometric of the leading edge are shown in Figures 9C3.11a and 9C3.11b. The client reinforced the earlier stated design goal for maximum transparency by directing the additional design and detail studies to achieve the minimal metal edge trim. An image of the vertical glass wall to glass roof intersection is shown in Figure 9C3.12.

Vertical Glass Enclosure

Insulated clear glass is supported at four corners with a custom profile through glass connection. The connection allows rotation at each glass connection point. Adjustment of the cables is accomplished with tensioners at the cable springs mounted below level 1. An image of the spring and cable tensioner is shown in Figure 9C3.13. Movement in the vertical glass enclosure is accomplished with a "slip" sill connection. The sill is fabricated from

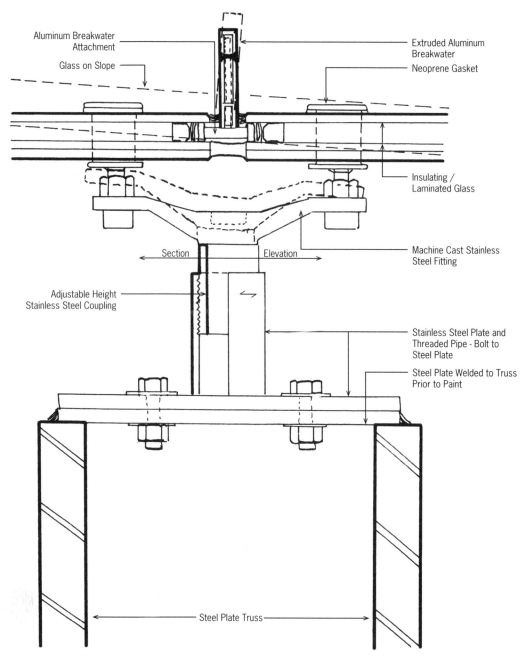

FIGURE 9C3.10 Glass roof connector detail. The glass assembly is insulating/laminated glass with a frit coating. An aluminum "breakwater" extrusion at glass joint diverts water to the perimeter. Insulating glass edge seals are recessed to allow installation of the breakwater without damaging the glass edge seals. Through glass fastener exterior surfaces are raised with a neoprene gasket weather seal.

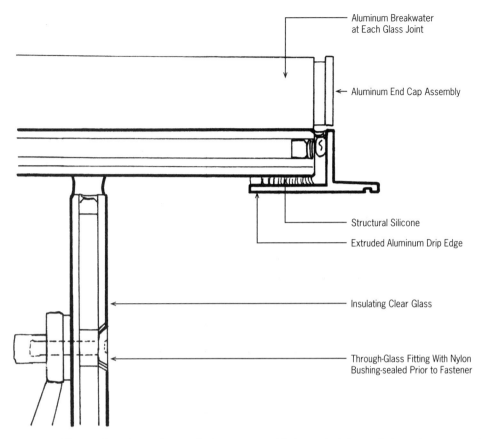

Aluminum Breakwater
at Each Glass Joint

Aluminum End Cap Assembly

Structural Silicone

Extruded Aluminum Drip Edge

Insulating Clear Glass

Through-Glass Fitting With Nylon
Bushing-sealed Prior to Fastener

FIGURE 9C3.11a   Glass roof panels cantilever at the intersection with the vertical glass wall. A continuous extruded aluminum profile provides a drip edge at the perimeter.

stainless steel plates in a deep "U" channel. Glass is supported from the cables and allowed to move vertically in the sill. The sill also serves as the end closure to a continuous reflecting pool along the east and west extent of the vertical glass wall. A sill detail is illustrated in Figure 9C3.14.

The entry vestibule and canopy are supported at level 1 in a freestanding structure. The vertical cable-supported glass is secured to the entry vestibule with similar adjustment devices as in the full-height vertical glass wall. A movement diagram identifying the location of the up/down movement in the vertical glass wall is shown in Figure 9C3.15.

Construction

The Lenovo/Raycom pavilion was tendered to a prescreened group of enclosure contractors with specific expertise in all-glass construction. The project design and details were presented to each tender contractor prior to tender preparation by the design team. After award, typical details of the roof glass and vertical glass wall, along with an erection sequence, were provided for owner and design team review and comment. After agreement on critical key details, full shop drawings were prepared.

A full-scale performance mock-up test was conducted to test for air and water infiltration, structural performance of the glass and glass fittings, and seismic drift. The test was fitted with steel tubes in lieu of the cables

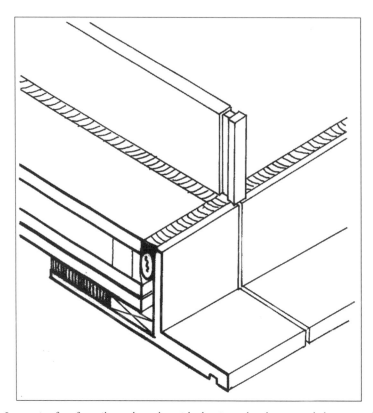

FIGURE 9C3.11b   Isometric of roof cantilever glass edge with aluminum breakwater and aluminum drip edge.

FIGURE 9C3.12   Completed glass roof to glass cable wall detail. The aluminum drip edge profile was developed in the design development phase and provides a minimal edge profile.   *Photo © Tim Griffith*

FIGURE 9C3.13 Detail image of cable adjustment device during construction.

for these tests. The cables were tested at a separate test facility for cable strength and performance. The cables were designed to deflection criteria of l/180 with maximum glass deflection at the center point of ¾″ (19 mm) under full load. Particular attention was given to the watertightness capability of the bushing of the through glass connection to the glass. The test apparatus is illustrated in Figure 9C3.16.

The roof glass to stainless steel fitting was also tested for water infiltration. The test apparatus consisted of a sealed frame with 4″ (100 mm) depth of water. The roof structure was designed to deflection criteria of l/200 with maximum glass deflection of ½″ (12 mm) under full load. The glass was measured for deflection between supports under this load. The test was conducted with water over the glass for four days. The continuous neoprene gasket was modified to a softer durometer to provide a positive seal between the glass surface and the cap fitting.

The on-site construction of the pavilion is illustrated in Figures 9C3.17 and 9C3.18.

Summary

The entry pavilion provides a spacious and light-filled arrival sequence for office tower tenants and access to the spaces at the lower levels. The pavilion and the office towers are illustrated in Figure 9C3.19. The nearly completed truss and cable supported glass roof is illustrated in Figure 9C3.20. The vertical clear glass enclosures are climate-controlled via insulating glass and an air supply at the sill along the continuous length of the cable-supported glass. An image of the completed east glass wall is shown in Figure 9C3.21.

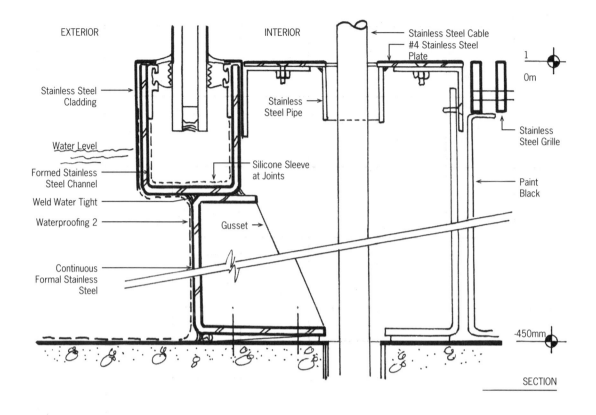

EXTERIOR   INTERIOR

Stainless Steel Cable
#4 Stainless Steel
Plate

1
0m

Stainless Steel
Cladding

Stainless
Steel Pipe

Water Level

Silicone Sleeve
at Joints

Stainless
Steel Grille

Formed Stainless
Steel Channel

Paint
Black

Weld Water Tight

Waterproofing 2

Gusset

Continuous
Formal Stainless
Steel

-450mm

SECTION

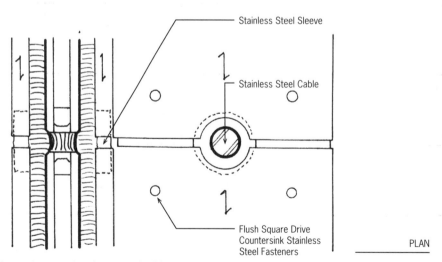

Stainless Steel Sleeve

Stainless Steel Cable

1   1

Flush Square Drive
Countersink Stainless
Steel Fasteners

PLAN

FIGURE 9C3.14   Sill plan and section detail at vertical cable-supported enclosure. Cable wall deflection is accommodated at the sill between the bottom of the glass edge and the bottom/top of sill. The stainless-steel-clad aluminum sill provides the reflection pool perimeter boundary.

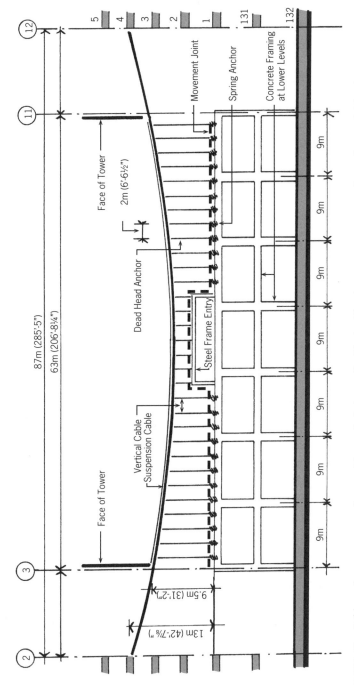

FIGURE 9C3.15 Cable enclosure structure diagram. The vertical glass wall cable dead head connection occurs at the spring connection below the ground-level slab.

FIGURE 9C3.16 Performance mock-up test chamber in China. Note the spacer in the insulting glass for the through-glass connector.

FIGURE 9C3.17 Construction progress of roof trusses prior to support cable installation.

FIGURE 9C3.18 Construction progress of vertical glass cable wall and glass roof.

FIGURE 9C3.19 Completed glass pavilion with adjacent supporting office towers. *Photo © Tim Griffith*

FIGURE 9C3.20 Glass roof with support cables and steel trusses.

FIGURE 9C3.21 Completed interior view of glass pavilion. *Photo © Tim Griffith*

Chapter 10
Realization

Bit by bit, / Putting it together. . . / Piece by piece— / Only way to make a work of art. / Every moment makes a contribution. / Every little detail plays a part. / Having just the vision's no solution, / Everything depends on execution: / Putting it together— / That's what counts.

STEPHEN SONDHEIM, SUNDAY IN THE PARK WITH GEORGE

Putting It All Together

Many building designs include more than one exterior enclosure system. Enclosure system descriptions and the associated case studies in Chapters 5–9 focused on visual and performance design particulars of their respective systems. Complete enclosure design incorporates singular or multiple exterior enclosure systems and transitions to adjacent building systems such as roofs and at grade conditions into a comprehensive building enclosure. Composing the design is a crucial aspect of creating the enclosure. However, it is simply not enough to have just a compelling vision and beautiful materials; these work together systematically to address the enclosure physics (structure, weather protection, thermal transfer,

light transmission, acoustics, and many more) to create a clear and comprehensive enclosure system approach. Thorough enclosure design integrates the visual design objectives of the overall visual composition and the performance composition of each enclosure system through a series of iterative studies, analysis, decision making, and details. Enclosure design functions on many levels. At the highest level is composition. The game within the game is "typical" detail development for each system and then the intersection of the system details within and between enclosure systems. It doesn't end there. Then comes composing the information into graphic and written narratives that can be understood by the multitude of participants who work together to create the built reality. Concurrent development of the details informs the design composition to achieve unity of visual and performance requirements at the multiple enclosure system intersections. The unification of visual and performance requirements with multiple systems into a complete enclosure design is the thesis statement of putting it all together.

COMPOSITION

Composition begins in the earliest design phase. Capture the essence through design composition. Develop a focus on materials and system(s). Keep the focus through development. Develop details to support the focus. The exterior enclosure is composed to a conceptual level with notional ideas to express the building's design aspirations and exterior identity. Even the most preliminary design will exhibit attitudes that begin to suggest applicable and suitable enclosure systems. Enclosure system selection must support and enhance visual design aspects in concert with technical design aspects. Details inform the overall composition of materials, intersections, and joinery as the enclosure design evolves and matures.

Composition is very dependent on the creator's style and response to the design opportunity at hand. Defining the appropriate enclosure system (or systems) is an art form and a science. The system design reflects the essential and defining factors, including composition, climate, use, system(s) complexity, performance requirements, cost parameters, contractor capabilities, and many others. Prior to evaluating these and other factors, it all begins with composition. Composition includes:

1. Overall composition: the portions visible to the public
2. Enclosure system composition: materials and components organized into system details
3. In designs consisting of more than one enclosure— the intersections

Overall exterior composition is the arrangement of elements and materials. Materials provide tactile and visual enrichment that expresses what the exterior enclosure design wants to be, and why. Rarely do the initial compositions remain exactly as first envisioned. There will be modifications and refinements, subtle and significant, throughout the design process. The goal is to maintain the design essence, limiting modifications and changes to the subtle-or-less category, allowing refinement of the design. This is achieved by identifying commonalities and differences, to assist in developing enclosure system(s) composition.

Enclosure system composition is organizing the materials and components into system details and zones that result in an envelope assembly. The envelope system assembly detail development and organization are influenced by material properties, weather protection principles, thermal requirements, fire resistance, and other performance requirements. System details are further informed by methods of fabrication, manufacture, assembly, construction, sequence of installation, and other logistical factors. System details are symbiotically developed to an appropriate level concurrent with the visual composition, from the initial design phases through documentation. Develop details with systems in mind. Additional levels of system detail are refined and applied when the enclosure moves into the construction phase.

As preliminary typical details of each enclosure system are developed, intersections between enclosure systems can be studied and evaluated—in plane, out of plane, and in other three-dimensional conditions. This is putting it all together. Success in putting systems together requires an understanding of system intersections and the associated visual and performance positives and negatives. Diagrammatic to detailed studies in drawings and models of the typical system details illustrate extents and edges of each enclosure. There is no manual of enclosure details that allows a "plug and play" approach. The details of each are project- and case-specific, achieved by merging the art of composition with a working knowledge of performance basics and tectonics. System composition studies begin to point to whether the enclosure intersections have continuity or boundary conditions between exterior systems and expressions.

CONTINUITY OR BOUNDARY

Jamb, head, and sill details contemplated for each enclosure system design will highlight commonalities and differences between adjacent systems. Creating the typical system details establishes rules and guiding principles to determine if a system and system intersections can provide continuity or require a termination, which creates boundary conditions for system structure, weather protection, thermal transfer, light transmission, fire protection, acoustics, and other performance items.

System cladding, cladding attachments, structure, and anchorage zones should be reviewed to determine whether intersections can be continuous or boundary. Exterior cladding materials may have similar expressed or concealed attachments. Cladding attachments (the same or different) may allow the same or similar depth or height requirements. The system cladding depth required to accommodate two separate cladding materials may be customized to utilize a constant system attachment. Structural supporting requirements may allow the same depth or height. System supports may be the same size or made the same size with localized reinforcement. System framing may be customized to utilize the same system anchor. System anchorage zone areas may be the same or different. Project specifics of intersections require study to determine if there is continuity or boundary between the different exterior expressions, materials, or systems.

CONTINUITY

Use of the term "continuity" means that enclosure supporting structural, weathertightness, and thermal principles are the same or similar enough to employ one system. In these cases, material components of the system continue the performance characteristics from one exterior expression to another. Different visible exterior materials do not necessarily dictate specifically different systems. On the contrary, many enclosures utilize the same system with a variety of exterior cladding materials and finishes. One example is curtain walls with different infill cladding, such as stone veneer, glass, and aluminum. This is illustrated in Figure 10.1.

This is one example. There are many more. The concept is simple. Exterior appearance may be dramatically distinct between materials, or in the visible exterior or interior composition. However, the performance characteristics are achieved with the same or similar material components in a similar approach, to achieve the project's visual and performance goals. For instance, if the enclosure system supports can achieve the required strength and deflection limit criteria for the respective cladding, and the weather protection principle can be tracked continuously, then the enclosure system can achieve a continuity approach, no matter the difference in the cladding material or exterior profile.

BOUNDARY

Use of the term "boundary" means that the enclosure systems' defining edges are stopped, and systems are contained within their respective limits and areas. Adjacent enclosure systems typically perform independently of each other. There are necessary details

and materials to address the boundary transition. Enclosure designs with boundary conditions usually require a higher level and quantity of detailing by the architect. Boundary condition projects require higher scrutiny for field coordination between multiple trades. Boundary conditions are more than a sealant joint separating systems. Examples include a metal framed and glass system adjacent to a brick masonry system. This is illustrated in Figure 10.2.

In a boundary approach, there are two or more independent enclosure systems at intersections. Structural performance characteristics are contained to each respective enclosure system. The same weather protection principle may bridge from the weather protection principle of one system to the adjacent system. Weather protection principles in adjacent systems may be completely different and require special design and details to terminate at a system and transition from one system to the other. This is often accomplished with a separate material. In some and more optimal cases, each system will provide its level of weather protection without relying on or contributing to the adjacent system. It is good design practice to collect, contain, and remove water within the areas of the respective systems at the boundary conditions. Providing a continuous primary air and water line between systems is the prime design objective. Locating this primary weather protection line completely between all adjacent systems is a three-dimensional design detail. It may occur in the same plane, or it may shift locations in plan, section, or elevation. In every case, the primary air and water line must be continuous on paper and must be achievable in construction.

STARTERS AND STOPPERS

As typical enclosure system details are developed, there are edge (also a boundary) conditions to be considered. The beginning of a system creates a "starter." Tops of a system create a "stopper." If there is more than one enclosure system, there may be stoppers, starters, and transition between systems.

STARTER

Enclosure system design details will inspire a fabrication sequence and, equally important, an installation

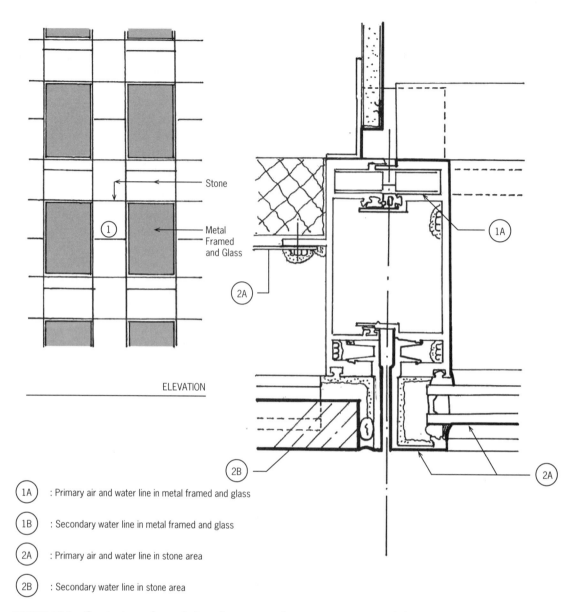

Stone

Metal
Framed
and Glass

①

ELEVATION

1A : Primary air and water line in metal framed and glass

1B : Secondary water line in metal framed and glass

2A : Primary air and water line in stone area

2B : Secondary water line in stone area

FIGURE 10.1 Continuity enclosure design relies on internal system components and their organization to continue the performance principles from one exterior expression to another.

sequence. Installations normally begin at the bottom and proceed vertically. The bottom may occur at or near the base of the building or within the body of the building. A starter is usually a horizontal condition. Each of the performance considerations discussed in Chapter 1, "Basics," needs to be addressed

in the starter details. Additionally, the functions and principles employed in the typical enclosure system details need to be accommodated in the starter boundary with interfaces to adjacent materials. This includes system structure, weather protection continuity, thermal, and others. This is one of many critical

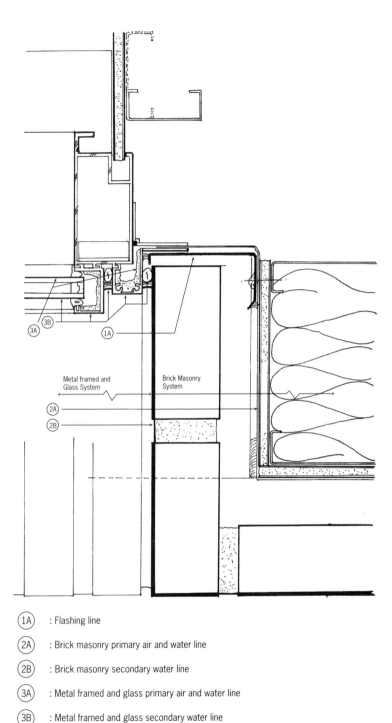

: Flashing line

2A   : Brick masonry primary air and water line

2B   : Brick masonry secondary water line

3A   : Metal framed and glass primary air and water line

3B   : Metal framed and glass secondary water line

FIGURE 10.2 Boundary enclosure design contains and terminates system performance items within each enclosure system. Transition materials provide performance continuity between enclosure systems.

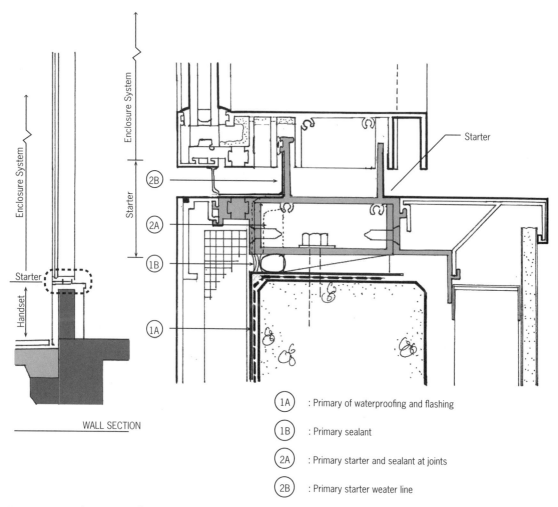

Enclosure System

Enclosure System

Starter

Starter

Handset

WALL SECTION

Starter

2B

2A

1B

1A

1A	: Primary of waterproofing and flashing
1B	: Primary sealant
2A	: Primary starter and sealant at joints
2B	: Primary starter weater line

FIGURE 10.3 A starter condition starts an enclosure system and transitions system performance to adjacent materials and systems. A curtain wall starter at a concrete curb with waterproofing and flashing and a hand-set aluminum panel is shown.

intersections to be designed and constructed. An example of a starter in a curtain wall type enclosure is illustrated in Figure 10.3.

STOPPER

Enclosure system details will also require terminations/transitions at the top and in some designs at the sides or edges. This is a stopper. Because of the interstitial space created by the top- or edges- of the enclosure, the space required for the system structure and anchorage, and the materials that are separate from the enclosure

details, there are bridging materials required to cap and transition the enclosure to either another enclosure system or a horizontal weatherproof system, such as a roof, skylight, or the like. The functional considerations discussed in Chapter 1, "Basics," also need to be addressed to maintain the continuity of each enclosure function and principle. As with the starter, performance principles must be connected between the enclosure and the other enclosure systems or roofs. An example of a top "stopper" coping condition is illustrated in Figure 10.4.

Another potential "stopper" condition may occur within the overall enclosure composition

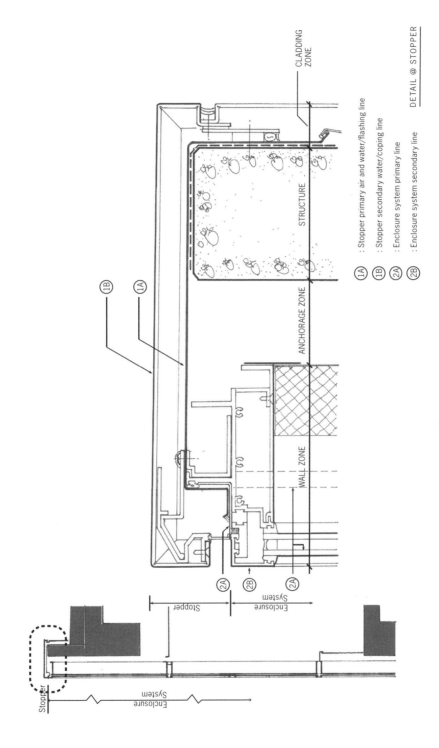

CLADDING ZONE

STRUCTURE

ANCHORAGE ZONE

WALL ZONE

1A : Stopper primary air and water/flashing line
1B : Stopper secondary water/coping line
2A : Enclosure system primary line
2B : Enclosure system secondary line

DETAIL @ STOPPER

FIGURE 10.4 A stopper condition terminates an enclosure system and transitions system performance to adjacent materials and systems. A curtain wall stopper at a concrete curb with waterproofing and flashing and a hand-set aluminum coping panel is shown.

between systems. These can and usually do create head, sill, and jamb "stopper" conditions.

EVALUATION

With the overall composition established, material components and zones organized into an enclosure system, and system transitions defined as either continuity or boundary, a series of critiques and evaluations is performed. Question and check the enclosure system details. See if these address the stated visual, as well as performance, goals. Mentally assemble, disassemble, and reassemble the system details to ascertain that there is "a way" to assembly the enclosure design. This is self-evaluation. Once there is a level of confidence with the design and detail approach, seek further evaluation from collaborating engineering discipline team members. Solicit structural, energy efficiency, energy consumption, thermal gain and loss, acoustic, and any other advice relating to the enclosure from design team disciplines. Additionally, run the enclosure design and details though each design team participant discipline to verify that the enclosure satisfies the performance needs, interactions, and interfaces of each discipline.

With the enclosure system details at this next development stage, seek evaluation from material suppliers. Question and determine if the materials proposed for use as indicated are proper and can be executed with a high level of certainty for a positive outcome. Once material suppliers have provided input, update the details and documents again.

Now is the time to review with builders. Contractor and builder evaluation provides a view from a different perspective. The specific enclosure builder entity is definitely tied to the enclosure design. If there is one system, consult several builders who provide this type of work. If the enclosure design is one with multiple systems, seek advice on each system and methods to terminate (boundary) and transition its enclosure type to the adjacent system. An architect's evaluation is predominantly a solution devised to support the design vision and goals. Collaborating disciplines are focused on specifics of the enclosure related to their engineering requirements. A contractor's evaluation provides constructability, logistics, and cost budgets. A builder is the best source for cost information. Who better to provide cost information than the entity actually performing the work? Contractor and builder insights into fabrication and installation methods often assist in finalizing technical details to unite with the visual and performance goals.

EVOLUTION VERSUS CHANGE

Development of enclosure system details is an evolutionary process by nature. Details don't just happen. Detailing can begin by working from the outside in, from the inside out, or from the middle working out in both directions. The argument can be made that since the enclosure is primarily viewed from the exterior, it is often designed from the exterior. Counterarguments claim that the enclosure is so integral to the comfort of the building user, the relationship to building service systems, and the specifics of the building's interior uses, that design from the inside out is required. Each design approach has its merits, and each approach depends on project-by-project influences. It is important that, no matter when the design initiates, a review be done from outside, from inside, and from the middle working out, prior to claiming design completion.

Cladding materials offer many methods of attachment. Each influences the final appearance. Visual appearance and system assembly can be significantly impacted by construction sequence. This cannot be ignored, nor can it be a dictating factor. Consult with those in the enclosure construction industry. Check typical and boundary details and conditions to determine if the seemingly preferred method works for all. Components in the structural zone are initially sized according to the level of knowledge of the design loads. Design loads are further refined as the process continues. Anchorages, while sometimes designed by the architect, are often left for final design by a builder or contractor. This is an area where dimensionally appropriate zones—not too small and not too big—are important to prevent change deep into the design or construction process.

Most enclosure system design and details will retain the same or a similar concept from the architectural drawings to the contractor's proposed method. Often there are slight to moderate material differences. While the finished exterior and interior appearance is the guiding principle for most architects, performance capabilities should have equal weight with visual design considerations. Each informs, respects, and coexists in harmony with the other. The enclosure should evolve to a development level commensurate with the design and construction phases. If the system detail development lags behind the project design, the stage is set for change. Enclosure design is an orderly layering of information on the design and detail foundation established in previous phases. The goal is design and detail evolution—not change.

Realization

Realization occurs on many levels at stages within the enclosure design process. While there are many, some primary realization moments are:

1. Paper (drawing completion—when do you realize you've got it)
2. Buy-in (participants get it)
3. First glimpse—seeing that mock-up or first installed assembly
4. Longevity and service—seeing the enclosure years later

Paper

Enclosure design is a cyclic process with back and forth development. This is hopefully a process of two steps forward and only one step back. There should and will come a time when there is a realization that the enclosure design and the details proposed are the correct solution. This is a "gut" realization, which only the enclosure author(s) can experience. No matter how many participants may agree with the enclosure solution, if the author does not believe it, then the realization is not positive, and the enclosure paper development is not complete. It must be positive and self-believed.

Buy-In

Collaboration (in the early design phases) and coordination (in the later design phases) with team participants should result in a "buy-in" realization

that each participant's requirements have been achieved. This realization should also be positive, with no items left unresolved or undocumented.

First Glimpse

One of the more, if not the most, dramatic realizations is the first glimpse of the finished enclosure. This may occur at a mock-up or in the early construction stages. There are few more exhilarating moments in architecture than the first impression of the built enclosure as reality. Months' or years' worth of bottled-up expectations result in a single moment of joy or despair. The goal is joy for all participants, but most importantly for the owner.

Longevity and Service

An overlooked and equally important realization is observing the enclosure several years after completion. Enclosures have a service life. The service life often extends beyond that initially envisioned. An enclosure should be timeless. It should still express itself visually in all of its original glory. It should still provide performance to original levels in all aspects, with minimal degradation of materials. For the architect and the team participants who have conceived and executed an enclosure—once a parent, always a parent.

Emerging Trends and Technology

The topics discussed so far have been the enclosure basics, participants, enclosure design process, enclosure construction process, select system descriptions/case studies, and putting it all together. This can also be summarized as preparation and current thinking. So what is the future of enclosure design and construction? This is emerging trends and technology.

Emerging trends and technologies are a subject with many topics that merit their own chapters or even books. To actively participate in emerging trends requires an understanding of the positives and shortcomings of present design and construction methodologies. Two will be discussed here. These are:

1. Practice
2. Emerging bricks and mortar

PRACTICE

The current state of knowledge in the architectural profession regarding the design and methods of construction of exterior enclosures is inconsistent. Continuing education for those in the architectural profession is paramount. All too often, the focus on enclosure design revolves around the hero image with slight or no recognition of how the enclosure was detailed and constructed, or of the guiding principles that created the solution. The basics and interrelationship of other discipline systems are necessary for "putting it all together" in design. The current state of the exterior enclosure construction and design industry appears to be a dwindling oasis of knowledge, craft, and talent. Neither of these observations is fatalistic. To solve a problem or make things better, existing conditions must be assessed so objectives for improved design, execution, and performance can be clearly identified.

There must be an increased level of education for architectural students. This begins in the professional architectural school curriculum. The study of enclosure design, the physics behind it, precedents and examples, and the art of visual composition exist in some curricula. However, it is uneven in depth and erratic. Just as professionals cannot be expected to know it all, it can't all be taught in schools. There is a need to address and teach the fundamentals, and to merge the teaching of overall design problem-solving skills with problem-solving skills for enclosure design. Enclosure examples and/or typologies can allow exposure to the subject. Every architectural graduate who enters the profession will have a hand, in some way, in the building design process. Every building has an enclosure. So why isn't this an area of study and focus in architectural schools?

Newer professional practice models, such as integrated design project delivery, attempt to mitigate the architect's inconsistency (or lack) of knowledge about enclosure design. The model includes bringing all participants in the building process—architects, engineers, and builders—together under one umbrella. On one hand, the reduction of traditional barriers between participants is a positive step. On the other hand, an architect without the basic knowledge and skill sets to guide the enclosure development may create an imbalanced situation with a low expectation for success.

There are several ways to improve the basic knowledge of students and the profession that can be integrated into the current routines. A few of these are:

1. Whenever the opportunity presents, tour a construction site with someone involved with an enclosure project.
2. Set up and attend presentations and information exchanges between students, architectural professionals, and enclosure builders and designers.
3. Tour fabrication facilities.
4. Stay in touch with and experience how things are made. This can take place on a plant tour, at a factory visit, or anywhere that people and machines are taking basic materials and fabricating finish assemblies.

EMERGING BRICKS AND MORTAR: TRENDS AND TECHNOLOGY

Walk Before You Run

Many project designs are implementing new materials, adding additional enclosure layers, and integrating multiple building systems strategies into exterior enclosures. This is refreshing and encouraging. However, physics doesn't change. New and additional complexities of advanced or enhanced materials and enclosure design strategies should never lose sight of the basics. Learn in steps; crawl before walking; walk before running. Architects who are involved with enclosure design should allocate time to study the basics. Assimilate a fundamental understanding of enclosure basics and system basics. Similar fundamentals are required in advanced enclosure designs. Advanced applications of new materials or new systems require an increased level of interdisciplinary and designer/material supplier/builder collaboration and involvement in the design phases, in order for the construction phases to achieve a successful outcome.

There is an increasing trend in both high-profile and lesser-known buildings to provide more than a single-layer enclosure. These are often touted as exemplary green or sustainable design strategies. Adding components and layers to an already high-performance enclosure provides design opportunities to respond in an even more dynamic manner to variable ambient conditions. Owners who support these efforts are to be commended for their vision and bravery. It is the responsibility of every team participant to maximize each opportunity to the fullest extent. This requires a level of informed risk taking. Push the envelope figuratively and literally to the maximum without busting it.

More Than a Single Skin

Multiple-layer building enclosure designs are becoming more prevalent as one possible solution, as energy consumption concerns and awareness—and energy costs—rise. Examples are more numerous, prevalent, and ubiquitous in regions with traditionally high energy costs. Europe has long led the way in this enclosure technology as a response to reduction of active energy consumption. Examples occur in the United States, but to a lesser extent. This has traditionally been attributed to low energy costs in the U.S. after the late 1940s. The U.S. energy crisis of the early 1970s was an initial wake-up call to owners and architects. Passive and active energy reduction strategies were the response, but of those that were implemented many have been forgotten. A period of low-cost energy and high-volume construction ensued from the late 1970s through the 1990s, with only a few examples of cutting-edge technology. Recent growth of modern enclosure design and construction in Asian countries, particularly China, notifies the world of their emergence as international players. The question is the same now as it has been for years: "Are sunscreens, double walls, and integrated technologies more environmentally responsible?" This is a debate that gives rise to the response of: "It is a great reason to get up and go to work to find out!"

CLASSIFICATIONS OF DESIGNS WITH MORE THAN A SINGLE ENCLOSURE SKIN INCLUDE:
Exterior Screens
There are hundreds of built examples of this trend. This is primarily due to the relatively low initial cost relative to the return on investment—or, basically, a bigger bang for the buck. Exterior screens provide shading in the hot time periods and admit direct or diffuse light in colder times. The applicability of the design is climate-dependent, and

precedents can be traced back to indigenous uses. These types of designs also need to consider the additional surfaces that are directly tied to maintenance and longevity. An architecture professor once told me: "There is nothing new in architecture—it is only how it is interpreted and applied properly." I remember being both offended and confused. It is only after years of practice that I realize that this is not a condemning statement at all. It is an acknowledgment of the basic tenets of building enclosures: Provide shelter and protection for the occupants to the most appropriate level possible. People who lived in an area before the advent of newer technologies lived closer to the local environment. They coexisted with nature in a less technology-assisted manner. Study the indigenous architecture, materials, and climate information of the region. It offers valuable clues to direct and static methods to incorporate exterior climate-controlling strategies for enclosures.

Exterior screens have been implemented using glass, metals, ceramics, and other materials in vertical, horizontal, and other geometric configurations. The performance overlays include solar angles and azimuths, interior views, and building use. A diagram of a horizontal sunscreen example is shown in Figure 10.5.

Design considerations include screen support locations, screen support load paths to the enclosure system structure, thermal transmission through the screen, screen attachments, screen materials, wind load resistance, and solar orientation. A finish installation of the horizontal glass sunscreen is illustrated in Figure 10.6.

Double Walls
There are many articles, publications, and entire books on this subject. Each carries its own definitions. A common trait of all types of double wall is an enclosure with a pair of enclosure "skins" separated by an air space. A diagram is shown in Figure 10.7. The assembly of each layer can be organized in a number of ways, with transparent (glass), opaque (metals, stone, or other), or a combination of component materials in each layer. The air space varies from a few inches (centimeters) to several feet (meters) in

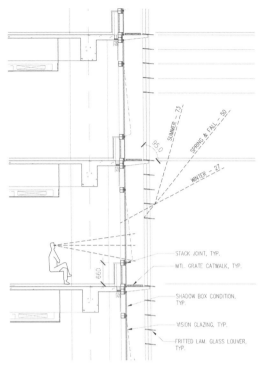

FIGURE 10.5 A section of a south-facing curtain wall in the northern hemisphere with horizontal sunscreens. The analysis identifies summer solstice, winter solstice, and interior view angles.

FIGURE 10.6 The completed south-facing curtain wall from Figure 10.5 with horizontal laminated and fritted glass sunscreens. ©*Tim Griffith*

depth. The focus is on the enclosure design and design process, so the questions that are initially posed are: When and why is this type of enclosure used in lieu of a single-layer, high-performance enclosure? What are the building use and climate conditions to merit the investigation and use of this type of enclosure technology? What are the additional system designs by other disciplines? What are the first and long-term operating costs and efficiencies? An understanding of double-wall classifications can assist in providing preliminary answers to the suitability of use. An abbreviated group of double-wall classifications are:

1. Single/double walls (AKA climate walls)

2. Independently supported double walls

Single/Double Wall (Climate Wall): This may appear an odd descriptor until it is studied in a graphic. A section is illustrated in Figure 10.8, which shows an enclosure with a system depth that is the same or similar to a single-layer enclosure. This approach is the next step up in enclosure design and construction complexity; it utilizes single-layer enclosure system depth with an additional layer or layers of cladding, increasing the air space depth, to enhance the performance. To use a clothing analogy, this is "layering" with an insulating sweater for colder periods, in a fabric that will breathe in hotter periods. This has been referred to in many publications as a "climate wall." Several curtain wall manufacturers offer versions of this system as a standard and custom variant within their product lines. These may be internally or externally ventilated, depending on the climate and building use. The zone within the "body" of the enclosure is the larger and deeper insulating area, particularly at vision glass zones. Design considerations are the methods of incorporating the inner glass assembly, controls for ventilation (manual or

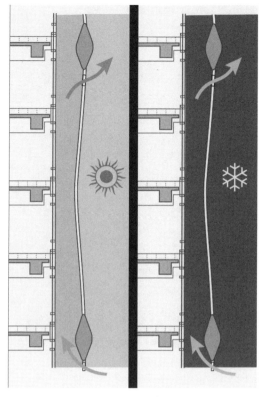

FIGURE 10.7 A common trait of double walls is a pair of enclosure system layers with an air space. *Skidmore, Owings & Merrill LLP*

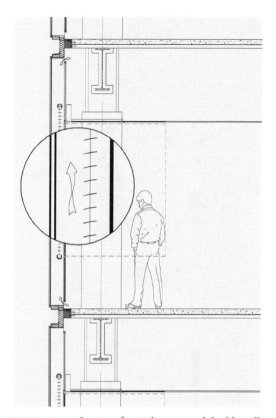

FIGURE 10.8 Section of a single supported double wall. Interior air is circulated in the cavity created by an exterior and interior layer of glass. *Skidmore, Owings & Merrill LLP*

motorized), and the interconnection with mechanical, electrical, and interior lighting systems. These systems are an expanded idea of an insulating glass lite with a deeper insulating cavity and options to control and customize temperature variations via additional devices, such as window coverings and solar controls. An example in the U.S. is illustrated in Figure 10.9.

Double Walls: There are static and dynamic versions of this enclosure type. The common organization characteristic is that two layers of enclosure are independently supported. This typically results in an air space/cavity with a larger/deeper dimension than a single/double wall. These may be sealed or ventilated. Subclassifications include:

1. Buffer walls
2. Externally ventilated
3. Internally ventilated

Each of these subclassifications can either be floor-to-floor or multifloor heights. Air volume, air circulation, external loads, and fire protection are some of the design considerations when contemplating design of these systems.

A buffer wall concept for commercial or institutional building is a new interpretation of a tried and true approach to increase insulation value and reduce acoustic transmission through the use of an air space. In the United States and other parts of the world, residential construction in particular has utilized storm windows installed outboard of operable windows for many decades. The concept of an air buffer that can be sealed or operable is a widespread and acceptable concept and is fairly easy to translate to larger-scale enclosures. Shading devices can be supplemented

FIGURE 10.9 Exterior view of the completed single-layer double wall from Figure 10.8. *Skidmore, Owings & Merrill LLP; photo: Peter Vanderwarker*

FIGURE 10.10 A completed multifloor double-layer buffer wall. An exterior glass wall is independently supported 5′0″ (1.5 m) from the interior glass curtain wall. The air cavity is vented at the bottom (2nd floor) and the top (12th floor). *© Tim Griffith*

in the buffer zone to further enhance the performance. In larger-scale projects, the buffer zone is commonly ventilated at the bottom for intake and at the top for exhaust. This can be done in multifloor or single-floor heights. An example of a multifloor example is illustrated in Figure 10.10. An example of a single-floor height approach is illustrated in Figure 10.11. In both examples the inner enclosure wall of the buffer assembly is the primary air and water protection line separating the building occupants from the elements. The outer enclosure wall is the enhancement for increased thermal, acoustic, and water infiltration protection performance. Methods and actual metrics of measurement to ascertain the actual increased level of performance are variable, but vital to understand and critically evaluate true performance.

Double ventilated walls provide exterior ventilation in the cavity created by the inner and outer enclosure systems. The inner wall is the primary air and water protection for the building occupants. Air circulation occurs at intervals of every floor or groups of floors by either natural convection circulation or through the use of mechanically induced air circulation. An example of natural air circulation in the double-wall cavity is illustrated in Figure 10.12.

Internally ventilated double walls employ ventilation between the inner enclosure wall and the cavity of the double wall. The level of engineering and interdisciplinary interface is much higher than with the methods described previously. Depending on the interior space requirements and the exterior temperature and humidity, "outside" air from the air cavity is introduced to the interior spaces through controlled openings in the inner

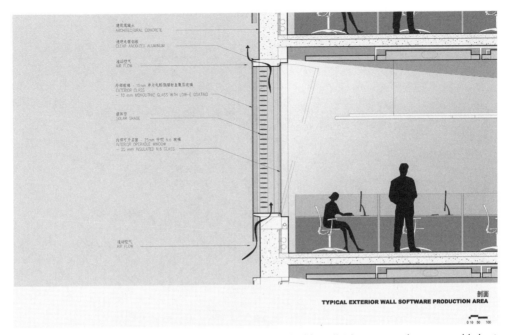

TYPICAL EXTERIOR WALL SOFTWARE PRODUCTION AREA

剖面

0 10   50   100

建筑混凝土
ARCHITECTURAL CONCRETE

透明电解铝板
CLEAR ANODIZED ALUMINUM

流动空气
AIR FLOW

外部玻璃 - 10mm 单片光能反射及覆层玻璃
EXTERIOR GLASS
- 10 mm MONOLITHIC GLASS WITH LOW-E COATING

遮阳板
SOLAR SHADE

内部可开启窗 - 25mm 中空 N.6 玻璃
INTERIOR OPERABLE WINDOW
- 25 mm INSULATED N.6 GLASS

流动空气
AIR FLOW

FIGURE 10.11 Section of a single-floor-high externally ventilated double wall. The air cavity has an operable horizontal sunscreen. The inner wall is operable for maintenance. *Skidmore, Owings & Merrill LLP*

FIGURE 10.12 A performance mock-up of a multifloor externally ventilated double wall. Intake and exhaust air for the double-wall cavity is achieved through the horizontal air slot.

FIGURE 10.13 Naturally ventilated double walls rely on air circulation in and through the air cavity. Air circulation, speed, temperature, and other design criteria can be dynamically modeled with computer software. *Skidmore, Owings & Merrill LLP*

enclosure wall. The interior spaces may be vented to the air cavity and/or the exterior. The air movement is dependent on the design objectives of the building use and the climate. The exterior double-wall layer can be fixed or operable and in this approach is the primary air and water protection between the exterior and interior. An example of this double-wall type is illustrated in the diagram in Figure 10.13.

EACH OF THESE CATEGORIES OF DOUBLE WALLS REQUIRES CASE-SPECIFIC DESIGN OBJECTIVES AND SOLUTIONS. THE CONSIDERATIONS COMMON TO ALL ARE:

1. Fire protection
2. Cleaning and maintenance
3. Daylight controls
4. First and long-term costs. First costs are the "bricks and mortar." Long-term costs are actual

energy consumption or reduction including maintenance.

Integrated Technologies

In the continual search to build a better mousetrap for exterior enclosures, new materials proliferate in the architectural market. New materials with increased performance and technologies, such as dynamic glass, photovoltaics, and others, are an attempt to integrate new technology into existing cladding and glazing materials.

DYNAMIC GLASS

This is a classification of materials in which the glass can change appearance or "state" through either electrical current or sunlight incident on coatings within the glass. The visual and performance design "balance" when considering these materials is the building use, occupant perception from the interior and exterior, and longevity of the materials.

BUILDING INTEGRATED PHOTO VOLTAIC (BIPV)

The concept of these products is fascinating. The application is limited only by the efficiency level of the BIPV and imagination. Harvesting sunlight and putting it to use is a quest as old as the human creation of shelters. The sun (in most climates) is dependable. The technology to harness and collect sunlight and convert it to usable power is in its infancy. Incorporating these technologies into enclosures should be done in a way that allows modifications with reasonable costs. BIPV is to building enclosure design, construction, and maintenance as computer technology is to any business venture. There are continual improvements and new product launches. Each significantly new level of material improvement brings into question the need to upgrade components and materials in the enclosure system. Enclosure systems that integrate these technologies should consider a plug-and-play approach to facilitate upgrades and if upgrades are incremental or replaced in total. BIPV is often suggested as a design approach that generates energy. The resulting perceived savings should be calculated based on the subtracted value of energy used to manufacture and build the generation device to yield the real savings on energy use.

Summary

New material technologies and advanced multilayer enclosures design should be embraced. Appropriate use should be balanced through research and testing. The design of exterior enclosures has advanced tremendously in the last 20–30 years. Common materials used today, such as insulating glass and high-performance glass coatings, were not readily available as recently as 30 years ago. Prefabricated systems, custom and standard, have decreased air and water infiltration to obtain higher performance. These are now common in the industry. This is the result of pioneering owners, architects, and builders who believed in a concept and had the courage to develop an approach to implement and try them out. Not all succeeded. However, the ones that did elevated design and performance to levels that we could hardly imagine being without today. The same is true of new materials and systems. These should be implemented to reduce energy consumption and provide higher-quality interior environments. The challenge for all in the building and enclosure design and construction industry is to learn from what is known and embark on a zealous and deliberate quest to merge new with existing high-performance technologies, to continue to achieve improvements.

Design with an open mind. Be ever mindful of the basics. Turn over new rocks in the quest for enhanced performance. Treat every design as if it is THE design you want to be remembered by.

Index

C